D0902435

Dodge Durango & Dakota Pick-ups Automotive Repair Manual

by John A. Wegmann and John H Haynes

Member of the Guild of Motoring Writers

Models covered:

Dodge Durango models - 2004 through 2006
Dodge Dakota models - 2005 and 2006

(9K1 - 30023)

ABCDE
FGHIJ
KLMNO
PQRS

Haynes Publishing Group
Sparkford Nr Yeovil
Somerset BA22 7JJ England

Haynes North America, Inc
861 Lawrence Drive
Newbury Park
California 91320 USA

Davie County Public Library
Mocksville, North Carolina

Acknowledgements

Technical writers who contributed to this project include Rob Maddox, Mike Stubblefield and Joe L. Hamilton. Wiring diagrams provided exclusively for Haynes North America, Inc by Solution Builders.

© **Haynes North America, Inc. 2006**

With permission from J.H. Haynes & Co. Ltd.

A book in the Haynes Automotive Repair Manual Series

Printed in the U.S.A.

All rights reserved. No part of this book may be reproduced or transmitted in any form or by any means, electronic or mechanical, including photocopying, recording or by any information storage or retrieval system, without permission in writing from the copyright holder.

ISBN-13: 978-1-56392-643-3
ISBN-10: 1-56392-643-1

Library of Congress Control Number 2006937274

While every attempt is made to ensure that the information in this manual is correct, no liability can be accepted by the authors or publishers for loss, damage or injury caused by any errors in, or omissions from, the information given.

Contents

Haynes mechanic and photographer with a 2006 Durango

About this manual

Its purpose

The purpose of this manual is to help you get the best value from your vehicle. It can do so in several ways. It can help you decide what work must be done, even if you choose to have it done by a dealer service department or a repair shop; it provides information and procedures for routine maintenance and servicing; and it offers diagnostic and repair procedures to follow when trouble occurs.

We hope you use the manual to tackle the work yourself. For many simpler jobs, doing it yourself may be quicker than arranging an appointment to get the vehicle into a shop and making the trips to leave it and pick it up. More importantly, a lot of money can be saved by avoiding the expense the shop must pass on to you to cover its labor and overhead costs. An added benefit is the sense of satisfaction and accomplishment that you feel after doing the job yourself.

Using the manual

The manual is divided into Chapters. Each Chapter is divided into numbered Sections, which are headed in bold type between horizontal lines. Each Section consists of consecutively numbered paragraphs.

At the beginning of each numbered Section you will be referred to any illustrations which apply to the procedures in that Section. The reference numbers used in illustration captions pinpoint the pertinent Section and the Step within that Section. That is, illustration 3.2 means the illustration refers to Section 3 and Step (or paragraph) 2 within that Section.

Procedures, once described in the text, are not normally repeated. When it's necessary to refer to another Chapter, the reference will be given as Chapter and Section number. Cross references given without use of the word "Chapter" apply to Sections and/or paragraphs in the same Chapter. For example, "see Section 8" means in the same Chapter.

References to the left or right side of the vehicle assume you are sitting in the driver's seat, facing forward.

Even though we have prepared this manual with extreme care, neither the publisher nor the author can accept responsibility for any errors in, or omissions from, the information given.

NOTE

A **Note** provides information necessary to properly complete a procedure or information which will make the procedure easier to understand.

CAUTION

A **Caution** provides a special procedure or special steps which must be taken while completing the procedure where the Caution is found. Not heeding a Caution can result in damage to the assembly being worked on.

WARNING

A **Warning** provides a special procedure or special steps which must be taken while completing the procedure where the Warning is found. Not heeding a Warning can result in personal injury.

Introduction to the Dodge Durango and Dodge Dakota pick-ups

Dodge Dakota pick-ups are available in standard, extended and Quad Cab body styles, in short-bed and long-bed models. The extended cab is a model of the Dakota with two smaller rear doors for access to the rear seat; the Quad Cab is a true four-door model. All cabs are single-welded unit construction and bolted to the frame. All models are available in two-wheel drive (2WD) and four-wheel drive (4WD) versions. The Dodge Durango is a four-door sport-utility vehicle.

Powertrain options include a 3.7L V6 engine, 4.7L V8 and 5.7L V8 Hemi (Durango models only) engines. Transmissions used are either a six-speed manual, or automatic transmission in either four-speed or five-speed versions. The Durango is available only with an automatic transmission.

Chassis layout is conventional, with the engine mounted at the front and the power being transmitted through either the manual or automatic transmission to a driveshaft and solid rear axle. On 4WD models a transfer case also transmits power to the front axle by way of a driveshaft.

Dakota models are equipped with an independent front suspension system with upper and lower control arms and coil-over shock absorber assemblies. Durango models are equipped with an independent front suspension system with upper and lower control arms, torsion bars and shock absorbers. The steering system on all models consists of a rack-and-pinion steering gear.

The rear suspension on Dakota models consists of two shock absorbers and two leaf springs. For the Durango models, there are coil springs, shock absorbers, control arms and a Watts link. Both models incorporate a stabilizer bar to control body roll.

All models are equipped with power assisted disc front brakes and either drum or disc rear brakes. Rear Wheel Anti-Lock (RWAL) brakes are standard, while a four-wheel Anti-lock Braking System (ABS) is used on some models.

Vehicle identification numbers

Modifications are a continuing and unpublicized process in vehicle manufacturing. Since spare parts manuals and lists are compiled on a numerical basis, the individual vehicle numbers are essential to correctly identify the component required.

Vehicle Identification Number (VIN)

This very important identification number is stamped on a plate attached to the left side of the dashboard just inside the windshield on the driver's side of the vehicle (see illustration). The VIN also appears on the Vehicle Certificate of Title and Registration. It contains information such as where and when the vehicle was manufactured, the model year and the body style.

VIN year and engine codes

Two particularly important pieces of information located in the VIN are the model year and engine codes. Counting from the left, the engine code is the eighth digit and the model year code is the 10th digit.

On the models covered by this manual the engine codes are:

K	3.7L V6
N	4.7L V8
J	4.7L V8 High Output Gasoline
2	5.7L V8 (Hemi)

On the models covered by this manual the model year codes are:

4	2004
5	2005
6	2006

Equipment identification plate

This plate is located on the left-front of the underside of the hood. It contains valu-

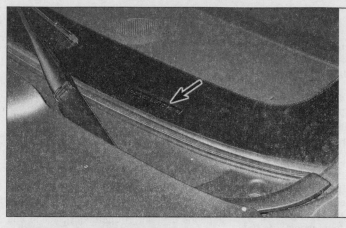

The VIN plate is visible from the outside of the vehicle, through the driver's side of the windshield

able information concerning the production of the vehicle as well as information on all production or optional equipment.

Vehicle Safety Certification label

The Safety Certification label is affixed to the left front door pillar or the end of the door (see illustration). The plate contains the name of the manufacturer, the month and year of production, the Gross Vehicle Weight Rating (GVWR) and the safety certification statement. This label also contains the original tire sizes and recommended pressures, and the paint code. It is especially useful for matching the color and type of paint during repair work.

Body Code Plate

All models have a Body Code plate, which contains information about the model, drivetrain, paint procedures, and other body information. There are seven lines of code, but you should be concerned with the lower three lines. If you need this information when purchasing parts or having paint work done, write down the numbers from the bottom three lines and show it to your dealer for decoding. On Dakota models, the plate is attached to the cab on the passenger side, behind the

rear trim panel. On Durango models, the plate is under the passenger seat, on the floorpan. To access the plate on Durango models, the seat must be removed, then remove the door-sill trim and pull the carpeting back to find the plate.

Engine identification number

The engine ID number on V6 and 4.7L V8 engines is located on a machined pad at the right-front of the engine. The identification number on Hemi engines is located at the right side of the engine block near the right side engine mount.

Transmission identification number

The ID number on manual transmissions is located on the left side of the case. On automatic transmissions, the number is stamped on the left side of the transmission case above the oil pan flange (see illustration).

Transfer case identification number

The transfer case identification plate is attached to the rear side of the case.

Typical Safety Certification label

Automatic transmission identification number pad location

Recall information

Vehicle recalls are carried out by the manufacturer in the rare event of a possible safety-related defect. The vehicle's registered owner is contacted at the address on file at the Department of Motor Vehicles and given the details of the recall. Remedial work is carried out free of charge at a dealer service department.

If you are the new owner of a used vehicle which was subject to a recall and you want to be sure that the work has been carried out, it's best to contact a dealer service department and ask about your individual vehicle - you'll need to furnish them your Vehicle Identification Number (VIN).

The table below is based on information provided by the National Highway Traffic Safety Administration (NHTSA), the body which oversees vehicle recalls in the United States. The recall database is updated constantly. For the latest information on vehicle recalls, check the NHTSA website at www.nhtsa.gov, or call the NHTSA hotline at 1-888-327-4236.

Recall date	Recall campaign number	Model(s) affected	Concern
Dec 07, 2004	04V578000	2004 Durango	On certain sport utility vehicles built with a 5.7L, 4.7L, or 3.7L engine, the positive battery cable may contact the front suspension upper control arm mounting bracket. This contact could abrade the cable and cause a short circuit, which may result in an underhood fire.
Jan 03, 2005	05V002000	2005 Dakota	On certain pickup trucks equipped with the optional side curtain air bag, the curtain fasteners may not have been properly tightened. This could result in an improper side air bag curtain deployment in certain side crash conditions, which can increase the risk of injury to vehicle occupants.
Feb 01, 2005	05V034000	2005 Durango	On certain sport utility vehicles, the fuel tank filler tube inlet check valve may not fully close at the end of refueling. This could allow some fuel to escape from the vehicle filler neck. Fuel leakage in the presence of an ignition source can result in a fire.
Oct 04, 2005	05V460000	2005 Dakota 2005 Durango	On certain pickup trucks and sport utility vehicles equipped with 42RLE automatic transmissions, the cup plug that retains the park pawl anchor shaft may be improperly installed. If the shaft moves out of position, the vehicle may not be able to achieve 'park' position. If this occurs and the parking brake is not applied, the vehicle may roll away and cause a crash without warning.
Dec 06, 2005	05V554000	2006 Durango	On certain sport utility vehicles with anti-lock brake system (ABS), the ABS control module software program may cause the rear brakes to lock up during certain braking conditions. This could result in a loss of vehicle control and a crash could occur without warning.
Feb 07, 2006	06V038000	2006 Dakota	On certain pickup trucks equipped with four-wheel antilock brake systems (ABS), the ABS electronic control unit (ECU) may cause a loss of front-to-rear brake balance, and the rear brakes could lock up prematurely during certain braking conditions. This could result in a loss of vehicle control and cause a crash without warning.
Feb 07, 2006	06V039000	2006 Dakota 2006 Durango	On certain pickup trucks and sport utility vehicles, a static electricity spark between the operator and the vehicle can cause the turn signal, headlamps or windshield wipers to malfunction without warning. This can impair the driver's vision and result in a crash.
Feb 07, 2006	06V044000	2006 Durango	Certain sport utility vehicles fail to conform to the requirements of Federal Motor Vehicle Safety Standard no. 208, 'Occupant Crash Protection.' the wrong occupant restraint controller (ORC) was installed on these vehicles. This can cause increased risk of injury to the driver and passenger(s) under certain crash conditions.
Mar 07, 2006	06V067000	2005 Durango	On certain sport utility vehicles, the front windshield wiper motor armature shaft may break. During certain operating conditions, loss of front windshield wiping capability could occur.
Jul 06, 2006	06V240000	2006 Durango	On certain sport utility vehicles, the left rear suspension Watts link may have been damaged during vehicle assembly and could fail. A failed Watts link could adversely affect vehicle handling and cause a crash without warning.

Buying parts

Replacement parts are available from many sources, which generally fall into one of two categories - authorized dealer parts departments and independent retail auto parts stores. Our advice concerning these parts is as follows:

Retail auto parts stores: Good auto parts stores will stock frequently needed components which wear out relatively fast, such as clutch components, exhaust systems, brake parts, tune-up parts, etc. These stores often supply new or reconditioned parts on an exchange basis, which can save a considerable amount of money. Discount auto parts stores are often very good places to buy materials and parts needed for general vehicle maintenance such as oil, grease, filters, spark plugs, belts, touch-up paint, bulbs, etc. They also usually sell tools and general accessories, have convenient hours, charge lower prices and can often be found not far from home.

Authorized dealer parts department: This is the best source for parts which are unique to the vehicle and not generally available elsewhere (such as major engine parts, transmission parts, trim pieces, etc.).

Warranty information: If the vehicle is still covered under warranty, be sure that any replacement parts purchased - regardless of the source - do not invalidate the warranty!

To be sure of obtaining the correct parts, have engine and chassis numbers available and, if possible, take the old parts along for positive identification.

Maintenance techniques, tools and working facilities

Maintenance techniques

There are a number of techniques involved in maintenance and repair that will be referred to throughout this manual. Application of these techniques will enable the home mechanic to be more efficient, better organized and capable of performing the various tasks properly, which will ensure that the repair job is thorough and complete.

Fasteners

Fasteners are nuts, bolts, studs and screws used to hold two or more parts together. There are a few things to keep in mind when working with fasteners. Almost all of them use a locking device of some type, either a lockwasher, locknut, locking tab or thread adhesive. All threaded fasteners should be clean and straight, with undamaged threads and undamaged corners on the hex head where the wrench fits. Develop the habit of replacing all damaged nuts and bolts with new ones. Special locknuts with nylon or fiber inserts can only be used once. If they are removed, they lose their locking ability and must be replaced with new ones.

Rusted nuts and bolts should be treated with a penetrating fluid to ease removal and prevent breakage. Some mechanics use turpentine in a spout-type oil can, which works quite well. After applying the rust penetrant, let it work for a few minutes before trying to loosen the nut or bolt. Badly rusted fasteners may have to be chiseled or sawed off or removed with a special nut breaker, available at tool stores.

If a bolt or stud breaks off in an assembly, it can be drilled and removed with a special tool commonly available for this purpose. Most automotive machine shops can perform this task, as well as other repair procedures, such as the repair of threaded holes that have been stripped out.

Flat washers and lockwashers, when removed from an assembly, should always be replaced exactly as removed. Replace any damaged washers with new ones. Never use a lockwasher on any soft metal surface (such as aluminum), thin sheet metal or plastic.

Fastener sizes

For a number of reasons, automobile manufacturers are making wider and wider use of metric fasteners. Therefore, it is important to be able to tell the difference between standard (sometimes called U.S. or SAE) and metric hardware, since they cannot be interchanged.

All bolts, whether standard or metric, are sized according to diameter, thread pitch and length. For example, a standard 1/2 - 13 x 1 bolt is 1/2 inch in diameter, has 13 threads per inch and is 1 inch long. An M12 - 1.75 x 25 metric bolt is 12 mm in diameter, has a thread pitch of 1.75 mm (the distance between threads) and is 25 mm long. The two bolts are nearly identical, and easily confused, but they are not interchangeable.

In addition to the differences in diameter, thread pitch and length, metric and standard bolts can also be distinguished by examining the bolt heads. To begin with, the distance across the flats on a standard bolt head is measured in inches, while the same dimension on a metric bolt is sized in millimeters (the same is true for nuts). As a result, a standard wrench should not be used on a metric bolt and a metric wrench should not be used on a standard bolt. Also, most standard bolts have slashes radiating out from the center of the head to denote the grade or strength of the bolt, which is an indication of the amount of torque that can be applied to it. The greater the number of slashes, the greater the strength of the bolt. Grades 0 through 5 are commonly used on automobiles. Metric bolts have a property class (grade) number, rather than a slash, molded into their heads to indicate bolt strength. In this case, the higher the number, the stronger the bolt. Property class numbers 8.8, 9.8 and 10.9 are commonly used on automobiles.

Strength markings can also be used to distinguish standard hex nuts from metric hex nuts. Many standard nuts have dots stamped into one side, while metric nuts are marked with a number. The greater the number of

dots, or the higher the number, the greater the strength of the nut.

Metric studs are also marked on their ends according to property class (grade). Larger studs are numbered (the same as metric bolts), while smaller studs carry a geometric code to denote grade.

It should be noted that many fasteners, especially Grades 0 through 2, have no distinguishing marks on them. When such is the case, the only way to determine whether it is standard or metric is to measure the thread pitch or compare it to a known fastener of the same size.

Standard fasteners are often referred to as SAE, as opposed to metric. However, it should be noted that SAE technically refers to a non-metric fine thread fastener only. Coarse thread non-metric fasteners are referred to as USS sizes.

Since fasteners of the same size (both standard and metric) may have different

strength ratings, be sure to reinstall any bolts, studs or nuts removed from your vehicle in their original locations. Also, when replacing a fastener with a new one, make sure that the new one has a strength rating equal to or greater than the original.

Tightening sequences and procedures

Most threaded fasteners should be tightened to a specific torque value (torque is the twisting force applied to a threaded component such as a nut or bolt). Overtightening the fastener can weaken it and cause it to break, while undertightening can cause it to eventually come loose. Bolts, screws and studs, depending on the material they are made of and their thread diameters, have specific torque values, many of which are noted in the Specifications at the beginning of each Chapter. Be sure to follow the torque recommendations closely. For fasteners not assigned a

Grade 1 or 2   Grade 5   Grade 8

Bolt strength marking (standard/SAE/USS; bottom - metric)

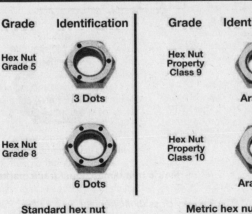

Grade	Identification
Hex Nut Grade 5	3 Dots
Hex Nut Grade 8	6 Dots

Standard hex nut strength markings

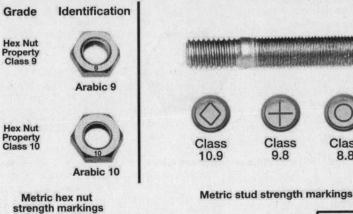

Grade	Identification
Hex Nut Property Class 9	Arabic 9
Hex Nut Property Class 10	Arabic 10

Metric hex nut strength markings

Class 10.9   Class 9.8   Class 8.8

Metric stud strength markings

00-1 HAYNES

specific torque, a general torque value chart is presented here as a guide. These torque values are for dry (unlubricated) fasteners threaded into steel or cast iron (not aluminum). As was previously mentioned, the size and grade of a fastener determine the amount of torque that can safely be applied to it. The figures listed here are approximate for Grade 2 and Grade 3 fasteners. Higher grades can tolerate higher torque values.

Fasteners laid out in a pattern, such as cylinder head bolts, oil pan bolts, differential cover bolts, etc., must be loosened or tightened in sequence to avoid warping the component. This sequence will normally be shown in the appropriate Chapter. If a specific pattern is not given, the following procedures can be used to prevent warping.

Initially, the bolts or nuts should be assembled finger-tight only. Next, they should be tightened one full turn each, in a crisscross or diagonal pattern. After each one has been tightened one full turn, return to the first one and tighten them all one-half turn, following the same pattern. Finally, tighten each of them one-quarter turn at a time until each fastener has been tightened to the proper torque. To loosen and remove the fasteners, the procedure would be reversed.

Component disassembly

Component disassembly should be done with care and purpose to help ensure that

Metric thread sizes	Ft-lbs	Nm
M-6	6 to 9	9 to 12
M-8	14 to 21	19 to 28
M-10	28 to 40	38 to 54
M-12	50 to 71	68 to 96
M-14	80 to 140	109 to 154
Pipe thread sizes		
1/8	5 to 8	7 to 10
1/4	12 to 18	17 to 24
3/8	22 to 33	30 to 44
1/2	25 to 35	34 to 47
U.S. thread sizes		
1/4 - 20	6 to 9	9 to 12
5/16 - 18	12 to 18	17 to 24
5/16 - 24	14 to 20	19 to 27
3/8 - 16	22 to 32	30 to 43
3/8 - 24	27 to 38	37 to 51
7/16 - 14	40 to 55	55 to 74
7/16 - 20	40 to 60	55 to 81
1/2 - 13	55 to 80	75 to 108

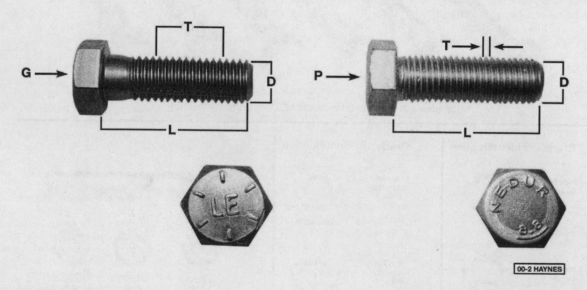

Standard (SAE and USS) bolt dimensions/grade marks   **Metric bolt dimensions/grade marks**

G	Grade marks (bolt strength)
L	Length (in inches)
T	Thread pitch (number of threads per inch)
D	Nominal diameter (in inches)

P	Property class (bolt strength)
L	Length (in millimeters)
T	Thread pitch (distance between threads in millimeters)
D	Diameter

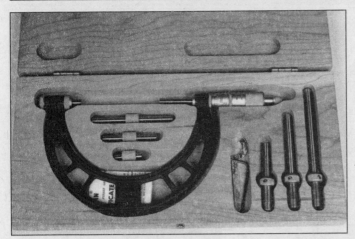

Micrometer set

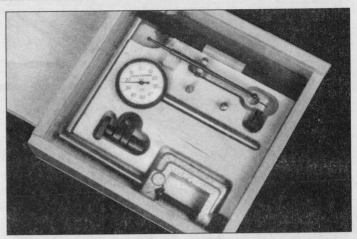

Dial indicator set

the parts go back together properly. Always keep track of the sequence in which parts are removed. Make note of special characteristics or marks on parts that can be installed more than one way, such as a grooved thrust washer on a shaft. It is a good idea to lay the disassembled parts out on a clean surface in the order that they were removed. It may also be helpful to make sketches or take instant photos of components before removal.

When removing fasteners from a component, keep track of their locations. Sometimes threading a bolt back in a part, or putting the washers and nut back on a stud, can prevent mix-ups later. If nuts and bolts cannot be returned to their original locations, they should be kept in a compartmented box or a series of small boxes. A cupcake or muffin tin is ideal for this purpose, since each cavity can hold the bolts and nuts from a particular area (i.e. oil pan bolts, valve cover bolts, engine mount bolts, etc.). A pan of this type is especially helpful when working on assemblies with very small parts, such as the carburetor, alternator, valve train or interior dash and trim pieces. The cavities can be marked with paint or tape to identify the contents.

Whenever wiring looms, harnesses or connectors are separated, it is a good idea to identify the two halves with numbered pieces of masking tape so they can be easily reconnected.

Gasket sealing surfaces

Throughout any vehicle, gaskets are used to seal the mating surfaces between two parts and keep lubricants, fluids, vacuum or pressure contained in an assembly.

Many times these gaskets are coated with a liquid or paste-type gasket sealing compound before assembly. Age, heat and pressure can sometimes cause the two parts to stick together so tightly that they are very difficult to separate. Often, the assembly can be loosened by striking it with a soft-face hammer near the mating surfaces. A regular hammer can be used if a block of wood is placed between the hammer and the part. Do

not hammer on cast parts or parts that could be easily damaged. With any particularly stubborn part, always recheck to make sure that every fastener has been removed.

Avoid using a screwdriver or bar to pry apart an assembly, as they can easily mar the gasket sealing surfaces of the parts, which must remain smooth. If prying is absolutely necessary, use an old broom handle, but keep in mind that extra clean up will be necessary if the wood splinters.

After the parts are separated, the old gasket must be carefully scraped off and the gasket surfaces cleaned. Stubborn gasket material can be soaked with rust penetrant or treated with a special chemical to soften it so it can be easily scraped off. **Caution:** *Never use gasket removal solutions or caustic chemicals on plastic or other composite components.* A scraper can be fashioned from a piece of copper tubing by flattening and sharpening one end. Copper is recommended because it is usually softer than the surfaces to be scraped, which reduces the chance of gouging the part. Some gaskets can be removed with a wire brush, but regardless of the method used, the mating surfaces must be left clean and smooth. If for some reason the gasket surface is gouged, then a gasket sealer thick enough to fill scratches will have to be used during reassembly of the components. For most applications, a non-drying (or semi-drying) gasket sealer should be used.

Hose removal tips

Warning: *If the vehicle is equipped with air conditioning, do not disconnect any of the A/C hoses without first having the system depressurized by a dealer service department or a service station.*

Hose removal precautions closely parallel gasket removal precautions. Avoid scratching or gouging the surface that the hose mates against or the connection may leak. This is especially true for radiator hoses. Because of various chemical reactions, the rubber in hoses can bond itself to the metal spigot that the hose fits over. To remove

a hose, first loosen the hose clamps that secure it to the spigot. Then, with slip-joint pliers, grab the hose at the clamp and rotate it around the spigot. Work it back and forth until it is completely free, then pull it off. Silicone or other lubricants will ease removal if they can be applied between the hose and the outside of the spigot. Apply the same lubricant to the inside of the hose and the outside of the spigot to simplify installation.

As a last resort (and if the hose is to be replaced with a new one anyway), the rubber can be slit with a knife and the hose peeled from the spigot. If this must be done, be careful that the metal connection is not damaged.

If a hose clamp is broken or damaged, do not reuse it. Wire-type clamps usually weaken with age, so it is a good idea to replace them with screw-type clamps whenever a hose is removed.

Tools

A selection of good tools is a basic requirement for anyone who plans to maintain and repair his or her own vehicle. For the owner who has few tools, the initial investment might seem high, but when compared to the spiraling costs of professional auto maintenance and repair, it is a wise one.

To help the owner decide which tools are needed to perform the tasks detailed in this manual, the following tool lists are offered: *Maintenance and minor repair, Repair/overhaul* and *Special*.

The newcomer to practical mechanics should start off with the *maintenance and minor repair* tool kit, which is adequate for the simpler jobs performed on a vehicle. Then, as confidence and experience grow, the owner can tackle more difficult tasks, buying additional tools as they are needed. Eventually the basic kit will be expanded into the *repair and overhaul* tool set. Over a period of time, the experienced do-it-yourselfer will assemble a tool set complete enough for most repair and overhaul procedures and will add tools from the special category when it is felt that the expense is justified by the frequency of use.

Dial caliper

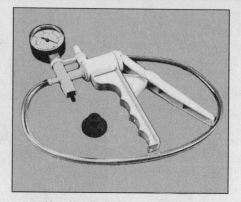

Hand-operated vacuum pump

Timing light

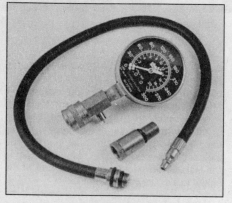

Compression gauge with spark plug hole adapter

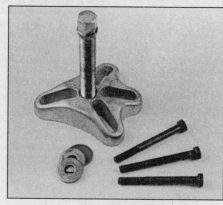

Damper/steering wheel puller

General purpose puller

Hydraulic lifter removal tool

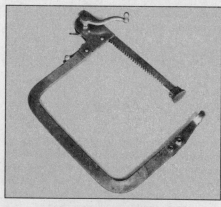

Valve spring compressor

Valve spring compressor

Ridge reamer

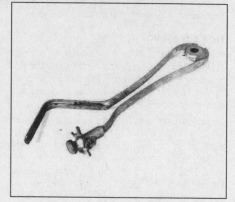

Piston ring groove cleaning tool

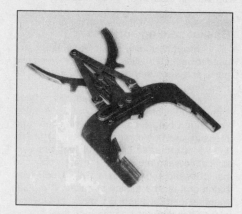

Ring removal/installation tool

Ring compressor

Cylinder hone

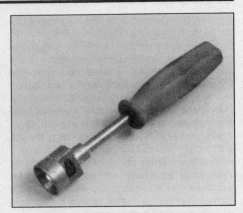
Brake hold-down spring tool

Torque angle gauge

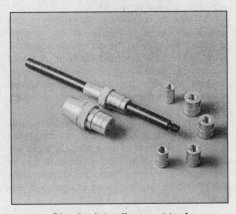
Clutch plate alignment tool

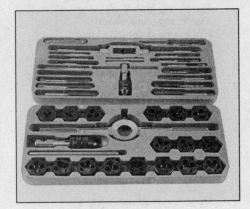
Tap and die set

Maintenance and minor repair tool kit

The tools in this list should be considered the minimum required for performance of routine maintenance, servicing and minor repair work. We recommend the purchase of combination wrenches (box-end and open-end combined in one wrench). While more expensive than open end wrenches, they offer the advantages of both types of wrench.

Combination wrench set (1/4-inch to 1 inch or 6 mm to 19 mm)
Adjustable wrench, 8 inch
Spark plug wrench with rubber insert
Spark plug gap adjusting tool
Feeler gauge set
Brake bleeder wrench
Standard screwdriver (5/16-inch x 6 inch)
Phillips screwdriver (No. 2 x 6 inch)
Combination pliers - 6 inch
Hacksaw and assortment of blades
Tire pressure gauge
Grease gun
Oil can
Fine emery cloth
Wire brush
Battery post and cable cleaning tool
Oil filter wrench
Funnel (medium size)
Safety goggles
Jackstands (2)
Drain pan

Note: *If basic tune-ups are going to be part of routine maintenance, it will be necessary to purchase a good quality stroboscopic timing light and combination tachometer/dwell meter. Although they are included in the list of special tools, it is mentioned here because they are absolutely necessary for tuning most vehicles properly.*

Repair and overhaul tool set

These tools are essential for anyone who plans to perform major repairs and are in addition to those in the maintenance and minor repair tool kit. Included is a comprehensive set of sockets which, though expensive, are invaluable because of their versatility, especially when various extensions and drives are available. We recommend the 1/2-inch drive over the 3/8-inch drive. Although the larger drive is bulky and more expensive, it has the capacity of accepting a very wide range of large sockets. Ideally, however, the mechanic should have a 3/8-inch drive set and a 1/2-inch drive set.

Socket set(s)
Reversible ratchet
Extension - 10 inch
Universal joint
Torque wrench (same size drive as sockets)
Ball peen hammer - 8 ounce
Soft-face hammer (plastic/rubber)
Standard screwdriver (1/4-inch x 6 inch)

Standard screwdriver (stubby - 5/16-inch)
Phillips screwdriver (No. 3 x 8 inch)
Phillips screwdriver (stubby - No. 2)
Pliers - vise grip
Pliers - lineman's
Pliers - needle nose
Pliers - snap-ring (internal and external)
Cold chisel - 1/2-inch
Scribe
Scraper (made from flattened copper tubing)
Centerpunch
Pin punches (1/16, 1/8, 3/16-inch)
Steel rule/straightedge - 12 inch
Allen wrench set (1/8 to 3/8-inch or 4 mm to 10 mm)
A selection of files
Wire brush (large)
Jackstands (second set)
Jack (scissor or hydraulic type)

Note: *Another tool which is often useful is an electric drill with a chuck capacity of 3/8-inch and a set of good quality drill bits.*

Special tools

The tools in this list include those which are not used regularly, are expensive to buy, or which need to be used in accordance with their manufacturer's instructions. Unless these tools will be used frequently, it is not very economical to purchase many of them. A consideration would be to split the cost and use between yourself and a friend or friends. In addition, most of these tools can be obtained from a tool rental shop on a temporary basis.

This list primarily contains only those tools and instruments widely available to the public, and not those special tools produced by the vehicle manufacturer for distribution to dealer service departments. Occasionally, references to the manufacturer's special tools are included in the text of this manual. Generally, an alternative method of doing the job without the special tool is offered. However, sometimes there is no alternative to their use. Where this is the case, and the tool cannot be purchased or borrowed, the work should be turned over to the dealer service department or an automotive repair shop.

Valve spring compressor
Piston ring groove cleaning tool
Piston ring compressor
Piston ring installation tool
Cylinder compression gauge
Cylinder ridge reamer
Cylinder surfacing hone
Cylinder bore gauge
Micrometers and/or dial calipers
Hydraulic lifter removal tool
Balljoint separator
Universal-type puller
Impact screwdriver
Dial indicator set
Stroboscopic timing light (inductive pick-up)
Hand operated vacuum/pressure pump
Tachometer/dwell meter
Universal electrical multimeter
Cable hoist
Brake spring removal and installation tools
Floor jack

Buying tools

For the do-it-yourselfer who is just starting to get involved in vehicle maintenance and repair, there are a number of options available when purchasing tools. If maintenance and minor repair is the extent of the work to be done, the purchase of individual tools is satisfactory. If, on the other hand, extensive work is planned, it would be a good idea to purchase a modest tool set from one of the large retail chain stores. A set can usually be bought at a substantial savings over the individual tool prices, and they often come with a tool box. As additional tools are needed, add-on sets, individual tools and a larger tool box can be purchased to expand the tool selection. Building a tool set gradually allows the cost of the tools to be spread over a longer period of time and gives the mechanic the freedom to choose only those tools that will actually be used.

Tool stores will often be the only source of some of the special tools that are needed,

but regardless of where tools are bought, try to avoid cheap ones, especially when buying screwdrivers and sockets, because they won't last very long. The expense involved in replacing cheap tools will eventually be greater than the initial cost of quality tools.

Care and maintenance of tools

Good tools are expensive, so it makes sense to treat them with respect. Keep them clean and in usable condition and store them properly when not in use. Always wipe off any dirt, grease or metal chips before putting them away. Never leave tools lying around in the work area. Upon completion of a job, always check closely under the hood for tools that may have been left there so they won't get lost during a test drive.

Some tools, such as screwdrivers, pliers, wrenches and sockets, can be hung on a panel mounted on the garage or workshop wall, while others should be kept in a tool box or tray. Measuring instruments, gauges, meters, etc. must be carefully stored where they cannot be damaged by weather or impact from other tools.

When tools are used with care and stored properly, they will last a very long time. Even with the best of care, though, tools will wear out if used frequently. When a tool is damaged or worn out, replace it. Subsequent jobs will be safer and more enjoyable if you do.

How to repair damaged threads

Sometimes, the internal threads of a nut or bolt hole can become stripped, usually from overtightening. Stripping threads is an all-too-common occurrence, especially when working with aluminum parts, because aluminum is so soft that it easily strips out.

Usually, external or internal threads are only partially stripped. After they've been cleaned up with a tap or die, they'll still work. Sometimes, however, threads are badly damaged. When this happens, you've got three choices:

1) *Drill and tap the hole to the next suitable oversize and install a larger diameter bolt, screw or stud.*
2) *Drill and tap the hole to accept a threaded plug, then drill and tap the plug to the original screw size. You can also buy a plug already threaded to the original size. Then you simply drill a hole to the specified size, then run the threaded plug into the hole with a bolt and jam nut. Once the plug is fully seated, remove the jam nut and bolt.*
3) *The third method uses a patented thread repair kit like Heli-Coil or Slimsert. These*

easy-to-use kits are designed to repair damaged threads in straight-through holes and blind holes. Both are available as kits which can handle a variety of sizes and thread patterns. Drill the hole, then tap it with the special included tap. Install the Heli-Coil and the hole is back to its original diameter and thread pitch.

Regardless of which method you use, be sure to proceed calmly and carefully. A little impatience or carelessness during one of these relatively simple procedures can ruin your whole day's work and cost you a bundle if you wreck an expensive part.

Working facilities

Not to be overlooked when discussing tools is the workshop. If anything more than routine maintenance is to be carried out, some sort of suitable work area is essential.

It is understood, and appreciated, that many home mechanics do not have a good workshop or garage available, and end up removing an engine or doing major repairs outside. It is recommended, however, that the overhaul or repair be completed under the cover of a roof.

A clean, flat workbench or table of comfortable working height is an absolute necessity. The workbench should be equipped with a vise that has a jaw opening of at least four inches.

As mentioned previously, some clean, dry storage space is also required for tools, as well as the lubricants, fluids, cleaning solvents, etc. which soon become necessary.

Sometimes waste oil and fluids, drained from the engine or cooling system during normal maintenance or repairs, present a disposal problem. To avoid pouring them on the ground or into a sewage system, pour the used fluids into large containers, seal them with caps and take them to an authorized disposal site or recycling center. Plastic jugs, such as old antifreeze containers, are ideal for this purpose.

Always keep a supply of old newspapers and clean rags available. Old towels are excellent for mopping up spills. Many mechanics use rolls of paper towels for most work because they are readily available and disposable. To help keep the area under the vehicle clean, a large cardboard box can be cut open and flattened to protect the garage or shop floor.

Whenever working over a painted surface, such as when leaning over a fender to service something under the hood, always cover it with an old blanket or bedspread to protect the finish. Vinyl covered pads, made especially for this purpose, are available at auto parts stores.

Jacking and towing

Jacking

The jack supplied with the vehicle should only be used for raising the vehicle when changing a tire or placing jackstands under the frame. NEVER work under the vehicle or start the engine when the vehicle supported only by a jack.

The vehicle should be parked on level ground with the wheels blocked, the parking brake applied and the transmission in Park (automatic) or Reverse (manual). If the vehicle is parked alongside the roadway, or in any other hazardous situation, turn on the emergency hazard flashers. If a tire is to be changed, loosen the lug nuts one-half turn before raising off the ground.

Place the jack under the vehicle in the indicated positions **(see illustrations)**. Operate the jack with a slow, smooth motion until the wheel is raised off the ground. Remove the lug nuts, pull off the wheel, install the spare and thread the lug nuts back on with the beveled side facing in. Tighten the lug nuts

snugly, lower the vehicle until some weight is on the wheel, tighten them completely in a criss-cross pattern and remove the jack. Note that some spare tires are designed for temporary use only - don't exceed the recommended speed, mileage or other restriction instructions accompanying the spare.

Towing

Equipment specifically designed for towing should be used and attached to the main structural members of the vehicle. Optional tow hooks may be attached to the frame at both ends of the vehicle; they are intended for emergency use only, for rescuing a stranded vehicle. Do not use the tow hooks for highway towing. Stand clear when using tow straps or chains, they may break causing serious injury.

Safety is a major consideration when towing and all applicable state and local laws must be obeyed. In addition to a tow bar, a safety chain must be used for all towing.

Two-wheel drive vehicles with an automatic transmission may be towed with four wheels on the ground for a distance of 15 miles or less, as long as the speed doesn't exceed 30 mph. If the vehicle has to be towed more than 15 miles, place the rear wheels on a towing dolly.

Two-wheel drive vehicles with a manual transmission can be towed without restrictions for a distance of 50 miles with the ignition lock in the Off (not "Lock") position and the transmission in Neutral.

Four-wheel drive vehicles should be towed on a flatbed or with all four wheels off the ground to avoid damage to the transfer case.

If any vehicle is to be towed with the front wheels on the ground and the rear wheels raised, the ignition key must be turned to the OFF position to unlock the steering column and a steering wheel clamping device designed for towing must be used or damage to the steering column lock may occur.

Front jacking position

Rear jacking position

Booster battery (jump) starting

Observe these precautions when using a booster battery to start a vehicle:

a) *Before connecting the booster battery, make sure the ignition switch is in the Off position.*
b) *Turn off the lights, heater and other electrical loads.*
c) *Your eyes should be shielded. Safety goggles are a good idea.*
d) *Make sure the booster battery is the same voltage as the dead one in the vehicle.*
e) *The two vehicles MUST NOT TOUCH each other!*
f) *Make sure the transaxle is in Park (automatic).*
g) *If the booster battery is not a maintenance-free type, remove the vent caps and lay a cloth over the vent holes.*

Connect the red jumper cable to the positive (+) terminals of each battery **(see illustration)**.

Connect one end of the black jumper cable to the negative (-) terminal of the booster battery. The other end of this cable should be connected to a good ground on the vehicle to be started, such as a bolt or bracket on the body.

Start the engine using the booster battery, then, with the engine running at idle speed, disconnect the jumper cables in the reverse order of connection.

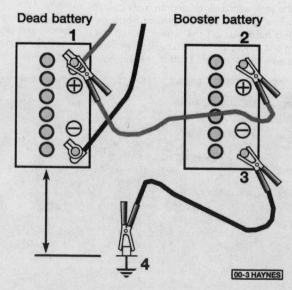

Make the booster battery cable connections in the numerical order shown (note that the negative cable of the booster battery is NOT attached to the negative terminal of the dead battery)

Automotive chemicals and lubricants

A number of automotive chemicals and lubricants are available for use during vehicle maintenance and repair. They include a wide variety of products ranging from cleaning solvents and degreasers to lubricants and protective sprays for rubber, plastic and vinyl.

Cleaners

Carburetor cleaner and choke cleaner is a strong solvent for gum, varnish and carbon. Most carburetor cleaners leave a dry-type lubricant film which will not harden or gum up. Because of this film it is not recommended for use on electrical components.

Brake system cleaner is used to remove brake dust, grease and brake fluid from the brake system, where clean surfaces are absolutely necessary. It leaves no residue and often eliminates brake squeal caused by contaminants.

Electrical cleaner removes oxidation, corrosion and carbon deposits from electrical contacts, restoring full current flow. It can also be used to clean spark plugs, carburetor jets, voltage regulators and other parts where an oil-free surface is desired.

Demoisturants remove water and moisture from electrical components such as alternators, voltage regulators, electrical connectors and fuse blocks. They are non-conductive and non-corrosive.

Degreasers are heavy-duty solvents used to remove grease from the outside of the engine and from chassis components. They can be sprayed or brushed on and, depending on the type, are rinsed off either with water or solvent.

Lubricants

Motor oil is the lubricant formulated for use in engines. It normally contains a wide variety of additives to prevent corrosion and reduce foaming and wear. Motor oil comes in various weights (viscosity ratings) from 0 to 50. The recommended weight of the oil depends on the season, temperature and the demands on the engine. Light oil is used in cold climates and under light load conditions. Heavy oil is used in hot climates and where high loads are encountered. Multi-viscosity oils are designed to have characteristics of both light and heavy oils and are available in a number of weights from 5W-20 to 20W-50.

Gear oil is designed to be used in differentials, manual transmissions and other areas where high-temperature lubrication is required.

Chassis and wheel bearing grease is a heavy grease used where increased loads and friction are encountered, such as for wheel bearings, balljoints, tie-rod ends and universal joints.

High-temperature wheel bearing grease is designed to withstand the extreme temperatures encountered by wheel bearings in disc brake equipped vehicles. It usually contains molybdenum disulfide (moly), which is a dry-type lubricant.

White grease is a heavy grease for metal-to-metal applications where water is a problem. White grease stays soft under both low and high temperatures (usually from -100 to +190-degrees F), and will not wash off or dilute in the presence of water.

Assembly lube is a special extreme pressure lubricant, usually containing moly, used to lubricate high-load parts (such as main and rod bearings and cam lobes) for initial start-up of a new engine. The assembly lube lubricates the parts without being squeezed out or washed away until the engine oiling system begins to function.

Silicone lubricants are used to protect rubber, plastic, vinyl and nylon parts.

Graphite lubricants are used where oils cannot be used due to contamination problems, such as in locks. The dry graphite will lubricate metal parts while remaining uncontaminated by dirt, water, oil or acids. It is electrically conductive and will not foul electrical contacts in locks such as the ignition switch.

Moly penetrants loosen and lubricate frozen, rusted and corroded fasteners and prevent future rusting or freezing.

Heat-sink grease is a special electrically non-conductive grease that is used for mounting electronic ignition modules where it is essential that heat is transferred away from the module.

Sealants

RTV sealant is one of the most widely used gasket compounds. Made from silicone, RTV is air curing, it seals, bonds, waterproofs, fills surface irregularities, remains flexible, doesn't shrink, is relatively easy to remove, and is used as a supplementary sealer with almost all low and medium temperature gaskets.

Anaerobic sealant is much like RTV in that it can be used either to seal gaskets or to form gaskets by itself. It remains flexible, is solvent resistant and fills surface imperfections. The difference between an anaerobic sealant and an RTV-type sealant is in the curing. RTV cures when exposed to air, while an anaerobic sealant cures only in the absence of air. This means that an anaerobic sealant cures only after the assembly of parts, sealing them together.

Thread and pipe sealant is used for sealing hydraulic and pneumatic fittings and vacuum lines. It is usually made from a Teflon compound, and comes in a spray, a paint-on liquid and as a wrap-around tape.

Chemicals

Anti-seize compound prevents seizing, galling, cold welding, rust and corrosion in fasteners. High-temperature ant-seize, usually made with copper and graphite lubricants, is used for exhaust system and exhaust manifold bolts.

Anaerobic locking compounds are used to keep fasteners from vibrating or working loose and cure only after installation, in the absence of air. Medium strength locking compound is used for small nuts, bolts and screws that may be removed later. High-strength locking compound is for large nuts, bolts and studs which aren't removed on a regular basis.

Oil additives range from viscosity index improvers to chemical treatments that claim to reduce internal engine friction. It should be noted that most oil manufacturers caution against using additives with their oils.

Gas additives perform several functions, depending on their chemical makeup. They usually contain solvents that help dissolve gum and varnish that build up on carburetor, fuel injection and intake parts. They also serve to break down carbon deposits that form on the inside surfaces of the combustion chambers. Some additives contain upper cylinder lubricants for valves and piston rings, and others contain chemicals to remove condensation from the gas tank.

Miscellaneous

Brake fluid is specially formulated hydraulic fluid that can withstand the heat and pressure encountered in brake systems. Care must be taken so this fluid does not come in contact with painted surfaces or plastics. An opened container should always be resealed to prevent contamination by water or dirt.

Weatherstrip adhesive is used to bond weatherstripping around doors, windows and trunk lids. It is sometimes used to attach trim pieces.

Undercoating is a petroleum-based, tar-like substance that is designed to protect metal surfaces on the underside of the vehicle from corrosion. It also acts as a sound-deadening agent by insulating the bottom of the vehicle.

Waxes and polishes are used to help protect painted and plated surfaces from the weather. Different types of paint may require the use of different types of wax and polish. Some polishes utilize a chemical or abrasive cleaner to help remove the top layer of oxidized (dull) paint on older vehicles. In recent years many non-wax polishes that contain a wide variety of chemicals such as polymers and silicones have been introduced. These non-wax polishes are usually easier to apply and last longer than conventional waxes and polishes.

Conversion factors

Length (distance)

Inches (in)	X	25.4	= Millimeters (mm)	X	0.0394	= Inches (in)
Feet (ft)	X	0.305	= Meters (m)	X	3.281	= Feet (ft)
Miles	X	1.609	= Kilometers (km)	X	0.621	= Miles

Volume (capacity)

Cubic inches (cu in; in^3)	X	16.387	= Cubic centimeters (cc; cm^3)	X	0.061	= Cubic inches (cu in; in^3)
Imperial pints (Imp pt)	X	0.568	= Liters (l)	X	1.76	= Imperial pints (Imp pt)
Imperial quarts (Imp qt)	X	1.137	= Liters (l)	X	0.88	= Imperial quarts (Imp qt)
Imperial quarts (Imp qt)	X	1.201	= US quarts (US qt)	X	0.833	= Imperial quarts (Imp qt)
US quarts (US qt)	X	0.946	= Liters (l)	X	1.057	= US quarts (US qt)
Imperial gallons (Imp gal)	X	4.546	= Liters (l)	X	0.22	= Imperial gallons (Imp gal)
Imperial gallons (Imp gal)	X	1.201	= US gallons (US gal)	X	0.833	= Imperial gallons (Imp gal)
US gallons (US gal)	X	3.785	= Liters (l)	X	0.264	= US gallons (US gal)

Mass (weight)

Ounces (oz)	X	28.35	= Grams (g)	X	0.035	= Ounces (oz)
Pounds (lb)	X	0.454	= Kilograms (kg)	X	2.205	= Pounds (lb)

Force

Ounces-force (ozf; oz)	X	0.278	= Newtons (N)	X	3.6	= Ounces-force (ozf; oz)
Pounds-force (lbf; lb)	X	4.448	= Newtons (N)	X	0.225	= Pounds-force (lbf; lb)
Newtons (N)	X	0.1	= Kilograms-force (kgf; kg)	X	9.81	= Newtons (N)

Pressure

Pounds-force per square inch (psi; lbf/in^2; lb/in^2)	X	0.070	= Kilograms-force per square centimeter (kgf/cm^2; kg/cm^2)	X	14.223	= Pounds-force per square inch (psi; lbf/in^2; lb/in^2)
Pounds-force per square inch (psi; lbf/in^2; lb/in^2)	X	0.068	= Atmospheres (atm)	X	14.696	= Pounds-force per square inch (psi; lbf/in^2; lb/in^2)
Pounds-force per square inch (psi; lbf/in^2; lb/in^2)	X	0.069	= Bars	X	14.5	= Pounds-force per square inch (psi; lbf/in^2; lb/in^2)
Pounds-force per square inch (psi; lbf/in^2; lb/in^2)	X	6.895	= Kilopascals (kPa)	X	0.145	= Pounds-force per square inch (psi; lbf/in^2; lb/in^2)
Kilopascals (kPa)	X	0.01	= Kilograms-force per square centimeter (kgf/cm^2; kg/cm^2)	X	98.1	= Kilopascals (kPa)

Torque (moment of force)

Pounds-force inches (lbf in; lb in)	X	1.152	= Kilograms-force centimeter (kgf cm; kg cm)	X	0.868	= Pounds-force inches (lbf in; lb in)
Pounds-force inches (lbf in; lb in)	X	0.113	= Newton meters (Nm)	X	8.85	= Pounds-force inches (lbf in; lb in)
Pounds-force inches (lbf in; lb in)	X	0.083	= Pounds-force feet (lbf ft; lb ft)	X	12	= Pounds-force inches (lbf in; lb in)
Pounds-force feet (lbf ft; lb ft)	X	0.138	= Kilograms-force meters (kgf m; kg m)	X	7.233	= Pounds-force feet (lbf ft; lb ft)
Pounds-force feet (lbf ft; lb ft)	X	1.356	= Newton meters (Nm)	X	0.738	= Pounds-force feet (lbf ft; lb ft)
Newton meters (Nm)	X	0.102	= Kilograms-force meters (kgf m; kg m)	X	9.804	= Newton meters (Nm)

Vacuum

Inches mercury (in. Hg)	X	3.377	= Kilopascals (kPa)	X	0.2961	= Inches mercury
Inches mercury (in. Hg)	X	25.4	= Millimeters mercury (mm Hg)	X	0.0394	= Inches mercury

Power

Horsepower (hp)	X	745.7	= Watts (W)	X	0.0013	= Horsepower (hp)

Velocity (speed)

Miles per hour (miles/hr; mph)	X	1.609	= Kilometers per hour (km/hr; kph)	X	0.621	= Miles per hour (miles/hr; mph)

Fuel consumption*

Miles per gallon, Imperial (mpg)	X	0.354	= Kilometers per liter (km/l)	X	2.825	= Miles per gallon, Imperial (mpg)
Miles per gallon, US (mpg)	X	0.425	= Kilometers per liter (km/l)	X	2.352	= Miles per gallon, US (mpg)

Temperature

Degrees Fahrenheit = (°C x 1.8) + 32   Degrees Celsius (Degrees Centigrade; °C) = (°F - 32) x 0.56

*It is common practice to convert from miles per gallon (mpg) to liters/100 kilometers (l/100km),
where mpg (Imperial) x l/100 km = 282 and mpg (US) x l/100 km = 235

DECIMALS to MILLIMETERS

Decimal	mm	Decimal	mm
0.001	0.0254	0.500	12.7000
0.002	0.0508	0.510	12.9540
0.003	0.0762	0.520	13.2080
0.004	0.1016	0.530	13.4620
0.005	0.1270	0.540	13.7160
0.006	0.1524	0.550	13.9700
0.007	0.1778	0.560	14.2240
0.008	0.2032	0.570	14.4780
0.009	0.2286	0.580	14.7320
		0.590	14.9860
0.010	0.2540		
0.020	0.5080		
0.030	0.7620		
0.040	1.0160	0.600	15.2400
0.050	1.2700	0.610	15.4940
0.060	1.5240	0.620	15.7480
0.070	1.7780	0.630	16.0020
0.080	2.0320	0.640	16.2560
0.090	2.2860	0.650	16.5100
		0.660	16.7640
0.100	2.5400	0.670	17.0180
0.110	2.7940	0.680	17.2720
0.120	3.0480	0.690	17.5260
0.130	3.3020		
0.140	3.5560		
0.150	3.8100		
0.160	4.0640	0.700	17.7800
0.170	4.3180	0.710	18.0340
0.180	4.5720	0.720	18.2880
0.190	4.8260	0.730	18.5420
		0.740	18.7960
0.200	5.0800	0.750	19.0500
0.210	5.3340	0.760	19.3040
0.220	5.5880	0.770	19.5580
0.230	5.8420	0.780	19.8120
0.240	6.0960	0.790	20.0660
0.250	6.3500		
0.260	6.6040		
0.270	6.8580	0.800	20.3200
0.280	7.1120	0.810	20.5740
0.290	7.3660	0.820	21.8280
		0.830	21.0820
0.300	7.6200	0.840	21.3360
0.310	7.8740	0.850	21.5900
0.320	8.1280	0.860	21.8440
0.330	8.3820	0.870	22.0980
0.340	8.6360	0.880	22.3520
0.350	8.8900	0.890	22.6060
0.360	9.1440		
0.370	9.3980		
0.380	9.6520		
0.390	9.9060		
		0.900	22.8600
0.400	10.1600	0.910	23.1140
0.410	10.4140	0.920	23.3680
0.420	10.6680	0.930	23.6220
0.430	10.9220	0.940	23.8760
0.440	11.1760	0.950	24.1300
0.450	11.4300	0.960	24.3840
0.460	11.6840	0.970	24.6380
0.470	11.9380	0.980	24.8920
0.480	12.1920	0.990	25.1460
0.490	12.4460	1.000	25.4000

FRACTIONS to DECIMALS to MILLIMETERS

Fraction	Decimal	mm	Fraction	Decimal	mm
1/64	0.0156	0.3969	33/64	0.5156	13.0969
1/32	0.0312	0.7938	17/32	0.5312	13.4938
3/64	0.0469	1.1906	35/64	0.5469	13.8906
1/16	0.0625	1.5875	9/16	0.5625	14.2875
5/64	0.0781	1.9844	37/64	0.5781	14.6844
3/32	0.0938	2.3812	19/32	0.5938	15.0812
7/64	0.1094	2.7781	39/64	0.6094	15.4781
1/8	0.1250	3.1750	5/8	0.6250	15.8750
9/64	0.1406	3.5719	41/64	0.6406	16.2719
5/32	0.1562	3.9688	21/32	0.6562	16.6688
11/64	0.1719	4.3656	43/64	0.6719	17.0656
3/16	0.1875	4.7625	11/16	0.6875	17.4625
13/64	0.2031	5.1594	45/64	0.7031	17.8594
7/32	0.2188	5.5562	23/32	0.7188	18.2562
15/64	0.2344	5.9531	47/64	0.7344	18.6531
1/4	0.2500	6.3500	3/4	0.7500	19.0500
17/64	0.2656	6.7469	49/64	0.7656	19.4469
9/32	0.2812	7.1438	25/32	0.7812	19.8438
19/64	0.2969	7.5406	51/64	0.7969	20.2406
5/16	0.3125	7.9375	13/16	0.8125	20.6375
21/64	0.3281	8.3344	53/64	0.8281	21.0344
11/32	0.3438	8.7312	27/32	0.8438	21.4312
23/64	0.3594	9.1281	55/64	0.8594	21.8281
3/8	0.3750	9.5250	7/8	0.8750	22.2250
25/64	0.3906	9.9219	57/64	0.8906	22.6219
13/32	0.4062	10.3188	29/32	0.9062	23.0188
27/64	0.4219	10.7156	59/64	0.9219	23.4156
7/16	0.4375	11.1125	15/16	0.9375	23.8125
29/64	0.4531	11.5094	61/64	0.9531	24.2094
15/32	0.4688	11.9062	31/32	0.9688	24.6062
31/64	0.4844	12.3031	63/64	0.9844	25.0031
1/2	0.5000	12.7000	1	1.0000	25.4000

Safety first!

Regardless of how enthusiastic you may be about getting on with the job at hand, take the time to ensure that your safety is not jeopardized. A moment's lack of attention can result in an accident, as can failure to observe certain simple safety precautions. The possibility of an accident will always exist, and the following points should not be considered a comprehensive list of all dangers. Rather, they are intended to make you aware of the risks and to encourage a safety conscious approach to all work you carry out on your vehicle.

Essential DOs and DON'Ts

DON'T rely on a jack when working under the vehicle. Always use approved jackstands to support the weight of the vehicle and place them under the recommended lift or support points.

DON'T attempt to loosen extremely tight fasteners (i.e. wheel lug nuts) while the vehicle is on a jack - it may fall.

DON'T start the engine without first making sure that the transmission is in Neutral (or Park where applicable) and the parking brake is set.

DON'T remove the radiator cap from a hot cooling system - let it cool or cover it with a cloth and release the pressure gradually.

DON'T attempt to drain the engine oil until you are sure it has cooled to the point that it will not burn you.

DON'T touch any part of the engine or exhaust system until it has cooled sufficiently to avoid burns.

DON'T siphon toxic liquids such as gasoline, antifreeze and brake fluid by mouth, or allow them to remain on your skin.

DON'T inhale brake lining dust - it is potentially hazardous (see *Asbestos* below).

DON'T allow spilled oil or grease to remain on the floor - wipe it up before someone slips on it.

DON'T use loose fitting wrenches or other tools which may slip and cause injury.

DON'T push on wrenches when loosening or tightening nuts or bolts. Always try to pull the wrench toward you. If the situation calls for pushing the wrench away, push with an open hand to avoid scraped knuckles if the wrench should slip.

DON'T attempt to lift a heavy component alone - get someone to help you.

DON'T *rush or take unsafe shortcuts to finish a job.*

DON'T allow children or animals in or around the vehicle while you are working on it.

DO wear eye protection when using power tools such as a drill, sander, bench grinder, etc. and when working under a vehicle.

DO keep loose clothing and long hair well out of the way of moving parts.

DO make sure that any hoist used has a safe working load rating adequate for the job.

DO get someone to check on you periodically when working alone on a vehicle.

DO carry out work in a logical sequence and make sure that everything is correctly assembled and tightened.

DO keep chemicals and fluids tightly capped and out of the reach of children and pets.

DO remember that your vehicle's safety affects that of yourself and others. If in doubt on any point, get professional advice.

Asbestos

Certain friction, insulating, sealing, and other products - such as brake linings, brake bands, clutch linings, torque converters, gaskets, etc. - may contain asbestos. Extreme care must be taken to avoid inhalation of dust from such products, since it is hazardous to health. If in doubt, assume that they do contain asbestos.

Fire

Remember at all times that gasoline is highly flammable. Never smoke or have any kind of open flame around when working on a vehicle. But the risk does not end there. A spark caused by an electrical short circuit, by two metal surfaces contacting each other, or even by static electricity built up in your body under certain conditions, can ignite gasoline vapors, which in a confined space are highly explosive. Do not, under any circumstances, use gasoline for cleaning parts. Use an approved safety solvent.

Always disconnect the battery ground (-) cable at the battery before working on any part of the fuel system or electrical system. Never risk spilling fuel on a hot engine or exhaust component. It is strongly recommended that a fire extinguisher suitable for use on fuel and electrical fires be kept handy in the garage or workshop at all times. Never try to extinguish a fuel or electrical fire with water.

Fumes

Certain fumes are highly toxic and can quickly cause unconsciousness and even death if inhaled to any extent. Gasoline vapor falls into this category, as do the vapors from some cleaning solvents. Any draining or pouring of such volatile fluids should be done in a well ventilated area.

When using cleaning fluids and solvents, read the instructions on the container carefully. Never use materials from unmarked containers.

Never run the engine in an enclosed space, such as a garage. Exhaust fumes contain carbon monoxide, which is extremely poisonous. If you need to run the engine, always do so in the open air, or at least have the rear of the vehicle outside the work area.

If you are fortunate enough to have the use of an inspection pit, never drain or pour gasoline and never run the engine while the vehicle is over the pit. The fumes, being heavier than air, will concentrate in the pit with possibly lethal results.

The battery

Never create a spark or allow a bare light bulb near a battery. They normally give off a certain amount of hydrogen gas, which is highly explosive.

Always disconnect the battery ground (-) cable at the battery before working on the fuel or electrical systems.

If possible, loosen the filler caps or cover when charging the battery from an external source (this does not apply to sealed or maintenance-free batteries). Do not charge at an excessive rate or the battery may burst.

Take care when adding water to a non maintenance-free battery and when carrying a battery. The electrolyte, even when diluted, is very corrosive and should not be allowed to contact clothing or skin.

Always wear eye protection when cleaning the battery to prevent the caustic deposits from entering your eyes.

Household current

When using an electric power tool, inspection light, etc., which operates on household current, always make sure that the tool is correctly connected to its plug and that, where necessary, it is properly grounded. Do not use such items in damp conditions and, again, do not create a spark or apply excessive heat in the vicinity of fuel or fuel vapor.

Secondary ignition system voltage

A severe electric shock can result from touching certain parts of the ignition system (such as the spark plug wires) when the engine is running or being cranked, particularly if components are damp or the insulation is defective. In the case of an electronic ignition system, the secondary system voltage is much higher and could prove fatal.

Troubleshooting

Contents

This section provides an easy reference guide to the more common problems that may occur during the operation of your vehicle. These problems and possible causes are grouped under various components or systems; i.e. Engine, Cooling System, etc., and also refer to the Chapter and/or Section that deals with the problem.

Remember that successful troubleshooting is not a mysterious black art practiced only by professional mechanics. It's simply the result of a bit of knowledge combined with an intelligent, systematic approach to the problem. Always work by a process of elimination, starting with the simplest solution and working through to the most complex - and never overlook the obvious. Anyone can forget to fill the gas tank or leave the lights on overnight, so don't assume that you are above such oversights.

Finally, always get clear in your mind why a problem has occurred and take steps to ensure that it doesn't happen again. If the electrical system fails because of a poor connection, check all other connections in the system to make sure that they don't fail as well. If a particular fuse continues to blow, find out why - don't just go on replacing fuses. Remember, failure of a small component can often be indicative of potential failure or incorrect functioning of a more important component or system.

Engine

1 Engine will not rotate when attempting to start

1 Battery terminal connections loose or corroded. Check the cable terminals at the battery. Tighten the cable or remove corrosion as necessary.
2 Battery discharged or faulty. If the cable connections are clean and tight on the battery posts, turn the key to the On position and switch on the headlights and/or windshield wipers. If they fail to function, the battery is discharged.
3 Automatic transmission not completely engaged in Park or Neutral or clutch pedal not completely depressed.
4 Broken, loose or disconnected wiring in the starting circuit. Inspect all wiring and connectors at the battery, starter solenoid and ignition switch.
5 Starter motor pinion jammed in flywheel ring gear. If manual transmission, place transmission in gear and rock the vehicle to manually turn the engine. Remove starter and inspect pinion and flywheel at earliest convenience (Chapter 5).
6 Starter solenoid faulty (Chapter 5).
7 Starter motor faulty (Chapter 5).
8 Ignition switch faulty (Chapter 12).

2 Engine rotates but will not start

1 Fuel tank empty, fuel filter plugged or fuel line restricted.
2 Fault in the fuel injection system (Chapter 4).
3 Battery discharged (engine rotates slowly). Check the operation of electrical components as described in the previous Section.
4 Battery terminal connections loose or corroded (see previous Section).
5 Fuel pump faulty (Chapter 4).
6 Excessive moisture on, or damage to, ignition components (see Chapter 5).
7 Worn, faulty or incorrectly gapped spark plugs (Chapter 1).
8 Broken, loose or disconnected wiring in the starting circuit (see previous Section).

3 Starter motor operates without rotating engine

1 Starter pinion sticking. Remove the starter (Chapter 5) and inspect.
2 Starter pinion or flywheel teeth worn or broken. Remove the flywheel/driveplate access cover and inspect.

4 Engine hard to start when cold

1 Battery discharged or low. Check as described in Section 1.
2 Fault in the fuel or electrical systems (Chapters 4 and 5).
3 Injector(s) leaking (Chapter 4).

5 Engine hard to start when hot

1 Air filter clogged (Chapter 1).
2 Fault in the fuel or electrical systems (Chapters 4 and 5).
3 Fuel not reaching the injectors (see Chapter 4).
4 Low cylinder compression (Chapter 2).
5 Malfunctioning EVAP system (Chapter 6).

6 Starter motor noisy or excessively rough in engagement

1 Pinion or flywheel gear teeth worn or broken. Remove the cover at the rear of the engine (if equipped) and inspect.
2 Starter motor mounting bolts loose or missing.

7 Engine starts but stops immediately

1 Loose or faulty electrical connection at the alternator.

2 Fault in the fuel or electrical systems (Chapters 4 and 5).
3 Vacuum leak at the gasket surfaces of the intake manifold or throttle body. Make sure all mounting bolts/nuts are tightened securely and all vacuum hoses connected to the manifold are positioned properly and in good condition.
4 Restricted intake or exhaust systems (Chapter 4)

8 Engine lopes while idling or idles erratically

1 Vacuum leakage. Check the mounting bolts/nuts at the throttle body and intake manifold for tightness. Make sure all vacuum hoses are connected and in good condition. Use a stethoscope or a length of fuel hose held against your ear to listen for vacuum leaks while the engine is running. A hissing sound will be heard. A soapy water solution will also detect leaks.
2 Fault in the fuel or electrical systems (Chapters 4 and 5).
3 Plugged PCV valve or hose (see Chapters 1 and 6).
4 Air filter clogged (Chapter 1).
5 Fuel pump not delivering sufficient fuel to the fuel injectors (see Chapter 4).
6 Leaking head gasket. Perform a compression check (Chapter 2).
7 Camshaft lobes worn (Chapter 2).

9 Engine misses at idle speed

1 Spark plugs worn, fouled or not gapped properly (Chapter 1).
2 Fault in the fuel or electrical systems (Chapters 4 and 5).
3 Vacuum leaks at intake or hose connections. Check as described in Section 8.
4 Uneven or low cylinder compression. Check compression as described in Chapter 2.

10 Engine misses throughout driving speed range

1 Fuel filter clogged and/or impurities in the fuel system (Chapter 1).
2 Faulty or incorrectly gapped spark plugs (Chapter 1).
3 Fault in the fuel or electrical systems (Chapters 4 and 5).
4 Faulty emissions system components (Chapter 6).
5 Low or uneven cylinder compression pressures. Remove the spark plugs and test the compression with a gauge (Chapter 2).
6 Vacuum leaks at the throttle body, intake manifold or vacuum hoses (see Section 8).

11 Engine stalls

1   Idle speed incorrect. Refer to the VECI label.
2   Fuel filter clogged and/or water and impurities in the fuel system (Chapter 1).
3   Fault in the fuel system or sensors (Chapters 4 and 6).
4   Faulty emissions system components (Chapter 6).
5   Faulty or incorrectly gapped spark plugs (Chapter 1).
6   Vacuum leak at the throttle body, intake manifold or vacuum hoses. Check as described in Section 8.

12 Engine lacks power

1   Fault in the fuel or electrical systems (Chapters 4 and 5).
2   Faulty or incorrectly gapped spark plugs (Chapter 1).
3   Faulty coil (Chapter 5).
4   Brakes binding (Chapter 1).
5   Automatic transmission fluid level incorrect (Chapter 1).
6   Clutch slipping (Chapter 8).
7   Fuel filter clogged and/or impurities in the fuel system (Chapter 1).
8   Emissions control system not functioning properly (Chapter 6).
9   Use of substandard fuel. Fill the tank with the proper fuel.
10   Low or uneven cylinder compression pressures. Test with a compression tester, which will detect leaking valves and/or a blown head gasket (Chapter 2).
11   Restriction in the intake or exhaust system (Chapter 4).

13 Engine backfires

1   Emissions system not functioning properly (Chapter 6).
2   Fault in the fuel or electrical systems (Chapters 4 and 5).
3   Faulty secondary ignition system (cracked spark plug insulator) (Chapters 1 and 5).
4   Fuel injection system problem (Chapter 4).
5   Vacuum leak at the throttle body, intake manifold or vacuum hoses. Check as described in Section 8.
6   Valves sticking (Chapter 2).

14 Pinging or knocking engine sounds during acceleration or uphill

1   Incorrect grade of fuel. Fill the tank with fuel of the proper octane rating.

2   Fault in the fuel or electrical systems (Chapters 4 and 5).
3   Improper spark plugs. Check the plug type against the VECI label located in the engine compartment. Also check the plugs for damage (Chapter 1).
4   Faulty emissions system (Chapter 6).
5   Vacuum leak. Check as described in Section 9.

15 Engine diesels (continues to run) after switching off

1   Idle speed too high. Refer to (Chapter 4).
2   Fault in the fuel or electrical systems (Chapters 4 and 5).
3   Excessive engine operating temperature. Probable causes of this are a low coolant level (see Chapter 1), malfunctioning thermostat, clogged radiator or faulty water pump (see Chapter 3).

Engine electrical system

16 Battery will not hold a charge

1   Drivebelt defective or not adjusted properly (Chapter 1).
2   Electrolyte level low or battery discharged (Chapter 1).
3   Battery terminals loose or corroded (Chapter 1).
4   Alternator not charging properly (Chapter 5).
5   Loose, broken or faulty wiring in the charging circuit (Chapter 5).
6   Short in the vehicle wiring causing a continuous drain on the battery (refer to Chapter 12 and the Wiring Diagrams).
7   Battery defective internally.

17 Alternator light fails to go out

1   Fault in the alternator or charging circuit (Chapter 5).
2   Alternator drivebelt defective or not properly adjusted (Chapter 1).

18 Alternator light fails to come on when key is turned on

1   Instrument cluster warning light bulb defective (Chapter 12).
2   Alternator faulty (Chapter 5).
3   Fault in the instrument cluster printed circuit, dashboard wiring or bulb holder (Chapter 12).

Fuel system

19 Excessive fuel consumption

1   Dirty or clogged air filter element (Chapter 1).
2   Emissions system not functioning properly (Chapter 6).
3   Fault in the fuel or electrical systems (Chapters 4 and 5).
4   Low tire pressure or incorrect tire size (Chapter 1).
5   Restricted exhaust system (Chapter 4).

20 Fuel leakage and/or fuel odor

1   Leak in a fuel feed or vent line (Chapter 4).
2   Tank overfilled. Fill only to automatic shut-off.
3   Evaporative emissions system canister clogged (Chapter 6).
4   Vapor leaks from system lines or injectors (Chapter 4).

Cooling system

21 Overheating

1   Insufficient coolant in the system (Chapter 1).
2   Drivebelt defective (Chapter 1).
3   Radiator core blocked or radiator grille dirty and restricted (see Chapter 3).
4   Thermostat faulty (Chapter 3).
5   Fan blades broken or cracked (Chapter 3).
6   Radiator cap not maintaining proper pressure. Have the cap pressure tested by a gas station or repair shop.

22 Overcooling

1   Thermostat faulty (Chapter 3).
2   Inaccurate temperature gauge (Chapter 12).

23 External coolant leakage

1   Deteriorated or damaged hoses or loose clamps. Replace hoses and/or tighten the clamps at the hose connections (Chapter 1).
2   Water pump seals defective. If this is the case, water will drip from the weep hole in the water pump body (Chapter 3).
3   Leakage from the radiator core or side tank(s). This will require the radiator to be professionally repaired (see Chapter 3 for removal procedures).
4   Engine drain plug(s) leaking (Chapter 1)

or water jacket core plugs leaking (see Chapter 2).
5　Leakage at the heater core. Signs of leakage should show up on interior carpeting (Chapter 3).

24　Internal coolant leakage

Note: *Internal coolant leaks can usually be detected by examining the oil. Check the dipstick and inside of the valve cover for water deposits and an oil consistency like that of a milkshake.*
1　Leaking cylinder head gasket. Have the cooling system pressure tested.
2　Cracked cylinder bore or cylinder head. Remove the head(s) and inspect (Chapter 2).
3　Leaking intake manifold gasket.

25　Coolant loss

1　Too much coolant in the system (Chapter 1).
2　Coolant boiling away due to overheating (see Section 15).
3　External or internal leakage (see Sections 23 and 24).
4　Faulty radiator cap. Have the cap pressure tested.

26　Poor coolant circulation

1　Inoperative water pump. A quick test is to pinch the top radiator hose closed with your hand while the engine is idling, then let it loose. You should feel the surge of coolant if the pump is working properly (see Chapter 1).
2　Restriction in the cooling system. Drain, flush and refill the system (Chapter 1). If necessary, remove the radiator (Chapter 3) and have it reverse flushed.
3　Drivebelt defective (Chapter 1).
4　Thermostat sticking (Chapter 3).
5　Drivebelt incorrectly routed, causing the pump to turn backward (Chapter 1).

Clutch

27　Fails to release (pedal pressed to the floor - shift lever does not move freely in and out of Reverse)

1　Leak in the clutch hydraulic system. Check the master cylinder, slave cylinder and lines (Chapters 1 and 8).
2　Clutch plate warped or damaged (Chapter 8).
3　Broken release bearing or fork (Chapter 8).

28　Clutch slips (engine speed increases with no increase in vehicle speed)

1　Clutch plate oil-soaked or lining worn. Remove clutch (Chapter 8) and inspect.
2　Clutch plate not seated. It may take 30 or 40 normal starts for a new one to seat.
3　Pressure plate worn (Chapter 8).

29　Grabbing (chattering) as clutch is engaged

1　Oil on clutch plate lining. Remove (Chapter 8) and inspect. Correct any leakage source.
2　Worn or loose engine or transmission mounts. These units move slightly when the clutch is released. Inspect the mounts and bolts (Chapter 2).
3　Worn splines on clutch plate hub. Remove the clutch components (Chapter 8) and inspect.
4　Warped pressure plate or flywheel. Remove the clutch components and inspect.

30　Squeal or rumble with clutch fully engaged (pedal released)

Release bearing binding on transmission bearing retainer. Remove clutch components (Chapter 8) and check bearing. Remove any burrs or nicks; clean and relubricate bearing retainer before installing.

31　Squeal or rumble with clutch fully disengaged (pedal depressed)

1　Worn, defective or broken release bearing (Chapter 8).
2　Worn or broken pressure plate springs (or diaphragm fingers) (Chapter 8).

32　Clutch pedal stays on floor when disengaged

1　Linkage or release bearing binding. Inspect the linkage or remove the clutch components as necessary.
2　Make sure proper pedal stop (bumper) is installed.

Manual transmission
Note: *All the following references are in Chapter 7A, unless noted.*

33　Noisy in Neutral with engine running

1　Input shaft bearing worn.

2　Damaged main drive gear bearing.
3　Worn countershaft bearings.
4　Worn or damaged countershaft endplay shims.

34　Noisy in all gears

1　Any of the above causes, and/or:
2　Insufficient lubricant (see the checking procedures in Chapter 1).

35　Noisy in one particular gear

1　Worn, damaged or chipped gear teeth for that particular gear.
2　Worn or damaged synchronizer for that particular gear.

36　Slips out of high gear

1　Transmission loose on clutch housing.
2　Dirt between the transmission case and engine or misalignment of the transmission.

37　Difficulty in engaging gears

1　Clutch not releasing completely (see clutch adjustment in Chapter 1).
2　Loose or damaged shifter. Make a thorough inspection, replacing parts as necessary.

38　Oil leakage

1　Excessive amount of lubricant in the transmission (see Chapter 1 for correct checking procedures). Drain lubricant as required.
2　Transmission oil seal in need of replacement.

Automatic transmission
Note: *Due to the complexity of the automatic transmission, it's difficult for the home mechanic to properly diagnose and service this component. For problems other than the following, the vehicle should be taken to a dealer service department or a transmission shop.*

39　General shift mechanism problems

Chapter 7B deals with checking and adjusting the shift cable on automatic transmissions. Common problems that may be attributed to poorly adjusted cable are:
a) *Engine starting in gears other than Park or Neutral.*

b) *Indicator on shifter pointing to a gear other than the one actually being selected.*
c) *Vehicle moves when in Park.*

40 Transmission will not downshift with accelerator pedal pressed to the floor

Since these transmissions are electronically controlled, check for any diagnostic trouble codes stored in the PCM. The actual repair will most likely have to be performed by a qualified repair shop with the proper equipment.

41 Transmission slips, shifts rough, is noisy or has no drive in forward or reverse gears

1   There are many probable causes for the above problems, but the home mechanic should be concerned with only one possibility - fluid level.
2   Before taking the vehicle to a repair shop, check the level and condition of the fluid as described in Chapter 1. Correct fluid level as necessary or change the fluid and filter if needed. If the problem persists, have a professional diagnose the probable cause.

42 Fluid leakage

1   Automatic transmission fluid is a deep red color. Fluid leaks should not be confused with engine oil, which can easily be blown by airflow to the transmission.
2   To pinpoint a leak, first remove all built-up dirt and grime from around the transmission. Degreasing agents and/or steam cleaning will achieve this. With the underside clean, drive the vehicle at low speeds so airflow will not blow the leak far from its source. Raise the vehicle and determine where the leak is coming from. Common areas of leakage are:
a) *Pan: Tighten the mounting bolts and/or replace the pan gasket as necessary (see Chapter 7B).*
b) *Filler pipe: Replace the rubber seal where the pipe enters the transmission case.*
c) *Transmission oil lines: Tighten the connectors where the lines enter the transmission case and/or replace the lines.*
d) *Vent pipe: Transmission overfilled and/or water in fluid (see checking procedures, Chapter 1).*
e) *Speedometer connector: Replace the O-ring where the speedometer sensor enters the transmission case (Chapter 7B).*

Transfer case

43 Transfer case is difficult to shift into the desired range

1   Speed may be too great to permit engagement. Stop the vehicle and shift into the desired range.
2   Shift linkage loose, bent or binding. Check the linkage for damage or wear and replace or lubricate as necessary (Chapter 7C).
3   If the vehicle has been driven on a paved surface for some time, the driveline torque can make shifting difficult. Stop and shift into two-wheel drive on paved or hard surfaces.
4   Insufficient or incorrect grade of lubricant. Drain and refill the transfer case with the specified lubricant. (Chapter 1).
5   Worn or damaged internal components. Disassembly and overhaul of the transfer case, by a qualified shop, may be necessary.

44 Transfer case noisy in all gears

Insufficient or incorrect grade of lubricant. Drain and refill (Chapter 1).

45 Noisy or jumps out of four-wheel drive Low range

1   Transfer case not fully engaged. Stop the vehicle, shift into Neutral and then engage 4L.
2   Shift linkage loose, worn or binding. Tighten, repair or lubricate linkage as necessary.
3   Shift fork cracked, inserts worn or fork binding on the rail. Disassemble and repair as necessary (Chapter 7C).

46 Lubricant leaks from the vent or output shaft seals

1   Transfer case is overfilled. Drain to the proper level (Chapter 1).
2   Vent is clogged or jammed closed. Clear or replace the vent.
3   Output shaft seal incorrectly installed or damaged. Replace the seal and check contact surfaces for nicks and scoring.

Driveshaft

47 Oil leak at seal end of driveshaft

Defective transmission or transfer case oil seal. See Chapter 7 for replacement procedures. While this is done, check the splined yoke for burrs or a rough condition that may be damaging the seal. Burrs can be removed with crocus cloth or a fine whetstone.

48 Knock or clunk when the transmission is under initial load (just after transmission is put into gear)

1   Loose or disconnected rear suspension components. Check all mounting bolts, nuts and bushings (see Chapter 10).
2   Loose driveshaft bolts. Inspect all bolts and nuts and tighten them to the specified torque.
3   Worn or damaged universal joint bearings. Check for wear (see Chapter 8).

49 Metallic grinding sound consistent with vehicle speed.

Pronounced wear in the universal joint bearings. Check as described in Chapter 8.

50 Vibration

Note: *Before assuming that the driveshaft is at fault, make sure the tires are perfectly balanced and perform the following test.*
1   Install a tachometer inside the vehicle to monitor engine speed as the vehicle is driven. Drive the vehicle and note the engine speed at which the vibration (roughness) is most pronounced. Now shift the transmission to a different gear and bring the engine speed to the same point.
2   If the vibration occurs at the same engine speed (rpm) regardless of which gear the transmission is in, the driveshaft is NOT at fault since the driveshaft speed varies.
3   If the vibration decreases or is eliminated when the transmission is in a different gear at the same engine speed, refer to the following probable causes.
4   Bent or dented driveshaft. Inspect and replace as necessary (see Chapter 8).
5   Undercoating or built-up dirt, etc. on the driveshaft. Clean the shaft thoroughly and recheck.
6   Worn universal joint bearings. Remove and inspect (see Chapter 8).
7   Driveshaft and/or companion flange out of balance. Check for missing weights on the shaft. Remove the driveshaft (see Chapter 8) and reinstall 180-degrees from original position, then retest. Have the driveshaft professionally balanced if the problem persists.

Axles

51 Noise

1   Road noise. No corrective procedures available.
2   Tire noise. Inspect tires and check tire

pressures (Chapter 1).
3   Rear wheel bearings loose, worn or damaged (Chapter 8).

52   Vibration

See probable causes under *Driveshaft*. Proceed under the guidelines listed for the driveshaft. If the problem persists, check the rear wheel bearings by raising the rear of the vehicle and spinning the rear wheels by hand. Listen for evidence of rough (noisy) bearings. Remove and inspect (see Chapter 8).

53   Oil leakage

1   Pinion seal damaged (see Chapter 8).
2   Axleshaft oil seals damaged (see Chapter 8).
3   Differential inspection cover leaking. Tighten the bolts or replace the gasket as required (see Chapters 1 and 8).

Driveaxles (4WD)

54   Clicking noise on turns

Worn or damaged outboard CV joints (Chapter 8).

55   Shudder or vibration during acceleration

1   Excessive toe-in. Have alignment checked.
2   Incorrect spring heights (Chapter 10).
3   Worn or damaged inboard or outboard CV joints (Chapter 8).
4   Sticking inboard CV joint assembly (Chapter 8).

56   Vibration at highway speeds

1   Out-of-balance front wheels and/or tires (Chapters 1 and 10).
2   Out-of-round front tires Chapters 1 and 10).
3   Worn CV joints (Chapter 8).

Brakes

Note: *Before assuming that a brake problem exists, make sure that the tires are in good condition and inflated properly (see Chapter 1), that the front-end alignment is correct and that the vehicle is not loaded with weight in an unequal manner.*

57   Vehicle pulls to one side during braking

1   Defective, damaged or oil contaminated disc brake pads or shoes on one side. Inspect as described in Chapter 9.
2   Excessive wear of brake shoe or pad material or drum/disc on one side. Inspect and correct as necessary.
3   Loose or disconnected front suspension components. Inspect and tighten all bolts to the specified torque (Chapter 10).
4   Defective drum brake or caliper assembly. Remove the drum or caliper and inspect for a stuck piston or other damage (Chapter 9).
5   Inadequate lubrication of front brake caliper slide rails. Remove caliper and lubricate slide rails (Chapter 9).

58   Noise (high-pitched squeal with the brakes applied)

1   Disc brake pads worn out. The noise comes from the wear sensor rubbing against the disc (does not apply to all vehicles) or the actual pad backing plate itself if the material is completely worn away. Replace the pads with new ones immediately (Chapter 9). If the pad material has worn completely away, the brake discs should be inspected for damage as described in Chapter 9.
2   Missing or damaged brake pad insulators (disc brakes). Replace pad insulators (see Chapter 9).
3   Linings contaminated with dirt or grease. Replace pads or shoes.
4   Incorrect linings. Replace with correct linings.

59   Excessive brake pedal travel

1   Partial brake system failure. Inspect the entire system (Chapter 9) and correct as required.
2   Insufficient fluid in the master cylinder. Check (Chapter 1), add fluid and bleed the system if necessary (Chapter 9).
3   Rear drum brakes not adjusting properly. Make a series of starts and stops while the vehicle is in Reverse. If this does not correct the situation, remove the drums and inspect the self-adjusters (Chapter 9).

60   Brake pedal feels spongy when depressed

1   Air in the hydraulic lines. Bleed the brake system (Chapter 9).
2   Faulty flexible hoses. Inspect all system hoses and lines. Replace parts as necessary.
3   Master cylinder mounting bolts/nuts loose.
4   Master cylinder defective (Chapter 9).

61   Excessive effort required to stop vehicle

1   Power brake booster not operating properly (see check in Chapter 1, repairs in Chapter 9).
2   Excessively worn linings or pads. Inspect and replace if necessary (Chapter 9).
3   One or more caliper pistons or wheel cylinders seized or sticking. Inspect and rebuild as required (Chapter 9).
4   Brake linings or pads contaminated with oil or grease. Inspect and replace as required (Chapter 9).
5   New pads or shoes installed and not yet seated. It will take a while for the new material to seat against the drum (or disc).

62   Pedal travels to the floor with little resistance

1   Little or no fluid in the master cylinder reservoir caused by leaking wheel cylinder(s), leaking caliper piston(s), loose, damaged or disconnected brake lines. Inspect the entire system and correct as necessary.
2   Worn master cylinder seals (Chapter 9).

63   Brake pedal pulsates during brake application

1   Caliper improperly installed. Remove and inspect (Chapter 9).
2   Disc or drum defective. Remove (Chapter 9) and check for excessive lateral runout and parallelism. Have the disc or drum resurfaced or replace it with a new one.

Suspension and steering systems

64   Vehicle pulls to one side

1   Tire pressures uneven or tires mismatched (Chapter 1).
2   Defective tire (Chapter 1).
3   Excessive wear in suspension or steering components (Chapter 10).
4   Front end in need of alignment.
5   Front brakes dragging. Inspect the brakes as described in Chapter 9.

65   Shimmy, shake or vibration

1   Tire or wheel out-of-balance or out-of-round. Have professionally balanced.
2   Loose, worn or out-of-adjustment front wheel bearings (Chapter 1).
3   Shock absorbers and/or suspension components worn or damaged (Chapter 10).

66   Excessive pitching and/or rolling around corners or during braking

1   Defective shock absorbers. Replace as a set (Chapter 10).
2   Broken or weak springs and/or suspension components. Inspect as described in Chapter 10.

67   Excessively stiff steering

1   Lack of fluid in power steering fluid reservoir (Chapter 1).
2   Incorrect tire pressures (Chapter 1).
3   Lack of lubrication at steering joints (see Chapter 1).
4   Front end out of alignment.
5   Lack of power assistance (see Section 69).

68   Excessive play in steering

1   Loose front wheel bearings (Chapters 1 and 10).

2   Excessive wear in suspension or steering components (Chapter 10).
3   Steering gearbox damaged or out of adjustment (Chapter 10).

69   Lack of power assistance

1   Drivebelt faulty (Chapter 1).
2   Fluid level low (Chapter 1).
3   Hoses or lines restricted. Inspect and replace parts as necessary.
4   Air in power steering system. Bleed the system (Chapter 10).

70   Excessive tire wear (not specific to one area)

1   Incorrect tire pressures (Chapter 1).
2   Tires out-of-balance. Have professionally balanced.
3   Wheels damaged. Inspect and replace as necessary.
4   Suspension or steering components excessively worn (Chapter 10).

71   Excessive tire wear on outside edge

1   Inflation pressures incorrect (Chapter 1).
2   Excessive speed in turns.
3   Front-end alignment incorrect. Have professionally aligned.
4   Suspension arm bent or twisted (Chapter 10).

72   Excessive tire wear on inside edge

1   Inflation pressures incorrect (Chapter 1).
2   Front-end alignment incorrect. Have professionally aligned.
3   Loose or damaged steering components (Chapter 10).

73   Tire tread worn in one place

1   Tires out-of-balance.
2   Damaged or buckled wheel. Inspect and replace if necessary.
3   Defective tire (Chapter 1).

Notes

Chapter 1
Tune-up and routine maintenance

Contents

Specifications

Recommended lubricants and fluids

Note: *Listed here are manufacturer recommendations at the time this manual was written. Manufacturers occasionally upgrade their fluid and lubricant specifications, so check with your local auto parts store for current recommendations.*

Engine oil type	API grade "certified for gasoline engines"
Engine oil viscosity	
2004 models (all)	SAE 5W-30
2005 and later models	
Dakota	SAE 5W-30
Durango	
3.7L V6 and 4.7L V8 engines	SAE 5W-30
5.7L V8 (Hemi) engine	SAE 5W-20
Automatic transmission fluid type	Mopar® ATF+4, automatic transmission fluid
Coolant	50/50 mixture of Mopar 5 year/100,000 mile Formula antifreeze/coolant with HOAT (Hybrid Organic Additive Technology) and water

Note: *Most models are filled with a 50/50 mixture of Mopar® 5 year/100,000 mile coolant that shouldn't be mixed with other coolants.*

Manual transmission lubricant type	Mopar® ATF+4, automatic transmission fluid
Transfer case lubricant type	Mopar® ATF+4, automatic transmission fluid
Differential lubricant type	
Rear axle	SAE 75W-140 Synthetic gear lubricant or equivalent*
Front axle (4WD models)	SAE 75W-90 Multi-purpose type, GL-5 gear lubricant or equivalent
Brake fluid type	DOT 3 brake fluid
Power steering fluid	Mopar® ATF+4, automatic transmission fluid

*Limited slip differential add 4 ounces Mopar® limited-slip additive friction modifier or equivalent, to the specified lubricant.

Capacities*

Cooling system	16.2 quarts
Engine oil (with filter change)	
V6 engine	5 quarts
4.7L V8 engine	6 quarts
5.7L V8 engine	7 quarts
Automatic transmission (drain and refill)	
42RLE	4 quarts
545RFE	
2WD	5.4 quarts
4WD	6.4 quarts
Manual transmission	
G238 (Dakota)	2.3 quarts
Transfer case	
NV144 (Durango)	1.8 pints
NV244 GENII (Durango)	3.4 pints
NV233 (Dakota)	2.5 pints
NV244 (Dakota)	2.85 pints
Front axle (4WD)	
C205F	1.75 quarts
Rear axle**	
8-1/4 inch	2.18 quarts
9-1/4 inch	2.25 quarts

*All capacities approximate. Add as necessary to bring up to the appropriate level.
**Add four ounces of friction modifier if equipped with a limited slip differential.

Ignition system

Spark plug type	
V6 engine	ZFR6F-11G (NGK)
4.7L V8 engine	RC12MCC4
5.7L V8 engine	Champion RE14MCC4
Spark plug gap	
V6 engine	0.042 inch
4.7L V8 engine	0.040 inch
5.7L V8 engine	0.045 inch
Firing order	
V6 engine	1-6-5-4-3-2
V8 engines (all)	1-8-4-3-6-5-7-2

Cylinder locations - 3.7L V6 engine

Brakes

Disc brake pad lining thickness (minimum)	1/8 inch
Parking brake shoe lining thickness (minimum)	1/16 inch

Torque specifications

Ft-lbs (unless otherwise specified)

Automatic transmission pan bolts	
42RLE transmission	165 in-lbs
545RFE transmission	105 in-lbs
Differential cover bolts	
Dakota	30
Durango	32
Drivebelt tensioner mounting bolt	30
Drivebelt tensioner pulley bolt (3.7L/4.7L engines)	45
Manual transmission drain/fill plug	37
Engine oil drain plug	25
Spark plugs	
V6 and 4.7L V8 engines	20
5.7L V8 engine (Hemi)	156 in-lbs
Transfer case drain/fill plug	15 to 25
Wheel lug nuts	85 to 115

Cylinder locations - 4.7L and 5.7L (Hemi) V8 engines

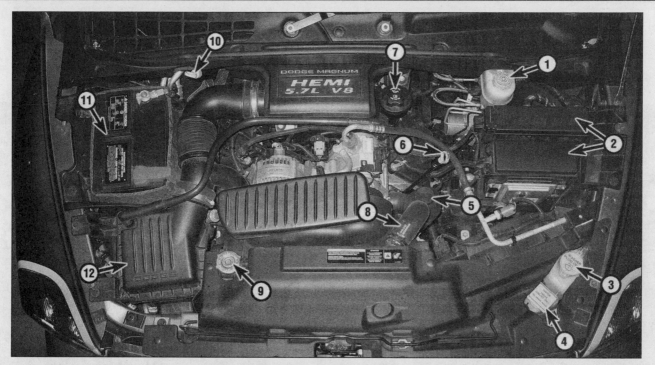

Durango engine compartment layout (5.7L V8 [Hemi] model shown)

1	Brake fluid reservoir	6	Engine oil dipstick	10	Automatic transmission fluid dipstick
2	Underhood fuse/relay blocks	7	Engine oil filler cap	11	Battery
3	Windshield washer fluid reservoir	8	Upper radiator hose	12	Air filter housing
4	Coolant reservoir	9	Radiator cap		
5	Power steering fluid reservoir				

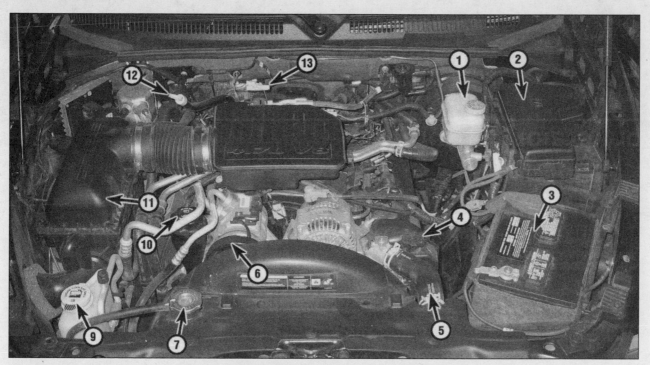

Dakota engine compartment layout (4.7L V8 model shown)

1	Brake fluid reservoir	6	Drivebelt	10	Engine oil filler cap
2	Underhood fuse/relay block	7	Radiator cap	11	Air filter housing
3	Battery	8	Windshield washer fluid reservoir	12	Automatic transmission fluid dipstick
4	Power steering fluid reservoir	9	Coolant reservoir	13	Engine oil dipstick
5	Upper radiator hose				

Typical engine compartment underside components (5.7L [Hemi] V8 shown, others similar)

1   Radiator drain fitting
2   Lower radiator hose
3   Engine oil filter
4   Front brake caliper
5   Front shock absorber
6   Engine oil drain plug
7   Automatic transmission pan

Typical rear underside components (Durango)

1	Rear brake caliper	3	Shock absorber	5	Fuel tank
2	Brake hose	4	Differential check/fill plug	6	Muffler

1 Dodge Dakota and Durango Maintenance schedule

The maintenance intervals in this manual are provided with the assumption that you, not the dealer, will be doing the work. These are the minimum maintenance intervals recommended by the factory for vehicles that are driven daily. If you wish to keep your vehicle in peak condition at all times, you may wish to perform some of these procedures even more often. Because frequent maintenance enhances the efficiency, performance and resale value of your car, we encourage you to do so. If you drive in dusty areas, tow a trailer, idle or drive at low speeds for extended periods or drive for short distances (less than four miles) in below freezing temperatures, shorter intervals are also recommended.

When your vehicle is new, it should be serviced by a factory authorized dealer service department to protect the factory warranty. In many cases, the initial maintenance check is done at no cost to the owner.

Every 250 miles or weekly, whichever comes first

Check the engine oil level (see Section 4)
Check the engine coolant level (see Section 4)
Check the brake and clutch fluid level (see Section 4)
Check the power steering fluid level (see Section 4)
Check the windshield washer fluid level (see Section 4)
Check the automatic transmission fluid level (see Section 4)
Check the tires and tire pressures (see Section 5)
Check the operation of all lights
Check the horn operation

Every 3,000 miles or 3 months, whichever comes first

All items listed above, plus:
Change the engine oil and filter (see Section 6)

Every 6,000 miles or 6 months, whichever comes first

All items listed above, plus:
Check the wiper blade condition (see Section 7)
Check and clean the battery and terminals (see Section 8)
Rotate the tires (see Section 9)
Check the seat belts (see Section 10)
Inspect underhood hoses (see Section 11)
Check the cooling system hoses and connections for leaks and damage (see Section 12)
Check the brake hoses (see Section 13)
Check the suspension, steering components and driveaxle boots (see Section 14)
Check the exhaust pipes and hangers (see Section 15)

Every 15,000 miles or 12 months, whichever comes first

All items listed above, plus:
Check the brake system (see Section 16)*
Check the drivebelts and replace if necessary (see Section 17)
Check the fuel system hoses and connections for leaks and damage (see Section 18)
Check the manual transmission lubricant level (see Section 19)
Check the transfer case lubricant level (see Section 19)
Check the differential lubricant level (Section 19)

Every 30,000 miles or 24 months, whichever comes first

All items listed above, plus:
Replace the air filter element (see Section 20)
Change the brake fluid (see Section 21)
Replace the spark plugs (see Section 22)
Check the ignition coils (see Section 23)

Every 60,000 miles or 48 months, whichever comes first

All items listed above, plus:
Check and replace, if necessary, the PCV valve (see Section 24)

Every 72,000 miles

Change the manual transmission lubricant (see Section 25)
Change the transfer case lubricant (see Section 25)
Change the differential lubricant (see Section 25)

Every 60 months (regardless of mileage)

Service the cooling system (drain, flush and refill) (see Section 26)

Every 100,000 miles

Change the automatic transaxle fluid and filter (Section 27)**

* This item is affected by "severe" operating conditions as described below. If your vehicle is operated under "severe" conditions, perform all maintenance indicated with an asterisk (*) at 3000 mile/3 month intervals (unless otherwise specified in the schedule). Severe conditions are indicated if you mainly operate your vehicle under one or more of the following conditions:

Operating in dusty areas
Towing a trailer
Idling for extended periods and/or low speed operation
Operating in extended temperatures below freezing (32-degrees F/0-degrees C)
If more the half of your driving is at high speeds in temperatures above 90-degrees F (32-degrees C)

**If operated under one or more of the following conditions, change the or automatic transaxle fluid lubricant every 30,000 miles:*

In heavy city traffic where the outside temperature regularly reaches 90-degrees F (32-degrees C) or higher
In hilly or mountainous terrain
Frequent towing of a trailer

2　Introduction

This Chapter is designed to help the home mechanic maintain the Dodge Dakota or Durango with the goals of maximum performance, economy, safety and reliability in mind.

Included is a master maintenance schedule, followed by procedures dealing specifically with each item on the schedule. Visual checks, adjustments, component replacement and other helpful items are included. Refer to the accompanying illustrations of the engine compartment and the underside of the vehicle for the locations of various components.

Servicing your vehicle in accordance with the mileage/time maintenance schedule and the step-by-step procedures will result in a planned maintenance program that should produce a long and reliable service life. Keep in mind that it's a comprehensive plan, so maintaining some items but not others at the specified intervals will not produce the same results.

As you service your vehicle, you will discover that many of the procedures can - and should - be grouped together because of the nature of the particular procedure you're performing or because of the close proximity of two otherwise unrelated components to one another.

For example, if the vehicle is raised for chassis lubrication, you should inspect the exhaust, suspension, steering and fuel systems while you're under the vehicle. When you're rotating the tires, it makes good sense to check the brakes since the wheels are already removed. Finally, let's suppose you have to borrow or rent a torque wrench. Even if you only need it to tighten the spark plugs, you might as well check the torque of as many critical fasteners as time allows.

The first step in this maintenance program is to prepare yourself before the actual work begins. Read through all the procedures you're planning to do, then gather up all the parts and tools needed. If it looks like you might run into problems during a particular job, seek advice from a mechanic or an experienced do-it-yourselfer.

Owner's Manual and VECI label information

Your vehicle owner's manual was written for your year and model and contains very specific information on component locations, specifications, fuse ratings, part numbers, etc. The Owner's Manual is an important resource for the do-it-yourselfer to have; if one was not supplied with your vehicle, it can generally be ordered from a dealer parts department.

Among other important information, the Vehicle Emissions Control Information (VECI) label contains specifications and procedures for applicable tune-up adjustments and, in some instances, spark plugs. The information on this label is the exact maintenance data recommended by the manufacturer. This data often varies by intended operating altitude, local emissions regulations, month of manufacture, etc.

This Chapter contains procedural details, safety information and more ambitious maintenance intervals than you might find in manufacturer's literature. However, you may also find procedures or specifications in your Owner's Manual or VECI label that differ with what's printed here. In these cases, the Owner's Manual or VECI label can be considered correct, since it is specific to your particular vehicle.

3　Tune-up general information

The term tune-up is used in this manual to represent a combination of individual operations rather than one specific procedure.

If, from the time the vehicle is new, the routine maintenance schedule is followed closely and frequent checks are made of fluid levels and high wear items, as suggested throughout this manual, the engine will be kept in relatively good running condition and the need for additional work will be minimized.

More likely than not, however, there will be times when the engine is running poorly due to lack of regular maintenance. This is even more likely if a used vehicle, which has not received regular and frequent maintenance checks, is purchased. In such cases, an engine tune-up will be needed outside of the regular routine maintenance intervals.

The first step in any tune-up or diagnostic procedure to help correct a poor running engine is a cylinder compression check. A compression check (see Chapter 2C) will help determine the condition of internal engine components and should be used as a guide for tune-up and repair procedures. If, for instance, a compression check indicates serious internal engine wear, a conventional tune-up will not improve the performance of the engine and would be a waste of time and money. Because of its importance, the compression check should be done by someone with the right equipment and the knowledge to use it properly.

The following procedures are those most often needed to bring a generally poor running engine back into a proper state of tune.

Minor tune-up

Check all engine-related fluids (Section 4)
Clean, inspect and test the battery (Section 8)
Check all underhood hoses (Section 11)
Check the cooling system (Section 12)

Major tune-up

All items listed under Minor tune-up, plus . . .
Check the drivebelt (Section 17)
Replace the air filter (Section 20)
Replace the spark plugs (Section 22)
Replace the PCV valve (Section 24)
Check the charging system (Chapter 5)

4   Fluid level checks (every 250 miles or weekly)

1   Fluids are an essential part of the lubrication, cooling, brake and windshield washer systems. Because the fluids gradually become depleted and/or contaminated during normal operation of the vehicle, they must be periodically replenished. See *Recommended lubricants and fluids* at the beginning of this Chapter before adding fluid to any of the following components. **Note:** *The vehicle must be on level ground when fluid levels are checked.*

Engine oil

Refer to illustrations 4.2a, 4.2b, 4.4, 4.6a and 4.6b

2   The oil level is checked with a dipstick, which is located at the rear or on the side of the engine **(see illustrations)**. The dipstick extends through a metal tube down into the oil pan.

3   The oil level should be checked before the vehicle has been driven, or about 5 minutes after the engine has been shut off. If the oil is checked immediately after driving the vehicle, some of the oil will remain in the upper part of the engine, resulting in an inaccurate reading on the dipstick.

4   Pull the dipstick out of the tube and wipe all the oil from the end with a clean rag or paper towel. Insert the clean dipstick all the

4.2a Engine oil dipstick location - 4.7L V8 engine (3.7L V6 similar)

way back into the tube and pull it out again. Note the oil at the end of the dipstick. At its highest point, the level should be between the ADD and FULL marks on the dipstick **(see illustration)**.

5   It takes one quart of oil to raise the level from the ADD mark to the FULL mark on the dipstick. Do not allow the level to drop below the ADD mark or oil starvation may cause engine damage. Conversely, overfilling the engine (adding oil above the FULL mark) may cause oil fouled spark plugs, oil leaks or oil seal failures.

4.2b Engine oil dipstick location - 5.7L V8 (Hemi) engine

6   To add oil, remove the filler cap **(see illustrations)**. After adding oil, wait a few minutes to allow the level to stabilize, then pull out the dipstick and check the level again. Add more oil if required. Install the filler cap and tighten it by hand only.

7   Checking the oil level is an important preventive maintenance step. A consistently low oil level indicates oil leakage through damaged seals, defective gaskets or past worn rings or valve guides. If the oil looks milky in color or has water droplets in it, the cylinder head gasket(s) may be blown or the head(s) or block may be cracked. The engine should be checked immediately. The condition of the oil should also be checked. Whenever you check the oil level, slide your thumb and index finger up the dipstick before wiping off the oil. If you see small dirt or metal particles clinging to the dipstick, the oil should be changed (see Section 6).

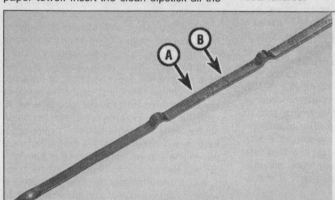

4.4 It takes about one quart of oil to raise the level from ADD mark (A) to the FULL mark (B)

Engine coolant

Refer to illustrations 4.8 and 4.9

Warning 1: *Do not allow antifreeze to come in contact with your skin or painted surfaces of the vehicle. Flush contaminated areas immediately with plenty of water. Don't store new coolant or leave old coolant lying around where it's accessible to children or pets - they're attracted by its sweet smell. Ingestion of even a small amount of coolant can be fatal! Wipe up garage floor and drip pan spills immediately. Keep antifreeze containers covered and repair cooling system leaks as soon as they're noticed.*

Warning 2: *Never remove the radiator cap when the engine is warm!*

8   All vehicles covered by this manual are equipped with a pressurized coolant recovery system. A plastic coolant reservoir, which catches coolant that escapes past the radiator cap, is located by the radiator in the engine compartment **(see illustration)**. When the engine cools down, the coolant is drawn back into the system.

9   The coolant level in the tank should be checked regularly. The level in the tank var-

4.6a Engine oil filler cap location - 4.7L V8 engine (3.7L V6 similar)

4.6b Engine oil filler cap location - 5.7L V8 (Hemi) engine

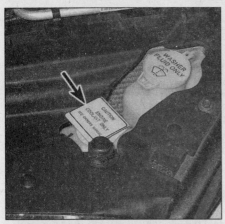

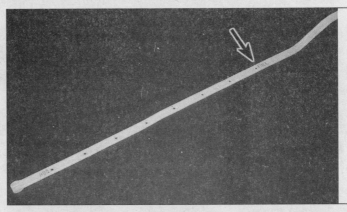

4.8 On Durango models the coolant reservoir is located in the left front corner of the engine compartment (on Dakota models it's at the right front)

4.9 When the engine is cold, the coolant level should be below the FULL mark on the dipstick (Durango models)

ies with the temperature of the engine. When the engine is cold, the coolant level should be below the FULL mark on the dipstick (Durango models) **(see illustration)**. On Dakota models the level can be viewed through the side of the reservoir. Once the engine has warmed up, the level should be at or near the FULL mark. If it isn't, remove the cap from the reservoir tank and add a 50/50 mixture of ethylene glycol based antifreeze and water.

10 Drive the vehicle and recheck the coolant level. If only a small amount of coolant is required to bring the system up to the proper level, water can be used. However, repeated additions of water will dilute the antifreeze and water solution. In order to maintain the proper ratio of antifreeze and water, always top up the coolant level with the correct mixture. Don't use rust inhibitors or additives. An empty plastic milk jug or bleach bottle makes an excellent container for mixing coolant.

11 If the coolant level drops consistently, there may be a leak in the system. Inspect the radiator, hoses, filler cap, drain plugs and water pump (see Section 12). If no leaks are noted, have the radiator cap or pressure tested by a service station.

12 If you have to remove the radiator cap, wait until the engine has cooled completely, then wrap a thick cloth around the cap and turn it to the first stop. If coolant or steam escapes, or if you hear a hissing noise, let the engine cool down longer, then remove the cap.

13 Check the condition of the coolant as well. It should be relatively clear. If it's brown or rust colored, the system should be drained, flushed and refilled. Even if the coolant appears to be normal, the corrosion inhibitors wear out, so it must be replaced at the specified intervals.

Brake and clutch fluid

Refer to illustration 4.15

14 The brake master cylinder is located in the driver's side of the engine compartment, near the firewall. The hydraulic clutch master cylinder used on manual transmission

vehicles is sealed at the factory and requires replacement if leaks develop.

15 To check the fluid level of the brake master cylinder, simply look at the MAX and MIN marks on the reservoir **(see illustration)**. The level should be within the specified distance from the maximum fill line.

16 If the level is low, wipe the top of the reservoir cover with a clean rag to prevent contamination of the brake system before lifting the cover.

17 Add only the specified brake fluid to the brake reservoir (refer to *Recommended lubricants and fluids* at the front of this Chapter or to your owner's manual). Mixing different types of brake fluid can damage the system. Fill the brake master cylinder reservoir only to the MAX line. **Warning:** *Use caution when filling either reservoir - brake fluid can harm your eyes and damage painted surfaces. Do not use brake fluid that is more than one year old or has been left open. Brake fluid absorbs moisture from the air. Excess moisture can cause a dangerous loss of braking.*

18 While the reservoir cap is removed, inspect the master cylinder reservoir for contamination. If deposits, dirt particles or water droplets are present, the system should be drained and refilled.

19 After filling the reservoir to the proper level, make sure the lid is properly seated to prevent fluid leakage and/or system pressure loss.

20 The fluid in the brake master cylinder will drop slightly as the brake pads at each wheel wear down during normal operation. If the master cylinder requires repeated replenishing to keep it at the proper level, this is an indication of leakage in the brake system, which should be corrected immediately. If the brake system shows an indication of leakage, check all brake lines and connections, along with the calipers and booster (see Section 16 for more information). If the hydraulic clutch system shows an indication of leakage, check all clutch lines and connections, along with the clutch release cylinder (see Chapter 8 for more information).

21 If, upon checking the brake master cylinder fluid level, you discover the reservoir empty or nearly empty, the system should be bled (see Chapter 9) and thoroughly inspected for leaks.

Power steering fluid

Refer to illustrations 4.23 and 4.27

22 Check the power steering fluid level periodically to avoid steering system problems, such as damage to the pump. **Caution:** *DO NOT hold the steering wheel against either stop (extreme left or right turn) for more than five seconds. If you do, the power steering pump could be damaged.*

23 The power steering reservoir, located at the left side of the engine compartment **(see illustration)**.

4.15 Never let the brake fluid level drop below the MIN mark

4.23 The power steering fluid reservoir is located on the left side of the engine

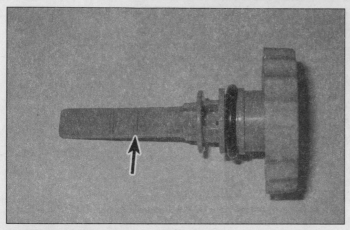

4.27 With the engine cold, the fluid level should be at the FULL COLD mark

4.30 On Durango models the windshield washer fluid reservoir is located at the left front corner of the engine compartment (on Dakota models it's at the right front)

24   For the check, the front wheels should be pointed straight ahead and the engine should be off.

25   Use a clean rag to wipe off the reservoir cap and the area around the cap. This will help prevent any foreign matter from entering the reservoir during the check.

26   Twist off the cap and check the temperature of the fluid at the end of the dipstick with your finger.

27   Wipe off the fluid with a clean rag, reinsert the dipstick, then withdraw it and read the fluid level. The fluid should be at the proper level, depending on whether it was checked hot or cold **(see illustration)**. Never allow the fluid level to drop below the lower mark on the dipstick.

28   If additional fluid is required, pour the specified type directly into the reservoir, using a funnel to prevent spills.

29   If the reservoir requires frequent fluid additions, all power steering hoses, hose connections, steering gear and the power steering pump should be carefully checked for leaks.

Windshield washer fluid

Refer to illustration 4.30

30   Fluid for the windshield washer system is stored in a plastic reservoir located at the left (Durango) or right (Dakota) front of the engine compartment **(see illustration)**.

31   In milder climates, plain water can be used in the reservoir, but it should be kept no more than 2/3 full to allow for expansion if the water freezes. In colder climates, use windshield washer system antifreeze, available at any auto parts store, to lower the freezing point of the fluid. Mix the antifreeze with water in accordance with the manufacturer's directions on the container. **Caution:** *Do not use cooling system antifreeze - it will damage the vehicle's paint.*

Automatic transmission

Refer to illustrations 4.34 and 4.37

32   The automatic transmission fluid level should be carefully maintained. Low fluid level can lead to slipping or loss of drive, while overfilling can cause foaming and loss of fluid.

33   With the parking brake set, start the engine, then move the shift lever through all the gear ranges, ending in Neutral. The fluid level must be checked with the vehicle level and the engine running at idle. **Note:** *Incorrect fluid level readings will result if the vehicle* has just been driven at high speeds for an extended period, in hot weather in city traffic, or if it has been pulling a trailer. If any of these conditions apply, wait until the fluid has cooled (about 30 minutes).

34   With the transmission at normal operating temperature, remove the dipstick from the filler tube. The dipstick is located at the rear of the engine compartment on the passenger's side **(see illustration)**. **Note:** *Normal operating temperature is reached after a few miles of driving.*

35   Wipe the fluid from the dipstick with a clean rag and push it back into the filler tube until the cap seats.

36   Pull the dipstick out again and note the fluid level.

37   At normal operating temperature, the fluid level should be between the two upper reference holes (HOT) **(see illustration)**. If additional fluid is required, add it a little at a time, directly into the tube using a funnel. **Caution:** *It's very important not to overfill the transmission.* Add the fluid a little at a time and keep checking the level until it's correct. **Note:** *Wait at least two minutes before rechecking the fluid level allowing the fluid to fully drain into the transmission.*

4.34 The automatic transmission fluid dipstick is located at the rear of the engine compartment

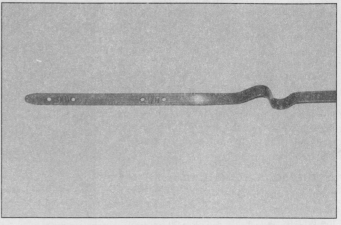

4.37 Check the fluid with the transmission at normal operating temperature - the level should be in the HOT range

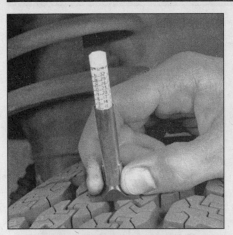

5.2 A tire tread depth indicator should be used to monitor tire wear - they are available at auto parts stores and service stations and cost very little

UNDERINFLATION

CUPPING

OVERINFLATION

Cupping may be caused by:
- Underinflation and/or mechanical irregularities such as out-of-balance condition of wheel and/or tire, and bent or damaged wheel.
- Loose or worn steering tie-rod or steering idler arm.
- Loose, damaged or worn front suspension parts.

INCORRECT TOE-IN
OR EXTREME CAMBER

FEATHERING DUE
TO MISALIGNMENT

5.3 This chart will help you determine the condition of your tires, the probable cause(s) of abnormal wear and the corrective action necessary

38   The condition of the fluid should also be checked along with the level. If the fluid at the end of the dipstick is a dark reddish-brown color, or if it smells burned, it should be changed. If you are in doubt about the condition of the fluid, purchase some new fluid and compare the two for color and smell.

5   Tire and tire pressure checks (every 250 miles or weekly)

Refer to illustrations 5.2, 5.3, 5.4a, 5.4b and 5.8

1   Periodic inspection of the tires may spare you the inconvenience of being stranded with a flat tire. It can also provide you with vital information regarding possible problems in the steering and suspension systems before major damage occurs.
2   The original tires on this vehicle are equipped with 1/2-inch wide bands that will appear when tread depth reaches 1/16-inch, at which point they can be considered worn out. Tread wear can be monitored with a simple, inexpensive device known as a tread depth indicator **(see illustration)**.
3   Note any abnormal tread wear **(see illustration)**. Tread pattern irregularities such as cupping, flat spots and more wear on one side than the other are indications of front end alignment and/or balance problems. If any of these conditions are noted, take the vehicle to a tire shop or service station to correct the problem.
4   Look closely for cuts, punctures and embedded nails or tacks. Sometimes a tire will hold air pressure for a short time or leak down very slowly after a nail has embedded itself in the tread. If a slow leak persists, check the valve stem core to make sure it is tight **(see illustration)**. Examine the tread for an object that may have embedded itself in the tire or for a plug that may have begun to leak (radial tire punctures are repaired with a plug that is installed in a puncture). If a puncture is suspected, it can be easily verified by spraying a solution of soapy water onto the puncture area **(see illustration)**. The soapy solution will bubble if there is a leak. Unless the puncture is unusually large, a tire shop or service station can usually repair the tire.
5   Carefully inspect the inner sidewall of each tire for evidence of brake fluid leakage. If you see any, inspect the brakes immediately.
6   Correct air pressure adds miles to the life span of the tires, improves mileage and enhances overall ride quality. Tire pressure cannot be accurately estimated by looking at a tire, especially if it's a radial. A tire pressure gauge is essential. Keep an accurate gauge in the glove compartment. The pressure gauges attached to the nozzles of air hoses at gas stations are often inaccurate.
7   Always check tire pressure when the tires are cold. Cold, in this case, means the vehicle has not been driven over a mile in the three hours preceding a tire pressure check. A pressure rise of four to eight pounds is not uncommon once the tires are warm.
8   Unscrew the valve cap protruding from the wheel or hubcap and push the gauge firmly onto the valve stem **(see illustration)**. Note the reading on the gauge and compare the figure to the recommended tire pressure

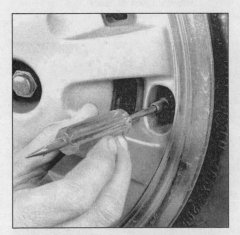

5.4a If a tire loses air on a steady basis, check the valve stem core first to make sure it's snug (special inexpensive wrenches are commonly available at auto parts stores)

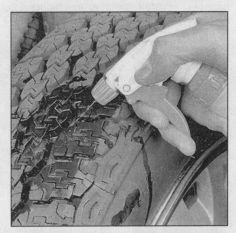

5.4b If the valve core is tight, raise the corner of the vehicle with the low tire and spray a soapy water solution onto the tread as the tire is turned slowly - slow leaks will cause small bubbles to appear

shown on the tire placard on the driver's side door. Be sure to reinstall the valve cap to keep dirt and moisture out of the valve stem mechanism. Check all four tires and, if necessary, add enough air to bring them up to the recommended pressure.

9   Don't forget to keep the spare tire inflated to the specified pressure (refer to the pressure molded into the tire sidewall).

6   Engine oil and filter change (every 3000 miles or 3 months)

Refer to illustrations 6.2, 6.7, 6.12 and 6.14

1   Frequent oil changes are the best preventive maintenance the home mechanic can give the engine, because aging oil becomes diluted and contaminated, which leads to premature engine wear.

2   Make sure you have all the necessary tools before you begin this procedure **(see illustration)**. You should also have plenty of rags or newspapers handy for mopping up any spills.

3   Access to the underside of the vehicle is greatly improved if the vehicle can be lifted on a hoist, driven onto ramps or supported by jackstands. **Warning:** *Do not work under a vehicle which is supported only by a bumper, hydraulic or scissors-type jack.*

4   If this is your first oil change, get under the vehicle and familiarize yourself with the locations of the oil drain plug and the oil filter. The engine and exhaust components will be warm during the actual work, so try to anticipate any potential problems before the engine and accessories are hot.

5   Park the vehicle on a level spot. Start the engine and allow it to reach its normal operating temperature. Warm oil and sludge will flow out more easily. Turn off the engine when it's warmed up. Remove the filler cap from the valve cover.

6   Raise the vehicle and support it securely on jackstands. **Warning:** *Never get beneath the vehicle when it is supported only by a*

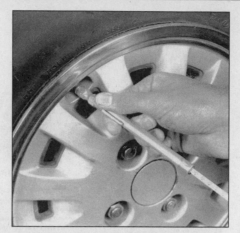

5.8 To extend the life of your tires, check the air pressure at least once a week with an accurate gauge (don't forget the spare!)

jack. The jack provided with your vehicle is designed solely for raising the vehicle to remove and replace the wheels. Always use jackstands to support the vehicle when it becomes necessary to place your body underneath the vehicle.

7   Being careful not to touch the hot exhaust components, place the drain pan under the drain plug in the bottom of the pan and remove the plug **(see illustration)**. You may want to wear gloves while unscrewing the plug the final few turns if the engine is hot.

8   Allow the old oil to drain into the pan. It may be necessary to move the pan farther under the engine as the oil flow slows to a trickle. Inspect the old oil for the presence of metal shavings and chips.

9   After all the oil has drained, wipe off the drain plug with a clean rag. Even minute metal particles clinging to the plug would immediately contaminate the new oil.

10   Clean the area around the drain plug opening, reinstall the plug and tighten it securely, but do not strip the threads.

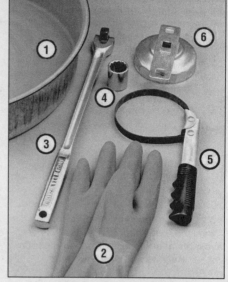

6.2 These tools are required when changing the engine oil and filter

1   **Drain pan** - *It should be fairly shallow in depth, but wide in order to prevent spills*

2   **Rubber gloves** - *When removing the drain plug and filter, it is inevitable that you will get oil on your hands (the gloves will prevent burns)*

3   **Breaker bar** - *Sometimes the oil drain plug is pretty tight and a long breaker bar is needed to loosen it*

4   **Socket** - *To be used with the breaker bar or a ratchet (must be the correct size to fit the drain plug)*

5   **Filter wrench** - *This is a metal band-type wrench, which requires clearance around the filter to be effective*

6   **Filter wrench** - *This type fits on the bottom of the filter and can be turned with a ratchet or beaker bar (different size wrenches are available for different types of filters)*

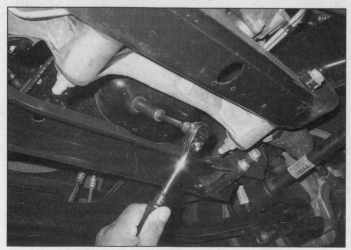

6.7 Use a socket to remove the oil drain plug and avoid rounding it off

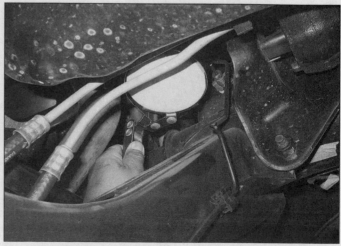

6.12 Use an oil filter wrench to remove the filter

11   Move the drain pan into position under the oil filter.

12   Loosen the oil filter **(see illustration)** by turning it counterclockwise with an oil filter wrench. Once the filter is loose, use your hands to unscrew it from the block. Keep the open end pointing up to prevent the oil inside the filter from spilling out. **Warning:** *The exhaust system may still be hot, so be careful.*

13   With a clean rag, wipe off the mounting surface on the block. If a residue of old oil is allowed to remain, it will smoke when the block is heated up. Also make sure that none of the old gasket remains stuck to the mounting surface. It can be removed with a scraper if necessary.

14   Compare the old filter with the new one to make sure they are the same type. Smear some clean engine oil on the rubber gasket of the new filter **(see illustration)**.

15   Attach the new filter to the engine, following the tightening directions printed on the filter canister or packing box. Most filter manufacturers recommend against using a filter wrench due to the possibility of overtightening and damaging the seal.

16   Remove all tools, rags, etc. from under the vehicle, being careful not to spill the oil in the drain pan, then lower the vehicle.

17   Add new oil to the engine through the oil filler cap in the valve cover. Use a funnel, if necessary, to prevent oil from spilling onto the top of the engine. Pour three quarts of fresh oil into the engine. Wait a few minutes to allow the oil to drain into the pan, then check the level on the oil dipstick (see Section 4). If the oil level is at or near the FULL mark on the dipstick, install the filler cap hand tight, start the engine and allow the new oil to circulate.

18   Allow the engine to run for about a minute. While the engine is running, look under the vehicle and check for leaks at the oil pan drain plug and around the oil filter. If either is leaking, stop the engine and tighten the plug or filter.

19   Wait a few minutes to allow the oil to trickle down into the pan, then recheck the level on the dipstick and, if necessary, add enough oil to bring the level to the FULL mark.

20   During the first few trips after an oil change, make it a point to check frequently for leaks and proper oil level.

21   The old oil drained from the engine cannot be reused in its present state and should be disposed of. Check with your local auto parts store, disposal facility or environmental agency to see if they will accept the oil for recycling. After the oil has cooled it can be drained into a container (capped plastic jugs, topped bottles, milk cartons, etc.) for transport to one of these disposal sites. Don't dispose of the oil by pouring it on the ground or down a drain!

6.14 Lubricate the oil filter gasket with clean engine oil before installing the filter on the engine

6   Attach the new wiper to the arm. Connection can be confirmed by an audible click.

7   Windshield wiper blade inspection and replacement (every 6000 miles or 6 months)

Refer to illustrations 7.5a and 7.5b

1   The windshield wiper and blade assembly should be inspected periodically for damage, loose components and cracked or worn blade elements.

2   Road film can build up on the wiper blades and affect their efficiency, so they should be washed regularly with a mild detergent solution.

3   The action of the wiping mechanism can loosen bolts, nuts and fasteners, so they should be checked and tightened, as necessary, at the same time the wiper blades are checked.

4   If the wiper blade elements are cracked, worn or warped, or no longer clean adequately, they should be replaced with new ones.

5   Lift the arm assembly away from the glass for clearance, press the release lever, then slide the wiper blade assembly out of the hook at the end of the arm **(see illustrations)**.

8   Battery check, maintenance and charging (every 6000 miles or 6 months)

Refer to illustrations 8.1, 8.6a, 8.6b, 8.7a and 8.7b

Warning: *Certain precautions must be followed when checking and servicing the battery. Hydrogen gas, which is highly flammable, is always present in the battery cells, so keep lighted tobacco and all other open flames and sparks away from the battery. The electrolyte inside the battery is actually diluted sulfuric acid, which will cause injury if splashed on your skin or in your eyes. It will also ruin clothes and painted surfaces. When removing the battery cables, always detach the negative cable first and hook it up last!*

1   A routine preventive maintenance program for the battery in your vehicle is the only way to ensure quick and reliable starts. But

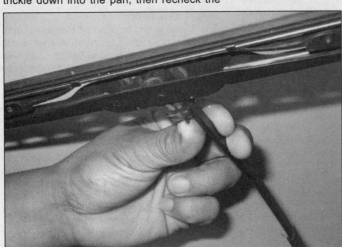

7.5a To release the blade holder, push the release lever . . .

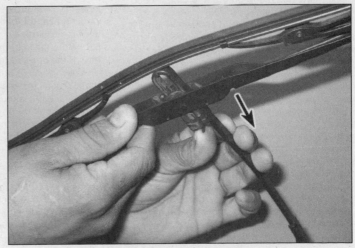

7.5b . . . and pull the wiper blade in the direction of the arrow to separate it from the arm

8.1 Tools and materials required for battery maintenance

1   **Face shield/safety goggles** - *When removing corrosion with a brush, the acidic particles can easily fly up into your eyes*

2   **Baking soda** - *A solution of baking soda and water can be used to neutralize corrosion*

3   **Petroleum jelly** - *A layer of this on the battery posts will help prevent corrosion*

4   **Battery post/cable cleaner** - *This wire brush cleaning tool will remove all traces of corrosion from the battery posts and cable clamps*

5   **Treated felt washers** - *Placing one of these on each post, directly under the cable clamps, will help prevent corrosion*

6   **Puller** - *Sometimes the cable clamps are very difficult to pull off the posts, even after the nut/bolt has been completely loosened. This tool pulls the clamp straight up and off the post without damage*

7   **Battery post/cable cleaner** - *Here is another cleaning tool which is a slightly different version of number 4 above, but it does the same thing*

8   **Rubber gloves** - *Another safety item to consider when servicing the battery; remember that's acid inside the battery!*

before performing any battery maintenance, make sure that you have the proper equipment necessary to work safely around the battery **(see illustration).**

2   There are also several precautions that should be taken whenever battery maintenance is performed. Before servicing the battery, always turn the engine and all accessories off and disconnect the cable from the negative terminal of the battery (see Chapter 5, Section 1).

3   The battery produces hydrogen gas,

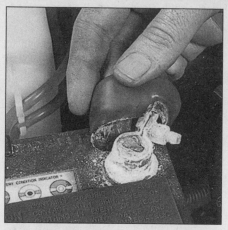

8.6a Battery terminal corrosion usually appears as light, fluffy powder

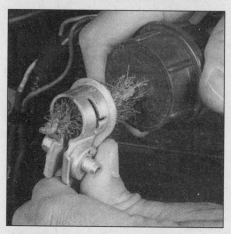

8.7a When cleaning the cable clamps, all corrosion must be removed

which is both flammable and explosive. Never create a spark, smoke or light a match around the battery. Always charge the battery in a ventilated area.

4   Electrolyte contains poisonous and corrosive sulfuric acid. Do not allow it to get in your eyes, on your skin on your clothes. Never ingest it. Wear protective safety glasses when working near the battery. Keep children away from the battery.

5   Note the external condition of the battery. If the positive terminal and cable clamp on your vehicle's battery is equipped with a rubber protector, make sure that it's not torn or damaged. It should completely cover the terminal. Look for any corroded or loose connections, cracks in the case or cover or loose hold-down clamps. Also check the entire length of each cable for cracks and frayed conductors.

6   If corrosion, which looks like white, fluffy deposits **(see illustration)** is evident, particularly around the terminals, the battery should be removed for cleaning. Loosen the cable clamp bolts with a wrench, being careful to remove the ground cable first, and slide them off the terminals **(see illustration).** Then disconnect the hold-down clamp bolt and nut, remove the clamp and lift the battery from the

8.6b Removing a cable from the battery post with a wrench - sometimes a pair of special battery pliers are required for this procedure if corrosion has caused deterioration of the nut hex (always remove the ground (-) cable first and hook it up last!)

8.7b Regardless of the type of tool used to clean the battery posts, a clean, shiny surface should be the result

engine compartment.

7   Clean the cable clamps thoroughly with a battery brush or a terminal cleaner and a solution of warm water and baking soda **(see illustration).** Wash the terminals and the top of the battery case with the same solution but make sure that the solution doesn't get into the battery. When cleaning the cables, terminals and battery top, wear safety goggles and rubber gloves to prevent any solution from coming in contact with your eyes or hands. Wear old clothes too - even diluted, sulfuric acid splashed onto clothes will burn holes in them. If the terminals have been extensively corroded, clean them up with a terminal cleaner **(see illustration).** Thoroughly wash all cleaned areas with plain water.

8   Make sure that the battery tray is in good condition and the hold-down clamp fasteners are tight. If the battery is removed from the tray, make sure no parts remain in the bottom of the tray when the battery is reinstalled.

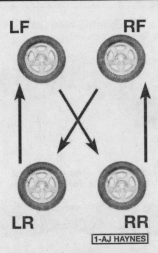

9.2 The recommended four-tire rotation pattern

When reinstalling the hold-down clamp bolts, do not overtighten them.

9   Information on removing and installing the battery can be found in Chapter 5. If you disconnected the cable(s) from the negative and/or positive battery terminals, see Chapter 5, Section 1. Information on jump starting can be found at the front of this manual. For more detailed battery checking procedures, refer to the *Haynes Automotive Electrical Manual.*

Cleaning

10   Corrosion on the hold-down components, battery case and surrounding areas can be removed with a solution of water and baking soda. Thoroughly rinse all cleaned areas with plain water.

11   Any metal parts of the vehicle damaged by corrosion should be covered with a zinc-based primer, then painted.

Charging

Warning: *When batteries are being charged, hydrogen gas, which is very explosive and flammable, is produced. Do not smoke or allow open flames near a charging or a recently charged battery. Wear eye protection when near the battery during charging. Also, make sure the charger is unplugged before connecting or disconnecting the battery from the charger.*

12   Slow-rate charging is the best way to restore a battery that's discharged to the point where it will not start the engine. It's also a good way to maintain the battery charge in a vehicle that's only driven a few miles between starts. Maintaining the battery charge is particularly important in the winter when the battery must work harder to start the engine and electrical accessories that drain the battery are in greater use.

13   It's best to use a one or two-amp battery charger (sometimes called a "trickle" charger). They are the safest and put the least strain on the battery. They are also the least expensive. For a faster charge, you can use

a higher amperage charger, but don't use one rated more than 1/10th the amp/hour rating of the battery. Rapid boost charges that claim to restore the power of the battery in one to two hours are hardest on the battery and can damage batteries not in good condition. This type of charging should only be used in emergency situations.

14   The average time necessary to charge a battery should be listed in the instructions that come with the charger. As a general rule, a trickle charger will charge a battery in 12 to 16 hours.

9   Tire rotation (every 6000 miles or 6 months)

Refer to illustration 9.2

1   The tires should be rotated at the specified intervals and whenever uneven wear is noticed.

2   The tires should be rotated in a specific pattern **(see illustration)**.

3   Refer to the information in *Jacking and towing* at the front of this manual for the proper procedures to follow when raising the vehicle and changing a tire. If the brakes are to be checked, don't apply the parking brake as stated. Make sure the tires are blocked to prevent the vehicle from rolling as it's raised.

4   Preferably, the entire vehicle should be raised at the same time. This can be done on a hoist or by jacking up each corner and then lowering the vehicle onto jackstands placed under the frame rails. Always use four jackstands and make sure the vehicle is safely supported.

5   After rotation, check and adjust the tire pressures as necessary. Tighten the lug nuts to the torque listed in this Chapter's Specifications.

10   Seat belt check (every 6000 miles or 6 months)

1   Check seat belts, buckles, latch plates and guide loops for obvious damage and signs of wear.

2   Where the seat belt receptacle bolts to the floor of the vehicle, check that the bolts are secure.

3   See if the seat belt reminder light comes on when the key is turned to the Run or Start position.

11   Underhood hose check and replacement (every 6000 miles or 6 months)

General

Caution: *Replacement of air conditioning hoses must be left to a dealer service department or air conditioning shop that has the equipment to depressurize the system safely*

and recover the refrigerant. Never remove air conditioning components or hoses until the system has been depressurized.

1   High temperatures in the engine compartment can cause the deterioration of the rubber and plastic hoses used for engine, accessory and emission systems operation. Periodic inspection should be made for cracks, loose clamps, material hardening and leaks. Information specific to the cooling system hoses can be found in Section 12.

2   Some, but not all, hoses are secured to their fittings with clamps. Where clamps are used, check to be sure they haven't lost their tension, allowing the hose to leak. If clamps aren't used, make sure the hose has not expanded and/or hardened where it slips over the fitting, allowing it to leak.

Vacuum hoses

3   It's quite common for vacuum hoses, especially those in the emissions system, to be color-coded or identified by colored stripes molded into them. Various systems require hoses with different wall thickness, collapse resistance and temperature resistance. When replacing hoses, be sure the new ones are made of the same material.

4   Often the only effective way to check a hose is to remove it completely from the vehicle. If more than one hose is removed, be sure to label the hoses and fittings to ensure correct installation.

5   When checking vacuum hoses, be sure to include any plastic T-fittings in the check. Inspect the fittings for cracks and the hose where it fits over the fitting for distortion, which could cause leakage.

6   A small piece of vacuum hose (1/4-inch inside diameter) can be used as a stethoscope to detect vacuum leaks. Hold one end of the hose to your ear and probe around vacuum hoses and fittings, listening for the "hissing" sound characteristic of a vacuum leak. **Warning:** *When probing with the vacuum hose stethoscope, be very careful not to come into contact with moving engine components such as the drivebelt, cooling fan, etc.*

Fuel hose

Warning: *There are certain precautions that must be taken when inspecting or servicing fuel system components. Work in a well-ventilated area and do not allow open flames (cigarettes, appliances, etc.) or bare light bulbs near the work area. Mop up any spills immediately and do not store fuel soaked rags where they could ignite. The fuel system is under high pressure, so if any fuel lines are to be disconnected, the pressure in the system must be relieved first (see Chapter 4 for more information).*

7   Check all rubber fuel lines for deterioration and chafing. Check especially for cracks in areas where the hose bends and just before fittings, such as where a hose attaches to the fuel filter.

8   High quality fuel line, made specifically for high-pressure fuel injection systems, must

be used for fuel line replacement. Never, under any circumstances, use unreinforced vacuum line, clear plastic tubing or water hose for fuel lines.

9   Spring-type clamps are commonly used on fuel lines. These clamps often lose their tension over a period of time, and can be "sprung" during removal. Replace all spring-type clamps with screw clamps whenever a hose is replaced.

Metal lines

10   Sections of metal line are routed along the frame, between the fuel tank and the engine. Check carefully to be sure the line has not been bent or crimped and that cracks have not started in the line.

11   If a section of metal fuel line must be replaced, only seamless steel tubing should be used, since copper and aluminum tubing don't have the strength necessary to withstand normal engine vibration.

12   Check the metal brake lines where they enter the master cylinder and brake proportioning unit for cracks in the lines or loose fittings. Any sign of brake fluid leakage calls for an immediate and thorough inspection of the brake system.

12   Cooling system check (every 6000 miles or 6 months)

Refer to illustration 12.4

1   Many major engine failures can be attributed to a faulty cooling system. If the vehicle is equipped with an automatic transmission, the cooling system also cools the transmission fluid and thus plays an important role in prolonging transmission life.

2   The cooling system should be checked with the engine cold. Do this before the vehicle is driven for the day or after it has been shut off for at least three hours.

3   Remove the cooling system pressure cap and thoroughly clean the cap, inside and out, with clean water. Also clean the filler neck on the radiator. All traces of corrosion should be removed. The coolant inside the radiator should be relatively transparent. If it is rust-colored, the system should be drained, flushed and refilled (see Section 26). If the coolant level is not up to the top, add additional antifreeze/coolant mixture (see Section 4).

4   Carefully check the large upper and lower radiator hoses along with the smaller diameter heater hoses that run from the engine to the firewall. Inspect each hose along its entire length, replacing any hose that is cracked, swollen or shows signs of deterioration. Cracks may become more apparent if the hose is squeezed **(see illustration)**. Regardless of condition, it's a good idea to replace hoses with new ones every two years.

5   Make sure all hose connections are tight. A leak in the cooling system will usually show up as white or rust-colored deposits on the areas adjoining the leak. If wire-type clamps

are used at the ends of the hoses, it may be a good idea to replace them with more secure screw-type clamps.

6   Use compressed air or a soft brush to remove bugs, leaves, etc. from the front of the radiator or air conditioning condenser. Be careful not to damage the delicate cooling fins or cut yourself on them.

7   Every other inspection, or at the first indication of cooling system problems, have the cap and system pressure tested. If you don't have a pressure tester, most repair shops will do this for a minimal charge.

13   Brake hose check (every 6000 miles or 6 months)

With the vehicle raised and supported securely on jackstands, the rubber hoses which connect the steel brake lines with the front and rear brake assemblies should be inspected for cracks, chafing of the outer cover, leaks, blisters and other damage. These are important and vulnerable parts of the brake system and inspection should be complete. A light and mirror will be helpful for a thorough check. If a hose exhibits any of the above conditions, replace it with a new one (see Chapter 9).

14   Suspension, steering and driveaxle boot check (every 6000 miles or 6 months)

Note: *The steering linkage and suspension components should be checked periodically. Worn or damaged suspension and steering linkage components can result in excessive and abnormal tire wear, poor ride quality and vehicle handling and reduced fuel economy. For detailed illustrations of the steering and suspension components, refer to Chapter 10.*

Shock absorber check

Refer to illustration 14.6

1   Park the vehicle on level ground, turn the engine off and set the parking brake. Check the tire pressures.

2   Push down at one corner of the vehicle, then release it while noting the movement of the body. It should stop moving and come to rest in a level position within one or two bounces.

3   If the vehicle continues to move up-and-down or if it fails to return to its original position, a worn or weak shock absorber is probably the reason.

4   Repeat the above check at each of the three remaining corners of the vehicle.

5   Raise the vehicle and support it securely on jackstands.

6   Check the shock absorbers for evidence of fluid leakage **(see illustration)**. A light film of fluid is no cause for concern. Make sure that any fluid noted is from the shocks and not from some other source. If leakage is noted,

Check for a chafed area that could fail prematurely.

Check for a soft area indicating the hose has deteriorated inside.

Overtightening the clamp on a hardened hose will damage the hose and cause a leak.

Check each hose for swelling and oil-soaked ends. Cracks and breaks can be located by squeezing the hose.

12.4 Hoses, like drivebelts, have a habit of failing at the worst possible time - to prevent the inconvenience of a blown radiator or heater hose, inspect them carefully as shown here

14.6 Check for signs of fluid leakage at this point on shock absorbers (rear shock shown)

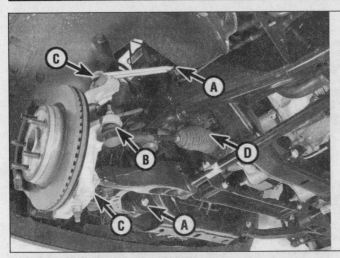

14.9 Examine the mounting points for the upper and lower control arms on the front suspension (A), the tie-rod ends (B), the balljoints (C), and the steering gear boots (D)

14.11 With the steering wheel in the locked position and the vehicle raised, grasp the front tire as shown and try to move it back-and-forth - if any play is noted, check the steering gear mounts and tie-rod ends for looseness

replace the shocks as a set.

7   Check the shocks to be sure that they are securely mounted and undamaged. Check the upper mounts for damage and wear. If damage or wear is noted, replace the shocks as a set (front or rear).

8   If the shocks must be replaced, refer to Chapter 10 for the procedure.

Steering and suspension check

Refer to illustrations 14.9 and 14.11

9   Visually inspect the steering and suspension components (front and rear) for damage and distortion. Look for damaged seals, boots and bushings and leaks of any kind. Examine the bushings where the control arms meet the chassis **(see illustration)**.

10   Clean the lower end of the steering knuckle. Have an assistant grasp the lower edge of the tire and move the wheel in-and-out while you look for movement at the steering knuckle-to-control arm balljoint. If there is any movement the suspension balljoint(s) must be replaced.

11   Grasp each front tire at the front and rear edges, push in at the front, pull out at the rear

and feel for play in the steering system components. If any freeplay is noted, check the idler arm and the tie-rod ends for looseness **(see illustration)**.

12   Additional steering and suspension system information and illustrations can be found in Chapter 10.

Driveaxle boot check (4WD models)

Refer to illustration 14.14

13   The driveaxle boots are very important because they prevent dirt, water and foreign material from entering and damaging the constant velocity (CV) joints. Oil and grease can cause the boot material to deteriorate prematurely, so it's a good idea to wash the boots with soap and water. Because it constantly pivots back and forth following the steering action of the front hub, the outer CV boot wears out sooner and should be inspected regularly.

14   Inspect the boots for tears and cracks as well as loose clamps **(see illustration)**. If there is any evidence of cracks or leaking lubricant, they must be replaced as described in Chapter 8.

15   Exhaust system check (every 6000 miles or 6 months)

Refer to illustrations 15.2a and 15.2b

1   With the engine cold (at least three hours after the vehicle has been driven), check the complete exhaust system from the manifold to the end of the tailpipe. Be careful around the catalytic converter, which may be hot even after three hours. The inspection should be done with the vehicle on a hoist to permit unrestricted access. If a hoist isn't available, raise the vehicle and support it securely on jackstands.

2   Check the exhaust pipes and connections for signs of leakage and/or corrosion indicating a potential failure. Make sure that all brackets and hangers are in good condition and tight **(see illustrations)**.

3   Inspect the underside of the body for holes, corrosion, open seams, etc. which may allow exhaust gasses to enter the passenger

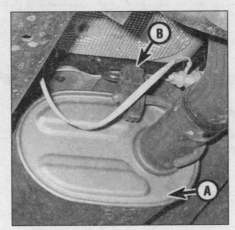

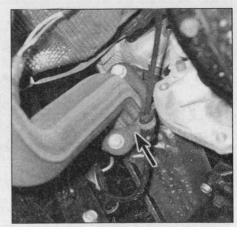

14.14 Inspect the inner and outer driveaxle boots on 4WD models for loose clamps, cracks or signs of leaking lubricant

15.2a Inspect the muffler (A) for signs of deterioration, and all hangers (B)

15.2b Inspect all flanged joints (arrow indicates pipe-to-manifold joint) for signs of exhaust gas leakage

16.7a With the wheel off, check the thickness of the inner pad through the inspection hole (front disc shown, rear disc caliper similar)

16.7b The outer pad is more easily checked at the edge of the caliper

compartment. Seal all body openings with silicone sealant or body putty.

4   Rattles and other noises can often be traced to the exhaust system, especially the hangers, mounts and heat shields. Try to move the pipes, mufflers and catalytic converter. If the components can come in contact with the body or suspension parts, secure the exhaust system with new brackets and hangers.

16   Brake system check (every 15,000 miles or 12 months)

Warning: *The dust created by the brake system is harmful to your health. Never blow it out with compressed air and don't inhale any of it. An approved filtering mask should be worn when working on the brakes. Do not, under any circumstances, use petroleum-based solvents to clean brake parts. Use brake system cleaner only!*
Note: *For detailed photographs of the brake*

system, refer to Chapter 9.
1   In addition to the specified intervals, the brakes should be inspected every time the wheels are removed or whenever a defect is suspected.
2   Any of the following symptoms could indicate a potential brake system defect: The vehicle pulls to one side when the brake pedal is depressed; the brakes make squealing or dragging noises when applied; brake pedal travel is excessive; the pedal pulsates; or brake fluid leaks, usually onto the inside of the tire or wheel.
3   Loosen the wheel lug nuts.
4   Raise the vehicle and place it securely on jackstands.
5   Remove the wheels (see *Jacking and towing* at the front of this book, or your owner's manual, if necessary).

Disc brakes

Refer to illustrations 16.7a, 16.7b and 16.9
6   There are two pads (an outer and an inner) in each caliper. The pads are visible with the wheels removed.
7   Check the pad thickness by looking

at each end of the caliper and through the inspection window in the caliper body **(see illustrations)**. If the lining material is less than the thickness listed in this Chapter's Specifications, replace the pads. **Note:** *Keep in mind that the lining material is riveted or bonded to a metal backing plate and the metal portion is not included in this measurement.*
8   If it is difficult to determine the exact thickness of the remaining pad material by the above method, or if you are at all concerned about the condition of the pads, remove the caliper(s), then remove the pads from the calipers for further inspection (refer to Chapter 9).
9   Once the pads are removed from the calipers, clean them with brake cleaner and re-measure them with a ruler or a vernier caliper **(see illustration).**
10   Measure the disc thickness with a micrometer to make sure that it still has service life remaining. If any disc is thinner than the specified minimum thickness, replace it (refer to Chapter 9). Even if the disc has service life remaining, check its condition. Look for scoring, gouging and burned spots. If these conditions exist, remove the disc and have it resurfaced (see Chapter 9).
11   Before installing the wheels, check all brake lines and hoses for damage, wear, deformation, cracks, corrosion, leakage, bends and twists, particularly in the vicinity of the rubber hoses at the calipers. Check the clamps for tightness and the connections for leakage. Make sure that all hoses and lines are clear of sharp edges, moving parts and the exhaust system. If any of the above conditions are noted, repair, reroute or replace the lines and/or fittings as necessary (see Chapter 9).

Drum brakes

Refer to illustration 16.15
12   On models with rear drum brakes, make sure the parking brake is off then tap on the outside of the drum with a rubber mallet to loosen it.

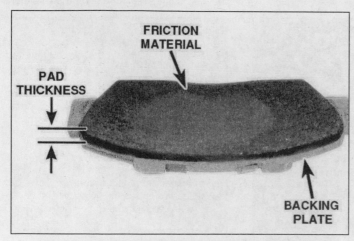

16.9 If a more precise measurement of pad thickness is necessary, remove the pads and measure the remaining friction material

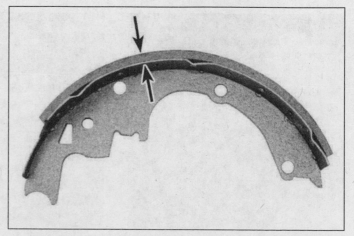

16.15 If the lining is bonded to the brake shoe, measure the lining thickness from the outer surface to the metal shoe. If the lining is riveted, measure from the lining outer surface to the rivet head

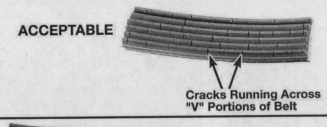

ACCEPTABLE

Cracks Running Across
"V" Portions of Belt

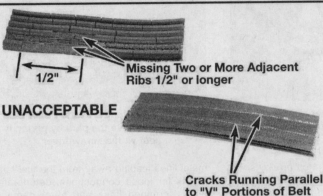

1/2"

**Missing Two or More Adjacent
Ribs 1/2" or longer**

UNACCEPTABLE

Cracks Running Parallel
to "V" Portions of Belt

**17.4 Here are some
of the more common
problems associated
with drivebelts
(check the belts
very carefully to
prevent an untimely
breakdown)**

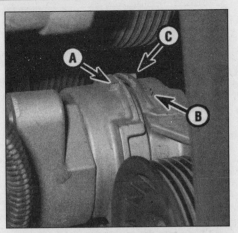

**17.5 Belt wear indicator marks are located
on the tensioner body - when the belt
reaches the maximum wear mark it
must be replaced**

A   *Stationary mark*
B   *When the belt is new, this mark will be
near the stationary mark*
C   *When this mark reaches the stationary
mark, the belt is worn out*

13   Remove the brake drums. If the drum still won't come off, refer to Chapter 9

14   With the drums removed, carefully clean the brake assembly with brake system cleaner. **Warning:** *Don't blow the dust out with compressed air and don't inhale any of it (it is harmful to your health).*

15   Note the thickness of the lining material on both front and rear brake shoes **(see illustration).** Compare the measurement with the limit given in this Chapter's Specifications; if any lining thickness is less than specified, then all of the brake shoes must be replaced (see Chapter 9). The shoes should also be replaced if they're cracked, glazed (shiny areas), or covered with brake fluid.

16   Make sure all the brake assembly springs are connected and in good condition.

17   Check the brake components for signs of fluid leakage. With your finger or a small screwdriver, carefully pry back the rubber cups on the wheel cylinder located at the top of the brake shoes. Any leakage here is an indication that the wheel cylinders should be replaced immediately (see Chapter 9). Also, check all hoses and connections for signs of leakage.

18   Wipe the inside of the drum with a clean rag and denatured alcohol or brake cleaner. Again, be careful not to breathe the dangerous asbestos dust.

19   Check the inside of the drum for cracks, score marks, deep scratches and "hard spots" which will appear as small discolored areas. If imperfections cannot be removed with fine emery cloth, the drum must be taken to an automotive machine shop for resurfacing.

20   Repeat the procedure for the remaining wheel. If the inspection reveals that all parts are in good condition, reinstall the brake drums, install the wheels and lower the vehicle to the ground.

Brake booster check

21   Sit in the driver's seat and perform the following sequence of tests.

22   With the brake fully depressed, start the engine - the pedal should move down a little when the engine starts.

23   With the engine running, depress the brake pedal several times - the travel distance should not change.

24   Depress the brake, stop the engine and hold the pedal in for about 30 seconds - the pedal should neither sink nor rise.

25   Restart the engine, run it for about a minute and turn it off. Then firmly depress the brake several times - the pedal travel should decrease with each application.

26   If your brakes do not operate as described, the brake booster has failed. Refer to Chapter 9 for the replacement procedure.

Parking brake

27   One method of checking the parking brake is to park the vehicle on a steep hill with the parking brake set and the transmission in Neutral (be sure to stay in the vehicle for this check!). If the parking brake cannot prevent the vehicle from rolling, it's in need of adjustment (see Chapter 9).

**17   Drivebelt check and replacement
(every 15,000 miles or 12
months)/tensioner replacement**

Drivebelt

1   The drivebelt is located at the front of the engine and plays an important role in the overall operation of the vehicle and its components. Due to its function and material make-up, the drivebelt is prone to failure after a period of time and should be inspected and

adjusted periodically to prevent major engine damage.

2   The vehicles covered by this manual are equipped with a single self-adjusting serpentine drivebelt, which is used to drive all of the accessory components such as the alternator, power steering pump, water pump and air conditioning compressor.

Inspection

Refer to illustrations 17.4 and 17.5

3   With the engine off, open the hood and locate the drivebelt at the front of the engine. Using your fingers (and a flashlight, if necessary), move along the belts checking for cracks and separation of the belt plies. Also check for fraying and glazing, which gives the belt a shiny appearance. Both sides of each belt should be inspected, which means you will have to twist the belt to check the underside.

4   Check the ribs on the underside of the belt. They should all be the same depth, with none of the surface uneven **(see illustration).**

5   The tension of the belt is automatically adjusted by the belt tensioner and does not require any adjustments. Drivebelt wear can be checked visually by inspecting the wear indicator marks located on the side of the tensioner body. Locate the belt tensioner at the front of the engine, then find the tensioner operating marks **(see illustration).** If the indicator mark is outside the operating range, the belt should be replaced.

Replacement

Refer to illustration 17.6

6   Disconnect the cable from the negative terminal of the battery (see Chapter 5, Section 1). Rotate the tensioner to relieve the

17.6 Rotate the tensioner arm to relieve belt tension

17.11 Drivebelt tensioner retaining bolt (3.7L V6 shown)

19.7 The differential has a rubber plug, you can remove the plug by prying it out with a screwdriver

tension on the belt **(see illustration)**. Some models have a square hole in the tensioner arm that will accept a breaker bar or ratchet. On other models, place a wrench on the tensioner pulley bolt.

7   Remove the belt from the auxiliary components and carefully release the tensioner.

8   Route the new belt over the various pulleys, again rotating the tensioner to allow the belt to be installed, then release the belt tensioner. Make sure the belt fits properly into the pulley grooves - it must be completely engaged. **Note:** *Most models have a drivebelt routing decal on the upper radiator panel to help during drivebelt installation.*

9   Reconnect the battery.

Tensioner replacement

Refer to illustration 17.11

10   Remove the drivebelt.

11   Remove the bolt that secures the drivebelt to the engine, then remove the tensioner **(see illustration)**.

12   If you're working on a 5.7L (Hemi) engine, separate the tensioner from the mounting bracket.

13   Installation is the reverse of removal. If you're working on a 3.7L V6 or a 4.7L V8 engine, align the slot on the back of the tensioner with the bolt head on the timing chain cover. Tighten the mounting bolt to the torque listed in this Chapter's Specifications.

18   Fuel system check (every 15,000 miles or 12 months)

Warning: *Gasoline is flammable, so take extra precautions when you work on any part of the fuel system. Don't smoke or allow open flames or bare light bulbs near the work area, and don't work in a garage where a gas-type appliance (such as a water heater or clothes dryer) is present. Since fuel is carcinogenic, wear fuel-resistant gloves when there's a possibility of being exposed to fuel, and, if you spill any fuel on your skin, rinse it off immedi-*

ately with soap and water. Mop up any spills immediately and do not store fuel-soaked rags where they could ignite. When you perform any kind of work on the fuel system, wear safety glasses and have a Class B type fire extinguisher on hand. The fuel system is under constant pressure, so, before any lines are disconnected, the fuel system pressure must be relieved (see Chapter 4).

1   If you smell fuel while driving or after the vehicle has been sitting in the sun, inspect the fuel system immediately.

2   Remove the fuel filler cap and inspect it for damage and corrosion. The gasket should have an unbroken sealing imprint. If the gasket is damaged or corroded, install a new cap.

3   Inspect the fuel feed line for cracks. Make sure that the connections between the fuel lines and the fuel injection system and between the fuel lines and the in-line fuel filter are tight. **Warning:** *Your vehicle is fuel injected, so you must relieve the fuel system pressure before servicing fuel system components. The fuel system pressure relief procedure is outlined in Chapter 4.*

4   Since some components of the fuel system - the fuel tank and part of the fuel feed and return lines, for example - are underneath the vehicle, they can be inspected more easily with the vehicle raised on a hoist. If that's not possible, raise the vehicle and support it on jackstands.

5   With the vehicle raised and safely supported, inspect the fuel tank and filler neck for punctures, cracks and other damage. The connection between the filler neck and the tank is particularly critical. Sometimes a rubber filler neck will leak because of loose clamps or deteriorated rubber. Inspect all fuel tank mounting brackets and straps to be sure that the tank is securely attached to the vehicle. **Warning:** *Do not, under any circumstances, try to repair a fuel tank (except rubber components). A welding torch or any open flame can easily cause fuel vapors inside the tank to explode.*

6   Carefully check all rubber hoses and

metal lines leading away from the fuel tank. Check for loose connections, deteriorated hoses, crimped lines and other damage. Repair or replace damaged sections as necessary (see Chapter 4).

19   Manual transmission, transfer case and differential lubricant level check (every 15,000 miles or 12 months)

Manual transmission

1   The manual transmission has a filler plug which must be removed to check the lubricant level. If the vehicle is raised to gain access to the plug, be sure to support it safely on jackstands - DO NOT crawl under a vehicle that is supported only by a jack! Be sure the vehicle is level or the check may be inaccurate.

2   Using the appropriate wrench, unscrew the plug from the side of the transmission.

3   Use your little finger to reach inside the housing to feel the lubricant level. The level should be at or near the bottom of the plug hole. If it isn't, add the recommended lubricant through the plug hole with a syringe or squeeze bottle.

4   Install and tighten the plug. Check for leaks after the first few miles of driving.

Transfer case (4WD models)

5   The transfer case lubricant level is checked by removing the fill plug.

6   After removing the plug, reach inside the hole. The lubricant level should be just at the bottom of the hole. If not, add the appropriate lubricant through the opening.

Differential

Refer to illustration 19.7

Note: *4WD vehicles have two differentials; one in the front as well as one in the rear - be sure to check the lubricant level in both differentials.*

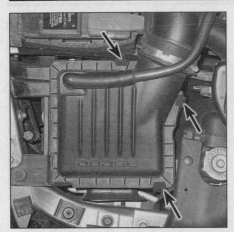

20.3a Release the spring clips and lift off the air filter housing cover

20.3b Remove the air filter element from the housing

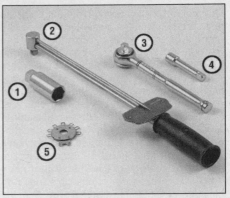

22.2 Tools required for changing spark plugs

1   *Spark plug socket* - *This will have special padding inside to protect the spark plug porcelain insulator*
2   *Torque wrench* - *Although not mandatory, use of this tool is the best way to ensure that the plugs are tightened properly*
3   *Ratchet* - *Standard hand tool to fit the plug socket*
4   *Extension* - *Depending on model and accessories, you may need special extensions and universal joints to reach one or more of the plugs*
5   *Spark plug gap gauge* - *This gauge for checking the gap comes in a variety of styles. Make sure the gap for your engine is included*

7   The differential lubricant level is checked by removing a filler plug from the differential cover **(see illustration)**. If the vehicle is raised to gain access to the plug, be sure to support it safely on jackstands - DO NOT crawl under a vehicle that is supported only by a jack! Be sure the vehicle is level or the check may be inaccurate.

8   With the differential cold, remove the fill plug. The lubricant should be level with the bottom of the fill plug hole.

9   If the level is low, add the recommended lubricant through the filler plug hole with a pump, syringe or squeeze bottle.

10   Install the plug and check for leaks after the first few miles of driving.

20 Air filter replacement (every 30,000 miles or 24 months)

Refer to illustrations 20.3a and 20.3b

1   At the specified intervals, the air filter element should be replaced with a new one.

2   On all models, the air filter is housed in a black plastic box mounted on the inner fenderwell on the right side of the engine compartment.

3   Detach the spring clips and pull the housing cover up, then lift the air filter element out of the housing **(see illustrations)**. Wipe out the inside of the air filter housing with a clean rag.

4   While the cover is off, be careful not to drop anything down into the air filter housing.

5   Place the new filter element in the air filter housing. Make sure it seats properly in the groove of the housing.

6   Installation is the reverse of removal.

21 Brake fluid change (every 30,000 miles or 24 months)

Warning: *Brake fluid can harm your eyes and damage painted surfaces, so use extreme caution when handling or pouring it. Do not*
use brake fluid that has been standing open or is more than one year old. Brake fluid absorbs moisture from the air. Excess moisture can cause a dangerous loss of braking effectiveness.

1   At the specified intervals, the brake fluid should be drained and replaced. Since the brake fluid may drip or splash when pouring it, place plenty of rags around the master cylinder to protect any surrounding painted surfaces.

2   Before beginning work, purchase the specified brake fluid (see *Recommended lubricants and fluids* at the beginning of this Chapter).

3   Remove the cap from the master cylinder reservoir.

4   Using a hand-held suction pump or similar device, withdraw the fluid from the master cylinder reservoir.

5   Add new fluid to the master cylinder until it rises to the base of the filler neck.

6   Bleed the brake system as described in Chapter 9 at all four brakes until new and uncontaminated fluid is expelled from the bleeder screw. Be sure to maintain the fluid level in the master cylinder as you perform the bleeding process. If you allow the master cylinder to run dry, air will enter the system.

7   Refill the master cylinder with fluid and check the operation of the brakes. The pedal should feel solid when depressed, with no sponginess. **Warning:** *Do not operate the vehicle if you are in doubt about the effectiveness of the brake system.*

22 Spark plug replacement (every 30,000 miles or 24 months)

Refer to illustrations 22.2, 22.5a, 22.5b, 22.6, 22.8, 22.10a and 22.10b

1   The spark plugs are threaded into the cylinder heads.

2   In most cases, the tools necessary for spark plug replacement include a spark plug socket which fits onto a ratchet (spark plug
sockets are padded inside to prevent damage to the porcelain insulators on the new plugs), various extensions and a gap gauge to check and adjust the gaps on the new plugs **(see illustration)**. A special plug wire removal tool is available for separating the wire boots from the spark plugs, but it isn't absolutely necessary. A torque wrench should be used to tighten the new plugs.

3   The best approach when replacing the spark plugs is to purchase the new ones in advance, adjust them to the proper gap and replace them one at a time. When buying the new spark plugs, be sure to obtain the correct plug type for your particular engine. This information can be found on the Emission Control Information label located under the hood, in the factory owner's manual and the Specifications at the front of this Chapter. If differences exist between the plug specified on the emissions label and in the owner's manual, assume that the emissions label is correct.

4   Allow the engine to cool completely before attempting to remove any of the plugs. While you're waiting for the engine to cool, check the new plugs for defects and adjust the gaps.

5   The gap is checked by inserting the proper-thickness gauge between the electrodes at the tip of the plug **(see illustration)**. The gap between the electrodes should be the same as the one specified on the Emissions Control Information label or in this

Chapter's Specifications. The gauge should just slide between the electrodes with a slight amount of drag. If the gap is incorrect, use the adjuster on the gauge body to bend the curved side electrode slightly until the proper gap is obtained **(see illustration)**. If the side electrode is not exactly over the center electrode, bend it with the adjuster until it is. Check for cracks in the porcelain insulator (if any are found, the plug should not be used).

6   All models are equipped with individual ignition coils which must be removed first to access the spark plugs **(see illustration)**.

7   If compressed air is available, use it to blow any dirt or foreign material away from the spark plug hole. The idea here is to eliminate the possibility of debris falling into the cylinder as the spark plug is removed.

8   Place the spark plug socket over the plug and remove it from the engine by turning it in a counterclockwise direction **(see illustration)**.

9   Compare the spark plug with the chart on the inside back cover of this manual to get an indication of the general running condition of the engine.

10   Apply a small amount of anti-seize compound to the spark plug threads **(see illustra-**

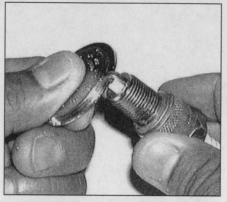

22.5a Using a tapered thickness gauge to check the spark plug gap - slide the thin side into the gap and turn it until the gauge just fills the gap, then read the thickness on the gauge - do not force the tool into the gap or use the tapered portion to widen a gap

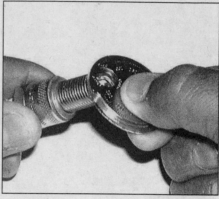

22.5b To change the gap, bend the side electrode only, using the adjuster hole in the tool, and be very careful not to crack or chip the porcelain insulator surrounding the center electrode

tion). Thread one of the new plugs into the hole until you can no longer turn it with your fingers, then tighten it with a torque wrench (if available) or the ratchet. It's a good idea to

slip a short length of rubber hose over the end of the plug to use as a tool to thread it into place **(see illustration)**. The hose will grip the plug well enough to turn it, but will start to slip if the plug begins to cross-thread in the hole - this will prevent damaged threads and the

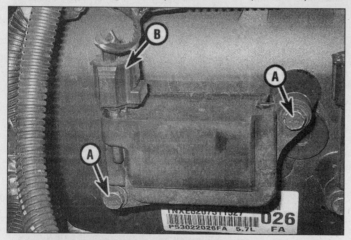

22.6a Remove the mounting bolts (A) and disconnect the electrical connector (B) . . .

22.6b . . . then remove the coil to access the spark plug

22.8 Use a socket and extension to unscrew the spark plugs

22.10a Apply a thin film of anti-seize compound to the spark plug threads to prevent damage to the cylinder head

22.10b A length of snug-fitting rubber hose will save time and prevent damaged threads when installing the spark plugs

24.1a On 3.7L V6 and 4.7L V8 engines, the PCV valve is located in the oil filler neck. To remove it, detach the hose, turn the valve 90-degrees counterclockwise and pull it out

24.1b On Hemi engines, the PCV valve is located in the top of the intake manifold. Twist it counterclockwise to remove it

accompanying repair costs.

11   Before pushing the ignition coil onto the end of the plug, inspect the ignition coil following the procedures outlined in Section 23.

12   Repeat the procedure for the remaining spark plugs.

23   Ignition coil check

1   Clean the coils with a dampened cloth and dry them thoroughly.

2   Inspect each coil for cracks, damage and carbon tracking. Make sure the coil fits securely onto the spark plug(s). If damage exists, replace the coil.

24   Positive Crankcase Ventilation (PCV) valve check and replacement (every 60,000 miles or 48 months)

Refer to illustration 24.1a and 24.1b

Note: *For additional information on the PCV system refer to Chapter 6.*

1   The PCV valve is located the in the neck of the oil filler tube on 3.7L V6 and 4.7L V8 engines. On Hemi engines, the PCV valve is located in the intake manifold **(see illustrations)**.

3.7L V6 and 4.7L V8 engines

2   With the engine idling at normal operating temperature, remove the PCV valve. Place your finger over the valve opening. If there's no vacuum at the valve, check for a plugged hose, manifold port, or the valve itself. Replace any plugged or deteriorated hoses.

3   Turn off the engine and shake the PCV valve, listening for a rattle. If the valve doesn't rattle, replace it with a new one.

4   To replace the valve, pull it from the end

of the hose, noting its installed position.

5   When purchasing a replacement PCV valve, make sure it's for your particular vehicle and engine size. Compare the old valve with the new one to make sure they're the same.

6   Push the valve into the end of the hose until it's seated.

7   Inspect the rubber grommet for damage and hardening. Replace it with a new one if necessary.

8   Install the PCV valve and hose securely into position.

5.7L Hemi engine

9   To replace the valve, twist the valve and pull it out from the intake manifold, noting its installed position.

10   When purchasing a replacement PCV valve, make sure it's for your particular vehicle and engine size. Compare the old valve with the new one to make sure they're the same.

11   Inspect the rubber O-rings for damage and hardening. Replace it with a new one if necessary.

12   Install the PCV valve securely into position.

25   Manual transmission, transfer case and differential lubricant change (every 72,000 miles)

Manual transmission

1   This procedure should be performed after the vehicle has been driven so the lubricant will be warm and therefore will flow out of the transmission more easily. Raise the vehicle and support it securely on jackstands.

2   Move a drain pan, rags, newspapers and wrenches under the transmission. Remove the fill plug from the side of the transmission case.

3   Remove the transmission drain plug at the bottom of the case and allow the lubricant

to drain into the pan.

4   After the lubricant has drained completely, reinstall the plug and tighten it securely.

5   Using a hand pump, syringe or funnel, fill the transmission with the specified lubricant until it begins to leak out through the hole. Reinstall the fill plug and tighten it securely.

6   Lower the vehicle.

7   Drive the vehicle for a short distance, then check the drain and fill plugs for leakage.

Transfer case (4WD models)

8   Drive the vehicle for at least 15 minutes to warm the lubricant in the case.

9   Raise the vehicle and support it securely on jackstands.

10   Remove the filler plug from the case.

11   Remove the drain plug from the lower part of the case and allow the old lubricant to drain completely.

12   After the lubricant has drained completely, reinstall the plug and tighten it securely.

13   Fill the case with the specified lubricant until it is level with the lower edge of the filler hole.

14   Install the filler plug and tighten it securely.

15   Drive the vehicle for a short distance and recheck the lubricant level. In some instances a small amount of additional lubricant will have to be added.

Differential

Refer to illustration 25.18, 25.19a, 25.19b, 25.19c and 25.21

16   This procedure should be performed after the vehicle has been driven so the lubricant will be warm and therefore will flow out of the differential more easily.

17   Raise the vehicle and support it securely on jackstands. If the differential has a bolt-on cover at the rear, it is usually easiest to

remove the cover to drain the lubricant (which will also allow you to inspect the differential). If there's no bolt-on cover, look for a drain plug at the bottom of the differential housing. If there's not a drain plug and no cover, you'll have to remove the lubricant through the filler plug hole with a suction pump. If you'll be draining the lubricant by removing the cover or a drain plug, move a drain pan, rags, newspapers and wrenches under the vehicle.

18   Remove the filler plug from the differential (see Section 19). If a suction pump is being used, insert the flexible hose. Work the hose down to the bottom of the differential housing and pump the lubricant out **(see illustration)**. If you'll be draining the lubricant through a drain plug, remove the plug and allow the lubricant to drain into the pan, then reinstall the drain plug.

19   If the differential is being drained by removing the cover plate, remove the bolts on the lower half of the plate. **Note:** *If you're working on a Durango, remove the Watts link bellcrank from the cover (see Chapter 10).* Loosen the bolts on the upper half and

use them to keep the cover loosely attached. Allow the oil to drain into the pan, then completely remove the cover **(see illustrations)**.

20   Using a lint-free rag, clean the inside of the cover and the accessible areas of the differential housing. As this is done, check for chipped gears and metal particles in the lubricant, indicating that the differential should be more thoroughly inspected and/or repaired.

21   Thoroughly clean the gasket mating surfaces of the differential housing and the cover plate. Use a gasket scraper or putty knife to remove all traces of old sealant **(see illustration)**.

22   Apply a bead of RTV sealant to the cover flange, then install the cover. Make sure the bolt holes align properly. **Note:** *The cover must be installed within three minutes of sealant application.*

23   Install the bolts and tighten them to the torque listed in this Chapter's Specifications.

24   Use a hand pump, syringe or funnel to fill the differential housing with the specified lubricant until it's level with the bottom of the plug hole.

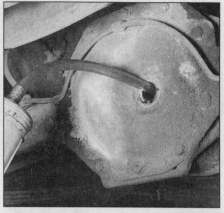

25.18 This is the easiest way to remove the lubricant: Work the end of the hose to the bottom of the differential housing and draw out the old lubricant with a hand pump or suction gun

25   Install the filler plug and make sure it is secure.

25.19a Remove the bolts from the lower edge of the cover . . .

25.19b . . . then loosen the top bolts and allow the lubricant to drain out

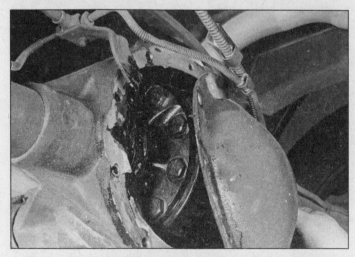

25.19c After the lubricant has drained, remove the remaining cover bolts and the cover

25.21 Carefully scrape the old gasket material off to ensure a leak-free seal

26.4 The radiator drain fitting is located at the lower corner of the radiator

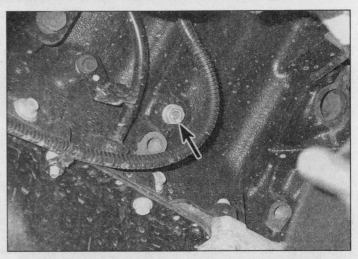

26.5 The block drain plugs are generally located about one to two inches above the oil pan - there is one on each side of the engine block

26 Cooling system servicing (draining, flushing and refilling) (every 60 months)

Warning: *Do not allow antifreeze to come in contact with your skin or painted surfaces of the vehicle. Rinse off spills immediately with plenty of water. Antifreeze is highly toxic if ingested. Never leave antifreeze lying around in an open container or in puddles on the floor; children and pets are attracted by it's sweet smell and may drink it. Check with local authorities about disposing of used antifreeze. Many communities have collection centers which will see that antifreeze is disposed of safely.*

1 Periodically, the cooling system should be drained, flushed and refilled to replenish the antifreeze mixture and prevent formation of rust and corrosion, which can impair the performance of the cooling system and cause engine damage. When the cooling system is serviced, all hoses and the expansion tank cap should be checked and replaced if necessary.

Draining

Refer to illustrations 26.4 and 26.5

2 Apply the parking brake and block the wheels. If the vehicle has just been driven, wait several hours to allow the engine to cool down before beginning this procedure.

3 Once the engine is completely cool, remove the radiator cap.

4 Move a large container under the radiator drain to catch the coolant. Attach a length of hose to the drain fitting to direct the coolant into the container, then open the drain fitting (a pair of pliers may be required to turn it) **(see illustration)**.

5 After the coolant stops flowing out of the radiator, move the container under the engine block drain plugs and allow the coolant in the block to drain **(see illustration)**.

6 While the coolant is draining, check the condition of the radiator hoses, heater hoses and clamps (refer to Section 12 if necessary). Replace any damaged clamps or hoses.

7 Apply thread sealant to the block drain plugs. Reinstall the drain plugs and tighten them securely.

Flushing

Refer to illustration 26.10

8 Once the system has completely drained, remove the thermostat housing from the engine (see Chapter 3), then reinstall the housing without the thermostat. This will allow the system to be thoroughly flushed.

9 Disconnect the upper hose from the radiator.

10 Place a garden hose in the upper radiator inlet and flush the system until the water runs clear at the upper radiator hose **(see illustration)**.

11 Severe cases of radiator contamination or clogging will require removing the radiator (see Chapter 3) and reverse flushing it. This involves inserting the hose in the bottom radiator outlet to allow the clean water to run against the normal flow, draining out through the top. A radiator repair shop should be consulted if further cleaning or repair is necessary.

12 When the coolant is regularly drained and the system refilled with the correct coolant mixture there should be no need to employ chemical cleaners or descalers.

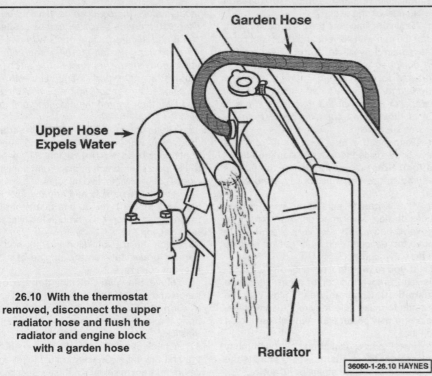

Garden Hose

Upper Hose Expels Water

26.10 With the thermostat removed, disconnect the upper radiator hose and flush the radiator and engine block with a garden hose

Radiator

36060-1-26.10 HAYNES

27.6 With the front bolts in place, but loose, pull the rear of the pan down to drain the fluid

27.9 Use a seal removal tool to remove the transmission filter seal from the valve body

27.11 Use an oil filter wrench to remove the transmission cooler return filter

27.12 On 545RFE transmissions, install the filter seal into the valve body first

Refilling

13   Close and tighten the radiator drain.

14   Place the heater temperature control in the maximum heat position.

15   Make sure to use the proper coolant listed in this Chapter's Specifications. Slowly fill the cooling system with the recommended mixture of antifreeze and water to the base of the filler neck. Then add coolant to the reservoir until it reaches the MAX mark on the reservoir dipstick. Wait five minutes and recheck the coolant level in the radiator, adding if necessary.

16   Leave the radiator cap off and run the engine in a well-ventilated area until the thermostat opens (coolant will begin flowing through the radiator and the upper radiator hose will become hot).

17   Turn the engine off and let it cool. Add more coolant mixture to bring the level between the MIN and MAX marks on the reservoir dipstick.

18   Squeeze the upper radiator hose to expel air, then add more coolant mixture if necessary. Replace the radiator cap.

19   Start the engine, allow it to reach normal operating temperature and check for leaks. Also, set the heater and blower controls to the maximum setting and check to see that the heater output from the air ducts is warm. This is a good indication that all air has been purged from the cooling system.

27   Automatic transmission fluid and filter change (every 100,000 miles)

Refer to illustrations 27.6, 27.9, 27.11 and 27.12

1   At the specified intervals, the transmission fluid should be drained and replaced. Since the fluid will remain hot long after driving, perform this procedure only after the engine has cooled down completely.

2   Before beginning work, purchase the specified transmission fluid (see *Recom-mended lubricants and fluids* at the front of this Chapter) and a new filter.

3   Other tools necessary for this job include a floor jack, jackstands to support the vehicle in a raised position, a drain pan capable of holding at least four quarts, newspapers and clean rags.

4   Raise the vehicle and support it securely on jackstands.

5   Place the drain pan underneath the transmission pan. Remove the rear and side pan mounting bolts, but only loosen the rear pan bolts approximately four turns.

6   Carefully pry the transmission pan loose with a screwdriver, allowing the fluid to drain **(see illustration)**.

7   Remove the remaining bolts, pan and gasket. Carefully clean the gasket surface of the transmission pan to remove all traces of the old gasket and sealant.

8   Drain the fluid from the transmission pan, clean the pan with solvent and dry it with compressed air, if available. **Note:** *Some models are equipped with magnets in the transmission pan to catch metal debris. Clean the magnet thoroughly. A small amount of metal material is normal at the magnet. If there is considerable debris, consult a dealer or transmission specialist.*

9   Remove the filter and seal from the valve body inside the transmission **(see illustration)**. **Note:** *On some models the filter is secured to the transmission by a mounting bolt.*

10   Use a gasket scraper to remove any traces of old gasket material that remain on the valve body. **Note:** *Be very careful not to gouge the delicate aluminum gasket surface on the valve body.*

11   If you're working on a 545RFE transmission, remove the cooler return filter **(see illustration)**. Compare the old filter with the new one to make sure they're the same type. Install the new cooler filter and tighten it to 84 inch-lbs.

12   Install a new gasket and filter. On many replacement filters, the gasket is attached to the filter to simplify installation. **Caution:** *On most models, the seal can be installed on the filter first, then the seal/filter can be pushed in place and secured. On models with 545RFE transmissions, install the filter seal into the valve body first, then install the filter **(see illustration)**. On models equipped with a filter secured by a mounting bolt, install the seal and filter then tighten the mounting bolt to 40 inch-lbs.*

13   Clean the pan and transmission surfaces thoroughly with lacquer thinner and apply a continuous bead of ATF-resistant RTV sealant to the pan, then bolt it in place and tighten to Specifications within five minutes.

14   Lower the vehicle and add the specified type and amount (minus one quart) of automatic transmission fluid through the filler tube (see Section 4).

15   With the transmission in Park and the parking brake set, run the engine at a fast idle, but don't race it.

16   Move the gear selector through each range and back to Park. Check the fluid level. It will probably be low. Add enough fluid to bring the level between the two holes on the dipstick.

17   Check under the vehicle for leaks during the first few trips. Check the fluid level again when the transmission is hot (see Section 4).

Chapter 2 Part A
3.7L V6 and 4.7L V8 engines

Contents

Specifications

General

Displacement	
3.7L V6	226 cubic inches
4.7L V8	287 cubic inches
Bore and stroke	
3.7L V6	3.66 x 3.40 inches
4.7L V8	3.66 x 3.40 inches
Cylinder numbers (front-to-rear)	
3.7L V6	
Left (driver's) side	1-3-5
Right side	2-4-6
Firing order	1-6-5-4-3-2
4.7L V8	
Left (driver's) side	1-3-5-7
Right side	2-4-6-8
Firing order	1-8-4-3-6-5-7-2
Cylinder compression pressure	See Chapter 2C

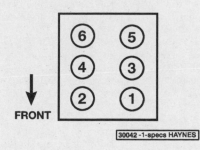

Cylinder locations - 3.7L V6 engine

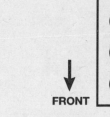

Cylinder locations - 4.7L V8 engine

Camshaft

Endplay	0.003 to 0.0079 inch
Camshaft bearing oil clearance	
Standard	0.001 to 0.0026 inch
Service limit	0.0026 inch
Camshaft journal diameter	1.0227 to 1.0235 inch
Camshaft bore diameter	1.0245 to 1.0252 inch

Timing chain

Idler gear endplay	0.004 to 0.010 inch

Oil pump

Cover warpage limit (maximum)	0.001 inch
Inner and outer rotor thickness	0.473 inch
Outer rotor diameter (minimum)	0.400 inch
Outer rotor-to-housing clearance (maximum)	0.009 inch
Inner rotor-to-outer rotor lobe clearance (maximum)	0.006 inch
Oil pump housing-to-rotor side clearance (maximum)	0.0038 inch

Torque specifications

	Ft-lbs (unless otherwise indicated)
Camshaft sprocket bolts (non-oiled)	90
Camshaft bearing cap bolts	100 in-lbs
Crankshaft pulley/vibration damper bolt	130
Cylinder head bolts	
3.7L V6 **(see illustration 11.19a)**	
Step 1 Bolts 1 through 8	20
Step 2	
Bolts 1 through 8	20 (recheck)
Bolts 9 through 12	120 in-lbs
Step 3	
Bolts 1 through 8	Tighten an additional 90-degrees
Step 4	
Bolts 1 through 8	Tighten an additional 90-degrees
Bolts 9 through 12	19
4.7L V8 **(see illustration 11.19b)**	
Step 1 Bolts 1 through 10	15
Step 2	
Bolts 1 through 10	35
Bolts 11 through 14	18
Step 3	
Bolts 1 through 10	Tighten an additional 90-degrees
Bolts 11 through 14	22
Driveplate bolts	
3.7L V6	70
4.7L V8	45
Exhaust manifold bolts	18
Exhaust manifold heat shield nuts	
Step 1	72 in-lbs
Step 2	Loosen 45-degrees
Flywheel bolts	70
Intake manifold bolts **(see illustrations 9.21a or 9.21b)**	105 in-lbs
Oil pan bolts	130 in-lbs
Oil pan drain plug	25
Oil pick-up tube mounting bolt/nut	250 in-lbs
Oil pump mounting bolts	250 in-lbs
Oil pump cover screws	105 in-lbs
Timing chain cover bolts	43
Timing chain guide bolts	250 in-lbs
Timing chain guide access plugs	60
Timing chain idler sprocket bolt	25
Timing chain tensioner arm pivot bolt	
3.7L V6 engine	250 in-lbs
4.7L V8 engine	150 in-lbs
Timing chain tensioner (secondary)	250 in-lbs
Timing chain tensioner (primary)	250 in-lbs
Transmission support brace bolts	40
Valve cover bolts	105 in-lbs
Water outlet housing	105 in-lbs

1   General information

This Part of Chapter 2 is devoted to in-vehicle repair procedures for the 3.7L V6 and 4.7L V8 single overhead camshaft (SOHC) engine. These engines utilize a cast iron engine block with cylinders arranged in a V shape at a 90-degree angle between the two banks. The overhead camshaft aluminum cylinder heads are equipped with replaceable valve guides and seats. Stamped steel rocker arms with an integral roller bearing actuate the valves.

Information concerning engine removal and installation and engine overhaul can be found in Part C of this Chapter.

The following repair procedures are based on the assumption that the engine is installed in the vehicle. If the engine has been removed from the vehicle and mounted on a stand, many of the steps outlined in this Part of Chapter 2 will not apply.

2   Engine identification

Engine identification on the 3.7L V6 and 4.7L V8 engines is accomplished by finding the engine code stamped on the engine block or by using the VIN number of the vehicle (8th position). Refer to the introductory pages in this manual for additional information.

3   Repair operations possible with the engine in the vehicle

Many major repair operations can be accomplished without removing the engine from the vehicle.

Clean the engine compartment and the exterior of the engine with some type of degreaser before any work is done. It will make the job easier and help keep dirt out of the internal areas of the engine.

Depending on the components involved, it may be helpful to remove the hood to improve access to the engine as repairs are performed (refer to Chapter 11, if necessary). Cover the fenders to prevent damage to the paint. Special pads are available, but an old bedspread or blanket will also work.

If vacuum, exhaust, oil or coolant leaks develop, indicating a need for gasket or seal replacement, the repairs can generally be made with the engine in the vehicle. The intake and exhaust manifold gaskets, oil pan gasket, crankshaft oil seals and cylinder head gaskets are all accessible with the engine in place.

Exterior engine components, such as the intake and exhaust manifolds, the oil pan, the oil pump, the water pump (see Chapter 3), the starter motor, the alternator and the fuel system components (see Chapter 4) can be removed for repair with the engine in place.

Since the cylinder heads can be removed without pulling the engine, valve component

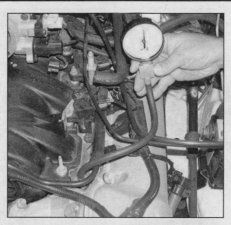

4.5 A compression gauge can be used in the number one spark plug hole to assist in finding TDC

servicing can also be accomplished with the engine in the vehicle. Replacement of the camshafts, timing chains and sprockets are also possible with the engine in the vehicle.

In extreme cases caused by a lack of necessary equipment, repair or replacement of piston rings, pistons, connecting rods and rod bearings is possible with the engine in the vehicle. However, this practice is not recommended because of the cleaning and preparation work that must be done to the components involved.

4   Top Dead Center (TDC) for number one piston - locating

Refer to illustrations 4.5 and 4.8

1   Top Dead Center (TDC) is the highest point in the cylinder that each piston reaches as it travels up the cylinder bore. Each piston reaches TDC on the compression stroke and again on the exhaust stroke, but TDC generally refers to piston position on the compression stroke.

2   Positioning the piston(s) at TDC is an essential part of many procedures such as valve timing, camshaft and timing chain/sprocket removal.

3   Before beginning this procedure, be sure to place the transmission in Neutral or Park and apply the parking brake or block the rear wheels. Also, remove the ignition coil packs and the spark plugs (see Chapter 1). If, in the next Step you will be using the starter motor to rotate the engine, disable the fuel pump by removing the fuel pump relay (see Chapter 4, Section 2).

4   In order to bring any piston to TDC, the crankshaft must be turned using one of the methods outlined below. When looking at the front of the engine, normal crankshaft rotation is clockwise.

a) *The preferred method is to turn the crankshaft with a socket and ratchet attached to the bolt threaded into the front of the crankshaft. Turn the bolt in a clockwise direction only. Never turn the*

4.8 Align the groove in the damper with the TDC mark on the timing chain cover

bolt counterclockwise.
b) *A remote starter switch, which may save some time, can also be used. Follow the instructions included with the switch. Once the piston is close to TDC, use a socket and ratchet as described in the previous paragraph.*
c) *If an assistant is available to turn the ignition switch to the Start position in short bursts, you can get the piston close to TDC without a remote starter switch. Make sure your assistant is out of the vehicle, away from the ignition switch, then use a socket and ratchet as described in Paragraph (a) to complete the procedure.*

5   Install a compression gauge in the number one spark plug hole. It should be a gauge with a screw-in fitting and a hose at least six inches long **(see illustration)**.

6   Rotate the crankshaft using one of the methods described above while observing for pressure on the compression gauge. The moment the gauge shows pressure indicates that the number one cylinder has begun the compression stroke.

7   Once the compression stroke has begun, TDC for the compression stroke is reached by bringing the piston to the top of the cylinder.

8   Continue turning the crankshaft until the notch in the crankshaft damper is aligned with the TDC mark on the timing chain cover **(see illustration)**. At this point, the number one cylinder is at TDC on the compression stroke. If the marks are aligned but there was no compression, the piston was on the exhaust stroke. Continue rotating the crankshaft 360-degrees (1-turn) and realign the marks. **Note:** *If a compression gauge is not available, you can simply place a blunt object over the spark plug hole and listen for compression as the engine is rotated. Once compression at the No.1 spark plug hole is noted, the remainder of the Step is the same.*

9   After the number one piston has been positioned at TDC on the compression stroke, TDC for any of the remaining cylinders can be located by turning the crankshaft in increments of 120-degrees for 3.7L V6 engines or 90-degrees for 4.7L V8 engines and following

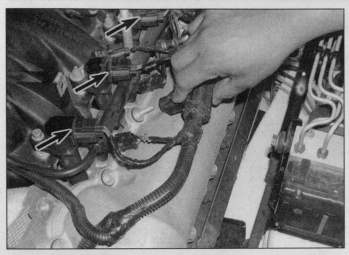

5.10 Detach the wiring harness from the valve cover studs, then disconnect the fuel injector electrical connectors and position the harness aside

5.12 Remove the valve cover bolts (left side shown)

the firing order (refer to the Specifications). For example on 3.7L V6 engines, rotating the engine 120-degrees past TDC #1 will put the engine at TDC compression for cylinder #6.

10   An even faster way to find TDC for any cylinder other than No. 1 is to make marks on the crankshaft damper 120-degree intervals from the TDC mark on the damper (V6 engine) or 90-degree intervals from the TDC mark on the damper (V8 engine). Install the compression gauge into the cylinder for which you want to find TDC, rotate the engine until compression begins to register on the gauge, then continue turning the crankshaft until the next mark on the damper aligns with the mark on the timing chain cover.

5   Valve covers - removal and installation

Refer to illustrations 5.10 and 5.12

Removal

1   Disconnect the cable from the negative terminal of the battery (see Chapter 5, Section 1).

Right (passenger's) side cover

Warning: *Wait until the engine is completely cool before beginning this procedure.*

2   Remove the air filter housing, the air intake duct and the throttle body resonator (see Chapter 4).

3   Drain the cooling system (see Chapter 1).

4   Disconnect the heater hoses at the firewall (see Chapter 3) and remove the heater hoses.

5   Remove the drivebelt (see Chapter 1) and the air conditioning compressor (see Chapter 3). Position the A/C compressor to the side without disconnecting the refrigerant lines from the compressor.

6   Disconnect and remove the PCV hose

(see Chapter 6) and the PCV breather tube located at the rear of the cylinder head.

7   Remove the oil filler tube.

Left (driver's) side cover

8   Remove the PCV breather tube located at the rear of the cylinder head. Detach the heater hoses from the clips and reposition them as necessary.

9   Remove the air intake duct and the throttle body resonator (see Chapter 4).

Either cover

10   Unclip the fuel injector wiring harness from the studs on the valve cover **(see illustration)**.

11   Disconnect the electrical connectors from the fuel injectors and ignition coil connectors on the side from which the valve cover is to be removed (see Chapter 4). If both valve covers are to be removed, disconnect all of the connectors from the fuel injectors.

12   Remove the valve cover bolts **(see illustration)**. Make a note of the locations of the bolts with studs before removal to ensure correct positioning during installation.

13   Detach the valve cover. **Note:** *If the cover sticks to the cylinder head, use a block of wood and a hammer to dislodge it. If the cover still won't come loose, pry on it carefully, but don't distort the sealing flange.*

Installation

14   The mating surfaces of each cylinder head and valve cover must be perfectly clean when the covers are installed. **Caution:** *Do not use harsh cleaners when cleaning the valve covers or damage to the covers may occur.* **Note:** *The valve cover gasket can be reused if it isn't hardened, cracked or otherwise damaged.*

15   Clean the mounting bolt or stud threads with a wire brush, if necessary, to remove any corrosion and restore damaged threads. Use a tap to clean the threaded holes in the heads.

16   Place the valve cover and gasket in position, then install the bolts in the correct locations from which they where removed. Tighten the bolts in several steps to the torque listed in this Chapter's Specifications.

17   Complete the installation by reversing the removal procedure. Refill the cooling system, if drained, by following the procedure in Chapter 1. Start the engine and check carefully for oil leaks.

6   Rocker arms and hydraulic lash adjusters - removal, inspection and installation

Refer to illustrations 6.5, 6.7 and 6.8

Warning: *Wait until the engine is completely cool before beginning this procedure.*

Note 1: *A special valve spring compressor available from most aftermarket specialty tool manufacturers will be required for this procedure. The only other alternative to accomplishing this task without the use of this special tool is to remove the timing chains and the camshafts, which requires major disassembly of the engine and surrounding components.*

Note 2: *This engine is a non-freewheeling (interference) engine and the pistons must be down in the cylinder bore before the valve and spring assembly can be compressed to allow rocker arm removal.*

1   Before beginning this procedure, be sure to place the transmission in Park and apply the parking brake or block the rear wheels. Also, remove the ignition coils and the spark plugs (see Chapter 1).

2   Remove the valve cover(s) (see Section 5).

3   Before the rocker arms and lash adjusters are removed, arrange to label and store them, so they can be kept separate and reinstalled on the same valve they were removed from.

4   Rotate the engine with a socket and

6.5 Using a special type valve spring compressor, depress the valve spring just enough to remove the rocker arm

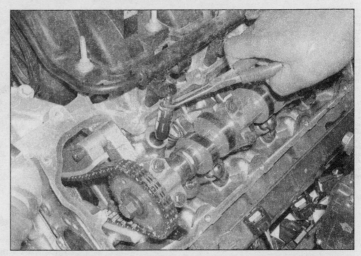

6.7 Pull the lash adjuster up and out of its bore to remove it from the cylinder head

ratchet in a clockwise direction by the crankshaft pulley/vibration damper bolt until the piston(s) are positioned correctly to remove the rocker arms from the corresponding cylinders as follows. Start the sequence from TDC number 1 on the compression stroke (see Section 4).

For the 3.7L V6 engine

a) With the No.1 piston at TDC on the compression stroke, remove the rocker arms from cylinders No. 2 and 6.

b) Rotate the crankshaft another 180-degrees (1/2-turn) from TDC on the compression stroke to bring the No. 1 piston to BDC on the firing stroke, then remove the rocker arms from cylinder No. 1.

c) Rotate the crankshaft another 180-degrees (1/2-turn) from BDC on the firing stroke to bring the No.1 piston to TDC on the exhaust stroke, then remove the rocker arms from cylinders No. 3 and 5.

d) Rotate the crankshaft another 180-degrees (1/2-turn) from TDC on the

exhaust stroke to bring the No.1 piston to BDC on the intake stroke, then remove the rocker arms from cylinder No. 4.

For the 4.7L V8 engine

a) With the No.1 piston at TDC on the compression stroke, remove the rocker arms from cylinders No. 2 and 8.

b) Rotate the crankshaft another 360-degrees (1-turn) from TDC on the compression stroke to bring the No.1 piston to TDC on the exhaust stroke, then remove the rocker arms from cylinders No. 3 and 5.

c) Position cylinder No. 3 at TDC on the compression stroke. Remove the rocker arms from cylinder No. 4 and 6.

d) Position cylinder No. 2 at TDC on the compression stroke. Remove the rocker arms from cylinder No. 1 and 7.

5   Hook the valve spring compressor around the base of the camshaft. Depress the valve spring just enough to release tension on the rocker arm to be removed. Once tension on the rocker arm is relieved, the rocker arm can be removed by simply pulling it out **(see illustration)**.

6   If you're removing or replacing only a few of the rocker arms or lash adjusters, locate the cylinder number of the rocker arm or lash adjuster you wish to remove in Step 4, then rotate the crankshaft to the corresponding position. Remember to keep the rocker arm and lash adjuster for each valve together so they can be reinstalled in the same locations. Refer to Section 3 as necessary to help position the designated cylinder at TDC.

7   Once the rocker arms are removed, the lash adjusters can be pulled out of the cylinder head and stored with the corresponding rocker arm **(see illustration)**.

8   Inspect each rocker arm for wear, cracks and other damage. Make sure the rollers turn freely and show no signs of wear. Also check the pivot area for wear, cracks and galling **(see illustration)**.

9   Inspect the lash adjuster contact surfaces for wear or damage. Make sure the lash adjusters move up and down freely in their bores in the cylinder head without excessive side-to-side play.

10   Installation is the reverse of removal with the following exceptions: Always install the lash adjuster first and make sure they're at least partially full of oil before installation. This is indicated by little or no lash adjuster plunger travel.

7   Timing chain and sprockets - removal, inspection and installation

Warning: Wait until the engine is completely cool before beginning this procedure.

Note 1: Special tools are necessary to complete this procedure. Read through the entire procedure and obtain the special tools before beginning work.

Note 2: These engines utilize three timing chains to produce proper valve timing. The primary timing chain runs around the crankshaft sprocket and the idler gear sprocket. This chain synchronizes the crankshaft and pistons with the idler gear, while two secondary timing chains run around the rear of the idler gear and up to the camshaft sprockets to synchronize the valve timing with the crankshaft. Refer to Step 24 for the in-vehicle timing chain inspection procedure prior to timing chain removal.

Removal

Refer to illustrations 7.7, 7.11, 7.13, 7.14, 7.15, 7.16a, 7.16b, 7.17 and 7.18

1   Position piston in cylinder No. 1 at Top Dead Center on the compression stroke (see Section 4). Disconnect the cable from the negative terminal of the battery (see Chapter 5, Section 1).

6.8 Inspect the rocker arms at the following locations

A   Valve stem seat
B   Roller
C   Lash adjuster pocket

7.7 Drivebelt tensioner retaining bolt

7.11 When the piston in cylinder no. 1 is at TDC on the exhaust stroke, the mark on the crankshaft damper is aligned with the mark on the timing chain cover and the V6 or V8 marks on the camshaft sprockets should be in the 12 o'clock position

2   Drain the cooling system (see Chapter 1).

3   Remove the drivebelt (see Chapter 1) and the engine cooling fan and fan shroud (see Chapter 3).

4   Detach the heater hoses and the lower radiator hose from the timing chain cover and position them aside.

5   Unbolt the power steering pump and set it aside without disconnecting the fluid lines (see Chapter 10).

6   Remove the alternator (see Chapter 5). Also unbolt the air conditioning compressor (if equipped) and position it aside without disconnecting the refrigerant lines.

7   Remove the accessory drivebelt tensioner from the timing chain cover **(see illustration)**.

8   Remove the valve covers (see Section 5) and the spark plugs (see Chapter 1).

9   Remove all of the rocker arms following the procedure outlined in Section 6. **Note:** *This step is not absolutely necessary, but it will help make alignment of the camshaft sprockets easier upon installation and also eliminate any possibility of the pistons contacting the valves during this procedure, since these are interference engines.*

10   Remove the camshaft position sen-

sor (CMP) from the right cylinder head (see Chapter 6).

11   Position the number one piston at TDC on the exhaust stroke (one revolution from TDC on the compression stroke). Visually confirm the engine is at TDC on the exhaust stroke by verifying that the timing mark on the crankshaft damper is aligned with the mark

on the timing chain cover and the V6 or V8 marks on the camshaft sprockets are pointing straight up in the 12 o'clock position **(see illustration 4.8 and the accompanying illustration)**.

12   Remove the crankshaft damper/pulley (see Section 12).

13   Remove the timing chain cover and the

7.13 Timing chain cover retaining bolts

7.14 Locking the primary timing chain tensioner in the retracted position

7.15 Secondary timing chain tensioner mounting bolts

7.16a Removing the left camshaft sprocket bolt while holding
the sprocket with a pin spanner wrench - note the chain
guide access plug

7.16b The right camshaft sprocket is identified by the camshaft
position sensor ring which is fastened to the rear of the sprocket
- be extremely careful not to damage or place a magnetic object
of any kind near the camshaft position sensor ring or a no
start condition may occur after installation

water pump as an assembly **(see illustration)**. Note that various types and sizes of bolts are used. They must be reinstalled in their original locations. Mark each bolt or make a sketch to help remember where they go.

14 Cover the oil pan opening with shop rags to prevent any components from falling into the engine. Collapse the primary timing chain tensioner with a pair of locking pliers and install a locking pin into the holes in the tensioner body to keep it in the retracted position **(see illustration)**.

15 Remove the secondary timing chain tensioners **(see illustration)**.

16 Remove the camshaft sprocket retaining bolts **(see illustrations)**. Pull the camshaft sprockets off the camshaft hubs one at a time. Lower the sprocket(s) into the cylinder head opening until the chain can be displaced from around the sprocket, then remove the camshaft sprockets from the engine and let the secondary chains fall down between the timing chain guides. **Caution 1:** *If the rocker*

arms were not removed as suggested in Step 9, it will be necessary to hold the camshafts from rotating with a set of locking pliers while the sprocket is being removed. Work on one camshaft and sprocket at a time starting with the left sprocket and proceeding to the right sprocket. After the sprocket is removed from the camshaft(s), let the camshaft slowly rotate to its neutral position. This is typically 15-degrees clockwise on the left camshaft sprocket and 45-degrees counterclockwise on the right camshaft. Pressure from the valve springs will make the camshafts rotate as the sprockets are removed. Sudden movement of the camshafts may allow the valves to strike the pistons. **Caution 2:** *Never install the locking pliers on a camshaft lobe as damage to the camshaft will occur. When using locking pliers, always rotate the camshaft with locking pliers by the shaft.* **Caution 3:** *Do not rotate the crankshaft or camshafts separately after the secondary timing chains are loosened or removed with*

the rocker arms installed in the engine as piston or valve damage may occur. The only exception to this rule is when the camshafts must be rotated slightly, to realign the camshaft sprockets with the camshafts during installation. **Caution 4:** *The right camshaft sprocket is identified by the camshaft position sensor ring which is fastened to the rear of the sprocket. Be extremely careful not to damage or place a magnetic object of any kind near the camshaft position sensor ring or a no start condition may occur after installation.*

17 Remove the idler sprocket bolt, then detach the idler sprocket, the crankshaft sprocket, the primary timing chain and the secondary timing chains as an assembly **(see illustration)**.

18 Remove the cylinder head access plugs **(see illustrations 7.16a and 7.16b)**. Also remove the oil fill tube (if not already removed) from the front of the right cylinder head. Detach the timing chain guides and tensioner arms **(see illustration)**.

7.17 Remove the primary timing chain and the secondary chains
as an assembly from the engine

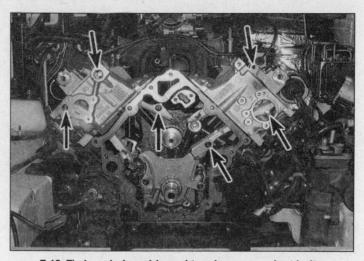

7.18 Timing chain guide and tensioner arm pivot bolts

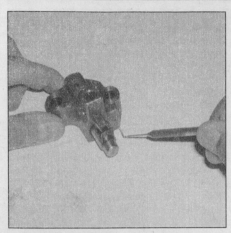

7.22 If excessive wear on the chain guides is evident, check the oil jet on the side of each secondary tensioner for clogging

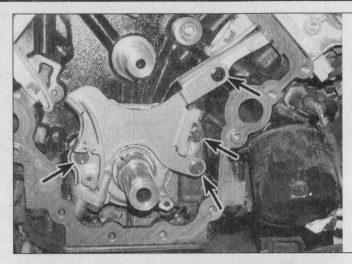

7.26 Primary timing chain tensioner/oil pump mounting bolts

Inspection

Refer to illustration 7.22

19   Inspect the camshaft and crankshaft sprockets for wear on the teeth and keyways.

20   Inspect the chains for cracks or excessive wear of the rollers.

21   Inspect the facings of the primary chain tensioner, secondary chain guides and tensioner arms for excessive wear. If any of the components show signs of excessive wear or the chain guides are grooved in excess of 0.039 inch deep, they must be replaced.

22   If any of the timing chain guides are excessively grooved or melted, the tensioner lube jet may be clogged. Be sure to remove the jet and clean it with a small metal pick, and then blow compressed air through it to remove any debris or foreign material **(see illustration)**.

23   Inspect the idler sprocket bushing, shaft and spline joint for wear.

24   Inspect the tensioner piston and ratchet assembly on both of the secondary chain tensioners. If it appears there has been heavy contact between the piston, and ratchet assembly, replace the tensioner arm and secondary timing chain. **Note:** *Secondary timing chain stretch can be checked by rotating the engine clockwise until the pistons in the secondary tensioners reach their maximum travel or extension. Using a machinist's ruler or a dial caliper, measure the piston protrusion or extension from the stepped ledge on the piston to the tensioner housing on each tensioner. If the maximum extension of either tensioner piston exceeds 0.590 inch, the secondary timing chains are worn beyond their limits and should be replaced.*

Installation

Refer to illustrations 7.26, 7.27, 7.31, 7.33, 7.39, 7.48 and 7.50

25   If removed, install the timing chain guides and tensioner pivot arms back onto the engine and tighten the bolts to the torque listed in this Chapter's Specifications. Apply

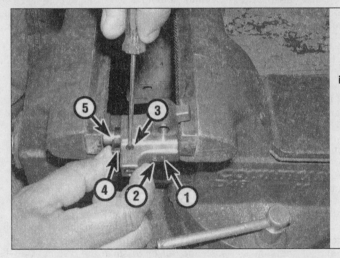

7.27 Locking the secondary tensioner(s) in the retracted position - note the identification mark on the side of the tensioner, as they are not interchangeable

1   *Insert locking pin*
2   *Identification mark*
3   *Ratchet pawl*
4   *Ratchet*
5   *Tensioner piston*

medium strength thread-locking compound to the tensioner pivot arm bolts before installing them. Note that the silver bolts retain the guides to the cylinder head and the black colored bolts retain the guides to the engine block.

26   If the primary timing chain tensioner was removed or replaced, install it back onto the engine in the locked position and tighten the lower two bolts to the torque listed in this Chapter's Specifications **(see illustration)**.

27   Working on one secondary timing chain tensioner at a time, compress the tensioner piston in a vise until the stepped edge is flush with the tensioner body **(see illustration)**. Insert a small scribe or other suitable tool into the side of the tensioner body and push the spring loaded ratchet pawl away from the ratchet mechanism, then push the ratchet down into the tensioner body until it's approximately 0.080 inch away from the tensioner body. Insert the end of a paper clip into the hole on the front of the tensioner to lock the tensioner in place.

28   After the two secondary tensioners have been compressed and locked into place, install them on the engine and tighten the bolts to the torque listed in this Chapter's Specifications. Make sure the tensioner with the R mark is installed on the right secondary chain

(passenger's side) and the tensioner with L mark is installed on the left secondary chain (driver's side). The secondary chain tensioners cannot be switched with one another. Also make sure the plate behind the left secondary chain tensioner is installed correctly.

29   If you purchased a new timing chain, verify that you have the correct timing chain for your vehicle by counting the number of links the chain has and comparing the new chain with the old chain. Also compare the position of the colored links in the new chain with the position of the colored links in the old chain.

30   Note that the idler sprocket has three sprockets and a gear incorporated into it. The front or forward facing sprocket (the largest of the three) is for the primary timing chain, the second or middle sprocket is for the left secondary chain, the third or rear sprocket is for the right secondary chain and the gear (3.7L V6 engines only) is for the counterbalance shaft (the 4.7 V8 doesn't have a counterbalance shaft). The next 5 Steps will involve assembling the timing chains onto the idler sprocket on a workbench.

31   Place the idler sprocket on a workbench with the mark on the front in the 12 o'clock position. Loop the right camshaft chain over the rear gear (farthest away from the primary chain gear) on the idler sprocket and position

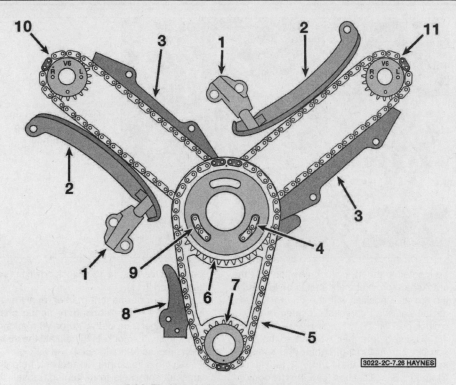

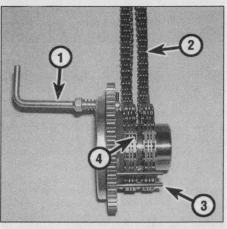

7.33 Install the secondary chain holding tool onto the idler sprocket with the plated links on the right camshaft chain in the 4 o'clock position and the left camshaft chain in the 8 o'clock position (typical)

1   *Secondary chain holding tool*
2   *Right camshaft timing chain*
3   *Secondary chain holding tool retaining pins*
4   *Left camshaft timing chain*

7.31 Timing chain installation details

1	*Secondary timing chain tensioner*	7	*Crankshaft sprocket*
2	*Secondary tensioner arm*	8	*Primary chain tensioner*
3	*Chain guide*	9	*Two plated links on left camshaft chain*
4	*Two plated links on right camshaft chain*	10	*Right camshaft sprocket and secondary chain*
5	*Primary chain*	11	*Left camshaft sprocket and secondary chain*
6	*Idler sprocket*		

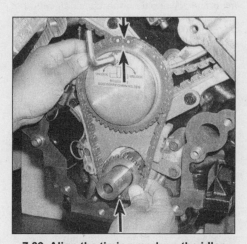

7.39 Align the timing mark on the idler sprocket gear with the timing mark on the counterbalance shaft, then install the idler sprocket, the crankshaft sprocket, the timing chains and the chain holding tool as an assembly onto the engine with the marks aligned as shown - feed the secondary chains up through the timing chain guides and loop them over the camshaft hubs, then push the primary chain assembly the rest of the way on the engine until it's seated against the block

it so that the two plated links on the chain are visible through the lower (4 o'clock) window in the idler sprocket **(see illustration)**.

32   Loop the left camshaft chain over the front of the idler sprocket and position it over the middle gear so that the two plated links on the chain are visible through the lower (8 o'clock) window in the idler sprocket. **Note:** *After the left chain is in position, the two plated links on the right chain will no longer be visible through the 4 o'clock window in the idler sprocket, so be sure that the right camshaft chain is installed correctly before installing the left camshaft chain.*

33   After the secondary (camshaft) chains have been installed properly on the idler sprocket, install the special secondary chain holding tool onto the idler sprocket **(see illustration)**. This tool serves as a third hand, to secure the camshaft chains to the idler sprocket during the installation of the idler sprocket onto the engine.

34   Install the primary timing chain onto the primary chain gear of the idler sprocket and align the double plated links with the mark on the front of the sprocket. The mark on the idler sprocket should still be in the 12 o'clock position.

35   Insert the teeth of the crankshaft sprocket into the primary timing chain with the mark on the crankshaft sprocket pointing down in

the 6 o'clock position and aligned with the single plated link on the chain.

36   Lubricate the idler shaft and bushing with clean engine oil.

37   Install the idler sprocket, the crankshaft sprocket and the timing chains with the chain holding tool as an assembly onto the engine. Slide the crankshaft sprocket over the keyway on the crankshaft and position the idler sprocket partially over the idler shaft (just enough to hold the primary chain in place). Then feed the secondary chains up through the chain guides and the cylinder head. **Note:** *It may be easier to bend a hook in the end of a coat hanger to help pull the secondary chains up through the timing chain guides and the cylinder head opening.*

38   Loop the secondary chains over the camshaft hubs and secure them with rubber bands to remove the slack from the chains.

39   Push the idler sprocket, primary timing chain and the crankshaft sprocket assembly back on to the engine until they're fully seated against the block **(see illustration)**. If you're working on a 3.7L V6 engine, you'll have to align the timing mark on the idler sprocket gear with the timing mark on the counterbalance shaft gear while doing this. **Note:** *On 3.7L V6 engines, make sure the single mark on the counterbalance shaft gear locks into position between the two marks on the idler*

sprocket gear.

40   Thoroughly clean the idler sprocket bolt. Make sure all oil is removed from the bolt threads before installation, as over-tightening of bolts may occur if oil is not removed, then lubricate the idler sprocket washer with small amount of clean engine oil making sure not to get oil on the bolt threads. Remove the secondary timing chain holding tool from the idler sprocket, then install the idler sprocket retain-

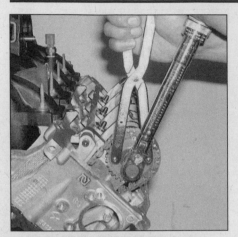

7.48 Tightening the left camshaft sprocket bolt

7.50 Timing chain cover tightening sequence

ing bolt and tighten it to the torque listed in this Chapter's Specifications.

41   Align the L mark on left camshaft sprocket with the plated link on the left camshaft chain and position the camshaft sprocket over the camshaft hub (**see illustration 7.31**). The camshaft may have to be rotated slightly to align the dowel pin on the camshaft with the slot on the sprocket.

42   Align the R mark on right camshaft sprocket with the plated link on the right camshaft chain and position the camshaft sprocket over the camshaft hub. The camshaft may have to be rotated slightly to align the dowel pin on the camshaft with the slot on the sprocket. **Note:** *If the rocker arms were not removed as suggested in Step 9, it will be necessary to rotate and hold the camshafts with a set of locking pliers while the sprocket is being installed. This is typically 15-degrees counterclockwise on the left camshaft sprocket and 45-degrees clockwise on the right camshaft (the exact opposite of removal). Work on one camshaft and sprocket at a time starting with the left sprocket and proceeding to the right sprocket and never rotate the camshaft by a camshaft lobe or damage to the camshaft will occur.*

43   Thoroughly clean the camshaft sprocket bolts. Make sure all oil is removed from the bolt threads before installation, as over-tightening of bolts may occur if oil is not removed, then lubricate the bolt washers with small amount of clean engine oil making sure not to get oil on the threads.

44   Install the camshaft sprocket bolts finger tight.

45   Verify that all the plated timing chain links are aligned with their corresponding marks (**see illustration 7.31**).

46   Remove the locking pins from the primary timing chain tensioner and the secondary timing chain tensioners. **Caution:** *Do not manually extend the tensioners; doing so will only over-extend the tensioners and lead to premature timing chain wear.*

47   Rotate the engine two complete revolutions and re-verify the position of the timing marks again. The idler sprocket mark should

be located in the 12 o'clock position and the crankshaft sprocket mark should be located in the 6 o'clock position with the V6 or V8 marks on the camshaft sprockets located in the 12 o'clock position.

48   Using a spanner wrench to hold the sprockets from turning, tighten the camshaft sprocket bolts to the torque listed in this Chapter's Specifications (**see illustration**).

49   Remove all traces of old sealant or gasket material from the timing chain cover and the engine block.

50   Place the timing chain cover and gasket in position on the engine and install the bolts in their original locations and tighten the bolts to the torque listed in this Chapter's Specifications. Follow the correct tightening sequence (**see illustration**).

51   The remainder of the installation is the reverse of removal. Be sure to use pipe sealant on the cylinder head plugs to prevent oil leaks.

52   Change the engine oil and filter and refill the cooling system (see Chapter 1).

8   Camshafts - removal, inspection and installation

Note 1: *Special tools are necessary to complete this procedure. Read through the entire procedure and obtain the special tools before beginning work.*
Note 2: *The camshafts should always be thoroughly inspected before installation and camshaft endplay should always be checked prior to camshaft removal (see Step 17).*

Removal

Refer to illustrations 8.6 and 8.9

1   Disconnect the cable from the negative terminal of the battery (see Chapter 5, Section 1).

2   Remove the valve covers (see Section 5).

3   Rotate the engine with a socket and ratchet (in a clockwise direction only) by the crankshaft pulley/vibration damper bolt until the V6 or V8 marks on the camshaft sprock-

ets are located in the 12 o'clock position (**see illustration 7.11**).

4   Using a permanent marker, apply alignment marks to the secondary timing chain links on either side of the V6 or V8 marks on both camshaft sprockets to help aid the installation process (4 marks total).

5   Using a spanner wrench to hold the camshaft sprockets from turning, loosen the camshaft sprocket bolts several turns, then retighten the bolts by hand until they're snug up against the sprocket. If the camshaft sprockets have rotated during the bolt-loosening process, rotate the engine clockwise until the V6 or V8 marks on the cam sprockets are realigned in the 12 o'clock position.

6   Install a timing chain tensioner wedge through the opening in the top of the cylinder head and force the wedge down between the narrowest section of the secondary chain (**see illustration**). If both camshafts are to be removed, two timing chain wedges will be necessary (one for the left camshaft chain and one for the right camshaft chain). The wedge is used to secure the chain and the secondary tensioner in place while the camshaft is removed. **Caution 1:** *Failure to use a timing chain wedge will allow the secondary tensioner to over-extend and require removal of the timing chain cover to reset the tensioners.* **Caution 2:** *Never force the wedge past the narrowest section of the secondary timing chain as damage to the tensioner will occur. If a timing chain wedge is not available, they may be fabricated using a block of wood that is 3/8 to 1/2-inch thick and a piece of wire to pull the wedge out of the cylinder head after installation.*

7   Remove the Camshaft Position Sensor (CMP) (see Chapter 6).

8   Remove the camshaft sprocket retaining bolt(s) and detach the camshaft sprocket(s) from the camshaft hub(s). Disengage the camshaft chain(s) from the sprocket(s) and remove the camshaft sprocket(s) from the engine.

9   Make note of the markings on the camshaft bearing caps. The caps are marked from 1 to 4 or 5 with arrow marks on the caps indicating the front of the engine (**see illustra-**

8.6 The timing chain tensioner wedge is pushed down between the chain strands to secure the secondary chain and the tensioner in place while the camshaft is removed - this wedge is fabricated from a block of wood and a piece of wire

8.9 Verify that the camshaft bearing caps are marked to ensure correct reinstallation - do not mix-up the caps from the left cylinder head with the caps from the right cylinder head

tion). If both camshafts are being removed, use a permanent marker to mark each bearing cap on the right cylinder head with an R and each bearing cap on the left cylinder head with an L to indicate from which cylinder head they came from. Loosen the camshaft bearing caps bolts a little at a time beginning with the bearing caps on the ends, then working inward. **Caution:** *Keep the caps in order. They must go back in the same location they were removed from.*

10   Detach the bearing caps. **Note:** *The rocker arms may slide out of position. Mark the rocker arms so that they will be installed in the same location.*

11   Remove the camshaft(s) from the cylinder head. Mark the camshaft(s) Left or Right to indicate which cylinder head it came from.

Inspection

Refer to illustrations 8.14, 8.15 and 8.18

12   Inspect the camshaft sprockets for wear on the teeth.

13   Inspect the chains for cracks or exces-

sive wear of the rollers. If any of the components show signs of excessive wear they must be replaced.

14   Visually check the camshaft bearing surfaces on the cylinder head(s) for pitting, score marks, galling and abnormal wear. If the bearing surfaces are damaged, the cylinder head may have to be replaced **(see illustration)**.

15   Measure the outside diameter of each camshaft bearing journal and record your measurements **(see illustration)**. Compare them to the journal outside diameter specified in this Chapter, then measure the inside diameter of each corresponding camshaft bearing and record the measurements. Subtract each cam journal outside diameter from its respective cam bearing bore inside diameter to determine the oil clearance for each bearing. Compare the results to the specified journal-to-bearing clearance. If any of the measurements fall outside the standard specified wear limits in this Chapter, either the camshaft or the cylinder head, or both, must be replaced.

16   Check camshaft runout by placing the

camshaft back into the cylinder head and set up a dial indicator on the center journal. Zero the dial indicator. Turn the camshaft slowly and note the dial indicator readings. Runout should not exceed 0.0010 inch. If the measured runout exceeds the specified runout, replace the camshaft.

17   Check the camshaft endplay by placing a dial indicator with the stem in line with the camshaft and touching the snout. Push the camshaft all the way to the rear and zero the dial indicator. Next, pry the camshaft to the front as far as possible and check the reading on the dial indicator. The distance it moves is the endplay. If it's greater than the Specifications listed in this Chapter, check the bearing caps for wear. If the bearing caps are worn, the cylinder head must be replaced.

18   Compare the camshaft lobe height by measuring each lobe with a micrometer **(see illustration)**. Measure each of the intake lobes and write the measurements and relative positions down on a piece of paper. Then measure of each of the exhaust lobes and record the

8.14 Inspect the cam bearing surfaces in each cylinder head for pits, score marks and abnormal wear - if wear or damage is noted, the cylinder head must be replaced

8.15 Measure the outside diameter of each camshaft journal and the inside diameter of each bearing to determine the oil clearance measurement

8.18 Measuring cam lobe height with a micrometer, make sure you move the micrometer to get the highest reading (top of cam lobe)

8.21 Camshaft bearing cap bolt tightening sequence - 4.7L V8 engine shown

9.1 Location of the cowl support brace (A) and the windshield wiper motor bracket (B)

measurements and relative positions also. This will let you compare all of the intake lobes to one another and all of the exhaust lobes to one another. If the difference between the lobes exceeds 0.005 inch the camshaft should be replaced. Do not compare intake lobe heights to exhaust lobe heights, as lobe lift may be different. Only compare intake lobes to intake lobes and exhaust lobes to exhaust lobes for this comparison.

Installation

Refer to illustration 8.21

19 Apply moly-based engine assembly lubricant to the camshaft lobes and journals and install the camshaft(s) into the cylinder head with the dowel pins in the 10 o'clock position. If the old camshafts are being used, make sure they're installed in the exact location from which they came.
20 Install the bearing caps and bolts and tighten them hand tight.
21 Tighten the bearing cap bolts a little at a time, to the torque listed in this Chapter's Specifications, starting with the middle bolts and working outward **(see illustration)**.
22 Engage the camshaft sprocket teeth with the camshaft drive chain links so that the V6 or V8 mark on the sprocket(s) is between the two marks made in Step 5 during removal, then position the sprocket over the dowel on the camshaft hub. At this point the chain marks and the V6 or V8 marks on the sprocket should be pointing up in the 12 o'clock position.
23 Thoroughly clean the camshaft sprocket bolts. Make sure all oil is removed from the bolt threads before installation, as over-tightening of bolts may occur if oil is not removed, then lubricate the bolt washers with a small amount of clean engine oil, making sure not to get oil on the threads.
24 Install the camshaft sprocket bolts and tighten them to the torque listed in this Chapter's Specifications **(see illustration 7.48)**.
25 Remove the timing chain wedge(s).

26 Install the camshaft position sensor (CPS) (see Chapter 6).
27 Install the valve covers (see Section 5).
28 Connect the cable to the negative terminal of the battery.

9   Intake manifold - removal and installation

Warning: *The engine must be completely cool before beginning this procedure.*

Removal

Refer to illustration 9.1

1   Remove the cowl (see Chapter 11). Remove the cowl support brace and the wiper motor support bracket **(see illustration)**.
2   Relieve the fuel system pressure (see Chapter 4).
3   Disconnect the cable from the negative terminal of the battery (see Chapter 5, Section 1).
4   Remove the resonator and intake air duct from the throttle body (see Chapter 4).
5   Label and disconnect the vacuum hoses leading to the intake manifold for the PCV valve, power brake booster, cruise control servo and evaporative emission control system.
6   Disconnect all of the electrical connectors leading to the intake manifold for the various sensors, the ignition coils and the Idle Air Control motor (IAC).
7   Disconnect the electrical connectors for the alternator and the air conditioning compressor.
8   Unbolt the ground straps attached to the intake manifold and the throttle body and the left and right radio suppressor straps.
9   Remove the engine oil dipstick nut from the stud on the intake manifold, then follow the dipstick tube to the rear of the engine block and remove the bolt securing the tube at the back of the block. Pull the dipstick tube up and out of the engine block to remove it.

10 Detach the throttle cable and the cruise control cable from the throttle body and the throttle cable bracket (see Chapter 4).
11 Remove the ignition coils (see Chapter 5).
12 Remove the fuel rails, then remove the throttle body and mounting bracket (see Chapter 4).
13 Refer to Chapter 1 and drain the cooling system, then remove the heater hoses from the front cover and heater core tubes.
14 Refer to Chapter 6 and remove the coolant temperature sensor. This step is necessary to allow clearance for the intake manifold as it is removed.
15 Remove the intake manifold mounting fasteners in the reverse order of the tightening sequence **(see illustrations 9.21a or 9.21b)**.
16 The manifold might be stuck to the cylinder heads and force may be required to break the gasket seal. **Caution:** *Don't pry between the manifold and the heads or damage to the gasket sealing surfaces may occur, leading to vacuum leaks.*
17 Label and detach any remaining hoses which would interfere with the removal of the intake manifold.
18 Lift the manifold straight up and remove it from the engine.

Installation

Refer to illustrations 9.21a and 9.21b

19 Clean and inspect the intake manifold-to-cylinder head sealing surfaces. Inspect the gaskets on the manifold for tears or cracks, replacing them if necessary. The gaskets can be reused if not damaged.
20 Position the manifold on the engine making sure the gaskets and manifold are aligned correctly over the cylinder heads, then install the intake manifold bolts hand tight.
21 Following the recommended tightening sequence, tighten the bolts to the torque listed in this Chapter's Specifications **(see illustrations)**.
22 The remainder of the installation is the

9.21a Intake manifold bolt tightening sequence - 3.7L V6

9.21b Intake manifold bolt tightening sequence - 4.7L V8

reverse of the removal procedure.

23   Fill the cooling system, run the engine and check for fuel, vacuum and coolant leaks.

10   Exhaust manifold - removal and installation

Warning: *The engine must be completely cool before beginning this procedure.*

Removal

1   Disconnect the cable from the negative terminal of the battery (see Chapter 5, Section 1).

2   Block the rear wheels, set the parking brake, raise the front of the vehicle and support it securely on jackstands.

3   Unbolt the exhaust pipe from the exhaust manifold.

Right side exhaust manifold, 4.7L V8 models

4   Remove the drivebelt (see Chapter 1).

5   Drain the engine coolant (see Chapter 1).

6   Remove the air inlet duct and air filter housing (see Chapter 4).

7   Remove the air conditioning compressor (see Chapter 3).

8   Remove the accumulator bracket.

9   Remove the heater hoses at the engine (see Chapter 3).

10   Remove the starter (see Chapter 5).

Either manifold, all models

11   Remove the exhaust manifold heat shields.

12   Remove the exhaust manifold mounting bolts and remove the manifold from the vehicle. Lower the exhaust manifold and remove it from under the vehicle.

Installation

13   Clean the mating surfaces to remove all traces of old gasket material, then inspect the manifold for distortion and cracks. Warpage can be checked with a precision straightedge held against the mating flange. If a feeler gauge thicker than 0.030-inch can be inserted between the straightedge and flange surface, take the manifold to an automotive machine shop for resurfacing.

14   Place the exhaust manifold in position with a new gasket and install the mounting bolts finger tight.

15   Starting in the middle and working out toward the ends, tighten the mounting bolts in several increments, to the torque listed in this Chapter's Specifications. Tighten the heat shield bolts to the torque listed in this Chapter's Specifications.

16   Install the remaining components in the reverse order of removal. If you're working on a right-side exhaust manifold on a 4.7L engine, refill the cooling system (see Chapter 1).

17   Start the engine and check for exhaust leaks between the manifold and cylinder head and between the manifold and exhaust pipe.

11   Cylinder head - removal and installation

Warning: *The engine must be completely cool before beginning this procedure.*
Note: *The following procedure describes how to remove the cylinder heads with the camshaft(s) and the exhaust manifold(s) still attached to the cylinder head.*

Removal

1   Remove the intake manifold (see Section 9).

2   Refer to Section 7 and remove the timing chains, sprockets and the timing chain guides.

3   Raise the front of the vehicle and support it securely on jackstands.

4   Unbolt the exhaust pipes from the exhaust manifolds.

5   Label and remove any remaining items attached to the cylinder head, such as coolant fittings, ground straps, cables, hoses, wires or brackets.

6   Using a breaker bar and the appropriate sized socket, loosen the cylinder head bolts in 1/4-turn increments until they can be removed by hand. Loosen the bolts in the reverse order of the tightening sequence **(see illustrations 11.19a or 11.19b)** to avoid warping or cracking the head.

7   Lift the cylinder head off the engine block with the camshaft in place and the exhaust manifold attached. If it's stuck, very carefully pry up at the front end of the cylinder head, beyond the gasket surface, at a casting protrusion.

8   Remove all external components from the head to allow for thorough cleaning and inspection.

Installation

Refer to illustrations 11.19a, 11.19b and 11.19c

9   The mating surfaces of the cylinder head and block must be perfectly clean when the head is installed.

10   Use a gasket scraper to remove all traces of carbon and old gasket material from the cylinder head and engine block being careful not to gouge the aluminum, then clean the mating surfaces with lacquer thinner or acetone. If there's oil on the mating surfaces when the head is installed, the gasket may not seal correctly and leaks could develop. When working on the block, stuff the cylinders with clean shop rags to keep out debris. Use a vacuum cleaner to remove material that falls into the cylinders.

11   Check the block and head mating surfaces for nicks, deep scratches and other damage. If damage is slight, it can be removed with a file; if it's excessive, machining may be the only alternative.

12   Use a tap of the correct size to chase the threads in the head bolt holes, then clean the

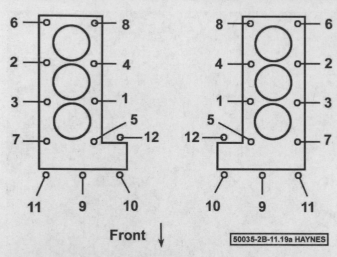

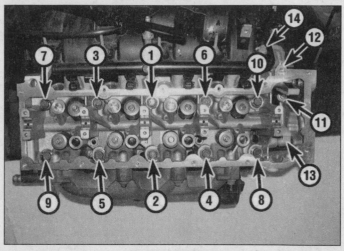

11.19a Cylinder head bolt tightening sequence - 3.7L V6

11.19b Cylinder head bolt tightening sequence - 4.7L V8

holes with compressed air - make sure that nothing remains in the holes. **Warning:** *Wear eye protection when using compressed air!*

13   With a straightedge, check each cylinder head bolt for stretching. If all threads do not contact the straightedge, replace the bolt.

14   Check the cylinder head for warpage. Check the head gasket, intake and exhaust manifold surfaces. Consult with an automotive machine shop.

15   Install any components that were removed from the head such as the lash adjusters, the exhaust manifold and the camshaft back onto the cylinder head.

16   Position the new cylinder head gasket over the dowel pins on the block noting which direction on the gasket faces up.

17   Carefully set the head over the dowels on the block without disturbing the gasket.

18   Before installing the M10 head bolts, apply a small amount of clean engine oil to the threads and hardened washers (if equipped). The chamfered side of the washers must face the bolt heads. Before installing the M8 head bolts, apply a small amount of thread sealant to the bolt threads.

19   Install the bolts in their original locations and tighten them finger tight. Then tighten them, following the proper sequence, to the torque and angle of rotation listed in this Chapter's Specifications **(see illustrations)**.

20   Install the timing chain guides, the timing chains and the timing chain sprockets as described in Section 7. The remaining installation steps are the reverse of removal.

21   Refill the cooling system and change the engine oil and filter (see Chapter 1).

22   Start the engine and check for oil and coolant leaks.

12   Crankshaft pulley/vibration damper - removal and installation

Refer to illustrations 12.4, 12.5 and 12.6

1   Disconnect the cable from the negative terminal of the battery (see Chapter 5, Section 1).

2   Refer to Chapter 3 and remove the cool-

ing fans and shroud assembly.

3   Remove the drivebelts (see Chapter 1) and position the belt tensioner away from the crankshaft pulley.

4   Use a strap wrench or chain wrench around the crankshaft pulley to hold it while using a breaker bar and socket to remove the crankshaft pulley center bolt **(see illustration)**.

5   Pull the damper off the crankshaft with a puller **(see illustration)**. **Caution:** *The jaws of the puller must only contact the hub of the pulley - not the outer ring. Also, the puller screw must not contact the threads in the nose of the crankshaft; it must either bear on the end of the crankshaft nose or a spacer must be inserted into the nose of the crankshaft to protect the threads.*

6   Check the surface on the pulley hub that the oil seal rides on. If the surface has been grooved from long-time contact with the seal, a press-on sleeve may be available to renew the sealing surface **(see illustration)**. This sleeve is pressed into place with a hammer and a block of wood and is commonly avail-

11.19c Using a torque angle gauge during the final stages of tightening

12.4 Use a strap wrench to hold the crankshaft pulley while removing the center bolt (a chain-type wrench may be used if you wrap a section of old drivebelt or a rag around the crankshaft pulley first)

12.5 The use of a three jaw puller will be necessary to remove the crankshaft pulley - always place the puller jaws around the pulley hub, not the outer ring

12.6 If the sealing surface of the pulley hub has a wear groove from contact with the seal, repair sleeves are available at most auto parts stores

13.2 Pry the seal out very carefully with a seal removal tool or screwdriver, being careful not to nick or gouge the seal bore or the crankshaft

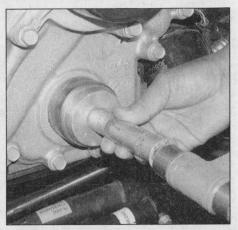

13.4 Use a seal driver or large-diameter socket to drive the new seal into the cover

able at auto parts stores for various applications.

7   Lubricate the pulley hub with clean engine oil. Align the slot in the pulley with the key on the crankshaft and push the crankshaft pulley on the crankshaft as far as it will go. Use a vibration damper installation tool to press the pulley the rest of the way onto the crankshaft.

8   Install the crankshaft pulley retaining bolt and tighten it to the torque listed in this Chapter's Specifications.

9   The remainder of installation is the reverse of the removal.

13   Crankshaft front oil seal - replacement

Refer to illustrations 13.2 and 13.4

1   Remove the crankshaft pulley from the engine (see Section 12).

2   Carefully pry the seal out of the cover with a seal removal tool or a large screwdriver **(see illustration). Caution:** *Be careful not to scratch, gouge or distort the area that the seal fits into or an oil leak will develop.*

3   Clean the bore to remove any old seal material and corrosion. Position the new seal in the bore with the seal lip (usually the side with the spring) facing IN (toward the engine). A small amount of oil applied to the outer edge of the new seal will make installation easier.

4   Drive the seal into the bore with a seal driver or a large socket and hammer until it's completely seated **(see illustration).** Select a socket that's the same outside diameter as the seal and make sure the new seal is pressed into place until it bottoms against the cover flange.

5   Lubricate the seal lips with engine oil and reinstall the crankshaft pulley.

6   The remainder of installation is the reverse of the removal. Run the engine and check for oil leaks.

14   Oil pan - removal and installation

Refer to illustrations 14.4 and 14.11

Removal

1   Disconnect the cable from the negative terminal of the battery (see Chapter 5, Section 1).

2   Apply the parking brake and block the rear wheels. Raise the front of the vehicle and place it securely on jackstands.

3   Drain the engine oil (see Chapter 1).

4   If equipped, remove the skidplate, then remove the transmission-to-oil pan support brace at the rear of the pan **(see illustration).**

5   Remove the transmission oil cooler line bracket.

6   Remove the front crossmember (see Chapter 10).

7   Remove the cowl (see Chapter 11). Remove the cowl support brace and the wiper motor support bracket (see Section 9).

8   Remove the engine cooling fan and shroud (see Chapter 3).

9   Attach an engine hoist or an engine support fixture to the lifting eyes on the engine, raise the engine just enough to take the weight of the engine off the engine mounts, then remove the engine mount through-bolts (see Section 18). **Note:** *If clearance is not sufficient for oil pan removal, it will be necessary to remove the intake manifold (see Section 9) and raise the engine slightly using the engine hoist.*

4WD 4.7L models

10   Remove the front axle assembly (see Chapter 8).

All models

11   Remove the bolts and nuts, noting the stud locations, then carefully separate the oil pan from the block. Don't pry between the block and the pan or damage to the sealing surfaces and gasket could occur and oil leaks

may develop. Instead, tap on the side of the oil pan with a rubber mallet if necessary to break the gasket seal **(see illustration).**

12   Remove the two nuts and one bolt that secures the oil pump pick-up tube and windage tray. Drop the pick-up tube into the oil pan, then remove the pick-up tube, windage tray and oil pan as a unit.

Installation

13   Clean the oil pan with solvent and remove any gasket material from the block and the pan mating surfaces. Clean the mating surfaces with lacquer thinner or acetone and make sure the bolt holes in the block are clear. Check the oil pan flange for distortion, particularly around the bolt holes.

14   Inspect the oil pan gasket for cuts and tears, replacing it if necessary. If the gasket is in good condition, it can be reused. **Note:** *The oil pan gasket and the windage tray are a one-piece design, therefore must be replaced together.*

15   Place the pick-up tube and oil pan gasket/windage tray in the oil pan and position the oil pan on the engine. **Note:** *Always use a new O-ring on the pick-up tube and tighten the pick-up tube-to-oil pump bolt first.*

16   After the fasteners are installed, tighten all the bolts in several steps, in a criss-cross pattern starting from the center and working out to the ends, to the torque listed in this Chapter's Specifications.

17   Place the transmission-to-oil pan support brace in position and install the vertically mounted bolts. Torque the vertically mounted bolts to 10 in-lbs, then install the horizontally mounted bolts. Torque the horizontally mounted bolts to 40 ft-lbs, then retorque the vertically mounted bolts to 40 ft-lbs **(see illustration 14.4).**

18   The remaining steps are the reverse of the removal procedure.

19   Refill the engine with oil (see Chapter 1), replace the oil filter, then run the engine until normal operating temperature is reached and check for leaks.

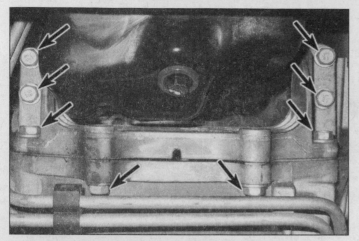

14.4 Remove the oil pan-to-transmission support brace

14.11 If the oil pan is stuck to the gasket, gently tap on the side of the oil pan to break the gasket seal

15 Oil pump - removal, inspection and installation

Removal

Refer to illustration 15.3

1   Refer to Section 7 and remove the timing chains and sprockets.

2   Remove the oil pan, windage tray and pick-up tube (see Section 14).

3   Remove the primary timing chain tensioner/oil pump bolts **(see illustration)**, then remove the tensioner.

4   Remove the remaining oil pump bolts, then gently pry the oil pump housing outward enough to clear the flats on the crankshaft and remove it from the engine.

Inspection

Refer to illustrations 15.5, 15.7a, 15.7b, 15.7c, 15.7d, 15.7e and 15.7f

5   Remove the screws holding the cover on the oil pump **(see illustration)**.

6   Clean all components with solvent, then inspect them for wear and damage. **Caution:** *The oil pressure relief valve and spring are an*

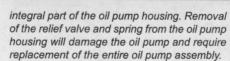

15.3 Oil pump housing/primary timing chain tensioner retaining bolts

integral part of the oil pump housing. Removal of the relief valve and spring from the oil pump housing will damage the oil pump and require replacement of the entire oil pump assembly.

7   Check the clearance of the following oil pump components with a straightedge and feeler gauge and a micrometer **(see illustrations)** and compare the measurement to the clearance specifications listed in this Chap-

ter's Specifications.

a) *Cover flatness*
b) *Outer rotor diameter and thickness*
c) *Inner rotor thickness*
d) *Outer rotor-to-body clearance*
e) *Inner rotor-to-outer rotor tip clearance*
f) *Cover-to-inner rotor side clearance*
g) *Cover-to-outer rotor side clearance*

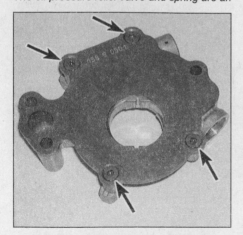

15.5 Remove the screws and lift the cover off

15.7a Place a straightedge across the oil pump cover and check it for warpage with a feeler gauge

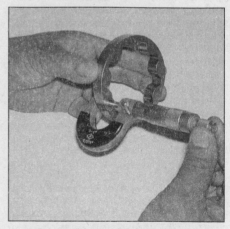

15.7b Use a micrometer to check the thickness and the diameter of the outer rotor

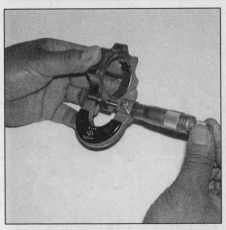

15.7c Use a micrometer or dial caliper to check the thickness of the inner rotor

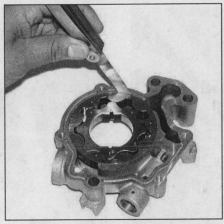

15.7d Check the outer rotor-to-housing clearance

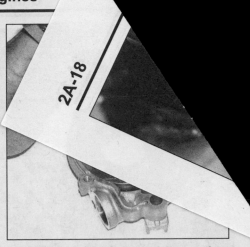

15.7e Check the clearance between the tips of the inner and outer rotors

If any clearance is excessive, replace the entire oil pump assembly.

8   Pack the oil pump rotor cavities with petroleum jelly to prime it. Assemble the oil pump and tighten all fasteners to the torque listed in this Chapter's Specifications.

Installation

9   To install the pump, turn the flats in the rotor so they align with the flats on the crankshaft and push the oil pump back into position against the block.

10   Position the primary timing chain tensioner over the oil pump and install the pump-to-block bolts. Tighten the oil pump/primary timing chain tensioner bolts to the torque listed in this Chapter's Specifications.

11   The remainder of installation is the reverse of removal.

16 Flywheel/driveplate - removal and installation

1   Raise the vehicle and support it securely on jackstands, then refer to Chapter 7 and remove the transmission.

2   Now would be a good time to check and replace the transmission front pump seal on automatic transmissions.

3   Use paint or a center-punch to make alignment marks on the flywheel/driveplate and crankshaft to ensure correct alignment during reinstallation.

4   Remove the bolts that secure the flywheel/driveplate to the crankshaft. If the crankshaft turns, wedge a screwdriver into the ring gear teeth to keep the crankshaft from turning.

5   Pull straight back on the flywheel/driveplate to detach it from the crankshaft.

6   Installation is the reverse of removal. Be sure to align the matching paint marks. Use thread locking compound on the bolt threads and tighten them in several steps, in a criss-cross pattern, to the torque listed in this Chapter's Specifications.

17 Rear main oil seal - replacement

Refer to illustration 17.2

1   These models use a one-piece rear main seal that is sandwiched between the engine block and the lower main bearing cap assembly, or "bed plate" as it's often referred to. Replacing this seal requires removal of the transmission (see Chapter 7) and flywheel/driveplate (see Section 16).

2   The seal can be removed by prying it out of the engine block with a screwdriver, being careful not to nick the crankshaft surface **(see illustration)**. Wrap the screwdriver tip with tape to avoid damage.

3   Thoroughly clean the seal bore in the block with a shop towel. Remove all traces of oil and dirt.

4   Lubricate the seal lip with clean engine oil and install the seal over the end of the crankshaft. Make sure the lip of the seal points toward the engine.

5   Preferably, a seal installation tool (available at most auto parts stores) should be used to press the new seal back into place.

15.7f Using a straightedge and feeler gauge, check the side clearance between the surface of the oil pump and the inner and outer rotors

Drive the new seal squarely into the seal bore and flush with the rear of the engine block.

6   The remainder of installation is the reverse of the removal procedure.

18 Engine mounts - check and replacement

1   There are three powertrain mounts on the vehicles covered by this manual: left and right engine mounts attached to the engine block and to the frame and a rear mount attached to the transmission and the frame. The rear transmission mount is covered in Chapter 7. Engine mounts seldom require attention, but broken or deteriorated mounts should be replaced immediately or the added strain placed on the driveline components may cause damage or wear.

Check

2   During the check, the engine must be raised slightly to remove the weight from the mounts.

3   Raise the vehicle and support it securely

17.2 Pry the seal out very carefully with a seal removal tool or screwdriver - if the crankshaft is damaged, the new seal will leak!

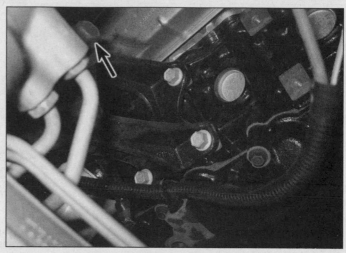

18.12a The engine mounts are secured by the through-bolt (arrow) and the mount-to-engine block bolts - left side mount shown

18.12b Location of the right side through bolt on a 4.7L V8 engine

on jackstands, then position a jack under the engine oil pan. Place a large wood block between the jack head and the oil pan, then carefully raise the engine just enough to take the weight off the mounts. **Warning:** *DO NOT place any part of your body under the engine when it's supported only by a jack!*

4   Check for relative movement between the inner and outer portions of the mount (use a large screwdriver or prybar to attempt to move the mounts). If movement is noted, lower the engine and tighten the mount fasteners.

5   Check the mounts to see if the rubber is cracked, hardened or separated from the metal casing which would indicate a need for replacement.

6   Rubber preservative should be applied to the mounts to slow deterioration.

Replacement

Refer to illustrations 18.12a and 18.12b

7   Disconnect the cable from the negative terminal of the battery (see Chapter 5, Section 1).

8   Remove the engine cooling fan and shroud (see Chapter 3). **Caution:** *Raising the engine with the cooling fan in place may damage the viscous clutch.*

9   Raise the front of the vehicle and support it securely on jackstands.

10   Support the engine with a lifting device from above. **Caution:** *Do not connect the lifting device to the intake manifold. Raise the engine just enough to take the weight off the engine mounts. If you're removing the driver's side engine mount, removal of the oil filter will be necessary.*

2WD models

11   Remove the engine mount-to-frame support bracket through-bolt.

12   Remove the mount-to-engine block bolts, then remove the mount and the heat shield, if equipped **(see illustrations)**.

13   Place the heat shield and the new mount in position, install the mount-to-engine block bolts and tighten all the bolts securely.

4WD models

14   Use a floor jack and jackstands to support the front axle. The front axle will be partially lowered to make additional clearance for the engine mount removal.

15   Remove the engine skidplate.

16   Remove the front crossmember (see Chapter 10).

17   Remove the bolts that support the engine mount to the front axle.

18   Remove the bolts that attach the front axle to the engine.

19   Remove the engine mount-to-frame support bracket through-bolt.

20   Remove the engine mount to engine support bracket bolt and nuts.

21   Install the engine mount onto the engine support bracket and tighten the bolts securely.

All models

22   After the engine mounts have been installed onto the engine, lower the engine while guiding the engine mount and through-bolt into the frame support bracket. Install the through-bolt nut and tighten it securely.

23   The remainder of the installation is the reverse of removal. Remove the engine hoist and the jackstands and lower the vehicle.

Chapter 2 Part B
5.7L V8 (Hemi) engine

Contents

Specifications

General

Firing order	1-8-4-3-6-5-7-2
Bore and stroke	3.91 x 3.58 inches
Displacement	5.7L (345 cubic inches)
Cylinder numbers (front-to-rear)	
Left (driver's) side	1-3-5-7
Right side	2-4-6-8
Compression	See Chapter 2C

30042 -1-specs HAYNES

**Cylinder locations on the
5.7L Hemi V8 engine**

Camshaft

Journal diameters	
No. 1	2.290 inches
No. 2	2.270 inches
No. 3	2.260 inches
No. 4	2.240 inches
No. 5	1.720 inches
Journal oil clearance	
No. 1, 3 and 5	0.0015 to 0.0030 inch
No. 2 and 4	0.0019 to 0.0035 inch
Endplay	0.0031 to 0.0114 inch

Torque specifications*

	Ft-lbs (unless otherwise indicated)
Camshaft sprocket bolt..	90
Camshaft thrust plate bolts...	21
Cylinder head bolts **(see illustration 10.16)**	
First step	
Large bolts...	25
Small bolts...	15
Second step	
Large bolts...	40
Small bolts...	15
Third step	
Large bolts...	Tighten an additional 90 degrees
Small bolts...	25
Drivebelt tensioner mounting bolt..	30
Drivebelt pulley mounting bolt...	45
Driveplate bolts...	70
Exhaust manifold bolts/nuts	18
Exhaust manifold heat shield nuts..	132 in-lbs
Exhaust pipe flange nuts	20
Flywheel bolts..	55
Intake manifold bolts	105 in-lbs
Oil pan bolts/studs	105 in-lbs
Oil pump pick-up tube bolts..	21
Oil pump mounting bolts...	21
Rear main seal retainer bolts	132 in-lbs
Rocker arm bolts..	16
Rocker arm lifter rail bolts..	106 in-lbs
Timing chain cover bolts...	21
Transmission brace mounting bolts **(see illustration 13.22)**	
Step 1...	50 to 100 in-lbs
Step 2...	40
Valve cover nuts/studs...	70 in-lbs
Vibration damper-to-crankshaft bolt	129
Water pump-to-timing chain cover bolts	21

*Note: *Refer to Part C for additional specifications*

1   General information

This part of Chapter 2 is devoted to in-vehicle repair procedures for the 5.7L V8 (Hemi) engine. All information concerning engine removal and installation and engine overhaul can be found in Part C of this Chapter.

Since the repair procedures included in this Part are based on the assumption that the engine is still installed in the vehicle, if they are being used during a complete engine overhaul (with the engine already out of the vehicle and on a stand) many of the steps included here will not apply.

These Hemi engines use a cast iron engine block with aluminum cylinder heads and intake manifold. The cylinder banks are positioned at a 90-degree angle with the camshaft mounted high in the engine block. The valvetrain includes roller lifters, with pushrods positioned between the camshaft and rocker arms in a nearly horizontal plane.

The camshaft can only be removed after the cylinder heads and valvetrain components (rocker arms, pushrods and lifters) have been removed.

2   Repair operations possible with the engine in the vehicle

Many major repair operations can be accomplished without removing the engine from the vehicle.

Clean the engine compartment and the exterior of the engine with some type of pressure washer before any work is done. A clean engine will make the job easier and will help keep dirt out of the internal areas of the engine.

Depending on the components involved, it may be a good idea to remove the hood to improve access to the engine as repairs are performed (refer to Chapter 11 if necessary).

If oil or coolant leaks develop, indicating

a need for gasket or seal replacement, the repairs can generally be made with the engine in the vehicle. The oil pan gasket, the cylinder head gaskets, intake and exhaust manifold gaskets, timing chain cover gaskets and the crankshaft front oil seal are all accessible with the engine in place.

Exterior engine components, such as the water pump, the starter motor, the alternator and the fuel injection components, as well as the intake and exhaust manifolds, can be removed for repair with the engine in place.

Since the cylinder heads can be removed without removing the engine, valve component servicing can also be accomplished with the engine in the vehicle.

Replacement of, repairs to or inspection of the timing chain and sprockets and the oil pump are all possible with the engine in place.

In extreme cases caused by a lack of necessary equipment, repair or replacement of piston rings, pistons, connecting rods and rod bearings is possible with the engine in the vehicle. However, this practice is not recom-

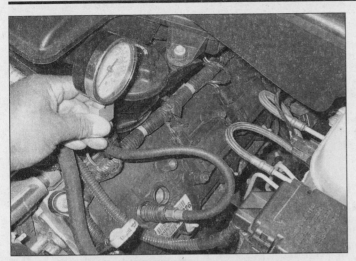

3.4a Install a compression gauge into one of the number one spark plug holes

3.4b Use a breaker bar and deep socket to rotate the crankshaft

mended because of the cleaning and preparation work that must be done to the components involved.

3 Top Dead Center (TDC) for number one piston - locating

Refer to illustrations 3.4a and 3.4b

1   Top Dead Center (TDC) is the highest point in the cylinder that each piston reaches as it travels up-and-down when the crankshaft turns. Each piston reaches TDC on the compression stroke and again on the exhaust stroke, but TDC generally refers to piston position on the compression stroke.

2   In order to bring any piston to TDC, the crankshaft must be turned using a breaker bar and socket on the vibration damper bolt. When looking at the front of the engine, normal crankshaft rotation is clockwise.

3   Disconnect the cable from the negative terminal of the battery (see Chapter 5, Section 1).

4   Remove one of the spark plugs from cylinder number 1, preferably the closest to the front of the engine, then thread a compression gauge into the spark plug hole **(see illustration)**. Turn the crankshaft with a large socket and breaker bar attached to the large bolt that is threaded into the vibration damper **(see illustration)**. When compression registers on the gauge, the number one piston is beginning its compression stroke. Stop turning the crankshaft and remove the gauge.

5   Insert a long dowel into the number one spark plug hole until it rests on top of the piston crown. Continue rotating the crankshaft slowly until the dowel levels off (piston reaches top of travel). This will be approximate TDC for number 1 piston.

6   These engines are not equipped with external components (vibration damper, flywheel, timing hole, etc.) that are marked to identify the position of number 1 TDC. Therefore the only method to double-check the exact location of TDC number 1 on Hemi engines is to remove the timing chain cover to access timing chain sprockets (see Section 9), or with the use of a degree wheel on the crankshaft vibration damper and a positive stop threaded into the spark plug hole, as you would use in the process of degreeing a camshaft (this procedure is described in detail in the *Haynes Chrysler Engine Overhaul Manual*).

4 Valve covers - removal and installation

Removal

Refer to illustrations 4.3a, 4.3b, 4.5, 4.6a and 4.6b

1   Disconnect the cable from the negative terminal of the battery (see Chapter 5, Section 1).

2   Remove the resonator, the air intake ducts and the air filter housing, if necessary. (see Chapter 4).

3   Remove the harness clips from the valve cover studs **(see illustrations)**.

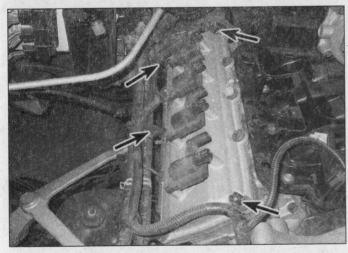

4.3a Location of the harness clips on the right side valve cover

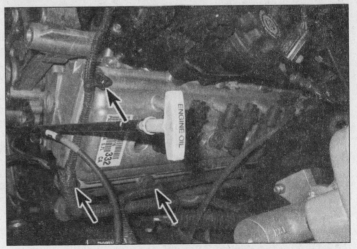

4.3b Location of the harness clips on the left side valve cover - some hidden from view

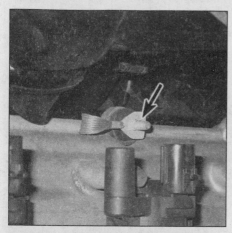

4.5 Remove the ground straps from the valve cover studs

4   Remove the ignition coils and ignition wires (see Chapter 5).

5   Remove the ground straps from the valve cover **(see illustration)**. Be sure to mark the location of each of the ground terminals for correct installation.

6   Remove the valve cover mounting bolts **(see illustrations)**.

7   Remove the valve cover. **Note:** *If the cover is stuck to the head, bump the cover with a block of wood and a hammer to release it. If it still will not come loose, try to slip a flexible putty knife between the head and cover to break the seal. Don't pry at the cover-to-head joint, as damage to the sealing surface and cover flange will result and oil leaks will develop.*

Installation

Refer to illustration 4.9

8   The mating surfaces of each cylinder head and valve cover must be perfectly clean when the covers are installed. Wipe the mating surfaces with a cloth saturated with lacquer thinner or acetone. If there is sealant or oil on the mating surfaces when the cover is installed, oil leaks may develop.

9   If the valve cover gasket isn't damaged or hardened, it can be re-used. If it is in need of replacement, install a new one into the valve cover perimeter and new rubber seals into the grooves in the valve cover that seal the spark plug tubes **(see illustration)**.

10   Carefully position the cover on the head and install the bolts, making sure the bolts with the studs are in the proper locations.

11   Tighten the bolts in three steps to the torque listed in this Chapter's Specifications. Start with the middle bolts and move to the outer bolts using a criss-cross pattern. **Caution:** *DON'T over-tighten the valve cover bolts.*

12   The remaining installation steps are the reverse of removal.

13   Start the engine and check carefully for oil leaks as the engine warms up.

5   Rocker arms and pushrods - removal, inspection and installation

Removal

Refer to illustrations 5.2 and 5.3

1   Remove the valve covers from the cylinder heads (see Section 4).

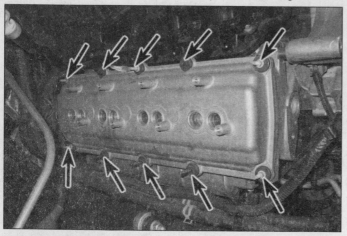

4.6a Location of the valve cover mounting bolts on the right-side valve cover

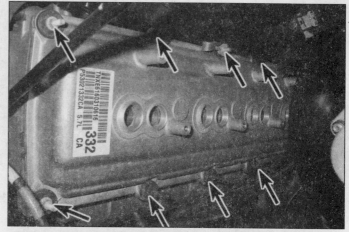

4.6b Location of the valve cover mounting bolts on the left-side valve cover (two bolts hidden from view)

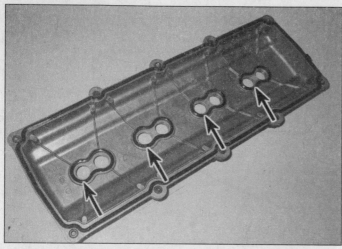

4.9 If they're damaged or hardened, replace the rubber gasket and spark plug tube seals with new ones (if they're OK, they can be re-used)

5.2 Remove the rocker arm shaft bolts - mark each rocker arm assembly and note that the upper rocker arms are the intake and the lower rocker arms are the exhaust

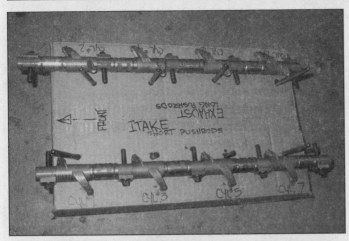

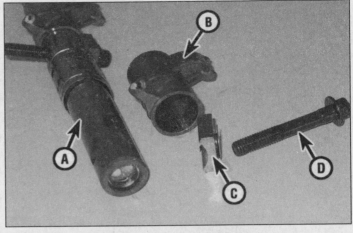

5.3 A perforated sheet of cardboard can be used to store the rocker arms and pushrods to ensure that they're reinstalled in their original locations - note the arrow indicating the front of the engine

5.4 Rocker arm component details

A   *Rocker arm shaft*   C   *Retainer*
B   *Rocker arm*   D   *Rocker shaft bolt*

2   Loosen the rocker arm shaft bolts, starting with the center bolts and working toward the outer bolts. When the bolts have been completely loosened, lift the rocker shaft assembly off the cylinder head **(see illustration)**.
3   Keep track of the rocker arm positions, since they must be returned to the same locations. Store each set of rocker components in such a way as to ensure that they're reinstalled in their original locations. Remove the pushrods and store them in order as well, to make sure they don't get mixed up during installation **(see illustration)**. **Note:** *The exhaust pushrods are slightly longer than the intake pushrods - they aren't interchangeable.*

Inspection

Refer to illustration 5.4
Caution: *If the cylinder heads have been removed and the surface milled for flatness, be sure to install correct length pushrods to compensate for the reduced distances of the rocker arms-to-camshaft dimensions. Consult with the machine shop for the correct length pushrods.*

4   Check each rocker arm for wear, cracks and other damage **(see illustration)**, especially where the pushrods and valve stems contact the rocker arm.
5   Check the rocker arm shafts and bores of the rocker arms for wear. Look for galling, stress cracks and unusual wear patterns. If the rocker arms are worn or damaged, replace them with new ones and install new shafts as well. **Note:** *Keep in mind that there is no valve adjustment on these engines, so excessive wear or damage in the valve train can easily result in excessive valve clearance, which in turn will cause valve noise when the engine is running.*
6   Make sure the hole at the pushrod end of each rocker arm is open.
7   Inspect the pushrods for cracks and excessive wear at the ends. Roll each pushrod across a piece of plate glass to see if it's bent (if it wobbles, it's bent).

Installation

8   Lubricate the lower end of each pushrod with clean engine oil or engine assembly lube and install them in their original locations. Make sure each pushrod seats completely in

the lifter socket.
9   Apply engine assembly lube to the ends of the valve stems and the upper ends of the pushrods to prevent damage to the mating surfaces on initial start-up.
10   Lubricate the rocker shafts with clean engine oil or engine assembly lube, then assemble the rocker shafts, with all of the components in their original positions. Install the rocker shafts onto the cylinder heads.
11   The rocker arm shafts must be tightened starting with the center bolt, then the center right bolt, the center left bolt, the outer right bolt and finally the outer left bolt. Follow this sequence in several steps until the torque listed in this Chapter's Specifications is reached. As the bolts are tightened, make sure the pushrods seat properly in the rocker arms. **Caution:** *Do not continue tightening the rocker arms if the rocker arm bolts become tight before the shaft is seated or the pushrods are binding. Remove the rocker arm shafts and inspect all the components carefully before proceeding.*
12   Refer to Section 4 and install the valve covers. Start the engine, listen for unusual valve train noises and check for oil leaks at the valve cover gaskets.

---

6   Intake manifold - removal and installation

Removal

Refer to illustrations 6.1 and 6.10
1   Remove the cowl cover (see Chapter 11). Remove the cowl support brace and the windshield wiper motor support bracket **(see illustration)**.
2   Relieve the fuel system pressure (see Chapter 4). Disconnect the cable from the negative terminal of the battery (see Chapter 5, Section 1).

6.1 Location of the cowl support brace (A) and the windshield wiper motor bracket (B)

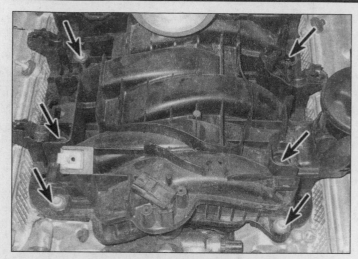

6.10 Location of the intake manifold bolts - four rear bolts not visible in photo

6.12 If necessary, replace the intake manifold O-rings with new ones. Make sure they seat properly in their grooves

3   Remove the air filter housing and the intake air duct (see Chapter 4).

4   Remove the ignition coils (see Chapter 5).

5   Disconnect the brake booster vacuum hose and the PCV hose.

6   Remove the fuel rails and injectors (see Chapter 4).

7   Remove the alternator (see Chapter 5).

8   Remove the air conditioning compressor, without disconnecting the refrigerant lines, and set it aside (see Chapter 3).

9   Refer to Chapter 6 and disconnect the electrical connectors from the IAT, MAP, TPS and ECT sensors.

10   Starting with the outer bolts and working to the inner bolts, loosen the intake manifold bolts in 1/4-turn increments until they can be removed by hand **(see illustration)**.

11   Remove the intake manifold. As the manifold is lifted from the engine, be sure to check for and disconnect anything still attached to the manifold.

Installation

Refer to illustrations 6.12 and 6.14

Note: *The mating surfaces of the cylinder heads and intake manifold must be perfectly clean when the manifold is installed.*

12   Check the O-rings on the intake manifold for damage or hardening. If they're OK, they can be re-used. If necessary, install new O-rings **(see illustration)**.

13   Carefully set the manifold in place. **Caution:** *Do not disturb the rubber seals and DO NOT move the manifold fore-and-aft after it contacts the cylinder heads or the seals could be pushed out of place and the engine may develop vacuum and/or oil leaks.*

14   Install the intake manifold bolts and tighten them following the recommended sequence **(see illustration)** to the torque listed in this Chapter's Specifications.

15   The remaining installation steps are the reverse of removal. Start the engine and check carefully for vacuum leaks at the intake manifold joints.

7   Exhaust manifolds - removal and installation

Removal

Refer to illustrations 7.3, 7.5a, and 7.5b

Warning: *Allow the engine to cool completely before performing this procedure.*

1   Disconnect the cable from the negative terminal of the battery (see Chapter 5, Section 1).

2   Raise the vehicle and support it securely on jackstands. Disconnect the exhaust pipe-to-manifold connections. It's a good idea to apply penetrating oil on the studs/bolts and let it soak in for about 10 minutes before attempting to remove them.

3   Lower the vehicle and remove the heat shield nuts and the heat shield **(see illustration)**.

4   Connect an engine support fixture or engine hoist to the engine. Remove the engine mount through-bolts and raise the

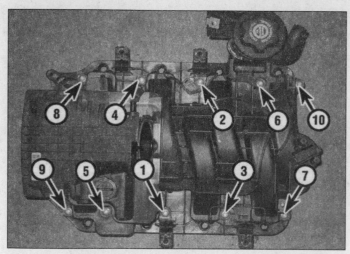

6.14 Tightening sequence for the intake manifold bolts

7.3 Location of the exhaust manifold heat shield nuts on the right-side exhaust manifold

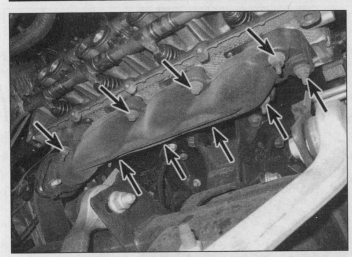 

7.5a Location of the mounting bolts on the right-side exhaust manifold

7.5b Location of the mounting bolts on the left-side exhaust manifold (not all are visible in this photo)

engine enough to allow removal of the manifold.

5   Remove the bolts retaining the exhaust manifold to the cylinder head **(see illustrations)**.

6   Remove the exhaust manifold(s).

Installation

7   Installation is the reverse of the removal procedure. Clean the manifold and head gasket surfaces and check for cracks and flatness. Replace the exhaust manifold gaskets.

8   Install the exhaust manifold(s) and fasteners. Tighten the bolts/nuts to the torque listed in this Chapter's Specifications. Work from the center to the ends and approach the final torque in three steps. Install the heat shields.

9   Apply anti-seize compound to the exhaust pipe-to-exhaust manifold bolts and tighten them securely.

8   Vibration damper and front oil seal - removal and installation

Refer to illustrations 8.4, 8.5, 8.6 and 8.8

Warning: *Wait until the engine is completely cool before beginning this procedure.*

1   Disconnect the cable from the negative terminal of the battery (see Chapter 5, Section 1).

2   Remove the engine drivebelt (see Chapter 1).

3   Drain the coolant (see Chapter 1), remove the upper radiator hose and remove the engine cooling fan (see Chapter 3).

4   Remove the large vibration damper-to-crankshaft bolt. To keep the crankshaft from turning, install a chain wrench around the circumference of the pulley. Be sure to use a piece of rubber (old drivebelt, old timing belt, etc.) under the chain wrench to protect the vibration damper from nicks or gouges **(see illustration)**.

5   Using the proper puller (commonly available from auto parts stores), detach the vibration damper **(see illustration)**. **Caution:** *Do not use a puller with jaws that grip the outer edge of the pulley. The puller must be the type that utilizes bolts or arms to apply force to the pulley hub only. Also, the puller screw must not contact the threads in the nose of the crankshaft; it must use an adapter that allows the puller screw to apply force to the end of the crankshaft nose or a spacer must be inserted into the nose of the crankshaft to protect the threads.*

6   If the seal is being removed while the cover is still attached to the engine block, carefully pry the seal out of the cover with a seal removal tool or a large screwdriver **(see illustration)**. **Caution:** *Be careful not to scratch, gouge or distort the area that the seal fits into or an oil leak will develop.*

7   Clean the bore to remove any old seal material and corrosion. Position the new seal in the bore with the seal lip (usually the side with the spring) facing IN (toward the engine). A small amount of oil applied to the outer edge

8.4 Use a chain wrench to lock the vibration damper - be sure to position a piece of an old timing belt or drivebelt underneath the chain wrench to prevent damaging the damper

8.5 Use a three-jaw puller to remove the vibration damper from the crankshaft

8.6 Use a seal puller to remove the front seal from the timing chain cover

8.8 Use a seal driver or a large socket to drive the new seal into the cover

9.10 Details of the idler pulleys and drivebelt tensioner on the timing chain cover

A   Idler pulley mounting bolt

B   Drivebelt tensioner mounting bolt

of the new seal will make installation easier.

8   Drive the seal into the bore with a seal driver or a large socket and hammer until it's completely seated **(see illustration)**. Select a socket that's the same outside diameter as the seal and make sure the new seal is pressed into place until it bottoms against the cover flange.

9   Check the surface of the damper that the oil seal rides on. If the surface has been grooved from long-time contact with the seal, replace the vibration damper.

10   Lubricate the seal lips with engine oil and reinstall the vibration damper, aligning the Woodruff key on the nose of the crankshaft with the keyway in the damper hub. Use a special installation tool (available at most auto parts stores) to press the vibration damper onto the crankshaft.

11   Install the vibration damper bolt and tighten it to the torque listed in this Chapter's Specifications.

12   The remainder of installation is the reverse of the removal process.

13   Refill the cooling system (see Chapter 1).

9   Timing chain cover, chain and sprockets - removal, inspection and installation

Warning: *Wait until the engine is completely cool before beginning this procedure.*

Removal

Refer to illustrations 9.10, 9.17, 9.19a, 9.19b, 9.19c, 9.20, 9.21a and 9.21b

1   Disconnect the cable from the negative terminal of the battery (see Chapter 5, Section 1).

2   Drain the cooling system (see Chapter 1).

3   Drain the engine oil (see Chapter 1).

4   Remove the air filter housing, the resonator and the air intake ducts (see Chapter 4).

5   Remove the drivebelt (see Chapter 1).

6   Remove the engine cooling fan and the upper and lower radiator hoses (see Chapter 3).

7   Remove the air conditioning compressor

without disconnecting the hoses (see Chapter 3). It is not necessary to evacuate the refrigerant from the air conditioning system for this procedure. Use rope or wire to tie the compressor away from the front of the engine with the air conditioning lines attached.

8   Remove the alternator (see Chapter 5).

9   Remove the coolant reservoir (see Chapter 3).

10   Remove the drivebelt tensioner **(see illustration)** and the idler pulleys.

11   Remove the vibration damper (see Section 8).

12   Remove the power steering pump (see Chapter 10) and set it aside without disconnecting the power steering lines.

13   Remove the dipstick tube.

14   Remove the oil pan and the pickup tube (see Section 13).

15   Disconnect the heater hoses from the front cover.

16   Remove the water pump (see Chapter 3).

17   Remove the timing chain cover bolts **(see illustration)** and the front cover.

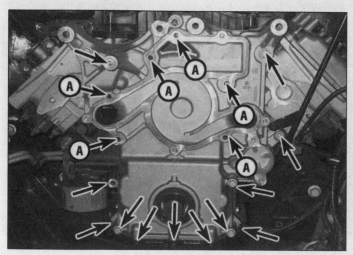

9.17 Location of the timing chain cover mounting bolts - the bolt holes marked with an (A) secure the water pump as well as the timing chain cover

9.19a Use a breaker bar and socket to rotate the crankshaft (clockwise) to TDC number 1 position

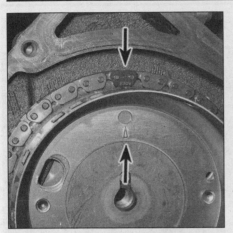

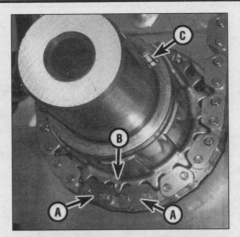

9.19b The single colored timing chain link should align with the camshaft sprocket timing mark . . .

9.19c . . . and the two colored timing chain links (A) should straddle the crankshaft sprocket timing dot (B) - note that the keyway (C) should be at the 2 o'clock position

9.20 Use a large pair of pliers to retract the tensioner until the hole in the tensioner aligns with the hole in the bracket (thrust plate), then install a drill bit through the hole to keep it in the retracted position

18 Remove the oil pump (see Section 14).

19 Reinstall the bolt into the end of the crankshaft and turn the crankshaft until the crankshaft sprocket timing mark is at the 6 o'clock position (with the crankshaft key at 2 o'clock) and the camshaft timing mark at the 12 o'clock position **(see illustrations)**.

20 Retract the tensioner until the hole in the tensioner aligns with the hole in the camshaft tensioner thrust plate **(see illustration)**. Install a suitable size drill bit to retain the tensioner in the retracted position. **Note:** *The timing chain tensioner is an integral component of the camshaft thrust plate. If necessary, the tensioner/thrust plate assembly must be replaced as a complete unit.*

21 Remove the camshaft sprocket bolt and remove the timing chain with the camshaft and crankshaft sprockets **(see illustrations)**.

22 Remove the camshaft tensioner thrust plate mounting bolts **(see illustration 11.9)** and separate the tensioner from the engine block.

Inspection

23 Inspect the camshaft sprocket for damage or wear. The camshaft sprocket is a steel sprocket, but the teeth can become grooved or worn enough to cause a poor meshing of the sprocket and the chain. **Note:** *Whenever a new timing chain is required, the entire set (chain, tensioner, camshaft and crankshaft sprockets) must be replaced as an assembly.*

24 Inspect the crankshaft sprocket for damage or wear. The crankshaft sprocket is a steel sprocket, but these teeth can also become grooved or worn enough to cause a poor meshing of the sprocket and the chain.

Installation

Refer to illustrations 9.27a, 9.27b and 9.34

Note: *Always replace the timing chain as a set with the camshaft sprocket, the crankshaft sprocket and the tensioner. Never install a new timing chain onto old sprockets.*

25 Stuff a shop rag into the opening at the front of the oil pan to keep debris out of the engine, then clean off all traces of old gasket material and sealant from the engine block. Wipe the sealing surfaces with a cloth saturated with lacquer thinner or acetone.

26 If the tensioner is not compressed (retracted position), compress the tensioner until the hole aligns with the bracket hole, then insert a suitable size drill bit through both holes to keep the tensioner locked in this position **(see illustration 9.20)**. Install the camshaft thrust plate and tighten the bolts to the torque listed in this Chapter's Specifications.

27 Assemble the timing chain and sprockets before installing them onto the engine. Loop the new chain over the camshaft sprocket with the single colored link (timing chain mark) aligned with the sprocket alignment mark **(see illustration)**. Mesh the chain with the crankshaft sprocket, with the crankshaft sprocket alignment mark between the two colored chain links **(see illustration)**.

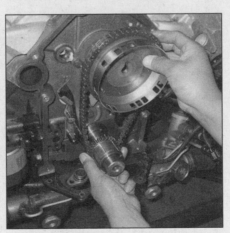

9.21a Use a breaker bar and socket to prevent the crankshaft from rotating while loosening the camshaft sprocket bolt

9.21b Remove the camshaft sprocket, crankshaft sprocket and timing chain as a complete assembly

9.27a The camshaft sprocket timing mark(s) must align with the single colored timing chain link . . .

9.27b . . . and the two colored timing chain links must straddle the crankshaft sprocket mark

9.34 Be sure to install a new rubber gasket into the timing chain cover groove

28   Align the sprocket with the Woodruff key in the end of the crankshaft and assemble the chain, camshaft sprocket and crankshaft sprocket onto the crankshaft and camshaft. Tap it gently into place until it is completely seated. **Caution:** *If resistance is encountered, do not hammer the sprocket onto the crankshaft. It may eventually move onto the shaft, but it may be cracked in the process and fail later, causing extensive engine damage.* When the timing chain components are installed, the timing marks MUST align as shown **in illustrations 9.19b and 9.19c.**

29   Apply a thread locking compound to the camshaft sprocket bolt threads and tighten the bolt to the torque listed in this Chapter's Specifications.

30   Lubricate the chain with clean engine oil.

31   Remove the drill bit from the tensioner and bracket. Make sure the tensioner has released and is pressing against the timing chain. Verify that the timing marks are still aligned properly.

32   Install the oil pump (see Section 14).

33   Install the oil pump pick-up tube to the bottom of the oil pump. Tighten the bolt to the torque listed in this Chapter's Specifications.

34   The timing chain cover rubber gasket can be re-used if it isn't damaged or hardened, but considering the amount of work that you've done to get to this point, it's a good idea to replace it. Double-check the surface of the timing chain cover and engine block. Make sure all old gasket material is removed and the surface is clean. Install a new rubber gasket into the groove in the timing chain cover **(see illustration).**

35   Apply a small amount of RTV sealant to the corner where the timing chain cover, engine block and oil pan meet.

36   Install the timing chain cover on the block **(see illustration 9.17)** and tighten the bolts, a little at a time, until you reach the torque listed in this Chapter's Specifications. **Note:** *Be sure to install the water pump onto the timing chain cover and tighten the timing chain cover bolts and the water pump bolts at the same time (see Chapter 3).*

37   Install the oil pan (see Section 13).

38   Lubricate the oil seal contact surface of the vibration damper hub with clean engine oil, then install the damper on the end of the crankshaft (see Section 8). Tighten the bolt to the torque listed in this Chapter's Specifications.

39   The remaining installation steps are the reverse of removal.

40   Add coolant and engine oil. Run the engine and check for oil and coolant leaks.

10   Cylinder heads - removal and installation

Warning: *Wait until the engine is completely cool before beginning this procedure.*

Removal

1   Relieve the fuel system pressure (see Chapter 4), then disconnect the cable from the negative terminal of the battery (see Chapter 5, Section 1).

2   Drain the cooling system (see Chapter 1).

3   Remove the intake manifold (see Section 6).

4   Remove the exhaust manifolds from the cylinder heads (see Section 7).

5   Remove the valve covers (see Section 4).

6   Remove the rocker arms and pushrods (see Section 5). **Caution:** *Again, as mentioned in Section 5, keep all the parts in order so they are reinstalled in the same locations.*

7   Loosen the head bolts in 1/4-turn increments in a pattern opposite of the tightening sequence **(see illustration 10.16)** until they can be removed by hand. **Note:** *There will be different-length head bolts for different locations, so store the bolts in order as they are removed. This will ensure that the bolts are reinstalled in their original holes.*

8   Lift the heads off the engine. If resistance is felt, do not pry between the head and block as damage to the mating surfaces will result. To dislodge the head, place a block of wood against the end of it and strike the wood block with a hammer, or lift on a casting protrusion. Store the heads on blocks of wood to prevent damage to the gasket sealing surfaces.

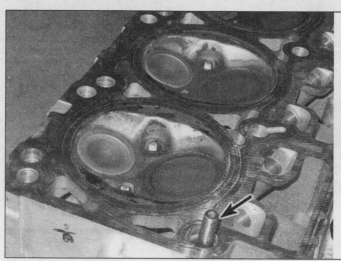

10.9 Make sure the cylinder head surface is perfectly clean, free from old gasket material, carbon deposits and dirt - note that the dowel is part of the cylinder head stand

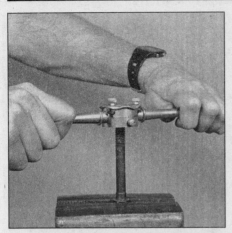

10.12 A die should be used to remove sealant and corrosion from the bolt threads prior to installation

Installation

Refer to illustrations 10.9, 10.12, 10.13 and 10.16

9   The mating surfaces of the cylinder heads and block must be perfectly clean when the heads are installed **(see illustration)**. Gasket removal solvents are available at auto parts stores and may prove helpful.

10   Use a gasket scraper to remove all traces of carbon and old gasket material, then wipe the mating surfaces with a cloth saturated with lacquer thinner or acetone. If there is oil on the mating surfaces when the heads are installed, the gaskets may not seal correctly and leaks may develop. When working on the block, cover the lifter valley with shop rags to keep debris out of the engine. Use a vacuum cleaner to remove any debris that falls into the cylinders.

11   Check the block and head mating surfaces for nicks, deep scratches and other damage. If damage is slight, it can be removed with emery cloth. If it is excessive, machining may be the only alternative.

12   Use a tap of the correct size to chase the threads in the head bolt holes in the block. Mount each bolt in a vise and run a die down the threads to remove corrosion and restore the threads **(see illustration)**. Dirt, corrosion, sealant and damaged threads will affect torque readings.

13   Position the new gaskets over the dowels in the block. Be sure the letter designations for the left (L) and right (R) cylinder heads and the top gasket surface (TOP) are correctly oriented **(see illustration)**.

14   Carefully position the heads on the block without disturbing the gaskets.

15   Before installing the head bolts, coat the threads with a small amount of engine oil.

16   Install the bolts in their original locations and tighten them finger tight. Following the recommended sequence **(see illustration)**, tighten the bolts in several steps to the torque listed in this Chapter's Specifications.

17   The remaining installation steps are the reverse of removal.

18   Add coolant and change the engine oil and filter (see Chapter 1). Start the engine and check for proper operation and coolant or oil leaks.

11   Multiple Displacement System (MDS) - general information and solenoid replacement

General information

1   2006 models are equipped with the Multiple Displacement System (MDS). The MDS selectively deactivates certain cylinders (numbers 1, 4, 6 and 7) to improve fuel economy during cruising and idling modes. The MDS uses a specialized camshaft, deactivating roller tappets, control solenoids for cylinders 1, 4, 6 and 7, an oil temperature sensor and the wiring harness.

2   The On-Board computer deactivates the exhaust and intake valves using the control solenoids on the designated cylinders allowing the piston to act as an air spring. The Powertrain Control Module (PCM) also cuts off fuel and spark to these cylinders, essentially converting the 8 cylinder engine into an economical 4 cylinder engine.

Solenoid replacement

3   Disconnect the cable from the negative terminal of the battery (see Chapter 5, Section 1).

4   Remove the intake manifold (see Section 6).

5   Disconnect the MDS control solenoid connectors.

6   Remove the MDS control solenoid mounting bolt.

7   Remove the MDS control solenoid.

8   Installation is the reverse of removal.

12   Camshaft and lifters - removal, inspection and installation

Warning: *Wait until the engine is completely cool before beginning this procedure.*
Note: *2006 models are equipped with the Multiple Displacement System (MDS) that uses a specialized camshaft. Replace the camshaft with ONLY the type used with the MDS design. Refer to Section 11 for a description of the MDS system.*

Removal

Refer to illustrations 12.6, 12.7a, 12.7b and 12.9

1   Relieve the fuel system pressure (see Chapter 4), then disconnect the cable from the negative terminal of the battery (see Chapter 5, Section 1).

2   Drain the cooling system (see Chapter 1).

3   Remove the timing chain cover, the timing chain and the sprockets (see Section 9).

4   Remove the cylinder heads (see Section 10).

5   Remove the radiator (see Chapter 3).

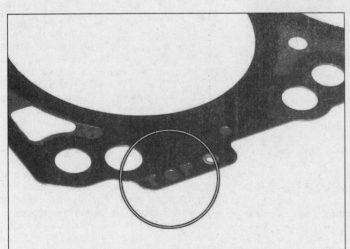

10.13 Make sure the head gaskets are installed on the correct cylinder banks, and the TOP marking is facing up

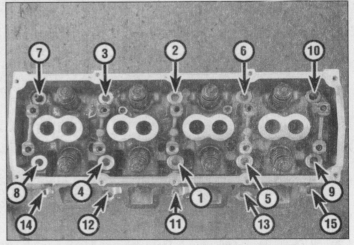

10.16 Cylinder head bolt tightening sequence

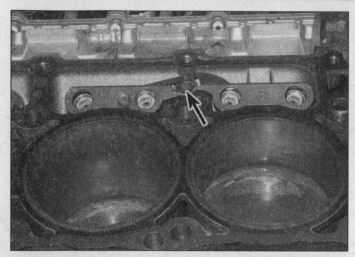

12.6 Each lifter rail is secured by one bolt

12.7a Remove the lifters from the lifter bores and install them into the lifter rail - each lifter must be installed into the same lifter bore and in the same direction (roller rotation)

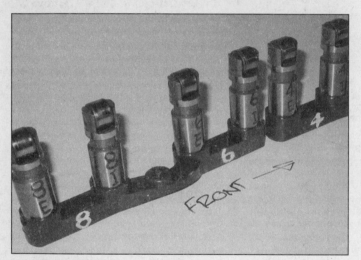

12.7b Install the lifters into the lifter rail and make sure the lifters are marked in their original positions with number designations for the cylinders and letter designations for the valve each one operates (intake or exhaust)

12.9 Location of the camshaft thrust plate mounting bolts

6   Remove the lifter rail mounting bolts **(see illustration)**.

7   Remove the lifters from the lifter bores in the engine block **(see illustration)**. Carefully place them in the correct location in the lifter rail. Each lifter must be installed into the same lifter bore and in the same direction (roller rotation) **(see illustration)**. Be sure to mark each lifter and lifter rail with a felt pen to designate the cylinder number and the type of lifter (intake or exhaust). There are several ways to extract the lifters from the bores. A special tool designed to grip and remove lifters is manufactured by many tool companies and is widely available, but it may not be required in every case. On newer engines without a lot of varnish buildup, the lifters can often be removed with a small magnet or even with your fingers. A machinist's scribe with a bent end can be used to pull the lifters out by positioning the point under the retainer ring inside the top of each lifter. **Caution:** *Do not use pliers to remove the lifters unless you intend to*

replace them with new ones (along with the camshaft). The pliers will damage the precision machined and hardened lifters, rendering them useless. Do not attempt to withdraw the camshaft with the lifters in place.

8   Before removing the camshaft, check the endplay. Mount a dial indicator so that it contacts the nose of the camshaft. Pry the camshaft forward and back using a long screwdriver with the tip taped to prevent damage to the camshaft. Record the movement of the dial indicator and compare the reading to the value given in this Chapter's Specifications. If the endplay is excessive, the camshaft must be replaced.

9   Unbolt and remove the camshaft thrust plate **(see illustration)**.

10   Thread a long bolt into the camshaft sprocket bolt hole to use as a handle when removing the camshaft from the block. Carefully pull the camshaft out. Support the cam near the block so the lobes do not nick or gouge the bearings as it is withdrawn.

Inspection

Refer to illustrations 12.12, 12.13, 12.14 and 12.18

11   After the camshaft has been removed from the engine, cleaned with solvent and dried, inspect the bearing journals for uneven wear, pitting and evidence of seizure. If the journals are damaged, the bearing inserts in the block are probably damaged as well. Both the camshaft and bearings will have to be replaced. **Note:** *Camshaft bearing replacement requires special tools and expertise that place it beyond the scope of the average home mechanic. The tools for bearing removal and installation are available at stores that carry automotive tools, possibly even found at a tool rental business. It is advisable though, if bearings are bad and the procedure is beyond your ability, remove the engine block and take it to an automotive machine shop to ensure that the job is done correctly.*

12   Measure the bearing journals with a

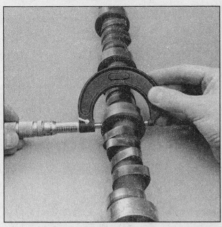

12.12 Check the diameter of each camshaft bearing journal to pinpoint excessive wear and out-of-round conditions

12.13 Measure the camshaft lobe height (greatest dimension) with a micrometer

12.14 Check the cam lobes for pitting, excessive wear and scoring. If scoring is excessive, as shown here, replace the camshaft

micrometer to determine if they are excessively worn or out-of-round **(see illustration)**.

13   Measure the lobe height of each cam lobe on the intake camshaft and record your measurements **(see illustration)**. Compare the measurements for excessive variations. If the lobe heights vary more than 0.005 inch (0.125 mm), replace the camshaft. Compare the lobe height measurements on the exhaust camshaft and follow the same procedure. Do not compare intake camshaft lobe heights with exhaust camshaft lobe heights, as they are different. Only compare intake lobes with intake lobes and exhaust lobes with other exhaust lobes.

14   Check the camshaft lobes for heat discoloration, score marks, chipped areas, pitting and uneven wear **(see illustration)**. If the lobes are in good condition and if the lobe lift variation measurements recorded earlier are within the limits, the camshaft can be reused.

15   Clean the lifters with solvent and dry them thoroughly without mixing them up.

16   Check each lifter wall, pushrod seat and foot for scuffing, score marks and uneven

wear. If the lifter walls are damaged or worn (which is not very likely), inspect the lifter bores in the engine block as well. If the pushrod seats are worn, check the pushrod ends.

17   If new lifters are being installed, a new camshaft must also be installed. If a new camshaft is installed, then use new lifters as well. Never install used lifters unless the original camshaft is used and the lifters can be installed in their original locations.

18   Check the rollers carefully for wear and damage and make sure they turn freely without excessive play **(see illustration)**.

Installation

Refer to illustration 12.19

19   Lubricate the camshaft bearing journals and cam lobes with camshaft installation lube **(see illustration)**.

20   Slide the camshaft slowly and gently into the engine. Support the cam near the block and be careful not to scrape or nick the bearings. Only install the camshaft far enough to install the camshaft thrust plate. Pushing it in too far could dislodge the camshaft plug at the

rear of the engine, causing an oil leak. Tighten the camshaft thrust plate mounting bolts to the torque listed in this Chapter's Specifications.

21   Install the timing chain and sprockets (see Section 9). Align the timing marks on the crankshaft and camshaft sprockets.

22   Lubricate the lifters with clean engine oil and install them in the block. If the original lifters are being reinstalled, be sure to return them to their original locations, and with the numbers facing UP (exactly as they were removed). Install the lifter rail and mounting bolts. Tighten the lifter rail mounting bolts to the torque listed in this Chapter's Specifications. **Note:** *Each lifter rail should be numbered and coincide with the correct cylinder numbers.*

23   The remaining installation steps are the reverse of removal.

24   Change the oil and install a new oil filter (see Chapter 1). Fill the cooling system with the proper type of coolant (see Chapter 1).

25   Start the engine and check for oil pressure and leaks. **Caution:** *Do not run the engine above a fast idle until all the hydraulic lifters have filled with oil and become quiet again.*

26   If a new camshaft and lifters have been installed, the engine should be brought to operating temperature and run at a fast idle for 15 to 20 minutes to "break in" the new components. Change the oil and filter again after 500 miles of operation.

13   Oil pan - removal and installation

Warning: *Wait until the engine is completely cool before beginning this procedure.*

Removal

Refer to illustrations 13.5 and 13.12

1   Disconnect the cable from the negative terminal of the battery (see Chapter 5, Section 1).

2   Drain the cooling system (see Chapter 1).

3   Raise the vehicle and support it securely

12.18 The roller on the roller lifters must turn freely - check for wear and excessive play as well

12.19 Be sure to apply camshaft installation lube to the cam lobes and bearing journals before installing the camshaft

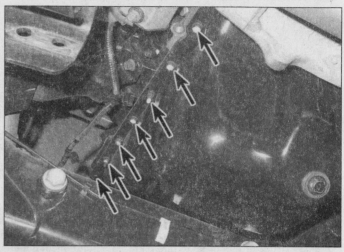

13.5 Remove the front crossmember mounting bolts and separate the crossmember from the chassis

13.12 Remove the oil pan mounting bolts from the perimeter of the oil pan - left side shown

on jackstands (see Chapter 1).

4   Drain the engine oil and replace the oil filter (see Chapter 1). Remove the engine oil dipstick.

5   Remove the crossmember beneath the oil pan **(see illustration)**.

6   Remove the brace between the oil pan and transmission **(see illustration 13.22)**.

7   Remove the engine cooling fan and shroud (see Chapter 3).

8   Support the engine from above with an engine hoist or an engine support fixture (see Chapter 2C), take a little weight off the engine mounts with the hoist or fixture, and remove the through-bolts from the engine mounts (see Section 17). Now raise the engine further. **Caution:** *Raise the engine slightly while observing the engine cooling fan and fan shroud. Do not allow the engine cooling fan to contact the shroud or the fan and/or shroud may be damaged. If necessary, remove the fan and shroud.*

4WD models

9   Unbolt the steering gear (see Chapter 10) and lower the assembly without disconnecting the power steering fluid lines.

10   Remove the front driveshaft (see Chapter 8).

11   Support the front axle using a pair of floor jacks and unbolt the mounts (see Chapter 8). Carefully lower the front axle.

All models

12   Remove all of the oil pan bolts **(see illustration)**, then lower the pan from the engine. The pan will probably stick to the engine, so strike the pan with a rubber mallet until it breaks the gasket seal. **Caution:** *Before using force on the oil pan, be sure all the bolts have been removed. Carefully slide the oil pan out, to the rear.*

13   Remove the windage tray from the engine block. **Note:** *The windage tray and gasket assembly must be replaced with new parts whenever the oil pan is removed from the engine block.*

Installation

Refer to illustration 13.22

14   Install a new gasket and windage tray.

15   Wash out the oil pan with solvent.

16   Thoroughly clean the mounting surfaces of the oil pan and engine block of old gasket material and sealer. If the oil pan is distorted at the bolt-hole areas, straighten the flange by supporting it from below on a 1x4 wood block and tapping the bolt holes with the rounded end of a ball-peen hammer. Wipe the gasket surfaces clean with a rag soaked in lacquer thinner or acetone.

17   Apply some RTV sealant to the corners where the timing chain cover meets the block and at the rear where the rear main oil seal retainer meets the block. Then attach the one-piece oil pan gasket to the engine block with contact-cement-type gasket adhesive.

18   Make sure the alignment studs are installed in the correct locations in the engine block.

19   Lift the pan into position, slipping it over the alignment studs and being careful not to disturb the gasket, install several bolts finger tight.

20   Check that the gasket isn't sticking out anywhere around the block's perimeter. When all the bolts are in place, install the oil pan nuts onto the studs.

21   Starting at the center and alternating from side-to-side towards the ends, tighten the fasteners to the torque listed in this Chapter's Specifications.

22   Install the transmission brace. The transmission brace must be tightened correctly or it may be damaged and cause engine noise **(see illustration)**.

  a) *Tighten bolts C and D to 50 to 100 inch-pounds.*

  b) *Tighten bolts A and B to 50 to 100 inch-pounds.*

  c) *Tighten bolts A to 40 ft-lbs.*

  d) *Tighten bolts B to 40 ft-lbs.*

  e) *Tighten bolts C and D to 40 ft-lbs.*

23   The remainder of the installation procedure is the reverse of removal.

24   Add the proper type and quantity of oil, and a new oil filter (see Chapter 1), start the engine and check for leaks before placing the vehicle back in service.

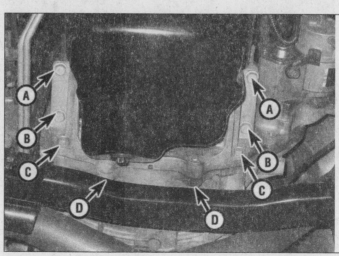

13.22 Transmission brace bolt identification (see text for tightening order)

14.5 Location of the oil pump pick-up tube retainer bolt (A) and the oil pump mounting bolts (B)

17.9a Location of the through-bolt on the right side engine mount

14   Oil pump - removal and installation

Warning: *Wait until the engine is completely cool before beginning this procedure.*

Caution: *The oil pressure relief valve must not be removed from the oil pump housing on this engine. If the oil pressure relief valve is removed from the housing, the entire oil pump assembly must be replaced with a new unit.*

Note: *The oil pump on the Hemi engine is available only as a complete unit.*

Removal

Refer to illustration 14.5

1   Disconnect the cable from the negative terminal of the battery (see Chapter 5, Section 1).
2   Drain the cooling system (see Chapter 1).
3   Remove the timing chain cover (see Section 9).
4   Remove the oil pan (see Section 13).
5   Remove the bolt from the pick-up tube assembly and lower it away from the oil pump **(see illustration)**.
6   Remove the oil pump mounting bolts and detach the pump from the engine block.

Installation

7   Position the pump on the engine. Make sure the pump rotor is aligned with the crankshaft drive. Install the oil pump mounting bolts and tighten them to the torque listed in this Chapter's Specifications.
8   Install a new O-ring onto the oil pump pick-up tube, connect the tube to the pump and tighten the bolt to the torque listed in this Chapter's Specifications.
9   The remainder of installation is the reverse of removal.
10 Fill the crankcase with the proper type and quantity of engine oil, and install a new oil filter (see Chapter 1). Fill the cooling system with the proper type of coolant (see

Chapter 1).
11 Run the engine and check for oil pressure and leaks.

15   Flywheel/driveplate - removal and installation

This procedure is essentially the same as for the 3.7L V6 and the 4.7L V8 engines. Refer to Part A and follow the procedure outlined there, but refer to the torque Specifications listed in this Chapter.

16   Rear main oil seal - replacement

This procedure is essentially the same as for the 3.7L V6 and the 4.7L V8 engines. Refer to Part A and follow the procedure outlined there but refer to the torque Specifications listed in this Chapter.

17   Engine mounts - check and replacement

1   Engine mounts seldom require attention, but broken or deteriorated mounts should be replaced immediately or the added strain placed on the driveline components may cause damage or wear.

Check

2   During the check, the engine must be raised slightly to remove the weight from the mounts.
3   Raise the vehicle and support it securely on jackstands, then position a jack under the engine oil pan. Place a large wood block between the jack head and the oil pan, then carefully raise the engine just enough to take the weight off the mounts. **Warning:** *DO NOT place any part of your body under the engine when it's supported only by a jack!*

4   Check the mount insulators to see if the rubber is cracked, hardened or separated from the metal in the center of the mount.
5   Check for relative movement between the mount and the engine or frame (use a large screwdriver or prybar to attempt to move the mounts).
6   If movement is noted, lower the engine and tighten the mount fasteners.

Replacement

7   Disconnect the cable from the negative terminal of the battery (see Chapter 5, Section 1). Raise the vehicle and support it securely on jackstands (if not already done). Support the engine as described in Step 3.

2WD models

Refer to illustrations 17.9a and 17.9b

8   Remove the through-bolts and raise the engine with the jack. Unscrew the mount fasteners and detach the mount.
9   Install the new mount(s), making sure it is correctly positioned in the bracket **(see illustrations)**. Install the fasteners and tighten them securely.

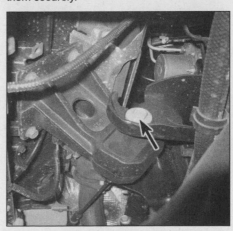

17.9b Location of the through-bolt on the left side engine mount

models

Remove the skidplate from below the engine compartment.

11 Remove the engine crossmember.

12 Remove the engine oil filter (see Chapter 1).

13 Install an engine hoist (see Chapter 2C) and raise the engine slightly to take the weight off the engine mounts.

14 Use a floor jack to support the front axle.

15 Remove the engine mount through-bolts.

16 Remove the bolts that attach the engine mounts to the front axle assembly.

17 Lower the front axle slightly (see Chapter 8).

18 Remove the engine mount(s) from the vehicle.

19 Install the new mount(s), making sure they are correctly positioned in the bracket. Install the fasteners and tighten them securely.

Chapter 2 Part C
General engine overhaul procedures

Contents

Specifications

General

Displacement
3.7L V6	226 cubic inches
4.7L V8	287 cubic inches
5.7L V8 (Hemi)	345 cubic inches

Bore and stroke
3.7L V6	3.66 x 3.40 inches
4.7L V8	3.66 x 3.40 inches
5.7L V8 (Hemi)	3.91 x 3.58 inches

Cylinder compression pressure
3.7L V6 and 4.7L V8
Minimum	170 psi
Maximum variation between cylinders	40 psi
5.7L V8 (Hemi)	not available, but pressure should not vary more than 40 psi between cylinders

Oil pump pressure
3.7L V6
Minimum pressure at curb idle	4 psi
Operating pressure	25 to 110 psi at 3,000 rpm

4.7L V8
Minimum pressure at curb idle	7 psi
Operating pressure	35 to 105 psi at 3,000 rpm

5.7L V8 (Hemi)
Minimum pressure at curb idle	4 psi
Operating pressure	25 to 110 psi at 3,000 rpm

Torque specifications

	Ft-lbs (unless otherwise indicated)
Connecting rod cap bolts	
3.7L V6 and 4.7L V8 engines	
Step 1	20
Step 2	Tighten an additional 90-degrees
5.7L V8 (Hemi) engine	
Step 1	15
Step 2	Tighten an additional 90-degrees
Main bearing cap bolts/bedplate assembly	
3.7L V6 bedplate fasteners **(see illustration 10.19a)**	
Step 1, bolts 4, 7 and 6..	Hand-tighten until bedplate contacts block mating surface
Step 2, bolts 1 through 10	40
Step 3, bolts 11 through 18..	60 in-lbs
Step 4, bolts 11 through 18..	Tighten an additional 90-degrees
Step 5, bolts 19 through 23	20
4.7L V8 bedplate fasteners **(see illustration 10.19b)**	
Step 1, bolts 1 through 12	40
Step 2, bolts 13 through 22	25 in-lbs
Step 3, bolts 13 through 22	Tighten an additional 90-degrees
Step 4, bolts 23 through 28	20
5.7L V8 (Hemi) engine* **(see illustration 10.19c)**	
Step 1, bolts 1 through 10	20
Step 2, bolts 1 through 10	Tighten an additional 90-degrees
Step 3, crossbolts 11 through 20	21
Step 4, crossbolts 11 through 20	21 (re-check)

Install a new washer/seal onto each crossbolt before tightening. First, install main bearing bolts and main bearing crossbolts all finger tight. Next torque the main bearing bolts completely (Steps 1 and 2) before torquing the crossbolts

1   General information - engine overhaul

Refer to illustrations 1.1, 1.2, 1.3, 1.4, 1.5 and 1.6

Included in this portion of Chapter 2 are general information and diagnostic testing procedures for determining the overall mechanical condition of your engine.

The information ranges from advice concerning preparation for an overhaul and the purchase of replacement parts and/or components to detailed, step-by-step procedures covering removal and installation.

The following Sections have been written to help you determine whether your engine needs to be overhauled and how to remove and install it once you've determined it needs to be rebuilt. For information concerning in-vehicle engine repair, see Chapter 2A or 2B.

The Specifications included in this Part are general in nature and include only those necessary for testing the oil pressure and engine compression, and bottom-end torque specifications. Refer to Chapter 2A or 2B for additional engine Specifications.

It's not always easy to determine when, or if, an engine should be completely overhauled, because a number of factors must be considered.

High mileage is not necessarily an indication that an overhaul is needed, while low mileage doesn't preclude the need for an overhaul. Frequency of servicing is probably the most important consideration. An engine that's had regular and frequent oil and filter changes, as well as other required maintenance, will most likely give many thousands of miles of reliable service. Conversely, a neglected engine may require an overhaul very early in its service life.

Excessive oil consumption is an indication that piston rings, valve seals and/or valve guides are in need of attention. Make sure that oil leaks aren't responsible before deciding that the rings and/or guides are bad. Perform a cylinder compression check to determine the extent of the work required (see Section 3). Also, check the vacuum readings under various conditions (see Section 4).

Check the oil pressure with a gauge installed in place of the oil pressure sending unit and compare it to this Chapter's Specifications (see Section 2). If it's extremely low, the bearings and/or oil pump are probably worn out.

Loss of power, rough running, knocking or metallic engine noises, excessive valve train noise and high fuel consumption rates may also point to the need for an overhaul, especially if they're all present at the same time. If a complete tune-up doesn't remedy the situation, major mechanical work is the only solution.

An engine overhaul involves restoring the internal parts to the specifications of a new engine. During an overhaul, the piston rings are replaced and the cylinder walls are reconditioned (rebored and/or honed) **(see illustrations 1.1 and 1.2)**. If a rebore is done by an automotive machine shop, new oversize pistons will also be installed. The main bearings, connecting rod bearings and camshaft bearings are generally replaced with new ones and, if necessary, the crankshaft may be reground to restore the journals **(see illustration 1.3)**. Generally, the valves are serviced as well, since they're usually in less-than-perfect condition at this point. While the engine is being overhauled, other components, such as

1.1 An engine block being bored. An engine rebuilder will use special machinery to recondition the cylinder bores

1.2 If the cylinders are bored, the machine shop will normally hone the engine on a machine like this

1.3 A crankshaft having a main bearing journal ground

1.4 A machinist checks for a bent connecting rod, using specialized equipment

1.5 A bore gauge being used to check the main bearing bore

the distributor, starter and alternator, can be rebuilt as well. The end result should be similar to a new engine that will give many trouble free miles. **Note:** *Critical cooling system components such as the hoses, drivebelts, thermostat and water pump should be replaced with new parts when an engine is overhauled. The radiator should be checked carefully to ensure that it isn't clogged or leaking (see Chapter 3). If you purchase a rebuilt engine or short block, some rebuilders will not warranty their engines unless the radiator has been professionally flushed. Also, we don't recommend overhauling the oil pump - always install a new one when an engine is rebuilt.*

Overhauling the internal components on today's engines is a difficult and time-consuming task which requires a significant amount of specialty tools and is best left to a professional engine rebuilder **(see illustrations 1.4, 1.5 and 1.6).** A competent engine rebuilder will handle the inspection of your old parts and offer advice concerning the reconditioning or replacement of the original engine, never purchase parts or have machine work done on other components until the block has been thoroughly inspected by a professional machine shop. As a general rule, time is the primary cost of an overhaul, especially since

the vehicle may be tied up for a minimum of two weeks or more. Be aware that some engine builders only have the capability to rebuild the engine you bring them while other rebuilders have a large inventory of rebuilt exchange engines in stock. Also be aware that many machine shops could take as much as two weeks time to completely rebuild your engine depending on shop workload. Sometimes it makes more sense to simply exchange your engine for another engine that's already rebuilt to save time.

2   Oil pressure check

Refer to illustrations 2.2a, 2.2b and 2.3

1   Low engine oil pressure can be a sign of an engine in need of rebuilding. A "low oil pressure" indicator (often called an "idiot light") is not a test of the oiling system. Such indicators only come on when the oil pressure is dangerously low. Even a factory oil pressure gauge in the instrument panel is only a relative indication, although much better for driver information than a warning light. A better test is with a mechanical (not electrical) oil

1.6 Uneven piston wear like this indicates a bent connecting rod

pressure gauge.
2   Locate the oil pressure indicator sending unit - it's located right above the oil filter **(see illustrations)**.
3   Unscrew and remove the oil pressure sending unit and then screw in the hose for your oil pressure gauge **(see illustration)**. If necessary, install an adapter fitting. Use Tef-

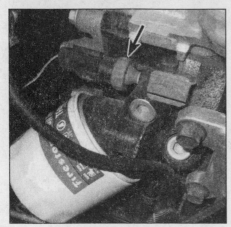

2.2a Location of the oil pressure sending unit on 3.7L V6 and 4.7L V8 engines

2.2b Location of the oil pressure sending unit on Hemi engines

2.3 Install an oil pressure gauge into the block after removing the oil pressure sending unit - Hemi engine shown

3.6 Use a compression gauge with a threaded fitting for the spark plug hole, not the type that requires hand pressure to maintain the seal

4.4 A simple vacuum gauge can be handy in diagnosing engine condition and performance

lon tape or thread sealant on the threads of the adapter and/or the fitting on the end of your gauge's hose.

4   Connect an accurate tachometer to the engine, according to the tachometer manufacturer's instructions.

5   Check the oil pressure with the engine running (normal operating temperature) at the specified engine speed, and compare it to this Chapter's Specifications. If it's extremely low, the bearings and/or oil pump are probably worn out.

3   Cylinder compression check

Refer to illustration 3.6

1   A compression check will tell you what mechanical condition the upper end of your engine (pistons, rings, valves, head gaskets) is in. Specifically, it can tell you if the compression is down due to leakage caused by worn piston rings, defective valves and seats or a blown head gasket. **Note:** *The engine must be at normal operating temperature and the battery must be fully charged for this check.*

2   Begin by cleaning the area around the spark plugs before you remove them (compressed air should be used, if available). The idea is to prevent dirt from getting into the cylinders as the compression check is being done.

3   Remove the ignition coil assemblies (see Chapter 5). Also disable the fuel pump by removing the fuel pump relay (see Chapter 4, Section 2).

4   If you're working on a 5.7L V8 (Hemi) engine, remove one spark plug from each cylinder; on all other engines, remove all of the spark plugs (see Chapter 1).

5   Block the throttle wide open.

6   Install a compression gauge in the spark plug hole **(see illustration)**.

7   Crank the engine over at least seven compression strokes and watch the gauge. The compression should build up quickly in a healthy engine. Low compression on the first stroke, followed by gradually increasing pressure on successive strokes, indicates worn piston rings. A low compression reading on the first stroke, which doesn't build up during successive strokes, indicates leaking valves or a blown head gasket (a cracked head could also be the cause). Deposits on the undersides of the valve heads can also cause low compression. Record the highest gauge reading obtained.

8   Repeat the procedure for the remaining cylinders and compare the results to this Chapter's Specifications.

9   Add some engine oil (about three squirts from a plunger-type oil can) to each cylinder, through the spark plug hole, and repeat the test.

10   If the compression increases after the oil is added, the piston rings are definitely worn. If the compression doesn't increase significantly, the leakage is occurring at the valves or head gasket. Leakage past the valves may be caused by burned valve seats and/or faces or warped, cracked or bent valves.

11   If two adjacent cylinders have equally low compression, there's a strong possibility that the head gasket between them is blown. The appearance of coolant in the combustion chambers or the crankcase would verify this condition.

12   If one cylinder is slightly lower than the others, and the engine has a slightly rough idle, a worn lobe on the camshaft could be the cause.

13   If the compression is unusually high, the combustion chambers are probably coated with carbon deposits. If that's the case, the cylinder head(s) should be removed and decarbonized.

14   If compression is way down or varies greatly between cylinders, it would be a good idea to have a leak-down test performed by an automotive repair shop. This test will pinpoint exactly where the leakage is occurring and how severe it is.

4   Vacuum gauge diagnostic checks

Refer to illustrations 4.4 and 4.6

A vacuum gauge provides inexpensive but valuable information about what is going on in the engine. You can check for worn rings or cylinder walls, leaking head or intake manifold gaskets, incorrect carburetor adjustments, restricted exhaust, stuck or burned valves, weak valve springs, improper ignition or valve timing and ignition problems.

Unfortunately, vacuum gauge readings are easy to misinterpret, so they should be used in conjunction with other tests to confirm the diagnosis.

Both the absolute readings and the rate of needle movement are important for accurate interpretation. Most gauges measure vacuum in inches of mercury (in-Hg). The following references to vacuum assume the diagnosis is being performed at sea level. As elevation increases (or atmospheric pressure decreases), the reading will decrease. For every 1,000 foot increase in elevation above approximately 2,000 feet, the gauge readings will decrease about one inch of mercury.

Connect the vacuum gauge directly to the intake manifold vacuum, not to ported (throttle body) vacuum **(see illustration)**. Some models are equipped with a vacuum fitting built into the brake booster vacuum hose grommet at the brake booster. Other models are equipped with a vacuum hose fitting on the intake manifold. Use a T-fitting to access the vacuum signal. Be sure no hoses are left disconnected during the test or false readings will result.

Before you begin the test, allow the engine to warm up completely. Block the wheels and set the parking brake. With the transmission in Park, start the engine and allow it to run at normal idle speed. **Warning:** *Keep your hands and the vacuum gauge clear of the fans.*

Read the vacuum gauge; an average,

healthy engine should normally produce about 17 to 22 in-Hg with a fairly steady needle (see illustration). Refer to the following vacuum gauge readings and what they indicate about the engine's condition:

1   A low, steady reading usually indicates a leaking gasket between the intake manifold and cylinder head(s) or throttle body, a leaky vacuum hose, late ignition timing or incorrect camshaft timing. Check ignition timing with a timing light and eliminate all other possible causes, utilizing the tests provided in this Chapter before you remove the timing chain cover to check the timing marks.

2   If the reading is three to eight inches below normal and it fluctuates at that low reading, suspect an intake manifold gasket leak at an intake port or a faulty fuel injector.

3   If the needle has regular drops of about two-to-four inches at a steady rate, the valves are probably leaking. Perform a compression check or leak-down test to confirm this.

4   An irregular drop or down-flick of the needle can be caused by a sticking valve or an ignition misfire. Perform a compression check or leak-down test and read the spark plugs.

5   A rapid vibration of about four in-Hg vibration at idle combined with exhaust smoke indicates worn valve guides. Perform a leak-down test to confirm this. If the rapid vibration occurs with an increase in engine speed, check for a leaking intake manifold gasket or head gasket, weak valve springs, burned valves or ignition misfire.

6   A slight fluctuation, say one inch up and down, may mean ignition problems. Check all the usual tune-up items and, if necessary, run the engine on an ignition analyzer.

7   If there is a large fluctuation, perform a compression or leak-down test to look for a weak or dead cylinder or a blown head gasket.

8   If the needle moves slowly through a wide range, check for a clogged PCV system, incorrect idle fuel mixture, throttle body or intake manifold gasket leaks.

9   Check for a slow return after revving the engine by quickly snapping the throttle open until the engine reaches about 2,500 rpm and let it shut. Normally the reading should drop to near zero, rise above normal idle reading (about 5 in-Hg over) and then return to the previous idle reading. If the vacuum returns slowly and doesn't peak when the throttle is snapped shut, the rings may be worn. If there is a long delay, look for a restricted exhaust system (often the muffler or catalytic converter). An easy way to check this is to temporarily disconnect the exhaust ahead of the suspected part and redo the test.

5   Engine rebuilding alternatives

The do-it-yourselfer is faced with a number of options when purchasing a rebuilt

Low, steady reading   Low, fluctuating needle   Regular drops

Irregular drops   Rapid vibration

Large fluctuation   Slow fluctuation

STD-O-OBR HAYNES

4.6 Typical vacuum gauge readings

engine. The major considerations are cost, warranty, parts availability and the time required for the rebuilder to complete the project. The decision to replace the engine block, piston/connecting rod assemblies and crankshaft depends on the final inspection results of your engine. Only then can you make a cost effective decision whether to have your engine overhauled or simply purchase an exchange engine for your vehicle.

Some of the rebuilding alternatives include:

Individual parts - If the inspection procedures reveal that the engine block and most engine components are in reusable condition, purchasing individual parts and having a rebuilder rebuild your engine may be the most economical alternative. The block, crankshaft and piston/connecting rod assemblies should all be inspected carefully by a machine shop first.

Short block - A short block consists of an engine block with a crankshaft and piston/connecting rod assemblies already installed. All new bearings are incorporated and all clearances will be correct. The existing camshafts, valve train components, cylinder head

and external parts can be bolted to the short block with little or no machine shop work necessary.

Long block - A long block consists of a short block plus an oil pump, oil pan, cylinder head, valve cover, camshaft and valve train components, timing sprockets and chain or gears and timing cover. All components are installed with new bearings, seals and gaskets incorporated throughout. The installation of manifolds and external parts is all that's necessary.

Low mileage used engines - Some companies now offer low mileage used engines which is a very cost effective way to get your vehicle up and running again. These engines often come from vehicles which have been in totaled in accidents or come from other countries which have a higher vehicle turn over rate. A low mileage used engine also usually has a similar warranty like the newly remanufactured engines.

Give careful thought to which alternative is best for you and discuss the situation with local automotive machine shops, auto parts dealers and experienced rebuilders before ordering or purchasing replacement parts.

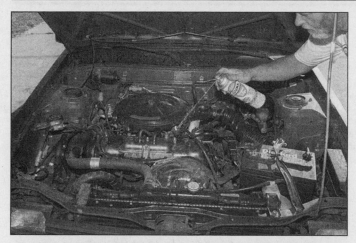

6.1 After tightly wrapping water-vulnerable components, use a spray cleaner on everything, with particular concentration on the greasiest areas, usually around the valve cover and lower edges of the block. If one section dries out, apply more cleaner

6.2 Depending on how dirty the engine is, let the cleaner soak in according to the directions and then hose off the grime and cleaner. Get the rinse water down into every area you can get at; then dry important components with a hair dryer or paper towels

6   Engine removal - methods and precautions

Refer to illustrations 6.1, 6.2, and 6.3

If you've decided that an engine must be removed for overhaul or major repair work, several preliminary steps should be taken. Read all removal and installation procedures carefully prior to committing to this job. These engines are removed by lowering the engine to the floor, along with the transmission, and then raising the vehicle sufficiently to slide the assembly out; this will require a vehicle hoist as well as an engine hoist.

Locating a suitable place to work is extremely important. Adequate work space, along with storage space for the vehicle, will be needed. If a shop or garage isn't available, at the very least a flat, level, clean work surface made of concrete or asphalt is required.

6.3 Get an engine stand sturdy enough to firmly support the engine while you're working on it. Stay away from three-wheeled models; they have a tendency to tip over more easily, so get a four-wheeled unit

Cleaning the engine compartment and engine before beginning the removal procedure will help keep tools clean and organized **(see illustrations 6.1 and 6.2).**

An engine hoist will also be necessary. Make sure the hoist is rated in excess of the combined weight of the engine and transmission. Safety is of primary importance, considering the potential hazards involved in removing the engine from the vehicle.

If you're a novice at engine removal, get at least one helper. One person cannot easily do all the things you need to do to remove a big heavy engine and transmission assembly from the engine compartment. Also helpful is to seek advice and assistance from someone who's experienced in engine removal.

Plan the operation ahead of time. Arrange for or obtain all of the tools and equipment you'll need prior to beginning the job **(see illustration 6.3).** Some of the equipment necessary to perform engine removal and installation safely and with relative ease are (in addition to a vehicle hoist and an engine hoist) a heavy duty floor jack (preferably fitted with a transmission jack head adapter), complete sets of wrenches and sockets as described in the front of this manual, wooden blocks, plenty of rags and cleaning solvent for mopping up spilled oil, coolant and gasoline.

Plan for the vehicle to be out of use for quite a while. A machine shop can do the work that is beyond the scope of the home mechanic. Machine shops often have a busy schedule, so before removing the engine, consult the shop for an estimate of how long it will take to rebuild or repair the components that may need work.

7   Engine - removal and installation

Warning 1: *Gasoline is extremely flammable, so take extra precautions when you work on any part of the fuel system. Don't smoke or* allow open flames or bare light bulbs near the work area, and don't work in a garage where a gas-type appliance (such as a water heater or clothes dryer) is present. Since gasoline is carcinogenic, wear fuel-resistant gloves when there's a possibility of being exposed to fuel, and, if you spill any fuel on your skin, rinse it off immediately with soap and water. Mop up any spills immediately and do not store fuel-soaked rags where they could ignite. The fuel system is under constant pressure, so, if any fuel lines are to be disconnected, the fuel pressure in the system must be relieved first (see Chapter 4 for more information). When you perform any kind of work on the fuel system, wear safety glasses and have a Class B type fire extinguisher on hand.*

Warning 2: *The air conditioning system is under high pressure. Do not loosen any hose fittings or remove any components until after the system has been discharged. Air conditioning refrigerant must be properly discharged into an EPA-approved recovery/recycling unit at a dealer service department or an automotive air conditioning repair facility. Always wear eye protection when disconnecting air conditioning system fittings.*

Warning 3: *The engine must be completely cool before beginning this procedure.*

Removal

Refer to illustrations 7.5 and 7.16

1   Have the air conditioning system discharged by an automotive air conditioning technician.

2   Relieve the fuel system pressure (see Chapter 4).

3   Disconnect the cable from the negative battery terminal (see Chapter 5, Section 1).

4   Remove the hood (see Chapter 11).

5   On Durango models, remove the cowl cover (see Chapter 11), then remove the cowl support brace and the wiper motor support bracket **(see illustration).**

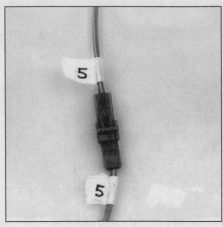

7.5 Location of the cowl support brace (A) and the windshield wiper motor bracket (B)

7.16 Label both ends of each wire or vacuum connection before disconnecting them

6   Remove the air filter housing and the intake air duct (see Chapter 4).

7   Drain the cooling system (see Chapter 1).

8   Remove the drivebelt (see Chapter 1).

9   Remove the radiator, shroud and engine cooling fan (see Chapter 3). Also remove the heater hoses.

10   Remove the air conditioning condenser (see Chapter 3) and, if equipped, the automatic transmission oil cooler (see Chapter 7A).

11   Remove the alternator (see Chapter 5).

12   Remove the power steering pump, without disconnecting the hoses, and tie it out of the way (see Chapter 10).

13   Disconnect the accelerator cable from the throttle body (see Chapter 4). **Note:** *This does not apply to models with the 5.7L V8 (Hemi) engine.*

14   Remove the PCV hose (see Chapter 6).

15   Remove the fuel rail (see Chapter 4).

16   Label and disconnect all wires from the engine **(see illustration)**. Masking tape and/or a touch-up paint applicator work well for marking items. **Note:** *Take instant photos or sketch the locations of components and brackets to help with reassembly.*

17   Label and remove all vacuum lines between the engine and the firewall (or other components in the engine compartment).

18   Remove the engine oil dipstick tube.

19   Remove the intake manifold (see Chapter 2A or 2B).

20   Raise the vehicle and support it securely on jackstands.

21   If you are working on a model with an automatic transmission, detach the transmission cooler lines from the engine brackets and the transmission (see Chapter 7B).

22   Disconnect the engine block heater, if equipped.

23   Disconnect the oxygen sensor and the crankshaft position sensor connector (see Chapter 6).

24   On 4WD models, remove the axle isolator bracket from the axle, engine and transmission. On 3.7L and 4.7L 4WD models, disconnect the driveshaft from the front differential (see Chapter 8). **Note:** *This is necessary*

for access to the starter and exhaust flange.

25   Remove the starter (see Chapter 5).

26   Drain the engine oil (see Chapter 1).

27   Disconnect the exhaust pipes from the exhaust manifolds. On Dakota models, remove the exhaust crossover pipe.

28   Support the engine from above with a hoist. Attach the hoist chain to the engine lifting brackets. If no brackets are present, you'll have to fasten the chains to some substantial part of the engine - one that is strong enough to take the weight, but in a location that will provide good balance. If you're attaching the chain to a stud on the engine, or are using a bolt passing through the chain and into a threaded hole, place a washer between the nut or bolt head and the chain, and tighten the nut or bolt securely.

29   Remove the transmission brace (see Chapter 2A or 2B).

30   On automatic transmission models, remove the torque converter-to-driveplate bolts (see Chapter 7B).

31   Use the hoist to take the weight off the engine mounts, then remove the engine mount through-bolts (see Chapters 2A or 2B).

32   Support the transmission with a floor jack. Place a block of wood on the jack head to protect the transmission.

33   Check to make sure everything is disconnected, then lift the engine out of the vehicle. The engine will probably need to be tilted and/or maneuvered as it's lifted out, so have an assistant handy. **Warning:** *Do not place any part of your body under the engine when it is supported only by a hoist or other lifting device.*

34   Remove the flywheel/driveplate and mount the engine on an engine stand or set the engine on the floor and support it so it doesn't tip over. Then disconnect the engine hoist.

Installation

35   Check the engine mounts. If they're worn or damaged, replace them (see Chapter 2A or 2B).

36   On manual transmission models, inspect the clutch components (see Chapter 8). On automatic transmission models, inspect the

front transmission fluid seal and bearing (see Chapter 7B).

37   On manual transmission models, apply a dab of grease to the pilot bearing.

38   Attach the hoist to the engine, remove the engine from the engine stand and install the flywheel or driveplate (see Chapter 2A or 2B).

39   Carefully guide the engine into place, lowering it slowly and moving it back into the engine compartment until the engine mounts can be secured.

40   Tighten the transmission-to-engine bolts to the torque listed in the Chapter 7A or 7B Specifications.

41   On automatic transmission models, install the torque converter-to-driveplate bolts (see Chapter 7B).

42   Tighten all the bolts on the engine mounts and remove the hoist and jack.

43   Reinstall the remaining components in the reverse order of removal.

44   Add coolant, oil, power steering and transmission fluid as needed (see Chapter 1).

45   Run the engine and check for proper operation and leaks. Shut off the engine and recheck the fluid levels.

8   Engine overhaul - disassembly sequence

1   It's much easier to remove the external components if it's mounted on a portable engine stand. A stand can often be rented quite cheaply from an equipment rental yard. Before the engine is mounted on a stand, the flywheel/driveplate should be removed from the engine.

2   If a stand isn't available, it's possible to remove the external engine components with it blocked up on the floor. Be extra careful not to tip or drop the engine when working without a stand.

3   If you're going to obtain a rebuilt engine, all external components must come off first, to be transferred to the replacement engine.

9.1 Before you try to remove the pistons, use a ridge reamer to remove the raised material (ridge) from the top of the cylinders

9.3 Checking the connecting rod endplay (side clearance)

These components include:

> *Flywheel/driveplate*
> *Ignition system components*
> *Emissions-related components*
> *Engine mounts and mount brackets*
> *Engine rear cover (spacer plate between flywheel/driveplate and engine block)*
> *Intake/exhaust manifolds*
> *Fuel injection components*
> *Oil filter*
> *Spark plug wires and spark plugs*
> *Thermostat and housing assembly*
> *Water pump*

Note: *When removing the external components from the engine, pay close attention to details that may be helpful or important during installation. Note the installed position of gaskets, seals, spacers, pins, brackets, washers, bolts and other small items.*

4   If you're going to obtain a short block (assembled engine block, crankshaft, pistons

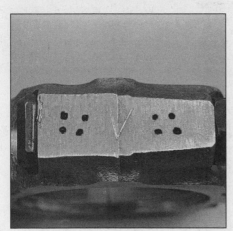

9.4 If the connecting rods or caps are not marked, use permanent ink or paint to mark the caps to the rods by cylinder number (for example, this would be number 4 cylinder connecting rod)

and connecting rods), then remove the timing chain, cylinder head, oil pan, oil pump pick-up tube, oil pump and water pump from your engine so that you can turn in your old short block to the rebuilder as a core. See *Engine rebuilding alternatives* for additional information regarding the different possibilities to be considered.

---

9   Pistons and connecting rods - removal and installation

Removal

Refer to illustrations 9.1, 9.3 and 9.4

Note: *Prior to removing the piston/connecting rod assemblies, remove the cylinder head and oil pan (see Chapter 2A or 2B).*

1   Use your fingernail to feel if a ridge has formed at the upper limit of ring travel (about 1/4-inch down from the top of each cylinder). If carbon deposits or cylinder wear have produced ridges, they must be completely removed with a special tool **(see illustration)**. Follow the manufacturer's instructions provided with the tool. Failure to remove the ridges before attempting to remove the piston/connecting rod assemblies may result in piston breakage.

2   After the cylinder ridges have been removed, turn the engine so the crankshaft is facing up.

3   Before the main bearing cap assembly and connecting rods are removed, check the connecting rod endplay with feeler gauges. Slide them between the first connecting rod and the crankshaft throw until the play is removed **(see illustration)**. Repeat this procedure for each connecting rod. The endplay is equal to the thickness of the feeler gauge(s). Check with an automotive machine shop for the endplay service limit (a typical endplay should measure between 0.005 to 0.015 inch [0.127 to 0.396 mm]). If the play

exceeds the service limit, new connecting rods will be required. If new rods (or a new crankshaft) are installed, the endplay may fall under the minimum allowable. If it does, the rods will have to be machined to restore it. If necessary, consult an automotive machine shop for advice.

4   Check the connecting rods and caps for identification marks. If they aren't plainly marked, use paint or marker **(see illustration)** to clearly identify each rod and cap (1, 2, 3, etc., depending on the cylinder they're associated with). Do not interchange the rod caps. Install the exact same rod cap onto the same connecting rod. **Caution:** *Do not use a punch and hammer to mark the connecting rods or they may be damaged.*

5   Loosen each of the connecting rod cap bolts or nuts 1/2-turn at a time until they can be removed by hand. **Note:** *New connecting rod cap bolts must be used when reassembling the engine, but save the old bolts for use when checking the connecting rod bearing oil clearance.*

6   Remove the number one connecting rod cap and bearing insert. Don't drop the bearing insert out of the cap.

7   Remove the bearing insert and push the connecting rod/piston assembly out through the top of the engine. Use a wooden or plastic hammer handle to push on the upper bearing surface in the connecting rod. If resistance is felt, double-check to make sure that all of the ridge was removed from the cylinder.

8   Repeat the procedure for the remaining cylinders.

9   After removal, reassemble the connecting rod caps and bearing inserts in their respective connecting rods and install the cap bolts finger tight. Leaving the old bearing inserts in place until reassembly will help prevent the connecting rod bearing surfaces from being accidentally nicked or gouged.

10   The pistons and connecting rods are now ready for inspection and overhaul at an automotive machine shop.

9.13 Install the piston ring into the cylinder then push it down into position using a piston so the ring will be square in the cylinder

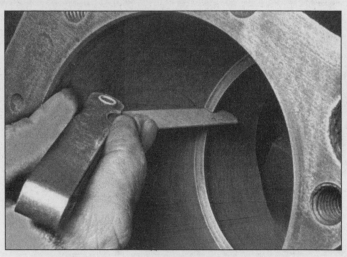

9.14 With the ring square in the cylinder, measure the ring end gap with a feeler gauge

Piston ring installation

Refer to illustrations 9.13, 9.14, 9.15, 9.19a, 9.19b and 9.22

11   Before installing the new piston rings, the ring end gaps must be checked. It's assumed that the piston ring side clearance has been checked and verified correct.

12   Lay out the piston/connecting rod assemblies and the new ring sets so the ring sets will be matched with the same piston and cylinder during the end gap measurement and engine assembly.

13   Insert the top (number one) ring into the first cylinder and square it up with the cylinder walls by pushing it in with the top of the piston **(see illustration)**. The ring should be near the bottom of the cylinder, at the lower limit of ring travel.

14   To measure the end gap, slip feeler gauges between the ends of the ring until a gauge equal to the gap width is found **(see illustration)**. The feeler gauge should slide between the ring ends with a slight amount of drag. A typical ring gap should fall between 0.010 and 0.020 inch [0.25 to 0.50 mm] for compression rings and up to 0.030 inch [0.76 mm] for the oil ring steel rails. If the gap is larger or smaller than specified, double-check to make sure you have the correct rings before proceeding.

15   If the gap is too small, it must be enlarged or the ring ends may come in contact with each other during engine operation, which can cause serious damage to the engine. If necessary, increase the end gaps by filing the ring ends very carefully with a fine file. Mount the file in a vise equipped with soft jaws, slip the ring over the file with the ends contacting the file face and slowly move the ring to remove material from the ends. When performing this operation, file only by pushing the ring from the outside end of the file towards the vise **(see illustration)**.

16   Excess end gap isn't critical unless it's greater than 0.040 inch (1.01 mm). Again, double-check to make sure you have the correct ring type.

17   Repeat the procedure for each ring that will be installed in the first cylinder and for each ring in the remaining cylinders. Remember to keep rings, pistons and cylinders matched up.

18   Once the ring end gaps have been checked/corrected, the rings can be installed on the pistons.

19   The oil control ring (lowest one on the piston) is usually installed first. It's composed of three separate components. Slip the spacer/expander into the groove **(see illustration)**. If an anti-rotation tang is used, make sure it's inserted into the drilled hole in the ring groove. Next, install the lower side rail in the same manner **(see illustration)**. Don't use a piston ring installation tool on the oil ring side rails, as they may be damaged. Instead, place one end of the side rail into the groove between the spacer/expander and the ring land, hold it firmly in place and slide a finger around the piston while pushing the rail into the groove. Finally, install the upper side rail.

20   After the three oil ring components have

9.15 If the ring end gap is too small, clamp a file in a vise as shown and file the piston ring ends - be sure to remove all raised material

9.19a Installing the spacer/expander in the oil ring groove

9.19b DO NOT use a piston ring installation tool when installing the oil control side rails

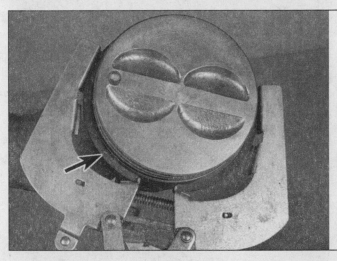

9.22 Use a piston ring installation tool to install the compression rings - on some engines the number two compression ring has a directional mark that must face toward the top of the piston

been installed, check to make sure that both the upper and lower side rails can be rotated smoothly inside the ring grooves.

21 The number two (middle) ring is installed next. It's usually stamped with a mark which must face up, toward the top of the piston. Do not mix up the top and middle rings, as they have different cross-sections. **Note:** *Always follow the instructions printed on the ring package or box - different manufacturers may require different approaches.*

22 Use a piston ring installation tool and make sure the identification mark is facing the top of the piston, then slip the ring into the middle groove on the piston **(see illustration)**. Don't expand the ring any more than necessary to slide it over the piston. **Note:** *Be careful not to confuse the number one and number two rings.*

23 Install the number one (top) ring in the same manner.

24 Repeat the procedure for the remaining pistons and rings.

Installation

25 Before installing the piston/connecting rod assemblies, the cylinder walls must be perfectly clean, the top edge of each cylinder

bore must be chamfered, and the crankshaft must be in place.

26 Remove the cap from the end of the number one connecting rod (refer to the marks made during removal). Remove the original bearing inserts and wipe the bearing surfaces of the connecting rod and cap with a clean, lint-free cloth. They must be kept spotlessly clean.

Connecting rod bearing oil clearance check

Refer to illustrations 9.30, 9.35, 9.37 and 9.41

27 Clean the back side of the new upper bearing insert, then lay it in place in the connecting rod.

28 Make sure the tab on the bearing fits into the recess in the rod. Don't hammer the bearing insert into place and be very careful not to nick or gouge the bearing face. Don't lubricate the bearing at this time.

29 Clean the back side of the other bearing insert and install it in the rod cap. Again, make sure the tab on the bearing fits into the recess in the cap, and don't apply any lubricant. It's critically important that the mating surfaces of the bearing and connecting rod are perfectly clean and oil free when they're assembled.

30 Position the piston ring gaps at the intervals around the piston as shown **(see illustration)**.

31 Lubricate the piston and rings with clean engine oil and attach a piston ring compressor to the piston. Leave the skirt protruding about 1/4-inch to guide the piston into the cylinder. The rings must be compressed until they're flush with the piston.

32 Rotate the crankshaft until the number one connecting rod journal is at BDC (bottom dead center) and apply a liberal coat of engine oil to the cylinder walls. Refer to the TDC locating procedure in Chapter 2A, or 2B for additional information.

33 With the "front" mark (letter F or arrow) on the piston facing the front (timing chain end) of the engine, gently insert the piston/connecting rod assembly into the number one cylinder bore and rest the bottom edge of the ring compressor on the engine block. **Note:** *Some engines have a letter "F" marking on the side of the piston near the wrist pin, others have an arrow, an "F" or a dimple or groove on the top of the piston. All of these are marks that indicate the front of the piston.*

34 Tap the top edge of the ring compressor to make sure it's contacting the block around its entire circumference.

35 Gently tap on the top of the piston with the end of a wooden or plastic hammer handle **(see illustration)** while guiding the end of the connecting rod into place on the crankshaft journal. The piston rings may try to pop out of the ring compressor just before entering the cylinder bore, so keep some downward pressure on the ring compressor. Work slowly, and if any resistance is felt as the piston enters the cylinder, stop immediately. Find out what's hanging up and fix it before proceeding. Do not, for any reason, force the piston into the cylinder - you might break a ring and/or the piston.

36 Once the piston/connecting rod assembly is installed, the connecting rod bearing oil clearance must be checked before the rod cap is permanently installed.

37 Cut a piece of the appropriate size Plastigage slightly shorter than the width of the connecting rod bearing and lay it in place on

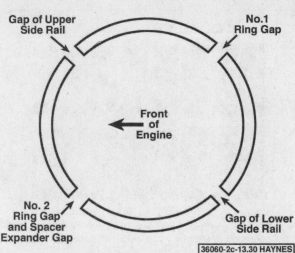

9.30 Position the piston ring end gaps as shown

Gap of Upper Side Rail

No.1 Ring Gap

Front of Engine

No. 2 Ring Gap and Spacer Expander Gap

Gap of Lower Side Rail

36060-2c-13.30 HAYNES

9.35 Use a plastic or wooden hammer handle to push the piston into the cylinder

ENGINE BEARING ANALYSIS

Debris

Babbitt bearing embedded with debris from machinings

Microscopic detail of debris

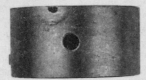

Microscopic detail of gouges

Overplated copper alloy bearing gouged by cast iron debris

Aluminum bearing embedded with glass beads

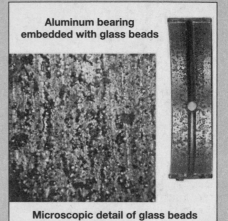

Microscopic detail of glass beads

Damaged lining caused by dirt left on the bearing back

Misassembly

Result of a lower half assembled as an upper - blocking the oil flow

Excessive oil clearance is indicated by a short contact arc

Polished and oil-stained backs are a result of a poor fit in the housing bore

Result of a wrong, reversed, or shifted cap

Overloading

Damage from excessive idling which resulted in an oil film unable to support the load imposed

Damaged upper connecting rod bearings caused by engine lugging; the lower main bearings (not shown) were similarly affected

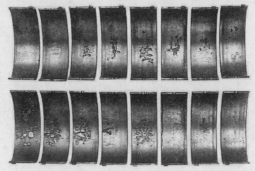

The damage shown in these upper and lower connecting rod bearings was caused by engine operation at a higher-than-rated speed under load

Misalignment

A poorly finished crankshaft caused the equally spaced scoring shown

A tapered housing bore caused the damage along one edge of this pair

A warped crankshaft caused this pattern of severe wear in the center, diminishing toward the ends

A bent connecting rod led to the damage in the "V" pattern

Lubrication

Result of dry start: The bearings on the left, farthest from the oil pump, show more damage

Result of a low oil supply or oil starvation

Severe wear as a result of inadequate oil clearance

Corrosion

Microscopic detail of corrosion

Corrosion is an acid attack on the bearing lining generally caused by inadequate maintenance, extremely hot or cold operation, or interior oils or fuels

Microscopic detail of cavitation

Example of cavitation - a surface erosion caused by pressure changes in the oil film

Damage from excessive thrust or insufficient axial clearance

Bearing affected by oil dilution caused by excessive blow-by or a rich mixture

© 1986 Federal-Mogul Corporation
Copy and photographs courtesy of Federal Mogul Corporation

9.37 Place Plastigage on each connecting rod bearing journal parallel to the crankshaft centerline

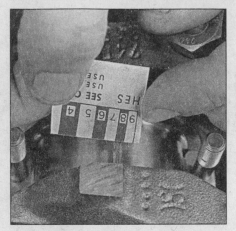

9.41 Use the scale on the Plastigage package to determine the bearing oil clearance - be sure to measure the widest part of the Plastigage and use the correct scale; it comes with both standard and metric scales

10.1 Checking crankshaft endplay with a dial indicator

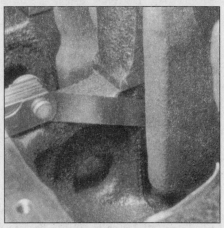

10.3 Checking crankshaft endplay with feeler gauges at the thrust bearing journal

the number one connecting rod journal, parallel with the journal axis **(see illustration)**.

38   Clean the connecting rod cap bearing face and install the rod cap. Make sure the mating mark on the cap is on the same side as the mark on the connecting rod **(see illustration 9.4)**.

39   Install the old rod bolts, at this time, and tighten them to the torque listed in this Chapter's Specifications. **Note:** *Use a thin-wall socket to avoid erroneous torque readings that can result if the socket is wedged between the rod cap and the bolt or nut. If the socket tends to wedge itself between the fastener and the cap, lift up on it slightly until it no longer contacts the cap.* DO NOT rotate the crankshaft at any time during this operation.

40   Remove the fasteners and detach the rod cap, being very careful not to disturb the Plastigage. Discard the cap bolts at this time as they cannot be reused. **Note:** *You MUST use new connecting rod bolts.*

41   Compare the width of the crushed Plastigage to the scale printed on the Plastigage envelope to obtain the oil clearance **(see illustration)**. The connecting rod bearing oil clearance is usually about 0.001 to 0.002 inch. Consult an automotive machine shop for the clearance specified for the rod bearings on your engine.

42   If the clearance is not as specified, the bearing inserts may be the wrong size (which means different ones will be required). Before deciding that different inserts are needed, make sure that no dirt or oil was between the bearing inserts and the connecting rod or cap when the clearance was measured. Also, recheck the journal diameter. If the Plastigage was wider at one end than the other, the journal may be tapered. If the clearance still exceeds the limit specified, the bearing will have to be replaced with an undersize bearing. **Caution:** *When installing a new crankshaft always use a standard size bearing.*

Final installation

43   Carefully scrape all traces of the Plastigage material off the rod journal and/or bear-

ing face. Be very careful not to scratch the bearing - use your fingernail or the edge of a plastic card.

44   Make sure the bearing faces are perfectly clean, then apply a uniform layer of clean moly-base grease or engine assembly lube to both of them. You'll have to push the piston into the cylinder to expose the face of the bearing insert in the connecting rod.

45   **Caution:** *Install new connecting rod cap bolts. Do NOT reuse old bolts - they have stretched and cannot be reused.* Slide the connecting rod back into place on the journal, install the rod cap, install the nuts or bolts and tighten them to the torque listed in this Chapter's Specifications. Again, work up to the torque in three steps.

46   Repeat the entire procedure for the remaining pistons/connecting rods.

47   The important points to remember are:

a) *Keep the back sides of the bearing inserts and the insides of the connecting rods and caps perfectly clean when assembling them.*

b) *Make sure you have the correct piston/ rod assembly for each cylinder.*

c) *The mark on the piston must face the front (timing chain end) of the engine.*

d) *Lubricate the cylinder walls liberally with clean oil.*

e) *Lubricate the bearing faces when installing the rod caps after the oil clearance has been checked.*

48   After all the piston/connecting rod assemblies have been correctly installed, rotate the crankshaft a number of times by hand to check for any obvious binding.

49   As a final step, check the connecting rod endplay again. If it was correct before disassembly and the original crankshaft and rods were reinstalled, it should still be correct. If new rods or a new crankshaft were installed, the endplay may be inadequate. If so, the rods will have to be removed and taken to an automotive machine shop for resizing.

10   Crankshaft - removal and installation

Removal

Refer to illustrations 10.1 and 10.3

Note: *The crankshaft can be removed only after the engine has been removed from the vehicle. It's assumed that the flywheel or drive-plate, crankshaft pulley, timing chain, oil pan, oil pump, oil filter and piston/connecting rod assemblies have already been removed. The rear main oil seal retainer must be unbolted and separated from the block before proceeding with crankshaft removal.*

1   Before the crankshaft is removed, measure the endplay. Mount a dial indicator with the indicator in line with the crankshaft and touching the end of the crankshaft **(see illustration)**.

2   Pry the crankshaft all the way to the rear and zero the dial indicator. Next, pry the crankshaft to the front as far as possible and check the reading on the dial indicator. The distance traveled is the endplay. A typical crankshaft endplay will fall between 0.003 to 0.010 inch (0.076 to 0.254 mm). If it is greater

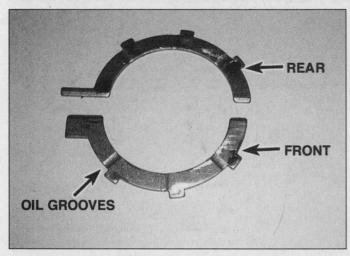

10.14a Thrust washer identification on the 3.7L V6 engine - 4.7L V8 similar

10.14b Insert the thrust washer into the machined surface between the crankshaft and the upper bearing saddle, then rotate it down into the block until it's flush with the parting line on the main bearing saddle - make sure the oil grooves on the thrust washer face the crankshaft

than that, check the crankshaft thrust washer/ bearing assembly surfaces for wear after it's removed. If no wear is evident, new main bearings should correct the endplay. Refer to Step 11 for the location of the thrust washer/ bearing assembly on each engine.

3   If a dial indicator isn't available, feeler gauges can be used. Gently pry the crankshaft all the way to the front of the engine. Slip feeler gauges between the crankshaft and the front face of the thrust bearing or washer to determine the clearance **(see illustration)**.

4   Loosen the main bearing cap/bedplate bolts 1/4-turn at a time each, until they can be removed by hand. **Note:** *The main bearing caps on the Hemi engine are each secured by four bolts, two of which are accessed from the sides of the engine block.*

5   Gently tap the main bearing caps/bedplate assembly with a soft-face hammer around the perimeter of the assembly. Pull the main bearing cap/bedplate assembly straight up and off the cylinder block. Try not to drop the bearing inserts if they come out with the assembly. **Note:** *The bedplate on 3.7L V6 and 4.7L V8 engines has built in pry points; don't pry anywhere else or damage to the bedplate will occur.*

6   Carefully lift the crankshaft out of the engine. It may be a good idea to have an assistant available, since the crankshaft is quite heavy and awkward to handle. With the bearing inserts in place inside the engine block and main bearing caps, reinstall the main bearing cap assembly onto the engine block and tighten the bolts finger tight. Make sure you install the main bearing cap assembly with the arrow facing the front of the engine.

Installation

7   Crankshaft installation is the first step in engine reassembly. It's assumed at this point that the engine block and crankshaft

have been cleaned, inspected and repaired or reconditioned.

8   Position the engine block with the bottom facing up.

9   Remove the mounting bolts and lift off the main bearing cap assembly.

10   If they're still in place, remove the original bearing inserts from the block and from the main bearing cap assembly. Wipe the bearing surfaces of the block and main bearing cap assembly with a clean, lint-free cloth. They must be kept spotlessly clean. This is critical for determining the correct bearing oil clearance.

Main bearing oil clearance check

Refer to illustrations 10.14a, 10.14b, 10.17, 10.18a, 10.18b, 10.19a, 19.19b, 10.19c and 10.21

11   Without mixing them up, clean the back sides of the new upper main bearing inserts (with grooves and oil holes) and lay one in each main bearing saddle in the block. Each upper bearing has an oil groove and oil hole in it. **Caution:** *The oil holes in the block must line up with the oil holes in the upper bearing inserts.* Clean the back sides of the lower main bearing inserts and lay them in the corresponding location in the main bearing cap. Make sure the tab on the bearing insert fits into the recess in the block or main bearing cap. The upper bearings with the oil holes are installed into the engine block while the lower bearings without the oil holes are installed in the caps or bedplate. **Caution:** *Do not hammer the bearing insert into place and don't nick or gouge the bearing faces. DO NOT apply any lubrication at this time.*

12   Clean the faces of the bearing inserts in the block and the crankshaft main bearing journals with a clean, lint-free cloth.

13   Check or clean the oil holes in the crank-

shaft, as any dirt here can go only one way - straight through the new bearings.

14   Once you're certain the crankshaft is clean, carefully lay it in position in the cylinder block. Locate the thrust washers.

   a) On 3.7L V6 engines, the thrust washers are located on the number 2 main journal **(see illustrations)**.

   b) On V8 engines, the thrust washers are located on the number 3 main journal.

The thrust washers must be installed in the correct journal. **Note:** *Install the thrust washers with the groove in the thrust washer facing the crankshaft with the smooth sides facing the main bearing saddle.*

15   Before the crankshaft can be permanently installed, the main bearing oil clearance must be checked.

16   Cut several strips of the appropriate size of Plastigage. They must be slightly shorter than the width of the main bearing journal.

17   Place one piece on each crankshaft main bearing journal, parallel with the journal axis as shown **(see illustration)**.

10.17 Place the Plastigage onto the crankshaft bearing journal as shown

COMMON ENGINE OVERHAUL TERMS

B

Backlash - The amount of play between two parts. Usually refers to how much one gear can be moved back and forth without moving gear with which it's meshed.

Bearing Caps - The caps held in place by nuts or bolts which, in turn, hold the bearing surface. This space is for lubricating oil to enter.

Bearing clearance - The amount of space left between shaft and bearing surface. This space is for lubricating oil to enter.

Bearing crush - The additional height which is purposely manufactured into each bearing half to ensure complete contact of the bearing back with the housing bore when the engine is assembled.

Bearing knock - The noise created by movement of a part in a loose or worn bearing.

Blueprinting - Dismantling an engine and reassembling it to EXACT specifications.

Bore - An engine cylinder, or any cylindrical hole; also used to describe the process of enlarging or accurately refinishing a hole with a cutting tool, as to bore an engine cylinder. The bore size is the diameter of the hole.

Boring - Renewing the cylinders by cutting them out to a specified size. A boring bar is used to make the cut.

Bottom end - A term which refers collectively to the engine block, crankshaft, main bearings and the big ends of the connecting rods.

Break-in - The period of operation between installation of new or rebuilt parts and time in which parts are worn to the correct fit. Driving at reduced and varying speed for a specified mileage to permit parts to wear to the correct fit.

Bushing - A one-piece sleeve placed in a bore to serve as a bearing surface for shaft, piston pin, etc. Usually replaceable.

C

Camshaft - The shaft in the engine, on which a series of lobes are located for operating the valve mechanisms. The camshaft is driven by gears or sprockets and a timing chain. Usually referred to simply as the cam.

Carbon - Hard, or soft, black deposits found in combustion chamber, on plugs, under rings, on and under valve heads.

Cast iron - An alloy of iron and more than two percent carbon, used for engine blocks and heads because it's relatively inexpensive and easy to mold into complex shapes.

Chamfer - To bevel across (or a bevel on) the sharp edge of an object.

Chase - To repair damaged threads with a tap or die.

Combustion chamber - The space between the piston and the cylinder head, with the piston at top dead center, in which air-fuel mixture is burned.

Compression ratio - The relationship between cylinder volume (clearance volume) when the piston is at top dead center and cylinder volume when the piston is at bottom dead center.

Connecting rod - The rod that connects the crank on the crankshaft with the piston. Sometimes called a con rod.

Connecting rod cap - The part of the connecting rod assembly that attaches the rod to the crankpin.

Core plug - Soft metal plug used to plug the casting holes for the coolant passages in the block.

Crankcase - The lower part of the engine in which the crankshaft rotates; includes the lower section of the cylinder block and the oil pan.

Crank kit - A reground or reconditioned crankshaft and new main and connecting rod bearings.

Crankpin - The part of a crankshaft to which a connecting rod is attached.

Crankshaft - The main rotating member, or shaft, running the length of the crankcase, with offset throws to which the connecting rods are attached; changes the reciprocating motion of the pistons into rotating motion.

Cylinder sleeve - A replaceable sleeve, or liner, pressed into the cylinder block to form the cylinder bore.

D

Deburring - Removing the burrs (rough edges or areas) from a bearing.

Deglazer - A tool, rotated by an electric motor, used to remove glaze from cylinder walls so a new set of rings will seat.

E

Endplay - The amount of lengthwise movement between two parts. As applied to a crankshaft, the distance that the crankshaft can move forward and back in the cylinder block.

F

Face - A machinist's term that refers to removing metal from the end of a shaft or the face of a larger part, such as a flywheel.

Fatigue - A breakdown of material through a large number of loading and unloading cycles. The first signs are cracks followed shortly by breaks.

Feeler gauge - A thin strip of hardened steel, ground to an exact thickness, used to check clearances between parts.

Free height - The unloaded length or height of a spring.

Freeplay - The looseness in a linkage, or an assembly of parts, between the initial application of force and actual movement. Usually perceived as slop or slight delay.

Freeze plug - See Core plug.

G

Gallery - A large passage in the block that forms a reservoir for engine oil pressure.

Glaze - The very smooth, glassy finish that develops on cylinder walls while an engine is in service.

H

Heli-Coil - A rethreading device used when threads are worn or damaged. The device is installed in a retapped hole to reduce the thread size to the original size.

I

Installed height - The spring's measured length or height, as installed on the cylinder head. Installed height is measured from the spring seat to the underside of the spring retainer.

J

Journal - The surface of a rotating shaft which turns in a bearing.

K

Keeper - The split lock that holds the valve spring retainer in position on the valve stem.

Key - A small piece of metal inserted into matching grooves machined into two parts fitted together - such as a gear pressed onto a shaft - which prevents slippage between the two parts.

Knock - The heavy metallic engine sound, produced in the combustion chamber as a result of abnormal combustion - usually detonation. Knock is usually caused by a loose or worn bearing. Also referred to as detonation, pinging and spark knock. Connecting rod or main bearing knocks are created by too much oil clearance or insufficient lubrication.

L

Lands - The portions of metal between the piston ring grooves.

Lapping the valves - Grinding a valve face and its seat together with lapping compound.

Lash - The amount of free motion in a gear train, between gears, or in a mechanical assembly, that occurs before movement can begin. Usually refers to the lash in a valve train.

Lifter - The part that rides against the cam to transfer motion to the rest of the valve train.

M

Machining - The process of using a machine to remove metal from a metal part.

Main bearings - The plain, or babbit, bearings that support the crankshaft.

Main bearing caps - The cast iron caps, bolted to the bottom of the block, that support the main bearings.

O

O.D. - Outside diameter.

Oil gallery - A pipe or drilled passageway in the engine used to carry engine oil from one area to another.

Oil ring - The lower ring, or rings, of a piston; designed to prevent excessive amounts of oil from working up the cylinder walls and into the combustion chamber. Also called an oil-control ring.

Oil seal - A seal which keeps oil from leaking out of a compartment. Usually refers to a dynamic seal around a rotating shaft or other moving part.

O-ring - A type of sealing ring made of a special rubberlike material; in use, the O-ring is compressed into a groove to provide the sealing action.

Overhaul - To completely disassemble a unit, clean and inspect all parts, reassemble it with the original or new parts and make all adjustments necessary for proper operation.

P

Pilot bearing - A small bearing installed in the center of the flywheel (or the rear end of the crankshaft) to support the front end of the input shaft of the transmission.

Pip mark - A little dot or indentation which indicates the top side of a compression ring.

Piston - The cylindrical part, attached to the connecting rod, that moves up and down in the cylinder as the crankshaft rotates. When the fuel charge is fired, the piston transfers the force of the explosion to the connecting rod, then to the crankshaft.

Piston pin (or wrist pin) - The cylindrical and usually hollow steel pin that passes through the piston. The piston pin fastens the piston to the upper end of the connecting rod.

Piston ring - The split ring fitted to the groove in a piston. The ring contacts the sides of the ring groove and also rubs against the cylinder wall, thus sealing space between piston and wall. There are two types of rings: Compression rings seal the compression pressure in the combustion chamber; oil rings scrape excessive oil off the cylinder wall.

Piston ring groove - The slots or grooves cut in piston heads to hold piston rings in position.

Piston skirt - The portion of the piston below the rings and the piston pin hole.

Plastigage - A thin strip of plastic thread, available in different sizes, used for measuring clearances. For example, a strip of plastigage is laid across a bearing journal and mashed as parts are assembled. Then parts are disassembled and the width of the strip is measured to determine clearance between journal and bearing. Commonly used to measure crankshaft main-bearing and connecting rod bearing clearances.

Press-fit - A tight fit between two parts that requires pressure to force the parts together. Also referred to as drive, or force, fit.

Prussian blue - A blue pigment; in solution, useful in determining the area of contact between two surfaces. Prussian blue is commonly used to determine the width and location of the contact area between the valve face and the valve seat.

R

Race (bearing) - The inner or outer ring that provides a contact surface for balls or rollers in bearing.

Ream - To size, enlarge or smooth a hole by using a round cutting tool with fluted edges.

Ring job - The process of reconditioning the cylinders and installing new rings.

Runout - Wobble. The amount a shaft rotates out-of-true.

S

Saddle - The upper main bearing seat.

Scored - Scratched or grooved, as a cylinder wall may be scored by abrasive particles moved up and down by the piston rings.

Scuffing - A type of wear in which there's a transfer of material between parts moving against each other; shows up as pits or grooves in the mating surfaces.

Seat - The surface upon which another part rests or seats. For example, the valve seat is the matched surface upon which the valve face rests. Also used to refer to wearing into a good fit; for example, piston rings seat after a few miles of driving.

Short block - An engine block complete with crankshaft and piston and, usually, camshaft assemblies.

Static balance - The balance of an object while it's stationary.

Step - The wear on the lower portion of a ring land caused by excessive side and back-clearance. The height of the step indicates the ring's extra side clearance and the length of the step projecting from the back wall of the groove represents the ring's back clearance.

Stroke - The distance the piston moves when traveling from top dead center to bottom dead center, or from bottom dead center to top dead center.

Stud - A metal rod with threads on both ends.

T

Tang - A lip on the end of a plain bearing used to align the bearing during assembly.

Tap - To cut threads in a hole. Also refers to the fluted tool used to cut threads.

Taper - A gradual reduction in the width of a shaft or hole; in an engine cylinder, taper usually takes the form of uneven wear, more pronounced at the top than at the bottom.

Throws - The offset portions of the crankshaft to which the connecting rods are affixed.

Thrust bearing - The main bearing that has thrust faces to prevent excessive endplay, or forward and backward movement of the crankshaft.

Thrust washer - A bronze or hardened steel washer placed between two moving parts. The washer prevents longitudinal movement and provides a bearing surface for thrust surfaces of parts.

Tolerance - The amount of variation permitted from an exact size of measurement. Actual amount from smallest acceptable dimension to largest acceptable dimension.

U

Umbrella - An oil deflector placed near the valve tip to throw oil from the valve stem area.

Undercut - A machined groove below the normal surface.

Undersize bearings - Smaller diameter bearings used with re-ground crankshaft journals.

V

Valve grinding - Refacing a valve in a valve-refacing machine.

Valve train - The valve-operating mechanism of an engine; includes all components from the camshaft to the valve.

Vibration damper - A cylindrical weight attached to the front of the crankshaft to minimize torsional vibration (the twist-untwist actions of the crankshaft caused by the cylinder firing impulses). Also called a harmonic balancer.

W

Water jacket - The spaces around the cylinders, between the inner and outer shells of the cylinder block or head, through which coolant circulates.

Web - A supporting structure across a cavity.

Woodruff key - A key with a radiused backside (viewed from the side).

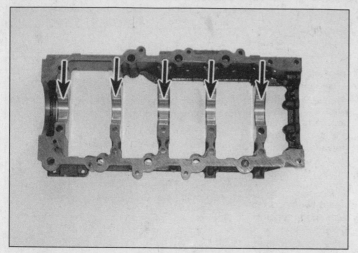

10.18a On the 3.7L V6 and 4.7L V8 engines, the bearings are installed into the corresponding saddles in the bedplate . . .

10.18b . . . then the bedplate is set over the crankshaft onto the dowels on the engine block

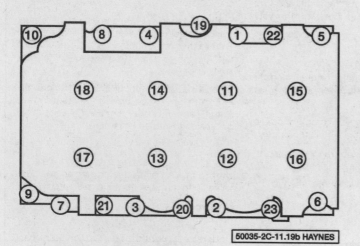

10.19a Main bearing cap/bedplate bolt tightening sequence on the 3.7L V6 engine

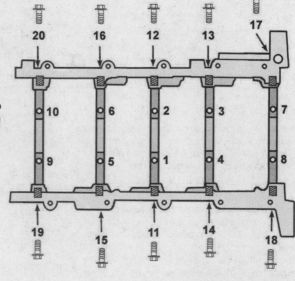

10.19b Main bearing cap/bedplate bolt tightening sequence on the 4.7L V8 engine

18   Clean the faces of the bearing inserts in the main bearing caps or bedplate assembly **(see illustrations)**. Hold the bearing inserts in place and install the assembly onto the crank-shaft and cylinder block. DO NOT disturb the Plastigage. Make sure you install the main bearing cap assembly with the arrow facing the front (timing chain end) of the engine.

19   Apply clean engine oil to all bolt threads prior to installation, then install all bolts fin-ger-tight. Tighten main bearing caps/bedplate assembly bolts in the sequence shown **(see illustrations)** progressing in steps, to the torque listed in this Chapter's Specifications. DO NOT rotate the crankshaft at any time during this operation.

20   Remove the bolts in the reverse order of the tightening sequence and carefully lift the main bearing cap assembly straight up and off the block. Do not disturb the Plastigage or rotate the crankshaft. If the main bearing cap assembly is difficult to remove, tap it gently from side-to-side with a soft-face hammer to loosen it.

10.19c Main bearing cap and crossbolt tightening sequence on the 5.7L V8 (Hemi) engine

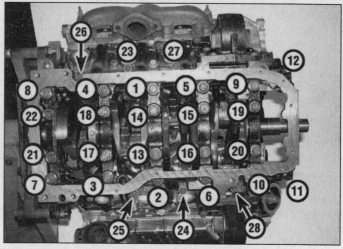

◄── **Front of Engine**

10.21 Use the scale on the Plastigage package to determine the bearing oil clearance - be sure to measure the widest part of the Plastigage and use the correct scale; it comes with both standard and metric scales

21   Compare the width of the crushed Plastigage on each journal to the scale printed on the Plastigage envelope to determine the main bearing oil clearance **(see illustration)**. A typical main bearing oil clearance should fall between 0.0015 and 0.0023-inch. Check with an automotive machine shop for the clearance specified for your engine.

22   If the clearance is not as specified, the bearing inserts may be the wrong size (which means different ones will be required). Before deciding if different inserts are needed, make sure that no dirt or oil was between the bearing inserts and the cap assembly or block when the clearance was measured. If the Plastigage was wider at one end than the other, the crankshaft journal may be tapered. If the clearance still exceeds the limit specified, the bearing insert(s) will have to be replaced with an undersize bearing insert(s). **Caution:** *When installing a new crankshaft always install a standard bearing insert set.*

23   Carefully scrape all traces of the Plastigage material off the main bearing journals and/or the bearing insert faces. Be sure to remove all residue from the oil holes. Use your fingernail or the edge of a plastic card - don't nick or scratch the bearing faces.

Final installation

Refer to illustrations 10 28a and 10.28b

24   Carefully lift the crankshaft out of the cylinder block.

25   Clean the bearing insert faces in the cylinder block, then apply a thin, uniform layer of moly-base grease or engine assembly lube to each of the bearing surfaces. Be sure to coat the thrust faces as well as the journal face of the thrust washers. **Note:** *Install the thrust washers after the crankshaft has been installed.*

26   Make sure the crankshaft journals are clean, then lay the crankshaft back in place in the cylinder block.

27   Clean the bearing insert faces and then apply the same lubricant to them. Clean the engine block thoroughly. The surfaces must be free of oil residue. Install the thrust washers.

28   On 3.7L V6 and 4.7L V8 models, apply a 2.5 mm bead of Mopar Engine RTV sealant or equivalent to the bedplate sealing area on the block **(see illustrations)**. Install each main bearing cap (or the bedplate) onto the crankshaft and cylinder block. On the 5.7L V8 engine, make sure the arrow on each main bearing cap faces the front of the engine.

29   Prior to installation, apply clean engine oil to all bolt threads wiping off any excess, then install all bolts finger-tight.

30   Tighten the main bearing cap bolts or bedplate assembly bolts to the torque listed in this Chapter's Specifications (in the proper sequence) **(see illustrations 10.19a, 10.19b and 10.19c)**.

31   Recheck crankshaft endplay with a feeler gauge or a dial indicator. The endplay should be correct if the crankshaft thrust faces aren't worn or damaged and if new bearings have been installed.

32   Rotate the crankshaft a number of times by hand to check for any obvious binding. It should rotate with a running torque of 50 in-lbs or less. If the running torque is too high, identify and correct the problem at this time.

33   Install the new rear main oil seal (see Chapter 2A and 2B).

11   Engine overhaul - reassembly sequence

1   Before beginning engine reassembly, make sure you have all the necessary new parts, gaskets and seals as well as the following items on hand:

Common hand tools
A 1/2-inch drive torque wrench
New engine oil
Gasket sealant
Thread locking compound

2   If you obtained a short block it will be necessary to install the cylinder head, the oil pump and pick-up tube, the oil pan, the water pump, the timing chain and timing cover, and the valve cover (see Chapter 2A or 2B). In order to save time and avoid problems, the external components must be installed in the following general order:

Thermostat and housing cover
Water pump
Intake and exhaust manifolds
Fuel injection components
Emission control components
Spark plugs
Ignition coils
Oil filter
Engine mounts and mount brackets
Flywheel/driveplate

12   Initial start-up and break-in after overhaul

Warning: *Have a fire extinguisher handy when starting the engine for the first time.*

1   Once the engine has been installed in the vehicle, double-check the engine oil and coolant levels.

2   With the spark plugs out of the engine and the ignition system and fuel pump dis-

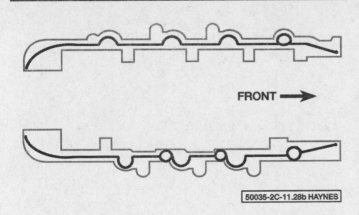

FRONT ➡

50035-2C-11.28b HAYNES

10.28a On 3.7L V6 engines, apply a 2.5 mm bead of RTV sealant to the engine block-to-bedplate sealing surface as shown

10.28b On 4.7L V8 engines, apply a 2.5 mm bead of RTV sealant to the engine block-to-bedplate sealing surface as shown

abled, crank the engine until oil pressure registers on the gauge or the light goes out.

3   Install the spark plugs and ignition coils, and reinstall the fuel pump relay.

4   Start the engine. It may take a few moments for the fuel system to build up pressure, but the engine should start without a great deal of effort.

5   After the engine starts, it should be allowed to warm up to normal operating temperature. While the engine is warming up, make a thorough check for fuel, oil and coolant leaks.

6   Shut the engine off and recheck the engine oil and coolant levels.

7   Drive the vehicle to an area with minimum traffic, accelerate from 30 to 50 mph, then allow the vehicle to slow to 30 mph with the throttle closed. Repeat the procedure 10 or 12 times. This will load the piston rings and cause them to seat properly against the cylinder walls. Check again for oil and coolant leaks.

8   Drive the vehicle gently for the first 500 miles (no sustained high speeds) and keep a constant check on the oil level. It is not unusual for an engine to use oil during the break-in period.

9   At approximately 500 to 600 miles, change the oil and filter.

10   For the next few hundred miles, drive the vehicle normally. Do not pamper it or abuse it.

11   After 2000 miles, change the oil and filter again and consider the engine broken in.

Chapter 3
Cooling, heating and air conditioning systems

Contents

Specifications

General
Coolant capacity	See Chapter 1
Drivebelt tension	See Chapter 1
Radiator cap pressure rating	19 to 23 psi (131 to 158 kPa)

Torque specifications
Ft-lbs (unless otherwise indicated)

Thermostat housing bolts	
3.7L V6 and 5.7L V8 (Hemi) engines	200 in-lbs
4.7L V8 engines	112 in-lbs
Water pump bolts	43
Fan clutch-to-engine cooling fan mounting bolts	17

1 General information

Refer to illustrations 1.1a and 1.1b

Engine cooling system

All vehicles covered by this manual employ a pressurized engine cooling system with thermostatically controlled coolant circulation (**see illustrations**). An impeller-type water pump mounted on the front of the block pumps coolant through the engine. The coolant flows around each cylinder and toward the rear of the engine. Cast-in coolant passages direct coolant around the intake and exhaust ports, near the spark plug areas and in close proximity to the exhaust valve guides. Because of the design of the accessories, pulleys and drivebelts, some engines are equipped with reverse rotating water pumps, cooling fans and viscous fan clutches. Always check with a parts department and install only components marked REVERSE on these components.

A wax-pellet type thermostat is located in a housing near the front of the engine. During warm up, the closed thermostat prevents coolant from circulating through the radiator. As the engine nears normal operating temperature, the thermostat opens and allows hot coolant to travel through the radiator, where it's cooled before returning to the engine.

These systems incorporate a pressure cap on top of the radiator that raises the boiling point of the coolant. If the system pressure exceeds the cap pressure-relief value, the excess pressure in the system forces the

1.1a Cooling system and air conditioning component locations on the Hemi engine

1	Radiator cap	4	Condenser cooling fan and shroud assembly
2	Radiator cover/radiator	5	Coolant reservoir
3	Upper radiator hose	6	Air conditioning compressor

1.1b Cooling system and air conditioning component locations on the 4.7L V8 engine

1	Radiator cap	3	Upper radiator hose	5	Air conditioning compressor
2	Radiator cover/radiator	4	Condenser	6	Coolant reservoir

2.3 An inexpensive hydrometer can be used to test the condition of your coolant

spring-loaded valve inside the cap off its seat. This allows either excess pressure or overheated coolant to escape through an overflow tube into a separate coolant reservoir.

The radiator cooling fan is mounted on the front of the water pump and is equipped with a viscous fan clutch.

Heating system

The heating system consists of a blower fan and a heater core located in the heater box, with hoses connecting the heater core to the engine cooling system. Hot engine coolant is circulated through the heater core. When the heater mode on the heater/air conditioning control head on the dashboard is activated, a flap door opens to expose the heater box to the passenger compartment. A fan switch on the control head activates the blower motor, which forces air through the core, heating the air. Some models are equipped with a rear heating/air conditioning system mounted in the right rear quarter panel.

Air conditioning system

The air conditioning system consists of

a condenser mounted in front of the radiator (Dakota models) or adjacent to the radiator (Durango models), an evaporator mounted adjacent to the heater core under the dash, a compressor mounted on the engine, an accumulator mounted in the engine compartment and the plumbing that connects all of these components.

A blower fan forces the warmer air of the passenger compartment through the evaporator core (sort of a radiator-in-reverse), transferring the heat from the air to the refrigerant. The liquid refrigerant boils off into low-pressure vapor, taking the heat with it when it leaves the evaporator.

2 Antifreeze/coolant - general information

Refer to illustration 2.3

Warning: *Do not allow antifreeze to come in contact with your skin or painted surfaces of the vehicle. Rinse off spills immediately with plenty of water. Antifreeze is highly toxic if ingested. Never leave antifreeze lying around in an open container or in puddles on the floor; children and pets are attracted by its sweet smell and may drink it. Check with local authorities about disposing of used antifreeze. Many communities have collection centers which will see that antifreeze is disposed of safely. Never dump used antifreeze on the ground or pour it into drains. Keep antifreeze containers covered and repair leaks in your cooling system as soon as they are noticed.*

These models use only Mopar 5 year/100,000 mile coolant or equivalent with a hybrid organic acid technology (HOAT) type antifreeze. Never mix different types or colors of coolants or damage to the cooling system can occur. Refer to the Specifications listed in Chapter 1 for the correct type of coolant.

Before adding antifreeze, check all hose connections, because antifreeze tends to leak through very minute openings. Engines don't normally consume coolant, so if the level goes down, find the cause and correct it.

The exact mixture of antifreeze-to-

water which you should use depends on the manufacturer's recommendation. Consult the mixture ratio chart on the antifreeze container before adding coolant. Hydrometers are available at most auto parts stores to test the coolant **(see illustration)**.

3 Thermostat - check and replacement

Warning: *Do not remove the radiator cap, drain the coolant or replace the thermostat until the engine has cooled completely.*

Check

1   Before assuming the thermostat is to blame for a cooling system problem, check the coolant level, drivebelt tension (see Chapter 1) and temperature gauge operation.
2   If the engine seems to be taking a long time to warm up (based on heater output or temperature gauge operation), the thermostat is probably stuck open. Replace the thermostat with a new one. **Note:** *It is very likely that the CHECK ENGINE light will illuminate on these models if the thermostat has failed. A diagnostic trouble code (DTC) will most likely be stored in the memory of the Powertrain Control Module (PCM). Refer to Chapter 6 for more information regarding DTCs.*
3   If the engine runs hot, use your hand to check the temperature of the radiator hose that leads from the thermostat to the radiator. If the hose isn't hot, but the engine is, the thermostat is probably stuck closed, preventing the coolant inside the engine from escaping to the radiator. Replace the thermostat. **Caution:** *Don't drive the vehicle without a thermostat. On some models the computer may stay in open-loop, potentially causing oil sludge, and excessive exhaust emissions/fuel consumption. On other models the engine will operate in "radiator bypass mode," which could cause it to overheat.*
4   If the inlet radiator hose is hot, it means that the coolant is flowing and the thermostat is open. Consult the *Troubleshooting* section at the front of this manual for cooling system diagnosis.

Replacement

5   Disconnect the cable from the negative battery terminal (see Chapter 5, Section 1).
6   Drain the cooling system (see Chapter 1). If the coolant is relatively new or in good condition, save it and reuse it (see Section 2).

3.7L V6 and 4.7L V8 engines

Refer to illustration 3.9

7   Raise the vehicle and support it securely on jackstands.
8   Remove the splash shield (see Chapter 11).
9   Follow the lower radiator hose to the engine to locate the thermostat housing **(see illustration)**.

3.9 Thermostat housing location on the 3.7L V6 engine (4.7L V8 similar) - view here is from below at the front of the engine

3.10 Thermostat housing location on the 5.7L V8 (Hemi) engine - the air conditioning compressor is removed for clarity

3.14 Location of the jiggle valve on the Hemi engine's thermostat

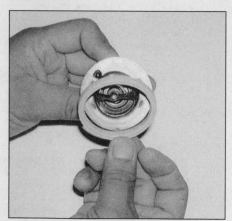

3.15a On 3.7L V6 engines, align the notch on the thermostat with the rubber tab on the gasket's inner groove . . .

3.15b . . . then align the tab (lower arrow) on the outer edge of the gasket with the notch in the thermostat housing (upper arrow) and insert the thermostat into the housing

3.15c On models without alignment notches, simply install a new rubber gasket around the perimeter of the thermostat

5.7L V8 (Hemi) engines

Refer to illustration 3.10

10   Follow the upper radiator hose to the engine to locate the thermostat housing **(see illustration)**. **Note:** *It may be necessary to partially move the air conditioning compressor for access to the thermostat housing.*

All models

Refer to illustrations 3.14, 3.15a, 3.15b and 3.15c

11   Squeeze the tabs on the hose clamp to loosen it from the hose(s), then reposition the clamp several inches back up the hose. Detach the hose(s) from the thermostat housing. **Note:** *Special hose clamp pliers are available at most auto parts stores. If the hose is stuck, grasp it near the end with a pair of adjustable pliers and twist it to break the seal, then pull it off. If the hose is old or deteriorated, cut it off and install a new one.*

12   If the outer surface of the thermostat housing that mates with the hose is deteriorated (corroded, pitted, etc.) it may be damaged further by hose removal. If it is, the ther-

mostat housing will have to be replaced.

13   Remove the thermostat housing from the engine. If the housing is stuck, tap it with a soft-face hammer to jar it loose. Be prepared for some coolant to spill as the gasket seal is broken.

14   Note how the thermostat is installed (which end is facing up, or out, and the position of the air bleed "jiggle valve," if equipped) and remove it from the engine **(see illustration)**.

15   Install a new rubber gasket around the thermostat. Be sure to align the rubber tab on the inside of the O-ring groove with the notch on the thermostat **(see illustration)**. Then align the rubber tab on the outside of the gasket with the notch on the thermostat housing and insert the thermostat and gasket into the thermostat housing **(see illustration)**. **Note:** *Some models are not equipped with alignment notches on the thermostat. Simply install the rubber gasket around the thermostat* **(see illustration)**.

16   Install the thermostat housing and bolts onto the engine. Tighten the bolts to the torque listed in this Chapter's Specifica-

tions. **Note:** *On Hemi V8 engines, install the thermostat housing with the word FRONT towards the front of the engine. This positions the slightly angled thermostat housing into the correct alignment.*

17   Reattach the hose(s) to the fitting(s) and tighten the hose clamp(s) securely.

18   Refill the cooling system (see Chapter 1).

19   Start the engine and allow it to reach normal operating temperature, then check for leaks and proper thermostat operation.

4   Engine and condenser cooling fan(s) - check and component replacement

Check

Warning: *Keep hands, tools and clothing away from the fan when the engine is running. To avoid injury or damage DO NOT operate the engine with a damaged fan. Do not attempt to repair fan blades - replace a damaged fan with a new one.*

4.6   Location of the condenser fan electrical connector (Durango models only)

4.14   Use a pin spanner to prevent the water pump pulley from turning, then loosen the fan clutch nut with an open-end wrench

Engine cooling fan

Warning 1: *While checking the fan, make sure that the engine is NOT started. If it is, you could be severely injured.*

Warning 2: *Before the fan clutch operation can be checked in Step 5, the engine must be warmed up to its normal operating temperature and then turned off. Even though the engine won't be running during this check, it's HOT! Make sure that you don't touch the engine itself during this check, or you could be burned.*

1   Symptoms of fan clutch failure are continuous noisy operation, looseness, vibration and/or silicone fluid leaking from the clutch.

Cold engine checks

2   Rock the fan back and forth by hand to check for excessive bearing play.

3   With the engine cold, turn the blades by hand. The fan should turn freely.

4   Visually inspect for substantial fluid leakage from the fan clutch assembly, a deformed bi-metal spring or grease leakage from the cooling fan bearing. If any of these conditions exist, replace the fan clutch.

Hot engine check

5   Start the engine and allow it to warm up to its normal operating temperature. When the engine is fully warmed up, turn off the engine. Turn the fan by hand. Some resistance should be felt. If the fan turns easily, replace the fan clutch.

Condenser cooling fan (Durango models only)

Refer to illustration 4.6

Note: *Dakota models are equipped with a condenser that is mounted in front of the radiator and are not equipped with an electric cooling fan.*

6   If the condenser cooling fan is not coming on when the air conditioning is selected, unplug the condenser fan motor electrical connector and connect one of the two terminals of the motor directly to the battery with a fused jumper wire **(see illustration)**. Connect the other terminal to ground using another fused jumper wire. If the fan motor doesn't come on, replace the motor. **Caution:** *Do not apply battery power to the harness side of the connector. Be sure to test the cooling fan motor only.*

7   If the condenser fan motor is okay, but it isn't coming on when the air conditioning is selected or the engine gets hot, the fan relay might be defective. A relay is used to control a circuit by turning it on and off in response to a control decision by the Powertrain Control Module (PCM). These control circuits are fairly complex, and checking them should be left to a dealer service department or other qualified repair shop. Sometimes, the control system can be fixed by simply identifying and replacing a bad relay.

8   Locate the fan relay in the engine compartment fuse/relay box.

9   Test the relay (see Chapter 12).

10   If the relay is okay, check all wiring and connections to the fan motor. If no obvious problems are found, the problem could be the engine coolant temperature (ECT) sensor or the Powertrain Control Module (PCM). Have the condenser cooling fan system and circuit diagnosed by a dealer service department or other repair shop with the proper diagnostic equipment.

Component replacement

Engine cooling fan

Refer to illustrations 4.14, 4.15 and 4.16

Warning: *To avoid possible injury or damage, DO NOT operate the engine with a damaged fan. Do not attempt to repair fan blades - replace a damaged fan with a new one.*

Caution 1: *Some models are equipped with reverse-direction engine cooling fans. On such models, be sure to install only cooling fans and fan clutches marked REVERSE or the engine may be overheated and may become damaged.*

Caution 2: *Do not store the cooling fan/viscous fan clutch assembly in the horizontal position. Fluid can leak into the bearing*

assembly and contaminate the bearing lubricant. Store the cooling fan/viscous fan clutch in the upright (vertical) position.

11   Partially drain the cooling system (see Chapter 1).

12   If you're working on a Durango model, remove the air filter housing (see Chapter 4).

13   Remove the upper radiator hose.

14   A special pin spanner wrench (obtainable at most auto parts stores) may be required to hold the water pump pulley while a large open-end wrench is used to loosen the fan clutch nut **(see illustration)**. Sometimes it is possible to hold the water pump pulley by applying considerable hand pressure to the serpentine belt while the large nut is loosened, but it may require the tool if the fan drive nut is excessively tight. **Note:** *On all models, turn the nut counterclockwise to loosen it. Carefully lower the fan and clutch assembly into the fan shroud. Be very careful not to damage the radiator fins while doing so.*

15   Remove the fan shroud mounting fasteners and, on models so equipped, pull the shroud up to detach the clips at the bottom of the shroud. Remove the fan shroud and the cooling fan together **(see illustration)**.

4.15   An engine cooling fan shroud mounting fastener on a Durango with a Hemi engine - other models similar

4.16 Remove the four bolts retaining the cooling fan to the fan clutch

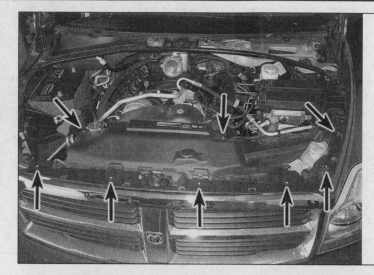

4.20 Fasteners for the radiator/ condenser cover

4.22a Upper refrigerant line fitting to the condenser

4.22b Lower refrigerant line fitting to the condenser

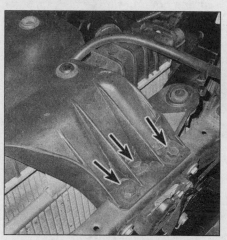

4.23 Radiator/condenser bracket and fasteners

16   Working on the bench, remove the cooling fan mounting bolts from the viscous fan clutch **(see illustration)**.

17   Installation is the reverse of removal. Tighten the fan clutch-to-cooling fan bolts to the torque Specifications listed in this Chapter. Tighten the fan clutch nut securely.

Condenser cooling fan (Durango models only)

Refer to illustrations 4.20, 4.22a, 4.22b, 4.23 and 4.24

Warning: *The air conditioning system is under high pressure. Do not loosen any hose fittings or remove any components until after the system has been discharged. Air conditioning refrigerant must be properly discharged into an EPA-approved recovery/recycling unit at a dealer service department or an automotive air conditioning repair facility. Always wear eye protection when disconnecting air conditioning system fittings.*

Note: *Dakota models are equipped with a condenser that is mounted in front of the radiator. These models are not equipped with an electric cooling fan.*

18   Have the air conditioning system discharged by an automotive air conditioning technician.

19   Disconnect the cable from the negative battery terminal (see Chapter 5, Section 1).

20   Remove the cover over the radiator support by removing the push pin fasteners **(see illustration)**.

21   Disconnect the electrical connector from the cooling fan **(see illustration 4.6)** and the air conditioning high pressure switch (see Section 17) and any other connectors attached to the fan shroud. Move the harness away from the shroud.

22   Disconnect the air conditioning lines at the condenser **(see illustrations)**. Install a piece of tape or special plugs into the openings to prevent dirt or contamination from entering.

23   Remove the top radiator/condenser mounting bracket **(see illustration)**.

24   Remove the condenser mounting fastener **(see illustration)**.

25   Move the radiator towards the engine for clearance and lift the condenser and cooling fan assembly from the engine compartment.

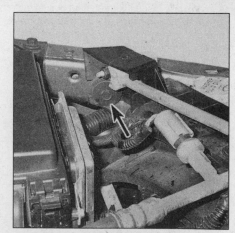

4.24 Location of the condenser mounting fastener

26   Remove the cooling fan/shroud assembly fasteners and separate it from the condenser.

27   Installation is the reverse of removal.

28   Have the air conditioning system evacuated, charged and leak tested by the shop that discharged it.

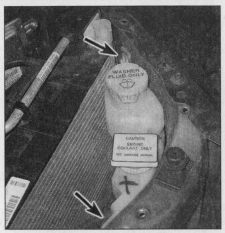

5.4 Reservoir mounting fasteners on the Durango (one lower fastener hidden)

6.6 Remove the mounting fasteners and detach the power steering cooler from the radiator

5 Coolant reservoir - removal and installation

Refer to illustration 5.4
Warning: *Wait until the engine is completely cool before beginning this procedure.*
Note: *The coolant reservoir is integrated with the windshield wiper fluid reservoir and is mounted on either side of the cooling fan shroud.*

1   On Durango models, remove the plastic cover over the radiator support **(see illustration 4.20)**
2   On Dakota models, remove the right-hand radiator seal by pulling out the plastic fasteners.
3   Disconnect the hose from the coolant reservoir. On Durango models, also detach the hose from the washer fluid reservoir and unplug the electrical connector for the washer pump.
4   Remove the mounting fasteners for the reservoir **(see illustration)**.
5   On Durango models, remove the reservoir from the bottom. On Dakota models,

remove the reservoir towards the front.
6   Installation is the reverse of removal.
7   Replace any lost coolant to the cooling system and, on Durango models, refill the windshield washer fluid (see Chapter 1).

6 Radiator - removal and installation

Warning: *Wait until the engine is completely cool before beginning this procedure.*

Removal

Refer to illustrations 6.6, 6.8a, 6.8b and 6.13

1   Disconnect the cable from the negative battery terminal (see Chapter 5, Section 1).
2   Drain the cooling system (see Chapter 1). If the coolant is relatively new or in good condition, save it and reuse it.
3   Remove the cover over the radiator support by removing the push-pin fasteners **(see illustration 4.20)**.
4   On Durango models, remove the air filter housing (see Chapter 4).
5   Detach the coolant reservoir hose from the radiator.

6   Remove the mounting fasteners and separate the power steering cooler from the radiator **(see illustration)**.
7   Disconnect the transmission cooler lines (see Chapter 7B).
8   Loosen the hose clamps, then detach the radiator hoses from the fittings on the radiator **(see illustrations)**. If they're stuck, grasp each hose near the end with a pair of adjustable pliers and twist it to break the seal, then pull it off - be careful not to distort the radiator fittings. If the hoses are old or deteriorated, cut them off and install new ones.
9   Remove the fan shroud from the radiator and move it over the cooling fan **(see illustration 4.15)**.
10   Remove the radiator mounting bracket from the radiator support **(see illustration 4.23)**.
11   On Dakota models, remove the seals on each side of the radiator.
12   Lift the radiator from the engine compartment. Don't spill coolant on the vehicle or scratch the paint. Also be careful not to damage the cooling fins of the transmission cooler or power steering cooler.
13   Whenever the radiator is removed from the vehicle, make note of the location of all rubber mounting cushions and their location

6.8a Location of the upper radiator hose clamp (Durango with a Hemi engine shown, others similar)

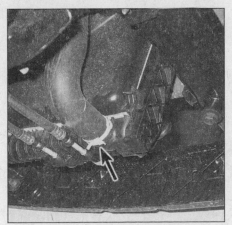

6.8b Location of the lower radiator hose spring tension clamp (Durango with a Hemi engine shown, others similar)

6.13 Inspect the radiator mounts for damage

(see illustration). If they're cracked, hardened or otherwise deteriorated, replace them.

Installation

14   With the radiator removed, it can be inspected for leaks and damage. If it needs repair, have a radiator shop or dealer service department perform the work, as special tools and techniques are required.

15   Bugs and dirt can be removed from the front of the radiator with a garden hose, followed by compressed air and a soft brush. Don't bend the cooling fins as this is done. When blowing out the core, direct the hose or air line only from the engine side out.

16   Inspect the radiator mounts for deterioration and make sure there's nothing in them when the radiator is installed.

17   Installation is the reverse of the removal procedure. Tighten the radiator mounting bracket fasteners securely.

18   After installation, fill the cooling system with the proper mixture of antifreeze and water and make sure that the automatic transmission and power steering fluid levels are correct (see Chapter 1).

19   Start the engine and check for leaks. Allow the engine to reach normal operating temperature, indicated by the inlet radiator hose becoming hot. Recheck the coolant level and add more if required.

7   Water pump - check

Refer to illustration 7.3

1   A failure in the water pump can cause serious engine damage due to overheating.

2   There are several ways to check the operation of the water pump while it's installed on the engine. If the pump is defective, it should be replaced with a new or rebuilt unit.

7.3 The water pump weep hole will drip coolant when the seal on the pump shaft fails (typical)

3   Water pumps are equipped with weep or vent holes. If a failure occurs in the pump seal, coolant will leak from the hole. In most cases you'll need a flashlight to find the hole on the water pump from underneath to check for leaks **(see illustration)**. **Note:** *The weep hole on some models is difficult to see because of the design of the pulleys and drivebelts.*

4   If the water pump shaft bearings fail there may be a howling sound at the front of the engine while it's running. Shaft wear can be felt if the water pump pulley is rocked up and down. Don't mistake drivebelt slippage, which causes a squealing sound, for water pump bearing failure.

5   It is possible for a water pump to be bad, even if it doesn't howl or leak water. Sometimes the fins on the back of the impeller can corrode away until the pump is no longer effective. The only way to check for this is to remove the pump for examination.

8   Water pump - removal and installation

Warning: *Wait until the engine is completely cool before beginning this procedure.*

Removal

Refer to illustrations 8.7, 8.8a and 8.8b

1   Disconnect the cable from the negative battery terminal (see Chapter 5, Section 1).

2   Drain the cooling system (see Chapter 1). If the coolant is relatively new or in good condition, save it and reuse it.

3   Remove the engine cooling fan and shroud (see Section 4).

4   Remove the drivebelt (see Chapter 1).

Hemi engines

5   Unbolt the air conditioning compressor and alternator and reposition them so they're out of the way. Remove the support bracket for these components from the engine. Don't disconnect the refrigerant lines from the compressor.

6   Remove the idler pulley and the drivebelt tensioner.

All engines

7   Detach the radiator hose(s) and the heater hose(s) from the water pump **(see illustration)**. If a hose sticks, grasp it near the end with a pair of adjustable pliers and twist it to break the seal, then pull it off. If the hose is deteriorated, cut it off and install a new one.

8   Remove the bolts and detach the water pump from the engine. Note the locations of the various lengths and different types of bolts as they're removed to ensure correct installation **(see illustrations)**.

Installation

Refer to illustration 8.13

9   Clean the bolt threads and the threaded

8.7 Location of the radiator hoses (A) and heater hoses (B) on the Hemi engine

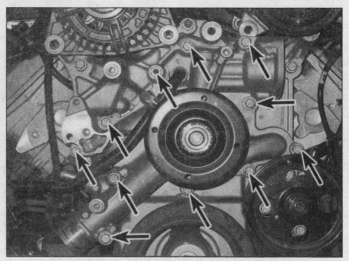

8.8a Water pump bolt locations on a Hemi engine

8.8b Water pump bolt locations and tightening sequence on 3.7L and 4.7L engines

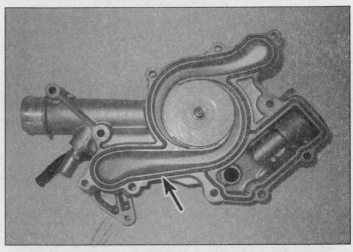

8.13 Make sure that the O-ring seal is properly seated in its groove on the water pump (Hemi shown)

holes in the engine to remove corrosion and sealant.

10   Compare the new pump to the old one to make sure they're identical. If the old pump is being reused, check the impeller blades on the backside for corrosion. If any fins are missing or badly corroded, replace the pump with a new one.

11   Remove all traces of old gasket material or the O-ring seal from the engine and water pump (if the same one is to be installed).

12   Clean the engine and water pump mating surfaces with lacquer thinner or acetone.

13   On water pumps equipped with an O-ring seal, apply a thin coat of RTV sealant to the new water pump O-ring and position it in the groove on the back of the water pump (see illustration). Caution: *Make sure the O-ring is correctly seated in the water pump groove to avoid a coolant leak.*

14   On water pumps equipped with a gasket, apply a thin film of RTV sealant to the gasket mating surface of the new pump, and position the gasket on the pump. Apply a thin film of RTV sealant to the engine-side of the gasket and slip a couple of bolts through the pump mounting holes to hold the gasket in place.

15   Carefully attach the pump and O-ring/gasket to the engine and thread the bolts into the holes finger tight.

16   Install the remaining bolts and tighten them in a criss-cross pattern to the torque listed in this Chapter's Specifications in 1/4-turn increments. Turn the water pump by hand to make sure it rotates freely.

17   Connect the hoses to the water pump and reinstall all parts removed for access to the pump.

18   Refill the cooling system (see Chapter 1). Run the engine and check for leaks.

9   Coolant temperature sending unit - check and replacement

Warning: *Wait until the engine is completely cool before beginning this procedure.*

Check

1   The coolant temperature indicator system consists of a warning light or a temperature gauge on the dash and a coolant temperature sending unit mounted on the engine. On the models covered by this manual, the Engine Coolant Temperature (ECT) sensor, which is an information sensor for the Powertrain Control Module (PCM), also functions as the coolant temperature sending unit (see Chapter 6).

2   If an overheating indication occurs, check the coolant level in the system and then make sure all connectors in the wiring harness between the sending unit and the indicator light or gauge are tight.

3   When the ignition switch is turned to START and the starter motor is turning, the indicator light (if equipped) should come on. This doesn't mean the engine is overheated; it just means that the bulb is good.

4   If the light doesn't come on when the ignition key is turned to START, the bulb might be burned out, the ignition switch might be faulty or the circuit might be open.

5   As soon as the engine starts, the indicator light should go out and remain off, unless the engine overheats. If the light doesn't go out, refer to Chapter 6 and check for any stored trouble codes in the Powertrain Control Module (PCM).

6   If the engine tends to overheat easily, check the coolant to make sure it's correctly mixed (see Chapter 1).

Replacement

7   See Chapter 6 for the ECT sensor replacement procedure.

10   Blower motor resistor and blower motor - replacement

Warning: *The models covered by this manual are equipped with a Supplemental Restraint System (SRS), more commonly known as* airbags. Always disarm the airbag system before working in the vicinity of any airbag system component to avoid the possibility of accidental deployment of the airbag, which could cause personal injury (see Chapter 12). Do not use a memory saving device to preserve the PCM's memory when working on or near airbag system components.

Front

Blower motor resistor

Refer to illustrations 10.3 and 10.4

Note: *Durango models with automatic temperature control utilize a power module instead of a blower motor resistor. It mounts virtually the same as a blower motor resistor and is replaced in the same manner.*

1   Disconnect the cable from the negative battery terminal (see Chapter 5, Section 1).

2   On Dakota models, remove the glove box (see Chapter 11).

3   On Durango models, remove the cover over the resistor, if equipped (see illustration).

10.3 Blower motor resistor cover mounting fasteners

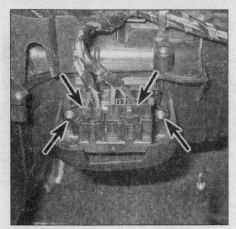

10.4 Blower motor resistor electrical connectors and mounting fasteners

10.8 Remove the electrical connector (A) and the mounting screws (B)

4 Disconnect the electrical connectors(s) from the blower motor resistor **(see illustration)**.
5 Remove the blower motor resistor mounting screws and remove it from the blower housing.
6 Installation is the reverse of removal.

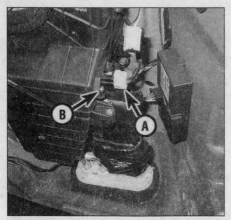

10.13 Remove the electrical connector (A) and the mounting screw (B) for the rear blower motor resistor

Blower motor
Refer to illustration 10.8
7 On Durango models, remove the right front kick panel.
8 Disconnect the electrical connector from the blower motor, then remove the mounting screws and lower the blower motor out of the housing **(see illustration)**.
9 If either the fan or motor is damaged, the entire unit must be replaced as an assembly.
10 Installation is the reverse of removal.

Rear (Durango only)
Blower motor resistor
Refer to illustration 10.13
11 Disconnect the cable from the negative battery terminal (see Chapter 5, Section 1).
12 Remove the right rear interior quarter panel (see Chapter 11).
13 Disconnect the electrical connector from the blower motor resistor **(see illustration)**.
14 Remove the blower motor resistor mounting screw and remove it from the blower housing.
15 Installation is the reverse of removal.

Blower motor
Refer to illustrations 10.18 and 10.21
Warning: *The air conditioning system is under high pressure. Do not loosen any hose fittings or remove any components until after the system has been discharged. Air conditioning*

refrigerant must be properly discharged into an EPA-approved recovery/recycling unit at a dealer service department or an automotive air conditioning repair facility. Always wear eye protection when disconnecting air conditioning system fittings.
Caution: *All models covered by this manual use environmentally friendly R-134a. This refrigerant (and its appropriate refrigerant oils) are not compatible with R-12 refrigerant system components and must never be mixed or the components will be damaged.*
Note: *Replacing the rear blower motor requires removing the rear heater/air conditioning housing.*
16 Have the air conditioning system discharged by an automotive air conditioning technician.
17 Disconnect the cable from the negative battery terminal (see Chapter 5, Section 1).
18 Remove the nut that secures the refrigerant line fitting under the vehicle and disconnect the fitting. Plug the lines and fittings to prevent contamination and moisture from entering the system **(see illustration)**.
19 Pinch-off the heater hoses that are under the vehicle and then remove the hoses from the hose fittings by removing the hose clamps **(see illustration 10.18)**.
20 Remove the right rear interior quarter panel (see Chapter 11).
21 Remove the air ducts that are attached to the heater/air conditioning housing **(see illustration)**.
22 Disconnect the electrical connector from

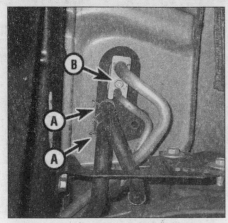

10.18 Heater hose (A) and refrigerant line (B) connections

10.21 Rear heater/air conditioning housing details:

1 *Air ducts*
2 *Mounting fasteners (two hidden from view - vicinities given)*

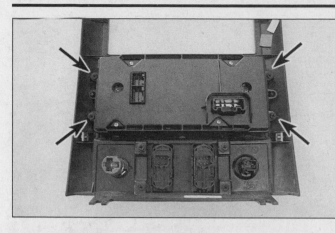

11.4 Heater/air conditioning control assembly mounting screws (Durango shown - Dakota models similar)

11.6 Pull the control assembly out of the rear console from the top . . .

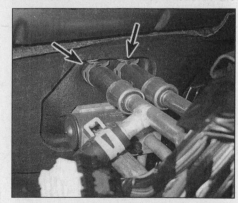

11.7 . . . then disconnect the electrical connector

the blower motor resistor and all other electrical connectors from the housing **(see illustration 10.13)**.

23 Remove the mounting fasteners for the housing, then lift it upward and remove it **(see illustration 10.21)**.

24 Disconnect the blower motor connector on the rear of the housing.

25 Remove the mounting screws on the rear of the blower motor housing and remove the blower motor.

26 Installation is the reverse of removal. Replace all O-rings with new ones specifically made for air conditioning system use and compatible with refrigerant R-134a. Lubricate them with the appropriate refrigerant oil.

27 Have the system evacuated, recharged and leak-tested by the shop that discharged it.

28 Check the coolant level (see Chapter 1).

11 Heater/air conditioning control assembly - removal and installation

Warning: *The models covered by this manual are equipped with a Supplemental Restraint System (SRS), more commonly known as airbags. Always disarm the airbag system before working in the vicinity of any airbag system component to avoid the possibility of accidental deployment of the airbag, which could cause personal injury (see Chapter 12). Do not use a memory saving device to preserve the PCM's memory when working on or near airbag system components.*

1 Disconnect the cable from the negative battery terminal (see Chapter 5, Section 1).

Front

Refer to illustration 11.4

2 Refer to Chapter 11 and remove the center trim bezel.

3 Pull the bezel forward and disconnect the electrical connectors.

4 Remove the mounting screws and detach the air conditioning and heater control assembly **(see illustration)**.

5 Installation is the reverse of the removal procedure.

Rear (Durango only)

Refer to illustrations 11.6 and 11.7

Note: *The manufacturer states that a scan tool is necessary to calibrate the rear heater/ air conditioning control assembly. If you are replacing the control assembly, you may have to drive the vehicle to a dealership to have the assembly calibrated after it is installed.*

6 Gently pull the top of the control assembly out from the back of the center console to release it.

7 Once released, disconnect the electrical connector in the rear and remove the assembly **(see illustration)**.

8 Installation is the reverse of the removal procedure.

12 Heater core - removal and installation

Warning 1: *The models covered by this manual are equipped with a Supplemental Restraint System (SRS), more commonly known as airbags. Always disarm the airbag system before working in the vicinity of any airbag system component to avoid the possibility of accidental deployment of the airbag, which could cause personal injury (see Chapter 12). Do not use a memory saving device to preserve the PCM's memory when working on or near airbag system components.*

Warning 2: *The air conditioning system is under high pressure. Do not loosen any hose fittings or remove any components until after the system has been discharged. Air conditioning refrigerant must be properly discharged into an EPA-approved recovery/recycling unit at a dealer service department or an automotive air conditioning repair facility. Always wear eye protection when disconnecting air conditioning system fittings.*

Warning 3: *Wait until the engine is completely cool before beginning this procedure.*

Note: *Heater core removal is a difficult task for the home mechanic. It can be done with slow, careful attention-to-detail, but many fasteners and wiring connectors are difficult to access behind the instrument panel. The entire instrument panel must be removed to allow the heater/air conditioning unit to be removed from the vehicle.*

Front

Removal

Refer to illustration 12.5

1 Have the air conditioning system discharged by an automotive air conditioning technician.

2 Disconnect the cable from the negative battery terminal (see Chapter 5, Section 1).

3 Drain the cooling system (see Chapter 1).

4 On Durango models, remove the inner fender splash shield from the right front wheel (see Chapter 11).

5 Disconnect the heater hoses at the

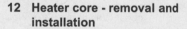

12.5 Slide the clamps away and detach the hoses from the heater core at the engine compartment firewall

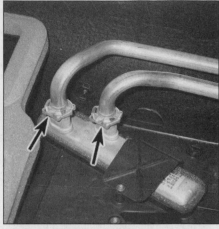

12.13 Heater core mounting details (Durango):

1 Heater core
2 Heater core retaining bracket
3 Heater/air conditioning housing bracket
4 Tube retaining bracket

12.15 Heater core tube retaining clips

heater core in the engine compartment at the firewall **(see illustration)**. Tape or plug all openings. **Note:** *On Dakota models, the heater hoses are on the driver's side of the firewall.*

6   On Dakota models, disconnect the refrigerant lines (just behind the accumulator) from the evaporator at the firewall.

7   Remove the instrument panel (see Chapter 11).

Dakota Models

8   Remove the three nuts on the firewall that hold heater/air conditioning housing in the engine compartment.

9   From inside the vehicle, disconnect any electrical connectors from the heater/air conditioning housing that are attached to electrical harnesses fastened to the chassis.

10   Remove the heater/air conditioning housing from the interior of the vehicle by pulling it away from the firewall.

11   Disassemble the heater/air conditioning housing to remove the heater core. Start by removing exterior components first along with any related electrical harnesses. **Note:** *The heater/air conditioning housing is made of two halves that must be separated in order to remove the heater core. Various components must be removed before separating the unit is possible.*

12   Remove the heater core from the heater/air conditioning housing. Replace any foam or rubber seals that are old or distorted before reassembling the housing.

Durango Models

Refer to illustrations 12.13 and 12.15

Note: *The heater core on Durango models can be removed from the top of the heater/air conditioning housing without removing the housing from the vehicle.*

13   Remove the heater/air conditioning housing bracket **(see illustration)**.

14   Remove the heater core tube retaining bracket at the firewall **(see illustration 12.13)**.

15   Release the heater core tube retaining clips and detach the tubes from the core and firewall **(see illustration)**. **Note:** *Discard the*

sealing rings from the tube fittings.

16   Remove the heater core retaining bracket and lift the core out of the housing **(see illustration 12.13)**.

Installation

17   Before installing the heater core, make sure all foam seals are in place on the heater core and evaporator.

18   Slide the heater core into the housing. On Dakota models, reassemble the entire heater/air conditioning housing.

19   Reinstall the remaining components in the reverse order of removal. **Note:** *When installing the heater/air conditioning housing, avoid pinching any wiring harnesses between the body and the housing.*

20   Refill the cooling system (see Chapter 1).

21   Start the engine and check for proper operation.

22   Have the air conditioning system evacuated, recharged and leak-tested by the shop that discharged it.

Rear

Refer to illustrations 12.31 and 12.32

Note: *Replacing the rear heater core requires removing the rear heater/air conditioning housing.*

12.31 Rear heater core mounting details (Durango):

1 Heater core
2 Heater core retaining bracket screw
3 Blend door actuator mounting fasteners

23   Have the air conditioning system discharged by an automotive air conditioning technician.

24   Disconnect the cable from the negative battery terminal (see Chapter 5, Section 1).

25   Remove the nut that secures the refrigerant line fitting under the vehicle and disconnect the fitting. Plug the lines and fittings to prevent contamination and moisture from entering the system **(see illustration 10.18)**.

26   Pinch-off the heater hoses that are under the vehicle, then remove the hoses from the hose fittings by removing the hose clamps **(see illustration 10.18)**.

27   Remove the right rear interior quarter panel.

28   Remove the air ducts that are attached to the heater/air conditioning housing **(see illustration 10.21)**.

29   Disconnect the electrical connector from the blower motor resistor and all other electrical connectors from the housing **(see illustration 10.13)**.

30   Remove the mounting fasteners for the housing and then lift it upward and carefully remove it **(see illustration 10.21)**.

31   Remove the blend door actuator **(see illustration)**.

32   Carefully remove the foam seal from the heater core and air conditioning evaporator

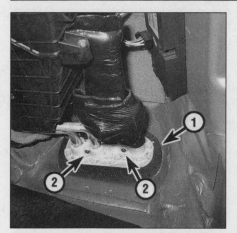

12.32 Air conditioning evaporator line details:

1   Foam seal
2   Line bracket screws

13.1 Check the evaporator housing drain tube for blockage (other components removed for clarity)

lines at the bottom of the housing **(see illustration)**.

33   Remove the two screws from the bracket that secures the lines and then remove the outer half of the bracket **(see illustration 12.32)**.

34   Remove the heater core retaining screw, then pull the heater core out of the housing **(see illustration 12.31)**.

35   Installation is the reverse of removal. Replace all O-rings with new ones specifically made for air conditioning system use and compatible with refrigerant R-134a. Lubricate them with the appropriate refrigerant oil.

36   Check the coolant level, adding as necessary (see Chapter 1).

37   Have the system evacuated, recharged and leak-tested by the shop that discharged it.

---

13   Air conditioning and heating system - check and maintenance

Air conditioning system

Refer to illustration 13.1

Warning: *The air conditioning system is under high pressure. Do not loosen any hose fittings or remove any components until after the system has been discharged. Air conditioning refrigerant must be properly discharged into an EPA-approved recovery/recycling unit at a dealer service department or an automotive air conditioning repair facility. Always wear eye protection when disconnecting air conditioning system fittings.*

Caution 1: *All models covered by this manual use environmentally friendly R-134a. This refrigerant (and its appropriate refrigerant oils) are not compatible with R-12 refrigerant system components and must never be mixed or the components will be damaged.*

Caution 2: *When replacing entire components, additional refrigerant oil should be added equal to the amount that is removed*

with the component being replaced. Be sure to read the can before adding any oil to the system, to make sure it is compatible with the R-134a system.

1   The following maintenance checks should be performed on a regular basis to ensure that the air conditioning continues to operate at peak efficiency.

a) *Inspect the condition of the drivebelt. If it is worn or deteriorated, replace it (see Chapter 1).*

b) *Inspect the system hoses. Look for cracks, bubbles, hardening and deterioration. Inspect the hoses and all fittings for oil bubbles or seepage. If there is any evidence of wear, damage or leakage, replace the hose(s).*

c) *Inspect the condenser fins for leaves, bugs and any other foreign material that may have embedded itself in the fins. Use a "fin comb" or compressed air to remove debris from the condenser.*

d) *Make sure the system has the correct refrigerant charge.*

e) *If you hear water sloshing around in the dash area or have water dripping on the carpet, check the evaporator housing drain tube **(see illustration)** and insert a piece of wire into the opening to check for blockage.*

2   It's a good idea to operate the system for about 10 minutes at least once a month, particularly during the winter. Long-term non-use can cause hardening, and subsequent failure, of the seals.

3   Leaks in the air conditioning system are best spotted when the system is brought up to temperature and pressure, by running the engine with the air conditioning ON for five minutes. Shut the engine off and inspect the air conditioning hoses and connections. Traces of oil usually indicate refrigerant leaks.

4   Because of the complexity of the air conditioning system and the special equipment necessary to service it, in-depth troubleshooting and repairs are not included in this manual. However, simple checks and component replacement procedures are provided in this Chapter.

5   If the air conditioning system doesn't operate at all, check the fuse panel and the air conditioning relay, located in the relay box in the engine compartment (see Chapter 12).

6   The most common cause of poor cooling is simply a low system refrigerant charge. If a noticeable drop in cool air output occurs, the following quick check will help you determine if the refrigerant level is low. For more complete information on the air conditioning system, refer to the Haynes *Automotive Heating and Air Conditioning Manual*.

Checking the refrigerant charge

7   Warm the engine up to normal operating temperature.

8   Place the air conditioning temperature selector at the coldest setting and put the blower at the highest setting. Open the doors (to make sure the air conditioning system doesn't cycle off as soon as it cools the passenger compartment).

9   With the compressor engaged, the clutch will make an audible click and the center of the clutch will rotate. Feel the evaporator inlet pipe between the fixed orifice tube or expansion valve and the evaporator with one hand, while placing your other hand on the metal portion of the hose between the evaporator and the condenser **(see illustration 18.1)**.

10   The pipe leading from the fixed orifice to the evaporator should be much colder than on the condenser side of the fixed orifice. If it isn't, the system charge is probably low. The earliest warning that a system is low on refrigerant is the air temperature coming out of the ducts inside the vehicle. If the air isn't as cold as it used to be, the system probably needs a charge. Further inspection or testing of the system requires special tools and techniques and is beyond the scope of this manual.

11   If the inlet pipe has frost accumulation or feels cooler than the accumulator surface, the refrigerant charge is low.

Adding refrigerant

Refer to illustrations 13.12, 13.15 and 13.18

12   Buy an automotive charging kit at an auto parts store. A charging kit includes a can

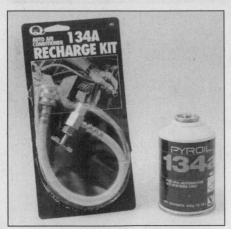

13.12 A basic charging kit for 134a systems is available at most auto parts stores - it must say 134a (not R-12) and so must the can of refrigerant

13.15 Add refrigerant to the system at the low-pressure port - Hemi model shown

13.18 If you have an accurate thermometer, you can place it in the center air conditioning duct inside the vehicle

of refrigerant, a tap valve and a short section of hose that can be attached between the tap valve and the system low side service valve **(see illustration)**. **Caution:** *Although the system will hold more than one can of refrigerant, don't add more than one can (you could overfill the system).*

13 Hook up the charging kit by following the manufacturer's instructions. **Warning:** *DO NOT hook the charging kit hose to the system high side! The fittings on the charging kit are designed to fit only on the low side of the system.*

14 Back off the valve handle on the charging kit and screw the kit onto the refrigerant can, making sure first that the O-ring or rubber seal inside the threaded portion of the kit is in place. **Warning:** *Wear protective eyewear when dealing with pressurized refrigerant cans.*

15 Remove the dust cap from the low-side charging port and attach the quick-connect fitting on the kit hose **(see illustration)**.

16 Warm up the engine and turn on the air conditioner. Keep the charging kit hose away from the fan and other moving parts. The charging process requires the compressor to be running.

17 Turn the valve handle on the kit until the stem pierces the can, then back the handle out to release the refrigerant. You should be able to hear the rush of gas. Add refrigerant to the low side of the system until both the accumulator surface and the evaporator inlet pipe feel about the same temperature. Allow stabilization time between each addition.

18 If you have an accurate thermometer, you can place it in the center air conditioning duct inside the vehicle **(see illustration)** and keep track of the outlet air temperature. A charged system that is working properly should cool to approximately 40-degrees F. If the ambient (outside) air temperature is very high, say 110-degrees F, or if the relative humidity is high, the duct air temperature may be as high as 60- to 70-degrees F, but gener-

ally the air conditioning is 30 to 50-degrees F cooler than the ambient air.

19 When the can is empty, turn the valve handle to the closed position and release the connection from the low-side port. Replace the dust cap.

20 Remove the charging kit from the can and store the kit for future use with the piercing valve in the UP position to prevent inadvertently piercing the can on the next use.

Eliminating air conditioning odors

Refer to illustration 13.24

21 Unpleasant odors that often develop in air conditioning systems are caused by the growth of a fungus, usually on the surface of the evaporator core. The warm, humid environment there is a perfect breeding ground for mildew to develop.

22 The evaporator core on most vehicles Is difficult to access, and factory dealerships have a lengthy, expensive process for eliminating the fungus by opening up the evaporator case and using a powerful disinfectant and rinse on the core until the fungus is gone. You can service your own system at home, but it takes something much stronger than basic household germ-killers or deodorizers.

23 Aerosol disinfectants for automotive air conditioning systems are available in most

auto parts stores, but remember when shopping for them that the most effective treatments are also the most expensive. The basic procedure for using these sprays is to start by running the system in the Recirculating mode for ten minutes with the blower on its highest speed. Use the highest heat mode to dry out the system - keep the compressor from engaging by disconnecting the wiring connector at the compressor (see Section 14).

24 Make sure that the disinfectant can comes with a long spray hose. Work the nozzle through the opening in the heater/air conditioning recirculation housing so that it protrudes inside and points toward the evaporator housing (towards the center of the instrument panel) **(see illustration)** and then spray according to the manufacturer's recommendations. Try to cover the whole surface of the evaporator core, by aiming the spray up, down and sideways. Follow the manufacturer's recommendations for the length of spray and waiting time between applications.

25 Once the evaporator has been cleaned, the best way to prevent the mildew from coming back again is to make sure your evaporator housing drain tube is clear **(see illustration 13.1)**.

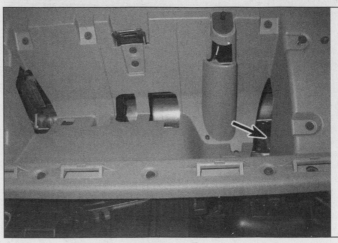

13.24 To disinfect the evaporator housing, insert the nozzle of the disinfectant can through the opening in the recirculation housing and point it toward the evaporator core (which is toward the left of the opening) - glove box removed for access

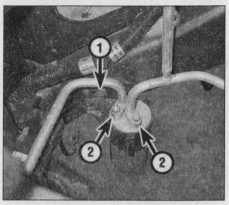

14.4 Air conditioning compressor details (Durango with a Hemi engine shown, others similar)

1   Compressor clutch electrical connector
2   High pressure line (discharge) fitting
3   Low pressure line (suction) fitting
4   Mounting fastener (others aren't visible in this photo)
5   High pressure switch

15.4 Air conditioning accumulator mounting details:

1   Mounting bracket fastener
2   Refrigerant line fittings

Heating system

26   If the carpet under the heater core is damp, or if antifreeze vapor or steam is coming through the vents, the heater core is leaking. Remove it (see Section 12) and install a new unit (most radiator shops will not repair a leaking heater core).

27   If the air coming out of the heater vents isn't hot, the problem could stem from any of the following causes:

a) *The thermostat is stuck open, preventing the engine coolant from warming up enough to carry heat to the heater core. Replace the thermostat (see Section 3).*

b) *There is a blockage in the system, preventing the flow of coolant through the heater core. Feel both heater hoses at the firewall. They should be hot. If one of them is cold, there is an obstruction in one of the hoses or in the heater core. Detach the hoses and back flush the heater core with a water hose. If the heater core is clear but circulation is still restricted, remove the two hoses and flush them out with a water hose.*

c) *If flushing fails to remove the blockage from the heater core, the core must be replaced (see Section 12).*

14 Air conditioning compressor - removal and installation

Refer to illustration 14.4

Warning: *The air conditioning system is under high pressure. Do not loosen any hose fittings or remove any components until after the system has been discharged. Air conditioning refrigerant must be properly discharged into an EPA-approved recovery/recycling unit at a dealer service department or an automotive air conditioning repair facility. Always wear eye protection when disconnecting air conditioning system fittings.*

Note: *The accumulator (see Section 15) should be replaced whenever the compressor is replaced.*

1   Have the air conditioning system dis-charged by an automotive air conditioning technician.

2   Disconnect the cable from the negative battery terminal (see Chapter 5, Section 1).

3   Remove the air intake duct resonator (see Chapter 4).

4   Disconnect the compressor clutch electrical connector **(see illustration)**.

5   Remove the drivebelt (see Chapter 1).

6   Disconnect the refrigerant lines from the compressor. Plug the open fittings to prevent entry of dirt and moisture and discard the O-ring seals.

7   Unbolt the compressor from the mounting brackets and lift it out of the vehicle. **Note:** *On Hemi engines, remove the alternator (see Chapter 5) and the alternator mounting bracket (which also supports the air conditioning compressor).*

8   If a new compressor is being installed, follow the directions with the compressor regarding the draining of excess oil prior to installation. **Note:** *Any replacement compressor used must be designated as compatible with refrigerant R-134a.*

9   The clutch may have to be transferred from the original to the new compressor.

10   Installation is the reverse of removal. Replace all O-rings with new ones specifically made for air conditioning system use and compatible with refrigerant R-134a. Lubricate them with refrigerant oil. Any refrigerant oil added must also be compatible with refrigerant R-134a.

11   Have the system evacuated, recharged and leak-tested by the shop that discharged it.

15 Air conditioning accumulator - removal and installation

Refer to illustration 15.4

Warning: *The air conditioning system is under high pressure. Do not loosen any hose fittings or remove any components until after the system has been discharged. Air conditioning refrigerant must be properly discharged into an EPA-approved recovery/recycling unit at a*

dealer service department or an automotive air conditioning repair facility. Always wear eye protection when disconnecting air conditioning system fittings.

1   Have the air conditioning system discharged by an automotive air conditioning technician.

2   Disconnect the cable from the negative battery terminal (see Chapter 5, Section 1).

3   Remove the air filter housing (see Chapter 4).

4   Disconnect the refrigerant line(s) from the accumulator **(see illustration)**.

5   On Dakota models, use a special tool to disconnect the accumulator line to the evaporator at the firewall.

6   Plug the open fittings to prevent entry of dirt and moisture.

7   Remove the accumulator and bracket. If a new accumulator is being installed, add 2 oz (60 ml) of new refrigerant oil (a type designated as compatible with refrigerant R-134a) to the new accumulator.

8   Installation is the reverse of removal. **Note:** *New R-134a compatible O-rings should be used in each fitting during reassembly.*

9   Take the vehicle back to the shop that discharged it. Have the air conditioning system evacuated, charged and leak tested.

16 Air conditioning condenser - removal and installation

Refer to illustration 16.5

Warning: *The air conditioning system is under high pressure. Do not loosen any hose fittings or remove any components until after the system has been discharged. Air conditioning refrigerant must be properly discharged into an EPA-approved recovery/recycling unit at a dealer service department or an automotive air conditioning repair facility. Always wear eye protection when disconnecting air conditioning system fittings.*

Note 1: *The accumulator (see Section 15) should be replaced whenever the condenser is replaced.*

16.5 The location of the refrigerant line fittings on the condenser

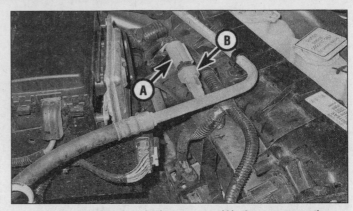

17.2 Unplug the electrical connector (A), then unscrew the switch (B)

Note 2: *On Durango models, the condenser is removed when removing the condenser cooling fan. Refer to Section 4 for condenser removal on Durango models.*

1   Have the air conditioning system discharged by an automotive air conditioning technician.

2   Disconnect the cable from the negative battery terminal (see Chapter 5, Section 1).

3   Remove the plastic cover over the radiator, the radiator mounting fasteners and then remove the radiator support and move it aside. **Note:** *It should not be necessary to remove the hood latch cable from the hood latch that is mounted to the radiator support.*

4   Remove the mounting fasteners for the power steering cooler (mounted to the front of the condenser) and move the cooler aside.

5   Disconnect the refrigerant lines from the condenser **(see illustration)**. Plug the lines and fittings to prevent the entry of moisture and contaminants.

6   Remove the fasteners that mount the condenser to the radiator (see Section 4).

7   Carefully move the radiator back, then remove the condenser by lifting it up and out of the engine compartment.

8   If the original condenser will be reinstalled, store it with the line fittings on top to prevent oil from draining out.

9   If a new condenser is being installed, pour 1 oz (30 ml) of refrigerant oil into it prior to installation (an oil designated as compatible with refrigerant R-134a). **Note:** *New R-134a compatible O-rings should be used in each fitting during reassembly.*

10 Install new O-rings onto the refrigerant lines.

11 Reinstall the components in the reverse order of removal.

12 Have the system evacuated, recharged and leak-tested by the shop that discharged it.

---

17   Air conditioning high pressure switch - replacement

Refer to illustration 17.2

Note: *It is not necessary to discharge the air*

conditioning system in order to replace the high pressure switch.

1   Disconnect the cable from the negative battery terminal (see Chapter 5, Section 1).

2   Unplug the electrical connector from the air conditioning pressure switch **(see illustration)**. **Note:** *The air conditioning high pressure switch is mounted on the high pressure line above the condenser on Durango models and near the coolant reservoir on Dakota models*

3   Unscrew the pressure cycling switch. Use a back-up wrench to prevent damaging the refrigerant line.

4   Lubricate the switch O-ring with clean refrigerant oil of the correct type.

5   Screw the new switch onto the refrigerant line until hand tight, and then tighten it securely using a back-up wrench to prevent damaging the refrigerant line.

6   Reconnect the electrical connector and the battery cable.

---

18   Air conditioning orifice tube (Dakota models) - removal and installation

---

Warning: *The air conditioning system is under high pressure. Do not loosen any hose fittings or remove any components until after the system has been discharged. Air conditioning refrigerant must be properly discharged into an EPA-approved recovery/recycling unit at a dealer service department or an automotive air conditioning repair facility. Always wear eye protection when disconnecting air conditioning system fittings.*

Note 1: *Durango models are not equipped with an orifice tube.*

Note 2: *After operating a fully-charged air conditioner for five minutes, the liquid line should be hot near the condenser (be careful - it can get very hot!) and it should be cold near the evaporator. If there isn't a significant temperature difference, the orifice tube may be plugged. If the system is checked with the appropriate gauges, and the high-pressure reads extremely high and the low-pressure reads almost a vacuum, the orifice tube is*

18.1 Air conditioning liquid line details:

1   *Liquid line*
2   *Line fitting fastener at condenser*

plugged. In either case, the liquid line, which contains the orifice tube, must be replaced.

Replacement

Refer to illustration 18.1

1   The fixed orifice tube is an inline metering restrictor that is located in the liquid line, between the condenser and the evaporator **(see illustration)**. Have the air conditioning system discharged by an automotive air conditioning technician.

2   Disconnect the cable from the negative battery terminal (see Chapter 5, Section 1).

3   Disconnect the air conditioning high pressure switch electrical connector (see Section 17).

4   Remove the air filter housing (see Chapter 4).

5   Disconnect the line fitting from the condenser. Cap or plug the refrigerant openings to prevent any dirt or moisture from entering the system.

6   Detach the line from the fasteners securing it in the engine compartment.

7   Using a special refrigerant line spring lock tool, disconnect the liquid line from the evaporator at the firewall.

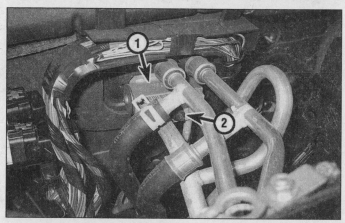

19.4 Front expansion valve details (Durango):

1   *Expansion valve*

2   *Refrigerant line fitting nut*

19.10 Rear expansion valve location

8   Remove the line from the engine compartment.

9   If you are replacing the line, remove the air conditioning pressure switch (see Section 17).

10   Installation is the reverse of removal.
Note: *New R-134a compatible O-rings should be used during reassembly.*

11   Have the system evacuated, recharged and leak-tested by the shop that discharged it.

---

19   Air conditioning expansion valve (Durango models) - removal and installation

Warning: *The air conditioning system is under high pressure. Do not loosen any hose fittings or remove any components until after the system has been discharged. Air conditioning refrigerant must be properly discharged into an EPA-approved recovery/recycling unit at a dealer service department or an automotive air conditioning repair facility. Always wear eye protection when disconnecting air conditioning system fittings.*

Note: *Dakota models are not equipped with an expansion valve.*

1   Have the air conditioning system discharged by an automotive air conditioning technician.

2   Disconnect the cable from the negative battery terminal (see Chapter 5, Section 1).

Front

Refer to illustration 19.4

3   Remove the inner fender splash shield from the right front wheel (see Chapter 11).

4   Disconnect the refrigerant lines at the firewall by removing the plastic retainer on the liquid line at the line fitting and the nut that secures the line fitting to the expansion valve **(see illustration)**. Cap or plug the refrigerant openings to prevent any dirt or moisture from entering the system.

5   Remove the two exposed mounting screws that secure the expansion valve.

6   Detach the expansion valve from the evaporator fitting and discard the O-rings.

7   Installation is the reverse of removal.
Note: *New R-134a compatible O-rings should be used during reassembly.*

8   Have the system evacuated, recharged and leak-tested by the shop that discharged it.

Rear

Refer to illustration 19.10

9   Remove the right rear interior quarter panel (see Chapter 11).

10   Carefully remove the insulation from around the expansion valve **(see illustration)**.

11   Remove the two bolts that secure the refrigerant line fitting and the expansion valve and detach the refrigerant lines from the top of the valve. Cap or plug the refrigerant openings to prevent any dirt or moisture from entering the system.

12   Detach the expansion valve from the evaporator fitting below it and discard the O-rings.

13   Installation is the reverse of removal.
Note: *New R-134a compatible O-rings should be used during reassembly.*

14   Have the system evacuated, recharged and leak-tested by the shop that discharged it.

Notes

Chapter 4
Fuel and exhaust systems

Contents

Specifications

General

Fuel pressure	56 to 60 psi
Fuel injector resistance	Not specified, but the injectors can still be checked with an ohmmeter to verify that the solenoid coils are not open or shorted

Torque specifications

Throttle body mounting bolts (all engines)	105 in-lbs
Fuel rail mounting nuts/bolts (all engines)	100 in-lbs

1   General information

Warning: *Gasoline is extremely flammable, so take extra precautions when you work on any part of the fuel system. Don't smoke or allow open flames or bare light bulbs near the work area, and don't work in a garage where a gas-type appliance (such as a water heater or a clothes dryer) is present. Since gasoline is carcinogenic, wear fuel-resistant gloves when there's a possibility of being exposed to fuel, and, if you spill any fuel on your skin, rinse it off immediately with soap and water. Mop up any spills immediately and do not store fuel-soaked rags where they could ignite. The fuel system is under constant pressure, so, if any fuel lines are to be disconnected, the fuel pressure in the system must be relieved first. When you perform any kind of work on the fuel system, wear safety glasses and have a Class B type fire extinguisher on hand.*

All models covered by this manual are equipped with a sequential multi-port fuel injection system. This type of fuel injection system uses timed impulses to sequentially inject the fuel directly into the intake ports of each cylinder in the same sequence as the firing order. The Powertrain Control Module (PCM) controls the injectors. The PCM monitors various engine parameters and delivers the exact amount of fuel, in firing order sequence, into the intake ports. For more information about the fuel injection system, see Section 10.

The fuel pump is located inside the fuel tank, and can be accessed by removing a locking ring on top of the tank. You must lower the fuel tank before you can remove this ring and pull the fuel pump out of the fuel tank. The fuel level sending unit is an integral component of the fuel pump and it must be accessed in the same manner. The fuel pump/fuel gauge sending unit consists of the fuel inlet strainer, the pump, an integral fuel filter, the fuel pressure regulator, the fuel gauge sending unit, the lockring that secures the fuel pump assembly to the fuel tank, and a gasket between the lockring and the tank.

The fuel pump/fuel gauge sending unit is not serviceable, i.e. if any component of the unit is defective, you must replace the entire fuel pump/fuel gauge sending unit.

There are two fuel filters. One is the nylon mesh fuel "sock" or strainer at the lower (inlet) end of the fuel pump/fuel level sending unit module, which is mounted in the roof of the fuel tank and protrudes down into the fuel inside. The main fuel filter is an integral part of the fuel pump/fuel gauge sending unit assembly. No external fuel filters are used on any of the vehicles covered by this manual. The fuel filters are extended-life parts and do not need to be replaced at scheduled maintenance intervals. They should only be replaced if diagnostic testing indicates the need to do so.

The exhaust system consists of the two exhaust manifolds, a pair of catalytic converters, an exhaust pipe and a muffler. All of these components are replaceable. For further information regarding the catalytic converters, refer to Chapter 6.

2   Fuel pressure relief procedure

Refer to illustration 2.2

Warning: *See the* **Warning** *in Section 1.*

1   Remove the fuel filler cap (this will relieve any pressure that has built-up in the tank).

2   On Durango models there are two fuse and relay boxes located on the left side of the engine compartment: the Integrated Power Module, which is the front unit, and the Power Distribution Center, which is right behind the Integrated Power Module. Open the cover of the Power Distribution Center and remove the fuel pump relay **(see illustration)**. On Dakota models there's only one fuse/relay box; open the cover and remove the fuel pump relay. **Note:** *The fuel pump relay might not be located in exactly the same spot on your vehicle. Verify the location of the fuel pump relay by looking at the relay guide printed on the underside of the Power Distribution Center cover.*

3   Turn the ignition key to START and crank over the engine for several seconds. It will either start momentarily and immediately stall, or it won't start at all.

4   Turn the ignition key to the OFF position.

5   Install the fuel pump relay.

6   Disconnect the cable from the negative battery terminal before beginning work on the fuel system (see Chapter 5, Section 1).

7   After all work on the fuel system has been completed, the CHECK ENGINE light or Malfunction Indicator Light (MIL) might come on during operation because the engine was cranked with the fuel pump relay unplugged. The light will likely go out after a period of normal operation. If it does not go out, refer to Chapter 6.

3   Fuel pump/fuel pressure - check

Warning: *See the* **Warning** *in Section 1.*

Preliminary check

1   The fuel pump is located inside the fuel tank, which muffles its sound when the engine is running. But you can actually hear the fuel pump. Turn the ignition key to ON (not START) and listen carefully for the soft whirring sound made by the fuel pump as it's briefly turned on by the PCM to pressurize the fuel system prior to starting the engine. You will only hear a soft whirring sound for a second or two, but that sound tells you that the pump is working. If you can't hear the pump from inside the vehicle, remove the fuel filler cap and have an assistant turn the ignition switch to ON while you listen for the sound of the pump. If the pump does not come on when the ignition key is turned to ON, check the fuel pump fuse and relay, both of which are located in the Power Distribution Center **(see illustration 2.2)**. If the fuse and relay are okay, check the wiring back to the fuel pump (see Section 5 if you need help locating the fuel pump electrical

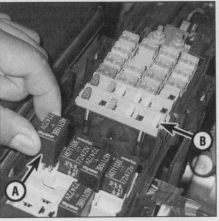

2.2 To depressurize the fuel system, remove the fuel pump relay (A) from the underhood fuse/relay box, then start the engine and let it stall. B is the fuel pump fuse (2006 Durango model shown; check the underside of the fuse/relay box cover for the relay and fuse locations on your vehicle)

connector). If the fuse, relay and wiring are okay, the fuel pump is probably defective. If the pump runs continuously with the ignition key in its ON position, the Powertrain Control Module (PCM) is probably defective. Have the PCM checked by a dealer service department or other qualified repair shop.

Pressure check

Refer to illustrations 3.3, 3.4 and 3.5

Note: *In order to perform the fuel pressure test, you will need a fuel pressure gauge capable of measuring high fuel pressure. You'll also need the right fittings or adapters to attach it to the fuel rail.*

2   Relieve the fuel system pressure (see Section 2).

3   For this check, you'll need to obtain a fuel pressure gauge with a hose and an adapter suitable for connecting it to the Schrader valve type test port on the injector fuel rail **(see illustration)**.

4   The test port is located on the fuel rail **(see illustration)**. If you have difficulty finding or accessing the fuel pressure test port, remove the air intake duct and, if necessary, the air resonator box (see Section 8).

5   Unscrew the threaded cap from the test port and connect the fuel pressure gauge hose to the test port **(see illustration)**.

6   Start the engine and check the pressure on the gauge, comparing your reading with the pressure listed in this Chapter's Specifications.

7   If the fuel pressure is not within specifications, check the following:

a) *If the pressure is lower than specified, check for a restriction in the fuel system (this includes the inlet strainer and the fuel filter at the fuel pump module). If no restrictions are found, replace the fuel pump/fuel gauge sending unit (see Section 7).*

3.3 To check the fuel pressure, you'll need to obtain a fuel pressure gauge capable of reading fuel pressure in excess of the specified operating system pressure, a hose to connect the gauge to the fuel pressure test port and an adapter suitable for connecting the hose to the test port

3.4 The fuel pressure test port is located on the fuel rail (4.7L V8 engine shown, other engines similar)

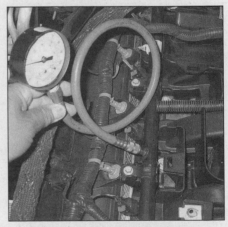

3.5 Unscrew the cap from the test port and, using an adapter that fits the Schrader valve type test port, connect the fuel pressure gauge hose to the test port

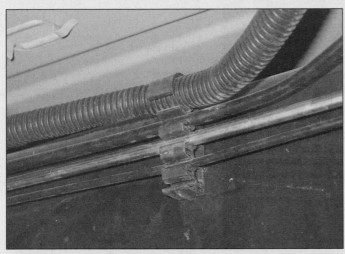

4.2a To free a line from this type of clip, pull the line out from the two retainers holding it in place. If you can't, pry the retainers apart (don't pry the line out, because you might kink it)

4.2b To free a line from a clamshell type of clip, pry open the front half of the clip with a screwdriver at both ends

b) *If the fuel pressure is higher than specified, replace the fuel pump/fuel gauge sending unit (see Section 7). (Even though the fuel pressure regulator is defective, but you can't replace the pressure regulator without replacing the fuel pump/fuel gauge sending unit assembly.)*

4   Fuel lines and fittings - repair and replacement

Refer to illustrations 4.2a and 4.2b
Warning: *See the* **Warning** *in Section 1.*
1   Always relieve the fuel pressure before servicing fuel lines or fittings on fuel-injected vehicles (see Section 2).
2   The fuel supply and return lines connect the fuel tank to the fuel rail on the engine. Be sure to inspect the fuel and the Evaporative Emission Control (EVAP) system lines for leaks, kinks and dents whenever you're servicing something underneath the vehicle. All of these lines are secured to the vehicle underbody by plastic clips **(see illustration).** To disengage fuel and/or vapor line(s) from the simpler style clip, simply pry the retainers apart and pull out the line(s). To disengage the lines from a clamshell style clip, pry open the clamshell "door" (the outer half of the clip) with a small screwdriver and swing the door open **(see illustration).**
3   Whenever you're working under the vehicle, be sure to inspect all fuel and EVAP lines for leaks, kinks, dents and other damage. Always replace a damaged fuel line or EVAP line immediately. Leaking fuel and EVAP lines will result in loss of fuel and excessive air pollution (leaking raw fuel emits unburned hydrocarbon vapors into the atmosphere).
4   If you find signs of dirt in the lines during disassembly, disconnect all lines and blow them out with compressed air. Also remove

the fuel pump (see Section 7) and inspect the fuel strainer for damage or plugging.

Steel tubing
5   Because fuel lines used on fuel-injected vehicles are under fairly high pressure, it is critical that they be replaced with lines of equivalent specification. If you have to replace a steel line, make sure that you use steel tubing that meets the manufacturer's specifications. Don't use copper or aluminum tubing to replace steel tubing. These materials cannot withstand normal vehicle vibration.
6   Some steel fuel lines have threaded fittings. When loosening these fittings to service or replace components:
   a) *Use a backup wrench on the stationary portion of the fitting while loosening and tightening the fitting nuts.*
   b) *If you're going to replace one of these fittings, use original equipment parts or parts that meet original equipment standards.*

Plastic tubing
7   If you ever have to replace a plastic line, use only the original equipment plastic tubing.
Caution: *When removing or installing plastic fuel line tubing, be careful not to bend or twist it too much, which can damage it. And damaged fuel lines MUST be replaced! Also, be aware that the plastic fuel tubing is NOT heat resistant, so keep it away from excessive heat. Nor is it acid-proof, so don't wipe it off with a shop rag that has been used to wipe off battery electrolyte. If you accidentally spill or wipe electrolyte on plastic fuel or emissions tubing, replace the tubing.*

Flexible hoses
Warning: *Use only original equipment replacement hoses or their equivalent. Unapproved hoses might fail when subjected to the high operating pressures of the fuel system.*

8   Don't route fuel hoses within four inches of exhaust system components or within ten inches of a catalytic converter. Make sure that no flexible hoses are installed directly against the vehicle, particularly in places where there is any vibration. If allowed to touch some vibrating part of the vehicle, a hose can easily become chafed and it might start leaking. A good rule of thumb is to maintain a minimum of 1/4-inch clearance around a hose (or metal line) to prevent contact with the vehicle underbody.

Fuel line and EVAP line quick-connect fittings
9   **Warning:** *ALWAYS relieve the fuel system pressure (see Section 2) before disconnecting a fuel line fitting.*
10   The vehicles covered in this manual use several kinds of fuel line quick-connect fittings for connections at the fuel pump, the EVAP canister and the fuel rail. The procedure for releasing each type of fuel line fitting is different. But a few rules of thumb apply to all fittings:
   a) *ALWAYS relieve the fuel system pressure (see Section 2) before disconnecting a fuel line fitting.*
   b) *Inspect the fitting for dirt. If the fitting is dirty, clean it off before disassembling it. The seals in the fitting will stick to the fuel line as they age. Twist the fitting on the line, then push and pull the fitting until it moves freely.*
   c) *Always disconnect all fuel line fittings from a fuel system component before removing the component.*
   d) *When disconnecting a quick-connect fitting, inspect the condition of the retainer before reconnecting the fitting. The best strategy with respect to retainers is to simply replace the retainer every time that you disconnect the fitting.*
   e) *When you disconnect a fitting with an*

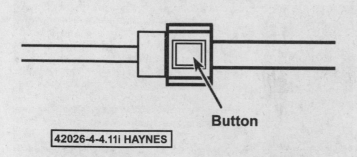

42026-4-4.11i HAYNES

4.11 Some quick-connect fittings have two buttons (one on each side of the fitting) that must be depressed to release the fitting. No tools are necessary

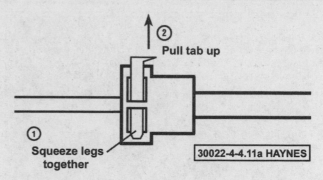

30022-4-4.11a HAYNES

4.15 To disconnect a single-tab type fitting, squeeze the legs of the tab together, pull up the tab and pull the fitting and fuel line or fuel component apart. Discard the old tab and substitute a new one for reassembly

O-ring inside, inspect the O-ring before reconnecting the fitting. Fuel line fittings are under the same pressure as the rest of the fuel system, so to avoid leaks (and fires!) make VERY SURE that the O-ring is in good condition. Even better, simply replace it.

f) *In most cases, the fitting itself is a non-removable part of the fuel line, so you might have to replace an entire fuel line if a fitting is damaged or defective.*

Two-button type fitting

Refer to illustration 4.11

11   This type of fitting has a pair of push buttons located on opposite sides of the fitting **(see illustration)**. No special tools are needed to disconnect a two-button fitting. Simply press on both buttons and pull the fitting off the fuel line or fuel component to which it's connected.

12   To reconnect a two-button fitting, push the fitting onto the fuel line or fuel system component until the raised "stop" on the fuel line or component is fully seated against the back of the fitting, then keep pushing until you feel a "click." Verify that the fitting is correctly reconnected by trying to pull the fuel line or component and the fitting in opposite directions.

Pinch-type fitting

13   Instead of push buttons, this type of fitting has two "finger tabs." Again, no special tools are needed to disconnect it. Simply pinch both tabs together and pull the fitting off the fuel line or fuel component to which it's connected.

14   To reconnect a pinch-type fitting, push it onto the fuel line or fuel component until the raised "stop" on the fuel line or component is fully seated against the back of the fitting. Then keep pushing until you feel a click. Verify that the fitting is correctly reconnected by trying to pull the fuel line or component and the fitting in opposite directions.

Single-tab type fitting

Refer to illustration 4.15

15   This type of fitting is locked into place by a single removable pull-tab **(see illustration)**. The only tool you might need to disconnect it is a small screwdriver. To disconnect the fitting, squeeze the legs of the tab together, pull up the tab (pry it up with a small screwdriver if necessary) and pull the fitting off the fuel line or fuel component to which it's connected. Remove and discard the old pull-tab, then install a new tab before reconnecting the fitting.

16   To reconnect a single-tab type fitting, install a new pull tab (but don't push it down into its locked position), push the fitting onto the fuel line or fuel component until the raised "stop" on the fuel line or component is seated against the back of the fitting, then keep pushing until you feel a click. When the fitting is fully seated, push the new tab down until it locks into place. Verify that the fitting is locked by firmly pulling the fuel line or component and the fitting in opposite directions.

Two-tab type fitting

Refer to illustrations 4.17a, 4.17b, and 4.18

17   This type of fitting is one of the more common ones used on Dodge pick-ups and SUVs. It uses a plastic retainer with two release tabs protruding from opposite sides of the fitting. To disconnect it, depress both release tabs with your fingers, then pull the fitting off the fuel line or fuel component **(see illustration)**. **Caution:** *Do NOT use a tool, such a pair of pliers, to squeeze the tabs together. Using anything besides your fingers might damage the plastic retainer. The retainer will remain on the fuel line or fuel component and the O-ring **(see illustration)** will remain inside the fitting. Inspect the condition of the O-ring. If it's cracked, torn, deteriorated or otherwise*

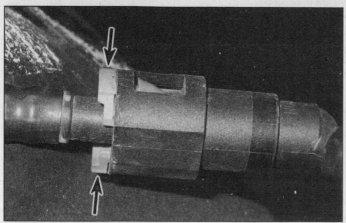

4.17a To disconnect a two-tab type fitting, depress both two tabs with your fingers then pull the fuel line and the fitting apart (the plastic retainer comes off with the fuel line)

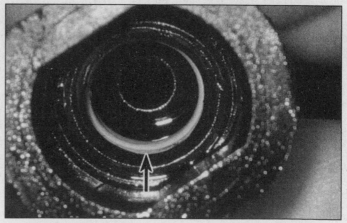

4.17b Inspect the O-ring inside the fitting. If it's cracked, torn, deteriorated or otherwise damaged in any way, replace it

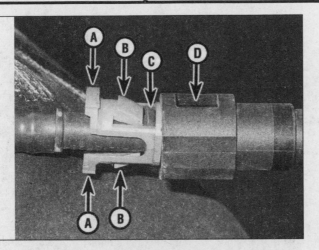

4.18 Before reconnecting a two-tab type fitting, be sure to position the plastic retainer correctly:

A   *Plastic retainer release tabs*

B   *Plastic retainer locking tabs (must be aligned with "window" in fitting)*

C   *Raised stop (must be visible through opening in plastic retainer)*

D   *Fitting "window" (must be aligned with locking tabs on plastic retainer)*

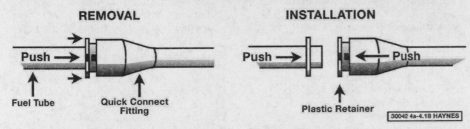

REMOVAL

Push →

Fuel Tube   Quick Connect Fitting

INSTALLATION

Push →   ← Push

Plastic Retainer

30042 4a-4.18 HAYNES

4.19 To disconnect a plastic retainer type fitting, push the plastic retainer ring and fitting body together and pull the line from the fitting. To reconnect, push the line into the fitting until you feel a click

damaged in any way, replace it.

18   To reconnect a two-tab type fitting, make sure that the retainer is correctly positioned on the fuel line or component, with the locking tabs of the retainer aligned with the "windows" in the fitting **(see illustration)**. When everything's correctly aligned, push the fitting onto the fuel line or fuel component until the raised stop on the fuel line or fuel component seats against the back of the fitting, then keep pushing until you feel a click. Verify that the fitting is locked into place by firmly pulling the fuel line or component and the fitting in opposite directions.

Plastic retainer ring type fitting

Refer to illustration 4.19

19   This type of fitting has a round plastic retainer ring, usually black in color, located inside the fitting. To disconnect a plastic retainer ring type fitting, push the fitting body toward the fuel line or fuel system component to which it's connected while firmly pushing the plastic retainer ring into the fitting, then while holding the retainer in its depressed position, pull the fuel line or fuel component out of the fitting **(see illustration)**. When disconnecting a plastic retainer type fitting, make sure that

the plastic retainer ring is pressed squarely into the fitting body. If the retainer becomes cocked in the fitting body it will be difficult or impossible to disconnect the fuel line or fuel system component from the fitting. One way to ensure that the retainer is depressed squarely into the fitting body is to depress the shoulder of the retainer with the flat face of an open-end wrench. After disconnecting the fuel line or fuel system component from the fitting, the plastic retainer ring will remain with quick-connect fitting connector body. Inspect the condition of the fitting body, the plastic retainer ring and the end of the fuel line or fuel system component for damage. Replace any damaged parts.

20   To reconnect a plastic retainer type fitting, push the fitting onto the fuel line or fuel system component until the raised stop on the fuel line or fuel component rests against the back of the fitting, then continue pushing until you feel a click. Verify that the two halves of the fitting are locked together by firmly pulling the fuel line and the fitting in opposite directions.

Metal collar type fittings with latch clips

Refer to illustrations 4.21, 4.22a, 4.22b and 4.23

Note 1: *You'll find these fittings at the connections between the fuel supply and return lines and the fuel rail.*

Note 2: *You'll need a special tool, available at most auto parts stores, to disconnect these fittings.*

21   To remove a latch clip, pull or pry the end of the latch off the fuel line, then disengage the other end of the latch from the female end of the metal collar fitting **(see illustration)**.

22   To disconnect a metal collar fitting (with either type of latch clip), release the locking fingers inside the fitting by inserting a special fuel line disconnection tool (available at most auto parts stores) into the metal collar **(see illustration)**. With the special tool still inserted, disconnect the metal collar from the fuel line or from the fuel system component **(see Illustration)**.

4.21 To remove latch clip from a metal collar fitting, pull or pry the end of the clip off the fuel line, then disengage the other end from the female side of the fitting

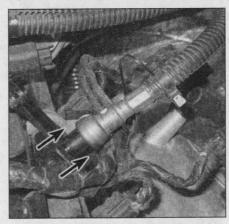

4.22a To release the locking fingers inside a metal collar type fitting, insert a special fuel line disconnection tool into the female side of the fitting until it releases the locking fingers . . .

4.22b . . . then pull the two halves of the fitting apart

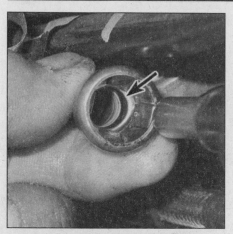

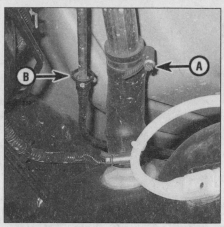

4.23 Inspect the old O-ring inside the female side of the metal collar fitting. If it's cracked, torn or otherwise deteriorated, replace it

5.4 To disconnect the fuel filler neck hose from the filler neck pipe, loosen this hose clamp (A). To disconnect the fuel EVAP vent tube quick-connect fitting (B) from the metal EVAP vent pipe, refer to the next illustration

5.5 To disconnect the vent tube quick-connect fitting from the metal EVAP vent pipe, squeeze these two flat spots together and pull the fitting off the pipe

23   Inspect the O-ring inside the metal collar fitting **(see illustration)**. If it's dried out, cracked, torn or otherwise deteriorated, replace it.

24   Apply a few drops of clean engine oil to the end of the fuel line or fuel system component, push the fitting onto the fuel line or component until the locking fingers snap into place. Verify that the fitting is correctly connected by pulling the fuel line or component and the fitting in opposite directions.

25   Install the latch clip until it snaps into position.

5   Fuel tank - removal and installation

Refer to illustrations 5.4, 5.5, 5.8, 5.9a and 5.9b

Warning: *See the* **Warning** *in Section 1.*

1   Relieve the fuel system pressure (see Section 2).

2   Disconnect the cable from the negative battery terminal (see Chapter 5, Section 1).

3   Raise the vehicle and place it securely on jackstands.

4   Loosen the hose clamp for the fuel filler neck hose **(see illustration)** and disconnect the fuel filler neck pipe from the filler neck hose.

5   Disconnect the EVAP fuel vent hose quick-connect fitting **(see illustration)** from the metal EVAP vent pipe.

6   If the fuel tank still has a lot of fuel in it, now is the time to siphon the remaining fuel from the tank through the rubber fuel filler neck hose. Using a siphoning kit (available at most auto part stores), siphon the fuel from the tank, through the filler neck pipe, into an approved gasoline container. **Warning:** *Never start the siphoning action by mouth!*

7   Support the fuel tank with a pair of floor jacks.

8   Remove the fuel tank retaining strap

bolts **(see illustration)** and remove both retaining straps. The hinged straps are secured with fasteners on the right side of the tank. To disengage the left end of each strap from its hinge, lift up the left end of the strap, then move it to the left.

9   Carefully lower the fuel tank just far enough to disconnect the electrical connector and fuel supply line from the fuel pump/fuel level sending unit module **(see illustration)**. At the front end of the fuel tank, locate the EVAP fitting **(see illustration)** and disconnect it. (This is a standard two-tab fitting. For help with disconnecting and reconnecting it, refer to Section 4.) Remove the fuel tank.

10   Installation is basically the reverse of removal. Please note the following guidelines:

a)   *If you're replacing the fuel tank, remove all components from the old fuel tank and install them on the new tank. If you need help with the EVAP lines, refer to Chapter 6.*

b)   *Tighten the fuel tank strap bolts securely.*

5.8 To detach the fuel tank from the underside of the vehicle, remove these two fuel tank strap bolts, then allow the fuel tank straps to swing down (they're hinged on the right side)

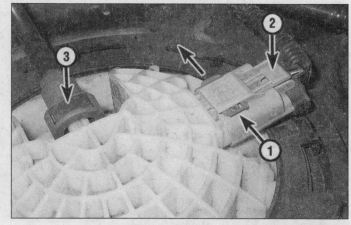

5.9a Lower the fuel tank just enough to access the fuel pump/fuel level sending unit, then slide the lock (1) to its released position, depress the release tab (2) and disconnect the electrical connector. To disconnect the fuel supply line fitting from the module, depress the button (3) and pull off the fitting

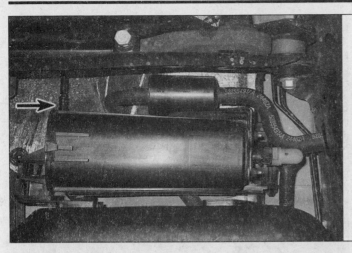

5.9b Locate the fitting at the upper right end of the EVAP canister and disconnect it (see illustration 4.17a), then lower the fuel tank the rest of the way to the ground

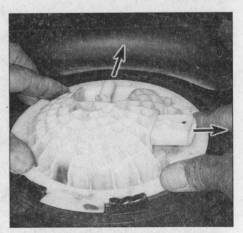

7.5 Using a hammer and brass drift, tap the fuel pump/fuel gauge sending unit lockring in a counterclockwise direction. When the lockring is loose, unscrew it

6 Fuel tank cleaning and repair - general information

1   The fuel tank installed in the vehicles covered by this manual is not repairable. If the fuel tank becomes damaged, it must be replaced.

2   Cleaning the fuel tank (due to fuel contamination) should be performed by a professional with the proper training to carry out this critical and potentially dangerous work. Even after cleaning and flushing, explosive fumes may remain inside the fuel tank.

3   If the fuel tank is removed from the vehicle, it should not be placed in an area where sparks or open flames could ignite the fumes coming out of the tank. Be especially careful inside a garage where a gas-type appliance is located.

7 Fuel pump/fuel gauge sending unit - removal and installation

Refer to illustrations 7.5, 7.6, 7.7 and 7.9

Warning: *See the* **Warning** *in Section 1.*

Note: *The fuel pump/fuel gauge sending unit module includes the fuel pump inlet strainer, the pump, an internal fuel filter, the fuel pressure regulator and the fuel gauge sending unit. This section covers the removal and installation of the complete module, which is removed as a complete assembly. You cannot replace any of the components (except the lockring gasket) separately. If any component is defective you must replace the entire assembly.*

1   Relieve the fuel system pressure (see Section 2).

2   Disconnect the cable from the negative battery terminal (see Chapter 5, Section 1).

3   Remove the fuel tank (see Section 5).

4   To prevent dirt from entering the fuel tank, clean the area surrounding the fuel pump/fuel gauge sending unit.

5   Using a hammer and a *brass* drift, tap on the lockring to turn it counterclockwise **(see illustration)**. When the lockring is loose, unscrew it. **Warning:** *Do NOT use a steel drift*

to loosen the lockring. Doing so could produce sparks, which could ignite fuel vapors from the tank.

6   Carefully remove the fuel pump/fuel gauge sending unit from the tank **(see illustration)**.

7   Remove the large rubber gasket **(see illustration)** and inspect it. If it's cracked, torn, deteriorated or otherwise damaged, replace it.

8   The fuel pump inlet filter is attached to the bottom of the fuel pump module. Anytime you remove the fuel pump for any reason, always inspect the inlet filter. If it's dirty, carefully scrub it with some clean solvent and an old toothbrush. Don't use a wire brush to clean the inlet filter - you'll damage It If you do. If you're unable to clean the inlet filter, replace the fuel pump/fuel gauge sending unit assembly.

9   When installing the fuel pump/fuel level sending unit module, position the module so that the electrical connector terminal is facing forward and the fuel outlet pipe is pointing toward the left (driver's side) of the vehicle **(see illustration)**.

10   Installation is otherwise the reverse of removal.

7.6 Carefully remove the fuel pump/fuel gauge sending unit module from the fuel tank. As you work the module through the hole, angle it to protect the float and the float arm from damage

7.7 Be sure to remove and inspect the large rubber gasket that seals the mounting hole for the pump/fuel gauge sending unit

7.9 When installing the fuel pump/fuel gauge sending unit module, make sure that the electrical connector terminal faces forward and the fuel outlet pipe faces to the left (driver's side)

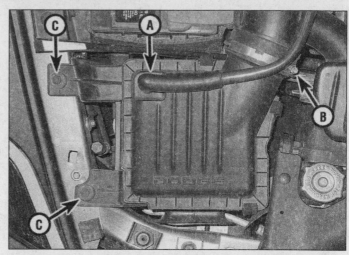

8.1 To remove the air intake duct, loosen the hose clamp screws at each end and disconnect the duct from the air filter housing and the air resonator box (Hemi engine shown, other engines similar)

8.4 Before removing the air filter housing, disconnect the Positive Crankcase Ventilation (PCV) fresh air inlet hose (A) from the air filter housing cover, loosen the hose clamp screw (B) that secures the air intake duct to the filter housing cover, and remove the filter housing mounting bolts (C)

8   Air filter housing, air intake duct and air resonator box - removal and installation

Air intake duct

Refer to illustration 8.1

1   Loosen the hose clamps (see illustration) and remove the air intake duct.

2   Inspect the condition of the air intake duct. Look for cracks, tears, deterioration and other damage. If the air intake duct is damaged in any way, replace it. A leaking air intake duct will allow the introduction of "false air" (unmetered air) into the air intake manifold, which will cause the air/fuel mixture to become excessively lean. A lean air/fuel mixture can cause rough running at idle, and

even misfires if the leak is big enough.

3   Installation is the reverse of removal.

Air filter housing

Refer to illustrations 8.4 and 8.7

Note: *The following procedure is for replacing the air filter housing, not for replacing the air filter element. If you want to replace the air filter element, refer to Chapter 1.*

4   Disconnect the air intake duct from the air filter housing (see illustration).

5   Disconnect the Positive Crankcase Ventilation (PCV) fresh air inlet hose from the air filter housing (see illustration 8.4).

6   Remove the air filter housing mounting bolts (see illustration 8.4).

7   To remove the air filter housing, grasp it firmly and lift it straight up to pull the locator

pin under the housing out of its grommet (see illustration).

8   Inspect the condition of the mounting grommet. If it's cracked, torn, deteriorated or otherwise damaged, replace it.

9   Installation is the reverse of removal.

Air resonator box

Refer to illustrations 8.11, 8.12a, 8.12b and 8.12c

10   Remove the air intake duct or disconnect it from the air resonator box (see illustration 8.1).

11   On Hemi engines, disconnect the electrical connector from the Intake Air Temperature (IAT) sensor (see illustration).

12   Remove the air resonator box mounting bolts (3.7L V6 and 4.7L V8 engines, see

8.7 To remove the air filter housing from the vehicle, grasp it firmly and lift it straight up to disengage the locator pin (A) from the grommet (B)

8.11 To detach the air resonator box from a Hemi engine, disconnect the electrical connector (1) from the Intake Air Temperature (IAT) sensor, remove the resonator mounting bolts (2), pull the box forward to disengage it from the throttle body, then lift it up slightly to disconnect the PCV fresh air inlet hose (3) from the underside

8.12a To detach the air resonator box from a 3.7L V6 or from a 4.7L V8 engine, remove this mounting bolt from the left side of the box . . .

8.12b . . . remove this mounting bolt from the right side of the box . . .

illustrations; Hemi engine, see illustration 8.11).

13   Grasp the air resonator box firmly and pull it forward to disengage it from the throttle body. Lift up the air resonator box slightly and disconnect the PCV fresh air inlet hose from the underside of the left front corner of the resonator **(see illustration 8.12c)**. Remove the air resonator box.

14   Installation is the reverse of removal.

9   Accelerator cable - replacement

Refer to illustrations 9.2, 9.3, 9.5 and 9.6

Note: *All engines use a conventional accelerator cable except for the Hemi. On Hemi engines, there is no accelerator cable. The throttle plate is electronically controlled by the Powertrain Control Module (PCM) in response to the signal from a potentiometer known as the Accelerator Pedal Position Sensor (APPS), which is located at and is an inte-*

gral part of, the accelerator pedal. The APPS and accelerator pedal are sold as a complete assembly. To replace the APPS, refer to Chapter 6.

1   Remove the air intake duct and, if equipped, the air resonator box (see Section 8).

2   Rotate the throttle lever to the wide-open position and detach the cable end **(see illustration)**. If you're replacing the cable on a Hemi model, disconnect the cable from the APPS (see *Accelerator Pedal Position Sensor - replacement* in Chapter 6).

3   Using a small screwdriver, press the tab to release the accelerator cable retainer from the cable bracket **(see illustration)** and slide the cable out of the bracket.

4   Trace the accelerator cable to the firewall and note its routing. Then detach the cable from any clamps, clips and/or brackets.

5   Working underneath the dash, disconnect the accelerator cable from the accelerator pedal **(see illustration)**.

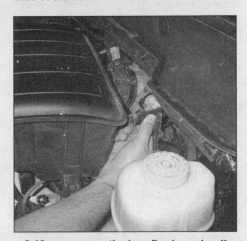

8.12c . . . grasp the box firmly and pull it forward slightly to disengage it from the throttle body, then reach around behind the left rear corner of the box and disconnect the PCV fresh air inlet hose from the box (4.7L V8 engine shown, 3.7L V6 similar)

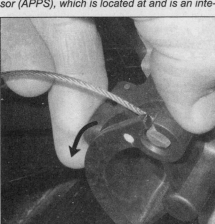

9.2 To disconnect the accelerator cable from the throttle lever, rotate the throttle lever to the wide-open position, then slide the cable end plug out of its socket in the throttle lever

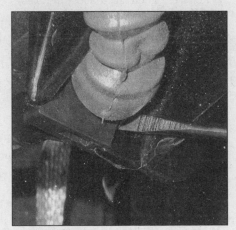

9.3 To disengage the accelerator cable from the cable bracket, use a small flat-blade screwdriver to press the tab to release the cable from the bracket

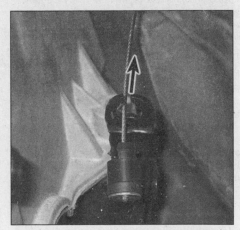

9.5 To disengage the cable from the accelerator pedal, push the upper end of the pedal forward and thread the cable through the slot in the top of the pedal

6   Remove the retaining clip **(see illustration)** that secures the cable housing to its hole in the firewall.

7   Pull the cable through the firewall and into the engine compartment.

8   Installation is the reverse of removal.

10   Fuel injection system - general information

The fuel injection systems used on all vehicles covered by this manual are the "sequential multiport" type. This means that there is a fuel injector in each intake port, and that these fuel injectors inject fuel into the intake ports in the cylinder firing order. The injectors are turned on and off by the Powertrain Control Module (PCM). When the engine is running, the PCM constantly monitors engine operating conditions with an array of information sensors, calculates the correct amount of fuel, then varies the interval of time during which the injectors are open. Sequential multiport systems provide much better control of the air/fuel mixture ratio than earlier fuel injection systems, and are therefore able to produce more power, better mileage and lower emissions.

The fuel injection system uses the PCM and an array of information sensors to determine and deliver the correct air/fuel ratio under all operating conditions. The fuel injection system consists of three sub-systems: air induction, electronic control and fuel delivery. The fuel injection system is also closely interrelated with PCM-controlled emission control systems. (For additional information about the PCM, the information sensors and the emission control systems, refer to Chapter 6.)

Air induction system

The air induction system consists of the air filter housing, the air intake duct, the resonator (if equipped), the throttle body and the intake manifold. The throttle body contains a throttle plate that regulates the amount of air entering the intake manifold. The throttle plate is opened and closed by a mechanical accelerator cable, except on Hemi models, on which the throttle plate is controlled by the PCM in response to input from the Accelerator Pedal Position Sensor (APPS). The lower part of the throttle body on some engines is heated by engine coolant to prevent icing in cold weather. The throttle body is also the location of the Throttle Position (TP) sensor, a potentiometer that monitors the opening angle of the throttle plate and sends a variable voltage signal to the Powertrain Control Module (PCM). The Manifold Absolute Pressure (MAP) sensor is also located on the throttle body. The MAP sensor measures intake manifold pressure and vacuum and generates a variable voltage signal that's proportional to the pressure or vacuum. The PCM uses this data to calculate the load on the engine. Another information sensor, the Intake Air Temperature (IAT) sensor, is located on the air intake duct or on

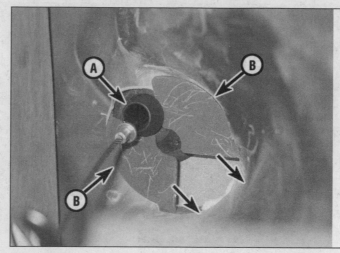

9.6 The accelerator cable housing (A) is secured to its hole in the firewall by this retaining clip (B). To access the clip, carefully peel back the rubber floor liner until you can see the entire clip

the intake manifold. The IAT sensor relays a voltage signal to the PCM that varies in accordance with the temperature of the incoming air in the manifold. The PCM uses this data to calculate how rich or lean the air/fuel mixture should be. All of the air induction components (air filter housing, air intake duct, air resonator box and throttle body) are covered in this Chapter, except for the intake manifold, which is covered in Chapter 2, and the information sensors, which are covered in Chapter 6.

When the engine is idling, the Idle Air Control (IAC) system maintains the correct idle speed by regulating the amount of air that bypasses the (closed) throttle plate in response to a command from the Powertrain Control Module (PCM). The IAC system consists of the IAC valve (located on or near the throttle body), the PCM, and several information sensors, including the Engine Coolant Temperature (ECT) sensor, the Intake Air Temperature (IAT) sensor, the Manifold Absolute Pressure (MAP) sensor, and the Power Steering Pressure (PSP) sensor.

Electronic control system

For more information about the electronic control system, i.e. the PCM, its information sensors and output actuators, refer to Chapter 6.

Fuel delivery system

The fuel delivery system consists of the fuel pump, the fuel filter/fuel pressure regulator, the fuel rail and fuel injectors, and the hoses, lines and pipes that carry fuel between all of these components. For more information about the fuel lines and the various types of fittings used on different models, refer to Section 4.

The fuel pump is an in-tank design. Fuel is drawn through a "sock" (or strainer) at the pump inlet, then pumped out the other end of the pump and through a fuel filter, which is an integral part of the fuel pressure regulator. The fuel filer/fuel pressure regulator, which is mounted on top of the fuel pump/fuel level sending unit module, maintains the fuel pressure within the specified operating range. When the operating pressure exceeds the

specified operating range, the pressure regulator opens and sends the excess fuel back into the fuel tank (there is no return fuel line from the fuel rail back to the tank). After the fuel has been filtered, it's pumped through a fuel supply line to the fuel rail on the engine.

The fuel rail, which is bolted to the intake manifold, functions as a reservoir for pressurized fuel so that there's always enough fuel available for acceleration and high speed operation. The upper end of each injector is inserted into the fuel rail and the lower end of each injector is inserted into the intake manifold. The upper and lower ends of each injector are sealed by O-rings.

Each fuel injector is a solenoid-actuated, pintle-type design consisting of a solenoid, plunger, ball or needle valve, and housing. When the engine is running, there is always voltage on the "hot" side of each injector terminal. Injector "drivers" inside the PCM turn the injectors on and off by switching their ground paths on and off. When the ground path for an injector is closed by the PCM, current flows through the solenoid coil, the ball or needle valve raises and pressurized fuel inside the injector housing squirts out the nozzle into the intake port directly above the intake valve(s). The quantity of fuel injected each time an injector opens is determined by its "pulse width," which is the interval of time during which the valve is open.

11   Fuel injection system - check

Refer to illustrations 11.7 and 11.8

Note: *The following procedure is based on the assumption that the fuel pressure is adequate (see Section 3).*

1   Inspect all electrical connectors that are related to the system. Check the ground wire connections on the intake manifold for tightness. Loose connectors and poor grounds can cause many problems that resemble more serious malfunctions.

2   Verify that the battery is fully charged, as the control unit and sensors depend on an accurate supply of voltage in order to properly meter the fuel.

11.7 Use a stethoscope to determine if the injectors are working properly - they should make a steady clicking sound that rises and falls with engine speed changes

11.8 If you discover an injector that doesn't appear to be operating, measure the resistance across the two terminals of the injector to see if the injector itself is defective

3   Inspect the air filter element (see Chapter 1). A dirty or partially blocked filter will severely impede performance and economy.

4   Check the related fuses. If a blown fuse is found, replace it and see if it blows again. If it does, search for a grounded wire in the harness.

5   Inspect the condition of all vacuum hoses connected to the intake manifold.

6   Remove the air intake duct and air resonator box (if equipped) and inspect the mouth of the throttle body for dirt, carbon or other residue build-up. If it's dirty, wipe it clean with a shop towel.

7   With the engine running, place an automotive stethoscope against each injector, one at a time, and listen for a clicking sound, indicating operation **(see illustration)**. If you don't have a stethoscope, place the tip of a screwdriver against the injector and listen through the handle.

8   If an injector doesn't make a clicking sound, disconnect the electrical connector

and measure the resistance of the injector **(see illustration)**. Compare the measurements with the resistance values listed in this Chapter's Specifications. If the resistance is within specification, the PCM or the injector wiring harness could be the cause of the injector not operating.

9   Any further testing of the fuel injection system should be performed at a dealer service department or other qualified repair shop.

10   For more information about the engine control system, refer to Chapter 6.

12   Throttle body - removal and installation

3.7L V6 and 4.7L V8 engines

Refer to illustration 12.3

1   Disconnect the cable from the negative

terminal of the battery (see Chapter 5, Section 1).

2   Remove the air intake duct and the air resonator box (see Section 8).

3   Disconnect the electrical connectors from the Throttle Position (TP) sensor and from the Idle Air Control motor **(see illustration)**.

4   Clearly label all vacuum hoses connected to the throttle body, then disconnect them. Be sure to inspect the vacuum hoses for cracks, tears and deterioration. If any of them are damaged, replace them.

5   Disconnect the accelerator cable and, if equipped, the cruise control cable from the throttle body (see Section 9). (Disconnect the cruise control cable using the same procedure you used to disconnect the accelerator cable.)

6   Remove the three mounting bolts and remove the throttle body.

7   Remove the throttle body O-ring and inspect it for cracks, tears and deterioration. If it's damaged, replace it.

8   Wipe off the gasket mating surfaces of the throttle body and the intake manifold. **Caution:** *Do NOT use spray carburetor cleaners or silicone lubricants on any part of the throttle body.*

9   Installation is the reverse of removal. Be sure to tighten the throttle body mounting bolts to the torque listed in this Chapter's Specifications.

Hemi engines

Refer to illustrations 12.12, 12.13, 12.14 and 12.15

10   Disconnect the cable from the negative terminal of the battery (see Chapter 5, Section 1).

11   Remove the air intake duct and the air resonator box (see Section 8).

12   Disconnect the electrical connector from the throttle body **(see illustration)**.

13   Remove the large rubber gasket that seals the connection between the throttle

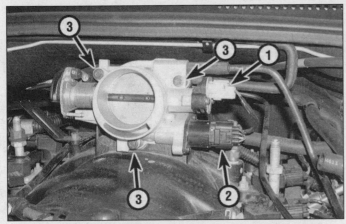

12.3 To remove the throttle body from a 3.7L V6 or a 4.7L V8 engine, disconnect the electrical connectors from the Throttle Position (TP) sensor (1) and the Idle Air Control (IAC) motor (2), label all vacuum lines connected to the throttle body and disconnect them, then remove the throttle body mounting bolts (3) (4.7L V8 engine shown, 3.7L V6 similar)

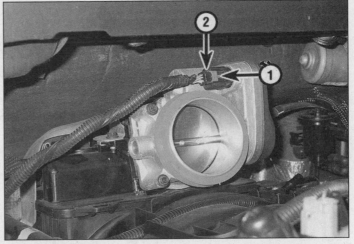

12.12 To disconnect the electrical connector from the electronic throttle body on a Hemi engine, push the red slide lock (1) away from the throttle body (toward the harness), then depress the release tabs (2) and pull off the connector

12.13 Remove and inspect the large rubber gasket that seals the connection between the air resonator box and the throttle body

12.14 To detach the electronic throttle body from the intake manifold, remove these four mounting bolts

12.15 Remove this O-ring type gasket that seals the connection between the throttle body and the intake manifold

body and the air resonator box **(see illustration)**. Inspect the gasket for cracks, tears and deterioration. If it's damaged, replace it.

14 Remove the four throttle body mounting bolts **(see illustration)** and remove the throttle body.

15 Remove the throttle body's O-ring type gasket **(see illustration)** and inspect it for cracks, tears and deterioration. If it's damaged, replace it.

16 Wipe off the gasket mating surfaces of the throttle body and the intake manifold. **Caution:** *Do NOT use spray carburetor cleaners or silicone lubricants on any part of the throttle body.*

17 Installation is the reverse of removal. Be sure to tighten the throttle body mounting bolts to the torque listed in this Chapter's Specifications. If you're installing a new throttle body, proceed to the next step.

Installing a NEW throttle body on a Hemi engine

18 If you *replace* the old throttle body with a new unit, a Diagnostic Trouble Code (DTC)

might be set by the Powertrain Control Module (PCM). If this happens, use a scan tool to clear any DTCs or, if you don't have a scan tool, have this service performed by a dealer service department.

---

13 Fuel rail and injectors - removal and installation

Warning 1: *See the* **Warning** *in Section 1.*
Warning 2: *The engine must be completely cool before beginning this procedure.*

3.7L V6 and 4.7L V8 engines

Refer to illustrations 13.7a, 13.7b, 13.9, 13.10a, 13.10b and 13.10c

1 Remove the fuel tank filler neck cap to relieve any pressure inside the fuel tank. Then relieve the fuel system pressure (see Section 2).

2 Disconnect the cable from the negative terminal of the battery (see Chapter 5, Section 1).

3 Remove the air intake duct and the air

box resonator (see Section 8).

4 Disconnect the fuel supply line from the fuel rail (see Section 4).

5 Clearly label any vacuum hoses that will interfere with fuel rail removal, then disconnect them from the throttle body and from the intake manifold.

6 Disconnect the electrical connectors from any information sensors mounted on the throttle body (see Section 12) and set the wiring harnesses for those sensors aside. Also disconnect the electrical connectors for any other wiring harnesses that will interfere with fuel rail removal and set the wiring harnesses aside.

7 Disconnect the fuel injector electrical connectors **(see illustrations)** and set the injector wiring harness aside. **Note:** *Each connector should be numbered with the corresponding cylinder number. If the number tag is obscured or missing, renumber the connectors.*

8 Remove all of the ignition coils from the engine (see Chapter 5).

9 Clean any debris from around the injectors. Remove the fuel rail mounting nuts/bolts

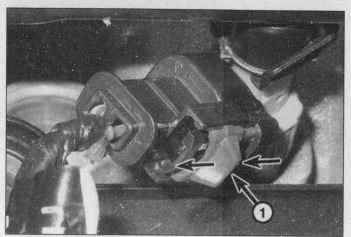

13.7a To disconnect the electrical connector from the injector on a 3.7L V6 or 4.7L V8, move the slider (1) up (away from the injector) . . .

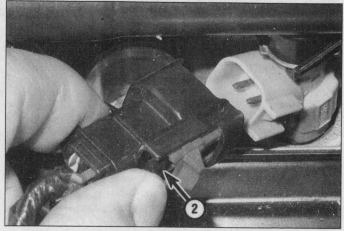

13.7b . . . then depress the tab (2) and pull the connector off of the injector

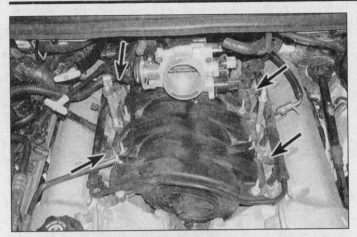

13.9 Fuel rail mounting bolts (4.7L V8 engine, shown, 3.7L V6 similar)

13.10a Using a screwdriver or pliers, remove the injector retaining clip . . .

13.10b . . . and withdraw the injector from the fuel rail

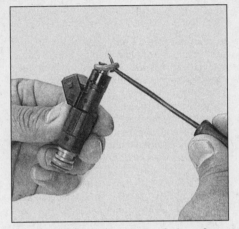

13.10c Carefully remove the O-rings from the injectors

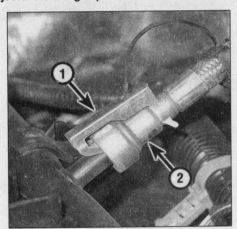

13.19 To disconnect the fuel supply line metal collar fitting from the fuel rail on a Hemi engine, remove the latch clip (1) from the metal collar fitting (2), then disconnect the fitting with a special fuel line disconnection tool (see Section 4)

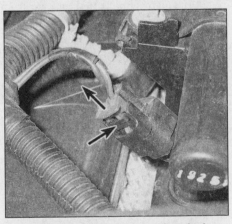

13.22 To disconnect the electrical connector from each fuel injector, pull up the sliding lock, then depress the release tab and pull off the connector

(see illustration). Gently rock the fuel rail and injectors to loosen the injectors and remove the fuel rail and fuel injectors as an assembly. **Caution:** *Do not attempt to separate the left and right fuel rails. Both sides are serviced together as an assembly.*

10 Remove the injectors from the fuel rail, then remove and discard the O-rings **(see illustrations)**. **Note:** *Whether you're replacing an injector or a leaking O-ring, it's a good idea to remove all the injectors from the fuel rail and replace all the O-rings.*

11 Coat the new O-rings with clean engine oil and install them on the injector(s), then insert each injector into its corresponding bore in the fuel rail. Install the injector retaining clip.

12 Clean the injector bores on the intake manifold.

13 Guide the injectors/fuel rail assembly into the injector bores on the intake manifold. Make sure the injectors are fully seated, then tighten the fuel rail mounting nuts/bolts to the torque listed in this Chapter's Specifications.

14 The remainder of installation is the reverse of removal.

15 After the injector/fuel rail assembly installation is complete, turn the ignition switch to ON, but don't operate the starter. This acti-

vates the fuel pump for about two seconds, which builds up fuel pressure in the fuel lines and the fuel rail. Repeat this step two or three times, then check the fuel lines, fuel rail and injectors for fuel leakage.

Hemi engine

Refer to illustrations 13.19, 13.22, 13.23 and 13.24

Note: *You'll need to obtain a special fuel line disconnection tool, available at auto parts stores or from automotive tool manufacturers, to disconnect the metal collar type fitting that connects the fuel supply line to the fuel rail.*

16 Remove the fuel tank filler neck cap to relieve any pressure inside the fuel tank. Then relieve the fuel system pressure (see Section 2).

17 Disconnect the cable from the negative terminal of the battery (see Chapter 5, Section 1).

18 Remove the air intake duct and the air resonator box (see Section 8).

19 Disconnect the fuel supply line fitting **(see illustration)** from the left fuel rail. If you're unfamiliar with this metal collar type fitting, refer to Section 4.

20 Disconnect the electrical connector from the throttle body **(see illustration 12.12).**

21 Disconnect the electrical connectors from all eight ignition coils (see Chapter 5).

22 Disconnect the electrical connectors from all eight fuel injectors **(see illustration)**.

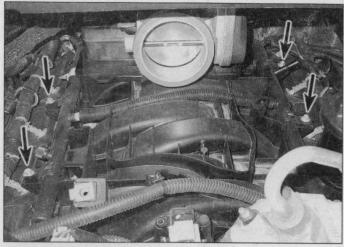

13.23 To detach the fuel rail from the intake manifold, remove these four bolts

13.24 Carefully lift the fuel rail and injectors off the engine as a single assembly

23　Remove the four fuel rail mounting bolts **(see illustration)**.

24　Starting with the left side of the fuel rail, carefully pull on the injectors while wiggling them from side to side at the same time until all four injectors start to clear their mounting holes. Then go the right side and repeat this step. Go back and forth between the two sides of the engine, gradually working the injectors out of their mounting holes, until all eight injectors are free. When all of the injectors are free, remove the fuel rail and injectors as a single assembly **(see illustration)**.

25　To remove an injector from the fuel rail, remove the injector retainer clip and pull the injector out of the fuel rail **(see illustrations 13.10a and 13.10b)**. **Note:** *Whether you're replacing an injector or a leaking O-ring, it's a good idea to remove all the injectors from the fuel rail and replace all the O-rings.*

26　Remove the O-rings from the injector **(see illustration 13.10c)**, discard them and install new O-rings. Be sure to lubricate the new O-rings with clean engine oil before installing the injector into the fuel rail.

27　Installation is the reverse of removal. Be sure to tighten the fuel rail mounting bolts to the torque listed in this Chapter's Specifications.

14　Exhaust system servicing - general information

Refer to illustrations 14.1 and 14.4

Warning: *The vehicle's exhaust system generates very high temperatures and must be allowed to cool down completely before touching any of the components. Be especially careful around the catalytic converter, which stays hot longer than other exhaust components.*

1　The exhaust system consists of the exhaust manifolds, the exhaust pipes, the catalytic converter(s), the muffler, the tailpipe, various exhaust heat shields and all connecting flanges and clamps. The exhaust system is isolated from the vehicle body and from chassis components by a series of rubber hangers **(see illustration)**. Inspect these hangers periodically for cracks or other signs of deterioration, and replace them as necessary. Some exhaust components are also supported by brackets bolted to the underside of the vehicle. Make sure that these brackets are tightly fastened to the exhaust system and to the vehicle and that they're neither cracked nor corroded.

2　Conduct regular inspections of the exhaust system to keep it safe and quiet. Look for any damaged or bent parts, open seams, holes, loose connections, excessive corrosion or other defects which could allow exhaust fumes to enter the vehicle. Do not repair deteriorated exhaust system components; replace them with new parts.

3　If the exhaust system components are extremely corroded, or rusted together, you'll need welding equipment and a cutting torch to remove them. The convenient strategy at this point is to have a muffler repair shop remove the corroded sections with a cutting torch. If you want to save money by doing it yourself, but you don't have a welding outfit and cutting torch, simply cut off the old components with a hacksaw. If you have compressed air, there are special pneumatic cutting chisels (available from specialty tool manufacturers) that can also be used. If you decide to tackle the job at home, be sure to wear safety goggles to protect your eyes from metal chips and wear work gloves to protect your hands.

4　Replacement of exhaust system components is basically a matter of removing the heat shields, disconnecting the component and installing a new one. The heat shields and exhaust system hangers must be reinstalled in the original locations or damage could result. Due to the high temperatures and exposed locations of the exhaust system components, rust and corrosion can seize parts together. Penetrating oils are available to help loosen frozen fasteners. However, in some cases it may be necessary to cut the pieces apart with a hacksaw or cutting torch. (Only persons experienced in this work should employ this latter method.) Here are some simple guidelines to follow when repairing the exhaust system:

a)　*Work from the back to the front when removing exhaust system components.*

b)　*Apply penetrating oil to the exhaust system component fasteners* **(see illustration)** *to make them easier to remove.*

14.1 Inspect the exhaust system rubber hangers for damage

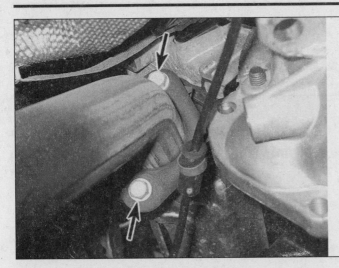

14.4 Exhaust pipe-to-exhaust manifold fasteners (shown) and exhaust pipe-to-catalytic converter fasteners can be extremely difficult to loosen because they're subjected to intense heat and to water, mud and road grime. If you're unable to loosen a fastener, apply a liberal amount of penetrant, wait for it to soak in, then try again

c) While you're waiting for the penetrant to loosen up the exhaust system fasteners, always disconnect the electrical connector for the downstream oxygen sensor and remove the sensor before removing the exhaust pipe section that includes the catalytic converter.

d) Use new gaskets, hangers and clamps when installing exhaust systems components.

e) Apply anti-seize compound to the threads of all exhaust system fasteners during reassembly.

f) Be sure to allow sufficient clearance between newly installed parts and all points on the underbody to avoid overheating the floor pan and possibly damaging the interior carpet and insulation. Pay particularly close attention to the catalytic converter and heat shield.

Notes

Chapter 5
Engine electrical systems

Contents

Specifications

General

Battery voltage
    Engine off .... 12.0 to 13.2 volts
    Engine running .... 13.5 to 15 volts
Firing order
    V6 engine 1-6-5-4-3-2
    V8 engines 1-8-4-3-6-5-7-2

Ignition system

Ignition coil resistance (approximate, at 70 to 80-degrees F)
    3.7L V6 and 4.7L V8 engines
        Primary resistance .... 0.6 to 0.9 ohms
        Secondary resistance .... 6 to 9 k-ohms
    Hemi engine
        Primary resistance .... 0.53 to 0.65 ohms
        Secondary resistance .... N/A

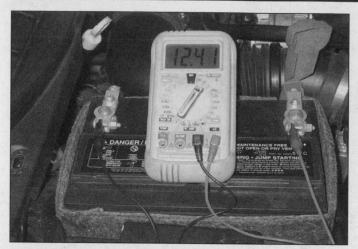

3.2 To test the open circuit voltage of the battery, connect a voltmeter to the battery terminals. A fully charged battery should have at least 12.4 volts

3.3 Connect a battery load tester to the battery and check the battery condition under load following the tool manufacturer's instructions

1   General information

The engine electrical systems include all ignition, charging and starting components. Because of their engine-related functions, these components are discussed separately from chassis electrical devices such as the lights, the instruments, etc. (which are included in Chapter 12).

Always observe the following precautions when working on the electrical systems:

a) *Be extremely careful when servicing engine electrical components. They are easily damaged if checked, connected or handled improperly.*

b) *Never leave the ignition switch on for long periods of time with the engine off.*

c) *Don't disconnect the battery cables while the engine is running.*

d) *Maintain correct polarity when connecting a battery cable from another vehicle during jump-starting.*

e) *Always disconnect the negative cable first and hook it up last or the battery may be shorted by the tool being used to loosen the cable clamps.*

It's also a good idea to review the safety-related information regarding the engine electrical systems located in the *Safety First!* Section near the front of this manual before beginning any operation included in this Chapter.

2   Battery - emergency jump starting

Refer to the *Booster battery (jump) starting* procedure at the front of this manual.

3   Battery - check, removal and installation

Warning: *Hydrogen gas is produced by the battery, so keep open flames and lighted cigarettes away from it at all times. Always wear eye protection when working around a battery. Rinse off spilled electrolyte immediately with large amounts of water.*
Caution: *Always disconnect the negative cable first and hook it up last or you might accidentally short the battery with the tool that you're using to loosen the cable clamps.*

Check

Refer to illustrations 3.2 and 3.3

1   To check the battery state of charge, look at the indicator eye on the top of the battery (the eye is the top of a hydrometer that's built into the battery). If the indicator eye is green, the battery is 75 to 100 percent charged. If the indicator eye is black, the battery is 0 to 75 percent charged. If the indicator eye is clear (or bright), the battery electrolyte level is low. All factory-installed batteries are the maintenance-free type, i.e. the cell caps cannot be removed, so no water can be added. If the indicator eye is clear on a maintenance-free battery, replace the battery. If the maintenance-free battery has been replaced by a low-maintenance battery with removable cell caps, remove the caps and add enough distilled water to bring it up to the correct level (which should be marked on the outside of the battery case. (If there are no MINIMUM and MAXIMUM lines on the battery case, add enough water to each cell so that the plates are fully immersed). Wait a few hours for the electrolyte in the plates to go back into solution, then charge the battery (see Chapter 1).
Note: *A low-electrolyte/low-water condition is often a symptom of overcharging, so after recharging the battery, check the alternator charging voltage (see Section 10) and, if necessary, replace the alternator. Otherwise, the same condition will reoccur.*

2   Perform an open-voltage circuit test using a voltmeter **(see illustration)**. **Note:** *To obtain an accurate voltage measurement, you must first remove the battery's surface charge. To remove the surface charge, turn* on the high beams for ten seconds, then turn them off and let the vehicle stand for two minutes. With the engine and all accessories off, touch the negative probe of the voltmeter to the negative terminal of the battery and the positive probe to the positive terminal of the battery. The battery voltage should be 12.4 volts or more. If the battery is less than the specified voltage, charge the battery before proceeding to the next test. Do not proceed with the battery load test unless the battery charge is correct.

3   Perform a battery load test. An accurate check of the battery condition can only be performed with a battery load tester (available at most auto parts stores). This test evaluates the ability of the battery to operate the starter and other accessories during periods of heavy amperage draw (load). Connect a battery load-testing tool to the terminals **(see illustration)**. Load test the battery according to the tool manufacturer's instructions. Typically a load of 50-percent of the cold

3.4 When disconnecting the battery cables, always disconnect the cable from the negative terminal (1) first, then the positive terminal (2). After the battery cables are disconnected, remove the thermal guard (3) from the battery

cranking amperage rating is applied during the test. The cold cranking amperage rating can usually be found on the battery label. Maintain the load on the battery for a maximum of 15 seconds. The battery voltage should not drop below 9.6 volts during the test. If the battery condition is weak or defective, the tool will indicate this condition immediately. **Note:** *Cold temperatures will cause the voltage readings to drop slightly. Follow the chart given in the tool manufacturer's instructions to compensate for cold climates. Minimum load voltage for freezing temperatures (32-degrees F) should be approximately 9.1 volts.*

Replacement
Battery

Refer to illustrations 3.4 and 3.5

4   Disconnect the cable from the negative battery terminal **(see illustration)**, then disconnect the cable from the positive terminal.
5   Remove the battery hold-down bolt **(see illustration)** and hold-down clamp.
6   Lift out the battery. Be careful - it's heavy. **Note:** *Battery straps and handlers are available at most auto parts stores for a reasonable price. They make it easier to remove and carry the battery.*
7   While the battery is out, inspect the tray for corrosion deposits. Clean the battery tray, then use a baking soda/water solution to neutralize any deposits to prevent further oxidation. If the metal around the tray is corroded, too, clean it as well and spray the area with a rust-inhibiting paint. (The tray is plastic, so it won't be damaged by corrosion, but once this corrosion leaks down past the tray onto metal parts, they will be.)
8   If corrosion has leaked down past the battery tray, remove the tray for further cleaning.
9   If you are replacing the battery, make sure you get one that's identical, with the

3.5 To detach the battery from the battery tray, remove the hold-down bolt and the hold-down clamp

same dimensions, amperage rating, cold cranking rating, etc.
10   Installation is the reverse of removal.

Battery tray
Durango models

Refer to illustrations 3.12 and 3.15

11   Remove the battery (see Steps 4 through 6).
12   Detach the heater hose, wiring harness and battery ground cable clips from the upper side of the battery tray **(see illustration)**.
13   Disconnect and remove, if applicable, the battery temperature sensor from the battery tray (see Chapter 6).
14   Loosen the right front wheel lug nuts, raise the front of the vehicle and place it securely on jackstands. Remove the right front wheel.
15   Detach the heater hose and electrical connector clips from the underside of the bat-

tery tray **(see illustration)**.
16   Remove the upper and lower battery tray mounting bolts and remove the battery tray.
17   Installation is the reverse of removal.

Dakota models

18   Remove the battery (see Steps 4 through 6).
19   Remove the lid from the underhood fuse/relay box, remove the nut that secures the B+ cable to its terminal, then detach the cable and move it aside.
20   Remove the two pushpin fasteners securing the fuse/relay box to the battery tray.
21   Disengage the two locking tabs and slide the fuse/relay box up, detaching it from the battery tray.
22   Remove the bolts and detach the ABS hydraulic control unit from the battery tray.
23   Remove the pushpins and detach the negative battery cable and the wiring harness from the battery tray.
24   Remove the left headlight (see Chapter 12).
25   Remove the six bolts retaining the upper portion of the battery tray.
26   Loosen the left front wheel lug nuts. Raise the front of the vehicle and support it securely on jackstands, then remove the left front wheel.
27   Remove the inner fender splash shield (see Chapter 11, Section 13).
28   Remove the two bolts retaining the lower portion of the battery tray, then remove the tray.
29   Installation is the reverse of removal.

---

4   Battery cables - check and replacement

Refer to illustrations 4.4a, 4.4b, 4.4c and 4.4d

1   Periodically inspect the entire length of each battery cable for damage, cracked or

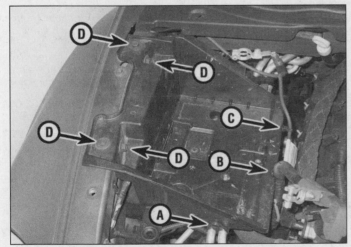

3.12 Topside battery tray mounting details (Durango)

A   Detach the heater hose clip
B   Detach the wiring harness clip
C   Detach the battery cable clip
D   Remove the upper battery tray mounting bolts

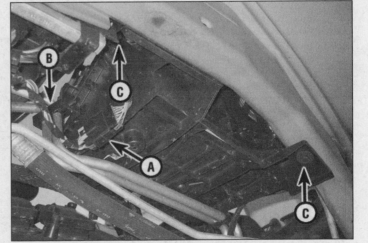

3.15 Underside battery tray mounting details (Durango)

A   Detach the wiring harness connector clip (clip, not visible in this photo, is between the connector body and the battery tray)
B   Detach the heater hose clip
C   Remove the lower battery tray mounting bolts

burned insulation and corrosion. Poor battery cable connections can cause starting problems and decreased engine performance.

2   Check the cable-to-terminal connections at the ends of the cables for cracks, loose wire strands and corrosion. The presence of white, fluffy deposits under the insulation at the cable terminal connection is a sign that the cable is corroded and should be replaced. Check the terminals for distortion, missing mounting bolts and corrosion.

3   When removing the cables, always disconnect the cable from the negative battery terminal first and hook it up last or the battery could be accidentally shorted by the tool you're using to loosen the cable clamps. Even if you're only replacing the cable for the positive terminal, be sure to disconnect the cable from the negative battery terminal first.

4   After disconnecting the old cables from the battery, trace each of them to their opposite ends and detach them from the starter solenoid and ground terminals **(see illustrations)**. Note the routing of each cable to ensure correct installation. If a cable is bundled with another wiring harness, cut the electrical tape tying them together, remove any protective sheathing and separate them.

5   If you are replacing either or both of the battery cables, take them with you when buying new cables. It is vitally important that you replace the cables with identical parts. Cables have characteristics that make them easy to identify: positive cables are usually red and larger in cross-section; ground cables are usually black and smaller in cross-section.

6   Clean the threads of the solenoid or ground connection with a wire brush to remove rust and corrosion. Apply a light coat of battery terminal corrosion inhibitor or petroleum jelly to the threads to prevent future corrosion.

7   Attach the cable to the solenoid or ground connection and tighten the mounting nut/bolt securely.

8   Before connecting a new cable to the battery, make sure that it reaches the battery post without having to be stretched.

9   Connect the positive cable first, followed by the negative cable.

5   Ignition system - general information

All engines are equipped with a distributorless ignition system. The ignition system consists of the battery, the ignition coils, the spark plugs, the two knock sensors (one on each cylinder head), the Camshaft Position (CMP) sensor, the Crankshaft Position (CKP) sensor, the Manifold Absolute Pressure (MAP) sensor, the Throttle Position (TP) sensor and the Powertrain Control Module (PCM). (For more information about the CMP sensor, CKP sensor, knock sensors, MAP sensor, TP sensor and PCM, refer to Chapter 6.) The PCM controls the base ignition timing and the ignition timing advance on all engines. The base

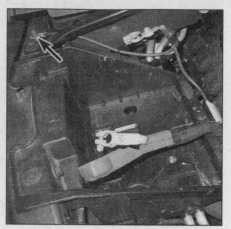

4.4a   To disconnect the upper ground cable from the right front fender, remove this bolt (Durango)

4.4b   To disconnect the lower ground cable from the boss on the right cylinder head, remove this nut (Durango)

ignition timing is not adjustable on any model.

The PCM controls the ignition system by opening and closing the ignition coil ground circuit. The computerized ignition system provides complete control of the ignition timing by determining the optimum timing in response to engine speed, coolant temperature, throttle position and vacuum pressure in the intake manifold. These parameters are relayed to the PCM by the camshaft position sensor, crankshaft position sensor, throttle position sensor, coolant temperature sensor and manifold absolute pressure sensor. The PCM and the crankshaft position sensor are very important components of the ignition system. The ignition system will not operate and the engine will not start if the PCM or the crankshaft position sensor are defective. Refer to Chapter 6 for additional information on the various sensors.

All engines use a coil-over-plug system, which consists of individual coils, one above each spark plug and connected directly to the spark plug. There are no spark plug wires on these engines. The secondary terminal of each coil, which is connected directly to its corresponding spark plug, is sealed by a rubber boot. The Automatic Shut Down (ASD) relay supplies battery voltage to the ignition

coil primary circuits. The PCM fires the coils in firing order sequence by turning the ground paths for their primary circuits on and off.

6   Ignition system - check

Refer to illustrations 6.5a and 6.5b

Warning 1: *Because of the high voltage generated by the ignition system, extreme care should be taken whenever an operation is performed involving ignition components. This not only includes the ignition coil, but also related components and test equipment.*

Warning 2: *The following procedure requires the engine to be cranked during testing. When cranking the engine, make sure that no test leads, loose clothing, long hair, etc. comes in contact with any moving parts (drivebelt, cooling fan, etc.).*

1   Before proceeding with the ignition system, check the following items:

a)   *Make sure the battery cable clamps, where they connect to the battery, are clean and tight.*

b)   *Test the condition of the battery (see Section 3). If it does not pass all the tests, replace it with a new battery.*

4.4c   To disconnect the battery cable from the alternator, remove this nut

4.4d   To disconnect the battery cable from the starter motor solenoid, remove this nut

6.5a To use a calibrated ignition tester on a 3.7L V6 or a 4.7L V6, remove an ignition coil and connect the tester to the spark plug boot, clip the tester to a convenient ground and crank over the engine (4.7L V8 shown, 3.7L V6 similar)

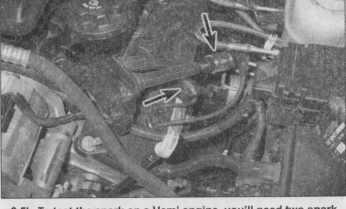

6.5b To test the spark on a Hemi engine, you'll need two spark testers - one for each spark plug. Detach each ignition coil from the valve cover and pull it up, then connect one end of each tester to the boots under the coil, connect the other ends of the testers to the spark plugs and crank over the engine

c) *Check the ignition system wiring and connections for tightness, damage, corrosion or any other signs of a bad connection.*

d) *Check the related fuses inside the engine compartment fuse and relay box (see Chapter 12). If they're burned, determine the cause and repair the circuit.*

2   If the engine turns over but won't start or has a severe misfire, perform the following steps using a calibrated ignition tester to make sure there is sufficient secondary ignition voltage to fire the spark plugs. (There are several different types of calibrated ignition testers available. A couple of them are shown in the accompanying photos. Either style will work on any of the engines covered in this manual.)

3   Disable the fuel system by removing the fuel pump relay, which is located in the engine compartment fuse and relay box (see Chapter 12).

4   Remove each ignition coil (see Sec-

tion 7) to test for spark to the plug(s) that it fires. **Note:** *On Hemi engines, you'll have to simultaneously test for spark at both coil high tension terminals, so you'll need two testers.*

5   Hook up the calibrated ignition system tester(s) (available at most auto parts stores) to the boot(s) underneath the coils **(see illustrations)**. Note whether the bulb within the tester body flashes.

6   If the tester emits a good spark or the tester body flashes during cranking (depending on tester type), sufficient voltage is reaching the plug to fire it. Repeat this test for each spark plug (or both plugs at each cylinder on Hemis) to verify that all the coils are OK.

7   If no sparks occur during cranking at any one cylinder, inspect the primary wire connection at the coil from which you're not getting any spark. Make sure that it's clean and tight.

8   If there's still no spark at any plug, or pair of plugs, the plug(s) might be fouled. So remove and inspect the plug(s) (see Chap-

ter 1), then retest.

9   If there is still no spark even after cleaning and inspecting the spark plug(s), the coil that fires the plug(s) might be defective (see Section 7).

10   If no sparks or intermittent sparks occur during cranking at all cylinders, the Powertrain Control Module (PCM) is probably defective. Have the PCM checked out by a dealer service department or other qualified repair shop (testing the PCM is beyond the scope of the do-it-yourselfer because it requires expensive special tools). Any additional testing of the ignition system must be done by a dealer service department or other repair shop with the right tools.

7   Ignition coil - check, removal and installation

3.7L V6 and 4.7L V8 engines
Check

Refer to illustrations 7.3 and 7.4

1   Remove the ignition coil (see Steps 6 through 9).

2   Clean the outer case and check it for cracks and other damage. Clean the coil primary terminals and check the coil tower terminal for corrosion. Clean it with a wire brush if any corrosion is found. Keeping all coil terminals clean and dry is essential for proper operation of the ignition system.

3   To check the coil primary resistance, attach the leads of an ohmmeter to the two terminals of the connector **(see illustration)**. Compare your measurement to the primary resistance value listed in this Chapter's Specifications. If the measured primary resistance value is not within the specified range, replace the ignition coil.

4   To check the coil secondary resistance, connect one of the ohmmeter leads to the positive terminal of the connector and the other ohmmeter lead to the high-tension terminal **(see illustration)**. Compare your mea-

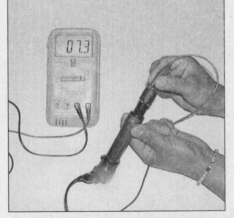

7.3 To check the primary resistance of a 3.7L V6 or 4.7L V8 ignition coil, measure the resistance across the two coil primary terminals and compare your measurement to the primary resistance listed in this Chapter's Specifications

7.4 To check the secondary resistance of a 3.7L V6 or 4.7L V8 ignition coil, measure the resistance between the positive terminal of the primary side and the high-tension terminal and compare your measurement to the secondary resistance listed in this Chapter's Specifications

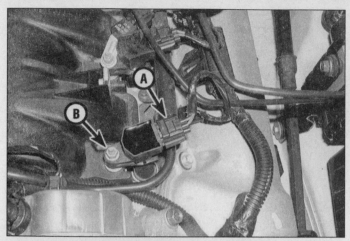

7.7 To remove an ignition coil from a 3.7L V6 or a 4.7L V8 engine, push down on the release lock on top of the electrical connector (A) and disconnect the connector, remove the coil mounting nut (B); then detach the coil from the spark plug by pulling it straight up

7.13 To check the primary resistance of a Hemi ignition coil, measure the resistance across these two coil primary terminals and compare your measurement to the primary resistance listed in this Chapter's Specifications

surements to the secondary resistance value listed in this Chapter's Specifications. If the measured secondary resistance value is not within the specified range, replace the ignition coil.

5   If the primary and secondary resistance values are within specification, but the coil seems to be misfiring or not firing at all, or is causing the PCM to set a Diagnostic Trouble Code (DTC) indicating a misfire, try swapping it with an adjacent coil. If the suspect coil was causing a DTC for one cylinder, it will likely set a misfire DTC for the cylinder to which it has been moved. If this is the case, the coil is probably defective because it's unlikely that the harnesses for two adjacent ignition coils would both be defective. At any rate, no further testing is possible at home. If you're not sure whether you should replace the coil at this point, consult a dealer service department or other qualified repair shop.

Removal and installation

Refer to illustration 7.7

6   Depending on which coil you're planning to check or replace, remove either the

air intake duct or the air intake resonator box (see Chapter 4).

7   Disconnect the electrical connector from the coil **(see Illustration)**. (To release the connector, push down on the release lock on top of the connector and pull off the connector.)

8   To prevent dirt and debris from falling down into the spark plug well, use compressed air to blow out the area around the base of the ignition coil.

9   Remove the ignition coil mounting nut and detach the coil from the spark plug **(see illustration 7.7)**.

10   Installation is the reverse of removal.

Hemi engine

Check

Refer to illustration 7.13

Note: *This procedure applies to all eight ignition coils.*

11   Remove the ignition coil (see Step 16).

12   Clean the outer case and check it for cracks and other damage. Clean the coil primary terminals and check the coil high-ten-

sion terminal for corrosion. If you find any corrosion, clean the high-tension terminal with a wire brush. Keeping the coil terminals and wires clean and dry is essential for proper operation of the ignition system.

13   To check the coil primary resistance, attach the leads of an ohmmeter to the two indicated terminals on the coil **(see illustration)**.

14   Compare your measurement to the primary resistance value listed in this Chapter's Specifications. If the measured resistance value is not within the specified range, replace the ignition coil.

15   There is no published secondary resistance value available for the ignition coils used on the Hemi engine. If the primary resistance is within specification, but the coil seems to be misfiring or not firing at all, or is causing the PCM to set a Diagnostic Trouble Code (DTC) that indicates a misfire, try swapping it with an adjacent coil. If the suspect coil was causing a DTC for one cylinder, it will likely set a misfire DTC for the cylinder to which it has been moved. If this is the case, the coil is probably defective because it's unlikely that the harnesses for two adjacent ignition coils would both be defective. At any rate, no further testing is possible at home. If you're not sure whether you should replace the coil at this point, have it checked by a dealer service department.

Removal and installation

Refer to illustration 7.17

16   To access the ignition coils for cylinder numbers 2, 4, 6 and/or 8, remove the air intake duct and the resonator box (see *Air filter housing - removal and installation* in Chapter 4). (The EGR tube is also routed directly across the top of the ignition coils. But there's enough room to remove any of these four coils without removing the EGR tube, because the spark plug boots on the underside of each coil are flexible rubber, so you don't really have

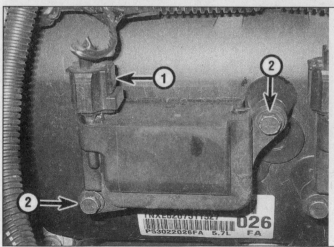

7.17 To detach an ignition coil from a Hemi engine, depress the release tab (1) on the electrical connector, disconnect the connector, then remove the two coil mounting bolts (2)

to lift up a coil very far to remove it from the valve cover.)

17   Disconnect the electrical connector from the ignition coil **(see illustration)**.

18   Remove the coil mounting bolts. To remove the coil, carefully pull it up with a back-and-forth motion to disengage the rubber spark plug boots from the plugs.

19   While the coil is removed, inspect the condition of the rubber spark plug boots. If they're cracked, torn or deteriorated, replace them.

20   Installation is the reverse of removal.

8   Charging system - general information and precautions

The charging system consists of the alternator, the Electronic Voltage Regulator (EVR) within the Powertrain Control Module (PCM), the ignition switch, the battery, a battery temperature sensor, a voltage gauge, a charge indicator light and the wiring between all the components. The charging system supplies electrical power for the ignition system, the lights, the radio, etc. The alternator is driven by a serpentine drivebelt at the front of the engine.

The charging system operates as long as the engine is running and the Automatic Shut Down (ASD) relay is energized. When the ASD relay is on, voltage is supplied to the ASD relay sense circuit at the Powertrain Control Module (PCM). This voltage is connected through the PCM and supplied to the alternator field terminal (GEN SOURCE +) on the backside of the alternator. The EVR's field control circuit inside the PCM regulates the current output of the alternator (there is no external voltage regulator). The field control circuit is connected in series with the second rotor field terminal and ground.

The battery temperature sensor, which (if used) is mounted on the underside of the battery tray, is a Negative Temperature Coefficient (NTC) thermistor that receives a 5-volt signal from the PCM and is grounded through a return wire. As the temperature of the battery increases, the resistance in the temperature sensor decreases and the detection voltage at the PCM increases. The PCM uses the signal from the battery temperature sensor and data from monitored line voltage to vary the battery charging rate. It does so by cycling the alternator's ground path, which controls the strength of the rotor's magnetic field. The PCM regulates the alternator's current output accordingly. System voltage is higher when the engine is cold and is gradually reduced to a lower voltage as the temperature increases. To replace the battery temperature sensor, refer to Chapter 6.

When the engine is running, the voltage gauge on the instrument cluster indicates electrical system voltage. The indicator needle should be within the normal range if the battery is charged. If the needle moves outside the normal range and stays there during nor-

10.2 After disconnecting the negative battery cable, remove the nut from the battery (B+) output terminal stud (A) and disconnect the battery cable from the stud, then disconnect the electrical connector (B) for the field terminals (4.7L V8 engine shown, 3.7L V6 engine similar)

mal driving, inspect the charging system (see Section 10). If the voltage gauge is defective, replace the instrument cluster (see Chapter 12). The voltage gauge cannot be serviced separately from the cluster.

The charging system doesn't ordinarily require periodic maintenance. However, you should inspect the drivebelt, the battery, the charging system wiring harness and all connections at the intervals outlined in Chapter 1. Be very careful when making electrical circuit connections to the alternator or the charging system circuit and note the following:

a)   *When reconnecting wires to the alternator from the battery, be sure to note the polarity.*

b)   *Before using arc-welding equipment to repair any part of the vehicle, disconnect the wires from the alternator and the battery terminals.*

c)   *Never start the engine with a battery charger connected.*

d)   *Always disconnect both battery cables before using a battery charger.*

e)   *The alternator is turned by an engine drivebelt, which could cause serious injury if your hands, hair or clothes become entangled in it with the engine running.*

f)   *Because the alternator is connected directly to the battery, it could arc or cause a fire if overloaded or shorted out.*

g)   *Wrap a plastic bag over the alternator and secure it with rubber bands before steam-cleaning the engine.*

9   Charging system - check

Note: *These vehicles are equipped with an On-Board Diagnostic-II (OBD-II) system that is useful for detecting charging system problems because it can provide you with the Diagnostic Trouble Code (DTC) that will indicate the general nature of the problem. Refer to Chapter 6 for a list of the DTCs used by the Powertrain Control Module (PCM) on these vehicles and for the procedure you'll need to use to obtain DTCs.*

1   If a malfunction occurs in the charging

circuit, do not immediately assume that the alternator is causing the problem. First check the following items:

a)   *The battery cables where they connect to the battery. Make sure the connections are clean and tight.*

b)   *The battery electrolyte specific gravity (by observing the charge indicator on the battery). If it is low, charge the battery.*

c)   *Inspect the external alternator wiring and connections.*

d)   *Check the drivebelt condition and tension (see Chapter 1).*

e)   *Check the alternator mounting bolts for tightness.*

f)   *Run the engine and check the alternator for abnormal noise.*

2   Using a voltmeter, check the battery voltage with the engine off. It should be approximately 12.4 to 12.6 volts with a fully charged battery.

3   Start the engine and check the battery voltage again. It should now be greater than the voltage recorded in Step 2, but should not read more than 15 volts.

4   If the indicated voltage reading is less or more than the specified charging voltage, have the charging system checked at a dealer service department or other properly equipped repair facility. The voltage regulator on these models is contained within the PCM and it cannot be adjusted, removed or tampered with in any way.

10   Alternator - removal and installation

3.7L V6 and 4.7L V8 engines

Refer to illustrations 10.2 and 10.4

1   Disconnect the cable from the negative terminal of the battery.

2   Disconnect the battery cable from the B+ output terminal and disconnect the field wire electrical connector from the field terminal **(see illustration)**.

3   Remove the drivebelt (see Chapter 1).

4   Remove the mounting bolts **(see illus-**

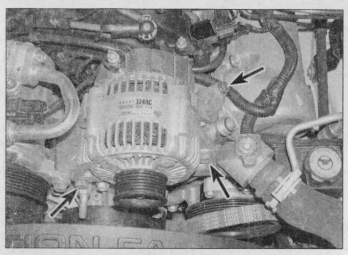

10.4 To detach the alternator from a 3.7L V6 or a 4.7L V8 engine, remove these mounting bolts (4.7L V8 engine shown, 3.7L V6 engine similar)

10.11 Disconnect the electrical connector (1) from the field terminal, then depress the two release tabs (2) on the plastic insulator cap, flip off the cap and remove the nut (3) that secures the battery cable to the B+ terminal (Hemi engines)

tration) and remove the alternator.

5   If you are replacing the alternator, take the old one with you when purchasing a replacement unit. Make sure the new/rebuilt unit looks identical to the old alternator. Look at the terminals - they should be the same in number, size and location as the terminals on the old alternator. Finally, look at the identification numbers - they will be stamped into the housing or printed on a tag attached to the housing. Make sure the numbers are the same on both alternators.

6   Many new and remanufactured alternators do not have a pulley installed, so you may have to switch the pulley from the old unit to the new/rebuilt one. When buying an alternator, find out the shop's policy regarding pulleys; some shops will perform this service free of charge.

7   Installation is the reverse of removal.

8   Install the drivebelt (see Chapter 1).

9   Check the charging voltage (see Section 10) to verify that the alternator is operating correctly.

Hemi engine

Refer to illustrations 10.11 and 11.13

10   Disconnect the cable from the negative terminal of the battery, then remove the drivebelt (see Chapter 1).

11   Disconnect the field wire electrical connector from the field terminal **(see illustration)**.

12   Unsnap the plastic insulator cap from the B+ output terminal, remove the battery cable retaining nut from the B+ output terminal and disconnect the battery cable from the B+ output terminal.

13   Remove the alternator mounting bolts **(see illustration)** and remove the alternator.

14   If you're replacing the alternator, take the old alternator with you to make sure that you obtain the correct unit. (You will probably have to exchange it as a core anyway.)

15   Installation is the reverse of removal.

11   Starting system - general description and precautions

General description

The starting system consists of the starter relay, the starter motor and starter solenoid assembly, the battery, the battery cables, the ignition switch and key lock cylinder, the Transmission Range (TR) sensor and the wiring connecting these components. All starter motors are located on the lower part of the engine, near the transmission bellhousing, where they can engage the ring gear on the flexplate.

The starting system has two separate circuits: A low-amperage control circuit, which operates on less than 20 amps, and a high-amperage supply circuit that delivers between 150 and 350 amps to the starter motor. The low-amp control circuit includes the ignition switch, the clutch pedal position switch or PNP switch, the starter relay, the coil inside the starter solenoid and the wire harness connecting these components. The high-amp supply circuit consists of the battery, the

battery cables, the contact disc in the starter solenoid and the starter motor itself.

The TR sensor is installed in series between the starter relay ground terminal and ground. The TR sensor is normally open to prevent the starter relay from being energized unless the shift lever is in the NEUTRAL or PARK position. When the ignition switch is turned to START, battery voltage is supplied through the low-amperage control circuit to the battery terminal of the starter relay coil if the shift lever is in the NEUTRAL or PARK position. If it isn't, the starter circuit remains open and the engine won't start.

When the starter relay coil is energized, the normally-open relay contacts close and connect the relay common supply terminal to the relay's normally-open terminal. The closed relay contacts energize the windings of the starter solenoid pull-in coil, which pulls in the solenoid plunger, which pulls the shift lever in the starter motor, which engages the starter's overrunning clutch and pinion gear with the starter's ring gear. As the solenoid plunger reaches the end of its travel, the solenoid contact disc completes the high-current

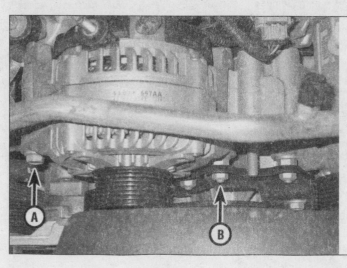

10.13 To remove the alternator from its mounting bracket, remove this bolt (A) and stud/bolt (B) (Hemi engine)

12.3 Use an inductive ammeter to measure starter current draw

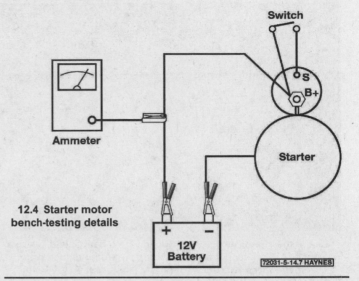

12.4 Starter motor
bench-testing details

starter supply circuit and energizes the sole-noid plunger hold-in coil. Current flows from the solenoid battery terminal to the starter motor and energizes the starter.

The starter motors used on the vehicles covered in this manual are not rebuildable because no parts are available. They're sold as complete new or remanufactured assemblies. If any part of the starter motor fails, including the starter solenoid, the entire assembly must be replaced.

Precautions

Always observe the following precautions when working on the starting system:

a) *Excessive cranking of the starter motor can overheat it and cause serious damage. Never operate the starter motor for more than 15 seconds at a time without pausing to allow it to cool for at least two minutes.*

b) *The starter is connected directly to the battery and could arc or cause a fire if mishandled, overloaded or shorted.*

c) *Always detach the cable(s) from the negative terminal of the battery before working on the starting system.*

12 Starter motor and circuit - check

Refer to illustrations 12.3 and 12.4

1   If a malfunction occurs in the starting circuit, do not immediately assume that the starter is causing the problem. First, check the following items:

a) *Make sure the battery cable clamps, where they connect to the battery, are clean and tight.*

b) *Check the condition of the battery cables (see Section 4). Replace any defective battery cables with new parts.*

c) *Test the condition of the battery (see Section 3). If it does not pass all the tests, replace it with a new battery.*

d) *Check the starter motor wiring and connections.*

e) *Check the starter motor mounting bolts for tightness.*

f) *Check the related fuses in the engine compartment fuse box (see Chapter 12). If they're blown, determine the cause and repair the circuit.*

g) *Check the ignition switch circuit for correct operation (see Chapter 12).*

h) *Check the starter relay (see Chapter 12).*

i) *Check the operation of the Transmission Range (TR) sensor (see Chapter 6). This system must operate correctly to provide battery voltage to the starter solenoid.*

2   If the starter does not activate when the ignition switch is turned to the start position, check for battery voltage to the starter solenoid. This will determine if the solenoid is receiving the correct voltage from the ignition switch. Connect a 12-volt test light or a volt-meter to the starter solenoid positive terminal. While an assistant turns the ignition switch to the start position, observe the test light or voltmeter. The test light should shine brightly or battery voltage should be indicated on the voltmeter. If voltage is not available to the starter solenoid, refer to the wiring diagrams in Chapter 12 and check the fuses and starter relay in series with the starting system. If voltage is available but there is no movement from the starter motor, remove the starter from the engine (see Section 13) and bench test the starter (see Step 4).

3   If the starter turns over slowly, check the starter cranking voltage and the current draw from the battery. This test must be performed with the starter assembly on the engine. Crank the engine over (for 10 seconds or less) and observe the battery voltage. It should not drop below 9.6 volts. Also, observe the current draw with an ammeter **(see illustration)**. Typically a starter should not exceed 160 amps. If the starter motor amperage draw is excessive, have it tested by a dealer service department or other qualified repair shop. There are several conditions that may affect the starter cranking potential. The battery must be in

good condition and the battery cold-cranking rating must not be under-rated for the particular application. Be sure to check the battery specifications carefully. The battery terminals and cables must be clean and not corroded. Also, in cases of extreme cold temperatures, make sure the battery and/or engine block is warmed before performing the tests.

4   If the starter is receiving voltage but does not activate, remove and check the starter motor assembly on the bench **(see illustration)**. Most likely the solenoid is defective. In some rare cases, the engine may be seized so be sure to try and rotate the crankshaft pulley (see Chapter 2) before proceeding. With the starter assembly mounted in a vise on the bench, install one jumper cable from the positive terminal of a test battery to the B+ terminal on the starter. Install another jumper cable from the negative terminal of the battery to the body of the starter. Install a starter switch and apply battery voltage to the solenoid S terminal (for 10 seconds or less) and observe the solenoid plunger, shift lever and overrunning clutch extend and rotate the pinion drive. If the pinion drive extends but does not rotate, the solenoid is operating but the starter motor is defective. If there is no movement but the solenoid clicks, the solenoid and/or the starter motor is defective. If the solenoid plunger extends and rotates the pinion drive, the starter assembly is operating properly.

13 Starter motor - removal and installation

1   Disconnect the cable from the negative terminal of the battery.

2   Raise the vehicle and support it securely on jackstands.

3.7L V6 and 4.7L V8 engines

Refer to illustrations 13.4 and 13.5

3   On 4WD models with certain transmissions, there's a support bracket between the front axle and the side of the transmission that

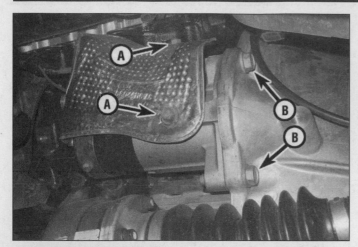

13.4 If the starter motor is equipped with a heat shield, remove bolts (A) to detach it from the starter. To remove the starter, remove these two bolts (B) (starter motor on 3.7L V6 with automatic and 4WD shown, starters on other 3.7L V6 engines and 4.7L V8 engines similar)

13.5 Disconnect the electrical connector (A) from the spade terminal on the solenoid, then remove the nut and disconnect the battery cable (B) from the terminal stud on the solenoid (starter motor on 3.7L V6 shown, starters on 4.7L V8 similar)

blocks access to the lower starter mounting bolt. If your vehicle has this support bracket, remove the two support bracket bolts at the transmission, then pry the support bracket aside enough to gain access to the lower starter mounting bolt. Additionally, on some 4WD models the driveshaft will have to be detached from the front differential companion flange for access to the starter mounting bolts.

4   Remove the heat shield, if equipped, from the starter motor **(see illustration)**.

5   Remove the nut that secures the battery cable to the terminal stud on the starter solenoid, disconnect the cable from the terminal stud and disconnect the electrical connector from the spade terminal on the solenoid **(see illustration)**. **Note:** *If you have difficulty disconnecting the battery cable or the electrical connector from the solenoid, leave them connected until you detach the starter from the transmission bellhousing and move it to a*

position where you can access the wiring connectors more easily.

6   Remove the two starter mounting bolts **(see illustration 13.4)**.

7   Move the starter motor toward the front of the vehicle until the nose of the starter pinion housing clears the transmission bellhousing, then tilt the nose down and, if you haven't already done so, lower the starter until you can disconnect the electrical connector and remove the nut that secures the battery cable to the terminal stud on the starter solenoid. Once everything is disconnected, remove the starter. **Caution:** *The starter motor is fairly heavy, so be sure to support it while removing it. Do NOT allow it to hang by the wiring harness.*

8   Installation is the reverse of removal.

Hemi engine

Refer to illustrations 13.12 and 13.13

9   Loosen the lug nuts on the right front

wheel. Raise the vehicle and place it securely on jackstands. Remove the right front wheel.

10 Remove the splash shield from the right front wheelhousing (see Chapter 11, Section 13).

11 On some 4WD models with certain transmissions, there's a support bracket between the front axle and the side of the transmission that blocks access to the lower starter mounting bolt. If your vehicle has this support bracket, remove the two support bracket bolts at the transmission, then pry the support bracket aside enough to gain access to the lower starter mounting bolt.

12   Disconnect the battery cable and electrical connector from the terminals on the starter motor solenoid **(see illustration)**.

13   Remove the two starter motor mounting bolts **(see illustration)** and remove the starter motor assembly.

14   Installation is the reverse of removal.

13.12 Disconnect the electrical connector (1) and the battery cable (2) from the starter solenoid. To detach the starter motor from the transmission, remove this upper bolt (3) . . .

13.13 . . . and this lower bolt (4) (Hemi engines)

Chapter 6
Emissions and engine control systems

Contents

Specifications

Torque specifications

Ft-lbs (unless otherwise noted)

Camshaft Position (CMP) sensor mounting bolt	106 in-lbs
EGR valve mounting bolts	20
EGR tube mounting flange bolts	20
Knock sensor mounting bolts	176 in-lbs
Oxygen sensors	22

1   General information

Refer to illustration 1.7

To prevent pollution of the atmosphere from incompletely burned and evaporating gases, and to maintain good driveability and fuel economy, a number of emission control systems are incorporated on the vehicles covered in this manual. These emission control systems and their components are an integral part of the engine management system. The engine management system also includes all the government mandated diagnostic features of the second generation of on-board diagnostics, which is known as On-Board Diagnostics II (OBD-II).

At the center of the engine management and OBD-II systems is the on-board computer, which is known as the Powertrain Control Module (PCM). Using a variety of information sensors, the PCM monitors all of the important engine operating parameters (temperature, speed, load, etc.). It also uses an array of output actuators - such as the ignition coils, the fuel injectors, the Idle Air Control (IAC) motor, the Torque Converter Clutch (TCC) and various solenoids and relays - to respond to and alter these parameters as necessary to maintain optimal performance, economy and emissions. The principal emission control systems used on the vehicles covered in this manual include the:

Catalytic converters
Evaporative Emission Control (EVAP) system
Exhaust Gas Recirculation (EGR) system
Positive Crankcase Ventilation (PCV) system
Torque Converter Clutch (TCC) system

The Sections in this Chapter include general descriptions and component replacement procedures for most of the information sensors and output actuators, as well as the important components that are part of the systems listed above. Refer to Chapter 4 for more information on the air induction, fuel delivery and injection systems and exhaust systems, and to Chapter 5 for information on the ignition system. Refer to Chapter 1 for any scheduled maintenance for emission-related systems and components.

The procedures in this Chapter are intended to be practical, affordable and within the capabilities of the home mechanic. The diagnosis of most engine and emission control functions and driveability problems requires specialized tools, equipment and training. When servicing emission devices or systems becomes too difficult or requires special test equipment, consult a dealer service department.

Although engine and emission control systems are very sophisticated on late-model vehicles, you can do most of the regular maintenance and some servicing at home with common tune-up and hand tools and relatively inexpensive digital multimeters. Because of the Federally mandated extended warranty that covers the emission control system, check with a dealer about warranty coverage before working on any emission-related systems. After the warranty has expired, you might want to perform some of the component replacement procedures in this Chapter to save money. Remember that the most frequent cause of emission and driveability problems is a loose electrical connector or a broken wire or vacuum hose, so before jumping to conclusions the first thing you should always do is to inspect all electrical connections, electrical wiring and vacuum hoses related to a system.

Pay close attention to any special precautions given in this Chapter. Remember that illustrations of various system components might not exactly match the component installed on the vehicle on which you're working because of changes made by the manufacturer during production or from year to year.

A Vehicle Emission Control Information (VECI) label **(see illustration)** is located in the engine compartment. This label contains emission-control and engine tune-up specifications and adjustment information. It also includes a vacuum hose routing diagram for emission-control components. When servicing the engine or emission systems, always check the VECI label in your vehicle. If any

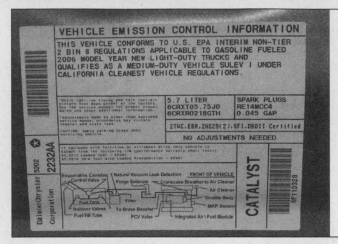

1.7 The Vehicle Emission Control Information (VECI) label, located in the engine compartment, contains information on the emission devices installed on your vehicle and a vacuum hose routing schematic

information in this manual contradicts what you read on the VECI label on your vehicle, always defer to the information on the VECI label.

2   On-Board Diagnostic (OBD) system and Diagnostic Trouble Codes (DTCs)

Scan tools

Refer to illustrations 2.1 and 2.2

1   Hand-held scanners are handy for analyzing the engine management systems used on late-model vehicles. Because extracting the Diagnostic Trouble Codes (DTCs) from an engine management system is now the first step in troubleshooting many computer-controlled systems and components, even the most basic generic code readers are capable of accessing a computer's DTCs **(see illustration)**. More powerful scan tools can also perform many of the diagnostics once associated with expensive factory scan tools. If you're planning to obtain a generic scan tool for your vehicle, make sure that it's compatible with OBD-II systems. If you don't plan to purchase a code reader or scan tool and don't have access to one, you can have the codes extracted by a dealer service department or

by an independent repair shop.

2   With the advent of the Federally mandated emission control system known as On-Board Diagnostics-II (OBD-II), specially designed scanners were developed. Several tool manufacturers have released OBD-II scan tools for the home mechanic **(see illustration)**.

OBD-II system

3   All vehicles covered by this manual are equipped with the OBD-II system. This system consists of the on-board computer, known as the Powertrain Control Module (PCM) and information sensors that monitor various functions of the engine and send a constant stream of data to the PCM during engine operation. Unlike earlier on-board diagnostics systems, the OBD-II system doesn't just monitor everything, store Diagnostic Trouble Codes (DTCs) and illuminate a Check Engine light or Malfunction Indicator Light (MIL) when there's a problem. (This warning light was referred to as the "Check Engine" light prior to OBD-II, and many do-it-yourselfers and professional technicians still use this term. However, its name was changed to "Malfunction Indicator

2.1 Simple code readers are an economical way to extract trouble codes when the CHECK ENGINE light comes on

2.2 Scanners like these from Actron and AutoXray are powerful diagnostic aids - they can tell you just about anything that you want to know about your engine management system

Light," or simply "MIL," as part of the Society of Automotive Engineers' standard terminology that was introduced in 1996 to encourage all manufacturers to use the same terms when referring to the same components. So in this manual we will refer to this warning light as the Malfunction Indicator Light, or MIL.)

4   The PCM is the "brain" of the electronically controlled OBD-II system. It receives data from a number of information sensors and switches. Based on the data that it receives from the sensors, the PCM constantly alters engine operating conditions to optimize driveability, performance, emissions and fuel economy. It does so by turning on and off and by controlling various output actuators such as relays, solenoids, valves and other devices. The PCM can only be accessed with an OBD-II scan tool plugged into the 16-pin Data Link Connector (DLC), which is located underneath the driver's end of the dashboard, near the steering column.

5   If your vehicle is still under warranty, virtually every fuel, ignition and emission control component in the OBD-II system is covered by a Federally mandated emissions warranty that is longer than the warranty covering the rest of the vehicle. Vehicles sold in California and in some other states have even longer emissions warranties than other states. Read your owner's manual for the terms of the warranty protecting the emission-control systems on your vehicle. It isn't a good idea to "do-it-yourself" at home while the vehicle emission systems are still under warranty because owner-induced damage to the PCM, the sensors and/or the control devices might void this warranty. So as long as the emission systems are still under warranty, take the vehicle to a dealer service department if there's a problem.

Information sensors

6   **Accelerator Pedal Position Sensor (APPS)** - The APPS, which is used on Hemi engines, is an integral component of the accelerator pedal assembly. The APPS provides the PCM with a variable voltage signal that's proportional to the position (angle) of the accelerator pedal. The PCM uses this data to control the position of the throttle plate inside the electronically controlled throttle body.

7   **Battery Temperature Sensor (BTS)** - The battery temperature sensor, if equipped, is located underneath the battery, in the battery tray. The BTS monitors the temperature of the battery. The Powertrain Control Module (PCM) uses this data, along with data from monitored line voltage, to control the battery's charging rate. The PCM keeps system voltage at a higher level in colder temperatures and at a lower level in warmer temperatures.

8   **Camshaft Position (CMP) sensor** - The CMP sensor is a Hall effect switching device (Dodge calls it a "sync signal generator"), which produces a square-wave (high voltage-low voltage) signal that the PCM uses to monitor the position of the camshaft. The CMP sensor is positioned adjacent to the cir-

cumference of a "tone wheel" mounted on the front end of the camshaft. The tone wheel has notches machined into it. When the engine is operating, the CMP sensor receives a 5-volt signal from the PCM, then switches back and forth from a high (5-volt) to a low (.3-volt) signal every time one of the notches in the tone wheel passes by it. This data enables the PCM to determine the position of the camshaft (and therefore the valve train) so that it can time the firing sequence of the fuel injectors. The PCM also uses the signal from the CMP sensor and the signal from the Crankshaft Position (CKP) sensor to distinguish between fuel injection and spark timing.

On 3.7L V6 and 4.7L V8 engines the CMP sensor is located on the outer side of the front end of the right cylinder head, just ahead of the exhaust manifold. On Hemi engines the CMP sensor is located on the upper right side of the timing chain cover.

9   **Crankshaft Position (CKP) sensor** - Like the CMP sensor, the CKP sensor is also a Hall effect device (see the explanation for how a Hall effect device works in the CMP sensor description above). And like the CMP sensor, the CKP sensor uses a "tone wheel" with notches machined into it to "flip" the CKP sensor's output from .3 volt to 5 volts every time a notch passes by it. The PCM uses data from the CKP sensor to calculate engine speed and crankshaft position, which enables it to synchronize ignition timing with fuel injector timing, to control spark knock and to detect misfires. The CKP sensor is located on the right rear side of the block on all engines.

10   **Engine Coolant Temperature (ECT) sensor** - The ECT sensor is a Negative Temperature Coefficient (NTC) "thermistor" (temperature-sensitive variable resistor). In an NTC-type thermistor, the resistance of the thermistor decreases as the coolant temperature increases, so the voltage output of the ECT sensor increases. Conversely, the resistance of the thermistor increases as the coolant temperature decreases, so the voltage of the ECT sensor decreases. The PCM uses this variable voltage signal to calculate the temperature of the engine coolant. The ECT sensor tells the PCM when the engine is sufficiently warmed up to go into closed-loop operation and helps the PCM control the air/fuel mixture ratio and ignition timing. On 3.7L V6 and 4.7L V8 engines the ECT sensor is located at the front of the intake manifold. On Hemi engines the ECT sensor is located at the front of the block, under the air conditioning compressor.

11   **Intake Air Temperature (IAT) sensor** - The IAT sensor is a Negative Temperature Coefficient (NTC) "thermistor" (temperature-sensitive variable resistor) that monitors the temperature of the air entering the engine and sends a variable voltage signal to the PCM. (See the explanation for how an NTC-type thermistor works in the ECT sensor description above.) The voltage signal from the IAT sensor is one of the parameters used by the PCM to determine injector pulse-width (the

duration of each injector's "on-time") and to adjust spark timing (to prevent spark knock). On 3.7L V6 and 4.7L V8 engines the IAT sensor is located on the left side of the intake manifold. On Hemi engines the IAT sensor is located on the front of the air resonator box.

12   **Knock Sensor (KS)** - The Knock Sensor (KS) is a "piezoelectric" crystal that oscillates in proportion to engine vibration. (The term piezoelectric refers to the property of certain crystals that produce a voltage when subjected to a mechanical stress.) The oscillation of the piezoelectric crystal produces a voltage output that is monitored by the PCM, which retards the ignition timing when the oscillation exceeds a certain threshold. When the engine is operating normally, the Knock Sensor (KS) oscillates consistently and its voltage signal is steady. When detonation occurs, engine vibration increases, and the oscillation of the Knock Sensor (KS) exceeds a design threshold. (Detonation is an uncontrolled explosion, after the spark occurs at the spark plug, which spontaneously combusts the remaining air/fuel mixture, resulting in a "pinging" or "slapping" sound.) If allowed to continue, the engine could be damaged. All engines covered by this manual are equipped with two knock sensors. On 3.7L V6 and 4.7L V8 engines, the knock sensors are located on top of the block, under the intake manifold. On Hemi engines the knock sensors are located on each side of the block, under the exhaust manifolds.

13   **Manifold Absolute Pressure (MAP) sensor** - As the altitude increases, the air becomes thinner. Because the air density changes with altitude, the PCM needs to know whether the vehicle is at sea level or at some higher elevation. Altitude and barometric pressure are inversely proportional: as the altitude increases, the barometric pressure decreases. The MAP sensor monitors the pressure or vacuum downstream from the throttle plate, inside the intake manifold. The MAP sensor measures intake manifold pressure and vacuum on the absolute scale, i.e. from zero psi, not from sea-level atmospheric pressure (14.7 psi). The MAP sensor converts the absolute pressure into a variable voltage signal that changes with the pressure or vacuum. The PCM uses this signal to calculate intake manifold pressure or vacuum, barometric pressure, engine load, injector pulse-width, spark advance, shift points, idle speed and deceleration fuel shut-off. On 3.7L V6 and 4.7L V8 engines the MAP sensor is located on the front of the intake manifold. On Hemi engines the MAP sensor is located on the front of the air resonator box.

14   **Oxygen sensors** - An oxygen sensor is a galvanic battery that generates a small variable voltage signal in proportion to the difference between the oxygen content in the exhaust stream and the oxygen content in the ambient air. The PCM uses the voltage signal from the upstream oxygen sensor to maintain a "stoichiometric" air/fuel ratio of 14.7:1 by constantly adjusting the "on-time" of

the fuel injectors. On vehicles with the Federal Emission Package, there are two oxygen sensors: the upstream (1/1) sensor is located just ahead of the catalytic converter, at the junction of the two exhaust downpipes from the exhaust manifolds. The downstream (1/2) oxygen sensor is located right behind the catalytic converter. On vehicles with the California Emission Package, there are four oxygen sensors: two upstream (1/1 and 2/1) and two downstream (1/2 and 2/2). The left upstream (1/1) sensor is located in the left exhaust downpipe, just ahead of the mini-converter; the left downstream (1/2) sensor is located right behind the mini-converter. The right upstream (2/1) sensor is located in the right exhaust downpipe, just ahead of the mini-converter; the right downstream (2/2) sensor is located right behind the mini-converter.

15   **Throttle Position (TP) sensor** - The TP sensor is a potentiometer that receives constant voltage input from the PCM and sends back a voltage signal that varies in relation to the opening angle of the throttle plate inside the throttle body. This voltage signal tells the PCM when the throttle is closed, half-open, wide open or anywhere in between. The PCM uses this data, along with information from other sensors, to calculate injector "pulse width" (the interval of time during which an injector solenoid is energized by the PCM). On 3.7L V6 and 4.7L V8 engines, the TP sensor is located on the throttle body, on the end of the throttle plate shaft. Hemi engines use an Electronic Throttle Control (ETC) system. The throttle body used in the ETC system has two TP sensors, but they're an integral part of the throttle body's ETC motor assembly and cannot be serviced separately.

16   **Transmission speed sensors** - There are two transmission speeds sensors on 45RFE and 545RFE automatic transmissions, the **Input Shaft Speed (ISS) sensor** and the **Output Shaft Speed (OSS) sensor**. Both sensors are located on the left side of the transmission housing. The ISS sensor is the unit closer to the front of the gear case. The OSS is the rear sensor. The ISS is a magnetic pick-up coil that generates an alternating current (AC) signal output to the Transmission Control Module (TCM) that's proportional to the speed of rotation of the input shaft. The OSS is also a magnetic pick-up coil that generates an AC signal output to the TCM that's proportional to the speed of rotation of the rear planetary carrier lugs (the TCM interprets this data as output shaft rpm). The TCM compares the ISS and OSS signals to determine the correct transmission gear ratio, to detect a speed ratio error, Torque Converter Clutch (TCC) slippage and to calculate parameters such as the torque converter element speed ratio. The ISS sensor is located on the left side of the overdrive gear case. There are two speed sensors on the left side of the transmission; the other one is the Output Shaft Speed (OSS) sensor (see Step 16).

17   **Transmission Range (TR) sensor** - The TR sensor is located at the end of the manual shaft, on the side of the automatic transaxle. The TR switch performs the same functions as a Park/Neutral Position (PNP) switch: it prevents the engine from starting in any gear other than Park or Neutral, and it closes the circuit for the back-up lights when the shift lever is moved to Reverse. But the TR switch is also connected to the PCM, which sends a voltage signal to the TR switch, which uses a series of step-down resistors that act as a voltage divider. The PCM monitors the voltage output signal from the switch, which corresponds to the position of the manual lever. Thus the PCM is able to determine the gear selected and is able to determine the correct pressure for the electronic pressure control system of the transaxle. On 45RFE and 545RFE transmissions, the TR sensor is an integral part of the shift solenoid module, which is on top of the valve body, inside the transmission. Replacing the TR sensors on either of these transmissions is beyond the scope of the home mechanic.

Powertrain Control Module (PCM)

18   The **PCM** is a computer. Think of it as the "brain" of the engine management system. Like all computers, the PCM receives data inputs, processes the data and outputs commands. The PCM receives data from all of the information sensors described above (input), compares the data to its program and calculates the appropriate responses (processing), then turns the output actuators on or off, or changes their *pulse width* or *duty cycle* (output) to keep everything running smoothly, cleanly and efficiently. The PCM is located in the right rear corner of the engine compartment, on the inner side of the right front fender. On some models, the PCM also houses the Transmission Control Module (TCM); on other models, the TCM is a separate component.

Output actuators

19   **EVAP canister purge solenoid** - The EVAP canister purge solenoid is a PCM-controlled solenoid that controls the purging of evaporative emissions from the EVAP canister to the intake manifold. The EVAP purge solenoid is never turned on during cold start warm-ups or during hot start time delays. But once the engine reaches a specified temperature and enters closed-loop operation the PCM will energize the canister purge solenoid between 5 and 10 times a second. When the solenoid is energized by the PCM, it allows the fuel vapors that are stored in the EVAP canister to be drawn into the intake manifold, where they're mixed with intake air, then burned along with the normal air/fuel mixture, under certain operating conditions. The PCM regulates the flow rate of the vapors by controlling the pulse-width of the solenoid (the length of time during which the solenoid is turned on) in accordance with operating conditions. The EVAP canister purge solenoid is located in the engine compartment, on the right side of the power brake booster.

20   **EVAP system Leak Detection Pump (LDP)** - Vehicles with a "Jeep Truck Engine Controller" (JTEC) utilize a Leak Detection Pump (LDP) to detect leaks in the EVAP system. The LDP pressurizes the EVAP system when the EVAP monitor tests the EVAP system for leaks. The LDP pressurizes the EVAP and fuel system components (the fuel tank, the EVAP canister, the canister purge solenoid and all of the EVAP lines) to test for leaks. It shuts off the EVAP system vent (which, when open, maintains atmospheric pressure inside the EVAP system) so that the EVAP system can be pressurized. The PCM monitors the pumping action of the LDP to determine whether the EVAP system's integrity has been compromised. If it has, then the PCM sets a Diagnostic Trouble Code (DTC) for a leak in the EVAP system. The LDP is located right in front of the EVAP canister, which is located under the vehicle, right in front of the fuel tank.

21   **EVAP Natural Vacuum Leak Detection (NVLD) system** - Vehicles with a current-generation PCM, referred to by Dodge as a "New Generation Controller" (NGC), use a Natural Vacuum Leak Detection (NVLD) system instead of a Leak Detection Pump (LDP). The NVLD system is based on the principle that the pressure inside a sealed system (such as the EVAP system) will change if the temperature changes, i.e. if the temperature goes up, so does the pressure, and vice versa. So if during a leak test the PCM notes that the pressure inside the EVAP system isn't proportional to the temperature, it sets a Diagnostic Trouble Code (DTC) for a leak. The NVLD unit is located right in front of the EVAP canister, which is located under the vehicle, right in front of the fuel tank.

22   **Fuel injectors** - The fuel injectors, which spray a fine mist of fuel into the intake ports, where it is mixed with incoming air, are inductive coils under PCM control. The injectors are installed between the fuel rail and the intake ports that connect the intake manifold runners to the combustion chambers. For more information about the injectors, see Chapter 4.

23   **Idle Air Control (IAC) motor** - The IAC motor controls the amount of air allowed to bypass the throttle plate when the throttle plate is at its (nearly closed) idle position. The IAC motor is controlled by the PCM. When the engine is placed under an additional load at idle (high power steering pressure or running the air conditioning compressor during low-speed maneuvers, for example), the engine can run roughly, stumble and even stall. To prevent this from happening, the PCM opens the IAC motor to increase the idle speed enough to overcome the extra load imposed on the engine. On 3.7L V6 and 4.7L V8 engines the IAC motor is mounted on the throttle body. There is no IAC motor on Hemi engines, because they're equipped with an Electronic Throttle Control (ETC) system, which uses the PCM to control the idle speed.

24   **Ignition coils** - The ignition coils are controlled by the Powertrain Control Module (PCM). There is no separate ignition control

module. This function is handled inside the PCM, which controls the ground path for the primary side of each coil. For more information about the ignition coils refer to Chapter 5.

Obtaining and clearing Diagnostic Trouble Codes (DTCs)

25 All models covered by this manual are equipped with on-board diagnostics. When the PCM recognizes a malfunction in a monitored emission control system, component or circuit, it turns on the Malfunction Indicator Light (MIL) on the dash. The PCM will continue to display the MIL until the problem is fixed and the Diagnostic Trouble Code (DTC) is cleared from the PCM's memory. You'll need a scan tool to access any DTCs stored in the PCM. Before outputting any DTCs stored in the PCM, thoroughly inspect ALL electrical connectors and hoses. Make sure that all electrical connections are tight, clean and free of corrosion. And make sure that all hoses are correctly connected, fit tightly and are in good condition (no cracks or tears).

Accessing the DTCs

Refer to illustration 2.26

26 On the vehicles covered in this manual, all of which are equipped with On-Board Diagnostic II (OBD-II) systems, the Diagnostic Trouble Codes (DTCs) can only be accessed with a scan tool. Simply plug the connector of the scan tool into the Data Link Connector (DLC), which is located under the lower edge of the dash, just to the left of the hood release handle **(see illustration)**. Then follow the instructions included with the scan tool to extract the DTCs.

27 Once you have outputted all of the stored DTCs, look them up on the accompanying DTC chart.

28 After troubleshooting the source of each DTC make any necessary repairs or replace the defective component(s).

Clearing the DTCs

29 Clear the DTCs with the scan tool in accordance with the instructions provided by the scan tool's manufacturer.

Diagnostic Trouble Codes

30 The accompanying tables are a list of the Diagnostic Trouble Codes (DTCs) that can be accessed by a do-it-yourselfer working at home (there are many more DTCs available to professional service technicians with proprietary scan tools and software, but those

2.26 The Data Link Connector (DLC), or diagnostic connector, is located under the instrument panel

codes cannot be accessed by a generic scan tool). If, after you have checked and repaired the connectors, wire harness and vacuum hoses (if applicable) for an emission-related system, component or circuit, the problem persists, have the vehicle checked by a dealer service department.

OBD-II Diagnostic Trouble Codes (DTCs) (includes transmission codes)

Note: *Not all trouble codes apply to all models.*

Code	Possible cause	Code	Possible cause
P0016	Crankshaft/camshaft timing misalignment	P0112	Intake Air Temperature (IAT) sensor circuit, low voltage
P0031	Oxygen sensor (1/1) heater circuit, low voltage	P0113	Intake Air Temperature (IAT) sensor circuit, high voltage
P0032	Oxygen sensor (1/1) heater circuit, high voltage	P0116	Engine Coolant Temperature (ECT) sensor circuit performance problem
P0037	Oxygen sensor (1/2) heater circuit, low voltage	P0117	Engine Coolant Temperature (ECT) sensor circuit, low voltage
P0038	Oxygen sensor (1/2) heater circuit, high voltage		
P0051	Oxygen sensor (2/1) heater circuit, low voltage	P0118	Engine Coolant Temperature (ECT) sensor circuit, high voltage
P0052	Oxygen sensor (2/1) heater circuit, high voltage	P0121	Throttle Position (TP) sensor/Accelerator Pedal Position (APP) sensor performance
P0057	Oxygen sensor (2/2) heater circuit, low voltage	P0122	Throttle Position (TP) sensor/Accelerator Pedal Position (APP) sensor circuit, low voltage
P0058	Oxygen sensor (2/2) heater circuit, high voltage		
P0068	Manifold pressure/throttle position correlation	P0123	Throttle Position (TP) sensor/Accelerator Pedal Position (APP) sensor circuit, high voltage
P0071	Ambient air temperature sensor performance	P0124	Throttle Position (TP) sensor/Accelerator Pedal Position (APP) sensor, intermittent
P0072	Ambient air temperature sensor circuit, low voltage		
P0073	Ambient air temperature sensor circuit, high voltage	P0125	Insufficient coolant temperature for closed-loop fuel control
P0107	Manifold Absolute Pressure (MAP) sensor circuit, low voltage	P0128	Thermostat rationality
P0108	Manifold Absolute Pressure (MAP) sensor circuit, high voltage	P0129	Barometric pressure out-of-range (too low)
P0111	Intake Air Temperature (IAT) sensor rationality	P0131	Oxygen sensor (1/1) circuit, low voltage

Code	Possible cause
P0132	Oxygen sensor (1/1) circuit, high voltage
P0133	Oxygen sensor (1/1), slow response
P0135	Oxygen sensor (1/1), heater performance problem
P0137	Oxygen sensor (1/2) circuit, low voltage
P0138	Oxygen sensor (1/2) circuit, high voltage
P0139	Oxygen sensor (/12) circuit, slow response
P0141	Oxygen sensor (1/2), heater performance problem
P0151	Oxygen sensor (2/1) circuit, low voltage
P0152	Oxygen sensor (2/1) circuit, high voltage
P0153	Oxygen sensor (2/1) circuit, slow response
P0155	Oxygen sensor (2/1), heater performance problem
P0157	Oxygen sensor (2/2) circuit, low voltage
P0158	Oxygen sensor (2/2) circuit, high voltage
P0159	Oxygen sensor (2/2) circuit, slow response
P0161	Oxygen sensor (2/2), heater performance problem
P0171	Fuel system too lean (cylinder bank no. 1)
P0172	Fuel system too rich (cylinder bank no. 1)
P0174	Fuel system too lean (cylinder bank no. 2)
P0175	Fuel system too rich (cylinder bank no. 2)
P0197	Engine oil temperature sensor circuit, low voltage
P0198	Engine oil temperature sensor circuit, high voltage
P0199	Fuel rail pressure sensor circuit, intermittent
P0201	Fuel injector circuit malfunction - cylinder no. 1
P0202	Fuel injector circuit malfunction - cylinder no. 2
P0203	Fuel injector circuit malfunction - cylinder no. 3
P0204	Fuel injector circuit malfunction - cylinder no. 4
P0205	Fuel injector circuit malfunction - cylinder no. 5
P0206	Fuel injector circuit malfunction - cylinder no. 6
P0207	Fuel injector circuit malfunction - cylinder no. 7
P0208	Fuel injector circuit malfunction - cylinder no. 8
P0218	High temperature operation activated
P0221	Throttle Position (TP) sensor no. 2 performance
P0222	Throttle Position (TP) sensor no. 2 circuit, low voltage
P0223	Throttle Position (TP) sensor no. 2 circuit, high voltage
P0300	Multiple cylinder misfire detected

Code	Possible cause
P0301	Cylinder no. 1 misfire detected
P0302	Cylinder no. 2 misfire detected
P0303	Cylinder no. 3 misfire detected
P0304	Cylinder no. 4 misfire detected
P0305	Cylinder no. 5 misfire detected
P0306	Cylinder no. 6 misfire detected
P0307	Cylinder no. 7 misfire detected
P0308	Cylinder no. 8 misfire detected
P0315	No Crankshaft Position (CKP) sensor learned
P0325	Knock sensor no. 1 circuit malfunction
P0330	Knock sensor no. 2 circuit malfunction
P0335	Crankshaft Position (CKP) sensor circuit malfunction
P0339	Crankshaft Position (CKP) sensor intermittent
P0340	Camshaft Position (CMP) sensor circuit malfunction
P0344	Camshaft Position (CMP) sensor intermittent
P0401	Exhaust Gas Recirculation (EGR) system, performance problem
P0403	Exhaust Gas Recirculation (EGR) solenoid circuit malfunction
P0404	Exhaust Gas Recirculation (EGR) position sensor rationality open
P0405	Exhaust Gas Recirculation (EGR) sensor circuit, low voltage
P0406	Exhaust Gas Recirculation (EGR) sensor circuit, high voltage
P0420	Catalyst system efficiency below threshold (cylinder bank no. 1)
P0430	Catalyst system efficiency below threshold (cylinder bank no. 2)
P0440	General Evaporative Emission Control (EVAP) system failure
P0441	Evaporative Emission Control (EVAP) purge system performance problem
P0442	Evaporative Emission Control (EVAP) purge system, medium leak detected
P0443	Evaporative Emission Control (EVAP) purge solenoid circuit malfunction
P0452	Natural Vacuum Leak Detection (NVLD) system, pressure switch stuck closed
P0453	Natural Vacuum Leak Detection (NVLD) system, pressure switch stuck open
P0455	Evaporative Emission Control (EVAP) system, large leak
P0456	Evaporative Emission Control (EVAP) system, small leak

Code	Possible cause
P0457	Loose fuel cap
P0461	Fuel level sensor no. 1, performance problem
P0462	Fuel level sensor no. 1, low voltage
P0463	Fuel level sensor no. 1, high voltage
P0480	Cooling fan no. 1, control circuit malfunction
P0481	Cooling fan no. 2, control circuit malfunction
P0498	Natural Vacuum Leak Detection (NVLD) canister vent valve solenoid, low voltage
P0499	Natural Vacuum Leak Detection (NVLD) canister vent valve solenoid, high voltage
P0501	Vehicle Speed Sensor (VSS) no. 1, performance problem
P0503	Vehicle Speed Sensor no. 1 circuit, erratic
P0506	Idle speed performance lower than expected
P0507	Idle speed performance higher than expected
P0508	Idle Air Control (IAC) valve sense circuit, low voltage
P0509	Idle Air Control (IAC) valve sense circuit, high voltage
P0513	Invalid Sentry Key Immobilizer System (SKIM) key
P0516	Battery temperature sensor circuit, low voltage
P0517	Battery temperature sensor circuit, high voltage
P0520	Engine oil pressure sensor circuit
P0521	Engine oil pressure sensor performance problem
P0522	Oil pressure too low
P0522	Engine oil pressure sensor circuit, low voltage (Hemi)
P0523	Engine oil pressure sensor circuit, high voltage
P0524	Engine oil pressure too low
P0532	A/C refrigerant pressure sensor, low voltage
P0533	A/C refrigerant pressure sensor, high voltage
P0551	Power Steering Pressure (PSP) switch performance problem
P0562	Battery voltage low
P0563	Battery voltage high
P0571	Brake switch no. 1 performance problem
P0572	Brake switch no. 1 stuck on
P0573	Brake switch no. 1 stuck off
P0579	Speed control switch no. 1 performance
P0580	Speed control switch no. 1 circuit, low voltage
P0581	Speed control switch no. 1 circuit, high voltage

Code	Possible cause
P0586	Speed control vent control circuit
P0591	Speed control switch no. 2 performance
P0592	Speed control switch no. 2, low voltage
P0593	Speed control switch no. 2, high voltage
P0594	Speed control servo power relay circuit
P0600	Serial communication link
P0601	Powertrain Control Module (PCM) internal memory checksum invalid
P0602	Powertrain Control Module (PCM) programming error or not programmed
P0604	Powertrain Control Module (PCM) Random Access Memory (RAM)
P0605	Powertrain Control Module (PCM) Read-Only Memory (ROM)
P0606	Internal Powertrain Control Module (PCM) processor
P060B	Electronic Throttle Control (ETC) analog-to-digital (A/D) ground performance problem
P060D	Electronic Throttle Control (ETC) level 2 Accelerator Pedal Position (APP) sensor performance problem
P060E	Electronic Throttle Control (ETC) level 2 Throttle Position (TP) sensor performance problem
P060F	Electronic Throttle Control (ETC) level 2 Engine Coolant Temperature (ECT) sensor performance problem
P061A	Electronic Throttle Control (ETC) level 2 torque performance problem
P061C	Electronic Throttle Control (ETC) level 2 rpm performance problem
P0613	Internal Transmission Control Module (TCM) or TCM processor
P0622	Generator field control circuit
P0627	Fuel pump relay circuit
P062C	Electronic Throttle Control (ETC) level 2 mph performance problem
P0630	Vehicle Identification Number (VIN) not programmed in Powertrain Control Module (PCM)
P0632	Odometer not programmed in Powertrain Control Module (PCM)
P0633	Sentry Key Immobilizer System (SKIM) secret key not stored in Powertrain Control Module (PCM)
P0642	Sensor reference voltage no. 1 circuit low
P0643	Primary 5-volt supply circuit, high voltage
P0645	Air conditioning clutch relay circuit

Code	Possible cause	Code	Possible cause
P0652	Sensor reference voltage no. 2 circuit low	P0750	LR shift solenoid circuit
P0653	Sensor reference voltage no. 2 circuit high	P0755	2/4 shift solenoid B circuit
P0685	Auto Shutdown (ASD) relay control circuit	P0760	OD shift solenoid circuit
P0688	Auto Shutdown (ASD) relay sense circuit low	P0765	UD shift solenoid circuit
P0689	Auto Shutdown (ASD) relay sense circuit low	P0770	4C shift solenoid circuit
P0690	Auto Shutdown (ASD) relay sense circuit high	P0841	LR pressure switch rationality
P0691	Cooling fan no. 1 relay control circuit low	P0845	2/4 or 2C hydraulic pressure test
P0692	Cooling fan no. 1 relay control circuit high	P0846	2/4 or 2C pressure switch rationality
P0693	Cooling fan no. 2 relay control circuit low	P0850	Park/Neutral switch performance
P0694	Cooling fan no. 1 relay control circuit high	P0868	Line pressure low
P0700	Transmission control system (Malfunction Indicator Light request)	P0869	Line pressure high
P0703	Brake switch no. 2 performance problem	P0870	OD hydraulic pressure test
P0706	Transmission Range (TR) sensor rationality	P0871	OD pressure switch rationality
P0707	Transmission range sensor circuit, low input	P0875	UD hydraulic pressure test
P0711	Transmission temperature sensor performance problem	P0876	UD pressure switch rationality
P0712	Transmission fluid temperature sensor circuit, low voltage	P0882	Transmission Control Module (TCM) input low
P0713	Transmission fluid temperature sensor circuit, high voltage	P0883	Transmission Control Module (TCM) input high
P0714	Transmission fluid temperature sensor circuit, intermittent voltage	P0884	Power up at speed
P0715	Input speed sensor no. 1 circuit	P0888	Transmission relay always off
P0720	Output speed sensor circuit	P0890	Switched battery
P0725	Engine speed sensor circuit	P0891	Transmission relay always on
P0731	Incorrect gear ratio, first gear	P0897	Transmission fluid deteriorated
P0732	Incorrect gear ratio, second gear	P0932	Line pressure sensor circuit
P0733	Incorrect gear ratio, third gear	P0934	Line pressure sensor circuit, low voltage
P0734	Incorrect gear ratio, fourth gear	P0935	Line pressure sensor circuit, high voltage
P0735	Incorrect gear ratio, fifth gear	P0944	Line pressure sensor circuit, low voltage
P0736	Incorrect gear ratio, reverse gear	P0987	4C hydraulic pressure test
P0740	Torque Converter Clutch (TCC) out of range	P0988	4C pressure switch rationality
		P0992	2/4 or OD hydraulic pressure test

3 Accelerator Pedal Position Sensor (APPS) - replacement

Warning: *The Accelerator Pedal Position Sensor (APPS) is an integral component of the accelerator pedal assembly. It's easy enough to remove. All you have to do to remove the APPS and the accelerator pedal assembly is disconnect the electrical connector and remove two mounting nuts. The problem is that when you install and connect the APPS again, the Powertrain Control Module (PCM) must relearn the operating parameters of the APPS. This was easy to do on earlier APPS units used on Dodge vehicles, but on the vehicles covered in this manual, you would need the factory scan tool to relearn the Electronic Throttle Control (ETC) parameters. We therefore recommend that, if the APPS must be replaced, that you have this procedure done at a dealer service department or other properly equipped repair shop. If you were to attempt this procedure at home, you won't just set Diagnostic Trouble Codes (DTCs); you will be driving a vehicle that might be dangerous.*

4 Battery temperature sensor - replacement

Refer to illustrations 4.3 and 4.4

Note: *The battery temperature sensor, if equipped, is located under the battery, in the battery tray.*

1   Disconnect the cable from the negative battery terminal (see Chapter 5, Section 1).

2   Remove the battery (see Chapter 5).

3   Disengage the battery temperature sensor from the battery tray (**see illustration**) and pull it straight up through its mounting hole in the tray.

4   Disconnect the electrical connector from the battery temperature sensor (**see illustration**) and remove the sensor.

5   Installation is the reverse of removal.

4.3 To detach the battery temperature sensor from the battery tray, squeeze these two locking tangs together . . .

5 Camshaft Position (CMP) sensor - replacement

1   Disconnect the cable from the negative battery terminal (see Chapter 5, Section 1).

3.7L V6 and 4.7L V8 engines

Refer to illustrations 5.3a and 5.3b

Note: *The CMP sensor is located on the outer side of the front end of the right cylinder head, just ahead of the exhaust manifold.*

2   Raise the front end of the vehicle and place it securely on jackstands.

3   Disconnect the electrical connector from the CMP sensor (**see illustrations**).

4   Remove the sensor mounting bolt and remove the CMP sensor.

5   Inspect the CMP sensor O-ring for cracks, tears and other deterioration. If it's damaged, replace it.

6   When installing the CMP sensor, apply a small dab of clean engine oil to the sensor O-ring, then use a slight rocking motion to work

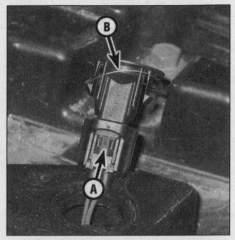

4.4 . . . then pull the battery temperature sensor up through the hole in the tray, depress the lock (A) and disconnect the electrical connector from the sensor. Make sure that the wave washer (B) is in place before you install the sensor

the O-ring into the sensor mounting bore. Do NOT use a twisting motion or you will damage the O-ring.

7   Make sure that the CMP sensor mounting flange is fully seated flat against the mounting surface around the sensor mounting hole. **Caution:** *If the CMP sensor is not fully seated against its mounting surface, the sensor mounting tang will be damaged when the sensor mounting bolt is tightened to the specified torque.*

8   Installation is otherwise the reverse of removal. Be sure to tighten the CMP sensor mounting bolt to the torque listed in this Chapter's Specifications.

Hemi engine

Refer to illustrations 5.9 and 5.11

Note: *The CMP sensor is located on the upper right side of the timing chain cover.*

9   Disconnect the electrical connector from

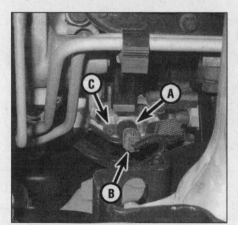

5.3a To detach the CMP sensor (A) from a 3.7L V6 engine, disconnect the electrical connector (B) and remove the sensor mounting bolt (C) (as seen from underneath the engine)

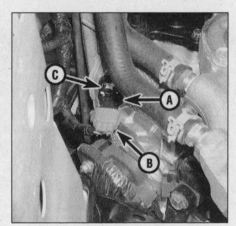

5.3b To detach the CMP sensor (A) from a 4.7L V8 engine, disconnect the electrical connector (B) and remove the sensor mounting bolt (C) (as seen from underneath the engine)

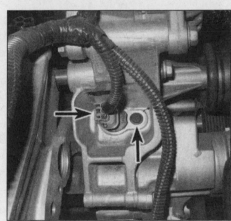

5.9 To detach the CMP sensor from the timing chain cover on a Hemi engine, disconnect the electrical connector and remove the sensor mounting bolt

5.11 Remove the old CMP sensor O-ring and inspect it for cracks, tears and deterioration. If it's damaged, replace it

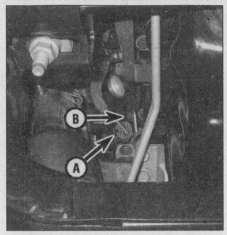

6.3a To detach the CKP sensor from the block on a 3.7L V6 engine, disconnect the electrical connector (A) and remove the sensor mounting bolt (B)

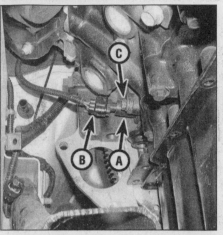

6.3b To detach the CKP sensor (A) from the block on a 4.7L V8 engine, disconnect the electrical connector (B) and remove the sensor mounting bolt (C)

the CMP sensor **(see illustration)**.

10   Remove the CMP sensor mounting bolt and remove the CMP sensor from the timing chain cover.

11   Remove the old CMP sensor O-ring **(see illustration)** and inspect it for cracks, tears and deterioration. If the old O-ring is damaged, replace it.

12   When installing the CMP sensor, apply a small dab of clean engine oil to the sensor O-ring, then use a slight rocking motion to work the O-ring into the sensor mounting bore. Do NOT use a twisting motion or you will damage the O-ring.

13   Make sure that the CMP sensor mounting flange is fully seated flat against the mounting surface around the sensor mounting hole. **Caution:** *If the CMP sensor is not fully seated against its mounting surface, the sensor mounting tang will be damaged when the sensor mounting bolt is tightened to the specified torque.*

14   Installation is otherwise the reverse of removal. Be sure to tighten the CMP sensor mounting bolt to the torque listed in this Chapter's Specifications.

6   Crankshaft Position (CKP) sensor - replacement

Refer to illustrations 6.3a, 6.3b and 6.3c

Note: *The CKP sensor is located on the right rear side of the block.*

1   Disconnect the cable from the negative battery terminal (see Chapter 5, Section 1).

2   Raise the front end of the vehicle and place it securely on jackstands.

3   Disconnect the electrical connector from the CKP sensor **(see illustrations)**.

4   Remove the CKP sensor mounting bolt and remove the sensor from the engine.

5   Remove the CKP sensor O-ring and inspect it for cracks, tears and deterioration. If it's damaged, replace it.

6   Apply a small amount of engine oil on the O-ring and, using a slight rocking motion, push the sensor into its mounting hole in the engine block until the sensor is fully seated.

7   Installation is otherwise the reverse of removal.

7   Engine Coolant Temperature (ECT) sensor - replacement

Warning: *Wait until the engine is completely cool before beginning this procedure.*

1   Partially drain the cooling system (see Chapter 1).

2   Disconnect the cable from the negative battery terminal (see Chapter 5, Section 1).

3.7L V6 and 4.7L V8 engines

Refer to illustrations 7.3a, 7.3b and 7.5

Note: *The ECT sensor is located at the front of the intake manifold.*

3   Disconnect the electrical connector from the ECT sensor **(see illustrations)**.

4   Using a deep socket, carefully unscrew the ECT sensor from the intake manifold.

5   To prevent leakage and thread corrosion, wrap the threads of the ECT sensor with Teflon sealing tape **(see illustration)** before installing the sensor. (Seal the sensor threads

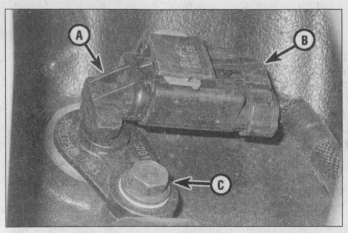

6.3c To detach the CKP sensor (A) from the right-rear side of the block on a Hemi engine, disconnect the electrical connector (B) and remove the sensor mounting bolt (C)

7.3a To remove the ECT sensor from the intake manifold on a 3.7L V6 engine, disconnect the electrical connector (A) and unscrew the sensor (B) from the manifold

7.3b To remove the ECT sensor from the intake manifold on a 4.7L V8 engine, disconnect the electrical connector and unscrew the sensor from the manifold

7.5 Before installing the ECT sensor, be sure to wrap the threads of the sensor with Teflon tape to prevent leaks

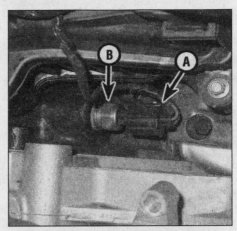

7.10 To remove the ECT sensor from the intake manifold on a Hemi engine, disconnect the electrical connector (A) and unscrew the sensor (B) from the manifold

8.2a On 3.7L V6 engines, the IAT sensor (A) is located on the left side of the intake manifold. The MAP sensor (B) is located at the front of the intake manifold

whether you're installing the old sensor or a new unit.)

6 Installation is otherwise the reverse of removal. Be sure to tighten the ECT sensor to the torque listed in this Chapter's Specifications.

7 Refill the cooling system (see Chapter 1).

Hemi engine

Refer to illustration 7.10

Note: *The ECT sensor is located at the front of the engine block, under the air conditioning compressor.*

8 Remove the drivebelt (see Chapter 1).

9 To access the ECT sensor, you'll need to unbolt the air conditioning compressor from the engine (see Chapter 3). It is NOT necessary to disconnect any air conditioning hoses from the compressor. Set the compressor aside and support it with a piece of rope or wire.

10 Disconnect the electrical connector from the ECT sensor **(see illustration)**.

11 Using a deep socket, carefully unscrew

the ECT sensor from the intake manifold.

12 To prevent leakage and thread corrosion, wrap the threads of the ECT sensor with Teflon sealing tape **(see illustration 7.5)** before installing the sensor. (Seal the sensor threads whether you're installing the old sensor or a new unit.)

13 Installation is otherwise the reverse of removal. Be sure to tighten the ECT sensor to the torque listed in this Chapter's Specifications.

14 When you're done, be sure to refill the cooling system (see Chapter 1).

8 Intake Air Temperature (IAT) sensor - replacement

Refer to illustrations 8.2a, 8.2b, 8.2c, 8.2d, 8.3 and 8.4

Note: *On 3.7L V6 and 4.7L V8 engines, the IAT sensor is located on the left side of the intake manifold. On Hemi engines the IAT sensor is located at the right front corner of the air resonator box.*

1 Disconnect the cable from the negative battery terminal (see Chapter 5, Section 1).

2 Disconnect the electrical connector from the IAT sensor **(see illustrations)**.

8.2b On 4.7L V8 engines the IAT sensor is also located on the left side of the intake manifold

8.2c On Hemi engines the IAT sensor is located at the right front corner of the air resonator box

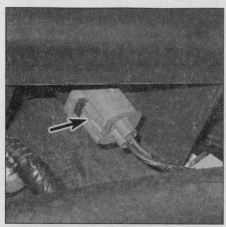

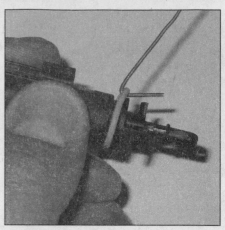

8.2d   To disconnect the electrical connector from an IAT sensor, depress the tab and pull off the connector (IAT sensor on Hemi engine shown, IAT sensor connectors on 3.7L V6 and 4.7L V8 are disconnected in a similar fashion)

8.3   To remove the IAT sensor, lift up the release tab slightly and rotate the sensor counterclockwise 1/4-turn and pull it out (IAT sensor on Hemi engine shown, 3.7L V6 and 4.7L V8 sensors are removed in a similar fashion)

8.4   Be sure to remove the O-ring from the IAT sensor and inspect it for cracks, tears and deterioration. If the O-ring is damaged, replace it

3   To remove the IAT sensor, lift up the release tab **(see illustration)** slightly, then turn the sensor 1/4-turn counterclockwise and pull it out.

4   Remove the old O-ring from the IAT sensor **(see illustration)** and inspect it for cracks, tears and deterioration. If the O-ring is damaged, replace it.

5   To install the IAT sensor, insert it into its mounting hole and rotate it clockwise 1/4-turn. Make sure that the release tab locks the sensor into place. Installation is otherwise the reverse of removal.

9   Knock sensor - replacement

3.7L V6 and 4.7L V8 engines

Note: *The two knock sensors are located on top of the block, in the valley between the cylinder heads, underneath the intake manifold. They must be replaced as a single assembly. They're not available separately.*

1   Disconnect the cable from the negative battery terminal (see Chapter 5, Section 1).

2   Disconnect the knock sensor electrical connector, which is located at the rear of the engine, behind the intake manifold. (If you can't find the knock sensor electrical connector, wait until you have removed the intake manifold, then locate the two knock sensors and trace their leads back to this common connector.)

3   Remove the intake manifold (see Chapter 2A).

4   Remove the knock sensor mounting bolts and remove the knock sensor assembly. **Note:** *The foam strips on the knock sensor mounting bolt threads are used to retain the bolts during vehicle assembly at the manufacturing plant. They have no other purpose. They are not some form of adhesive, thread sealant or locking compound. Do NOT use any type of adhesive, thread sealant or locking compound when installing these bolts again.*

5   Make sure that the holes for the knock sensor mounting bolts are thoroughly cleaned before installing the knock sensor mounting bolts.

6   Note that the left knock sensor is identified by an identification tag (LEFT) and that

it has a larger mounting bolt. Do NOT switch the knock sensors, i.e. do not install the left knock sensor in the right sensor mounting position and vice versa. The PCM assumes that the knock sensors are installed in their correct locations. **Caution:** *Switching the sensor locations will confuse the PCM and cause it to set a Diagnostic Trouble Code.*

7   Installation is otherwise the reverse of removal. Be sure to tighten the knock sensor mounting bolts to the torque listed in this Chapter's Specifications. **Caution:** *Over- or under-tightening the knock sensor mounting bolts will affect knock sensor performance, which might affect the PCM's spark control ability.*

Hemi engine

Refer to illustration 9.9

Note: *There are two knock sensors. One is located on the left side of the block, below the exhaust manifold, and the other is located in the same place on the right side of the block.*

8   Raise the front of the vehicle and place it securely on jackstands.

9   Disconnect the electrical connector from the knock sensor **(see illustration)**.

10   Remove the knock sensor mounting bolt and remove the knock sensor from the engine. **Note:** *The foam strips on the knock sensor mounting bolt threads are used to retain the bolts during vehicle assembly at the manufacturing plant. They have no other purpose. They are not some form of adhesive, thread sealant or locking compound. Do NOT use any type of adhesive, thread sealant or locking compound when installing these bolts again.*

11   Installation is the reverse of removal. Be sure to tighten the knock sensor mounting bolts to the torque listed in this Chapter's Specifications. **Caution:** *Over- or under-tightening the knock sensor mounting bolts will affect knock sensor performance, which might affect the PCM's spark control ability.*

9.9   To detach a knock sensor from the block on a Hemi engine, disconnect the electrical connector (A) and remove the knock sensor mounting bolt (B)

10.2 On 4.7L V8 engines the MAP sensor is located on the front of the intake manifold (3.7L V6 similar)

10.6 To disconnect the electrical connector from the MAP sensor on a Hemi engine, slide the release lock (1) away from the sensor (toward the harness), then depress the release tab (2) and pull off the connector

10.7 To remove the MAP sensor from the intake manifold on a Hemi engine, rotate it 1/4-turn counterclockwise and pull it out of its mounting hole. Be sure to inspect the MAP sensor O-ring

10   Manifold Absolute Pressure (MAP) sensor - replacement

1   Disconnect the cable from the negative battery terminal (see Chapter 5, Section 1).

3.7L V6 and 4.7L V8 engines

Refer to illustration 10.2

Note: *The MAP sensor is located on the front of the intake manifold.*

2   Disconnect the electrical connector from the MAP sensor **(see illustration)**.

3   Remove the two MAP sensor mounting screws and remove the MAP sensor from the intake manifold.

4   Remove the MAP sensor O-ring and inspect it for cracks, tears and deterioration. If the O-ring is damaged, replace it.

5   Installation is the reverse of removal.

Hemi engine

Refer to illustrations 10.6 and 10.7

Note: *The MAP sensor is located on the front of the intake manifold.*

6   Disconnect the electrical connector from the MAP sensor **(see illustration)**.

7   Remove the MAP sensor from the intake manifold **(see illustration)**.

8   Remove the old MAP sensor O-ring **(see illustration 10.7)** and inspect it for cracks, tears and deterioration. If it's damaged, replace it.

9   To install the MAP sensor, place it in position, insert it into the mounting hole in the intake manifold and turn it 1/4-turn clockwise.

10   Installation is otherwise the reverse of removal.

11   Oxygen sensors - general description and replacement

Description

1   The oxygen in the exhaust reacts with the elements inside the oxygen sensor to produce

a voltage output that varies from 0.1 volt (high oxygen, lean mixture) to 0.9 volt (low oxygen, rich mixture). The pre-converter oxygen sensor (mounted in the exhaust system before the catalytic converter) provides a feedback signal to the PCM that indicates the amount of leftover oxygen in the exhaust. The PCM monitors this variable voltage continuously to determine the required fuel injector pulse width and to control the engine air/fuel ratio. A mixture ratio of 14.7 parts air to 1 part fuel is the ideal ratio for minimum exhaust emissions, as well as the best combination for fuel economy and engine performance. Based on oxygen sensor signals, the PCM tries to maintain this air/fuel ratio of 14.7:1 at all times.

2   The post-converter oxygen sensor (mounted in the exhaust system after the catalytic converter) has no effect on PCM control of the air/fuel ratio. However, the post-converter sensor is identical to the pre-converter sensor and operates in the same way. The PCM uses the post-converter signal to monitor the efficiency of the catalytic converter. A post-converter oxygen sensor will produce a slower fluctuating voltage signal that reflects the lower oxygen content in the post-catalyst exhaust.

3   Oxygen sensor configuration varies depending on the model and on where it is sold, i.e. "Federal" (49-State) model or "California" model. On vehicles equipped with the Federal (49-State) emissions package and on some California models, there is one upstream and one downstream oxygen sensor. On these vehicles, the upstream oxygen sensor is located in the exhaust pipe ahead of the catalyst and the downstream sensor is located on the pipe behind the catalyst. On some vehicles equipped with the California emissions package (those with two catalysts, one for each cylinder bank) there are two upstream sensors (one in each exhaust pipe between the exhaust manifold and the catalyst) and two downstream sensors (one

behind each catalyst).

4   An oxygen sensor produces no voltage when it is below its normal operating temperature of about 600-degrees F. During this warm-up period, the PCM operates in an open-loop fuel control mode. It does not use the oxygen sensor signal as a feedback indication of residual oxygen in the exhaust. Instead, the PCM controls fuel metering based on the inputs of other sensors and its own programs.

5   An oxygen sensor depends on four conditions in order to operate correctly:

  a) **Electrical** - *The low voltage generated by the sensor requires good, clean connections. Always check the connectors whenever an oxygen sensor problem is suspected or indicated.*

  b) **Outside air supply** - *The sensor needs air circulation to the internal portion of the sensor. Whenever the sensor is installed, make sure that the air passages are not restricted.*

  c) **Correct operating temperature** - *The PCM will not react to the sensor signal until the sensor reaches approximately 600-degrees F. This factor must be considered when evaluating the performance of the sensor.*

  d) **Unleaded fuel** - *Unleaded fuel is essential for correct sensor operation.*

6   The PCM can detect several different oxygen sensor problems and set Diagnostic Trouble Codes (DTCs) to indicate the specific fault (see Section 2). When an oxygen sensor DTC occurs, the PCM disregards the oxygen sensor signal voltage and reverts to open-loop fuel control as described previously.

Replacement

Refer to illustrations 11.8, 11.9a and 11.9b

Warning: *Be careful not to burn yourself during the following procedure.*

Note: *Since the exhaust pipe contracts when cool, the oxygen sensor may be hard to*

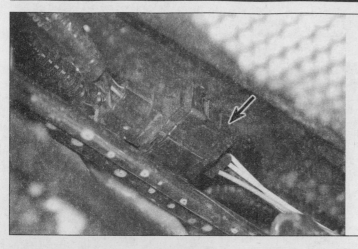

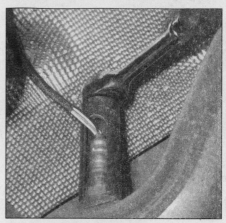

11.8 On California models, there are four oxygen sensors - two upstream and two downstream. To disconnect one of these connectors, depress this release tab and pull apart the connector halves

11.9a Each upstream oxygen sensor is located ahead of the catalytic converter. To find the electrical connector, trace the electrical lead from the sensor to the connector and disconnect it. To remove the sensor, unscrew it with either an oxygen sensor socket or with a wrench

loosen. To make sensor removal easier, start the engine and let it run for a minute or two, then turn it off.

7   Raise the vehicle and place it securely on jackstands.

8   Locate the upstream or downstream oxygen sensor, trace the sensor's electrical lead to the sensor electrical connector (see illustration) and disconnect it.

9   Remove the upstream or downstream oxygen sensor. On some models you can remove the sensor with a wrench (see illustrations). On others, you will have to use an oxygen sensor socket (available at most auto parts stores).

10   Clean the threads inside the sensor mounting hole in the exhaust pipe with an appropriate tap.

11   If you're installing the old sensor, clean off the threads, then apply a coat of anti-seize compound to the threads before installing the sensor. If you're installing a new sensor, do NOT apply anti-seize compound; new sensors are already coated with anti-seize.

12   Installation is otherwise the reverse of removal. Be sure to tighten the oxygen sensor to the torque listed in this Chapter's Specifications.

12   Throttle Position (TP) sensor - replacement

Refer to illustrations 12.3 and 12.4

Note: This procedure applies to 3.7L V6 and 4.7L V8 engines. It does not apply to Hemi engines, which are equipped with the Electronic Throttle Control (ETC) system. The ETC system doesn't use a removable TP sensor.

1   Disconnect the cable from the negative battery terminal (see Chapter 5, Section 1).

2   Remove the air intake duct and the air resonator box (see Chapter 4).

3   Disconnect the electrical connector from the TP sensor (see illustration), remove the TP sensor mounting screws and remove the TP sensor from the throttle body.

4   When installing the TP sensor on the throttle body, align the sensor so that the locating tangs on the backside of the TP sensor fit over each side of the flat end of the throttle shaft (see illustration). If the sensor fits flush against the throttle body and you're able to rotate the TP sensor a few degrees in order to align the sensor mounting holes with the mounting holes in the throttle body, then you've installed the sensor correctly. If

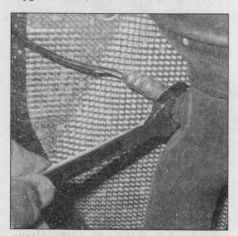

11.9b Each downstream oxygen sensor is located behind the catalyst. First, trace the electrical lead up to the sensor connector and disconnect it, then remove the sensor with either an oxygen sensor socket or with a wrench

12.3 Locations of the TP sensor (A) and IAC motor (B) on 3.7L V6 and 4.7L V8 engines. To disconnect the TP sensor electrical connector, slide the lock tab (1) away from the sensor, then depress the tab (2) and pull off the connector. To disconnect the electrical connector from the IAC motor, depress the tab (3) and pull off the connector

12.4 When installing the TP sensor, make sure that the flat end of the throttle shaft (A) fits between the two locating tangs (B) on the backside of the TP sensor (3.7L V6 shown, 4.7L V8 similar)

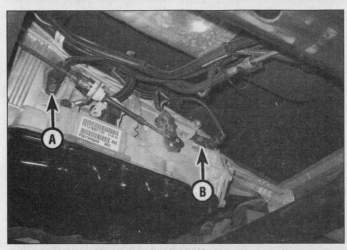

13.3 The ISS sensor (A) and OSS sensor (B) are located on the left side of 45RFE and 545RFE automatic transmissions

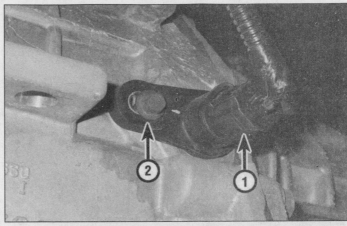

13.4 To remove an ISS or OSS sensor from the transmission, disconnect the electrical connector (1), then remove the sensor mounting bolt (2)

the sensor doesn't fit flush against the throttle body and/or you're unable to rotate it a few degrees to align the mounting holes, then pull it off, verify that the locating tangs are correctly positioned above and below the flat end of the throttle shaft and try again.

5   Installation is otherwise the reverse of removal.

13 Transmission speed sensors - replacement

Refer to illustrations 13.3 and 13.4

Note: *The Input Shaft Speed (ISS) and Output Shaft Speed (OSS) sensors are located on the left side of the transmission.*

1   Disconnect the cable from the negative battery terminal (see Chapter 5, Section 1).

2   Raise the vehicle and place it securely on jackstands.

3   The ISS and OSS sensors **(see illustration)** are identical in appearance (and are replaced exactly the same way), so make

sure that you've correctly identified the sensor that you wish to replace.

4   Disconnect the electrical connector from the ISS or OSS sensor **(see illustration)**.

5   Place a drain pan underneath the sensor that you're going to replace. Remove the sensor mounting bolt and pull out the sensor.

6   Installation is the reverse of removal.

7   When you're done, check the transmission fluid level (see Chapter 1) and add fluid as necessary.

14 Powertrain Control Module (PCM) - removal and installation

Caution: *Avoid static electricity damage to the Powertrain Control Module (PCM) by grounding yourself to the body of the vehicle before touching the PCM and using a special anti-static pad on which to store the PCM once it's removed.*

Note 1: *The PCM is located in right rear corner of the engine compartment, on the inner*

side of the right front fender.

Note 2: *Anytime the PCM is replaced with a new unit, it must be reprogrammed with a scan tool by a dealership service department or other properly equipped repair shop.*

Note 3: *Anytime the battery is disconnected, stored operating parameters may be lost from the PCM, causing the engine to run rough for a period of time while the PCM relearns the information.*

1   Disconnect the cable from the negative battery terminal (see Chapter 5, Section 1).

Durango models

Refer to illustrations 14.5, 14.6, 14.7, 14.8 and 14.9

2   Remove the wiper arms (see *Windshield wiper motor, linkage and mounting bracket - removal and installation* in Chapter 12).

3   Remove the cowl grille (see Chapter 11).

4   Remove the air intake duct and the resonator box (see Chapter 4).

5   Remove the plastic trim cover from the

14.5 Unclip and remove this plastic trim cover from the right side of the cowl area

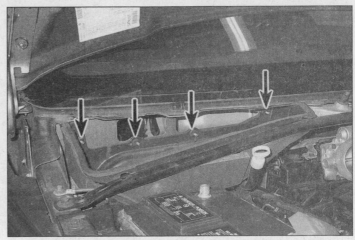

14.6 To detach the cowl box below the plastic trim cover, remove these four nuts

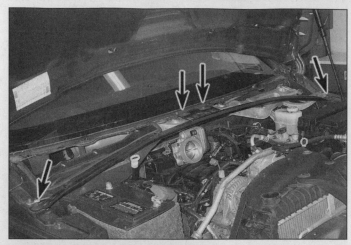

14.7 To remove the cowl support brace, remove these four bolts

14.8 To disconnect each PCM electrical connector, slide the red lock (1) away from the PCM (toward the harness), depress the release tab (2) and pull off the connector

right side of the cowl **(see illustration)**.

6   Remove the cowl box below the plastic trim cover **(see illustration)**.

7   Remove the cowl support brace **(see illustration)**.

8   Disconnect the electrical connectors from the PCM **(see illustration)**. Note that the electrical connectors are color-coded to prevent mix-ups during installation.

9   Remove the PCM mounting bolts **(see illustration)** and carefully remove the PCM.

10   Installation is the reverse of removal. Make sure that you plug each connector into the same color terminal as the connector.

Dakota models

Refer to illustration 14.11

11   The Powertrain Control Module (PCM) on Dakota models is located in the right rear corner of the engine compartment, near the accumulator **(see illustration)**.

12   Remove the air filter housing (see Chapter 4).

13   Disconnect the electrical connectors from the PCM **(see illustration 14.8)**.

14   Remove the three mounting bolts (one at the top and two at the bottom) and remove the PCM.

15   Installation is the reverse of the removal procedure. Don't forget to secure the ground strap with the lower front mounting bolt.

---

15   Idle Air Control (IAC) motor - replacement

Note: *This procedure applies to 3.7L V6 and 4.7L V8 engines. It does not apply to Hemi engines, which are equipped with the Electronic Throttle Control (ETC) system. The ETC system doesn't use an IAC motor.*

1   Disconnect the cable from the negative battery terminal (see Chapter 5, Section 1).

2   Remove the air intake duct and the air resonator box (see Chapter 4).

3   Disconnect the electrical connector from

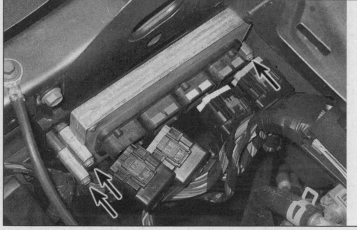

14.9 To detach the PCM from the fender, remove these three bolts

the IAC motor **(see illustration 12.3)**.

4   Remove the two IAC motor mounting screws and remove the IAC motor from the throttle body.

5   Installation is the reverse of removal.

---

16   Catalytic converter - description, check and replacement

Note: *Because of a Federally-mandated extended warranty which covers emission-related components such as the catalytic converter, check with a dealer service department before replacing the converter at your own expense.*

General description

1   A catalytic converter (or catalyst) is an emission control device in the exhaust system that reduces certain pollutants in the exhaust gas stream. There are two types of converters. An oxidation catalyst reduces hydrocarbons (HC) and carbon monoxide (CO). A reduction catalyst reduces oxides of nitrogen (NOx). A catalyst that can reduce all three pollutants is known as a "Three-Way Catalyst" (TWC). All models covered by this manual are equipped with TWCs.

Check

2   The test equipment for a catalytic converter (a "loaded-mode" dynamometer and a 5-gas analyzer) is expensive. If you suspect that the converter on your vehicle is malfunctioning, take it to a dealer or authorized emission inspection facility for diagnosis and repair.

14.11 The Powertrain Control Module (PCM) on Dakota models is located in the right rear corner of the engine compartment, near the accumulator

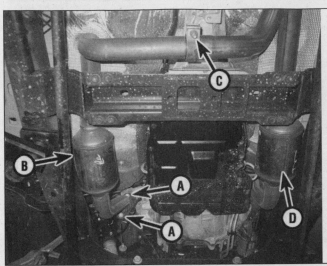

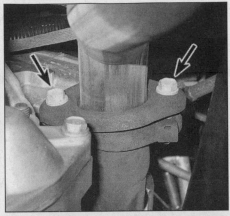

16.6 A typical catalytic converter setup on a Hemi with a California Emissions Package (other models similar)

A   Exhaust manifold-to-exhaust pipe bolts/nuts (always replace)
B   Left catalytic converter
C   Clamp, bolt and nut that secures two sides of crossover pipe (always replace)
D   Right catalytic converter

16.8 To disconnect the exhaust pipe ahead of the catalyst from the exhaust manifold, remove these two bolts (right exhaust manifold-to-exhaust pipe bolts shown, left side identical). When reconnecting the exhaust pipes to the exhaust manifolds, be sure to use a new gasket and new bolts

16.9 To disconnect the two sides of the crossover pipe, back off this nut and slide the two halves of the crossover apart. When reconnecting this slip joint, Dodge recommends that you replace the clamp assembly

16.10 If you're removing or replacing the right catalytic converter, back off his nut and pull the exhaust pipe and the pre-muffler pipe apart. When reconnecting a slip joint, Dodge recommends that you replace the clamp assembly

3   Whenever you raise the vehicle to service underbody components, inspect the converter for leaks, corrosion, dents and other damage. Carefully inspect the welds and/or flange bolts and nuts that attach the front and rear ends of the converter to the exhaust system. If you note any damage, replace the converter.

4   Although catalytic converters don't break too often, they can become clogged or even plugged up. The easiest way to check for a restricted converter is to use a vacuum gauge to diagnose the effect of a blocked exhaust on intake vacuum.

a) Connect a vacuum gauge to an intake manifold vacuum source (see Chapter 2).
b) Warm the engine to operating temperature, place the transaxle in Park (automatic models) or Neutral (manual models) and apply the parking brake.
c) Note the vacuum reading at idle and jot it down.

d) Quickly open the throttle to near its wide-open position and then quickly get off the throttle and allow it to close. Note the vacuum reading and jot it down.
e) Do this test three more times, recording your measurement after each test.
f) If your fourth reading is more than one in-Hg lower than the reading that you noted at idle, the exhaust system might be restricted (the catalytic converter could be plugged, OR an exhaust pipe or muffler could be restricted).

Replacement

Refer to illustrations 16.6, 16.8, 16.9 and 16.10

Warning: *Make sure that the exhaust system is completely cooled down before proceeding. If the vehicle has just been driven, the catalytic converter can be hot enough to cause serious burns.*

5   Raise the vehicle and place it securely on jackstands.

6   Spray a liberal amount of penetrant onto the threads of the exhaust pipe-to-exhaust manifold bolts, the clamp bolt that connect the two parts of the crossover pipe and the clamp bolt that connects pipe behind the right catalyst to the muffler (see illustration). Wait awhile for the penetrant to loosen things up.

7   While you're waiting for the penetrant to do its work, disconnect the electrical connectors for the upstream and downstream oxygen sensor and remove both oxygen sensors (see Section 11).

8   Unscrew the upper exhaust pipe-to-exhaust manifold flange bolts (see illustration). If they're still difficult to loosen, spray the threads with some more penetrant, wait awhile and try again.

9   To loosen the clamp (see illustration) that secures the slip joint between the two sides of the crossover pipe between the two catalysts, back off the nut. If it's still difficult to loosen, spray the threads with some more penetrant, wait awhile and try again.

10   If you're removing or replacing the right catalytic converter, you'll also have to loosen the clamp that secures the slip joint between the right exhaust pipe and the pre-muffler (see illustration). Again, if it's still difficult to remove, spray the threads with more penetrant, then wait awhile and try again.

11   Remove the catalytic converter assembly. Remove and discard the old flange gasket.

12   Installation is the reverse of removal. Be sure to use a new flange gasket and new bolts at each exhaust manifold mounting flange. Dodge also recommends using new clamps at the slip joints. Coat the threads of the clamp and the exhaust manifold bolts with anti-seize compound to facilitate future removal. Tighten the fasteners securely.

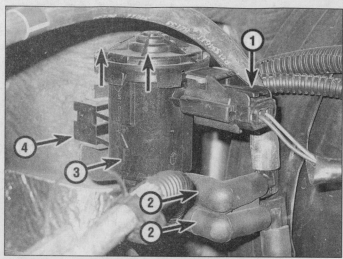

17.9 To remove the EVAP canister purge solenoid, disconnect the electrical connector (1), label and disconnect the EVAP hoses (2) and disengage the solenoid (3) from its mounting bracket (4) by pulling it straight up

17.14 Natural Vacuum Leak Detection (NVLD) filter, EVAP canister and NVLD pump mounting details:

A EVAP canister	D NVLD filter-to-NVLD pump
B NVLD filter	hose
C NVLD filter air inlet hose	E EVAP hose (from fuel tank)

17 Evaporative Emissions Control (EVAP) system - description and component replacement

General description

1   The Evaporative Emissions Control (EVAP) system prevents fuel system vapors (which contain unburned hydrocarbons) from escaping into the atmosphere. On warm days, vapors trapped inside the fuel tank expand. When the pressure reaches a certain threshold, these vapors are routed from the fuel tank through the fuel vapor vent valve and the fuel vapor control valve to the EVAP canister, where they're stored temporarily, until they can be consumed by the engine during normal operation. Under certain conditions (engine warmed up, vehicle up to speed, moderate or heavy loads, etc.) the Powertrain Control Module (PCM) opens the canister purge solenoid, which allows intake vacuum to pull fuel vapors from the EVAP canister into the intake manifold, where they mix with the air/fuel mixture before being consumed in the combustion chambers. This system is complex and virtually impossible to troubleshoot without the right tools and training. However, the following description should give you a good idea of how the system works and where the components are located:

2   The EVAP canister, which contains activated charcoal, stores fuel vapors produced by gasoline as it heats up inside the fuel tank. You'll have to raise the vehicle to inspect or replace the canister, but the canister is designed to be maintenance-free and should last the life of the vehicle. The EVAP canister is located underneath the vehicle, just in front of the fuel tank.

3   The Natural Vacuum Leak Detection (NVLD) pump is located at the upper left end in front of the EVAP canister. The NVLD pump monitors the temperature of the unburned

hydrocarbon vapors inside the EVAP system. As the temperature increases, so does the pressure; as the temperature decreases, so does the pressure. But this effect can occur only if the system is fully sealed. If there's a leak, the relationship between pressure and temperature will diverge from the pressure-temperature relationship that the Powertrain Control Module (PCM) is programmed to expect. When this divergence between the pressure and the temperature of the fuel occurs, the PCM concludes that the system is leaking and it sets a Diagnostic Trouble Code (DTC) indicating either a small, medium or large leak in the EVAP system. Diagnosis of the NVLD pump and detection system is beyond the scope of the home mechanic. If a DTC indicates a problem with the NVLD system, have a dealer service department or other qualified repair shop repair the vehicle. But a defective NVLD pump is easy to replace, and you'll find the instructions to do so later in this section.

4   The EVAP canister purge solenoid, which is under the control of the Powertrain Control Module (PCM), regulates the flow of vapors being purged from the EVAP canister into the intake manifold. The canister purge solenoid is normally closed. It opens only when directed to do so by the PCM, which uses the availability of intake manifold vacuum and data from various information sensor inputs to determine when and how long to open the valve. The interval of time during which the purge valve is opened by the PCM is known as its "duty cycle." The canister purge solenoid valve is located in the engine compartment, to the right of the power brake booster.

General system checks

5   The most common symptom of a faulty EVAP system is a strong fuel odor (particularly during hot weather). If you smell fuel while driving or (more likely) right after you park the vehicle and turn off the engine, check the

fuel filler cap first. Make sure that it's screwed onto the fuel filler neck all the way. If the odor persists, inspect all EVAP hose connections, both in the engine compartment and under the vehicle. You'll have to raise the vehicle and place it securely on jackstands to inspect most of the EVAP system, since it's located under the vehicle. Be sure to inspect each hose attached to the canister for damage and leakage along its entire length. Repair or replace as necessary. Inspect the canister for damage and look for fuel leaking from the bottom. If fuel is leaking or the canister is otherwise damaged, replace it.

6   Poor idle, stalling, and poor driveability can be caused by a defective fuel vapor vent valve or canister purge solenoid, a damaged canister, cracked hoses, or hoses connected to the wrong tubes. Fuel loss or fuel odor can be caused by fuel leaking from fuel lines or hoses, a cracked or damaged canister, or a defective vapor valve.

7   To check for excessive fuel vapor pressure in the fuel tank, remove the gas cap and listen for the sound of pressure release. If the fuel tank emits a "whooshing" sound when you open the filler cap, fuel tank vapor pressure is excessive. Inspect the canister vapor hoses and the canister inlet port for blockage or collapsed hoses. Also inspect the hose for the EVAP canister vent valve. A complete test can only be done with a proprietary OBD-II scan tool (see Section 2), which will run a series of checks to detect excessive pressure. You'll have to take the vehicle to a dealer service department to have the EVAP system professionally diagnosed.

Component replacement

EVAP canister purge solenoid

Refer to illustration 17.9

Note: *The EVAP canister purge solenoid is located in the engine compartment, to the right of the power brake booster.*

8   Disconnect the cable from the negative battery terminal (see Chapter 5, Section 1).
9   Disconnect the electrical connector from the EVAP canister purge solenoid (see illustration).
10   Clearly label the EVAP hoses, then disconnect them from the EVAP canister purge solenoid.
11   Disengage the EVAP canister purge solenoid from its mounting bracket.
12   Installation is the reverse of removal.

NVLD filter, EVAP canister and NVLD pump

Refer to illustration 17.14

Note: *The NVLD filter, EVAP canister and NVLD pump assembly is located right in front of the fuel tank. You can remove the NVLD filter without removing the EVAP canister, but you'll have to remove the EVAP canister in order to remove the NVLD pump.*

13   Raise the vehicle and place it securely on jackstands.
14   Locate the NVLD filter on the front side of the EVAP canister (see illustration).

NVLD filter

Refer to illustration 17.16

Note: *The NVLD filter is located in front of the EVAP canister assembly, which is located right in front of the fuel tank.*

15   Clearly label the EVAP hoses connected to the NVLD filter (see illustration 17.14), then disconnect them from the filter.
16   To detach the NVLD filter from its mounting bracket, remove the mounting screw, then disengage the filter mounting tab from its mounting slot in the canister mounting bracket (see illustration).
17   Installation is the reverse of removal.

EVAP canister

Refer to illustrations 17.18, 17.19, 17.21a and 17.21b

18   Disconnect the EVAP hose from the EVAP canister (see illustration).
19   Disconnect the electrical connector from the NVLD pump (see illustration).

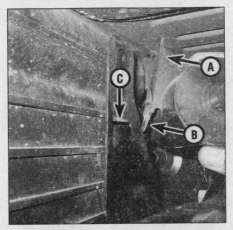

17.16 To detach the NVLD filter from the EVAP canister mounting bracket, pull out the push-pin fastener (A) from the upper part of the filter mounting bracket, then lift up the filter to disengage the mounting tab (B) from the mounting slot (C) in the canister bracket

20   Disconnect the NVLD hose from the NVLD pump.
21   Disengage the EVAP canister from the two right canister mounting brackets (see

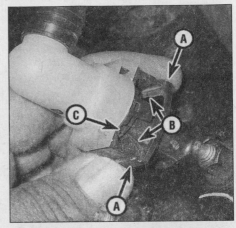

17.18 To disconnect the EVAP hose from the EVAP canister, squeeze the inner edges (A) of the release tabs together to release the locking teeth (B) from the raised ridge (C) on the EVAP canister pipe and pull the connector off the pipe

illustration), then disengage the canister mounting slot from its mounting tab on the left canister bracket (see illustration) and remove the canister assembly.
22   Installation is the reverse of removal.

17.19 To disconnect the electrical connector from the NVLD pump, push the sliding lock (1) to its released position (away from the pump, toward the harness), then depress the release tab (2) and pull off the connector. Then disconnect the NVLD filter hose (3) from the NVLD pump

17.21a To disengage the EVAP canister from the two right mounting brackets, depress the upper and lower locking tabs (lower tab shown) with a screwdriver . . .

17.21b . . . swing out the right end of the canister and disengage the canister mounting slot (A) from the mounting tab (B) on the left canister mounting bracket

NVLD pump

Refer to illustration 17.24

Note: *The NVLD pump is mounted on the upper left end of the EVAP canister. You have to remove the canister to remove the NVLD pump.*

23   Remove the EVAP canister assembly (see Steps 18 through 21).

24   To remove the NVLD pump from the EVAP canister, squeeze the locking tab on the side of the pump and rotate the pump counterclockwise to disengage its bayonet-type mounting system **(see illustration)**, then pull the pump off the canister.

25   Installation is the reverse of removal.

---

18   Exhaust Gas Recirculation (EGR) system - description and component replacement

EGR valve

Refer to illustration 18.2

Note: *The EGR valve, if equipped, is located on the front of the right cylinder head.*

1   Remove the air intake duct and the air filter housing (see *Air filter housing - removal and installation* in Chapter 4).

2   Disconnect the electrical connector from the EGR valve **(see illustration)**.

3   Remove the EGR tube mounting flange bolts **(see illustration 18.2)**.

4   Remove the EGR valve mounting bolts **(see illustration 18.2)** and remove the EGR valve. Remove and discard the old gasket.

5   Installation is the reverse of removal. Be sure to use new gaskets between the EGR valve and the cylinder head and between the EGR tube mounting flange and the EGR valve and tighten the EGR valve and EGR tube mounting bolts to the torque listed in this Chapter's Specifications.

EGR tube

Refer to illustration 18.8

6   Remove the air intake duct and the air filter housing (see *Air filter housing - removal and installation* in Chapter 4).

7   Remove the EGR tube mounting flange bolts **(see illustration 18.2)**.

8   Remove the wire retaining clip **(see illustration)** that secures the other end of the EGR pipe to the throttle body.

9   Installation is the reverse of removal. Be sure to tighten the EGR tube mounting flange bolts to the torque listed in this Chapter's Specifications.

---

19   Positive Crankcase Ventilation (PCV) system - description and check

Description

Refer to illustrations 19.2, 19.3a and 19.3b

Note: *For specific information on how to replace the PCV valves on the engines covered by this manual, see Chapter 1.*

1   The Positive Crankcase Ventilation (PCV) system reduces hydrocarbon emissions by scavenging crankcase vapors, which

17.24 To remove the NVLD pump from the EVAP canister, squeeze the locking tab on the side of the pump, rotate the pump counterclockwise to disengage its bayonet-type mounting system and pull off the pump

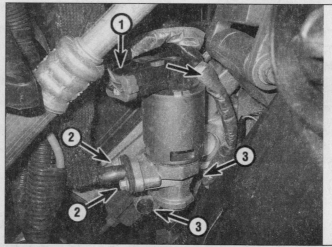

18.2 To remove the EGR valve, slide the red lock on top of the electrical connector forward, depress the release tab (1) and pull off the connector, remove the EGR tube mounting flange bolts (2), remove the EGR valve mounting bolts (3), then remove the valve. Be sure to remove and discard the old EGR tube and EGR valve gaskets

18.8 To remove the wire retainer clip that secures the EGR tube to the intake manifold, insert a pair of needle-nose pliers through the upper bend of the retainer and lever it straight up

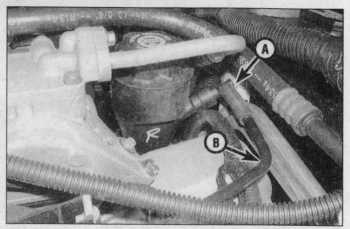

19.2 On 3.7L V6 and 4.7L V8 engines, the PCV valve (A) is located on the side of the engine oil filler tube. The crankcase ventilation hose (B) connects the PCV valve to the intake manifold (4.7L V8 shown, 3.7L V6 similar)

19.3a On Hemi engines, the PCV fresh air inlet hose (A) connects the air filter housing (B) to the oil filler tube (C)

19.3b On Hemi engines, the PCV valve is located in the right rear corner of the intake manifold

are rich in unburned hydrocarbons. A PCV valve regulates the flow of gases into the intake manifold in proportion to the amount of intake vacuum available. At idle, when intake vacuum is very high, the PCV valve restricts the flow of vapors so that the engine doesn't run poorly. As the throttle plate opens and intake vacuum begins to diminish, the PCV valve opens more to allow vapors to flow more freely.

2   On 3.7L V6 and 4.7L V8 engines, the PCV system consists of a fresh air inlet hose that connects a pipe at the left rear corner of the air resonator box to a pair of breather pipes at the inner rear corner of each valve cover; the PCV valve **(see illustration)**, which is located on the oil filler tube; and the crankcase ventilation hose that connects the PCV valve to the intake manifold.

3   On Hemi engines, the PCV system consists of a fresh air inlet hose **(see illustration)** that connects the air filter housing to the oil filler tube, and the PCV valve **(see illustration)**, which is located to the right of the throttle body, on the right rear corner of the intake manifold. There is no external crankcase ventilation hose (PCV hose) on these models; an internal passage connects the PCV valve to the crankcase.

Inspection

4   An engine that is operated without a properly functioning crankcase ventilation system can be damaged. So anytime you're servicing the engine, be sure to inspect the PCV system hose(s) for cracks, tears, deterioration and other damage. Disconnect the hose(s) and inspect it/them for damage and

obstructions. If a hose is clogged, clean it out. If you're unable to clean it satisfactorily, replace it.

5   A plugged PCV hose might cause any or all of the following conditions: A rough idle, stalling or a slow idle speed, oil leaks or sludge in the engine. So if the engine is running roughly, stalling and idling at a lower than normal speed, or is losing oil, or has oil in the throttle body or air intake manifold plenum, or has a build-up of sludge, a PCV system hose might be clogged. Repair or replace the hose(s) as necessary.

6   A leaking PCV hose might cause any or all of the following conditions: a rough idle, stalling or a high idle speed. So if the engine is running roughly, stalling and idling at a higher than normal speed, a PCV system hose might be leaking. Repair or replace the hose(s) as necessary.

7   Here's an easy functional check of the PCV system on a vehicle with a fresh air inlet hose and a crankcase ventilation hose with a PCV valve in it:

a) *Disconnect the crankcase ventilation hose (the crankcase ventilation hose, or simply "the PCV hose," is the hose that connects the PCV valve to the intake manifold).*

b) *Start the engine and let it warm up to its normal idle.*

c) *Verify that there is vacuum at the PCV hose. If there is no vacuum, look for a plugged hose or a clogged port or pipe on the intake manifold. Also look for a hose that collapses when it's blocked (i.e. when vacuum is applied). Replace clogged or deteriorated hoses.*

d) *Remove the engine oil dipstick and install a vacuum gauge on the upper end of the dipstick tube.*

e) *Pinch off or plug the PCV system's fresh air inlet hose.*

f) *Run the engine at 1500 rpm for 30 seconds, then read the vacuum gauge while the engine is running at 1500 rpm.*

g) *If there's vacuum present, the crankcase ventilation system is operating correctly.*

h) *If there's NO vacuum present, the engine might be drawing in outside air. The PCV system won't function correctly unless the engine is a sealed system. Inspect the valve cover(s), oil pan gasket or other sealing areas for leaks.*

i) *If the vacuum gauge indicates positive pressure, look for a plugged hose or engine blow-by.*

8   If the PCV system is functioning correctly, but there's evidence of engine oil in the throttle body or air filter housing, it could be caused by excessive crankcase pressure. Have the crankcase pressure tested by a dealer service department.

9   In the PCV system, excessive blow-by (caused by worn rings, pistons and/or cylinders, or by constant heavy loads) is discharged into the intake manifold and consumed. If you discover heavy sludge deposits or a dilution of the engine oil, even though the PCV system is functioning correctly, look for other causes (see the *Troubleshooting* section at the front of this manual and Chapter 2C) and correct them as soon as possible.

Notes

Chapter 7 Part A
Manual transmission

Contents

Specifications

General
Transmission lubricant type .... See Chapter 1

Torque specifications   Ft-lbs (unless otherwise indicated)
Back-up light switch .... 88 In-lbs
Shift tower-to-transmission bolts .... 88 in-lbs
Structural dust cover bolts 40
Transmission-to-engine mounting bolts
    Transmission-to-engine bolts (no washers) 30
    Engine-to-transmission bolts (washers) 50

1   General information

The vehicles covered by this manual are equipped with a six-speed manual or a four- or five speed automatic transmission. Information on the manual transmission is included in this Part of Chapter 7. Information on the automatic transmission can be found in Part B of this Chapter. And if you're looking for the transfer case, you'll find it in Chapter 7C.

Vehicles equipped with a manual trans-mission use the Getrag 238. The Getrag 238 is a six-speed transmission.

Depending on the cost of having a trans-mission overhauled, it might be a better idea to replace it with a used or rebuilt unit. Your local auto parts store, dealer or transmission shop should be able to supply information concerning cost, availability and exchange policy. Regardless of how you decide to rem-edy a transmission problem, you can still save a lot of money by removing and installing the unit yourself.

2   Extension housing oil seal - replacement

Refer to illustrations 2.4 and 2.6
Note: *This procedure also applies to the transfer case extension housing seal on 4WD models.*

1   Oil leaks at the extension housing oil seal are usually caused by a worn seal lip. Replac-ing this seal is relatively easy, since you can do so without removing the transmission from

2.4 Use a hammer and chisel to dislodge the rear seal from the extension housing on 2WD models (shown) or, on 4WD models, from the transfer case

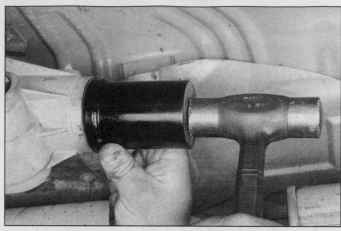

2.6 Use a large socket or a seal driver to drive the new seal into the extension housing or transfer case (2WD model shown). The outside diameter of the socket must be slightly smaller than the outside diameter of the seal, just enough to clear the edges of the seal bore

the vehicle. The extension housing oil seal is located at the rear tip of the transmission extension housing, where the driveshaft is attached. (If the vehicle is a 4WD model, there is no extension housing. Instead, the transfer case is bolted to the rear of the transmission housing. But the following procedure applies to replacing the rear seal on 4WD models too.)

2   If you suspect that the extension housing seal is leaking (because you've seen puddles right below the extension housing seal and/or because the transmission seems to be losing lubricant all the time), raise the vehicle and support it securely on jackstands. If the seal is leaking, gear lube will be oozing or dripping from the rear of the transmission, coating the forward end of the driveshaft and leaking onto the ground.

3   Remove the driveshaft (see Chapter 8).

4   Some seals have a metal casing with a lip. With this type of seal you can use a chisel and hammer to carefully pry the oil seal out of the rear of the transmission **(see illustration)**. Do not damage the splines on the transmission output shaft.

5   If the seal doesn't have a metal lip, obtain a special oil seal removal tool (available at most auto parts stores) to do the job.

6   Using a seal driver or a very large socket as a drift, install the new oil seal **(see illustration)**. Drive it into the bore squarely and make sure that it's completely seated.

7   Lubricate the splines of the transmission output shaft and the outside of the driveshaft yoke with lightweight grease, then install the driveshaft (see Chapter 8). Be careful not to damage the lip of the new seal.

3   Shift lever - removal and installation

1   If equipped, remove the center console (see Chapter 11). With the parking brake on and the wheels blocked, place the shift lever in Neutral.

2   Carefully pry the lock tabs for the shift lever boot and slide the shift lever boot up the shift lever.

3   Remove the four shift tower mounting bolts and remove the shift lever and tower from the transmission as a single assembly.

4   Disassemble the shift lever assembly, clean the parts in solvent, blow everything dry with compressed air, then coat all friction surfaces with clean multi-purpose grease and reassemble.

5   Installation is the reverse of removal. Be sure to tighten the shift tower mounting bolts to the torque listed in this Chapter's Specifications.

4   Back-up light switch - check and replacement

Check

1   The back-up light switch is located on the side of the transmission case.

2   Turn the ignition key to the ON position, move the shift lever to the REVERSE position and verify that the back-up lights come on.

3   If the back-up lights don't go on, check the back-up light fuse, which is located in the engine compartment fuse and relay box (see Chapter 12).

4   If the fuse is blown, troubleshoot the back-up light circuit for a short circuit.

5   If the fuse is okay, put the shift lever in REVERSE, then raise the vehicle and support it securely on jackstands.

6   Working under the vehicle, disconnect the electrical connector from the back-up light switch. Using an ohmmeter, check for continuity across the terminals of the switch (not the connector). There should be continuity.

7   If there is no continuity between the switch terminals with the shift lever in

REVERSE, replace the switch.

8   If there is continuity at the switch, check for voltage at the electrical connector. One of the two terminals should have battery voltage present with the ignition key in the ON position.

9   If there is no voltage at the switch electrical connector, troubleshoot the circuit between the engine compartment fuse and relay box and the back-up light switch connector for an open circuit condition.

10   If there is voltage at the switch electrical connector, trace the back-up light circuit between the electrical connector and the back-up light bulbs for an open circuit condition. **Note:** *Although not very likely, the back-up light bulbs could both be burned out, but don't rule out this possibility.*

Replacement

11   Raise the vehicle and support it securely on jackstands, if not already done.

12   Disconnect the electrical connector from the back-up light switch.

13   Using a wrench, unscrew the back-up light switch mounting bolt from the transmission case.

14   Install the switch in the transmission case and tighten it to the torque listed in this Chapter's Specifications.

15   The remainder of installation is the reverse of removal.

5   Transmission - removal and installation

Refer to illustrations 5.21a and 5.21b

Removal

1   Disconnect the cable from the negative battery terminal (see Chapter 5, Section 1).

2   Put the transmission shift lever into the NEUTRAL position.

3   Carefully pry the lock tabs for the shift

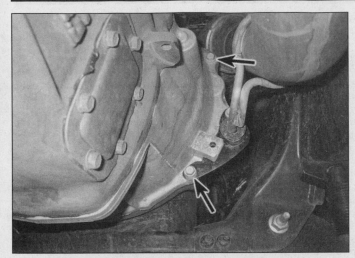

5.21a Right-side transmission mounting bolts (not all bolts are visible in this photo)

5.21b Left-side transmission mounting bolts (not all bolts are visible in this photo)

lever boot and slide the boot up the shift lever. Remove the shift tower and lever assembly (see Section 3).

4   Raise the vehicle and support it securely on jackstands.

5   Remove the skid plate, if equipped.

6   Disconnect the electrical connector from the back-up light switch and detach the wiring harness from any clips on the transmission.

7   Drain the transmission lubricant (see Chapter 1).

8   Remove the driveshaft (see Chapter 8).

9   Detach the exhaust pipe(s) between the exhaust manifolds and the catalytic converter(s) and remove them. Remove any other exhaust system components that are routed under the transmission and/or transfer case.

10   On 4WD models, remove the transfer case shift linkage, then remove the transfer case (see Chapter 7C).

11   Detach the clutch release cylinder from the clutch housing (see Chapter 8), then move the cylinder aside for clearance. If you're careful, you should be able to set the release cylinder aside without actually disconnecting the clutch hydraulic line from the release cylinder.

12   Remove the starter motor (see Chapter 5).

13   Remove the structural dust cover bolts at the transmission. Do not remove the structural dust cover from the engine block or it will have to be aligned properly (see Chapter 2A or 2B).

14   Remove the clutch hydraulic cylinder dust shield.

15   Remove the suspension crossmember.

16   Support the engine from above with an engine hoist, or place a jack (with a block of wood as an insulator) under the engine oil pan. The engine must remain supported at all times while the transmission is out of the vehicle.

17   Support the transmission with a transmission jack (available at auto parts stores and at tool rental yards) or with a large heavy-duty floor jack. If you're going to use a floor jack to support the transmission, make sure

that you use a transmission jack adapter head (also available at auto parts stores and at tool rental yards). These transmissions are very heavy, so it's a good idea to have someone help you lower the transmission to make sure that it doesn't fall off the jack.

18   Raise the transmission slightly, then disconnect and remove the transmission mount between the extension housing and the crossmember.

19   Remove the bolts and nuts attaching the crossmember to the frame rails, then remove the crossmember.

20   After the crossmember has been removed, lower the jack slightly so that the transmission is still supported but neither raised nor lowered by the jack.

21   Remove the bolts attaching the transmission to the engine and the engine to the transmission **(see illustrations)**.

22   Make a final inspection for any wiring harness or hoses that might still be connected to the transmission.

23   Keeping the transmission level, roll the jack toward the rear of the vehicle until the transmission input shaft clears the splined hub in the clutch disc.

24   Once the input shaft is clear, lower the transmission to the floor and remove it from under the vehicle.

25   While the transmission is removed, be sure to remove and inspect all clutch components (see Chapter 8). Always install new clutch components whenever you have to remove the transmission.

Installation

26   Apply a light coat of high-temperature bearing grease (or a suitable equivalent) to the following components:

Pilot bearing (in the rear end of the crankshaft)
Driveshaft slip yoke
Input shaft splines
Release bearing bore
Release bearing sliding surface
Release fork ballstud

After lubricating the above components, install the clutch components (see Chapter 8).

27   Raise the transmission into position and carefully slide it forward, engaging the input shaft with the clutch plate hub. Do not use excessive force to install the transmission - if the input shaft does not slide into place, readjust the angle of the transmission so it is level and/or turn the input shaft so the splines engage properly with the clutch.

28   Install the transmission-to-engine bolts and tighten them to the torque listed in this Chapter's Specifications. **Caution:** *Don't use the bolts to draw the transmission to the engine. If the transmission doesn't slide forward easily and mate with the engine block, find out why before proceeding.*

29   Raise the transmission extension housing just high enough to clear the crossmember, install the crossmember and attach it to the frame rails. Install the transmission mount between the extension housing and the crossmember. Carefully lower the transmission extension housing onto the mount and the crossmember. When everything is properly aligned, tighten all nuts and bolts securely.

30   Remove the jacks supporting the transmission and the engine.

31   On 4WD models install the transfer case and shift linkage (see Chapter 7C).

32   Install the various components previously removed:

Clutch release cylinder (see Chapter 8)
Driveshaft (see Chapter 8)
Exhaust system components (see Chapter 4)
Starter motor (see Chapter 5)

33   Reconnect the electrical connector for the back-up light switch. Also reconnect any other wiring harness connectors that you might have disconnected. And make sure that any harnesses that were attached to clips or cable guides on the transmission housing are reattached.

34   Remove the jackstands and lower the vehicle.

35   Install the shift tower and shift lever assembly (see Section 3).

36   Fill the transmission to the correct level with the specified lubricant (see Chapter 1).

37   Reconnect the cable to the negative battery terminal.

38   Road test the vehicle for proper operation and check for leakage.

6   Transmission overhaul - general information

Overhauling a manual transmission is a difficult job for the do-it-yourselfer. It involves the disassembly and reassembly of many small parts. Numerous clearances must be precisely measured and, if necessary, changed with select fit spacers and snap-rings. As a result, if transmission problems arise, it can be removed and installed by a competent do-it-yourselfer, but overhaul should be left to a transmission repair shop. Rebuilt transmissions might be available. Check with your dealer parts department and auto parts stores. At any rate, the time and money involved in an overhaul is almost sure to exceed the cost of a rebuilt unit.

Nevertheless, it's not impossible for an inexperienced mechanic to rebuild a transmission if the special tools are available and the job is done in a deliberate step-by-step manner so nothing is overlooked.

The tools necessary for an overhaul include internal and external snap-ring pliers, a bearing puller, a slide hammer, a set of pin punches, a dial indicator and possibly a hydraulic press. In addition, a large, sturdy workbench and a vise or transmission stand will be required.

During disassembly of the transmission, make careful notes of how each piece comes off, where it fits in relation to other pieces and what holds it in place. If you note how each part is installed before removing it, getting the transmission back together again will be much easier.

Before taking the transmission apart for repair, it will help if you have some idea what area of the transmission is malfunctioning. Certain problems can be closely tied to specific areas in the transmission, which can make component examination and replacement easier. Refer to the *Troubleshooting* section at the front of this manual for information regarding possible sources of trouble.

Chapter 7 Part B
Automatic transmission

Contents

Specifications

General
Transmission fluid type .... See Chapter 1

Torque specifications
Ft-lbs (unless otherwise indicated)

Torque converter-to-driveplate bolts

42RLE .... 65 in-lbs

545RFE 23

Transmission-to-engine bolts 50

1   General information

The vehicles covered in this manual are equipped with a six-speed manual transmission or a four-speed or five-speed automatic transmission. Information on manual transmissions is in Part A of this Chapter. You'll also find extension housing oil seal replacement, which is a virtually identical procedure for both automatic and manual transmissions, in Part A. Information on automatic transmissions is included in this Part of Chapter 7. If you're looking for information on the transfer case, refer to Part C of this Chapter.

Vehicles with an automatic transmission are equipped with a 42RLE four-speed automatic transmission or a 545RFE five-speed automatic transmission. All transmissions are equipped with a Torque Converter Clutch (TCC) system that increases fuel economy. The TCC engages in Drive and Overdrive modes. The TCC system consists of a solenoid, controlled by the Powertrain Control Module (PCM), that locks the torque converter when the vehicle is cruising on level ground and the engine is fully warmed up.

All automatic transmissions covered in this Chapter are equipped with an external air-to-oil transmission oil cooler, which is located in front of the radiator.

All vehicles with an automatic transmission are equipped with a Brake Transmission Shift Interlock (BTSI) system that locks the shift lever in the PARK position and prevents the driver from shifting out of PARK unless the brake pedal is depressed. The BTSI system also prevents the ignition key from being turned to the LOCK or ACCESSORY position unless the shift lever is in the PARK position.

Due to the complexity of the automatic transmissions covered in this manual and the need for specialized equipment to perform most service operations, this Chapter is limited to general diagnosis, routine maintenance, adjustments and removal and installation procedures.

If the transmission requires major repair work, leave it to a dealer service department or a transmission repair shop. However, even if a transmission shop does the repairs, you can save some money by removing and installing the transmission yourself.

2   Diagnosis - general

Note: *Automatic transmission malfunctions may be caused by five general conditions: poor engine performance, incorrect adjustments, hydraulic malfunctions, mechanical malfunctions or malfunctions in the computer or its signal network. Diagnosis of these problems should always begin with a check of the easily repaired items: fluid level and condition (see Chapter 1) and shift cable adjustment. Next, perform a road test to determine if the problem has been corrected or if more diagnosis is necessary. If the problem persists after the preliminary tests and corrections are completed, additional diagnosis should be done by a dealer service department or transmission repair shop. Refer to the Troubleshooting section at the front of this manual for information on symptoms of transmission problems.*

Preliminary checks

1   Drive the vehicle to warm up the transmission to its normal operating temperature.
2   Check the fluid level as described in Chapter 1:

a) *If the fluid level is unusually low, add enough fluid to bring the level within the area between the high and low marks on the dipstick (see Section 4 in Chapter 1), then check for external leaks (see below).*

b) *If the fluid level is abnormally high, it might have been overfilled. Drain off the excess.*

c) *If the fluid is foaming, drain it and refill the transmission, then check for coolant in the fluid or a high fluid level.*

3   Check the engine idle speed. **Note:** *If the engine is malfunctioning, do not proceed with the preliminary checks until it has been repaired and runs normally.*
4   Inspect the shift cable (see Section 3). Make sure it's properly adjusted and that it operates smoothly.

Fluid leak diagnosis

5   Most fluid leaks are usually easy to locate because they leave a visible stain and/or wet spot. Most repairs are simply a matter of replacing a seal or gasket. If a leak is more difficult to find, the following procedure will help.
6   Identify the fluid. Make sure that it's transmission fluid, not engine oil or brake fluid. One way to positively identify Automatic Transmission Fluid (ATF) is by its red color.
7   Try to pinpoint the source of the leak. Drive the vehicle several miles, then park it over a large sheet of cardboard. After a minute or two, you should be able to locate the leak by determining the source of the fluid dripping onto the cardboard.
8   Make a careful visual inspection of the suspected component and the area immediately around it. Pay particular attention to gasket mating surfaces. A flashlight and mirror

are often helpful for finding leaks in areas that are hard to see.
9   If you still can't find the leak, thoroughly clean the suspected area with a degreaser or solvent, then dry it off.
10   Drive the vehicle for several miles at normal operating temperature and varying speeds. After driving the vehicle, visually inspect the suspected component again.
11   Once you have located the leak, you must determine the source before you can repair it properly. For example, if you replace a pan gasket but the sealing flange is warped or bent, the new gasket won't stop the leak. The flange must first be straightened.
12   Before attempting to repair a leak, verify that the following conditions are corrected or they might cause another leak. **Note:** *Some of the following conditions cannot be fixed without highly specialized tools and expertise. Such problems must be referred to a transmission repair shop or a dealer service department.*

Gasket leaks

13   Inspect the pan periodically. Make sure that the bolts are tight, that no bolts are missing, that the gasket is in good condition and that the pan is flat (dents in the pan might indicate damage to the valve body inside).
14   If the pan gasket is leaking, the fluid level or the fluid pressure might be too high, the vent might be plugged, the pan bolts might be too tight, the pan sealing flange might be warped, the sealing surface of the transmission housing might be damaged, the gasket might be damaged or the transmission casting might be cracked or porous. If sealant instead of gasket material has been used to form a seal between the pan and the transmission housing, it may be the wrong type sealant.

Seal leaks

15   If a transmission seal is leaking, the fluid level or pressure might be too high, the vent might be plugged, the seal bore might be damaged, the seal itself might be damaged or incorrectly installed, the surface of the shaft protruding through the seal might be damaged or a loose bearing might be causing excessive shaft movement.
16   Make sure that the dipstick tube seal is in good condition and that the tube is correctly seated.

Case leaks

17   If the case itself appears to be leaking, the casting is porous. A porous casting must be repaired or replaced.
18   Make sure that the oil cooler hose fittings are tight and in good condition.

Fluid comes out vent pipe or fill tube

19   If this condition occurs, the transmission is overfilled, there is coolant in the fluid, the case is porous, the dipstick is incorrect, the vent is plugged or the drain-back holes are plugged.

3   Shift cable - check, adjustment and replacement

Check

1   Firmly apply the parking brake and try to momentarily operate the starter in each shift lever position. The starter should only operate when the shift lever is in the PARK OR NEUTRAL positions. If the starter operates in any position other than PARK or NEUTRAL, adjust the shift cable (see below). If, after adjustment, the starter still operates in positions other than PARK or NEUTRAL, the Transmission Range (TR) sensor is defective (see Chapter 6).

Adjustment

Refer to illustrations 3.4 and 3.6

Note: *Do not confuse adjusting the shift cable with adjusting the Brake Transmission Shift Interlock (BTSI) system. The shift cable adjuster lock tab and the BTSI lock tab are just inches apart and they both work on the same shift cable. But their functions are different. The purpose of adjusting the shift cable is to make sure that it shifts the transmission correctly and that the engine can be started only in PARK or NEUTRAL. The purpose of adjusting the BTSI system is to ensure that the shift lever cannot be moved from PARK or NEUTRAL unless the brake pedal is depressed. Although adjusting the shift cable is part of adjusting the BTSI system (see Section 4), you can adjust the shift cable without disturbing the BTSI system.*

2   Place the shift lever in the PARK position.
3   Remove the knee bolster (see Section 25 in Chapter 11).
4   Release the shift cable adjuster lock tab **(see illustration)**.
5   Raise the vehicle and support it securely

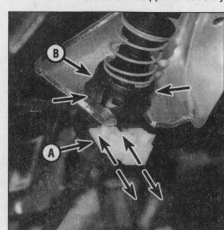

3.4 To release the shift cable adjuster lock tab (A), pull it away from the cable to its released position; to apply the lock tab, push it toward the cable until it snaps into place. To release the cable housing (B) from the cable bracket, depress the two tangs on the cable housing

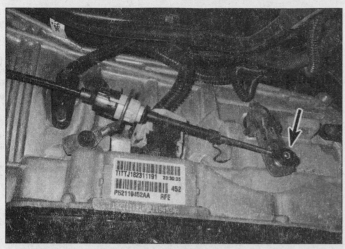

3.6 Use a screwdriver to pry the shift cable off the shift lever at the transmission

3.20 To disconnect the electrical connector (A) from the Brake Transmission Shift Interlock (BTSI) solenoid, slide the sliding lock toward you, then depress the button (B) on the slide lock and pull off the connector

on jackstands. **Note:** *The rear of the vehicle must also be raised, so the driveshaft can be turned in Step 8 (to verify that the transmission is completely engaged in PARK).*

6 Working at the transmission end of the cable, pry the cable end off the manual shift lever **(see illustration)**.

7 Verify that the manual shift lever on the transmission is all the way to the rear, in the last detent. (This is the PARK position.)

8 Verify that the park lock pawl inside the transmission is engaged by trying to rotate the driveshaft. The driveshaft will not rotate if the transmission is correctly engaged in PARK.

9 Reconnect the shift cable to the manual shift lever on the transmission.

10 Lower the vehicle.

11 With the parking brake firmly applied make sure the engine starts (don't move the shift lever from PARK yet).

12 Push the cable adjuster lock tab until it snaps into place (which indicates that the locking tangs have re-engaged the cable).

13 If the linkage appears to be adjusted correctly, but the starter still operates in any other position(s) besides PARK and NEUTRAL, replace the Transmission Range (TR) sensor (see Chapter 6).

Replacement

Refer to illustrations 3.20, 3.21 and 3.22

14 Make sure the shift lever is in the PARK position.

15 Raise the vehicle and place it securely on jackstands.

16 Working at the transmission end of the cable, pry the cable end off the manual shift lever **(see illustration 3.6)**.

17 Lower the vehicle.

18 Remove the knee bolster (see Section 23 in Chapter 11) and the steering column covers (see Section 25 in Chapter 11).

19 Remove the shift cable grommet **(see illustration 3.22)** from the firewall.

20 Disconnect the electrical connector from the Brake Transmission Shift Interlock (BTSI)

solenoid **(see illustration)**.

21 Pry the cable end off the lever on the steering column **(see illustration)**.

22 To disengage the cable assembly from the lower steering column bracket, squeeze the two tangs on the cable housing together **(see illustration 3.4)**, then pull the cable assembly straight down **(see illustration)**.

23 Installation is the reverse of removal. When you're done, adjust the cable (see Steps 2 through 13).

---

4 Brake Transmission Shift Interlock (BTSI) system - description, check and adjustment

---

Description

1 The Brake Transmission Shift Interlock (BTSI) system is a solenoid-operated device, located on the shift cable, that locks the shift

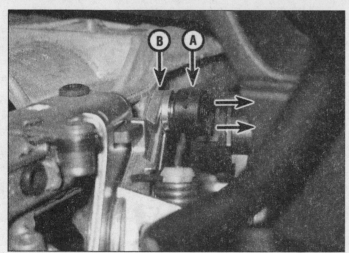

3.21 To disconnect the shift cable (A) from the shift lever pin (B), insert a flat blade screwdriver between them and pry them apart

3.22 To disengage the shift cable assembly from its mounting bracket, squeeze the two tangs on the cable housing together (see illustration 3.4), then pull the cable assembly straight down. To remove the cable assembly, disengage the grommet (A) from the cable hole in the firewall, then pull the cable through the hole into the cab

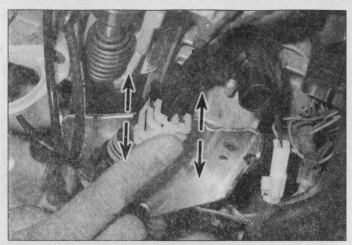

4.11 To release the Brake Transmission Shift Interlock (BTSI) cable lock tab, pull it away from the cable; to apply the lock tab, push it toward the cable

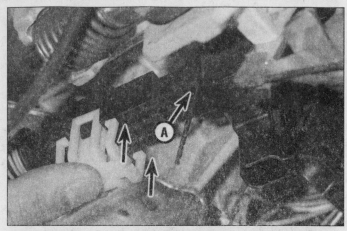

4.17 Slide the BTSI assembly up or down the shift cable as necessary until you can insert a small drill bit into the alignment hole (A) and up through the assembly, then push the BTSI lock tab toward the cable until it snaps into place and remove the drill bit

lever into the PARK position when the ignition key is in the LOCK or ACCESSORY position. When the ignition key is in the RUN position, a magnetic holding device, inline with the park lock cable, is energized. When the system is functioning correctly, the only way to unlock the shift lever and move it out of PARK is to depress the brake pedal. The BTSI system also prevents the ignition key from being turned to the LOCK or ACCESSORY position unless the shift lever is fully locked into the PARK position.

Check

2   Verify that the ignition key can be removed only in the PARK position.

3   When the shift lever is in the PARK position and the shift lever Overdrive Off ("O/D OFF") button is not activated, you should be able to rotate the ignition key from OFF to LOCK. But when the shift lever is in any gear position other than PARK (including NEUTRAL), you should not be able to rotate the ignition key to the LOCK position.

4   You should not be able to move the shift lever out of the PARK position when the ignition key is turned to the OFF position.

5   You should not be able to move the shift lever out of the PARK position when the ignition key is turned to the RUN or START position until you depress the brake pedal.

6   You should not be able to move the shift lever out of the PARK position when the ignition key is turned to the ACC or LOCK position.

7   Once in gear, with the ignition key in the RUN position, you should be able to move the shift lever between gears, or put it into NEUTRAL or PARK, without depressing the brake pedal.

8   If the BTSI system doesn't operate as described, try adjusting it as follows.

Adjustment

Refer to illustrations 4.11 and 4.17

Note: *Do not confuse adjusting the shift*

cable with adjusting the Brake Transmission Shift Interlock (BTSI) system. The shift cable adjuster lock tab and the BTSI lock tab are just inches apart and they both work on the same shift cable. But their functions are different. The purpose of adjusting the shift cable is to make sure that it shifts the transmission correctly and that the engine can be started only in PARK or NEUTRAL. The purpose of adjusting the BTSI system is to ensure that the shift lever cannot be removed from PARK or NEUTRAL unless the brake pedal is depressed. Although adjusting the shift cable is part of adjusting the BTSI system, you can adjust the shift cable without disturbing the BTSI system (see Section 3).

9   Remove the knee bolster (see Chapter 11).

10   Put the shift lever in the PARK position.

11   Release the BTSI lock tab **(see illustration)** and the shift cable adjuster lock tab **(see illustration 3.4)**.

12   Make sure that the shift lever is in the PARK position.

13   Raise the vehicle and place it securely on jackstands. (Make sure that the rear wheels are off the ground so that you can rotate the rear wheels or the driveshaft in the next step.)

14   Verify that the transmission park lock is positively engaged by trying to rotate the driveshaft (the driveshaft will not rotate when the park lock is correctly engaged).

15   Turn the ignition key to the LOCK position. (Make SURE that the ignition key is in the LOCK position, because the cable cannot be correctly adjusted with the key in any other position.)

16   Make sure that the shift cable is free to self-adjust itself by pushing it to the rear and releasing it. Then push the shift cable lock tab **(see illustration 3.4)** toward the cable until it snaps into place (which indicates that the locking tangs have re-engaged the cable).

17   Locate the BTSI alignment hole **(see illustration)** on the underside of the BTSI mechanism, between the BTSI lock tab and

the electrical terminal for the BTSI solenoid. Slide the BTSI assembly up or down on the shift cable until you can insert an appropriate size drill bit into the alignment hole and through the mechanism.

18   Push the BTSI lock tab toward the shift cable **(see illustration 4.17)** until it snaps into place, then remove the drill bit.

19   Install the knee bolster (see Chapter 11).

---

5   Transmission oil cooler - removal and installation

Refer to illustration 5.4

Note: *All vehicles with an automatic transmission are equipped with an external air-to-oil cooler and an internal oil-to-coolant cooler as standard or optional equipment. All external transmission oil coolers are mounted in front of the radiator in a similar fashion, although they vary in size and in the location and number of mounting bolts used.*

1   Disconnect the cable from the negative battery terminal.

2   Put a drain pan underneath the oil cooler line fittings to catch any spilled transmission fluid.

3   Raise the front of the vehicle and place it securely on jackstands.

4   Using a quick-connect release tool (available at most auto parts stores), disconnect the transmission oil cooler line fittings **(see illustration)**. Plug the lines to prevent fluid spills.

5   Detach the transmission oil cooler lines from the radiator side tank (optional equipment) or from the transmission.

6   Remove the upper radiator panel cover and support (see Chapter 3) to access the cooler.

7   Remove the transmission oil cooler mounting bolts and remove the cooler. Be careful not to damage the oil cooler tubes or the radiator cooling fins.

8   If you removed the cooler in order to flush it after a transmission failure, have it

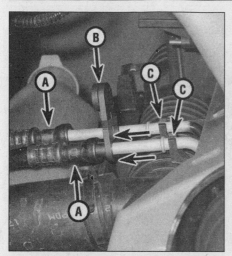

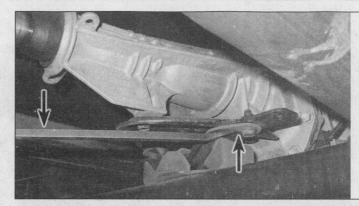

6.2 To check the transmission mount, insert a large screwdriver between the extension housing and the crossmember and try to lever the transmission up

5.4 To disconnect each transmission oil cooler line fitting (A), insert the special quick-connect release tool (B) into each fitting, push the tool into the fitting until it releases the locking fingers inside the fitting, then pull the two sides of the fitting apart. Once both fittings are disconnected, detach both lines from the clips (C) on the radiator side tank

flushed by a dealer service department or by a transmission shop. A number of special tools are needed to flush the cooler correctly.

9   Installation is the reverse of removal. When you're done, check the transmission fluid level and add some if necessary (see Chapter 1).

6   Transmission mount - check and replacement

Check

Refer to illustration 6.2

1   Raise the vehicle and support it securely on jackstands.

2   Insert a large screwdriver or prybar into the space between the transmission exten-sion housing and the crossmember and try to pry the transmission up slightly **(see illustra-tion)**.

3   The transmission should not move much at all and the rubber in the center of the mount should fully insulate the center of the mount from the mount bracket around it.

Replacement

4   To replace the mount, remove the bolts or nuts attaching the mount to the crossmember and the bolts attaching the mount to the trans-mission.

5   Raise the transmission slightly with a jack and remove the mount.

6   Installation is the reverse of the removal procedure. Be sure to tighten all fasteners securely.

7   Automatic transmission - removal and installation

Removal

Refer to illustrations 7.10, 7.11, 7.12, 7.13, 7.19, 7.21 and 7.24

Caution: *The transmission and torque con-verter must be removed as a single assem-bly. If you try to leave the torque converter attached to the driveplate, the converter driveplate, pump bushing and oil seal will be* *damaged. The driveplate is not designed to support the load, so none of the weight of the transmission should be allowed to rest on the plate during removal.*

1   Disconnect the cable from the negative battery terminal (see Chapter 5, Section 1).

2   Raise the vehicle and support it securely on jackstands.

3   On 4WD models, remove the skid plate.

4   Remove all exhaust components that interfere with transmission removal (see Chapter 4). **Note:** *On models equipped with the 42RLE transmission, remove the exhaust crossover pipe and mounting brackets.*

5   Remove the oil pan, drain the transmis-sion fluid and reinstall the pan (see Chap-ter 1).

6   Disconnect the output speed sensor and input speed sensor connectors (see Chap-ter 6).

7   Remove the starter motor (see Chap-ter 5).

8   Mark the yokes and remove the driveshaft (see Chapter 8). On 4WD models, remove both driveshafts.

9   Remove the Crankshaft Position (CKP) sensor, which is located at the rear of the engine block near the driveplate (see Chap-ter 6).

10   Remove the transmission brace **(see illustration)**.

11   Remove the torque converter access cover, if equipped **(see illustration)**.

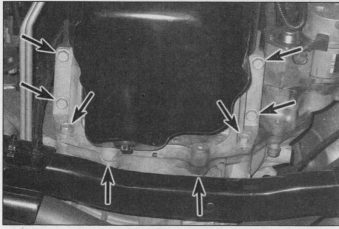

7.10 To remove the transmission brace, remove these bolts (Hemi engine shown, other transmission braces similar)

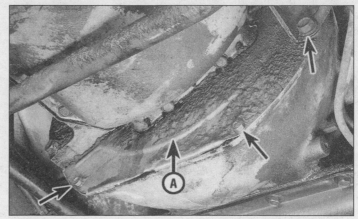

7.11 To remove the torque converter access cover (A), remove all the retaining bolts and pull it off. The number and location of the cover bolts varies with the engine-transmission combination

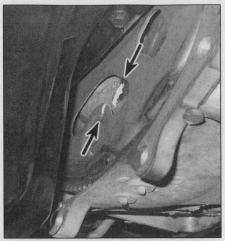

7.12 If you're going to re-use the old torque converter, mark the relationship of the torque converter to the driveplate to ensure that their dynamic balance is preserved when the torque converter is reattached

7.13 To remove the torque converter-to-driveplate bolts, turn the crankshaft to access each bolt

12   Mark the relationship of the torque converter to the driveplate **(see illustration)** to ensure that their dynamic balance is maintained when the converter is reattached to the driveplate.

13   Remove the torque converter-to-driveplate bolts **(see illustration)**. Turn the crankshaft for access to each bolt.

14   Disconnect all electrical connectors from the transmission. Generally speaking, the connectors to various electrical and/or electronic devices on the transmission are different in shape, color and the number of terminals, so there's little danger of accidentally reconnecting a connector to the wrong device. The wiring harness is also designed so that each connector will only reach the device to which it's supposed to be connected. However, if any of the connectors look identical or look like they could be accidentally reconnected

to the wrong device, be sure to mark them to prevent mix-ups.

15   Disconnect the shift cable from the transmission (see Section 3).

16   On 4WD models, disconnect the shift rod from the transfer case shift lever (see Chapter 7C).

17   Support the rear end of the transmission with a floor jack, then raise the transmission slightly to take the weight off the crossmember.

18   Unbolt the transmission mounting bracket from the transmission and from the crossmember and remove the bracket.

19   Unbolt and remove the transmission crossmember **(see illustration)**.

20   On 4WD models, remove the transfer case (see Chapter 7C). **Note:** *If you are not planning to replace the transmission, but are removing it in order to gain access to other components such as the torque converter, it isn't really necessary to remove the transfer case. However, the two components are awkward and heavy when removed and installed as a single assembly. They're much easier to maneuver off and on as separate units. If you*

decide to leave the transfer case attached, disconnect the shift rod from the transfer case shift lever, or remove the shift lever from the transfer case and tie the rod and lever to the chassis (see Chapter 7C). **Warning:** *If you decide to remove the transfer case and transmission as a single assembly, use safety chains to help stabilize them and to prevent them from falling off the jack head, which could cause serious damage to the transmission and/or transfer case and serious bodily injury to you.*

21   Using a flare-nut wrench, disconnect the transmission cooler lines from the transmission **(see illustration)**. Plug the ends of the lines to prevent fluid from leaking out after you disconnect them.

22   Remove the oil filler tube bracket bolts and withdraw the tube from the transmission. Don't lose the filler tube seal (unless it's damaged, in which case you should replace it). On 4WD models, remove the bolt that attaches the transfer case vent tube to the converter housing (unless you already did so when removing the transfer case).

23   Support the transmission with a trans-

7.19 Location of the crossmember mounting bolts and the transmission mount fasteners

7.21 To prevent damage to the lines, use a back-up wrench on the stationary fittings when unscrewing the transmission cooler line fittings

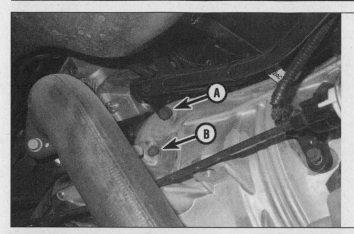

7.24 To detach the transmission from the engine, remove all transmission-to-engine bolts (A) and engine-to-transmission bolts (B) (left side shown, right side similar; not all bolts visible in this photo)

mission jack (available at most equipment rental facilities) and secure the transmission to the jack with safety chains. Support the engine with a jack. Use a block of wood under the oil pan to spread the load.

24   Remove the bolts securing the transmission to the engine **(see illustration)**. A long extension and a U-joint socket will greatly simplify this step. **Note:** *The upper bolts are easier to remove after the transmission has been lowered (see the next Step). Also, on some models, you might have to remove the oil filter (see Chapter 1) before you can remove the lower right (passenger's side) bolt.*

25   Lower the engine and transmission slightly and clamp a pair of locking pliers onto the lower portion of the transmission case, just in front of the torque converter. The pliers will prevent the torque converter from falling out while you're removing the transmission.

26   Move the transmission to the rear to disengage it from the engine block dowel pins and make sure the torque converter is detached from the driveplate. Lower the transmission with the jack.

Installation

27   Prior to installation, make sure the torque converter is securely engaged in the pump. If you've removed the converter, spread transmission fluid on the torque converter rear hub, where the transmission front seal rides. With the front of the transmission facing up,

rotate the converter back and forth. It should drop down into the transmission front pump in stages. To make sure the converter is fully engaged, lay a straightedge across the transmission-to-engine mating surface and make sure the converter lugs are at least 1/2-inch below the straightedge. Reinstall the locking pliers to hold the converter in this position.

28   With the transmission secured to the jack, raise it into position. Connect the transmission fluid cooler lines.

29   Turn the torque converter to line up the holes with the holes in the driveplate. The marks on the torque converter and driveplate made during removal must line up.

30   Move the transmission forward carefully until the dowel pins and the transmission are engaged. Make sure the transmission mates with the engine with no gap. If there's a gap, make sure there are no wires or other objects pinched between the engine and transmission and also make sure the torque converter is completely engaged in the transmission front pump. Try to rotate the converter - if it doesn't rotate easily, it's probably not fully engaged in the pump. If necessary, lower the transmission and install the converter fully.

31   Install the transmission-to-engine bolts and tighten them to the torque listed in this Chapter's Specifications, if applicable (if there's no torque specification for the transmission that you're servicing, tighten the bolts securely). As you're tightening the bolts, make sure that the engine and transmission mate

completely at all points. If not, find out why. Never try to force the engine and transmission together with the transmission-to-engine bolts or you'll break the transmission case!

32   Install the torque converter-to-driveplate bolts. Tighten them to the torque listed in this Chapter's Specifications, if applicable (if there's no torque specification for the transmission that you're servicing, tighten the bolts securely). **Caution:** *Using the correct length bolts for bolting the converter to the driveplate is critical. A number of different converters are used on the vehicles covered by this manual. If the bolts are too long, they will damage the converter. If you're planning to use new bolts, make sure you obtain original equipment replacement bolts of the same length.* **Note:** *Install all of the bolts before tightening any of them.*

33   Install the transmission brace and tighten the bolts to the torque listed in the Chapter 2 Specifications, in the sequence indicated in *Oil pan - removal and installation.*

34   The remainder of installation is the reverse of removal.

35   When you're done, refill the transmission with the specified fluid (see Chapter 1), run the engine and check for fluid leaks.

8   Automatic transmission overhaul - general information

In the event of a fault occurring, it will be necessary to establish whether the fault is electrical, mechanical or hydraulic in nature, before repair work can be contemplated. Diagnosis requires detailed knowledge of the transmission's operation and construction, as well as access to specialized test equipment, and so is deemed to be beyond the scope of this manual. It is therefore essential that problems with the automatic transmission are referred to a dealer service department or other qualified repair facility for assessment.

Note that a faulty transmission should not be removed before the vehicle has been assessed by a knowledgeable technician equipped with the proper tools, as troubleshooting must be performed with the transmission installed in the vehicle.

Notes

Chapter 7 Part C
Transfer case

Contents

Specifications

Torque specifications

	Ft-lbs
Electric shift motor mounting bolts	12 to 18
Transfer case-to-transmission bolts/nuts	20 to 25
Companion flange nut	90 to 130

1   General information

The transfer case is a device which transmits power from the transmission to the front and rear driveshafts. The models covered by this manual may be equipped with any one of the following transfer cases, all of them manufactured by New Venture (NV):

a) *The NV144 transfer cases*
b) *The NV244 GEN II transfer case*
c) *The NV233 and NV244 transfer cases*

We don't recommend trying to rebuild any of these transfer cases at home. They're difficult to overhaul without special tools, and rebuilt units may even be available (on an exchange basis) for less than it would cost to rebuild your own. However, there are a number of components that you can check, adjust and/or replace - and those items are covered in this Chapter.

2   Shift range selector switch - replacement

1   Disconnect the cable from the negative battery terminal (see Chapter 5, Section 1).
2   Remove the center instrument panel bezel (see Chapter 11, *Dashboard trim panels - removal and installation*).
3   Disconnect the switch assembly electrical connectors.
4   Separate the shift range selector switch from the panel bezel.
5   Installation is the reverse of the removal.

3   Electric shift motor - replacement

Note: *New shift motors are packaged with the shift motor positioned in the 2WD/AWD mode. The transfer case must be selected for 2WD/AWD before the shift motor can be installed.*
1   Disconnect the cable from the negative battery terminal (see Chapter 5, Section 1).
2   Raise the vehicle and support it securely on jackstands.
3   Disconnect the shift motor and the mode sensor connectors.
4   Remove the shift motor and mode sensor assembly mounting bolts and separate the unit from the transfer case.
5   Installation is the reverse of removal. Replace the shift sector O-ring with a new part. If the sector shaft does not align with the

4.9 Use a seal removal tool to pry the transfer case seal out of the housing

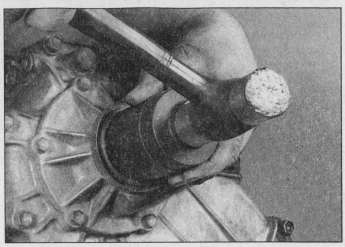

4.11 The new seal can be driven into place using a seal installer tool or a large socket

shift motor, manually shift the transfer case to the correct position.

6   Tighten the electric shift motor mounting bolts to the torque Specifications listed in this Chapter.

4   Oil seal - replacement

1   Disconnect the cable from the negative battery terminal (see Chapter 5, Section 1).
2   Raise the vehicle and support it securely on jackstands.
3   Remove the skid plate, if equipped.
4   Drain the transfer case lubricant (see Chapter 1).

Front (output shaft) seal

Refer to illustrations 4.9 and 4.11

5   Remove the front driveshaft (see Chapter 8).
6   On models equipped with a companion flange, it will be necessary to remove the companion flange nut and flange from the transfer case. Tap the companion flange off the output shaft with a brass or plastic hammer.
7   On models not equipped with the com-

panion flange, remove the front driveshaft seal boot clamp and slide the boot from the transfer case slinger.

8   Carefully bend the slinger away from the transfer case and remove it from the shaft. It may be necessary to tap on the slinger using a punch and hammer to jar it loose from the transfer case shaft.

9   Carefully pry out the old seal with a screwdriver or a seal removal tool **(see illustration)**. Make sure you don't scratch or gouge the seal bore.

10   Lubricate the lips and the outer diameter of the new seal with multi-purpose grease. Place the seal in position, square to the bore, making sure the garter spring faces toward the inside of the transfer case.

11   Use a seal driver or a suitable equivalent to drive the seal into place. A large deep socket **(see illustration)** with an outside circumference slightly smaller than the circumference of the new seal will work fine. Start the seal in the bore with light hammer taps. Continue tapping the seal into place until it is recessed the correct amount.

12   Install the seal slinger and driveshaft seal boot. Secure the boot with a new clamp.

13   Install the companion flange, if equipped,

onto the transfer case output shaft. Install the flange nut and tighten the nut to the torque listed in this Chapter's Specifications.

14   Install the front driveshaft (see Chapter 8).

15   Remove the jackstands and lower the vehicle.

Extension housing seal

16   This procedure is identical to the extension housing seal replacement procedure for the transmission (see Chapter 7A).

5   Transfer case - removal and installation

Note: *Before starting this procedure, shift the transfer case into 2WD or AWD.*

Removal

Refer to illustration 5.11

1   Disconnect the cable from the negative battery terminal (see Chapter 5, Section 1).
2   Raise the vehicle and support it securely on jackstands.
3   Remove the skid plate, if equipped.
4   Drain the transfer case lubricant (see Chapter 1).
5   Detach all vacuum/vent lines, if equipped, and electrical connectors from the transfer case.
6   Disconnect the transfer case shift motor and transfer case sensor connectors.
7   Remove the front and rear driveshafts (see Chapter 8).
8   On some models, it may be necessary to remove the rear crossmember.
9   Support the transmission with a transmission jack.
10   Support the transfer case with a transmission jack. Secure the transfer case to the transmission jack with safety chains.
11   Remove the transfer case-to-transmission bolts/nuts **(see illustration)**.

5.11 Remove the transfer case bolts/nuts from the transmission - remaining bolts/nuts hidden from view

12   Make a final check that all wires and hoses have been disconnected from the transfer case, then move the transfer case and jack toward the rear of the vehicle until the transfer case is clear of the transmission. Keep the transfer case level as this is done.

13   Once the input shaft is clear, lower the transfer case and remove it from under the vehicle.

Installation

14   Remove all gasket material from the rear of the transmission. Apply RTV sealant to both sides of the transfer-case-to-transmission gasket and position the gasket on the mating surface of the transmission.

15   With the transfer case secured to the jack as on removal, raise it into position behind the transmission and then carefully slide it forward, engaging the input shaft with the transmission output shaft. Do not use excessive force to install the transfer case - if the input shaft does not slide into place, readjust the angle so it is level and/or turn the input shaft so the splines engage properly with the transmission.

16   Install the transfer case-to-transmission bolts/nuts, tightening them to the torque listed in this Chapter's Specifications.

17   Remove the safety chains and remove the jack supporting the transfer case.

18   Install the rear crossmember, if removed.

19   Remove the transmission jack from under the transmission.

20   Install the driveshafts (see Chapter 8).

21   Reattach all vacuum and/or vent lines. Plug in all electrical connectors.

22   Connect the transfer case shift motor and transfer case sensor electrical connectors.

23   Refill the transfer case with lubricant (see Chapter 1). If the vehicle has a manual transmission, this is also a good time to check the lubricant level for the transmission (see Chapter 1).

24   Install the skid plate, if equipped.

25   Remove the jackstands and lower the vehicle.

26   Connect the negative battery cable.

27   Road test the vehicle for proper operation and check for leakage.

6   Transfer case overhaul - general information

Overhauling a transfer case is a difficult job for the do-it-yourselfer. It involves the disassembly and reassembly of many small parts. Numerous clearances must be precisely measured and, if necessary, changed with select fit spacers and snap-rings. As a result, if transfer case problems arise, it can be removed and installed by a competent do-it-yourselfer, but overhaul should be left to a transmission repair shop. Rebuilt transfer cases may be available - check with your dealer parts department and auto parts stores. At any rate, the time and money involved in an overhaul is almost sure to exceed the cost of a rebuilt unit.

Nevertheless, it's not impossible for an inexperienced mechanic to rebuild a transfer case if the special tools are available and the job is done in a deliberate step-by-step manner so nothing is overlooked.

The tools necessary for an overhaul include internal and external snap-ring pliers, a bearing puller, a slide hammer, a set of pin punches, a dial indicator and possibly a hydraulic press. In addition, a large, sturdy workbench and a vise or transmission stand will be required.

During disassembly of the transfer case, make careful notes of how each piece comes off, where it fits in relation to other pieces and what holds it in place. Note how parts are installed when you remove them; this will make it much easier to get the transfer case back together.

Before taking the transfer case apart for repair, it will help if you have some idea what area of the transfer case is malfunctioning. Certain problems can be closely tied to specific areas in the transfer case, which can make component examination and replacement easier. Refer to the *Troubleshooting* section in the introductory pages of this manual for information regarding possible sources of trouble.

Notes

Chapter 8
Clutch and driveline

Contents

Specifications

General

Clutch hydraulic fluid type	See Chapter 1
Clutch disc lining thickness	1/16 inch (above rivet)

Torque specifications

Ft-lbs (unless otherwise indicated)

Clutch

Pressure plate-to-flywheel bolts	
5/16-inch diameter bolts	17
3/8-inch diameter bolts	30
Clutch release cylinder mounting nuts	17
Clutch master cylinder mounting nuts	40
Clutch fluid reservoir mounting screws	40 in-lbs
Flywheel bolts	
V6 and 5.2L/5.9L V8	55
4.7L V8	70

Driveshaft

Front driveshaft-to-differential companion flange	85
Front driveshaft-to-transfer case companion flange (2006 Dakota)	30
Rear driveshaft-to-differential companion flange	85
Rear driveshaft-to-manual transmission companion flange	85
Center support bearing bolts	40

Torque specifications (continued)

Ft-lbs (unless otherwise indicated)

Driveaxles (4WD models)
Driveaxle/hub nut 185

Rear axle
Pinion shaft lock bolt
    Durango models... 18.5
    Dakota models .... 96 in-lbs
Pinion nut initial torque 210

Front axle (4WD models)
Front axle assembly mounting fasteners
    Durango models... 70
    Dakota models 85

---

1   General information

The information in this Chapter deals with the components from the rear of the engine to the rear wheels, except for the transmission (and transfer case, if equipped), which is dealt with in the previous Chapter. For the purposes of this Chapter, these components are grouped into three categories: clutch, driveshaft and axles. Separate Sections within this Chapter offer general descriptions and checking procedures for components in each of the three groups.

Since nearly all the procedures covered in this Chapter involve working under the vehicle, make sure it's securely supported on sturdy jackstands or on a hoist where the vehicle can be easily raised and lowered.

---

2   Clutch - description and check

1   All vehicles with a manual transmission use a single dry plate, diaphragm spring type clutch. The clutch disc has a splined hub which allows it to slide along the splines of the transmission input shaft. The clutch and pressure plate are held in contact by spring pressure exerted by the diaphragm in the pressure plate.

2   The clutch release system is operated by hydraulic pressure. The hydraulic release system consists of the clutch pedal, a master cylinder and fluid reservoir, the hydraulic line, a release (or slave) cylinder which actuates the clutch release lever and the clutch release (or throwout) bearing.

3   When pressure is applied to the clutch pedal to release the clutch, hydraulic pressure is exerted against the outer end of the clutch release lever. As the lever pivots, the shaft fingers push against the release bearing. The bearing pushes against the fingers of the diaphragm spring of the pressure plate assembly, which in turn releases the clutch plate.

4   Terminology can be a problem when discussing the clutch components because common names are in some cases different from those used by the manufacturer. For example, the driven plate is also called the clutch plate or disc, the clutch release bearing is sometimes called a throwout bearing, the release cylinder is sometimes called the operating or slave cylinder.

5   Other than to replace components with obvious damage, some preliminary checks should be performed to diagnose clutch problems.

a) *The first check should be of the fluid level in the clutch master cylinder. If the fluid level is excessively low, add fluid as necessary and inspect the hydraulic sys-tem for leaks (fluid level will actually rise as the clutch wears).*

b) *To check "clutch spin down time," run the engine at normal idle speed with the transmission in Neutral (clutch pedal up - engaged). Disengage the clutch (pedal down), wait several seconds and shift the transmission into Reverse. No grinding noise should be heard. A grinding noise would most likely indicate a problem in the pressure plate or the clutch disc.*

c) *To check for complete clutch release, run the engine (with the parking brake applied to prevent movement) and hold the clutch pedal approximately 1/2-inch from the floor. Shift the transmission between First gear and Reverse several times. If the shift is hard or the transmission grinds, component failure is indicated. Check the release cylinder pushrod travel. With the clutch pedal depressed completely, the release cylinder pushrod should extend substantially. If it doesn't, check the fluid level in the clutch master cylinder (see Chapter 1).*

d) *Visually inspect the pivot bushing at the top of the clutch pedal to make sure there is no binding or excessive play.*

e) *Crawl under the vehicle and make sure the clutch release lever is solidly mounted on the ball stud.*

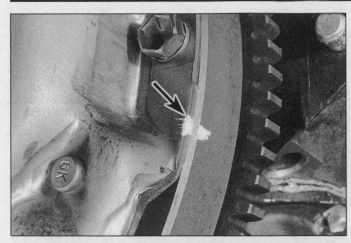

4.6 Be sure to mark the pressure plate and flywheel in order to insure proper alignment during installation (this won't be necessary if a new pressure plate is to be installed)

4.9 Check the flywheel for cracks, hot spots and other obvious defects (slight imperfections can be removed by a machine shop)

3 Clutch release system - removal and installation

Note: *The clutch release system is serviced as a complete unit and has been bled of air at the factory, as individual components or rebuild kits are not available separately. There are no provisions for adjustment of clutch pedal height or freeplay.*

Removal

1   Disconnect the cable from the negative battery terminal (see Chapter 5, Section 1).

Master cylinder

2   Remove the clip that attaches the clutch master cylinder pushrod to the clutch pedal.
3   Slide the clutch master cylinder pushrod off the clutch pedal pin.
4   Inspect the condition of the bushing on the pushrod and replace it if it's worn or damaged.
5   Unplug the electrical connector from the clutch pedal position switch.
6   To avoid spillage during removal, verify that the cap on the clutch fluid reservoir is tight.
7   Remove the nuts attaching the clutch fluid reservoir to the engine firewall.
8   Working inside the vehicle, unscrew the clutch master cylinder mounting nuts, then detach the cylinder from the firewall in the engine compartment. Using a piece of wire, secure the cylinder and reservoir to a nearby component while the release cylinder is removed.

Release cylinder

9   Raise the vehicle and support it securely on jackstands.
10   Remove the two release cylinder mounting nuts.
11   Detach the release cylinder from the transmission.
12   If the entire system is being removed or replaced, carefully lift the system from the engine compartment.

Installation

13   Installation is the reverse of removal. If the fluid level is extremely low, fill the clutch master cylinder reservoir with the fluid recommended in the Chapter 1 Specifications Section. Don't add too much, though, because the fluid level actually rises as the clutch components wear.

4 Clutch components - removal, inspection and installation

Warning: *Dust produced by clutch wear and deposited on clutch components is hazardous to your health. DO NOT blow it out with compressed air and DO NOT inhale it. DO NOT use gasoline or petroleum-based solvents to remove the dust. Brake system cleaner should be used to flush the dust into a drain pan. After the clutch components are wiped clean with a rag, dispose of the contaminated rags and cleaner in a covered, marked container.*

Removal

Refer to illustration 4.6

1   Access to the clutch components is normally accomplished by removing the transmission, leaving the engine in the vehicle. If, of course, the engine is being removed for major overhaul, then check the clutch for wear and replace worn components as necessary. However, the relatively low cost of the clutch components compared to the time and trouble spent gaining access to them warrants their replacement anytime the engine or transmission is removed, unless they are new or in near perfect condition. The following procedures are based on the assumption the engine will stay in place.
2   Unbolt the release cylinder and position it out of the way (see Section 3).
3   Referring to Chapter 7 Part A, remove the transmission from the vehicle. Support the engine while the transmission is out. Prefer-

ably, an engine hoist should be used to support it from above. However, if a jack is used underneath the engine, make sure a piece of wood is positioned between the jack and oil pan to spread the load. **Caution:** *The pickup for the oil pump is very close to the bottom of the oil pan. If the pan is bent or distorted in any way, engine oil starvation could occur.*
4   The clutch fork and release bearing can remain attached to the bellhousing for the time being.
5   To support the clutch disc during removal, install a clutch alignment tool through the clutch disc hub.
6   Carefully inspect the flywheel and pressure plate for indexing marks. The marks are usually an X, an O or a white letter. If they cannot be found, scribe marks yourself so the pressure plate and the flywheel will be in the same alignment during installation **(see illustration)**.
7   Turning each bolt only 1/4-turn at a time, loosen the pressure plate-to-flywheel bolts. Work in a criss-cross pattern until all spring pressure is relieved. Then hold the pressure plate securely and completely remove the bolts, followed by the pressure plate and clutch disc.

Inspection

Refer to illustrations 4.9, 4.11, 4.13a and 4.13b

8   Ordinarily, when a problem occurs in the clutch, it can be attributed to wear of the clutch driven plate assembly (clutch disc). However, all components should be inspected at this time.
9   Inspect the flywheel for cracks, heat checking, grooves and other obvious defects **(see illustration)**. If the imperfections are slight, a machine shop can machine the surface flat and smooth, which is highly recommended regardless of the surface appearance. Refer to Chapter 2 for the flywheel removal and installation procedure.
10   Inspect the pilot bearing (see Section 6).
11   Inspect the lining on the clutch disc.

There should be at least 1/16-inch of lining above the rivet heads. Check for loose rivets, distortion, cracks, broken springs and other obvious damage **(see illustration)**. As mentioned above, ordinarily the clutch disc is routinely replaced, so if in doubt about the condition, replace it with a new one.

12   The release bearing should also be replaced along with the clutch disc (see Section 5).

13   Check the machined surfaces and the diaphragm spring fingers of the pressure plate **(see illustrations)**. If the surface is grooved or otherwise damaged, replace the pressure plate. Also check for obvious damage, distortion, cracking, etc. Light glazing can be removed with sandpaper or emery cloth. If a new pressure plate is required, new and factory-rebuilt units are available.

Installation

Refer to illustration 4.15

14   Before installation, clean the flywheel and pressure plate machined surfaces with brake system cleaner. It's important that no oil or grease is on these surfaces or the lining of the clutch disc. Handle the parts only with clean hands.

15   Position the clutch disc and pressure plate against the flywheel with the clutch held in place with an alignment tool **(see illustra-**

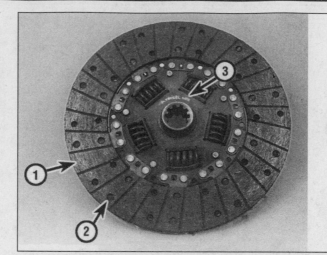

4.11 The clutch plate

1   *Lining - This will wear down in use*
2   *Rivets - These secure the lining and will damage the flywheel or pressure plate if allowed to contact the surfaces*
3   *Markings - "Flywheel side" or something similar*

tion). Make sure it's installed properly (most replacement clutch plates will be marked "flywheel side" or something similar - if not marked, install the clutch disc with the damper springs toward the transmission).

16   Tighten the pressure plate-to-flywheel bolts only finger tight, working around the pressure plate.

17   Center the clutch disc by ensuring the alignment tool extends through the splined hub and into the pilot bearing in the crankshaft. Wiggle the tool up, down or side-to-side

as needed to bottom the tool in the pilot bearing. Tighten the pressure plate-to-flywheel bolts a little at a time, working in a criss-cross pattern to prevent distorting the cover. After all of the bolts are snug, tighten them to the torque listed in this Chapter's Specifications. Remove the alignment tool.

18   Using high-temperature grease, lubricate the inner groove of the release bearing. Also place grease on the release lever contact areas and the transmission input shaft bearing retainer.

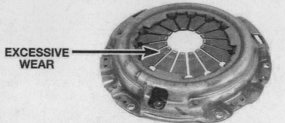

EXCESSIVE WEAR

NORMAL FINGER WEAR   **EXCESSIVE FINGER WEAR**   **BROKEN OR BENT FINGERS**

4.13a Replace the pressure plate if excessive wear is noted

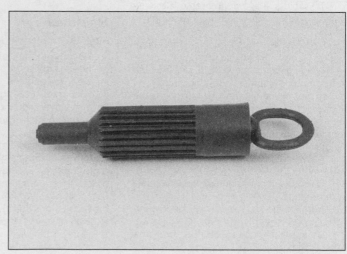

4.13b Examine the pressure plate friction surface for score marks, cracks and evidence of overheating

4.15 Center the clutch disc using a clutch alignment tool

5.3 To detach the release bearing from the release fork, slide the bearing down and disengage the wire retainers from their slots in the fork

5.4 To check the release bearing, hold the hub in one hand and turn the bearing with the other; if it feels rough or dry, replace it

5.5 Remove the wire retainer clip for the pivot ball and check to make sure it still fits tightly; if it's loose, replace it

19   Install the clutch release bearing as described in Section 5.

20   Install the transmission, release cylinder and all components removed previously. Tighten all fasteners to the proper torque specifications.

5   Clutch release bearing - removal, inspection and installation

Warning: *Dust produced by clutch wear and deposited on clutch components is hazardous to your health. DO NOT blow it out with compressed air and DO NOT inhale it. DO NOT use gasoline or petroleum-based solvents to remove the dust. Brake system cleaner should be used to flush the dust into a drain pan. After the clutch components are wiped clean with a rag, dispose of the contaminated rags and cleaner in a covered, marked container.*

Removal

Refer to illustration 5.3

1   Disconnect the cable from the negative battery terminal (see Chapter 5, Section 1).

2   Remove the transmission and bellhousing (see Chapter 7, Part A).

3   Remove the clutch release fork from the pivot stud, then remove the bearing and sleeve from the fork **(see illustration).**

Inspection

Refer to illustrations 5.4 and 5.5

4   Hold the center of the bearing and rotate the outer portion while applying pressure **(see illustration).** If the bearing doesn't turn smoothly or if it's noisy, remove it from the sleeve and replace it with a new one. Wipe the bearing with a clean rag and inspect it for damage, wear and cracks. Don't immerse the bearing in solvent - it's sealed for life and to do so would ruin it. Also check the release

fork for cracks and other damage.

5   Check the wire retainer clip on the release fork to make sure it still fits tightly on the pivot ball; if not, replace it **(see illustration).**

Installation

Refer to illustrations 5.6a and 5.6b

6   Apply a light coat of high-temperature grease to the release fork pivot ball, the contact points of the release fork, the bore of the release bearing, the splines of the transmission input shaft and the release bearing sliding surface on the input shaft bearing retainer **(see illustrations).**

7   Attach the release bearing and sleeve to the release fork.

8   Apply a light coat of high-temperature grease to the face of the release bearing, where it contacts the pressure plate diaphragm fingers.

9   The remainder of installation is the reverse of the removal procedure.

5.6a Using high-temperature grease, lubricate the inner groove of the release bearing

6   Pilot bearing - inspection and replacement

Refer to illustrations 6.5 and 6.6

1   The clutch pilot bearing is pressed into the rear of the crankshaft. It is greased at the factory and does not require additional lubrication. Its primary purpose is to support the front of the transmission input shaft. The pilot bearing should be inspected whenever the clutch components are removed from the engine. Due to its inaccessibility, if you are in doubt as to its condition, replace it with a new one. **Note:** *If the engine has been removed from the vehicle, disregard the following steps which do not apply.*

2   Remove the transmission (refer to Chapter 7 Part A).

3   Remove the clutch components (see Section 4).

4   Inspect for any excessive wear, scoring, lack of grease, dryness or obvious damage. If

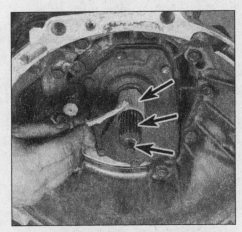

5.6b Lightly lubricate the bearing retainer surface on which the release bearing slides, the input shaft splines and the nose of the input shaft that is supported by the pilot bearing

any of these conditions are noted, the bearing should be replaced. A flashlight will be helpful to direct light into the recess.

5   Removal can be accomplished with a slide hammer fitted with a puller attachment **(see illustration),** which are available at most auto parts stores or equipment rental yards.

6   To install the new bearing, lightly lubricate the outside surface with multi-purpose grease, then drive it into the recess with a hammer and bearing/bushing driver **(see illustration).** Make sure the bearing seal faces toward the transmission. If you don't have a bearing driver, carefully tap it into place with a hammer and a socket. **Caution:** *Be careful not to let the bearing become cocked in the bore.*

7   Install the clutch components, transmission and all other components removed previously, tightening all fasteners properly.

7   Clutch pedal position switch - check and replacement

Check

1   The clutch pedal position switch, which is part of the starter relay circuit, is mounted on the clutch master cylinder pushrod. The switch closes the starter relay circuit only when the clutch pedal is fully depressed.

2   To test the switch, verify that the engine will not crank over when the clutch pedal is in the released position, and that it does crank over with the pedal depressed.

3   If the engine starts without depressing the clutch pedal, replace the switch.

Replacement

4   The switch is an integral part of the clutch master cylinder pushrod and can't be serviced separately. If the switch must be replaced, so must the clutch hydraulic release system (see Section 3).

8   Driveshaft(s) - general information

The driveshaft is of tubular construction and may be of a one or two-section type. The front driveshaft on 4WD models is bolted to a flange at the front axle pinion, while attachment to the transfer case may include a bolted flange or a splined sliding sleeve connecting it to the output shaft. The attachment of the rear driveshaft to the rear axle pinion flange is connected by bolted flange, while attachment to the transmission or transfer case may include a bolted flange or a splined sliding sleeve connecting it to the output shaft. The type of connection used depends on the transmission type. Where a two-section shaft is used, the shaft is supported near its forward end on a ball bearing which is flexibly mounted in a bracket attached to the frame crossmember.

The driveshaft is finely balanced during manufacture and it is recommended that care be used when universal joints are replaced

6.5 A small slide-hammer puller is handy for removing the pilot bearing

to help maintain this balance. It is sometimes better to have the universal joints replaced by a dealership or shop specializing in this type of work. If you replace the joints yourself, mark each individual yoke in relation to the one opposite in order to maintain the balance. Do not drop the assembly during servicing operations.

9   Driveshaft(s) - removal and installation

Note: *The manufacturer recommends replacing driveshaft fasteners with new ones when installing the driveshaft.*

Rear driveshaft

Removal

Refer to illustrations 9.2 and 9.3

Note: *Where a two-piece driveshaft is involved, the rear shaft must be removed before the front shaft.*

1   Raise the vehicle and support it securely on jackstands.

2   Use chalk or a scribe to "index" the relationship of the driveshaft to the differential

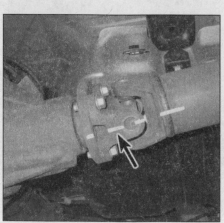

9.2 Mark the relationship of the driveshaft to the pinion flange

6.6 If available, use a bearing driver to install the pilot bearing

axle assembly mating flange. This ensures correct alignment when the driveshaft is reinstalled **(see illustration).**

3   Remove the bolts securing the driveshaft flange to the differential pinion flange **(see illustration).** Turn the driveshaft (or wheels) as necessary to bring the bolts into the most accessible position.

4   Pry the universal joint away from its mating flange or yoke and remove the shaft from the flange. Be careful not to let the caps fall off of the universal joint (which would cause contamination and loss of the needle bearings).

5   Lower the rear of the driveshaft. If the driveshaft is a one-piece unit, slide the front end of the driveshaft out of the transmission extension housing; if it's a two-piece driveshaft, mark the relationship of the center support bearing to the support bracket, then unbolt the center support bearing and slide the front end of the front driveshaft out of the extension housing.

6   Wrap a plastic bag over the extension housing and hold it in place with a rubber band. This will prevent loss of fluid and protect against contamination while the driveshaft is out.

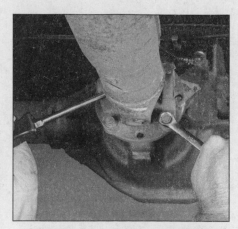

9.3 Insert a screwdriver through the driveshaft yoke to prevent the shaft from turning when you loosen the bolts

Installation

7   Remove the plastic bag from the transmission or transfer case extension housing and wipe the area clean. Inspect the oil seal carefully. If it's leaking, now is the time to replace it (see Chapter 7).

8   Inspect the center support bearing, if equipped. If it's rough or noisy, replace it (see Section 10).

9   Insert the front end of the driveshaft assembly into the transmission or transfer case extension housing.

10   If the driveshaft is a one-piece unit, raise the rear of the driveshaft into position, checking to be sure the marks are in alignment. If not, turn the pinion flange until the marks line up.

11   If the driveshaft is a two-piece unit, raise the center support bearing and bolt it loosely into place, raise the rear end of the rear shaft into position and make sure the alignment marks are in alignment. If not, turn the pinion flange until they do.

12   Remove the tape securing the bearing caps and install the clamps, if equipped, and fasteners. Tighten the fasteners center support bearing bolts to the torque listed in this Chapter's Specifications.

Front (4WD)

Removal

13   Raise the vehicle and support it securely on jackstands.

14   If equipped, remove the skid plate.

15   If necessary, remove the exhaust crossover pipe (see Chapter 4).

16   Use chalk or a scribe to mark the relationship of the driveshaft to the differential axle assembly mating flange (see illustration 9.2). This ensures correct alignment when the driveshaft is reinstalled.

17   Remove the bolts that secure the front end of the driveshaft to the differential mating flange.

18   On models equipped with a transfer case flange, make alignment marks on the driveshaft and transfer case flanges. Unbolt the flange that secures the driveshaft universal joint to the transfer, then

12.2   A pair of needle-nose pliers can be used to remove the universal joint snap-rings

remove the driveshaft.

19   On models equipped with a splined sliding sleeve, remove the dust boot clamp, then slide the end of the driveshaft out of the transfer case.

Installation

20   Installation is the reverse of removal. If the shaft cannot be lined up due to the components of the differential or transfer case having been rotated, put the vehicle in Neutral or rotate one wheel to allow the original alignment to be achieved. Make sure the universal joint caps are properly placed in the flange seat. Tighten the fasteners to the torque listed in this Chapter's Specifications.

---

10   Driveshaft center support bearing - removal and installation

---

1   Raise the vehicle and support it securely on jackstands.

2   Remove the driveshaft assembly (see Section 9). Mark the relationship of the front portion of the driveshaft to the rear portion of the driveshaft.

3   Loosen the slip-joint boot clamp and pull back the boot on the front of the rear driveshaft.

4   Pull the rear driveshaft out of the center bearing.

5   Take the front driveshaft and center bearing to an automotive machine shop and have the old bearing pressed off and a new bearing pressed on.

6   Installation is the reverse of removal. Be sure the match marks line up so the driveshaft is properly "phased."

---

11   Universal joints - general information and check

---

1   Universal joints are mechanical couplings which connect two rotating components that meet each other at different angles.

2   These joints are composed of a yoke on each side connected by a crosspiece called a trunnion. Cups at each end of the trunnion contain needle bearings which provide smooth transfer of the torque load. Snap-rings, either inside or outside of the bearing cups, hold the assembly together.

3   Wear in the needle roller bearings is characterized by vibration in the driveline, noise during acceleration, and in extreme cases of lack of lubrication, metallic squeaking and ultimately grating and shrieking sounds as the bearings disintegrate.

4   It is easy to check if the needle bearings are worn with the driveshaft in position, by trying to turn the shaft with one hand, the other hand holding the rear axle flange when the rear universal joint is being checked, and the front half coupling when the front universal joint is being checked. Any movement between the driveshaft and the front half couplings, and around the rear half couplings,

is indicative of considerable wear. Another method of checking for universal joint wear is to use a prybar inserted into the gap between the universal joint and the driveshaft or flange. Leave the vehicle in gear and try to pry the joint both radially and axially. Any looseness should be apparent with this method. A final test for wear is to attempt to lift the shaft and note any movement between the yokes of the joints.

5   If any of the above conditions exist, replace the universal joints with new ones.

---

12   Universal joints - replacement

Single-cardan U-joints

Refer to illustrations 12.2, 12.4 and 12.9

Note: *A press or large vise will be required for this procedure. It may be advisable to take the driveshaft to a local dealer service department, service station or machine shop where the universal joints can be replaced for you, normally at a reasonable charge.*

1   Remove the driveshaft as outlined in Section 9.

2   On U-joints with external snap-rings, use a small pair of pliers to remove the snap-rings from the spider (see illustration).

3   Supporting the driveshaft, place it in position on a workbench equipped with a vise.

4   Place a piece of pipe or a large socket, having an inside diameter slightly larger than the outside diameter of the bearing caps, over one of the bearing caps. Position a socket with an outside diameter slightly smaller than that of the opposite bearing cap against the cap (see illustration) and use the vise or press to force the bearing cap out (inside the pipe or large socket). Use the vise or large pliers to work the bearing cap the rest of the way out.

5   Transfer the sockets to the other side and press the opposite bearing cap out in the same manner.

6   Pack the new universal joint bearings with grease. Ordinarily, specific instructions

12.4   To press the universal joint out of the driveshaft yoke, set it up in a vise with the small socket pushing the joint and bearing cap into the large socket

12.9 If the snap-ring will not seat in the groove, strike the yoke with a brass hammer - this will relieve the tension that has set up in the yoke and slightly spring the yoke ears (this should also be done if the joint feels tight when assembled)

for lubrication will be included with the universal joint servicing kit and should be followed carefully.

7   Position the spider in the yoke and partially install one bearing cap in the yoke.

8   Start the spider into the bearing cap and then partially install the other cap. Align the spider and press the bearing caps into position, being careful not to damage the dust seals.

9   Install the snap-rings. If difficulty is encountered in seating the snap-rings, strike the driveshaft yoke sharply with a hammer. This will spring the yoke ears slightly and allow the snap-rings to seat in the groove **(see illustration).**

10   Install the grease fitting and fill the joint with grease. Be careful not to overfill the joint, as this could blow out the grease seals.

11   Install the driveshaft (see Section 9).

Double-cardan U-joints

12   Use the above procedure, but note that it will have to be repeated because the double-cardan joint is made up of two single-cardan joints. Also pay attention to how the spring, centering ball and bearing are arranged. **Note:** *Both U-joints in the double-cardan assembly must be replaced at the same time, even if only half of it is worn out.*

13   Front and rear axles - description and check

Description

1   The rear axle assembly is a hypoid, semi-floating type (the centerline of the pinion gear is below the centerline of the ring gear). The differential carrier is a casting with a pressed steel cover and the axle tubes are made of steel, pressed and welded into the carrier.

2   An optional locking rear axle is also

14.2a Remove the pinion shaft lock bolt . . .

available. This differential allows for normal operation until one wheel loses traction. The unit utilizes multi-disc clutch packs which lock both axleshafts together, applying equal rotational power to both wheels, when one wheel loses traction.

3   On 4WD models, a fully independent front axle assembly is used. This consists of a differential, two axleshafts (similar to the rear axleshafts) and a pair of driveaxles. Each driveaxle has an inner and outer Constant Velocity (CV) joint. Because the differential - like the transfer case - is offset to the left, the distance between the differential and the right front wheel is greater than the distance from the differential to the left wheel. In order to use two equal-length driveaxles, an extended axleshaft is employed on the right side to make up the difference.

Check

4   Many times a problem is suspected in an axle area when, in fact, it lies elsewhere. For this reason, a thorough check should be performed before assuming an axle problem.

5   The following noises are those commonly associated with axle diagnosis procedures:

a) *Road noise is often mistaken for mechanical faults. Driving the vehicle on different surfaces will show whether the road surface is the cause of the noise. Road noise will remain the same if the vehicle is under power or coasting.*

b) *Tire noise is sometimes mistaken for mechanical problems. Tires which are worn or low on pressure are particularly susceptible to emitting vibrations and noises. Tire noise will remain about the same during varying driving situations, where axle noise will change during coasting, acceleration, etc.*

c) *Engine and transmission noise can be deceiving because it will travel along the driveline. To isolate engine and transmission noises, make a note of the engine speed at which the noise is most pronounced. Stop the vehicle and place the transmission in Neutral and run the*

14.2b . . . then carefully remove the pinion shaft from the differential case (don't turn the wheels or the case after the shaft has been removed, or the pinion gears may fall out)

engine to the same speed. If the noise is the same, the axle is not at fault.

6   Overhaul and general repair of the front or rear axle differential is beyond the scope of this manual due to the many special tools and critical measurements required. Thus, the procedures listed here will involve axleshaft removal and installation, axleshaft oil seal replacement, axleshaft bearing replacement and removal of the entire unit for repair or replacement. Information on differential overhaul can be found in the Haynes *Suspension, Steering and Driveline Manual.*

14   Rear axleshaft - removal and installation

Refer to illustrations 14.2a, 14.2b and 14.3

1   Loosen the wheel lug nuts, raise the vehicle and support it securely on jackstands. Remove the wheel, brake caliper, caliper mounting bracket and rotor (refer to Chapter 9).

2   Remove the cover from the differential housing and allow the oil to drain into a container (see Chapter 1). Remove the lock bolt from the differential pinion shaft. Remove the pinion shaft **(see illustration).**

3   Push the outer (flanged) end of the axleshaft in and remove the C-lock from the inner end of the shaft **(see illustration).**

4   Withdraw the axleshaft, taking care not to damage the oil seal in the end of the axle housing as the splined end of the axleshaft passes through it (unless, of course, you are going to replace the seal anyway).

5   Installation is the reverse of removal. Apply a non-hardening thread-locking compound to the threads of the lock bolt, then tighten the lock bolt to the torque listed in this Chapter's Specifications. When installing the axleshaft, be sure to lubricate the seal lip and the bore in the axle bearing with clean differential lubricant.

14.3 Push the axle flange in, then remove the C-lock from the inner end of the axleshaft

6   Clean off all traces of old gasket material from the differential cover and axle housing, then apply a bead of RTV sealant to the cover. Install the cover and bolts, tightening the bolts to the torque listed in this Chapter's Specifications.

7   Refill the axle with the correct quantity and grade of lubricant (see Chapter 1).

8   Tighten the wheel lug nuts to the torque listed in the Chapter 1 Specifications.

15   Rear axleshaft oil seal - replacement

Refer to illustrations 15.2a, 15.2b and 15.3

1   Remove the axleshaft (see Section 14).

2   Pry the oil seal out of the end of the axle housing with a seal removal tool or the inner end of the axleshaft **(see illustrations)**.

3   Apply high-temperature grease to the oil seal recess and tap the new seal evenly into place with a hammer and seal installation tool **(see illustration)**, large socket or piece of pipe so the lips are facing in and the metal face is visible from the end of the axle housing. When correctly installed, the face of the oil seal should be flush with the end of the axle housing.

4   Install the axleshaft (see Section 14).

16   Rear axle bearing - replacement

Refer to illustrations 16.2, 16.3 and 16.4

1   Remove the axleshaft (see Section 14)

15.2a Using a seal removal tool to remove the old seal from the rear axle housing

and the oil seal (see Section 15).

2   A bearing puller which grips the bearing from behind will be required for this job **(see illustration)**.

3   Attach a slide hammer to the puller and extract the bearing and seal from the axle housing **(see illustration)**.

4   Clean out the bearing recess and drive in the new bearing with a bearing installer or

15.2b You can use the end of the axleshaft to pry out the old seal

15.3 Use a seal driver (shown) or a large socket to install the new seal

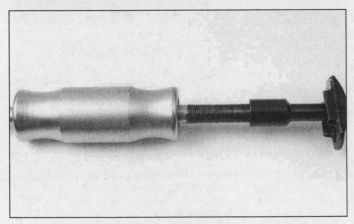

16.2 A typical slide hammer and axleshaft bearing removal attachment

16.3 Using the slide hammer and puller attachment to remove the axleshaft bearing

16.4 Use a special bearing installer tool or a large socket to tap the bearing evenly into the axle housing

18.6 Remove the snap-ring from the groove in the end of the axleshaft

18.12 Wrap the driveshaft splines with electrical tape to prevent damaging the boot as it's slid onto the shaft

a large socket positioned against the outer bearing race **(see illustration)**. Make sure the bearing is tapped in to the full depth of the recess and the numbers on the bearing are visible from the outer end of the axle housing.
5   Install a new oil seal (see Section 15), then install the axleshaft (see Section 14).

17   Driveaxle (4WD models) - removal and installation

1   Loosen the wheel lug nuts, raise the vehicle and support it securely on jackstands. Remove the wheel(s).
2   Remove the caliper and brake disc as outlined in Chapter 9, then disconnect the ABS sensor and secure the sensor and wire harness aside.
3   Remove the driveaxle/hub nut. Place a prybar between two of the wheel studs to prevent the hub from turning while loosening the nut.
4   Remove the hub bearing and brake shield (see Chapter 10).
5   Using a prybar or slide hammer with CV joint adapter, pry the inner CV joint assembly from the front differential. Be careful not to damage the front differential. Guide the driveaxle out from under the vehicle.
6   Installation is the reverse of the removal procedure, noting the following points:
a) *Thoroughly clean the splines and bearing shield on the outer CV joint. This is very important, as the bearing shield protects the wheel bearings from water and contamination. Also clean the wheel bearing area of the steering knuckle.*
b) *Thoroughly clean the splines and oil seal sealing surface on the inner tripod CV joint. Apply a film of multi-purpose grease around the oil seal contact surface of the inner CV joint.*
c) *When installing the driveaxle, hold the driveaxle straight out, then push it in sharply to seat the set-ring on the splines of the inner CV joint. To make sure the set-ring is properly seated, attempt to*

pull the inner CV joint housing out of the differential by hand. If the set-ring is properly seated, the inner joint will not move out.
d) *Tighten the hub bearing mounting bolts to the torque listed in the Chapter 10 Specifications.*
e) *Tighten the driveaxle/hub nut to the torque listed in this Chapter's Specifications.*
f) *Install the wheel and lug nuts, lower the vehicle and tighten the lug nuts to the torque listed in the Chapter 1 Specifications.*

18   Driveaxle boot (4WD models) - replacement

Note: *If the CV joints exhibit wear, indicating the need for an overhaul (usually due to torn boots), explore all options before beginning the job. Complete rebuilt driveaxles may be available on an exchange basis, which eliminates a lot of time and work. Whatever is decided, check on the cost and availability of parts before disassembling the joints.*
1   Loosen the wheel lug nuts. Raise the vehicle and support it securely on jackstands, then remove the wheel.
2   Remove the driveaxle (see Section 17).

Inner CV joint

Refer to illustrations 18.6, 18.12, 18.19 and 18.20

Disassembly

3   Mount the driveaxle in a bench vise with wood blocks to protect it. **Caution:** *Do not overtighten the vise.*
4   Remove the boot retaining clamps and slide the inner boot back onto the shaft.
5   Pull the inner CV joint housing off the shaft and tripod.
6   Use a pair of snap-ring pliers and remove the snap-ring from the end of the shaft.
7   Mark the end of the shaft and the tripod, then remove the tripod from the shaft.
8   Remove the boot from the shaft.

9   Clean the housing and the tripod with solvent.
10   Check the tripod components and the housing for excessive wear and/or damage.
11   If any components are worn or damaged, the entire joint must be replaced.

Assembly

12   Wrap the splines of the shaft with tape to prevent damage to the boot, then install the small boot clamp and boot onto the shaft **(see illustration)**.
13   Install the tripod onto the end of the shaft, with the mark you made facing the end of the shaft (and aligned with the mark on the shaft).
14   Install the snap-ring, making sure it is completely seated in its groove.
15   Apply CV joint grease to the tripod and interior of the housing. **Note:** *If grease was not included with the new boot, obtain some CV joint grease - don't use any other type of grease.*
16   Apply the remainder of the grease into the boot, then insert the shaft and tripod into the housing.
17   Position the large-diameter end of the boot over the edge of the housing and seat the lip of the boot into the locating groove at the edge of the housing. Insert the lip of the small-diameter end of the boot into the locating groove on the shaft.
18   Adjust the length of the joint by positioning it mid-way through its travel.
19   Insert a small screwdriver between the boot and the housing to equalize the pressure inside the boot **(see illustration)**.
20   Tighten the boot clamps **(see illustration)**.

Outer CV joint

Refer to illustrations 18.23, 18.27, 18.28, 18.30, 18.31, 18.34a, 18.34b and 18.40

Disassembly

21   Mount the axleshaft in a vise with wood blocks to protect it, remove the boot clamps and push the boot back.

22   Wipe the grease from the joint.
23   Using a pair of snap-ring pliers, expand the snap-ring retaining the outer joint to the shaft, then remove the joint (see illustration).
24   Slide the boot off the driveaxle.
25   Clean the axle spline area and inspect for wear, damage, corrosion and broken splines.
26   Clean the outer CV joint bearing assembly with a clean cloth to remove excess grease.
27   Mark the relative position of the bearing cage, inner race and housing (see illustration).
28   Mount the CV joint in the vise with wood blocks to protect the stub shaft. Push down one side of the cage and remove the ball bearing from the opposite side (see illustration). The balls may have to be pried out.
29   Repeat this procedure until all of the balls are removed. If the joint is tight, tap on the inner race (not the cage) with a hammer and brass drift.
30   Remove the bearing assembly from the housing by tilting it vertically and aligning two opposing cage windows in the area between

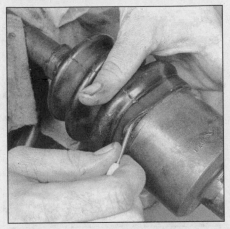

18.19 After positioning the joint mid-way through its travel, equalize the pressure inside the boot by inserting a small, dull screwdriver between the boot and the CV joint housing

18.20 Depending on the type of clamps furnished with the replacement boot, you'll most likely need a special pair of clamp tightening pliers (most auto parts stores carry these)

the ball grooves (see illustration).
31   Turn the inner race 90-degrees to the cage and align one of the spherical lands with

an elongated cage window. Raise the land into the window and swivel the inner race out of the cage (see illustration).

18.23 After expanding the snap-ring, the outer joint assembly can be removed

18.27 Mark the bearing cage, inner race and housing relationship after removing the grease

18.28 With the cage and inner race tilted, the balls can be removed one at a time

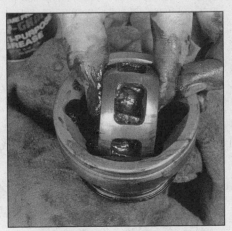

18.30 Align one of the elongated windows in the cage with one of the lands on the housing (outer race), then rock the cage and inner race out of the housing

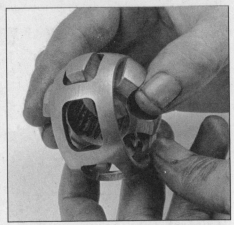

18.31 Tilt the inner race 90-degrees, align the race lands with the windows in the cage, then separate the two components

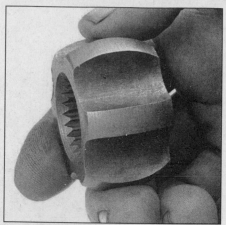

18.34a Check the inner race lands and grooves for pitting and score marks

18.34b Check the cage for cracks, pitting and score marks (shiny spots are normal and don't affect operation)

18.40 Apply grease through the splined hole, then insert a wooden dowel into the hole and push down - the dowel will force the grease into the joint

32   Clean all of the parts with solvent and dry them with compressed air (if available).

33   Inspect the housing, splines, balls and races for damage, corrosion, wear and cracks.

34   Check the inner race for wear and scoring. If any of the components are not serviceable, the entire CV joint assembly must be replaced with a new one **(see illustrations)**.

Assembly

35   Apply a thin film of oil to all CV joint components before beginning reassembly.

36   Align the marks and install the inner race in the cage so one of the race lands fits into the elongated window **(see illustration 18.31)**.

37   Rotate the inner race into position in the cage and install the assembly in the CV joint housing, again using the elongated window for clearance **(see illustration 18.30)**.

38   Rotate the inner race into position in the housing. Be sure the large counterbore of the inner race faces out. The marks made during disassembly should face out and be aligned.

39   Pack the lubricant from the kit into the ball races and grooves.

40   Install the balls into the holes, one at a time, until they are all in position. Fill the joint with grease through the splined hole, then insert a wooden dowel into the splined hole to force the grease into the joint **(see illustration)**.

41   Place the driveaxle in the vise and slide the inner clamp and boot over it (wrap the shaft splines with tape to prevent damaging the boot **(see illustration 18.12)**.

42   Place the CV joint housing in position on the axle, align the splines and push it into place. If necessary, tap it on with a soft-face hammer. Make sure it is seated on the snapring by attempting to pull it from the shaft.

43   Make sure the boot is not distorted, then install and tighten the clamps **(see illustration 18.20)**.

19   Pinion oil seal - replacement

Refer to illustrations 19.3, 19.5, 19.8 and 19.9

Note: *This procedure applies to the front and rear pinion oil seals.*

1   Loosen the wheel lug nuts. Raise the front (for front differential) or rear (for rear differential) of the vehicle and support it securely on jackstands. Block the opposite set of wheels to keep the vehicle from rolling off the stands. Remove the wheels.

2   Disconnect the driveshaft from the differential pinion flange and support it out of the way with a piece of wire or rope (see Section 9).

3   Rotate the pinion a few times by hand. Use a beam-type or dial-type inch-pound torque wrench to check the torque required to rotate the pinion **(see illustration)**. Record it for use later.

4   Mark the relationship of the pinion flange to the shaft then count and write down the number of exposed threads on the shaft.

5   A special tool, available at most auto parts stores, can be used to keep the companion flange from moving while the self-locking pinion nut is loosened. A chain wrench can also be used to immobilize the flange **(see illustration)**.

6   Remove the pinion nut.

7   Withdraw the flange. It may be necessary to use a two-jaw puller engaged behind the flange to draw it off. Do not attempt to pry

19.3 Use an inch-pound torque wrench to check the torque necessary to rotate the pinion shaft

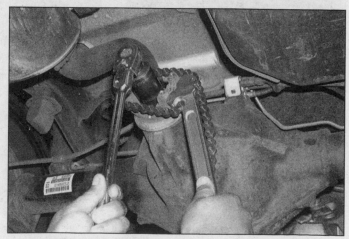

19.5 A chain wrench can be used to hold the pinion flange while the nut is loosened

19.8 Use a seal removal tool or a large screwdriver to remove the pinion seal (be careful not to disturb the pinion while doing this)

19.9 A large socket with a diameter the same as that of the new seal can be used to drive the pinion seal into the differential housing

or hammer behind the flange or hammer on the end of the pinion shaft.

8   Pry out the old seal and discard it (see illustration).

9   Lubricate the lips of the new seal and fill the space between the seal lips with wheel bearing grease, then tap it evenly into position with a seal installation tool or a large socket (see illustration). Make sure it enters the housing squarely and is tapped in to its full depth.

10   Install the pinion flange, lining up the marks made in Step 4. If necessary, tighten the pinion nut to draw the flange into place. Do not try to hammer the flange into position.

11   Apply a bead of RTV sealant to the ends of the splines visible in the center of the flange so oil will be sealed in.

12   Install the washer and a new pinion nut. Tighten the nut until the number of threads recorded in Step 4 are exposed.

13   Measure the torque required to rotate the pinion and tighten the nut in small increments (no more than 5 ft-lbs) until it matches the figure recorded in Step 3. To compensate for the drag of the new oil seal, the nut should be tightened a little more until the rotational torque of the pinion exceeds the earlier recording by 5 in-lbs.

14   Reinstall all components removed previously by reversing the removal Steps, tightening all fasteners to their specified torque values.

20   Axle assembly - removal and installation

Rear axle assembly

Removal

1   Raise the rear of the vehicle and support it with jackstands placed under the frame rails.

2   Remove the rear wheels.

3   Disconnect the driveshaft from the rear axle (see Section 9).

4   Disconnect the ABS sensor.

5   Disconnect the parking brake cable from the parking brake lever (see Chapter 9).

6   Unscrew the vent hose fitting to detach the brake line junction block from the axle tube.

7   Disconnect the brake lines from the clips and brackets on the axle housing. Remove the rear brake calipers (see Chapter 9). **Caution:** *Tie the calipers up with wire to keep any strain off the flexible brake lines.*

8   Support the rear axle with a floor jack. If the rear differential is offset to one side, you'll have to use two jacks - one placed under each axle tube.

9   On Durango models, remove the Watts link bellcrank bolt (see Chapter 10).

10   Remove the stabilizer bar clamp bolts (see Chapter 10).

11   Remove the lower mounting bolts securing the rear shocks to the axle (see Chapter 10).

12   On Durango models, remove the upper control arms from the axle brackets (see Chapter 10), then with the jack(s) supporting the axle assembly, lower the axle assembly and remove the coil springs. Remove the lower control arms from the axle brackets, then lower the axle assembly and remove it from under the vehicle.

13   On Dakota models, with the jack(s) supporting the axle, remove the nuts and U-bolts securing the axle to the springs, then lower the axle assembly and remove it from under the vehicle.

Installation

14   Installation is the reverse of the removal procedure, noting the following points:

a) *On Durango models, be sure to tighten all suspension fasteners to the torque*

listed in the Chapter 10 Specifications after the vehicle has been lowered to the ground.

b) *On Dakota models, tighten the U-bolt nuts to the torque listed in the Chapter 10 Specifications.*

c) *On all models, tighten the caliper mounting bolts to the torque listed in the Chapter 9 Specifications. Tighten the lug nuts to the torque listed in the Chapter 1 Specifications, and if necessary, check and fill the axle with the specified lubricant (see Chapter 1).*

Front axle assembly (4WD models)

15   Raise the front of the vehicle and support it with jackstands placed under the frame rails.

16   Remove the front wheels.

17   Remove the driveaxles (see Section 17).

18   Remove the crossmember mounting bolts, then remove the crossmember.

19   Disconnect the driveshaft from the differential pinion flange and support it out of the way with a piece of wire or rope (see Section 9).

20   Disconnect the vent tube from the differential cover.

21   Support the axle assembly with a floor jack under the differential.

22   At the left engine mount, remove the fasteners securing the axle assembly to the mount.

23   At the pinion nose bracket, remove the fasteners securing the axle assembly to the pinion nose bracket.

24   Remove the remaining mounting bolts for the axle assembly at the right engine mount.

25   Lower the jack slowly, then remove the axle assembly from under the vehicle.

26   Installation is the reverse of removal.

Notes

Chapter 9   Brakes

Contents

Specifications

General

Brake fluid type.. See Chapter 1

Disc brakes

Brake pad minimum thickness	See Chapter 1
Disc lateral runout limit	0.005 inch
Disc minimum thickness	Cast into disc

Torque specifications

Ft-lbs (unless otherwise indicated)

Brake hose-to-caliper banjo bolt	21
Caliper mounting bolts	
Front	
Dakota	26
Durango	24
Rear	132 in-lbs
Caliper mounting bracket bolts	
Front	130
Rear	100
Master cylinder mounting nuts	90 in-lbs
Wheel cylinder	139 in-lbs
Power brake booster mounting nuts	21

1   General information

The vehicles covered by this manual are equipped with hydraulically operated front and rear brake systems. The front brakes are disc type, the rear brakes are either drum or disc type. Both the front and rear brakes are self adjusting; disc brakes automatically compensate for pad wear while the rear drum brakes incorporate an adjustment mechanism which is activated as the brakes are applied when the vehicle is driven in reverse.

Hydraulic system

The hydraulic system consists of two separate circuits. The master cylinder has separate reservoirs for the two circuits, and, in the event of a leak or failure in one hydraulic circuit, the other circuit will remain operative.

Power brake booster

The power brake booster uses engine manifold vacuum to provide assistance to the brakes. It is mounted on the firewall in the engine compartment, directly behind the master cylinder.

Parking brake

The parking brake pedal mechanically operates the rear brakes only. On models with rear drum brakes, the parking brake cables pull on a lever attached to the brake shoe assembly, causing the shoes to expand against the drum. Models with rear disc brakes incorporate a parking brake shoe assembly (similar to a drum brake) inside of the hub portion of each rear brake disc.

Service

After completing any operation involving disassembly of any part of the brake system, always test drive the vehicle to check for proper braking performance before resuming normal driving. When testing the brakes, perform the tests on a clean, dry, flat surface. Conditions other than these can lead to inaccurate test results.

Test the brakes at various speeds with both light and heavy pedal pressure. The vehicle should stop evenly without pulling to one side or the other.

Tires, vehicle load and wheel alignment are factors which also affect braking performance.

Precautions

There are some general cautions and warnings involving the brake system on this vehicle:

a) *Use only brake fluid conforming to DOT 3 specifications.*
b) *The brake pads and linings contain fibers which are hazardous to your health if inhaled. Whenever you work on brake system components, clean all parts with brake system cleaner. Do not allow the fine dust to become airborne. Also, wear an approved filtering mask.*

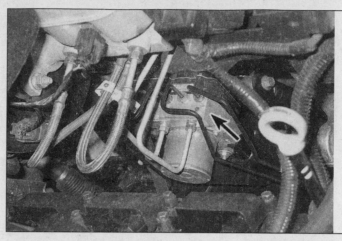

2.2 This ABS hydraulic unit is mounted beneath the master cylinder

c) *Safety should be paramount whenever any servicing of the brake components is performed. Do not use parts or fasteners which are not in perfect condition, and be sure that all clearances and torque specifications are adhered to. If you are at all unsure about a certain procedure, seek professional advice. Upon completion of any brake system work, test the brakes carefully in a controlled area before putting the vehicle into normal service. If a problem is suspected in the brake system, don't drive the vehicle until it's fixed.*

2   Anti-lock Brake System (ABS) - general information

General information

Refer to illustration 2.2

1   The anti-lock brake system is designed to maintain vehicle steerability, directional stability and optimum deceleration under severe braking conditions on most road surfaces. It does so by monitoring the rotational speed of each wheel and controlling the brake line pressure to each wheel during braking. This prevents the wheels from locking up.

2   The ABS system has three main components - the wheel speed sensors, the anti-lock brake control module and the hydraulic control unit **(see illustration)**. Wheel speed sensors - one at each wheel or one located on the rear differential for the rear wheels - send a variable voltage signal to the control unit, which monitors these signals, compares them to its program and determines whether a wheel is about to lock up. When a wheel is about to lock up, the control unit signals the hydraulic unit to reduce hydraulic pressure (or not increase it further) at that wheel's brake caliper. Pressure modulation is handled by electrically operated solenoid valves.

3   If a problem develops within the system, an ABS warning light will glow on the dashboard. Sometimes, a visual inspection of the ABS system can help you locate the problem. Carefully inspect the ABS wiring harness. Pay

particularly close attention to the harness and connections near each wheel. Look for signs of chafing and other damage caused by incorrectly routed wires. If a wheel sensor harness is damaged, the sensor must be replaced. **Warning:** *Do NOT try to repair an ABS wiring harness. The ABS system is sensitive to even the smallest changes in resistance. Repairing the harness could alter resistance values and cause the system to malfunction. If the ABS wiring harness is damaged in any way, it must be replaced.* **Caution:** *Make sure the ignition is turned off before unplugging or reattaching any electrical connections.*

4   If a dashboard warning light comes on and stays on while the vehicle is in operation, the ABS system requires attention. Although special electronic ABS diagnostic testing tools are necessary to properly diagnose the system, you can perform a few preliminary checks before taking the vehicle to a dealer service department.

a) *Check the brake fluid level in the reservoir.*
b) *Verify that the computer electrical connectors are securely connected.*
c) *Check the electrical connectors at the hydraulic control unit.*
d) *Check the fuses.*
e) *Follow the wiring harness to each wheel and verify that all connections are secure and that the wiring is undamaged.*

5   If the above preliminary checks do not rectify the problem, the vehicle should be diagnosed by a dealer service department or other qualified repair shop. Due to the complex nature of this system, all actual repair work must be done by a qualified automotive technician.

Wheel speed sensor - removal and installation

Refer to illustrations 2.9a, 2.9b and 2.9c

6   Loosen the wheel lug nuts, raise the vehicle and support it securely on jackstands. Remove the wheel.

7   Make sure the ignition key is turned to the Off position.

8   Trace the wiring back from the sensor, detaching all brackets and clips while noting

2.9a Front wheel speed sensor

2.9b Rear wheel speed sensor

2.9c Differential-mounted rear wheel speed sensor

3.5 Before removing the caliper, be sure to depress the piston into the bottom of its bore in the caliper with a large C-clamp to make room for the new pads

3.6a Always wash the brakes with brake cleaner before disassembling anything

its correct routing, then disconnect the electrical connector.

9 Remove the mounting fastener and carefully pull the sensor out from the hub, the knuckle or rear differential **(see illustrations)**.

10 Installation is the reverse of the removal procedure. Tighten the mounting fastener securely.

11 Install the wheel and lug nuts, tightening them securely. Lower the vehicle and tighten the lug nuts to the torque listed in the Chapter 1 Specifications.

3 Disc brake pads - replacement

Refer to illustrations 3.5 and 3.6a through 3.6o

Warning: *Disc brake pads must be replaced on both front or rear wheels at the same time - never replace the pads on only one wheel. Also, the dust created by the brake system is harmful to your health. Never blow it out with compressed air and don't inhale any of it. An approved filtering mask should be worn when*

working on the brakes. Do not, under any circumstances, use petroleum-based solvents to clean brake parts. Use brake system cleaner only!

Note: *This procedure applies to the front and rear brake pads.*

1 Remove the cap from the brake fluid reservoir.

2 Loosen the wheel lug nuts, raise the end of the vehicle you're working on and support it securely on jackstands. Block the wheels at the opposite end.

3 Remove the wheels. Work on one brake assembly at a time, using the assembled brake for reference if necessary.

4 Inspect the brake disc carefully as outlined in Section 5. If machining is necessary, follow the information in that Section to remove the disc, at which time the pads can be removed as well.

5 Push the piston back into its bore to provide room for the new brake pads. A C-clamp can be used to accomplish this **(see illustration)**. As the piston is depressed to the bottom of the caliper bore, the fluid in the master cylinder will rise. Make sure that it doesn't overflow. If necessary, siphon off

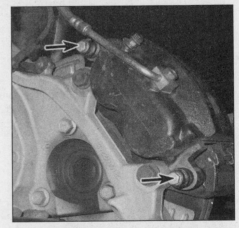

3.6b Remove the brake caliper mounting bolts (front caliper shown, rear caliper similar)

some of the fluid.

6 Follow the accompanying photos **(illustrations 3.6a through 3.6o)**, for the actual pad replacement procedure. Be sure to stay in order and read the caption under each illustration.

3.6c Remove the caliper . . .

3.6d . . . and use a piece of wire to tie it to the control arm - never let the caliper hang by the brake hose

3.6e Remove the inner pad . . .

3.6f . . . then remove the outer pad from the caliper mounting bracket

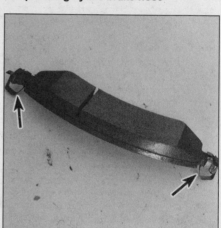

3.6g On Dakota models, the anti-rattle clips are attached to the ends of the each brake pad

7   After the job has been completed, firmly depress the brake pedal a few times to bring the pads into contact with the disc. Check the level of the brake fluid, adding some if necessary. Check the operation of the brakes carefully before placing the vehicle into normal service.

4   Disc brake caliper - removal and installation

Refer to illustration 4.2
Warning: *The dust created by the brake system is harmful to your health. Never blow it out with compressed air and don't inhale any of*

it. An approved filtering mask should be worn when working on the brakes. Do not, under any circumstances, use petroleum-based solvents to clean brake parts. Use brake system cleaner only!
Note: *This procedure applies to the front and rear disc brake calipers.*

3.6h Remove the anti-rattle clips, paying close attention to how they're installed in the mounting bracket

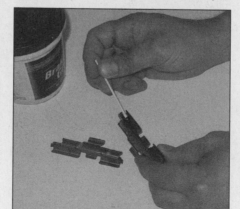

3.6i Lubricate the anti-rattle clips with multi-purpose grease . . .

3.6j . . . then install the clips

3.6k Install the inner pad . . .

3.6l . . . and outer pad into the mounting bracket - make sure both pads are fully seated . . .

3.6m . . . then place the caliper into position

3.6n Pull out both bushings and inspect them for corrosion and wear; if either bushing is damaged, replace it

Removal

1   Loosen the front or rear wheel lug nuts, raise the front or rear of the vehicle and place it securely on jackstands. Block the wheels at the opposite end. Remove the front or rear wheel.

2   Remove the brake hose-to-caliper banjo bolt and disconnect the brake hose from the caliper (**see illustration**). Discard the old sealing washers. Plug the brake hose immediately to keep contaminants and air out of the brake system and to prevent losing any more brake fluid than is necessary. **Note:** *If you are simply removing the caliper for access to other components, leave the brake hose connected and suspend the caliper with a length of wire - don't let it hang by the hose* (**see illustration 3.6d**).

3   Remove the caliper mounting bolts and detach the caliper from the mounting bracket (**see illustration 3.6b**).

Installation

4   Installation is the reverse of removal. Don't forget to use new sealing washers on each side of the brake hose fitting and be sure to tighten the banjo bolt and the caliper mounting bolts to the torque listed in this Chapter's Specifications.

5   Bleed the brake system (see Section 9). **Note:** *If the brake hose was not disconnected, bleeding won't be required. Make sure there are no leaks from the hose connections. Test the brakes carefully before returning the vehicle to normal service.*

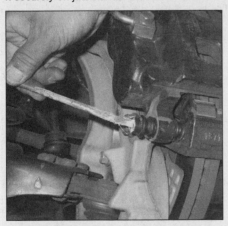

3.6o Lubricate the bushings with high-temperature grease, then install the bushings and mounting bolts. Tighten the bolts to the torque listed in this Chapter's Specifications

4.2 To disconnect the brake hose, remove the brake hose-to-caliper banjo bolt (rear caliper shown, front caliper similar)

5   Brake disc - inspection, removal and installation

Inspection

Refer to illustrations 5.2, 5.3, 5.4a and 5.4b

1   Loosen the wheel lug nuts, raise the vehicle and support it securely on jackstands. Apply the parking brake. Remove the wheels.

2   Visually inspect the disc surface for score marks and other damage **(see illustration)**. Light scratches and shallow grooves are normal after use and won't affect brake operation. Deep grooves require disc removal and refinishing by an automotive machine shop. Be sure to check both sides of the disc.

3   To check disc runout, place a dial indicator at a point about 1/2-inch from the outer edge of the disc **(see illustration)**. Install the lug nuts, with the flat sides facing in, and tighten them securely to hold the disc in place. Set the indicator to zero and turn the disc. The indicator reading should not exceed the runout limit listed in this Chapter's Specifications. If it does, the disc should be refinished by an automotive machine shop. If you elect not to have the discs resurfaced, deglaze them with sandpaper or emery cloth.

4   The disc must not be machined to a thickness less than the specified minimum thickness, which is cast into the disc **(see illustration)**. The disc thickness can be checked with a micrometer **(see illustration)**.

Removal and installation

Refer to illustrations 5.6 and 5.7

5   Remove the brake caliper (don't disconnect the brake hose) and hang it out of the way (see Section 4).

6   Remove the caliper mounting bracket **(see illustration)**.

7   Remove the lug nuts installed in Step 3 and pull the disc off the hub. If the disc is held in place by pressed on washer-like retainers, cut them off **(see illustration)**.

8   Installation is the reverse of removal. Tighten the caliper mounting bracket fasteners to the torque listed in this Chapter's Specifications.

9   Lower the vehicle and tighten the wheel lug nuts to the torque listed in the Chapter 1 Specifications.

5.2 The brake pads on this vehicle were obviously neglected - they wore down completely and cut deep grooves into the disc (wear this severe means the disc must be replaced)

5.3 Measure the brake disc runout with a dial indicator

5.4a The minimum (discard) thickness of the brake disc is cast into the disc

5.4b Measure the brake disc thickness at several points with a micrometer

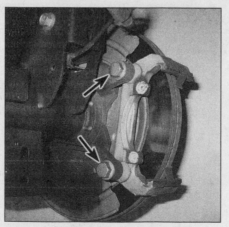

5.6 The caliper mounting bracket is retained by two bolts (rear shown, front similar)

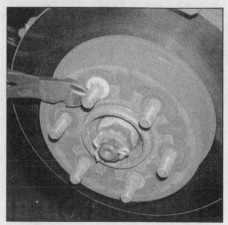

5.7 Cut off any retainers holding the disc onto the hub and discard them (there is no need to reinstall them)

6.2 Fuse and relay box tray mounting fasteners (one hidden in photo)

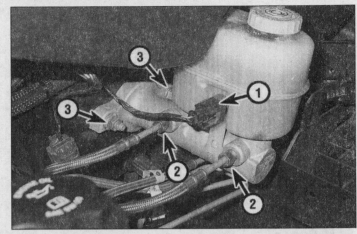

6.5 Brake master cylinder mounting details:

1	Brake fluid switch electrical connector	2	Brake lines
		3	Mounting nuts

6 Master cylinder - removal and installation

Removal

Refer to illustrations 6.2 and 6.5

1 The master cylinder is located in the engine compartment, mounted to the power brake booster.

2 On Durango models with ESP (electronic stability program), remove the inner fender splash shield (see Chapter 11). Remove the fasteners for the fuse and relay box tray to move it slightly forward for clearance when removing the master cylinder **(see illustration)**.

3 Remove as much fluid as you can from the reservoir with a syringe, such as an old turkey baster. **Warning:** *If a baster is used, never again use it for the preparation of food.*

4 Place rags under the fluid fittings and prepare caps or plastic bags to cover the ends of the lines once they are disconnected. **Caution:** *Brake fluid will damage paint. Cover all painted surfaces around the work area and be careful not to spill fluid during this procedure.*

5 Loosen the fittings at the ends of the brake lines where they enter the master cylinder **(see illustration)**. To prevent rounding off the corners on these nuts, the use of a flare-nut wrench, which wraps around the nut, is preferred. Pull the brake lines slightly away from the master cylinder and plug the ends to prevent contamination.

6 Disconnect the electrical connector at the brake fluid level switch on the master cylinder reservoir, then remove the nuts attaching the master cylinder to the power booster. Keep the master cylinder level while carefully pulling it off the studs and out of the engine compartment. **Note:** *Make sure that the power booster output rod is not disturbed while removing the master cylinder as it is seated inside the booster and could become dislodged.*

7 If a new master cylinder is being installed,

remove the fastener securing the reservoir to the master cylinder then pull up on the reservoir to remove it from the master cylinder. Transfer the reservoir to the new master cylinder. **Note:** *Be sure to install new seals when transferring the reservoir.*

Installation

Refer to illustration 6.9

8 Bench bleed the new master cylinder before installing it. Mount the master cylinder in a vise, with the jaws of the vise clamping on the mounting flange.

9 Attach a pair of master cylinder bleeder tubes to the outlet ports of the master cylinder **(see illustration)**.

10 Fill the reservoir with brake fluid of the recommended type (see Chapter 1).

11 Slowly push the pistons into the master cylinder (a large Phillips screwdriver can be used for this) - air will be expelled from the pressure chambers and into the reservoir. Because the tubes are submerged in fluid, air can't be drawn back into the master cylinder when you release the pistons.

12 Repeat the procedure until no more air bubbles are present.

13 Remove the bleed tubes, one at a time, and install plugs in the open ports to prevent fluid leakage and air from entering. Install the reservoir cap.

14 Install the master cylinder over the studs on the power brake booster and tighten the attaching nuts only finger tight at this time. **Note:** *Confirm that the output rod of the power brake booster is aligned with the master cylinder before attempting to install it.*

15 Thread the brake line fittings into the master cylinder. Since the master cylinder is still a bit loose, it can be moved slightly in order for the fittings to thread in easily. Do not strip the threads as the fittings are tightened.

16 Fully tighten the mounting nuts, then the brake line fittings. Tighten the nuts to the torque listed in this Chapter's Specifications.

17 Connect the brake fluid switch electrical connector.

18 Fill the master cylinder reservoir with fluid, then bleed the master cylinder and the brake system as described in Section 9. To bleed the cylinder on the vehicle, have an assistant depress the brake pedal and hold the pedal to the floor. Loosen the fitting to allow air and fluid to escape. Repeat this pro-

6.9 The best way to bleed air from the master cylinder before installing it on the vehicle is with a pair of bleeder tubes that direct brake fluid into the reservoir during bleeding

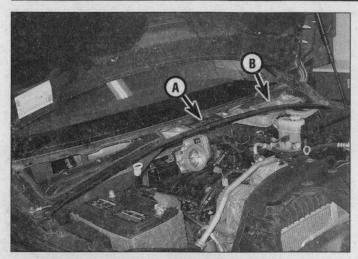

7.8 Remove the cowl support brace (A) and the wiper arm bracket assembly (B)

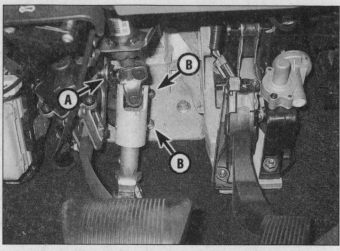

7.10 Remove the retaining clip (A) and the mounting fasteners (B) (two fasteners are not visible in photo)

cedure on both fittings until the fluid is clear of air bubbles. **Caution:** *Have plenty of rags on hand to catch the fluid - brake fluid will ruin painted surfaces. After the bleeding procedure is completed, rinse the area under the master cylinder with clean water.*

19   On Durango models with ESP, replace the fuse and relay box tray and the fender splash shield.

20   Test the operation of the brake system carefully before placing the vehicle into normal service. **Warning:** *Do not operate the vehicle if you are in doubt about the effectiveness of the brake system. It is possible for air to become trapped in the anti-lock brake system hydraulic control unit, so, if the pedal continues to feel spongy after repeated bleedings or the BRAKE or ANTI-LOCK light stays on, have the vehicle towed to a dealer service department or other qualified shop to be bled with the aid of a scan tool.*

7   Power brake booster - check, removal and installation

1   The power brake booster unit requires no special maintenance apart from periodic inspection of the vacuum hose and the case.

2   The power unit is not repairable. If a problem develops, it must be replaced.

Operating check

3   Depress the brake pedal several times with the engine off and make sure that there is no change in the pedal reserve distance.

4   Depress the pedal and start the engine. If the pedal goes down slightly, operation is normal.

Airtightness check

5   Start the engine and turn it off after one or two minutes. Depress the brake pedal several times slowly. If the pedal goes down farther the first time but gradually rises after the second or third depression, the

booster is airtight.

6   Depress the brake pedal while the engine is running, then stop the engine with the pedal depressed. If there is no change in the pedal reserve travel after holding the pedal for 30 seconds, the booster is airtight.

Removal

Refer to illustrations 7.8 and 7.10

7   Remove the master cylinder (see Section 6).

8   On Durango models, remove the cowl cover (see Chapter 11), the cowl support brace and the windshield wiper arm bracket assembly **(see illustration)**. **Note:** *Be sure to disconnect the wiper arm motor electrical connector.*

9   Disconnect the vacuum hose from the power brake booster. **Note:** *Do not remove the check valve from the booster, only the vacuum hose.*

10   Working under the dash, disconnect the power brake pushrod from the top of the brake pedal by prying off the clip **(see illustration)**.

11   Remove the nuts attaching the booster to the firewall **(see illustration 7.10)**.

12   Carefully lift the booster unit away from the firewall and out of the engine compartment. Be sure to note how gaskets and any spacer blocks are placed between the booster and firewall.

Installation

13   To install the booster, place it into position and tighten the retaining nuts to the torque listed in this Chapter's Specifications.

14   Connect the booster pushrod to the brake pedal.

15   Install the master cylinder (see Section 6).

16   Connect the vacuum hose to the brake booster assembly.

17   Bleed the brake system (see Section 9).

18   Carefully test the operation of the brakes before placing the vehicle in normal operation.

8   Brake hoses and lines - inspection and replacement

Inspection

1   Whenever the vehicle is raised and supported securely on jackstands, the rubber hoses which connect the steel brake lines with the front and rear brake assemblies should be inspected for cracks, chafing of the outer cover, leaks, blisters and other damage. These are important and vulnerable parts of the brake system and inspection should be thorough. A light and mirror will be helpful for a complete check. If a hose exhibits any of the above conditions, replace it immediately.

Flexible hose replacement

Refer to illustrations 8.3a and 8.3b

2   Clean all dirt away from the hose fittings.

3   Using a flare-nut wrench, disconnect the metal brake line from the hose fitting **(see illustrations)**. Be careful not to bend the line. If the threaded fitting is corroded, spray it with penetrating oil and allow it to soak in for about 10 minutes, then try again. If you try to break loose a fitting nut that's frozen, you will kink the metal line, which will then have to be replaced.

4   Disconnect the brake hose from the frame or bracket by removing the U-clip. Immediately plug the metal line to prevent excessive leakage and contamination.

5   Unscrew the banjo bolt at the caliper and remove the hose, discarding the sealing washers on either side of the fitting.

6   Attach the new brake hose to the caliper. **Note:** *When connecting a brake hose to a caliper, always use new sealing washers. Tighten the banjo bolt to the torque listed in this Chapter's Specifications.*

7   Place the end of the hose fitting into the frame or bracket. Making sure it is routed the same way as the original one and then secure it with the U-clip. Thread the metal line to the hose (or hose fitting) and tighten the brake

8.3a Flexible hose line and line fitting at the caliper

8.3b Line fitting details:

1	Brake tube fitting nut	3	Line fitting
2	U-Clip		

tube fitting nut securely.

8   Carefully check to make sure the suspension or steering components don't make contact with the hose. Have an assistant push down on the vehicle while you watch to see whether the hose interferes with suspension operation. If you're replacing a front hose, have your assistant turn the steering wheel lock-to-lock while you make sure the hose doesn't interfere with the steering linkage or the steering knuckle.

9   After installation, bleed the brakes (see Section 9). Check the master cylinder fluid level and add fluid as necessary. Carefully test brake operation before returning the vehicle to normal service.

Metal brake lines

10   When replacing brake lines, be sure to use the correct parts. Do not use copper tubing for any brake system components. Purchase steel brake lines from a dealer parts department or auto parts store.

9.8 When bleeding the brakes, a hose is connected to the bleed screw at the caliper and submerged in brake fluid - air will be seen as bubbles in the tube and container (all air must be expelled before moving to the next wheel)

11   Prefabricated brake line, with the tube ends already flared and fittings installed, is available at auto parts stores and dealer parts departments. If it is necessary to bend a line, use a tubing bender to prevent kinking the line.

12   When installing the new line make sure it's well supported in the brackets and has plenty of clearance between moving or hot components. Make sure you tighten the fittings securely.

13   After installation, check the master cylinder fluid level and add fluid as necessary. Bleed the brakes (see Section 9). Carefully test brake operation before resuming normal operation.

9   Brake hydraulic system - bleeding

Refer to illustration 9.8

Warning 1: *The following procedure is a manual bleeding procedure. This is the only bleeding procedure which can be performed at home without special tools. However, if air has found its way into the hydraulic control unit, the entire system must be bled manually, then with a scan tool, then manually a second time. If the brake pedal feels "spongy" even after bleeding the brakes, or the ABS light on the instrument panel does not go off, or if you have any doubts whatsoever about the effectiveness of the brake system, have the vehicle towed to a dealer service department or other repair shop equipped with the necessary tools for bleeding the system.*

Warning 2: *Wear eye protection when bleeding the brake system. If the fluid comes in contact with your eyes, immediately rinse them with water and seek medical attention.*

Note: *Bleeding the hydraulic system is necessary to remove any air that manages to find its way into the system when it's been opened during removal and installation of a hydraulic component or line.*

1   It will be necessary to bleed the complete system if air has entered the system due to low fluid level, or if the brake lines have been disconnected at the master cylinder.

2   If a brake line was disconnected only at a wheel, then only that caliper must be bled.

3   If a brake line is disconnected at a fitting located between the master cylinder and any of the brakes, that part of the system served by the disconnected line must be bled. The following procedure describes bleeding the entire system, however.

4   Remove any residual vacuum (or hydraulic pressure) from the brake power booster by applying the brake several times with the engine off.

5   Remove the cap from the master cylinder reservoir and fill the reservoir with brake fluid. Reinstall the cap. **Note:** *Check the fluid level often during the bleeding operation and add fluid as necessary to prevent the fluid level from falling low enough to allow air bubbles into the master cylinder.*

6   Have an assistant on hand, as well as a supply of new brake fluid, a clear container partially filled with clean brake fluid, a length of clear tubing to fit over the bleeder valve and a wrench to open and close the bleeder valve.

7   Beginning at the right rear wheel, loosen the bleeder screw slightly, then tighten it to a point where it's snug but can still be loosened quickly and easily.

8   Place one end of the tubing over the bleeder screw fitting and submerge the other end in brake fluid in the container **(see illustration)**.

9   Have the assistant slowly depress the brake pedal and hold it in the depressed position.

10   While the pedal is held depressed, open the bleeder screw just enough to allow a flow of fluid to leave the valve. Watch for air bubbles to exit the submerged end of the tube. When the fluid flow slows after a couple of seconds, tighten the screw and have your assistant release the pedal.

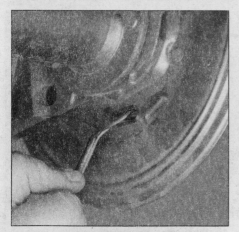

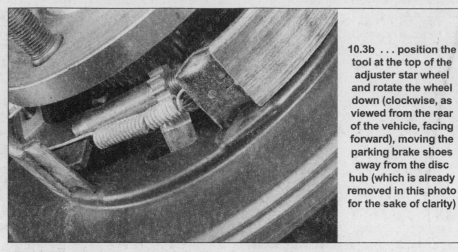

10.3b . . . position the tool at the top of the adjuster star wheel and rotate the wheel down (clockwise, as viewed from the rear of the vehicle, facing forward), moving the parking brake shoes away from the disc hub (which is already removed in this photo for the sake of clarity)

10.3a Remove the plug from the hole in the brake backing plate, insert a brake adjuster tool through the hole . . .

11   Repeat Steps 9 and 10 until no more air is seen leaving the tube, then tighten the bleeder screw and proceed to the left rear wheel, the right front wheel and the front left wheel, in that order, and perform the same procedure. Be sure to check the fluid in the master cylinder reservoir frequently.

12   Never use old brake fluid. It contains moisture which can boil, rendering the brake system inoperative.

13   Refill the master cylinder with fluid at the end of the operation.

14   Check the operation of the brakes. The pedal should feel solid when depressed, with no sponginess. If necessary, repeat the entire process. **Warning:** *Do not operate the vehicle if you are in doubt about the effectiveness of the brake system. It is possible for air to become trapped in the anti-lock brake system hydraulic control unit, so, if the pedal continues to feel spongy after repeated bleedings or the BRAKE or ANTI-LOCK light stays on, have the vehicle towed to a dealer service department or other qualified shop to be bled with the aid of a scan tool.*

10   Parking brake shoes (models with rear disc brakes)- replacement

Refer to illustrations 10.3a, 10.3b and 10.4a through 10.4p

Warning: *Dust created by the brake system is harmful to your health. Never blow it out with compressed air and don't inhale any of it. An approved filtering mask should be worn when working on the brakes. Do not, under any circumstances, use petroleum-based solvents to clean brake parts. Use brake system cleaner only!*

Note: *Although the procedure illustrated here is shown with the axle still in place, it takes some dexterity to work behind the axle flange while replacing the parking brake shoes. If this proves difficult, you can remove the axle for better access (see Chapter 8).*

1   Loosen the wheel lug nuts, release the parking brake, raise the rear of the vehicle and support it securely on jackstands. Block the front wheels to keep the vehicle from rolling. Remove the rear wheels.

2   Remove the rear brake caliper (see Section 4) and hang it with a length of wire, then remove the caliper mounting bracket (see Section 5).

3   Remove the brake disc (see Section 5). **Note:** *If the brake disc cannot be easily pulled off the axle and shoe assembly, make sure that the parking brake is completely released, then apply some penetrating oil at the hub-to-disc joint. Allow the oil to soak in and try to pull the disc off. If the disc still cannot be pulled off, the parking brake shoes will have to be retracted. This is accomplished by first removing the plug from the backing plate. With the plug removed, turn the adjusting wheel with a narrow screwdriver or brake adjusting tool, moving the shoes away from the braking surface* **(see illustration)**. *The disc should now come off.*

4   Clean the parking brake shoe assembly with brake system cleaner, then follow the accompanying illustrations **(10.4a through 10.4p)** for the parking brake shoe replacement procedure. Be sure to stay in order and read the caption under each illustration. **Note:** *All four parking brake shoes must be replaced at the same time, but to avoid mixing up parts, work on only one brake assembly at a time.*

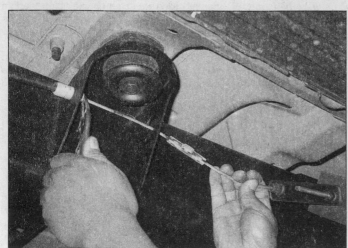

10.4a Pull down on the parking brake cable, then clamp a pair of locking pliers on the cable to retain slack . . .

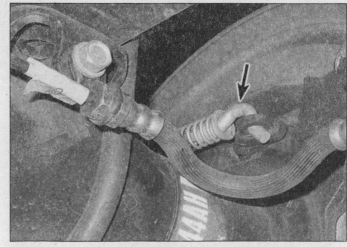

10.4b . . . then release the cable from the lever behind the brake backing plate

10.4c Pushing on the pin from the backing plate side with your finger, pry the front hold-down clip loose, then pull the pin out

10.4d Remove the rear hold-down clip and pin the same way

10.4e Disengage the lower spring from the parking brake shoes

5   Before reinstalling the disc, check the parking brake surfaces of the disc hub for cracks, score marks, deep scratches and hard spots, which will appear as small discolored areas. If hard spots or any of the other conditions listed above cannot be removed with sandpaper or emery cloth, the disc must be replaced.

6   Once all of the new parking brake shoes are in place, install the brake discs (see Section 5) and the brake calipers (see Section 4).

7   Remove the rubber plugs from the brake backing plates, insert a narrow screwdriver or brake adjusting tool through the adjustment hole and turn the star wheel until the shoes drag slightly as the disc is turned. Turn

10.4f Remove the adjuster

10.4g Disengage the upper spring from the rear parking brake shoe

10.4h Remove both parking brake shoes

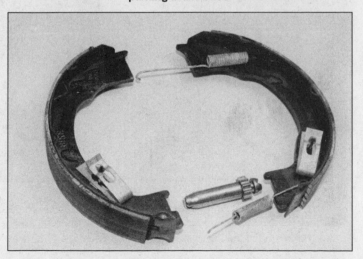

10.4i Here's how the shoes, springs and adjuster go together

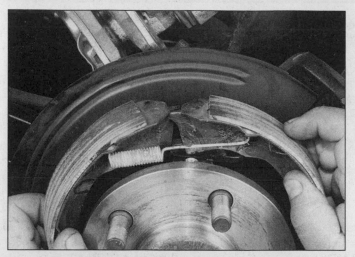

10.4j Holding them together with the upper spring, install the new shoes

10.4k Spread the upper ends of the shoes apart and engage them with the anchor as shown

the star wheel in the opposite direction until the disc turns freely. Install the backing plate plugs.

8   Install the rear wheels and lug nuts, lower the vehicle and tighten the lug nuts to the torque listed in the Chapter 1 Specifications.

9   Operate the parking brake lever several times to release the lockout spring and adjust the cables.

10   Carefully check the operation of the brakes before placing the vehicle in normal service.

---

11   Drum brake shoes - replacement

Refer to illustrations 11.2, 11.3, 11.4a through 11.4v and 11.5

Warning: *Drum brake shoes must be replaced on both wheels at the same time - never replace the shoes on only one wheel. Also, the dust created by the brake system is harmful to your health. Never blow it out with compressed air and don't inhale any of it. An approved filtering mask should be worn when working on the brakes. Do not, under any cir-*

10.4l Install the adjuster

cumstances, use petroleum-based solvents to clean brake parts. Use brake system cleaner only!

Caution: *Whenever the brake shoes are replaced, the return and hold-down springs should also be replaced. Due to the continu-*

10.4m Make sure the adjuster is engaged with the shoes as shown

ous heating/cooling cycle that the springs are subjected to, they lose their tension over a period of time and may allow the shoes to drag on the drum and wear at a much faster rate than normal.

10.4n Install the lower spring

10.4o Install the front pin and hold-down clip as shown, with the head of the pin firmly seated into the lower, smaller part of the hole in the clip

10.4p Install the rear pin and hold-down clip the same way

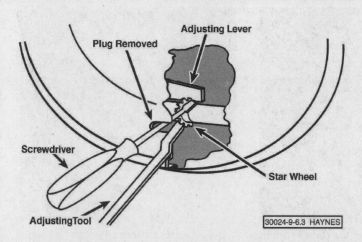

11.2 Use a thin screwdriver to push the lever away, then use an adjusting tool or another screwdriver to back-off the star wheel

11.3 Before disassembling the brake shoe assembly, spray it with brake cleaner to remove brake dust; DO NOT blow brake dust off with compressed air - collect the contaminated fluid in a suitable container and dispose of it properly!

1   Loosen the wheel lug nuts, raise the rear of the vehicle and support it securely on jackstands. Block the front wheels to keep the vehicle from rolling. Release the parking brake. Remove the wheel. **Note:** *To avoid mixing up parts, work on only one brake assembly at a time.*

2   Use wire cutters to remove any retainers on the wheel studs holding the drum on (if equipped) and remove the brake drum. If the drum will not come off, retract the brake shoes by using the adjuster port in the brake backing plate **(see illustration)**. **Note:** *Use a screwdriver to reach the star wheel (through the port) and turn it. If the star wheel stops turning and the brake drum will not move, turn the star wheel in the other direction until the brake drum becomes loose and can be removed from the hub.*

3   Clean the brake shoe assembly with brake system cleaner before beginning work **(see illustration).**

4   Follow the accompanying illustrations for the brake shoe replacement procedure **(see illustrations 11.4a through 11.4v).** Be sure

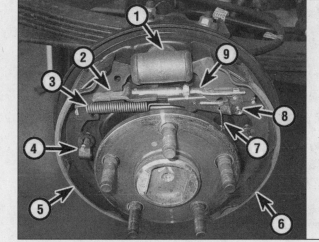

11.4a Rear drum brake details:

1   *Wheel cylinder*
2   *Parking brake actuating lever*
3   *Outer top return spring (inner top return spring not visible in this photo)*
4   *Hold-down spring clip and pin*
5   *Primary brake shoe*
6   *Secondary brake shoe*
7   *Adjuster lever spring*
8   *Adjuster lever*
9   *Automatic adjuster*

to stay in order and read the caption under each illustration.

5   Before reinstalling the drum, carefully examine it for cracks, score marks, deep scratches and hard spots, which will appear as small discolored areas. If the hard spots

cannot be removed with fine emery cloth or if any of the other conditions listed above exist, the drum must be taken to an automotive machine shop to have it resurfaced. **Note:** *Professionals recommend resurfacing the drums whenever a brake job is performed.*

11.4b Disconnect the adjuster lever spring from the brake shoe

11.4c Remove the adjuster lever

11.4d Remove the outer top return spring

11.4e Remove the bottom return spring

11.4f Remove the inner top return spring from the secondary shoe

11.4g Depress the spring clips on each shoe with a screwdriver and remove them and the hold-down pins . . .

11.4h . . . and then remove the secondary shoe, noting the small pin installed on it for the adjuster lever

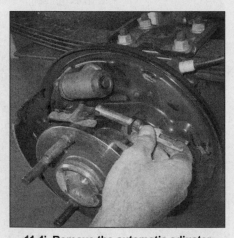

11.4i Remove the automatic adjuster

11.4j Separate the parking brake actuating lever from the primary shoe and remove the shoe and the inner top return spring

Resurfacing will eliminate the possibility of out-of-round drums. If the drums are worn so much that they can't be resurfaced without exceeding the maximum allowable diameter (see illustration), then new ones will be required. At the very least, if you elect not to

have the drums resurfaced, remove the glazing from the surface with emery cloth or sandpaper using a swirling motion.
6   Install the brake drum onto the hub flange. Remove the rubber plug covering the adjuster port (see illustration 11.2). Insert a screwdriver into the adjusting port in the

brake backing plate and turn the gear on the adjuster until the brake shoes drag on the drum as it's rotated. Back off the adjustment enough so that the shoes don't drag when the drum is turned. Reinstall the rubber plug into the backing plate.

11.4k Clean, then lubricate the automatic adjuster screw threads with high-temperature grease

11.4l Lubricate the contact surfaces of the backing plate with high-temperature grease

11.4m Engage the parking brake actuating lever with the primary brake shoe

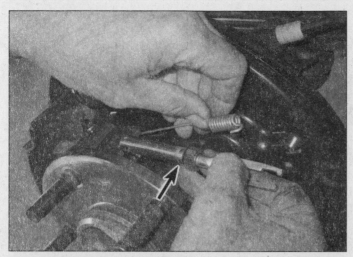

11.4n Place the inner top return spring on the back of the primary shoe and the automatic adjuster onto the parking brake actuating lever (the end of the spring with the most coils is attached to the primary shoe and the small notch on the adjuster faces outward)

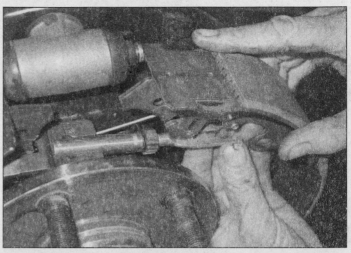

11.4o Hook the inner top return spring to the secondary shoe and then pull it enough to engage the automatic adjuster to the shoe (an assistant might be helpful to hold the primary shoe in place while this is being done)

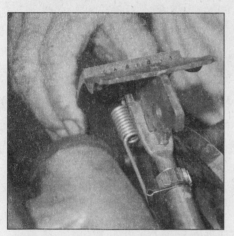

11.4p Make sure that the inner top return spring is correctly placed beneath the automatic adjuster

11.4q Seat the bottom of the brake shoes to the bracket on the backing plate

11.4r Place the hold-down pin through each shoe and install the spring clips

11.4s Install the bottom return spring

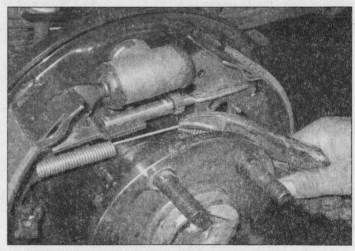

11.4t Making sure that the top of the brake shoes are positioned correctly on each side of the wheel cylinder, install the outer top return spring

11.4u Install the adjuster lever and spring

11.4v Install the adjuster spring between the lever and the secondary shoe

7   Mount the wheel and install the lug nuts. Lower the vehicle and tighten the lug nuts to the torque listed in the Chapter 1 Specifications.

8   Make a number of forward and reverse stops and operate the parking brake to adjust the brakes until satisfactory pedal action is obtained.

9   Check the operation of the brakes carefully before driving the vehicle.

12   Wheel cylinder - removal and installation

Warning: *The dust created by the brake system is harmful to your health. Never blow it out with compressed air and don't inhale any of it. An approved filtering mask should be worn when working on the brakes. Do not, under any circumstances, use petroleum-based solvents to clean brake parts. Use brake system cleaner only!*

Note: *If replacement is indicated (usually because of fluid leakage or sticky operation), it is recommended that the wheel cylinders be replaced, not overhauled. Always replace the wheel cylinders in pairs - never replace just one of them.*

Removal

Refer to illustration 12.4

1   Raise the rear of the vehicle and support it securely on jackstands. Block the front wheels to keep the vehicle from rolling.

2   Remove the brake shoe assembly (see Section 11).

3   Remove all dirt and foreign material from around the wheel cylinder.

4   Disconnect the brake line **(see illustration)**. Don't pull the brake line away from the wheel cylinder.

5   Remove the wheel cylinder mounting bolts.

6   Detach the wheel cylinder from the brake backing plate and immediately plug the brake line to prevent fluid loss and contamination.

Installation

7   Apply a small amount of RTV sealant between the backing plate and wheel cylinder, then place the wheel cylinder in position and install the bolts finger tight. Connect the brake line to the cylinder, being careful not to cross thread the fitting. Tighten the wheel cylinder mounting bolts to the torque listed in this Chapter's Specifications. Now tighten the brake line fitting securely.

8   Install the brake shoe assembly (see Section 11).

9   Bleed the brakes (see Section 9).

10   Check the operation of the brakes carefully before driving the vehicle.

13   Parking brake - adjustment

Refer to illustration 13.2

1   Raise the rear of the vehicle and support it securely on jackstands. Block the front wheels to prevent the vehicle from rolling.

11.5 The maximum allowable diameter is cast into the drum (typical)

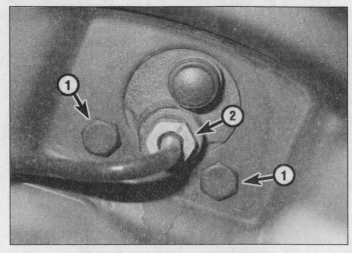

12.4 Wheel cylinder mounting details:

1   Mounting bolt   *2   Brake line fitting*

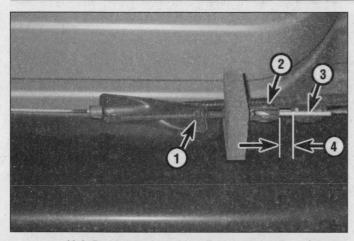

13.2 Parking brake cable adjustment details:

1   Adjuster nut
2   Tensioner
3   Tensioner rod
4   1/4 inch mark

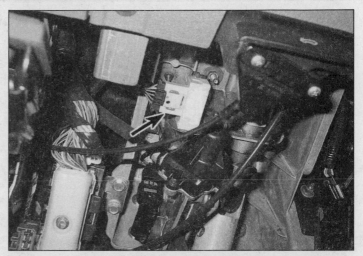

14.1 The brake light switch is attached to a bracket near the top of the brake pedal

2   Adjust the parking brake shoes as described in Section 10. Loosen the adjusting nut at the equalizer enough to create slack in the cables **(see illustration)**.

3   Verify that the drums rotate freely without drag, then fully apply the parking brake.

4   Mark the tensioner rod about 1/4-inch from the tensioner.

5   Tighten the adjusting nut at the tensioner bracket until the mark on the tensioner rod moves into alignment with the tensioner. **Caution:** *Do NOT loosen or tighten the tensioner adjusting nut after completing this adjustment.*

6   Release the parking brake pedal and verify that the rear wheels rotate freely without any drag.

7   Remove the jackstands and lower the vehicle.

8   Test the operation of the parking brake on an incline (be sure to remain in the vehicle for this check!).

14   Brake light switch - replacement

Refer to illustration 14.1

Caution: *Do not move the small lever on the replacement switch until it has been installed or the switch will have to be replaced again.*

Note: *Once the switch is removed, it must be replaced with a new one. The switch can only be installed once.*

1   The brake ligvht switch is mounted on a bracket supporting the steering column. The switch is secured in the bracket by means of an integral retainer on the switch body **(see illustration)**.

2   Depress the brake pedal and hold it down.

3   Rotate the switch about 30-degrees in a clockwise direction to unlock the switch retainer, then pull the switch out of its bracket.

4   Unplug the switch electrical connector and remove the switch.

5   Plug in the electrical connector to the new switch.

6   Press and hold the brake pedal in its fully-applied position.

7   Align the tab on the switch with the notch in the switch bracket, then insert the switch in the bracket and turn it counterclockwise about 30-degrees to lock it into place.

8   Move the small lever on the switch to a horizontal position (this will connect the contacts inside the switch).

9   Try the brakes and verify that the switch is operating properly.

Notes

Chapter 10
Suspension and steering systems

Contents

Specifications

Torque specifications

Ft-lbs (unless otherwise noted)

Front suspension

Hub bearing mounting bolts	120
Shock absorber	
Upper mounting nut(s)	75
Lower mounting nut	60
Stabilizer bar	
Link nut	
Upper	27
Lower	125
Bracket bolts	45
Upper control arm	
Arm-to-frame pivot bolts	75
Balljoint-to-steering knuckle nut	55
Lower control arm	
Arm-to-frame pivot bolts	180
Balljoint-to-steering knuckle nut	
Dakota	55
Durango	70

Torque specifications (continued)   **Ft-lbs** (unless otherwise noted)

Rear suspension - Dakota

Rear shock absorber mounting bolts/nuts	75
Stabilizer bar	
Link nut	
Upper	27
Lower	75
Bracket bolts	75
Leaf spring-to-axle U-bolt nuts	110
Leaf spring-to-front and rear spring hanger nut and bolt	120
Rear shackle-to-frame bracket nut and bolt	120

Rear suspension - Durango

Rear shock absorber mounting bolts/nuts	75
Stabilizer bar	
Bracket bolts	45
Link nut	
Upper	75
Lower	75
Watts links nuts/bolts	80
Bellcrank mounting bolt	185

Steering

Airbag module-to-steering wheel screws	90 in-lbs
Front crossmember (Durango)	75
Steering wheel bolt	45
Steering column nuts	20
Intermediate shaft pinch bolts	
Upper coupler (to steering column shaft)	28
Lower coupler (to steering gear input shaft)	36
Steering gear mounting bolts	190
Tie-rod-to-steering knuckle nut	55
Wheel lug nuts	See Chapter 1

1   General information

Front suspension

Refer to illustrations 1.1 and 1.2

Dakota models are equipped with an independent front suspension system with upper and lower control arms and shock absorbers/coil spring assemblies. A stabilizer bar controls body roll. Each steering knuckle is positioned by a pair of balljoints in the ends of the upper and lower control arms **(see illustration)**.

Durango models are equipped with an independent front suspension system with upper and lower control arms, torsion bars and shock absorbers. A stabilizer bar controls body roll. Each steering knuckle is positioned by a pair of balljoints in the ends of the upper and lower control arms **(see illustration)**.

Rear suspension

Refer to illustrations 1.3a and 1.3b

The rear suspension on Dakota models consists of two shock absorbers and two leaf springs **(see illustration)**. For the Durango models, there are coil springs, shock absorbers, control arms and a Watts link **(see illustration)**. Both models incorporate a stabilizer bar to control body roll.

Steering

The steering system consists of a rack-and-pinion steering gear and two adjustable tie-rods. Power assist is standard.

Frequently, when working on the suspension or steering system components, you may come across fasteners which seem impossible to loosen. These fasteners on the underside of the vehicle are continually subjected to water, road grime, mud, etc., and can become rusted or "frozen," making them extremely difficult to remove. In order to unscrew these stubborn fasteners without damaging them (or other components), be sure to use lots of penetrating oil and allow it to soak in for a while. Using a wire brush to clean exposed threads will also ease removal of the nut or bolt and prevent damage to the threads. Sometimes a sharp blow with a hammer and punch is effective in breaking the bond between a nut and bolt threads, but care must be taken to prevent the punch from slipping off the fastener and ruining the threads. Heating the stuck fastener and surrounding area with a torch sometimes helps too, but isn't recommended because of the obvious dangers associated with fire. Long breaker bars and extension, or "cheater," pipes will increase leverage, but never use an extension pipe on a ratchet - the ratcheting mechanism could be damaged. Sometimes, turning the nut or bolt in the tightening (clockwise) direction first will help to break it loose. Fasteners that require drastic measures to unscrew should always be replaced with new ones.

Since most of the procedures that are dealt with in this Chapter involve jacking up the vehicle and working underneath it, a good pair of jackstands will be needed. A hydraulic floor jack is the preferred type of jack to lift the vehicle, and it can also be used to support certain components during various operations. **Warning:** *Never, under any circumstances, rely on a jack to support the vehicle while working on it. Also, whenever any of the suspension or steering fasteners are loosened or removed they must be inspected and, if necessary, be replaced with new ones of the same part number or of original equipment*

1.1 Front suspension and steering components (Dakota)

1	*Stabilizer bar*	*3*	*Steering knuckle*	*5*	*Lower control arm*
2	*Tie-rod end*	*4*	*Lower balljoint*		

1.2 Front suspension and steering components (Durango)

1	*Stabilizer bar*	*4*	*Stabilizer bar link*	*7*	*Lower control arm*
2	*Shock absorber*	*5*	*Steering knuckle*	*8*	*Torsion bar*
3	*Upper balljoint*	*6*	*Lower balljoint*		

1.3a Rear suspension components (Dakota)

1   Leaf springs
2   Shock absorber (one shown, the other
    is not visible in this photo)
3   Spring plates
4   Spring plate U-bolts
5   Rear axle

1.3b Rear suspension components (Durango)

1   Watts link
2   Bellcrank
3   Coil spring
4   Shock absorber
5   Lower control arm
6   Upper control arm
7   Rear axle

2.3a Upper shock absorber fasteners for Dakota models

2.3b Shock absorber fasteners for Durango models

quality and design. Torque specifications must be followed for proper reassembly and component retention. Never attempt to heat or straighten any suspension or steering components. Instead, replace any bent or damaged part with a new one.

2 Shock absorber (front) - removal and installation

Note: Dakota models have a shock absorber/ coil spring assembly. It is possible to replace the shocks or springs individually but the unit will have to be disassembled by a qualified repair shop with the proper equipment. This will add considerable cost to the project. You can compare the cost of replacing the complete assemblies yourself to the cost of replacing individual components (with the help of a shop).

Removal

Refer to illustrations 2.3a and 2.3b

1   Loosen the front wheel lug nuts. Raise the vehicle and support it securely on jackstands. Remove the front wheels.
2   Support the outer end of the control arm using a floor jack or equivalent.
3   Remove the fasteners that attach the upper end of the shock to the frame **(see illustrations)**.
4   Disconnect the stabilizer bar link from the lower control arm (see Section 3).
5   Remove the fasteners attaching the lower end of the shock absorber to the lower control arm.
6   Remove the shock absorber.
7   Inspect the shock absorber for leaking fluid, dents, cracks and other damage. Inspect the coil spring for chips and cracks which could cause premature failure. Inspect the spring seats for hardness and general deterioration. If any of the components of the assembly are worn or damaged, have the unit serviced by a qualified repair shop or replace it.

Installation

8   Installation is the reverse of removal. Be sure to tighten the fasteners to the torque listed in this Chapter's Specifications. **Note 1:** *On Dakota models, install the lower shock fasteners so that the head of the bolt is facing the rear of the vehicle.* **Note 2:** *The shock absorber lower mounting fasteners should be tightened with the vehicle at normal ride height. This can be done after the vehicle has been lowered to the ground (on vehicles with adequate clearance), or can be simulated by raising the lower control arm with a floor jack.*
9   Tighten the wheel lug nuts to the torque listed in the Chapter 1 Specifications.

3 Stabilizer bar and bushings (front) - removal and installation

Refer to illustration 3.1
Note: *The manufacturer states that the vehicle must be at curb height when installing the stabilizer bar.*
1   Remove the upper nut from the stabilizer bar link and separate it from the bar **(see illustration)**. **Note:** *The stabilizer bar link can*

be separated from the lower control arm by removing the lower nut on the link.
2   Remove the stabilizer bar bracket fasteners and remove the brackets.
3   Remove the stabilizer bar. Remove the rubber bushings from the stabilizer bar.
4   Inspect all rubber bushings for wear and damage. If any of the rubber parts are cracked, torn or generally deteriorated, replace them.
5   Installation is the reverse of removal. Be sure to tighten all the fasteners to the torque listed in this Chapter's Specifications. Tighten the wheel lug nuts to the torque listed in the Chapter 1 Specifications.

4 Torsion bar - removal and installation

Refer to illustrations 4.2a and 4.2b
Warning: *Removing a torsion bar is potentially dangerous and utmost attention must be directed to the job, or serious injury may result. The following procedure requires the use of a tool specifically designed to unload the tension on the torsion bar. Carefully follow the instructions furnished with the tool.*
Note 1: *Torsion bars are utilized on Durango*

3.1 Remove the stabilizer bar link upper nut (A) and the stabilizer bar bracket nuts (B)

4.2a Mark the relationship of the torsion bar to the lower control arm

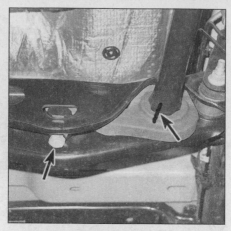

4.2b Mark the relationship of the torsion bar to the anchor and mark the adjustment bolt threads where it meets the anchor adjuster nut

Adjustment

10   Drive the vehicle back-and-forth a few times to settle the suspension.

11   Make sure the tires are properly inflated and the vehicle is unloaded and parked on level ground. Measure the vehicle's ride height on each side, from equal points on the frame to the ground. If the side that has been worked on is higher or lower than the other side, turn the torsion bar adjustment bolt accordingly until the vehicle sits level. This may take a few tries, and it's important to roll the vehicle back and forth between adjustments, to settle the suspension and get an accurate reading.

12   Have the front end alignment checked, and if necessary, adjusted.

models only.

Note 2: *The torsion bars are marked L for left and R for right; they aren't interchangeable.*

Removal

1   Loosen the front wheel lugs nuts, raise the vehicle and support it securely on jackstands placed under the frame rails. Remove the wheel.

2   Mark the relationship of the torsion bar to the lower control arm and to the torsion bar anchor **(see illustrations)**.

3   Make a mark on the adjustment bolt where it goes into the nut that bears on the anchor, or count the number of threads showing between the nut and the bolt head.

4   Install the special tool on the crossmember; make sure the tool's center bolt is positioned on the dimple in the torsion bar anchor, then tighten the center bolt until the load is removed from the adjustment bolt and nut.

5   Unscrew the adjustment bolt and nut, then carefully unscrew the tool, allowing the torsion bar to unload.

6   Remove the anchor from the torsion bar

and pull the torsion bar out of the lower control arm to remove it.

Installation

7   Installation is the reverse of removal. Be sure to clean out the hexagonal hole in the lower control arm and lube it with multi-purpose grease before inserting the torsion bar into the arm. Also apply some grease to the hex ends of the torsion bar, to the top of the anchor and to the adjustment bolt. Make sure that the marks you made on the rear end of the torsion bar and the crossmember and on the front end of the torsion bar and the control arm line up. And make sure that the torsion bar adjustment bolt is tightened until the same number of threads are showing between the bolt head and nut that were showing before removal.

8   Install the wheel, remove the jackstands and lower the vehicle.

9   Tighten the wheel lug nuts to the torque listed in the Chapter 1 Specifications.

5   Upper control arm (front) - removal and installation

Warning: *If you're working on a Durango model, the shock absorber must remain in place when removing the control arm. If for some reason the shock absorber has already been removed, support the lower control arm with a floor jack.*

Removal

Refer to illustrations 5.2 and 5.3

1   Loosen the wheel lug nuts, raise the vehicle and support it securely on jackstands placed under the frame rails. Remove the wheel.

2   Loosen (but don't remove) the nut on the upper balljoint stud, then disconnect the balljoint from the steering knuckle with a balljoint removal tool **(see illustration)**. **Note:** *If you don't have the proper balljoint removal tool, a "picklefork" type balljoint separator can be used, but keep in mind that this type of tool will probably destroy the balljoint boot.*

3   Remove the control arm mounting fasteners **(see illustration)**. Pull the upper arm from its frame brackets.

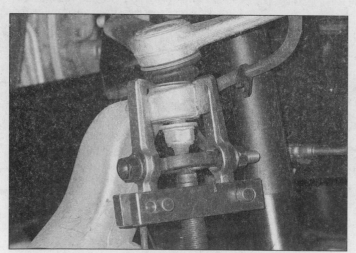

5.2 Back off the nut a few turns, then separate the balljoint from the steering knuckle (leaving the nut on the ballstud will prevent the balljoint from separating abruptly)

5.3 Upper control arm fasteners (Durango shown - Dakota model is similar)

Installation

4   Installation is the reverse of removal. Be sure to tighten all fasteners to the torque values listed in this Chapter's Specifications, but don't tighten the pivot bolt nuts until the vehicle is sitting at normal ride height. If it's too hard to get to the nuts with the wheel on, normal ride height can be simulated by raising the outer end of the lower control arm with a floor jack.

5   Install the wheel and lug nuts. Lower the vehicle and tighten the lug nuts to the torque listed in the Chapter 1 Specifications. Have the front end alignment checked and, if necessary, adjusted.

6   Lower control arm (front) - removal and installation

Removal

Refer to illustrations 6.7a, 6.7b, 6.7c and 6.8

1   Loosen the wheel lug nuts, raise the vehicle and support it securely on jackstands placed under the frame rails. Remove the wheel. **Note:** *On 4WD models, loosen the driveaxle/hub nut before raising the vehicle* (see Chapter 8).

2   Remove the brake disc and disconnect the wheel speed sensor (see Chapter 9).

3   Support the outer end of the lower control arm with a floor jack. Remove the lower mounting fasteners that attach the shock absorber to the lower control arm (see Section 2).

4   On Durango models, remove the torsion bar (see Section 4).

5   Separate the stabilizer bar end link from the control arm (see Section 3).

6   On 4WD models, remove the driveaxle (see Chapter 8).

7   Mark the relationship of the control arm mounting fasteners to the frame then remove them **(see illustrations)**. Pull the upper arm from its frame brackets. **Note:** *Marking the*

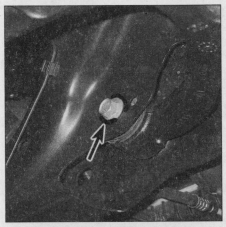

6.7a Mark the relationship of each individual fastener to the frame before removing them (Durango)

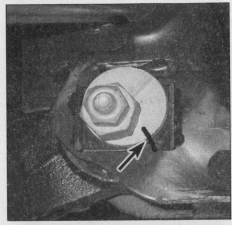

6.7b Mark the position of each individual cam-type adjuster before removing them (Dakota)

fastener positions (on each individual fastener) in relation to the frame is crucial to preserving the wheel alignment.

8   Loosen (but don't remove) the nut on the lower balljoint stud, then disconnect the balljoint from the steering knuckle with a balljoint removal tool **(see illustration)**. **Note:** *If you don't have the proper balljoint removal tool, a "picklefork" type balljoint separator can be used, but keep in mind that this type of tool will probably destroy the balljoint boot.*

Installation

9   Installation is the reverse of removal. Be sure to tighten all fasteners to the torque values listed in this Chapter's Specifications, but don't tighten the pivot bolt nuts until the vehicle is sitting at normal ride height. If it's too hard to get to the nuts with the wheel on, normal ride height can be simulated by raising the outer end of the lower control arm with a floor jack.

10   Install the wheel and lug nuts. Lower the vehicle and tighten the lug nuts to the torque listed in the Chapter 1 Specifications. Have

the front end alignment checked and, if necessary, adjusted.

11   On Durango models, be sure to check and adjust the ride height as a result of removing the torsion bar (see Section 4).

7   Balljoints - check and replacement

1   Inspect the control arm balljoints for looseness anytime either of them is separated from the steering knuckle. See if you can turn the ballstud in its socket with your fingers. If the balljoint is loose, or if the ballstud can be turned, replace the balljoint. You can also check the balljoints with the suspension assembled as follows.

Upper balljoint

2   Loosen the front wheel lug nuts, raise the front of the vehicle and support it securely on jackstands, then remove the wheel. Raise the lower control arm with a floor jack to simulate normal ride height (or close to it).

6.7c Remove the nuts and the upper control arm pivot bolts (turn the nuts, not the bolts)

6.8 Back off the nut a few turns, then separate the balljoint from the steering knuckle (leaving the nut on the ballstud will prevent the balljoint from separating violently)

3   Using a large prybar inserted between the upper control arm and the steering knuckle, pry upwards on the upper control arm. The manufacturer specifies up to 0.020-inch movement is allowed; a dial indicator can be used to check for play. If you are unable to accurately measure balljoint play, have the balljoint checked at an automotive repair shop.

4   If replacement is indicated, replace the upper control arm (see Section 5); the balljoint cannot be replaced separately.

Lower balljoint

Refer to illustration 7.7

5   Raise the vehicle and support it securely on jackstands.

6   Place a floor jack under the lower control arm, near the outer end, and raise it until the upper control arm lifts off its rebound bumper.

7   Now, insert the prybar between the top of the balljoint and the steering knuckle and pry down **(see illustration)**. The manufacturer specifies up to 0.020-inch movement is allowed; a dial indicator can be used to check for play. If you are unable to accurately measure balljoint play, have the balljoint checked at an automotive repair shop.

8   If replacement is indicated, remove the lower control arm (see Section 6); the balljoint is press fit in the lower control arm, which necessitates the use of a special press tool and receiver cup to remove and install the balljoint. Equipment rental yards and some auto parts stores have these tools available for rent. If you don't have access to this tool, take the vehicle (or the lower control arm) to an automotive machine shop or other qualified repair facility to have the balljoint replaced. **Note:** *Some balljoint replacement tools are similar to a big, heavy-duty C-clamp. With this type of tool it is only necessary to separate the balljoint from the steering knuckle.*

8   Hub and bearing assembly (front) - removal and installation

Refer to illustration 8.3

Warning: *The dust created by the brake system is harmful to your health. Never blow it out with compressed air and don't inhale any of it. Do not, under any circumstances, use petroleum-based solvents to clean brake parts. Use brake system cleaner only.*
Note: *The hub and bearing assembly is sealed-for-life. If worn or damaged, it must be replaced as a unit.*

Removal

1   Loosen the wheel lug nuts, raise the vehicle and support it securely on jackstands placed under the frame rails. Remove the wheel. **Note:** *On 4WD models, loosen the driveaxle/hub nut before raising the vehicle (see Chapter 8).*

2   Remove the brake disc and disconnect

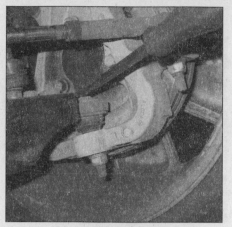

7.7 Pry down on the balljoint to check for wear

the wheel speed sensor (see Chapter 9).

3   Working from the back side of the steering knuckle, remove the hub retaining bolts from the steering knuckle **(see illustration)**.

4   Remove the hub from the steering knuckle. Remove the disc shield. **Note:** *On 4WD models, remove the driveaxle/hub nut and then remove the hub from the steering knuckle. If the hub is stuck to the driveaxle, use a two-jaw puller to remove it.*

Installation

5   Clean the mating surfaces on the steering knuckle, bearing flange and knuckle bore.

6   Position the disc shield, insert the hub and bearing assembly into the steering knuckle and install the bolts, tightening them to the torque listed in this Chapter's Specifications.

7   Installation is the reverse of removal, noting the following points:

a) *If you're working on a 4WD model, tighten the driveaxle/hub nut to the torque listed in the Chapter 8 Specifications.*

b) *Tighten the brake caliper mounting bracket and brake caliper mounting bolts to the torque listed in the Chapter 9 Specifications.*

c) *Install the wheel, lower the vehicle and tighten the lug nuts to the torque listed in the Chapter 1 Specifications.*

9   Steering knuckle - removal and installation

1   If you're working on a 4WD model, remove the driveaxle/hub nut (see Chapter 8).

2   Loosen the wheel lug nuts, raise the vehicle and support it securely on jackstands. Remove the wheel.

3   Remove the brake disc and wheel speed sensor (see Chapter 9).

4   Disconnect the tie-rod from the steering knuckle (see Section 18).

5   Support the lower control arm with a

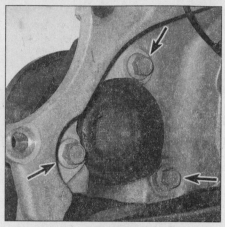

8.3 Hub mounting fasteners

10.2 Rear shock absorber fasteners

floor jack. The jack must remain in this position throughout the entire procedure.

6   Separate the upper control arm from the steering knuckle (see Section 5).

7   Separate the lower control arm from the steering knuckle (see Section 7).

8   Carefully inspect the steering knuckle for cracks, especially around the steering arm and spindle mounting area. Also inspect the balljoint stud holes. If they're elongated, or if you find any cracks in the knuckle, replace the steering knuckle.

9   Installation is the reverse of removal. Be sure to tighten all suspension fasteners to the torque listed in this Chapter's Specifications. Refer to the Chapter Specifications listed in Chapter's 8 and 9 for those related fasteners.

10   Shock absorber (rear) - removal and installation

Refer to illustration 10.2

1   Raise the rear of the vehicle and support it securely on jackstands placed under the frame rails. Support the rear axle with a floor jack placed under the axle tube on the side being worked on. Don't raise the axle - just support its weight. **Note:** *On Durango models,*

11.2 The stabilizer bar link fasteners (A) and the stabilizer bar bracket fasteners (B)

12.2 Rear upper control arm mounting fasteners

lower the spare tire if you are removing the left shock absorber.

2   Remove the nut and bolt that attach the upper end of the shock absorber to the frame **(see illustration)**. If the nut won't loosen because of rust, apply some penetrating oil and allow it to soak in for awhile.

3   Remove the nut and bolt that attach the lower end of the shock to the axle bracket. Again, if the nut is frozen, apply some penetrating oil, wait awhile and try again.

4   Extend the new shock absorber as far as possible. Install new rubber grommets into the shock absorber eyes (if they are not already present).

5   Installation is the reverse of removal. Be sure to tighten the shock absorber mounting fasteners to the torque listed in this Chapter's Specifications.

11 Stabilizer bar and bushings (rear) - removal and installation

Refer to illustration 11.2

1   Raise the vehicle and support it securely on jackstands.

2   Remove the nuts from the stabilizer bar link and separate it from the bar **(see illustration)**.

3   Remove the stabilizer bar bracket fasteners and remove the brackets **(see illustration 11.2)**.

4   Remove the stabilizer bar. Remove the rubber bushings from the stabilizer bar.

5   Inspect all rubber bushings for wear and damage. If any of the rubber parts are cracked, torn or generally deteriorated, replace them.

6   Installation is the reverse of removal. Be sure to tighten all the fasteners to the torque listed in this Chapter's Specifications and to reinstall the parking brake cable bracket (if equipped). Tighten the wheel lug nuts to the torque listed in the Chapter 1 Specifications.

12 Control arms (rear) - removal and installation

Note: *Rear control arms are utilized on Durango models only.*

1   Raise the rear of the vehicle and support it securely on jackstands.

Upper control arm

Refer to illustration 12.2

2   Remove the control arm fasteners at the axle **(see illustration)**.

3   Remove the control arm fasteners at the frame and then remove the upper control arm.

Lower control arm

Refer to illustration 12.5

4   Remove the parking brake cable bracket (left arm only).

5   Remove the control arm fasteners at the axle **(see illustration)**.

6   Remove the control arm fasteners at the frame and then remove the lower control arm.

Both arms

7   Inspect all rubber bushings for wear and damage. If any of the rubber parts are cracked, torn or generally deteriorated, replace them.

8   Installation is the reverse of removal. Be sure to tighten all fasteners to the torque values listed in this Chapter's Specifications, but don't tighten the fasteners until the vehicle is sitting at normal ride height.

13 Coil spring (rear) - removal and installation

Note: *Rear coil springs are utilized on Durango models only.*

1   Raise the rear of the vehicle and support it securely on jackstands placed under the frame rails. Support the rear axle with a floor jack placed under the axle tube on the side being worked on. Don't raise the axle - just support its weight.

2   Remove the lower shock absorber fastener (see Section 10). Also detach the stabilizer bar links from the stabilizer bar (see Section 11).

12.5 Rear lower control arm mounting fasteners

14.2 Watts link and bellcrank mounting details:

1   Watts link fasteners
2   Bellcrank mounting bolt

15.2 The U-bolt mounting nuts and spring plate

3   Remove the bellcrank mounting bolt on the rear differential cover (see Section 14).
4   Lower the jack to lower the rear axle and then remove the coil spring
5   Installation is the reverse of removal. Be sure to tighten all fasteners to the torque listed in this Chapter's Specifications.

14 Watts links and bellcrank - removal and installation

Refer to illustration 14.2
Note: *Watts links with a bellcrank are utilized on Durango models only.*
1   Raise the rear of the vehicle and support it securely on jackstands.
2   Remove the fasteners that attach the upper ends of the Watts links to the frame **(see illustration)**.
3   Remove the fasteners that attach the lower ends of the Watts links to the bellcrank **(see illustration 14.2)**.
4   To remove the bellcrank, remove its mounting bolt **(see illustration 14.2)**.
5   Inspect all rubber bushings for wear and damage. If any of the rubber parts are cracked, torn or generally deteriorated, replace them.

6   Installation is the reverse of removal. Be sure to tighten the all mounting fasteners to the torque listed in this Chapter's Specifications.

15 Leaf spring - removal and installation

Removal

Refer to illustrations 15.2, 15.3 and 15.4
Note: *Leaf springs are utilized on Dakota models only.*
1   Loosen the wheel lug nuts, raise the rear of the vehicle and support it securely on jackstands placed under the frame rails. Remove the wheel and support the rear axle with a floor jack placed under the axle tube. Don't raise the axle - just support its weight.
2   Remove the nuts, U-bolts and spring plate that clamp the leaf spring to the axle **(see illustration)**.
3   Remove the leaf spring shackle-to-frame bracket mounting fasteners (rear) **(see illustration)**.
4   Remove the leaf spring-to-frame mounting fasteners (front) **(see illustration)** then

remove the leaf spring from the vehicle. **Note:** *The shackle can be removed from the leaf spring if necessary.*

Installation

5   Install the rear shackle to the spring (if removed) but leave the fasteners finger tight.
6   Position the spring on the axle tube so that it is centered correctly.
7   Line up the eye at the front of the spring with the mounting bracket and install the mounting fasteners but leave them finger tight.
8   Install the rear shackle to the frame and leave the fasteners finger tight.
9   Install the U-bolts and the spring plate. Tighten the nuts to the torque listed in the Chapter 1 Specifications.
10   Install the wheel and lug nuts. Remove the jackstands and lower the vehicle. Tighten the lug nuts to the torque listed in the Chapter 1 Specifications.
11   Tighten the front spring fasteners and rear shackle fasteners to the torque listed in this Chapter's Specifications with the vehicle sitting at normal ride height.

15.3 Remove the shackle mounting fastener (A) and loosen the shackle fastener (B)

15.4 To detach the front end of the leaf spring from the forward bracket, remove this bolt (the nut is a flag nut and can be removed through the hole in the mount after the bolt has been removed)

16.3 Remove the airbag module retaining screws

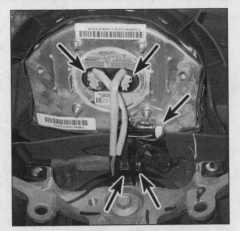

16.4 Lift the airbag off the steering wheel and unplug the electrical connectors for the airbag, horn, etc.

16.5 After removing the bolt, mark the relationship of the wheel to the shaft

16 Steering wheel - removal and installation

Warning: *These models are equipped with airbags. Always disable the airbag system whenever working in the vicinity of any airbag system component to avoid the possibility of accidental airbag deployment, which could cause personal injury (see Chapter 12).*

Removal

Refer to illustrations 16.3, 16.4, 16.5, 16.7 and 16.8

1 Park the vehicle with the front wheels in the straight-ahead position. **Warning:** *Do NOT turn the steering shaft during or after steering wheel removal. If the shaft is turned while the steering wheel is removed, a mechanism known as the clockspring can be damaged. The clockspring, which maintains a continuous electrical circuit between the wiring harness and the airbag module, consists of a flat, ribbon-like electrically conductive tape which winds and unwinds as the steering wheel is turned.*

2 Disconnect the cable from the negative battery terminal, (see Chapter 5, Section 1).

3 Remove the two airbag module retaining screws **(see illustration)** and lift off the airbag module. **Warning:** *Carry the airbag module with the trim cover (upholstered side) facing away from you, and set the airbag module in a safe location with the trim cover facing up.*

4 Unplug the electrical connectors for the airbag, horn and other components (if equipped) **(see illustration)**.

5 Remove the steering wheel bolt and mark the relationship of the steering wheel hub to the steering shaft **(see illustration)**.

6 Reinstall the steering wheel bolt and leave a generous gap between the head of the bolt and the steering wheel.

7 Use a puller to remove the steering wheel **(see illustration)**. **Caution 1:** *Don't thread the bolts of the puller into this steering wheel more than five turns, as they could contact the airbag clockspring and damage it.* **Caution 2:** *Any attempt to remove the steering wheel without using a puller can damage the steering column.* Make certain that all electrical connectors are disconnected before lifting the steering wheel off the hub.

8 If it is necessary to remove the clockspring, remove the steering column covers (see Chapter 11), unplug the electrical connectors for the clockspring, remove the mounting screws and lift the clockspring from the steering column **(see illustration)**.

Installation

9 When installing the clockspring, make absolutely sure that the airbag clockspring is centered with the arrows on the clockspring rotor and case lined up. **Note:** *The Durango models do not have arrows; just make certain that the alignment dowel that engages the steering wheel is down and the pigtail wire is at the top* **(see illustration 16.8)**. This shouldn't be a problem as long as you have not turned the steering shaft while the wheel was removed. If for some reason the shaft was turned, center the clockspring as follows:

a) *Rotate the clockspring clockwise until it stops (don't apply too much force, though).*

b) *Rotate the clockspring counterclockwise about 2-1/2 turns until the arrows on the clockspring rotor and case line up.*

16.7 Remove the steering wheel with a steering wheel puller

16.8 Disconnect the clockspring electrical connectors on the backside of the clockspring (A), then remove the mounting screws (B)

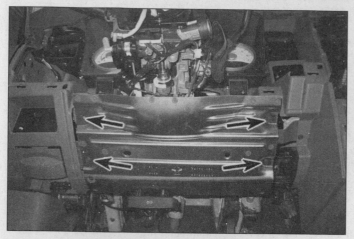

17.4 Knee bolster reinforcement plate fasteners

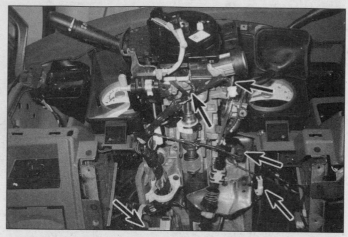

17.6 Remove any wiring harnesses and connectors that would interfere with the column removal

10 Installation is the reverse of removal, noting the following points:

a) *Make sure the airbag clockspring is centered before installing the steering wheel (see Step 9).*

b) *When installing the steering wheel, align the marks on the shaft and the steering wheel hub.*

c) *Install a NEW steering wheel bolt and tighten it to the torque listed in this Chapter's Specifications.*

d) *Install the airbag module on the steering wheel and tighten the mounting screws to the torque listed in this Chapter's Specifications.*

e) *Enable the airbag system (see Chapter 12).*

17 Steering column - removal and installation

Warning: *These models are equipped with airbags. Always disable the airbag system whenever working in the vicinity of any airbag system component to avoid the possibility of* accidental airbag deployment, which could cause personal injury (see Chapter 12).
Note: *The manufacturer states that a new shaft coupler bolt is necessary for installation.*

Removal

Refer to illustrations 17.4, 17.6, 17.7 and 17.9

1 Park the vehicle with the wheels pointing straight ahead. Disconnect the cable(s) from the negative battery terminal(s), (see Chapter 5, Section 1). Wait at least two minutes before proceeding (to allow the backup power supply for the airbag system to become depleted).

2 Remove the steering wheel (see Section 14), then turn the ignition key to the LOCK position to prevent the steering shaft from turning. **Caution:** *If this is not done, the airbag clockspring could be damaged.*

3 Remove the steering column covers (see Chapter 11), then remove the airbag clockspring to prevent accidental damage (see Section 16).

4 Remove the knee bolster (see Chapter 11) and the reinforcement plate underneath it **(see illustration).**

5 Remove the shift cable from the shift lever and column bracket (see Chapter 7B).

6 Detach the electrical connectors from the ignition and multi-function switches (see Chapter 12). Unplug any other electrical connectors that would interfere with column removal **(see illustration).**

7 Remove the shaft coupler bolt **(see illustration).** Separate the intermediate shaft from the steering shaft.

8 Remove the brake light switch and discard it (see Chapter 9).

9 Remove the steering column mounting nuts **(see illustration),** lower the column and pull it to the rear, making sure nothing is still connected.

Installation

10 Guide the steering column into position and install the mounting nuts, but don't tighten them yet.

11 Connect the intermediate shaft to the steering column. Install a new coupler bolt, then tighten the nut to the torque listed in this Chapter's Specifications.

12 Tighten the column mounting nuts to the

17.7 Mark the relationship of the steering shaft to the intermediate shaft (A) and then remove the coupler bolt (B)

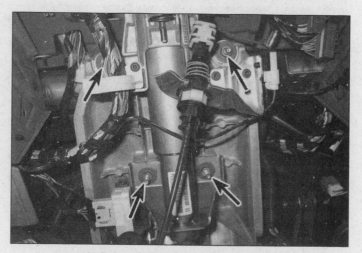

17.9 Steering column mounting nuts

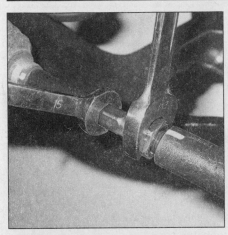

18.2 Hold the tie-rod end with a wrench while loosening the jam nut

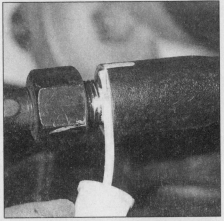

18.3 Mark the position of the tie-rod end in relation to the threads

18.4 Back-off the ballstud nut a few turns, then separate the tie-rod end from the steering knuckle with a puller (leaving the nut on the ballstud will prevent the tie-rod end from separating violently)

torque listed in this Chapter's Specifications.
13 The remainder of installation is the reverse of removal. Adjust the shift cable following the procedures described in Chapter 7B and replace the brake light switch (see Chapter 9).

18 Tie-rod ends - removal and installation

Removal

Refer to illustrations 18.2, 18.3, and 18.4

1 Loosen the wheel lug nuts, raise the vehicle and support it securely on jackstands. Apply the parking brake. Remove the wheel.
2 Loosen the tie-rod end jam nut **(see illustration)**.
3 Mark the relationship of the tie-rod end to the threaded portion of the tie-rod. This will ensure the toe-in setting is restored when reassembled **(see illustration)**.
4 Loosen (but don't remove) the nut on the tie-rod end ballstud and disconnect the tie-rod end from the steering knuckle arm with a puller **(see illustration)**. **Note:** *If the ballstud turns while loosening the nut, hold the ball-*

stud with a wrench while removing the nut.
5 If you're replacing the tie-rod end, unscrew the tie-rod end from the tie-rod, then thread the new tie-rod end onto the tie-rod to the marked position.

Installation

6 Connect the tie-rod end to the steering knuckle arm. Install the nut on the ballstud and tighten it to the torque listed in this Chapter's Specifications. Install the wheel. Lower the vehicle and tighten the lug nuts to the torque listed in the Chapter 1 Specifications.
7 Have the front end alignment checked and, if necessary, adjusted.

19 Steering gear boots - replacement

Refer to illustration 19.3

1 Loosen the wheel lug nuts, raise the vehicle and support it securely on jackstands. Remove the wheel.
2 Remove the tie-rod end and jam nut (see Section 18).
3 Remove the steering gear boot clamps

and slide the boot off. **Note:** *Check for the presence of power steering fluid in the boot. If there is a substantial amount, it means the rack seals are leaking and the power steering gear should be replaced with a new or rebuilt unit.*
4 Before installing the new boot, wrap the threads and serrations on the end of the steering rod with a layer of tape so the small end of the new boot isn't damaged.
5 Slide the new boot into position on the steering gear until it seats in the grooves, then install new clamps.
6 Remove the tape and install the tie-rod end (see Section 18).
7 Install the wheel and lug nuts. Lower the vehicle and tighten the lug nuts to the torque listed in the Chapter 1 Specifications.
8 Have the front end alignment checked and, if necessary, adjusted.

20 Steering gear - removal and installation

Refer to illustrations 20.3, 20.7 and 20.8
Warning: *Make sure the steering column shaft is not turned while the steering gear is removed or you could damage the airbag system clockspring. To prevent the shaft from turning, turn the ignition key to the lock position before beginning work, and run the seat belt through the steering wheel and clip it into its latch.*
1 Park the vehicle with the wheels pointing straight ahead. Loosen the front wheel lug nuts, raise the front of the vehicle and support it securely on jackstands. Apply the parking brake. Remove the wheels.
2 Detach the tie-rod ends from the steering knuckles (see Section 18).
3 Mark the relationship of the intermediate shaft coupler to the steering gear input shaft, remove the pinch bolt and separate the coupler from the input shaft **(see illustration)**.

19.3 Remove both clamps to remove the steering gear boot

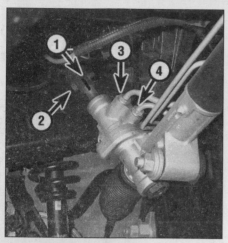

20.3 Steering gear details: (Dakota model shown, Durango similar)

1   *Mark on steering input shaft and coupler*
2   *Coupler pinch bolt*
3   *Pressure line fitting*
4   *Return hose fitting*

4   Position a drain pan under the steering gear. Using a flare-nut wrench, disconnect the power steering pressure and return lines from the steering gear **(see illustration 20.3)**. Cap the lines to prevent leakage.

5   Turn the steering gear to the right as far as it will go.

6   On Durango models with 3.7L and 4.7L engines, remove the exhaust Y-pipe.

7   On Durango models, remove the crossmember mounted in front of the steering gear **(see illustration)**.

8   Remove the mounting bolts, then maneuver the steering gear out of the vehicle **(see illustration)**.

9   Inspect all rubber bushings for wear and damage. If any of the rubber parts are cracked, torn or generally deteriorated, replace them.

10   Installation is the reverse of removal, noting the following points:

a) *Tighten the steering gear mounting bolts and the intermediate shaft coupler pinch bolt to the torque values listed in this Chapter's Specifications.*

b) *Tighten the wheel lug nuts to the torque listed in the Chapter 1 Specifications.*

c) *Check the power steering fluid level and add some, if necessary (see Chapter 1) and then bleed the system as described in Section 22.*

d) *Re-check the power steering fluid level.*

21   Power steering pump - removal and installation

Refer to illustration 21.3

1   Remove the drivebelt (see Chapter 1).

2   Using a large syringe or suction gun, suck as much fluid out of the power steering fluid reservoir.

3   Position a drain pan under the power steering pump, then disconnect the pressure line from the pump and the return hose from the reservoir **(see illustration)**. Plug the openings to prevent excessive fluid loss and the entry of contaminants.

4   Remove the pump mounting bolts. The bolts can be accessed through the holes in the power steering pump pulley.

5   Lift the pump from the engine compartment, being careful not to let any power steering fluid drip on the vehicle's paint.

6   Installation is the reverse of removal. Be sure to tighten all fasteners securely. Fill the power steering reservoir with the recommended fluid (see Chapter 1) and bleed the system following the procedure described in Section 22. Re-check the power steering fluid level.

22   Power steering system - bleeding

1   The power steering system must be bled whenever a line is disconnected. Bubbles can

be seen in power steering fluid that has air in it and the fluid will often have a milky appearance. Low fluid level can cause air to mix with the fluid, resulting in a noisy pump as well as foaming of the fluid.

2   Open the hood and check the fluid level in the reservoir, adding the specified fluid necessary to bring it up to the proper level (see Chapter 1).

3   Start the engine and slowly turn the steering wheel several times from left-to-right and back again. Do not turn the wheel completely from lock-to-lock. Check the fluid level, topping it up as necessary until it remains steady and no more bubbles are visible.

23   Wheels and tires - general information

Refer to illustration 23.1

Most models covered by this manual are equipped with radial tires **(see illustration)**, or inch-pattern light truck tires. Use of other size or type of tires may affect the ride and handling of the vehicle. Don't mix different types of tires, such as radials and bias belted tires, on the same vehicle - handling may be seriously affected. It's recommended that tires be replaced in pairs on the same axle, but if only one tire is being replaced, be sure it's the same size, structure and tread design as the other tire on the same axle.

Because tire pressure has a substantial effect on handling and wear, the pressure of all tires should be checked at least once a month or before any extended trips are taken (see Chapter 1).

Wheels must be replaced if they are bent, dented, leak air, have elongated bolt holes, are heavily rusted, out of vertical symmetry or if the lug nuts won't stay tight. Wheel repairs that use welding or peening are not recommended.

Tire and wheel balance are important to the overall handling, braking and performance of the vehicle. Unbalanced wheels can

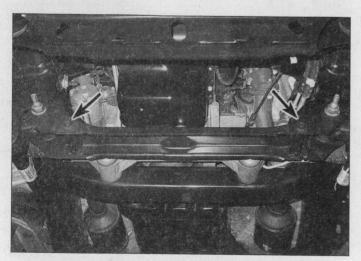

20.7 Crossmember mounting fasteners (Durango only)

20.8 Steering gear mounting fasteners

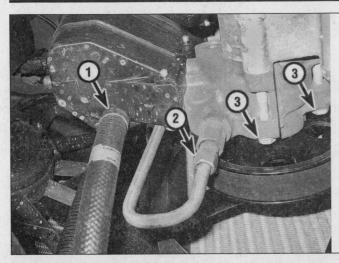

21.3 Power steering pump details:

1 *Reservoir return hose*
2 *Pressure line fitting*
3 *Mounting fasteners*

adversely affect handling and ride characteristics as well as tire life. Whenever a tire is installed on a wheel, the tire and wheel should be balanced by a shop with the proper equipment and expertise.

24 Wheel alignment - general information

Refer to illustration 24.1

Note: *Since wheel alignment requires special equipment and techniques it is beyond the scope of this manual. This section is intended only to familiarize the reader with the basic terms used and procedures followed during a typical wheel alignment.*

The three basic checks made when aligning a vehicle's front wheels are camber, caster and toe-in **(see illustration)**.

Camber and caster are the angles at which the wheels and suspension are inclined in relation to a vertical centerline. Camber is the angle of the wheel in the lateral, or side-to-side plane, while caster is the tilt between the steering axis and the vertical plane, as viewed from the side. Camber angle affects the amount of tire tread which contacts the road and compensates for changes in suspension geometry as the vehicle travels around curves and over bumps. Caster angle affects the self-centering action of the steering, which governs straight-line stability.

Toe-in is the amount the front wheels are angled in relationship to the center line

of the vehicle. For example, in a vehicle with zero toe-in, the distance measured between the front edges of the wheels and the distance measured between the rear edges of the wheels are the same. In other words, the wheels are running parallel with the centerline of the vehicle. Toe-in is adjusted by lengthening or shortening the tie-rods. Incorrect toe-in will cause the tires to wear improperly by allowing them to "scrub" against the road surface.

Proper wheel alignment is essential for safe steering and even tire wear. Symptoms of alignment problems are pulling of the steering to one side or the other and uneven tire wear. If these symptoms are present, check for the following before having the alignment adjusted:

a) *Loose steering gear mounting bolts*
b) *Damaged or worn steering gear mounts*
c) *Worn or damaged wheel bearings*
d) *Bent tie-rods*
e) *Worn balljoints*
f) *Improper tire pressures*
g) *Mixing tires of different construction*

Front wheel alignment should be left to an alignment shop with the proper equipment and experienced personnel.

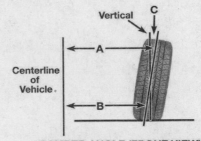

CAMBER ANGLE (FRONT VIEW)

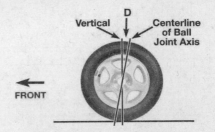

CASTER ANGLE (SIDE VIEW)

METRIC TIRE SIZES

P 185 / 80 R 13

TIRE TYPE
P-PASSENGER
T-TEMPORARY
C-COMMERCIAL

SECTION WIDTH
(MILLIMETERS)
185
195
205
ETC

ASPECT RATIO
(SECTION HEIGHT)
(SECTION WIDTH)
70
75
80

CONSTRUCTION TYPE
R-RADIAL
B-BIAS - BELTED
D-DIAGONAL (BIAS)

RIM DIAMETER
(INCHES)
13
14
15

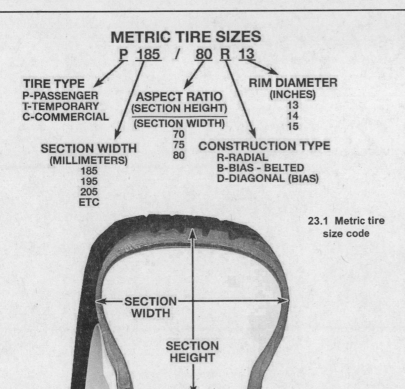

SECTION WIDTH

SECTION HEIGHT

23.1 Metric tire size code

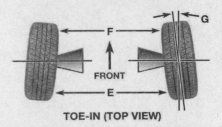

TOE-IN (TOP VIEW)

24.1 Front wheel alignment details

A minus B = C (degrees camber)
D = degrees caster
E minus F = toe-in (measured in inches)
G = toe-in (expressed in degrees)

Notes

Chapter 11 Body

Contents

1 General information

The vehicles covered by this manual are built with body-on-frame construction. The frame is a ladder-type, consisting of two C-sectioned steel side rails joined by crossmembers. The front 1/3 portion of the frame is boxed for extra rigidity in powertrain and suspension mounting. A number of lateral crossmembers are used, with some being welded or riveted to the side rails. Crossmembers designed for removal (such as the transmission crossmember) are bolted to the side rails. The Durango frame is of three sections formed to fit together and then welded.

The Dakota body is in two separate sections, the cab and the bed, while the Durango body incorporates the cab, back-seat area and cargo compartment in one unitized structure. Certain components are particularly vulnerable to accident damage and can be unbolted and repaired or replaced. Among these parts are the body moldings, bumpers, hood, fenders, doors, tailgate and all glass.

Only general body maintenance practices and body panel repair procedures within the scope of the do-it-yourselfer are included in this Chapter.

2 Body - maintenance

1 The condition of your vehicle's body is very important, because the resale value depends a great deal on it. It's much more difficult to repair a neglected or damaged body than it is to repair mechanical components. The hidden areas of the body, such as the wheel wells, the frame and the engine compartment, are equally important, although they don't require as frequent attention as the rest of the body.
2 Once a year, or every 12,000 miles, it's a good idea to have the underside of the body steam cleaned. All traces of dirt and oil will be removed and the area can then be inspected carefully for rust, damaged brake lines, frayed electrical wires, damaged cables and other problems. The front suspension components should be greased after completion of this job.
3 At the same time, clean the engine and the engine compartment with a steam cleaner or water soluble degreaser.
4 The wheel wells should be given close attention, since undercoating can peel away and stones and dirt thrown up by the tires can cause the paint to chip and flake, allowing rust to set in. If rust is found, clean down to the bare metal and apply an anti-rust paint.
5 The body should be washed about once a week. Wet the vehicle thoroughly to soften the dirt, then wash it down with a soft sponge and plenty of clean soapy water. If the surplus dirt is not washed off very carefully, it can wear down the paint.
6 Spots of tar or asphalt thrown up from the road should be removed with a cloth soaked in solvent.
7 Once every six months, wax the body and chrome trim. If a chrome cleaner is used to remove rust from any of the vehicle's plated parts, remember that the cleaner also removes part of the chrome, so use it sparingly.

These photos illustrate a method of repairing simple dents. They are intended to supplement *Body repair - minor damage* in this Chapter and should not be used as the sole instructions for body repair on these vehicles.

1 If you can't access the backside of the body panel to hammer out the dent, pull it out with a slide-hammer-type dent puller. In the deepest portion of the dent or along the crease line, drill or punch hole(s) at least one inch apart . . .

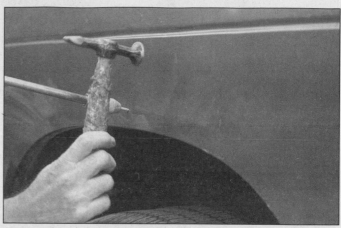

2 . . . then screw the slide-hammer into the hole and operate it. Tap with a hammer near the edge of the dent to help 'pop' the metal back to its original shape. When you're finished, the dent area should be close to its original contour and about 1/8-inch below the surface of the surrounding metal

3 Using coarse-grit sandpaper, remove the paint down to the bare metal. Hand sanding works fine, but the disc sander shown here makes the job faster. Use finer (about 320-grit) sandpaper to feather-edge the paint at least one inch around the dent area

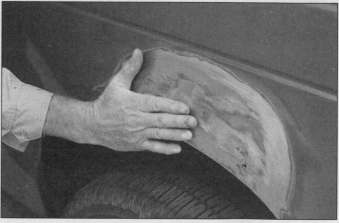

4 When the paint is removed, touch will probably be more helpful than sight for telling if the metal is straight. Hammer down the high spots or raise the low spots as necessary. Clean the repair area with wax/silicone remover

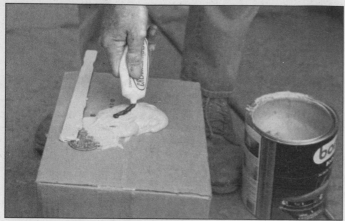

5 Following label instructions, mix up a batch of plastic filler and hardener. The ratio of filler to hardener is critical, and, if you mix it incorrectly, it will either not cure properly or cure too quickly (you won't have time to file and sand it into shape)

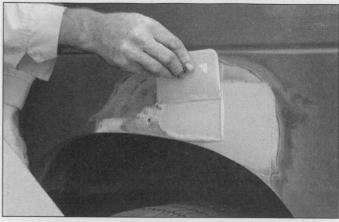

6 Working quickly so the filler doesn't harden, use a plastic applicator to press the body filler firmly into the metal, assuring it bonds completely. Work the filler until it matches the original contour and is slightly above the surrounding metal

7 Let the filler harden until you can just dent it with your fingernail. Use a body file or Surform tool (shown here) to rough-shape the filler

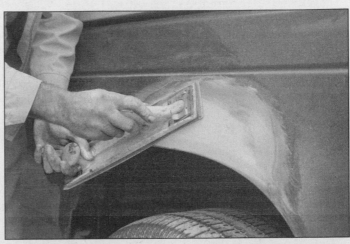

8 Use coarse-grit sandpaper and a sanding board or block to work the filler down until it's smooth and even. Work down to finer grits of sandpaper - always using a board or block - ending up with 360 or 400 grit

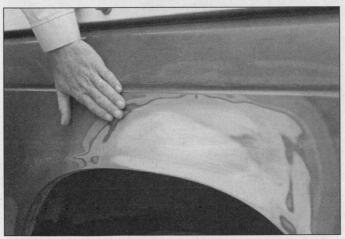

9 You shouldn't be able to feel any ridge at the transition from the filler to the bare metal or from the bare metal to the old paint. As soon as the repair is flat and uniform, remove the dust and mask off the adjacent panels or trim pieces

10 Apply several layers of primer to the area. Don't spray the primer on too heavy, so it sags or runs, and make sure each coat is dry before you spray on the next one. A professional-type spray gun is being used here, but aerosol spray primer is available inexpensively from auto parts stores

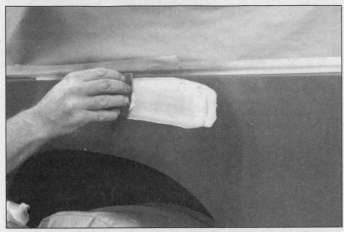

11 The primer will help reveal imperfections or scratches. Fill these with glazing compound. Follow the label instructions and sand it with 360 or 400-grit sandpaper until it's smooth. Repeat the glazing, sanding and respraying until the primer reveals a perfectly smooth surface

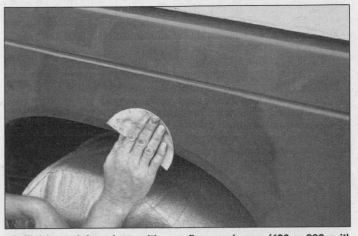

12 Finish sand the primer with very fine sandpaper (400 or 600-grit) to remove the primer overspray. Clean the area with water and allow it to dry. Use a tack rag to remove any dust, then apply the finish coat. Don't attempt to rub out or wax the repair area until the paint has dried completely (at least two weeks)

3   Vinyl trim - maintenance

Don't clean vinyl trim with detergents, caustic soap or petroleum-based cleaners. Plain soap and water works just fine, with a soft brush to clean dirt that may be ingrained. Wash the vinyl as frequently as the rest of the vehicle.

After cleaning, application of a high quality rubber and vinyl protectant will help prevent oxidation and cracks. The protectant can also be applied to weatherstripping, vacuum lines and rubber hoses (which often fail as a result of chemical degradation) and to the tires.

4   Upholstery and carpets - maintenance

1   Every three months remove the carpets or mats and clean the interior of the vehicle (more frequently if necessary). Vacuum the upholstery and carpets to remove loose dirt and dust.
2   Leather upholstery requires special care. Stains should be removed with warm water and a very mild soap solution. Use a clean, damp cloth to remove the soap, then wipe again with a dry cloth. Never use alcohol, gasoline, nail polish remover or thinner to clean leather upholstery.
3   After cleaning, regularly treat leather upholstery with a leather wax. Never use car wax on leather upholstery.
4   In areas where the interior of the vehicle is subject to bright sunlight, cover leather seats with a sheet if the vehicle is to be left out for any length of time.

5   Body repair - minor damage

See photo sequence

Repair of minor scratches

1   If the scratch is superficial and does not penetrate to the metal of the body, repair is very simple. Lightly rub the scratched area with a fine rubbing compound to remove loose paint and built-up wax. Rinse the area with clean water.
2   Apply touch-up paint to the scratch, using a small brush. Continue to apply thin layers of paint until the surface of the paint in the scratch is level with the surrounding paint. Allow the new paint at least two weeks to harden, then blend it into the surrounding paint by rubbing with a very fine rubbing compound. Finally, apply a coat of wax to the scratch area.
3   If the scratch has penetrated the paint and exposed the metal of the body, causing the metal to rust, a different repair technique is required. Remove all loose rust from the bottom of the scratch with a pocket knife, then apply rust inhibiting paint to prevent the formation of rust in the future. Using a rubber or nylon applicator, coat the scratched

area with glaze-type filler. If required, the filler can be mixed with thinner to provide a very thin paste, which is ideal for filling narrow scratches. Before the glaze filler in the scratch hardens, wrap a piece of smooth cotton cloth around the tip of a finger. Dip the cloth in thinner and then quickly wipe it along the surface of the scratch. This will ensure that the surface of the filler is slightly hollow. The scratch can now be painted over as described earlier in this Section.

Repair of dents

4   When repairing dents, the first job is to pull the dent out until the affected area is as close as possible to its original shape. There is no point in trying to restore the original shape completely as the metal in the damaged area will have stretched on impact and cannot be restored to its original contours. It is better to bring the level of the dent up to a point which is about 1/8-inch below the level of the surrounding metal. In cases where the dent is very shallow, it is not worth trying to pull it out at all.
5   If the back side of the dent is accessible, it can be hammered out gently from behind using a soft-face hammer. While doing this, hold a block of wood firmly against the opposite side of the metal to absorb the hammer blows and prevent the metal from being stretched.
6   If the dent is in a section of the body which has double layers, or some other factor makes it inaccessible from behind, a different technique is required. Drill several small holes through the metal inside the damaged area, particularly in the deeper sections. Screw long, self-tapping screws into the holes just enough for them to get a good grip in the metal. Now the dent can be pulled out by pulling on the protruding heads of the screws with locking pliers.
7   The next stage of repair is the removal of paint from the damaged area and from an inch or so of the surrounding metal. This is done with a wire brush or sanding disk in a drill motor, although it can be done just as effectively by hand with sandpaper. To complete the preparation for filling, score the surface of the bare metal with a screwdriver or the tang of a file, or drill small holes in the affected area. This will provide a good grip for the filler material. To complete the repair, see the subsection on filling and painting later in this Section.

Repair of rust holes or gashes

8   Remove all paint from the affected area and from an inch or so of the surrounding metal using a sanding disk or wire brush mounted in a drill motor. If these are not available, a few sheets of sandpaper will do the job just as effectively.
9   With the paint removed, you will be able to determine the severity of the corrosion and decide whether to replace the whole panel, if possible, or repair the affected area. New body panels are not as expensive as most

people think and it is often quicker to install a new panel than to repair large areas of rust.
10   Remove all trim pieces from the affected area except those which will act as a guide to the original shape of the damaged body, such as headlight shells, etc. Using metal snips or a hacksaw blade, remove all loose metal and any other metal that is badly affected by rust. Hammer the edges of the hole in to create a slight depression for the filler material.
11   Wire brush the affected area to remove the powdery rust from the surface of the metal. If the back of the rusted area is accessible, treat it with rust inhibiting paint.
12   Before filling is done, block the hole in some way. This can be done with sheet metal riveted or screwed into place, or by stuffing the hole with wire mesh.
13   Once the hole is blocked off, the affected area can be filled and painted. See the following subsection on filling and painting.

Filling and painting

14   Many types of body fillers are available, but generally speaking, body repair kits which contain filler paste and a tube of resin hardener are best for this type of repair work. A wide, flexible plastic or nylon applicator will be necessary for imparting a smooth and contoured finish to the surface of the filler material. Mix up a small amount of filler on a clean piece of wood or cardboard (use the hardener sparingly). Follow the manufacturer's instructions on the package, otherwise the filler will set incorrectly.
15   Using the applicator, apply the filler paste to the prepared area. Draw the applicator across the surface of the filler to achieve the desired contour and to level the filler surface. As soon as a contour that approximates the original one is achieved, stop working the paste. If you continue, the paste will begin to stick to the applicator. Continue to add thin layers of paste at 20-minute intervals until the level of the filler is just above the surrounding metal.
16   Once the filler has hardened, the excess can be removed with a body file. From then on, progressively finer grades of sandpaper should be used, starting with a 180-grit paper and finishing with 600-grit wet-or-dry paper. Always wrap the sandpaper around a flat rubber or wooden block, otherwise the surface of the filler will not be completely flat. During the sanding of the filler surface, the wet-or-dry paper should be periodically rinsed in water. This will ensure that a very smooth finish is produced in the final stage.
17   At this point, the repair area should be surrounded by a ring of bare metal, which in turn should be encircled by the finely feathered edge of good paint. Rinse the repair area with clean water until all of the dust produced by the sanding operation is gone.
18   Spray the entire area with a light coat of primer. This will reveal any imperfections in the surface of the filler. Repair the imperfections with fresh filler paste or glaze filler and once more smooth the surface with sandpa-

9.2 Before removing the hood, draw a mark around the hinge plate

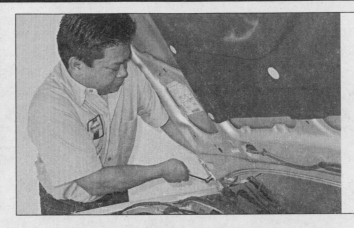

9.4 Support the hood with your shoulder while removing the hood bolts

per. Repeat this spray-and-repair procedure until you are satisfied that the surface of the filler and the feathered edge of the paint are perfect. Rinse the area with clean water and allow it to dry completely.

19   The repair area is now ready for painting. Spray painting must be carried out in a warm, dry, windless and dust free atmosphere. These conditions can be created if you have access to a large indoor work area, but if you are forced to work in the open, you will have to pick the day very carefully. If you are working indoors, dousing the floor in the work area with water will help settle the dust which would otherwise be in the air. If the repair area is confined to one body panel, mask off the surrounding panels. This will help minimize the effects of a slight mismatch in paint color. Trim pieces such as chrome strips, door handles, etc., will also need to be masked off or removed. Use masking tape and several thickness of newspaper for the masking operations.

20   Before spraying, shake the paint can thoroughly, then spray a test area until the spray painting technique is mastered. Cover the repair area with a thick coat of primer. The thickness should be built up using several thin layers of primer rather than one thick one. Using 600-grit wet-or-dry sandpaper, rub down the surface of the primer until it is very smooth. While doing this, the work area should be thoroughly rinsed with water and the wet-or-dry sandpaper periodically rinsed as well. Allow the primer to dry before spraying additional coats.

21   Spray on the top coat, again building up the thickness by using several thin layers of paint. Begin spraying in the center of the repair area and then, using a circular motion, work out until the whole repair area and about two inches of the surrounding original paint is covered. Remove all masking material 10 to 15 minutes after spraying on the final coat of paint. Allow the new paint at least two weeks to harden, then use a very fine rubbing compound to blend the edges of the new paint into the existing paint. Finally, apply a coat of wax.

6   Body repair - major damage

1   Major damage must be repaired by an auto body shop specifically equipped to perform these repairs. Most shops have the specialized equipment required to do the job properly.

2   If the damage is extensive, the body must be checked for proper alignment or the vehicle's handling characteristics may be adversely affected and other components may wear at an accelerated rate.

3   Due to the fact that all of the major body components (hood, fenders, etc.) are separate and replaceable units, any seriously damaged components should be replaced rather than repaired. Sometimes the components can be found in a wrecking yard that specializes in used vehicle components, often at considerable savings over the cost of new parts.

7   Hinges and locks - maintenance

Once every 3000 miles, or every three months, the hinges and latch assemblies on the doors, hood and trunk should be given a few drops of light oil or lock lubricant. The door latch strikers should also be lubricated with a thin coat of grease to reduce wear and ensure free movement. Lubricate the door and trunk locks with spray-on graphite lubricant.

8   Windshield and fixed glass - replacement

Replacement of the windshield and fixed glass requires the use of special fast-setting adhesive/caulk materials and some specialized tools. It is recommended that these operations be left to a dealer or a shop specializing in glass work.

9   Hood - removal, installation and adjustment

Note: *The hood is heavy and somewhat awkward to remove and install - at least two people should perform this procedure.*

Removal and installation
Refer to illustrations 9.2 and 9.4

1   Use blankets or pads to cover the cowl area of the body and fenders. This will protect the body and paint as the hood is lifted off.

2   Make marks or scribe a line around the hood hinge to ensure proper alignment during installation **(see illustration)**.

3   Disconnect any cables or wires that will interfere with removal.

4   Have an assistant support one side of the hood while you support the other. Simultaneously remove the hinge-to-hood nuts **(see illustration)**.

5   Lift off the hood.

6   Installation is the reverse of removal.

Adjustment
Refer to illustrations 9.10 and 9.11

7   Fore-and-aft and side-to-side adjustment of the hood is done by moving the hinge plate slot after loosening the bolts or nuts.

8   Mark around the each hinge plate so you can determine the amount of movement **(see illustration 9.2)**.

9   Loosen the bolts or nuts and move the hood into correct alignment. Move it only a little at a time. Tighten the hinge bolts and carefully lower the hood to check the position.

10   If necessary after installation, the hood latch can be adjusted up-and-down as well as

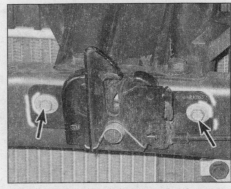

9.10 Make a mark around the latch to use as a reference point. To adjust the hood latch, loosen the retaining bolts, move the latch and retighten bolts, then close the hood to check the fit

11.1 Remove the fasteners securing the upper condenser/radiator seal

9.11 Adjust the hood closing height by turning the hood bumpers in or out

from side-to-side on the radiator support so the hood closes securely and flush with the fenders. To make the adjustment, scribe a line or mark around the hood latch mounting bolts to provide a reference point, then loosen them and reposition the latch, as necessary **(see illustration)**. Following adjustment, retighten the mounting bolts.

11   Finally, adjust the hood bumpers on the radiator support so the hood, when closed, is flush with the fenders **(see illustration)**.

12   The hood latch assembly, as well as the hinges, should be periodically lubricated with white, lithium-base grease to prevent binding and wear.

---

10   Hood latch and release cable - removal and installation

Latch

1   Scribe a line around the latch to aid alignment when reinstalling the latch assembly.

2   Remove the latch retaining bolts securing the latch to the radiator support **(see illustration 9.10)** and remove the latch.

3   Disconnect the hood release cable by disengaging the cable from the back of the latch assembly.

4   Installation is the reverse of the removal procedure. **Note:** *Adjust the latch so the hood engages securely when closed and the hood bumpers are slightly compressed.*

Cable

5   Remove the hood latch as described earlier in this Section, then detach the cable from the latch.

6   If you're working on a Durango model, remove the radiator grille (see Section 11), then remove the left-side headlight housing (see Chapter 12).

7   Attach a length of wire to the end of the cable (in the engine compartment). This will be used to pull the new cable back into the engine compartment.

8   Working in the engine compartment, detach the cable from all of its retaining clips. It may be necessary to cut some of the clips to free the cable.

9   Working under the instrument panel, remove the screws and detach the hood release handle. Dislodge the grommet and pull the cable through the firewall and into the cab.

10   Detach the wire from the old cable, then attach it to the end of the new cable. **Note:** *Make sure the new cable is equipped with a grommet.*

11   Pull the new cable through the firewall and into the engine compartment. Seat the grommet in the firewall.

12   The remainder of installation is the reverse of removal.

---

11   Radiator grille - removal and installation

Durango models

Refer to illustrations 11.1, 11.2, 11.3 and 11.4

1   Remove the upper condenser/radiator seal **(see illustration)**.

2   Remove the fasteners securing the upper part of the grille **(see illustration)**.

3   Separate the clips securing the sides of the grille **(see illustration)**. **Note:** *It may be necessary to remove the headlight housing to gain access to the clips securing the sides of the grille - refer to Chapter 12 for the removal procedure.*

4   Remove the fasteners securing the bot-

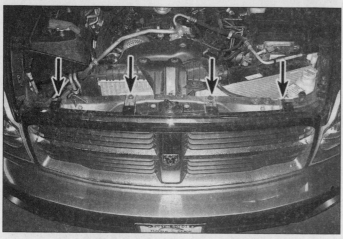

11.2 Radiator grille upper mounting fasteners

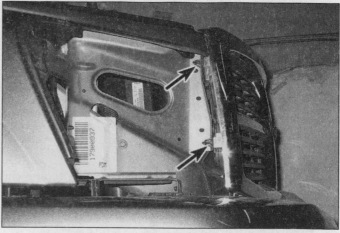

11.3 Separate the clips securing the sides of the grille

11.4 Remove the fasteners securing the bottom of the grille

12.6 Release the tabs along the top of the bumper cover (Durango models)

tom of the grille and carefully lift it away from the bumper **(see illustration).**

5   Installation is the reverse of removal.

Dakota models

6   Open the hood.

7   Remove the mounting screws and nuts, then detach the grille assembly from the bracket.

8   Remove the screws attaching the support bracket to the hood and detach it from the hood.

9   Installation is the reverse of removal.

12 Bumpers - removal and installation

1   Front bumpers on all models are composed of a plastic fascia, or bumper cover, fascia support and a structural beam. Rear bumpers on Durango models on also have a plastic fascia.

Front bumper

Bumper cover

Refer to illustration 12.6

2   Remove the radiator grille (see Sec-

tion 11).

3   Remove the headlight housings (see Chapter 12).

4   Working in the front wheelwell, remove the fasteners securing the ends of the bumper.

5   On Dakota models, remove the bumper cover upper mounting fasteners and remove

12.11 Remove the two fasteners near the fog lamps

the bumper cover.

6   On Durango models, release the tabs along the top of the bumper cover and remove the bumper cover **(see illustration).**

7   Installation is the reverse of removal.

Bumper cover support

Refer to illustration 12.11

8   Remove the bumper cover.

9   Disconnect the fog lamps, if equipped.

10   On Dakota models, remove the three fasteners along the top and the six fasteners along the front of the support. Remove the bumper cover support.

11   On Durango models, remove the fasteners near the fog lamps, then remove the bumper cover support **(see illustration).**

12   Installation is the reverse of removal.

Rear bumper

Bumper cover (Durango models)

Refer to illustrations 12.14, 12.15a and 12.15b

13   Open the liftgate.

14   Remove the upper mounting fasteners **(see illustration).**

15   Remove the fasteners securing the bottom of the bumper cover **(see illustrations).**

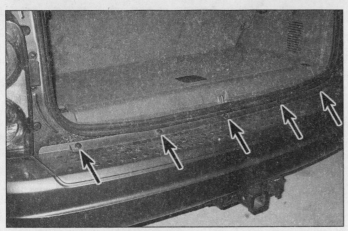

12.14 Remove the fasteners securing the top of the rear bumper cover

12.15a Remove the fasteners securing the bottom . . .

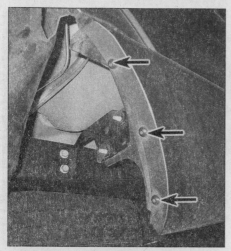

12.15b ... and the sides of the rear bumper cover

16 Remove the rear bumper cover from the vehicle.

17 Installation is the reverse of removal.

13.7a Fender upper mounting bolts

13.2 Remove the pin retainers from the inner fender splash shield

Dakota models

18 Unplug any electrical connectors which would interfere with bumper removal.

19 Remove the bolts retaining the center of the bumper to the trailer hitch or crossmember.

20 With an assistant supporting the bumper, remove the bolts retaining the bumper to the trailer hitch or frame rails, or the nuts retaining the bumper to the brackets.

21 Installation is the reverse of removal.

13 Front fender - removal and installation

Refer to illustrations 13.2, 13.7a, 13.7b and 13.7c

1 Raise the vehicle and support it securely on jackstands and remove the front wheel.

2 Remove the fasteners retaining the fender inner splash shield **(see illustration)**.

3 Remove the headlight housing (see Chapter 12).

4 On Dakota models, remove the radiator grille (see Section 11).

5 Remove the cowl cover (see Section 29).

6 If you're removing the right fender, remove the battery, battery tray (see Chapter 5) and the fasteners securing the air filter housing (see Chapter 4). If you're removing the left fender, remove the fasteners securing the power distribution center to the fender.

7 Remove the fender mounting bolts **(see illustrations)**.

8 Detach the fender. It's a good idea to have an assistant support the fender while it's being moved away from the vehicle to prevent damage to the surrounding body panels. If you're removing the right-side fender, disconnect the antenna (see Chapter 12).

9 Installation is the reverse of removal.

14 Door trim panels - removal and installation

Removal

Refer to illustrations 14.1, 14.2a, 14.2b, 14.5 and 14.6

1 Remove the power window control

13.7b Fender lower mounting bolts

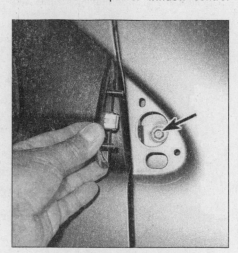

13.7c Fender-to-door pillar bolt

14.1 Using a trim stick, carefully pry up the power window control switch to release the clips

14.2a Remove the fastener at the bottom of the door panel

14.2b Remove the handle retaining screw

switch **(see illustration).**

2   Remove all door trim panel retaining screws **(see illustrations).**

3   Pull upward to release the door panel hooks from the door.

4   Once all of the hooks are disengaged, raise the trim panel up and off the door. Disconnect any wiring harness connectors.

5   Disconnect the handle link rod **(see illustration),** then remove the trim panel from the vehicle.

6   For access to the inner door, carefully

peel back the plastic watershield **(see illustration).**

Installation

7   Connect the wiring harness connectors and place the panel in position on the door. Connect the handle link rod. Press the trim panel straight against the door until the clips on the trim panel align with all the holes in the door, then push down on the panel until the clips are seated.

8   The remainder of installation is the reverse of removal.

---

15   Door - removal, installation and adjustment

Refer to illustrations 15.3 and 15.5

1   Open the door and disconnect the door wire harness electrical connector at the A-pillar.

2   Place a jack under the door or have an assistant on hand to support it when the hinge fasteners are removed. **Note:** *If a jack is used, place a few rags between it and the door to protect the door's painted surfaces.*

14.5 Disconnect the handle link rod

3   Scribe around the hinges with a marking pen, remove the fasteners and carefully lift off the door **(see illustration).**

4   Installation is the reverse of removal, making sure to align the hinge with the marks made during removal before tightening the fasteners.

5   Following installation of the door, check

14.6 Peel the plastic watershield carefully away from the door, taking care not to tear it

15.3 Mark their locations, then remove the fasteners at each hinge

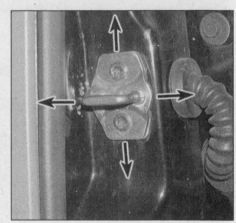

15.5 The latch striker on the door jamb can be adjusted slightly up/down or in/out

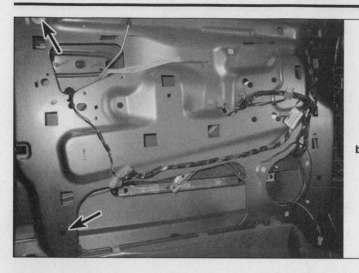

16.2 Remove the rear glass run channel mounting bolts, then move the channel for more working room

16.4 Remove the latch mounting screws

the alignment and adjust the hinges, if necessary. Adjust the door lock striker, centering it in the door latch **(see illustration).**

6   Rear doors are removed and installed as described above for front doors, except that the door is attached to the body "B" pillar.

16   Door latch, lock cylinder and handle - removal and installation

Latch

Refer to illustrations 16.2 and 16.4

1   Raise the window completely and remove the door trim panel and watershield (see Section 14).

2   Remove the fasteners at the rear glass run channel and move the channel away from the latch **(see illustration).** This provides a little extra working room in the latch area inside the door.

3   Rotate the plastic retaining clips off the rods, then detach the latch links. Disconnect the electrical connector.

4   Remove the three mounting screws (it may be necessary to use an impact-type screwdriver to loosen them), then remove the latch from the door **(see illustration).**

5   Place the latch in position and install the screws. Tighten the screws securely.

6   Connect the link rods and electrical connector to the latch.

7   The remainder of installation is the reverse of removal.

Lock cylinder

8   Remove the outside door handle (see Step 10). Disconnect the link, remove the mounting screw and withdraw the lock cylinder from the door handle.

9   Installation is the reverse of removal.

Outside handle

10   Remove the door trim panel (see Section 14). Disconnect the link rods from the outside handle, remove the mounting nuts and carefully detach the handle from the door.

11   Place the handle in position, attach the link and install the nuts. Tighten the nuts securely.

17   Door window glass - removal and installation

Front

Refer to illustration 17.5

1   Remove the door trim panel and watershield (see Section 14).

2   Lower the window.

3   Pry the inner weather seal out of the door glass opening.

4   Remove the door speaker (see Chapter 12).

5   Raise the window for access to the glass retaining nuts, then remove the two fasteners **(see illustration).**

6   Remove the window by tilting it forward, then lifting it out of the door.

7   To install, lower the glass into the door, slide it into position and install the nuts.

8   The remainder of installation is the reverse of removal.

Rear

9   The rear doors are serviced similarly to

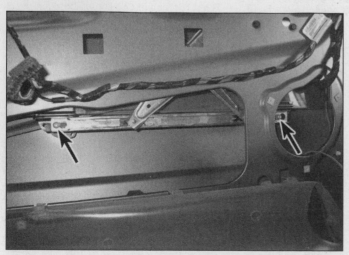

17.5 Align the window so that the nuts can be removed from the glass track

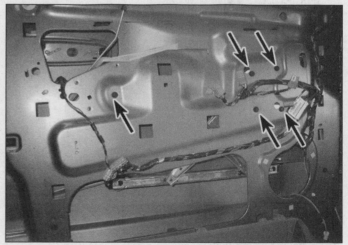

18.3 Door window regulator mounting bolt locations

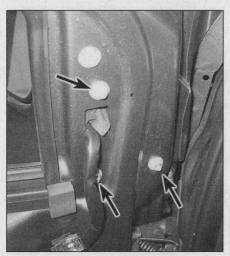

19.3 Remove the three outside mirror mounting nuts

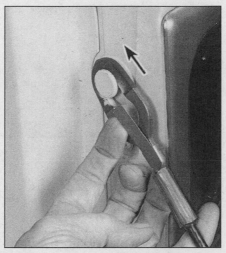

20.1 Lift the spring retainer up and slide the cable end off the pin

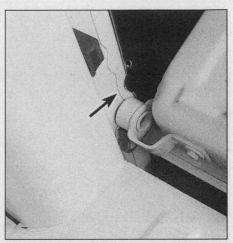

20.2 Align the flat on the right side hinge pin with the slot in the hinge pocket and lift the tailgate off the vehicle

the front doors, except that there is both a moving window glass and a stationary glass. **Note:** *On Quad-Cab Dakota models, the rear door quarter glass is difficult to remove from the door without damage to the trim panel. It's recommended that these windows should be removed/installed only at a professional auto glass shop.*

18 Door window glass regulator - removal and installation

Refer to illustration 18.3

1   Remove the door trim panel and watershield (see Section 14).
2   Unbolt the window glass from the regulator (see Section 17). Push the glass all the way up and tape it to the door frame.
3   Remove the window regulator-to-door and track mounting fasteners **(see illustration).**
4   Unplug the electrical connector.
5   Remove the regulator from the door.
6   Installation is the reverse of removal.

19 Mirrors - removal and installation

Outside mirrors

Refer to illustration 19.3

1   Remove the door trim panel (see Section 14).
2   On power mirrors, unplug the electrical connector.
3   Remove the nuts and detach the mirror from the door **(see illustration).**
4   Installation is the reverse of removal.

Inside mirror

5   Remove the setscrew, then slide the mirror up off the support base on the windshield. On models with optional automatic day/night mirror, disconnect the electrical connector.
6   Installation is the reverse of removal.
7   If the support base for the mirror has come off the windshield, it can be reattached with a special mirror adhesive kit available at auto parts stores. Clean the glass and support base thoroughly and follow the directions on the adhesive package.

20 Tailgate (Dakota models) - removal and installation

Refer to illustrations 20.1 and 20.2

1   Open the tailgate and detach the retaining cables **(see illustration).**
2   Lower the tailgate until the flat on the right side hinge-pin aligns with the slot in the hinge pocket. Lift the tailgate out of the pocket **(see illustration).** With the help of an assistant to support the weight, withdraw the left hinge pin from the body and remove the tailgate from the vehicle.
3   Installation is the reverse of removal.

21 Tailgate latch and handle (Dakota models) - removal and installation

Refer to illustrations 21.1, 21.2 and 21.4

1   Remove the handle retaining screws **(see illustration).**
2   Pull the handle out far enough to rotate the plastic retaining clips off the control rods

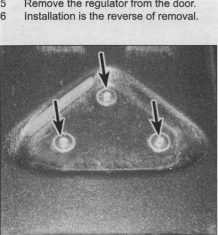

21.1 Remove the three handle retaining screws

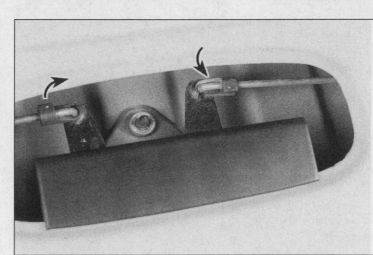

21.2 Rotate the plastic retaining clips off the control rods and detach the rods from the handle

21.4 Latch-to-tailgate mounting screws

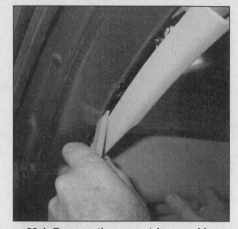

23.1 Remove the upper trim panel by pulling it outward carefully to free it from the spring clips

23.2a Remove the fasteners securing the liftgate trim panel . . .

and detach the rods from the handle **(see illustration)**.
3   Detach the handle from the tailgate.
4   Remove the screws and withdraw the latch assembly from the end of the tailgate **(see illustration)**.
5   Installation is the reverse of removal. Tighten all fasteners securely.

22 Liftgate (Durango models) - removal and installation

1   Open the liftgate and cover the upper body area around the opening with pads or cloths to protect the painted surfaces when the liftgate is removed.
2   Using a trim stick, remove the upper headliner trim panel, then disconnect the body-to-liftgate electrical connectors.
3   Paint or scribe alignment marks around the liftgate hinge flanges.
4   While an assistant supports the liftgate, detach the support struts (see Section 23).
5   Remove the hinge bolts and detach the

liftgate from the vehicle.
6   Installation is the reverse of removal.
7   After installation, close the liftgate and make sure it's in proper alignment with the surrounding body panels.
8   If the liftgate needs to be adjusted, loosen the hinge bolts slightly, gently close the liftgate and verify that it's centered (the striker should center it). Then carefully open the liftgate and retighten the hinge bolts.

23 Liftgate panels, outside handle, latch and support struts (Durango models) - removal and installation

Interior trim panels
Refer to illustrations 23.1, 23.2a and 23.2b
1   Remove the upper trim panel by pulling it outward carefully to free it from the spring clips **(see illustration)**.
2   The upper trim panel must be removed for access to the two upper mounting screws

of the lower (larger) liftgate trim panel. Remove the screws at the top and the bottom edge of the lower panel **(see illustrations)**.
3   With the lower panel pulled away from the liftgate, disconnect the electrical connectors at the courtesy lights.
4   Installation is the reverse of the removal procedure.

Outside handle
Refer to illustration 23.6
5   Remove the interior liftgate panels.
6   Remove the handle-to-latch rod, then the handle mounting fasteners **(see illustration)**.
7   Installation is the reverse of the removal procedure.

Latch
Refer to illustration 23.10
8   Remove the interior liftgate panels.
9   From inside, disconnect the electrical connector and handle-to-latch rod.
10   From below, remove the latch mounting fasteners **(see illustration)**.
11   Installation is the reverse of the removal procedure.

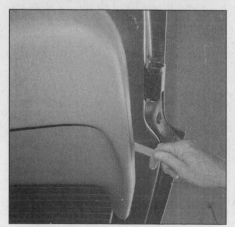

23.2b . . . then, using a trim stick, carefully pry around the outside of the trim panel to release the clips

23.6 Liftgate handle mounting bolts

23.10 Liftgate latch mounting fasteners

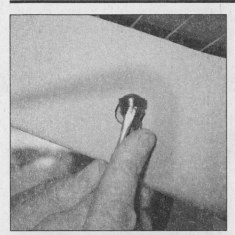

23.13 Use a small screwdriver to detach the retaining clip at the top end of the support strut

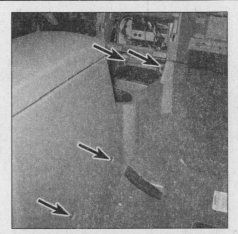

24.2 Remove the fasteners at the side and at the front of the console

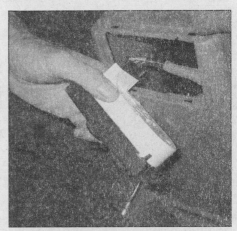

24.4 Disconnect the electrical connector for the rear blower

Support struts

Refer to illustration 23.13

12   Open the liftgate and prop it securely in the full open position.

13   Using a small screwdriver, detach the retaining clip at the top end of the support strut. Then pry or pull sharply to detach it from the vehicle **(see illustration)**.

14   Remove the support strut mounting screw at the bottom end of the strut, then remove the strut.

15   Installation is the reverse of the removal procedure.

24   Center console - removal and installation

Refer to illustrations 24.2 and 24.4

Warning: *The models covered by this manual are equipped with Supplemental Restraint Systems (SRS), more commonly known as airbags. Always disable the airbag system before working in the vicinity of any airbag system components to avoid the possibility of accidental deployment of the airbags, which*

could cause personal injury (see Chapter 12).

1   On Dakota models, open the console lid, remove the tray and remove the bolts securing the console to the floorpan.

2   On Durango models, remove the fasteners at the side and at the front of the console **(see illustration)**.

3   Remove the inserts from the cup holders (on Dakota models, there is only the front cup holder, while Durango models have a front and a rear) and remove the front and rear console mounting bolts.

4   On Durango models with rear heat/air, disconnect the electrical connector for the rear blower **(see illustration)**.

5   Unplug any electrical connectors and remove the console from the vehicle.

6   Installation is the reverse of removal.

25   Dashboard trim panels - removal and installation

Warning: *The models covered by this manual are equipped with Supplemental Restraint Systems (SRS), more commonly known as airbags. Always disable the airbag system before working in the vicinity of any airbag*

system component to avoid the possibility of accidental deployment of the airbags, which could cause personal injury (see Chapter 12).

Instrument cluster bezel

Refer to illustration 25.1

1   On models with automatic transmission and column shift, apply the parking brake and put the shift lever in the Low position. If equipped with a tilt steering column, lower the column. Remove the screws above the instrument cluster **(see illustration)**.

2   Remove the knee bolster (see Step 7).

3   Use a trim removal tool or a flat-blade screwdriver with the tip taped to pry around the complete edge of the instrument cluster bezel.

4   Grasp the bezel securely and pull out sharply to detach the retaining clips from the instrument panel.

5   Pull the panel out far enough to disconnect all electrical connectors.

6   Installation is the reverse of removal.

Knee bolster

Refer to illustration 25.7

7   Remove the screws at the bottom of

25.1 Remove the two screws above the instrument cluster

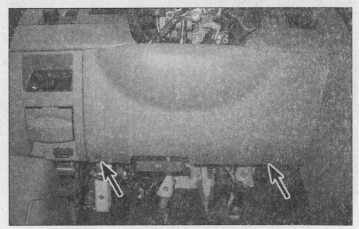

25.7 Remove the knee bolster mounting screws

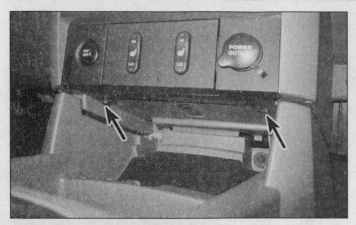

25.10 Remove the two screws at the bottom of the center bezel

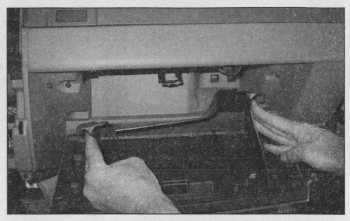

25.14 Push on the rear of the glove box until the stop clears the instrument panel

the driver's knee bolster, then use a dull, flat-bladed tool around the top of the panel to release it from the clips at the top **(see illustration)**.

8   If the knee bolster reinforcement panel needs to be removed for any reason, disconnect the electrical harness clips then remove the bolts.

9   Installation is the reverse of removal.

Center instrument panel bezel

Refer to illustration 25.10

10   Remove the screws at the bottom of the bezel **(see illustration)**.

11   Pull the panel away from the instrument panel enough to disconnect the electrical connectors behind it.

12   Installation is the reverse of removal.

Glove box

Refer to illustration 25.14

13   Open the glove box door.

14   Squeeze the two sides of the glove compartment bin together and pull the door down until the bumpers on the bin have cleared the stops **(see illustration)**.

15   Pull the glove box door away from the

instrument panel until the three hinge clips on the glove box door clear the pins in the instrument panel.

16   Installation is the reverse of removal.

Instrument panel top cover

Refer to illustrations 25.17 and 25.18

17   Remove the trim from the A-pillars **(see illustration)**.

18   Carefully pry around the complete edge of the top cover to release the clips **(see illustration)**.

19   Remove the panel.

20   Installation is the reverse of removal.

---

26   Steering column covers - removal and installation

Refer to illustration 26.2

Warning: *The models covered by this manual are equipped with Supplemental Restraint Systems (SRS), more commonly known as airbags. Always disable the airbag system before working in the vicinity of any airbag system component to avoid the possibility of accidental deployment of the airbags, which*

could cause personal injury (see Chapter 12).

1   Refer to Section 25 and remove the driver's knee bolster.

2   Remove the screws securing the upper cover to the lower cover **(see illustration)**.

3   Remove the tilt lever, then pull the upper cover up until the snaps are released, then remove the cover.

4   Installation is the reverse of the removal procedure.

---

27   Instrument panel - removal and installation

Refer to illustrations 27.2, 27.12, 27.13, 27.15a, 27.15b and 27.15c

Warning: *The models covered by this manual are equipped with Supplemental Restraint Systems (SRS), more commonly known as airbags. Always disable the airbag system before working in the vicinity of any airbag system components to avoid the possibility of accidental deployment of the airbags, which could cause personal injury (see Chapter 12).*

Note: *This is a difficult procedure for the home mechanic. There are many hidden fasteners, difficult angles to work in and many electrical*

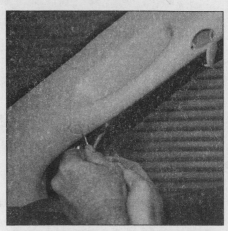

25.17 The A-pillar trim is secured by two screws (right side shown, left side similar)

25.18 Carefully pry around the complete edge of the top cover to release the clips

26.2 Detach the tilt lever handle, then remove the column cover fasteners

27.2 Use a trim panel tool to remove the instrument panel end caps

27.12 Disconnect the harness connectors from the Occupant Restraint Controller

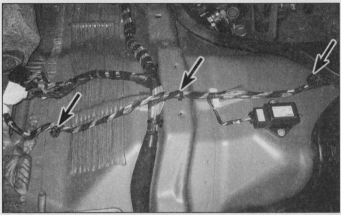

27.13 Release the clips to disconnect the wire harness from the floor pan

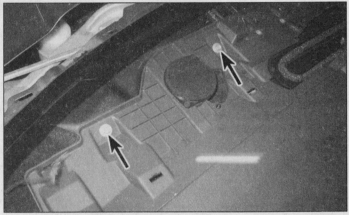

27.15a Remove the fasteners along the top of the instrument panel (left side shown, right side similar)

connectors to tag and disconnect/connect. *We recommend that this procedure be done at a dealership or qualified shop.*

1   Turn the front wheels to the straight-ahead position and lock the steering column, disconnect the negative battery cable and disable the airbag system (see Chapter 12).

2   Remove the right and left side cowl trim ("kick") panels. To access the rear screw on each kick panel, pry up the front end of the door sill plates with a trim tool. Remove the instrument panel end caps **(see illustration)**.

3   Refer to Section 25 and remove the instrument panel top cover, glove box, instrument cluster bezel, bolster, and knee bolster reinforcement. Remove the instrument cluster (see Chapter 12).

4   Remove steering column covers (see Section 26).

5   Refer to Chapter 10 and lower the steering column. **Note:** *There will be more working room if the front seats are moved back as far as possible, and even more room if the driver's seat is removed* (see Section 28).

6   Under the driver's side of the instrument panel, disconnect the large electrical bulkhead connector (by removing the screw in the center), and the two large connectors (without screws) on either side of the main bulkhead connector.

7   While working under that side of the instrument panel, tag and disconnect all other electrical connectors connected to the instrument panel. **Note:** *Watch for ground straps bolted to the cowl or the area behind the kick panels.*

8   Refer to Chapter 9 and release the parking brake rod from the release lever, which is part of the instrument panel.

9   Remove the brake light switch (see Chapter 9).

10   At the pedal support bracket, remove the three mounting bolts.

11   Remove the center console (see Section 24).

12   Disconnect the harness connectors from the Occupant Restraint Controller **(see illustration)**.

13   Pull back the carpet and disconnect the wire harness from the floor pan **(see illustration)**.

14   Working on the passenger's side of the instrument panel, disconnect the antenna connector and remove the amplifier (see Chapter 12).

15   Disconnect any remaining electrical connectors, then remove the instrument panel

27.15b Remove the left side . . .

27.15c . . . and right side instrument panel mounting bolts

28.3a Remove the front bolts from the front seat . . .

retaining fasteners **(see illustrations).**
16   Remove the instrument panel from the vehicle.
17   Installation is the reverse of removal.

28 Seats - removal and installation

Warning: *Some models are equipped with seat belt pre-tensioners, which are pyrotechnic (explosive) devices that tighten the seat belts during an impact of sufficient force. Always disable the airbag system before working in the vicinity of any restraint system component to avoid the possibility of accidental deployment of the airbag(s) and seat belt pre-tensioners, which could cause personal injury (see Chapter 12).*

Front seat

Refer to illustrations 28.3a and 28.3b
Warning: *The front passenger seat is equipped with a weight sensor module, which is an integral component of the Occupant Classification System (OCS), which is part of the front passenger airbag circuit. The seat weight sensor is a calibrated unit that calculates the weight of the passenger seat occupant. The weight of the person sitting in the passenger seat is a CRITICAL factor in airbag*

deployment. If you have to remove the front passenger seat for any reason, make sure that you DO NOT ALLOW ANYONE TO SIT IN THE PASSENGER SEAT UNTIL AFTER YOU HAVE DRIVEN THE VEHICLE TO A DEALER SERVICE DEPARTMENT AND HAVE HAD THE AIRBAG SYSTEM AND THE OCCUPANT CLASSIFICATION SYSTEM VERIFIED. Failure to do so could result in serious injury or death to the passenger seat occupant in the event of an accident.
1   In the Dakota pickup models, there are three styles of front seats: bench, split-bench and bucket seats. Durango models have bucket seats with either a console or center seat cushion between the bucket seats. All are removed in a similar fashion.
2   Remove the screws and the plastic covers over the outer tracks.
3   Remove the seat track-to-floor bolts and remove the front seat assembly **(see illustrations). Note:** *This is a job for two people.*
4   If the bucket seats need to be separated from each other for repair, turn the assembly over, preferably onto a blanket for protection of the upholstery. Remove the four bolts securing the center seat cushion to the two inside tracks of the bucket seats.
5   Installation is the reverse of removal. When reassembling the two bucket seats to the center cushion, make sure the alignment

is as it was, or the seat track-to-floor bolts may not line up properly.

2nd seat (Durango models)

6   Fold the left and right seat backs forward, then release the catch behind each unit and flip the seat and bottom forward.
7   On each side, remove the two bolts holding the tube-and-bracket to the floor, and the one seat belt bolt on each side of the center cushion.
8   Remove the seat assembly as a unit.
Note: *This is a job for two people.*
9   Installation is the reverse of removal.

29 Cowl cover - removal and installation

Refer to illustration 29.2
1   Remove the windshield wiper arms (see Chapter 12).
2   Remove the fasteners securing the cowl cover **(see illustration).**
3   Disconnect the windshield washer hose.
4   Installation is the reverse of removal.

28.3b . . . then remove the rear bolts

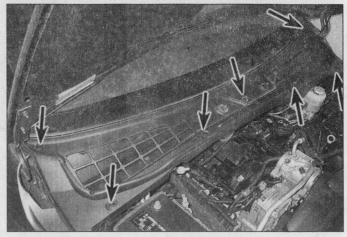

29.2 Remove the cowl cover retaining screws and pushpins

Chapter 12
Chassis electrical system

Contents

1 General information

The electrical system is a 12-volt, negative ground type. A lead/acid-type battery that is charged by the alternator supplies power for the lights and all electrical accessories.

This Chapter covers repair and service procedures for the various electrical components not associated with the engine. Information on the battery, alternator, distributor and starter motor can be found in Chapter 5. **Warning:** *When working on the electrical system, disconnect the cable from the negative battery terminal to prevent electrical shorts and/or fires (see Chapter 5, Section 1).*

2 Electrical troubleshooting - general information

Refer to illustrations 2.5a, 2.5b, 2.6, 2.9 and 2.15

A typical electrical circuit consists of an electrical component, any switches, relays, motors, fuses, fusible links or circuit breakers related to that component and the wiring and connectors that link the component to both the battery and the chassis. To help you pinpoint an electrical circuit problem, wiring diagrams are included at the end of this Chapter.

Before tackling any troublesome electrical circuit, first study the appropriate wiring diagrams to get a complete understanding of what makes up that individual circuit. You can often narrow down trouble spots, for instance, by noting whether other components related to the circuit are operating correctly. If several components or circuits fail at one time, chances are that the problem is in a fuse or ground connection, because several circuits are often routed through the same fuse and ground connections.

Electrical problems usually stem from simple causes, such as loose or corroded connections, a blown fuse, a melted fusible link or a failed relay. Visually inspect the condition of all fuses, wires and connections in a problem circuit before troubleshooting the circuit.

If test equipment and instruments are going to be utilized, use the diagrams to plan ahead of time where you will make the necessary connections in order to accurately pinpoint the trouble spot.

For electrical troubleshooting you'll need a circuit tester or voltmeter, a continuity tester, which includes a bulb, battery and set of test leads, and a jumper wire, preferably with a circuit breaker incorporated, which can be used to bypass electrical components **(see illustrations)**. Before attempting to locate a problem with test instruments, use the wiring

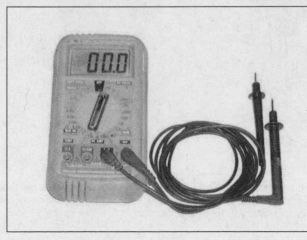

2.5a The most useful tool for electrical troubleshooting is a digital multimeter that can check volts, amps, and test continuity

diagram(s) to decide where to make the connections.

Voltage checks

Voltage checks should be performed if a circuit is not functioning properly. Connect one lead of a circuit tester to either the negative battery terminal or a known good ground. Connect the other lead to a connector in the circuit being tested, preferably nearest to the battery or fuse **(see illustration)**. If the bulb of the tester lights, voltage is present, which means that the part of the circuit between the connector and the battery is problem free. Continue checking the rest of the circuit in the same fashion. When you reach a point at which no voltage is present, the problem lies between that point and the last test point with voltage. Most of the time the problem can be traced to a loose connection. **Note:** *Keep in mind that some circuits receive voltage only when the ignition key is in the ACC or RUN position.*

Finding a short

One method of finding shorts in a circuit is to remove the fuse and connect a test light or voltmeter to the fuse terminals. There should be no voltage present in the circuit when it is turned off. Move the wiring harness from side-to-side while watching the test light. If the bulb goes on, there is a short to ground somewhere in that area, probably where the insulation has rubbed through. The same test can be performed on each component in the circuit, even a switch.

Ground check

Perform a ground test to check whether a component is properly grounded. Disconnect the battery and connect one lead of a continuity tester or multimeter (set to the ohm scale), to a known good ground. Connect the other lead to the wire or ground connection being tested. If the resistance is low (less than

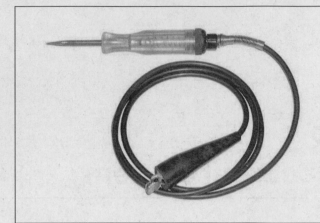

2.5b A simple test light is a very handy tool for testing voltage

5 ohms), the ground is good. If the bulb on a self-powered test light does not go on, the ground is not good.

Continuity check

A continuity check determines whether there are any breaks in a circuit, i.e. whether it's conducting electricity correctly. With the circuit off (no power in the circuit), use a self-powered continuity tester or multimeter to check the circuit. Connect the test leads to both ends of the circuit (or to the "power" end and a good ground). If the test light comes on, the circuit is conducting current correctly **(see illustration)**. If the resistance is low (less than 5 ohms), there is continuity; if the reading is 10,000 ohms or higher, there is a break somewhere in the circuit. The same procedure can be used to test a switch, by connecting the continuity tester to the switch terminals. With the switch turned on, the test light should come on (or low resistance should be indicated on a meter).

Finding an open circuit

When diagnosing for possible open circuits, it is often difficult to locate them by sight because the connectors hide oxidation or terminal misalignment. Merely wiggling a connector on a sensor or in the wiring harness may correct the open circuit condition. Remember this when an open circuit is indicated when troubleshooting a circuit. Intermittent problems may also be caused by oxidized or loose connections.

Electrical troubleshooting is simple if you keep in mind that all electrical circuits are basically electricity running from the battery, through the wires, switches, relays, fuses and fusible links to each electrical component (light bulb, motor, etc.) and to ground, from which it is passed back to the battery. Any electrical problem is an interruption in the flow of electricity to and from the battery.

Connectors

Most electrical connections on these vehicles are made with multi-wire plastic connectors. The mating halves of many connectors are secured with locking clips molded into the plastic connector shells. The mating halves of large connectors, such as some of those under the instrument panel, are held together by a bolt through the center of the connector.

2.6 In use, a basic test light's lead is clipped to a known good ground, then the pointed probe can test connectors, wires or electrical sockets - if the bulb lights, battery voltage is present at the test point

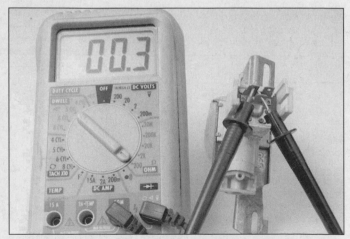

2.9 With a multimeter set to the ohm scale, resistance can be checked across two terminals - when checking for continuity, a low reading indicates continuity, a very high or infinite reading indicates lack of continuity

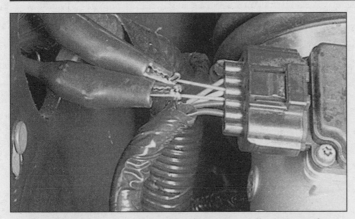

2.15 To backprobe a connector, insert a small, sharp probe (such as a straight-pin) into the back of the connector alongside the desired wire until it contacts the metal terminal inside; connect your meter leads to the probes - this allows you to test a functioning circuit

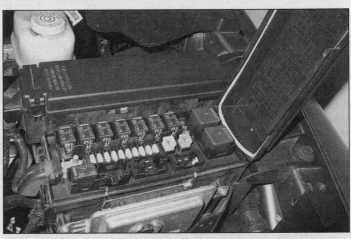

3.1a The Integrated Power Module (fuse and relay box) is located on the left side of the engine compartment, just in front of the Power Distribution Center (Durango)

To separate a connector with locking clips, use a small screwdriver to pry the clips apart carefully, then separate the connector halves. Pull only on the shell, never pull on the wiring harness as you may damage the individual wires and terminals inside the connectors. Look at the connector closely before trying to separate the halves. Often the locking clips are engaged in a way that is not immediately clear. Additionally, many connectors have more than one set of clips.

Each pair of connector terminals has a male half and a female half. When you look at the end view of a connector in a diagram, be sure to understand whether the view shows the harness side or the component side of the connector. Connector halves are mirror images of each other, and a terminal shown on the right side end-view of one half will be on the left side end view of the other half.

It is often necessary to take circuit voltage measurements with a connector connected. Whenever possible, carefully insert a small straight pin (not your meter probe) into the rear of the connector shell to contact the terminal inside, then clip your meter lead to the pin. This kind of connection is called "backprobing" (see illustration). When insert-

ing a test probe into a male terminal, be careful not to distort the terminal opening. Doing so can lead to a poor connection and corrosion at that terminal later. Using the small straight pin instead of a meter probe results in less chance of deforming the terminal connector.

3   Fuses and fusible links - general information

Fuses

Refer to illustrations 3.1a, 3.1b, 3.1c and 3.3

The electrical circuits of the vehicle are protected by a combination of fuses and relays. The engine compartment fuse and relay box(es) are located on the left side of the engine compartment **(see illustrations)**. On Durango models there are two boxes: the Power Distribution Center and the Integrated Power Module. On Dakota models there is only one fuse and relay box. You'll find handy fuse and relay guides on the underside of the cover(s). (There is also a fuse and relay guide in your owner's manual.) On Durango models there's also a Junction Block, located inside

the vehicle, behind the left kick panel (the triangular-shaped trim panel located below the left end of the instrument panel. You can access the Junction Block by opening the access door in the kick panel.

Each of the fuses is designed to protect a specific circuit, and the various circuits are identified (in a highly abbreviated way) on the fuse panel itself. Different sizes of fuses are employed. There are "mini" and "maxi" sizes, with the larger located in the fuse and relay box. The maxi fuses can be removed with your fingers, but the mini fuses require the use of pliers or the small plastic fuse-puller tool found in most fuse boxes. If an electrical component fails, always check the fuse first. The best way to check the fuses is with a test light. Check for power at the exposed terminal

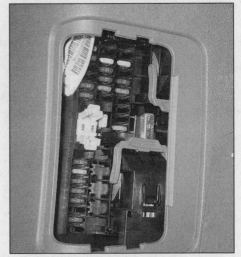

3.1b The Power Distribution Center (fuse and relay box) is located on the left side of the engine compartment, just behind the Integrated Power Module (Durango)

3.1c The Junction Block is located behind a small access panel (removed in this photo) in the left kick panel. To locate a fuse or relay, refer to the fuse and relay guide imprinted on the backside of the access panel. There is also a handy fuse removal tool on the backside of the access panel (Durango)

tips of each fuse. If power is present at one side of the fuse but not the other, the fuse is blown. A blown fuse can also be identified by visually inspecting it (**see illustration**).

Be sure to replace blown fuses with the correct type. Fuses of different ratings are physically interchangeable, but only fuses of the proper rating should be used. Replacing a fuse with one of a higher or lower value than specified is not recommended. Each electrical circuit needs a specific amount of protection. The amperage rating of each fuse is molded into the fuse body.

If the replacement fuse immediately fails, don't replace it again until the cause of the problem is isolated and corrected. In most cases, the cause will be a short circuit in the wiring caused by a broken or deteriorated wire.

Fusible links

The wiring between the battery and the alternator is protected by a fusible link. This link functions like a fuse, in that it melts when the circuit is overloaded, but resembles a large-gauge wire. To replace a fusible link, first disconnect the negative cable from the battery. Disconnect the burned-out link and replace it with a new one (available from your dealer or auto parts store). Always determine the cause for the overload that melted the fusible link before installing a new one.

4   Circuit breakers - general information

Circuit breakers protect certain heavy-

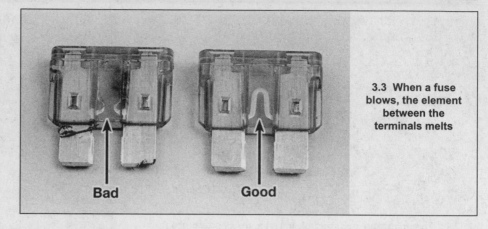

3.3 When a fuse blows, the element between the terminals melts

load circuits. Depending on the vehicle's accessories, there might be one to three circuit breakers located in one or more of the three fuse and relay boxes (**see illustrations 3.1a, 3.1b and 3.1c**).

Because the circuit breakers reset automatically, an electrical overload in a circuit-breaker-protected system will cause the circuit to fail momentarily, then come back on. If the circuit does not come back on, check it immediately.

For a basic check, pull the circuit breaker up out of its socket on the fuse panel, but just far enough to probe with a voltmeter. The breaker should still contact the sockets.

With the voltmeter negative lead on a good chassis ground, touch each end prong of the circuit breaker with the positive meter probe. There should be battery voltage at each end. If there is battery voltage only at one end, the circuit breaker must be replaced.

5   Relays - general information and testing

1   Many electrical accessories in the vehicle utilize relays to transmit current to the component. If the relay is defective, the component won't operate properly.
2   Most relays are located in the engine compartment fuse and relay box (**see illustration 3.1a or 3.1b**).
3   Some relays are located in other parts of the vehicle, such as the Junction Block inside the vehicle (**see illustration 3.1c**), or in various wiring harnesses underneath the instrument panel.
4   If a faulty relay is suspected, it can be removed and tested using the procedure below or by a dealer service department or a repair shop. Defective relays must be replaced as a unit.

Testing

Refer to illustrations 5.5a and 5.5b

5   Most of the relays used in these vehicles are of a type often called "ISO" relays, which refers to the International Standards Organization. The terminals of ISO relays are numbered to indicate their usual circuit connections and functions. There are two basic layouts of terminals on the relays used in the vehicles covered by this manual (**see illustrations**).

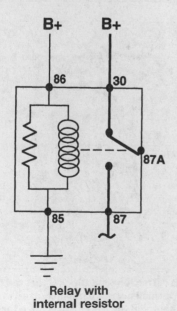

Relay with internal resistor

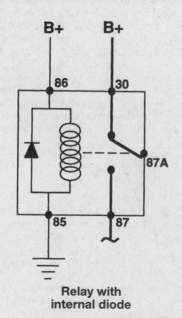

Relay with internal diode

24053-12-5.2a HAYNES

5.5a Typical ISO relay designs, terminal numbering and circuit connections

Control circuits   **Power circuits**

5.5b Most relays are marked on the outside to easily identify the control circuit and power circuits - this one is of the four-terminal type

6.4 To disconnect the larger electrical connector from the multi-function switch, slide the lock away from the connector (toward the harness), depress it and pull off the connector. To disconnect the smaller upper connector, depress the release tab and pull off the connector

6.5a To remove the multi-function switch, remove these two mounting screws . . .

6   Refer to the wiring diagram for the circuit to determine the proper connections for the relay you're testing. If you can't determine the correct connection from the wiring diagrams, however, you may be able to determine the test connections from the information that follows.

7   Two of the terminals are the relay control circuit and connect to the relay coil. The other relay terminals are the power circuit. When the relay is energized, the coil creates a magnetic field that closes the larger contacts of the power circuit to provide power to the circuit loads.

8   Terminals 85 and 86 are normally the control circuit. If the relay contains a diode, terminal 86 must be connected to battery positive (B+) voltage and terminal 85 to ground. If the relay contains a resistor, terminals 85 and 86 can be connected in either direction with respect to B+ and ground.

9   Terminal 30 is normally connected to the battery voltage (B+) source for the circuit loads. Terminal 87 is connected to the ground side of the circuit, either directly or through a load. If the relay has several alternate terminals for load or ground connections, they usually are numbered 87A, 87B, 87C, and so on.

10   Use an ohmmeter to check continuity through the relay control coil.

 a) *Connect the meter according to the polarity shown in* **illustration 5.5a** *for one check; then reverse the ohmmeter leads and check continuity in the other direction.*

 b) *If the relay contains a resistor, resistance will be indicated on the meter, and should be the same value with the ohmmeter in either direction.*

 c) *If the relay contains a diode, resistance should be higher with the ohmmeter in the forward polarity direction than with the meter leads reversed.*

 d) *If the ohmmeter shows infinite resistance in both directions, replace the relay.*

11   Remove the relay from the vehicle and use the ohmmeter to check for continuity

6.5b . . . then carefully pull out the switch assembly

between the relay power circuit terminals. There should be no continuity between terminal 30 and 87 with the relay de-energized.

12   Connect a fused jumper wire to terminal 86 and the positive battery terminal. Connect another jumper wire between terminal 85 and ground. When the connections are made, the relay should click.

13   With the jumper wires connected, check for continuity between the power circuit terminals. Now there should be continuity between terminals 30 and 87.

14   If the relay fails any of the above tests, replace it.

6   Multi-function switch - replacement

Refer to illustrations 6.4, 6.5a and 6.5b

Warning: *The models covered by this manual are equipped with a Supplemental Restraint System (SRS), more commonly known as airbags. Always disarm the airbag system before working in the vicinity of any airbag system component to avoid the possibility of accidental deployment of the airbag, which could cause personal injury (see Section 25).*

Do not use a memory-saving device to preserve the PCM's memory when working on or near airbag system components.

1   Disconnect the cable from the negative battery terminal (see Chapter 5, Section 1).

2   Remove the steering wheel (see Chapter 10).

3   Remove the steering column covers (see Chapter 11).

4   Disconnect the electrical connector from the multi-function switch **(see illustration)**.

5   Remove the multi-function switch mounting screws and remove the switch **(see illustrations)**.

6   Installation is the reverse of removal. Before reinstalling the steering wheel, make sure the airbag clockspring is centered (see Chapter 10, Section 16).

7   Key lock cylinder and ignition switch - replacement

Warning: *The models covered by this manual are equipped with a Supplemental Restraint System (SRS), more commonly known as airbags. Always disarm the airbag system before working in the vicinity of any airbag* system component to avoid the possibility of accidental deployment of the airbag, which could cause personal injury (see Section 25). Do not use a memory-saving device to preserve the PCM's memory when working on or near airbag system components.

Note: If the key is difficult to turn, the problem might not be in the ignition switch or the key lock cylinder. The transmission shift cable might be out of adjustment (see Chapter 7A).

Key lock cylinder

Refer to illustrations 7.4 and 7.5

1   Disconnect the cable from the negative battery terminal (see Chapter 5, Section 1).
2   Remove the upper and lower steering column covers (see Chapter 11).
3   Insert the ignition key into the key lock cylinder and put the shift lever in the PARK position.
4   Turn the ignition key to the RUN position, then insert a small punch into the hole for the key lock cylinder retaining pin, depress the retaining pin and pull the key lock cylinder out of the steering column **(see illustration)**.
5   Before installing the key lock cylinder, make sure that the ignition key is still in the RUN position. Then align the inner end of the key lock cylinder with the flats **(see illustration)** in the receptacle at the inner end of the lock cylinder bore and push the lock cylinder into the ignition switch until it clicks into place.
6   Installation is otherwise the reverse of removal.

Ignition switch

Refer to illustrations 7.11, 7.12, 7.13, 7.14 and 7.15

7   Disconnect the cable from the negative battery terminal (see Chapter 5, Section 1).
8   Disable the airbag system (see Section 25).
9   Remove the upper and lower steering column covers (see Chapter 11).
10   Remove the ignition key lock cylinder

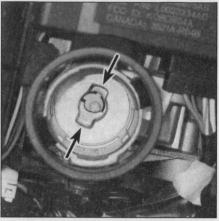

7.4 To remove the key lock cylinder, turn the ignition key to the RUN position, insert a small punch, drill bit or screwdriver into this hole and depress the retaining pin, then pull the lock cylinder out of the steering column

7.5 When installing the key lock cylinder into the steering column, be sure to align the end of the cylinder with these two flats inside the small receptacle in the floor of the lock cylinder mounting bore

7.11 Disconnect these two electrical connectors from the clockspring

(see Steps 1 through 4).
11   Disconnect the electrical connectors from the clockspring **(see illustration)**, then set the clockspring wiring harness aside.

12   Remove the tilt lever mounting bracket screws **(see illustration)**.
13   Disconnect the electrical connector from the ignition switch **(see illustration)**.

7.12 To detach the tilt lever assembly, remove these two mounting bracket screws

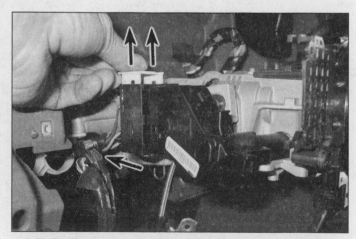

7.13 To disconnect the electrical connector from the ignition switch, pull up the white plastic lock on top of the switch, push the red sliding lock underneath the switch forward, then pull the connector out of the switch

7.14 To detach the ignition switch from the steering column, remove these two mounting screws

7.15 To remove the ignition switch from the steering column, pry this locking tab away from the column, then pull off the switch

14   Remove the ignition switch mounting screws **(see illustration)**.

15   Carefully pry the small locking tab away from the steering column **(see illustration)** and remove the ignition switch.

16   Installation is the reverse of removal.

8   Headlight switch - replacement

Refer to illustration 8.3

1   Disconnect the cable from the negative battery terminal (see Chapter 5, Section 1).

2   Remove the instrument cluster bezel (see Chapter 11).

3   To detach the headlight switch from the instrument cluster bezel, remove the switch mounting screws **(see illustration)**.

4   Installation is the reverse of removal.

9   Instrument cluster - removal and installation

Refer to illustrations 9.3 and 9.4

1   Disconnect the cable from the negative

8.3 To detach the headlight switch from the instrument cluster bezel, remove these three screws

battery terminal (see Chapter 5, Section 1).

2   Remove the instrument cluster bezel (see Chapter 11).

3   Remove the four instrument cluster mounting screws **(see illustration)**.

4   Pull out the cluster and disconnect the electrical connectors from the backside of cluster **(see illustration)**.

5   Installation is the reverse of removal.

10   Wiper motors - replacement

Windshield wiper motor

Refer to illustrations 10.2, 10.3, 10.5, 10.6, 10.7, 10.8 and 10.9

1   Disconnect the cable from the negative battery terminal (see Chapter 5, Section 1).

9.3 To detach the instrument cluster from the instrument panel, remove these four screws

9.4 Pull out the cluster and disconnect the electrical connectors from the backside of the cluster (left connector shown, right connector not visible in this photo)

10.2 To detach each windshield wiper arm from its shaft(s), remove the retaining nut(s) (right windshield wiper arm, shown, has two retaining nuts; left arm has only one retaining nut)

10.3 Before the removing either windshield wiper arm from its shaft, mark the relationship of the arm to the shaft

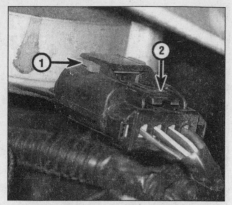

10.5 To disconnect the electrical connector from the windshield wiper motor, push the slide lock (1) to the right, then depress the release tab (2) and pull off the connector

2   Remove the wiper arm retaining nuts **(see illustration)**.
3   Mark the relationship of the wiper arms to their shafts **(see illustration)**, then remove the wiper arms.
4   Remove the cowl cover (see Chapter 11).
5   Disconnect the electrical connector from the windshield wiper motor **(see illustration)**.

6   Disengage the socket bushing of the right wiper drive link from the ballstud on the wiper motor crank arm **(see illustration)**.
7   Disengage the sleeve bushing of the left wiper drive link from the ballstud on the wiper motor crank arm **(see illustration)**.
8   Remove the crank arm retaining nut from the windshield wiper motor shaft **(see illustration)**. Before detaching the crank arm

from the motor shaft, be sure to make alignment marks on the arm and on the shaft to ensure correct alignment when installing the crank arm on the shaft.
9   Remove the windshield wiper motor mounting bolts **(see illustration 10.8)** and remove the windshield wiper motor **(see illustration)**.
10   Installation is the reverse of removal.

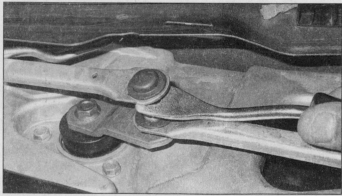

10.6 To disengage the socket bushing of the right wiper drive link from the ballstud on the wiper motor crank arm, carefully pry them apart with a trim removal tool (shown) or with a prybar or big screwdriver

10.7 To disengage the sleeve bushing of the left wiper drive link from the ballstud on the wiper motor crank arm, carefully pry them apart with a trim removal tool (shown) or a screwdriver

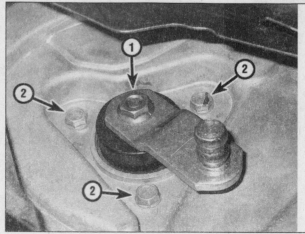

10.8 To remove the crank arm from the windshield wiper motor, remove this retaining nut (1) and pull the arm off the motor shaft. To detach the wiper motor from its mounting bracket, remove these three bolts (2) . . .

10.9 . . . then remove the windshield wiper motor from the underside of the wiper motor mounting bracket

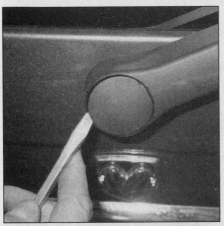

10.12 Carefully pry the trim cap from the rear wiper arm

10.13 Remove the rear wiper arm retaining nut

10.14 Remove the washer, then mark the relationship of the rear wiper arm to the wiper motor shaft

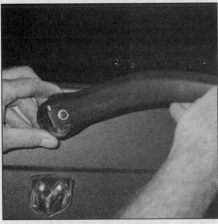

10.15 Release spring tension by hinging the wiper arm toward you, then remove the rear wiper arm from the wiper motor shaft

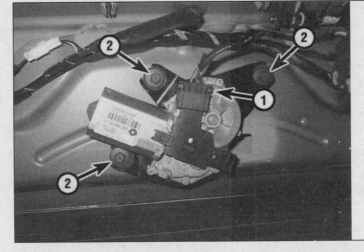

10.17 Disconnect the electrical connector (1) from the rear wiper motor, then remove the three wiper motor mounting bolts (2) and remove the wiper motor from the rear liftgate

Rear wiper motor

Refer to illustrations 10.12, 10.13, 10.14, 10.15 and 10.17

11   Disconnect the cable from the negative battery terminal (see Chapter 5, Section 1).
12   Remove the trim cap from the rear wiper arm **(see illustration)**.
13   Remove the rear wiper arm retaining nut **(see illustration)**.
14   Remove the washer **(see illustration)**, then mark the relationship of the wiper arm to the wiper motor shaft.
15   The wiper arm is still secured to the wiper motor shaft by spring tension. To release tension, hinge the wiper arm toward you **(see illustration)**, then remove the arm from the motor shaft.
16   Remove the rear liftgate trim panel (see Chapter 11).
17   Disconnect the electrical connector from the rear wiper motor, remove the mounting bolts, then detach the motor from the liftgate **(see illustration)**.

11   Radio and speakers - removal and installation

Radio

Refer to illustrations 11.3 and 11.4

Note: *The photographs accompanying this section depict the optional satellite navigation radio. The regular radio unit has only two mounting screws, but the procedure for removing either unit is otherwise identical.*

1   Disconnect the cable from the negative battery terminal (see Chapter 5, Section 1).
2   Remove the instrument panel center bezel (see Chapter 11).
3   Remove the radio mounting screws **(see illustration)** and pull the radio out of the dash.

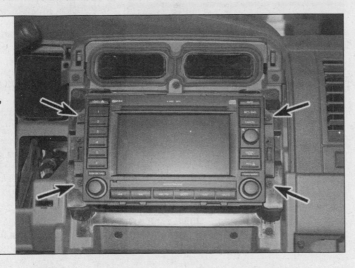

11.3 To detach the radio from the dash, remove these four mounting screws (on models without satellite navigation, there are two screws)

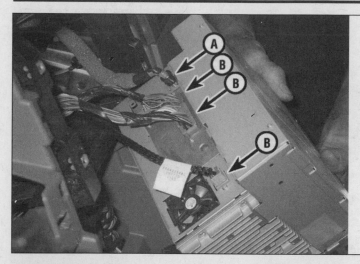

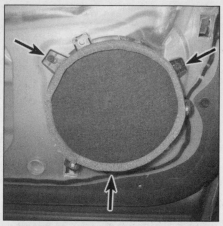

11.4 Pull the radio out of the dash far enough to disconnect the antenna cable (A) and the electrical connectors (B)

11.8 To detach the speaker from the front door, remove these three mounting screws (lower screw not visible in this photograph) (rear door speakers similar)

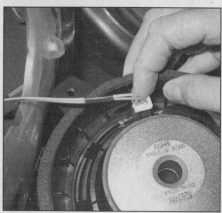

11.9 Pull the speaker out of the door and disconnect the electrical connector

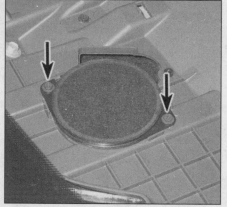

11.13 To detach an instrument panel speaker, simply remove these two mounting screws, pull out the speaker and disconnect the electrical connector

11.18 To detach the subwoofer, remove these six mounting screws, then pull out the subwoofer and disconnect the electrical connector

4   Disconnect the antenna cable and the electrical connectors from the radio **(see illustration)**.

5   Installation is the reverse of removal.

Speakers

Door speakers

Refer to illustrations 11.8 and 11.9

Note: *The photographs accompanying this section depict a front door speaker, but this procedure also applies to the rear door speakers and tweeters, both of which are removed exactly the same way as a front door speaker.*

6   Disconnect the cable from the negative battery terminal (see Chapter 5, Section 1).

7   Remove the door trim panel (see Chapter 11).

8   Remove the three speaker mounting screws **(see illustration)**.

9   Pull out the speaker and disconnect the electrical connector **(see illustration)**.

10   Installation is the reverse of removal.

Instrument panel speakers

Refer to illustration 11.13

11   Disconnect the cable from the negative battery terminal (see Chapter 5, Section 1).

12   Remove the instrument panel top cover (see Chapter 11).

13   Remove the speaker mounting screws **(see illustration)**.

14   Pull out the speaker and disconnect the electrical connector.

15   Installation is the reverse of removal.

12.1 To remove the antenna mast from the antenna mounting base, simply unscrew it with an open-end wrench

Subwoofer

Refer to illustration 11.18

Note: *On SUVs, the subwoofer (if equipped) is located at the left rear corner of the vehicle, behind the left rear quarter panel trim.*

16   Disconnect the cable from the negative battery terminal (see Chapter 5, Section 1).

17   Remove the left rear quarter panel trim (see Chapter 11).

18   Remove the speaker mounting screws **(see illustration)**.

19   Pull out the speaker and disconnect the electrical connector.

20   Installation is the reverse of removal.

---

12   Antenna and cable - replacement

Antenna mast

Refer to illustration 12.1

1   Unscrew the antenna mast from the mounting base **(see illustration)**.

2   Installation is the reverse of removal.

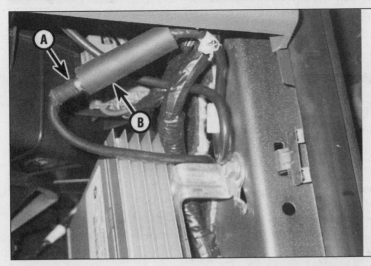

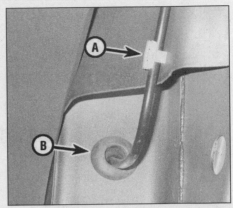

12.4 Disconnect the antenna mast's coaxial connector (A) from the instrument panel antenna cable connector (B)

12.7 To detach this antenna cable clip (A) from the vehicle, simply pull it straight out with a pair of needle-nose pliers. Before pulling out the antenna cable, remove this grommet (B)

Antenna cables

Note: *There are actually two antenna cables: The antenna mast cable connects the antenna mast to the instrument panel antenna cable underneath the right end of the instrument panel, and the instrument panel antenna cable goes from there, through the instrument panel, to the radio.*

Antenna mast cable

Refer to illustrations 12.4, 12.7, 12.8 and 12.9

3   Remove the right-side kick panel (see Chapter 11).

4   Reach under the right end of the instrument panel and disconnect the antenna mast cable's coaxial connector from the instrument panel antenna cable connector **(see illustration)**.

5   Loosen the right front wheel lug nuts. Raise the vehicle and place it securely on jackstands. Remove the right front wheel.

6   Remove the splash shield from the right front wheelhousing (see Chapter 11).

7   Detach the antenna mast cable clip from this panel **(see illustration)**.

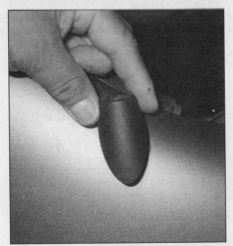

12.9 Remove the antenna mounting base adapter from the top of the fender

8   Using an antenna wrench (available at auto parts stores), unscrew the cap nut from the antenna mounting base **(see illustration)** and remove the base.

9   Remove the antenna mounting base adapter from the top of the fender **(see illustration)**.

10   Push the antenna mounting base down through the mounting hole in the fender.

11   Remove the grommet **(see illustration 12.7)**, then pull out the antenna cable.

12   Installation is the reverse of removal.

Instrument panel antenna cable

Refer to illustration 12.14

13   Disconnect the instrument panel antenna cable from the antenna mast cable (see Steps 3 and 4).

14   Using a flashlight and a mirror, reach up under the instrument panel and disengage the old instrument panel antenna cable from the clips on the backside of the glove box **(see illustration)**.

15   Remove the radio and disconnect the instrument panel antenna cable from the backside of the radio (see Section 11).

16   Pull the old instrument panel antenna cable out through the radio mounting hole.

17   Installation is the reverse of removal.

12.8 Using an antenna nut wrench, unscrew the cap nut from the antenna mounting base

13   Rear window defogger - check and repair

1   The rear window defogger consists of a number of horizontal heating elements baked onto the inside surface of the glass. Power is supplied through a relay and fuse from the interior fuse/relay box. A defogger switch on the instrument panel controls the defogger grid.

12.14 Using a flashlight and a mirror, reach up under the instrument panel and disengage the old instrument panel antenna cable from these clips on the backside of the glove box (instrument panel removed for clarity)

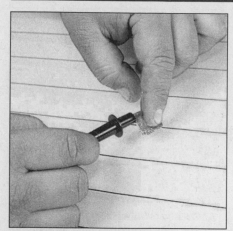

13.5 When measuring voltage at the rear window defogger grid, wrap a piece of aluminum foil around the positive probe of the voltmeter and press the foil against the wire with your finger

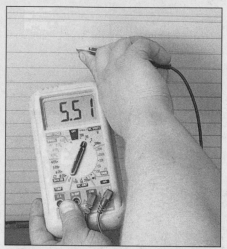

13.6 To determine if a heating element has broken, check the voltage at the center of each element - if the voltage is 6-volts, the element is unbroken

13.8 To find the break, place the voltmeter negative lead against the defogger ground terminal, place the voltmeter positive lead with the foil strip against the heat wire at the positive terminal end and slide it toward the negative terminal end. The point at which the voltmeter deflects from several volts to zero volts is the point at which the wire is broken

2   Small breaks in the element can be repaired without removing the rear window.

Check

Refer to illustrations 13.5, 13.6 and 13.8

3   Turn the ignition and defogger switches to the ON position.

4   Using a voltmeter, place the positive probe against the defogger grid positive side and the negative probe against the ground side. If battery voltage is not indicated, check that the ignition switch is On and that the feed and ground wires are properly connected. Check the two fuses, defogger switch, defogger relay and related wiring. The dealer can scan the body control module if necessary. If voltage is indicated, but all or part of the defogger doesn't heat, proceed with the following tests.

5   When measuring voltage during the next two tests, wrap a piece of aluminum foil around the tip of the voltmeter positive probe and press the foil against the heating element with your finger **(see illustration)**. Place the negative probe on the defogger grid ground terminal.

6   Check the voltage at the center of each heating element **(see illustration)**. If the voltage is 5 to 6 volts, the element is okay (there is no break). If the voltage is 0 volts, the element is broken between the center of the element and the positive end. If the voltage is 10 to 12 volts, the element is broken between the center of the element and the ground side. Check each heating element.

7   If none of the elements are broken, connect the negative probe to a good chassis ground. The voltage reading should stay the same, if it doesn't the ground connection is bad.

8   To find the break, place the voltmeter negative probe against the defogger ground terminal. Place the voltmeter positive probe with the foil strip against the heating element at the positive side and slide it toward the

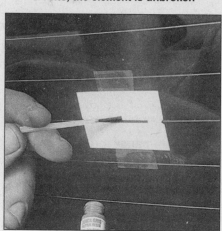

13.14 To use a defogger repair kit, apply masking to the inside of the window at the damaged area, then brush on the special conductive coating

negative side. The point at which the voltmeter deflects from several volts to zero is the point where the heating element is broken **(see illustration)**.

Repair

Refer to illustration 13.14

9   Repair the break in the element using a repair kit specifically for this purpose, such as DuPont paste No. 4817 (or equivalent). The kit includes conductive plastic epoxy.

10   Before repairing a break, turn off the system and allow it to cool for a few minutes.

11   Lightly buff the element area with fine steel wool; then clean it thoroughly with rubbing alcohol.

12   Use masking tape to mask off the area being repaired.

13   Thoroughly mix the epoxy, following the kit instructions.

14   Apply the epoxy material to the slit in the masking tape, overlapping the undamaged

area about 3/4-inch on either end **(see illustration)**.

15   Allow the repair to cure for 24 hours before removing the tape and using the system.

14   Headlight bulb - replacement

Refer to illustrations 14.2a, 14.2b, 14.3 and 14.4

Warning: *Halogen bulbs are gas-filled and under pressure and they can shatter if the surface is scratched or the bulb is dropped. Wear eye protection and handle the bulbs carefully, grasping only the base whenever possible. Don't touch the surface of the bulb with your fingers because the oil from your skin could cause it to overheat and fail prematurely. If you do touch the bulb surface, clean it with rubbing alcohol.*

Note: *The following procedure simplifies headlight bulb replacement by showing how to replace a headlight bulb without removing the headlight housing. However, if your hands are too big, remove the headlight housing first (see Section 15), then replace the bulb.*

1   Start the engine and turn the front wheels all the way to the left or right to provide some room to work. (As an alternative, you could also loosen the front wheel lug nuts, raise the front of the vehicle, place it securely on jackstands and remove the wheel.)

2   Working inside the wheelhousing, remove the access panel for the headlight housing electrical connectors **(see illustrations)**.

3   Remove the bulb socket from the headlight housing **(see illustration)**.

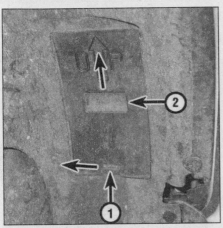

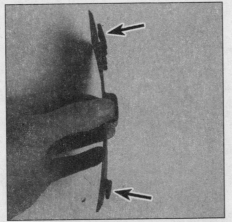

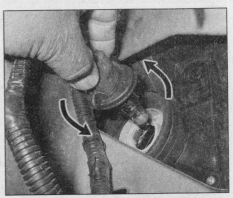

14.3 To remove the headlight socket from the headlight housing, rotate it counterclockwise and pull it out of the housing

14.2a To remove the access panel for the headlight housing electrical connectors:

A   *Insert a screwdriver into the slot (1) at the bottom of the panel and pry out the lower end of the panel until the two lower mounting tabs are disengaged from the lower edge of the hole*

B   *Using the recessed pull cup (2) for leverage, slide the panel up until it stops*

C   *Pull out the lower edge of the access panel, slide the panel down and disengage the upper mounting tabs from the upper edge of the hole*

4   Disconnect the electrical connector from the headlight bulb holder (**see illustration**).

5   Installation is the reverse of removal.

14.2b The backside of the access panel has four mounting tabs: two larger upper tabs and two smaller lower tabs. When installing the panel, make sure that the larger tabs are at the top and the smaller tabs are at the bottom

14.4 To disconnect the electrical connector from the headlight bulb holder, release the sliding lock by pushing it out (away from the connector, toward the harness), then depress the release tab on top and pull off the connector

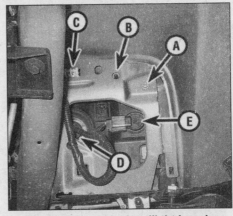

15.3a To remove the headlight housing:

A   *Remove this nut*

B   *Locator pin*

C   *Pull the headlight mounting stud out of this plastic clip*

D   *Headlight bulb electrical connector (disconnect after you pull out the headlight)*

E   *Front park/turn signal/sidemarker light bulb electrical connector (disconnect after you pull out the headlight housing)*

15 Headlight housing - removal and installation

Refer to illustrations 15.3a, 15.3b and 15.4 and 15.5

1   Start the engine and turn the front wheels all the way to the left or right to provide some room to work. (As an alternative, you could also loosen the front wheel lug nuts, raise the front of the vehicle, place it securely on jackstands and remove the wheel.)

2   Working inside the wheelhousing, remove the access panel for the headlight housing electrical connectors (**see illustra-**

tions 14.2a and 14.2b).

3   Remove the headlight mounting nut and mounting bolts (**see illustrations**).

4   Pull out the headlight housing far enough to remove the bulb sockets for the headlight bulb and for the front park/turn signal/sidemarker light bulbs (**see illustration**). Remove the headlight housing.

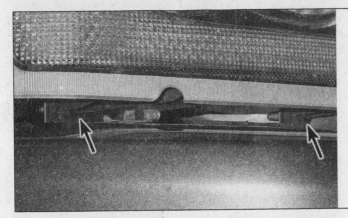

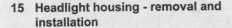

15.3b Working at the front side of the headlights, remove these two mounting bolts

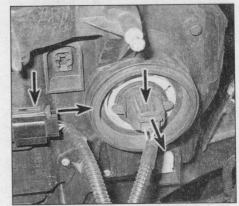

15.4 To disconnect the electrical connectors for the headlight and front park/turn signal/sidemarker light bulbs, pull out the slide locks, depress the release tabs and pull off the connectors

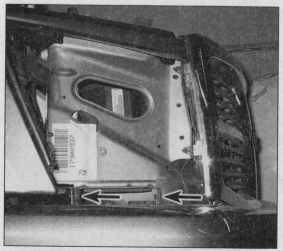

15.5 Before installing the headlight housing, make sure that these two U-nuts are correctly positioned on the small mounting tabs that are part of the front fender

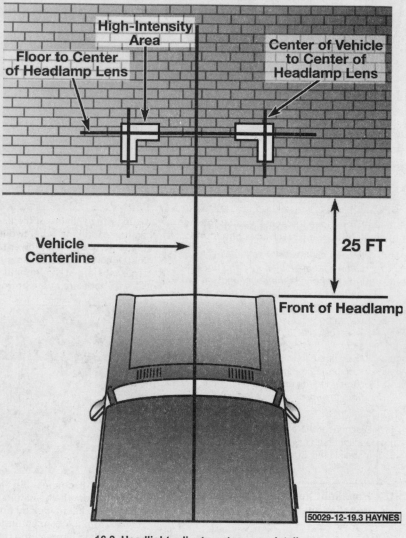

16.2 Headlight adjustment screen details

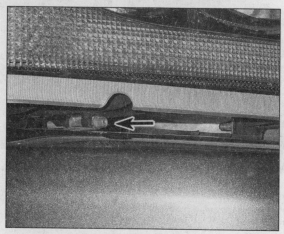

16.1 Headlight vertical adjustment screw location

5 Installation is the reverse of removal. The two lower front mounting bolts are screwed into U-nuts mounted on small mounting tabs that are part of the front fender **(see illustration)**. Make sure that these U-nuts are correctly positioned on the mounting tabs before installing the front mounting bolts.

16 Headlights - adjustment

Warning: *The headlights must be aimed correctly. If adjusted incorrectly, they could temporarily blind the driver of an oncoming vehicle and cause an accident or seriously reduce your ability to see the road. The headlights should be checked for proper aim every 12 months and any time a new headlight is installed or front-end bodywork is performed. The following procedure is only intended to provide temporary adjustment until you can have the headlights professionally adjusted by a dealer service department.*

Headlights

Refer to illustrations 16.1 and 16.2

1 Each headlight has an adjusting screw for vertical adjustment **(see illustration)**. (There is no horizontal adjustment screw.)
2 There are several ways to adjust the headlights. The simplest method requires an open area with a blank wall and a level floor **(see illustration)**.
3 Position masking tape vertically on the wall in reference to the vehicle centerline and the centerlines of both headlights.
4 Position a horizontal tape line in reference to the centerline of the headlights. **Note:** *It might be easier to position the tape on the wall with the vehicle parked only a few inches away.*
5 Adjustment should be made with the vehicle parked 25 feet from the wall, sitting level, the gas tank full and no unusually heavy load in the vehicle.
6 The high intensity zone should be vertically centered with the exact center about three inches below the horizontal line.
7 Have the headlights adjusted by a qualified technician at the earliest opportunity.

Fog lights

Note: *This procedure applies only to vehicles equipped with optional fog lights.*
8 Park the vehicle 25 feet from the wall.
9 Tape a horizontal line on the wall that represents the height of the fog lights and tape another line four inches below that line.
10 Using the adjusting screw on each fog light, adjust the pattern on the wall so that the top of the fog light beam meets the lower line on the wall.
11 Repeat the procedure for the other fog light.

Light bar

Note: *This procedure applies only to trucks equipped with an optional light bar.*
12 Park the vehicle 25 feet from the wall.
13 Attach a horizontal piece of tape to

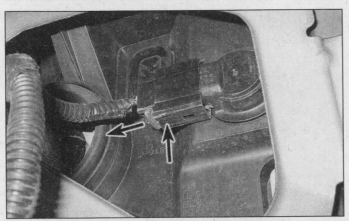

17.3 To disconnect the electrical connector from the socket for the front park/turn signal/sidemarker light bulb, slide the lock out of the connector (toward the harness), then depress the release tab and pull off the connector

17.4 To remove the bulb socket for the front park/turn signal/ sidemarker light bulb from the headlight housing, rotate the socket counterclockwise and pull it out of the housing

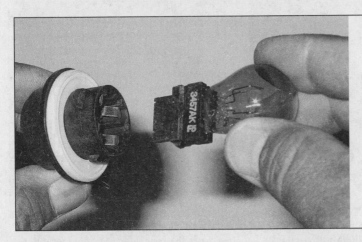

17.5 To remove the front park/turn signal/sidemarker light bulb from its socket, simply pull it straight out of the socket

17.7 To disconnect the electrical connector from the fog light bulb socket, pry the two connector locking tabs away from the terminal, depress the two release tabs on the sides of the connector and pull off the connector

the wall at seven feet, nine inches from the ground.

14   Cover three of the four lights and aim the fourth using the adjustment screw in the rear. The center of its high intensity zone should be on the tape line.

15   Repeat the procedure for the other light(s).

17 Bulb replacement

Exterior lights

Front park/turn signal/sidemarker light bulbs

Refer to illustrations 17.3, 17.4 and 17.5

1   Start the engine and turn the front wheels all the way to the left or right to provide some room to work. (As an alternative, you could also loosen the front wheel lug nuts, raise the front of the vehicle, place it securely on jackstands and remove the wheel.)

2   Working inside the wheelhousing, remove the access panel for the headlight housing electrical connectors **(see illustrations 14.2a and 14.2b)**.

3   Disconnect the electrical connector from

the socket for the front park/turn signal/side-marker light bulb **(see illustration)**.

4   Remove the front park/turn signal/side-marker light bulb socket from the headlight housing **(see illustration)**.

5   Remove the front park/turn signal/side-marker light bulb from its socket by simply pulling it straight out of the socket **(see illustration)**. To install a new bulb, push it straight into the bulb socket until it seats fully.

6   Installation is the reverse of removal.

Fog light bulbs (optional)

Refer to illustrations 17.7 and 17.8

Warning: *The fog light bulbs are gas-filled and under pressure and they can shatter if the surface is scratched or the bulb is dropped. Wear eye protection and handle the bulbs carefully, grasping only the base whenever possible. Don't touch the surface of the bulb with your fingers because the oil from your skin could cause it to overheat and fail prematurely. If you do touch the bulb surface, clean it with rubbing alcohol.*

7   Disconnect the electrical connector from the fog light socket **(see illustration)**.

8   Remove the fog light bulb socket **(see illustration)**.

9   Remove the fog light bulb from its socket

17.8 To remove the fog light bulb socket, rotate it counterclockwise and pull it out of the housing

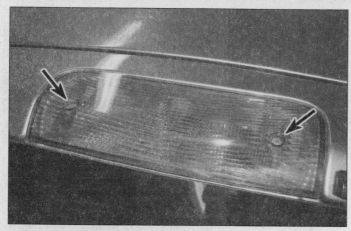

17.11 To detach the center high-mounted brake light housing from the liftgate, remove these two screws

17.12 To disconnect the electrical connector from the center high-mounted brake light bulb socket, push the slide lock toward the wiring harness, then depress the release tab and pull off the connector

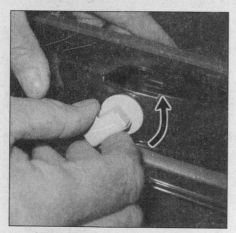

17.13 To remove the center high-mounted brake light bulb socket, rotate it counterclockwise and pull it out of the housing

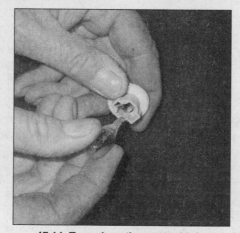

17.14 To replace the center high-mounted brake light bulb, pull it straight out of the socket

17.16 To detach the taillight housing from the rear quarter panel, carefully pry out these two push-pin fasteners, then pull the outer edge of the taillight housing far enough back to disengage the two ballstuds on the housing from their grommets in the rear quarter panel

by simply pulling it straight out of the socket **(see illustration 17.5)**. To install a new bulb, push it straight into the bulb socket. Make sure that the bulb is fully seated in the socket.

10   Installation is the reverse of removal.

Center high-mounted brake light bulb

Refer to illustrations 17.11, 17.12, 17.13 and 17.14

11   Remove the center high-mounted brake light housing **(see illustration)**.

12   Disconnect the electrical connector from the center high-mounted brake light bulb socket **(see illustration)**.

13   Remove the center high-mounted bulb socket from the center high-mounted brake light housing **(see illustration)**.

14   To replace the center high-mounted brake light bulb, simply pull it straight out of the socket **(see illustration)**. To install a new bulb, push it straight into the bulb socket. Make sure that the bulb is fully seated in the socket.

15   Installation is the reverse of removal.

Taillight bulbs

Refer to illustrations 17.16, 17.17, 17.18, 17.19a and 17.19b

Note: *The rear taillight assembly consists of four bulbs: the sidemarker bulb, the taillight/ brake light bulb, the taillight/turn signal bulb and the back-up light bulb.*

16   Open the liftgate, then remove the two push-pin fasteners that secure the taillight housing to the rear quarter panel **(see illustration)**. Then pull the outer edge of the taillight housing far enough back to disengage the two ballstuds on the outer edge of the housing from their grommets in the rear quarter panel.

17   Disconnect the electrical connector from the taillight assembly **(see illustration)**.

18   Remove the bulb socket plate from the taillight housing **(see illustration)**.

19   To remove the bulb that you want to replace, pull it straight out of its socket **(see illustrations)**. To install a new bulb, insert it into the socket and push it in until it's fully seated.

20   Installation is the reverse of removal.

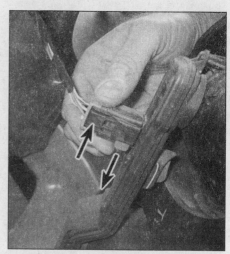

17.17 To disconnect the electrical connector from the taillight assembly, push out the red lock, then depress the release tab and pull off the connector

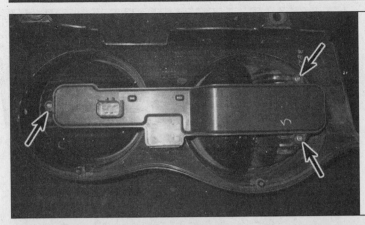

17.18 To detach the bulb socket plate from the taillight housing, remove these three screws

17.19a Backup light bulb (A) and taillight/turn signal bulb (B)

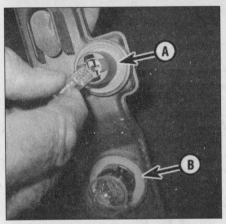

17.19b Sidemarker light bulb (A) and taillight/brake light bulb (B)

17.21 To detach the license plate light housing, remove these two screws

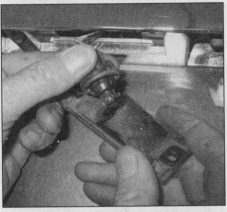

17.22 To remove the license plate light bulb socket, rotate it counterclockwise and pull it out of the housing

License plate light bulb

Refer to illustrations 17.21 and 17.22

21   Remove the license plate light housing retaining screws **(see illustration)** and pull the housing out of the liftgate.

22   Remove the license plate light bulb socket from the housing **(see illustration)**.

23   Remove the license plate light bulb from its socket by pulling it straight out.

24   To install a new bulb, insert it into the socket and push it in until it's fully seated.

25   Installation is the reverse of removal.

Interior lights

Warning: *The models covered by this manual are equipped with a Supplemental Restraint System (SRS), more commonly known as airbags. Always disarm the airbag system before working in the vicinity of any airbag system component to avoid the possibility of accidental deployment of the airbag, which could cause personal injury (see Section 25). Do not use a memory-saving device to preserve the PCM's memory when working on or near airbag system components.*

Reading light bulbs

Refer to illustrations 17.26, 17.27 and 17.28

Note: *There are two reading lights, one for the driver and one for the passenger. The following procedure, which depicts replacement of the driver's side bulb, also applies to the*

passenger side reading light.

26   Using a small, thin-blade screwdriver, carefully pry the switch housing loose from the reading light bezel **(see illustration)**, disconnect the switch electrical connectors and remove the switch housing.

27   Using the small screwdriver again, carefully pry loose the reading light lens **(see illustration)**.

17.26 Using a small, thin-blade screwdriver, carefully pry the switch housing loose from the reading light bezel, then disconnect the switch electrical connector and remove the switch housing

17.27 To pry off the reading light lens, insert the same small screwdriver between the outer edge of the lens and the reading light bezel, then lever the lens toward the center of the vehicle until it unsnaps

17.28 To remove a reading light bulb, pull it straight down. To install a new bulb, push it back into the terminals until its snaps into place

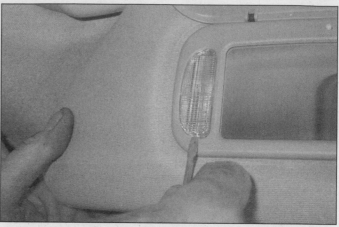

17.31 To remove a vanity light lens from the visor, carefully pry the lens out with a small, thin-blade screwdriver

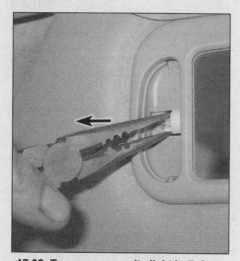

17.32 To remove a vanity light bulb from the housing, carefully pull it out of the housing with small needle-nose pliers. Caution: *Pull only on the plastic portion - not the glass!*

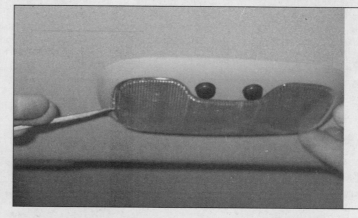

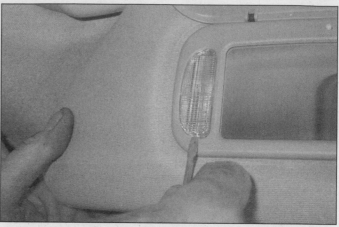

17.35a To remove the dome light lens, insert a small flat-blade screwdriver into the notch on the left side of the lens and pop the lens loose from the dome light housing . . .

Vanity lights bulbs

Refer to illustrations 17.31 and 17.32

31   Using a small, thin-blade screwdriver, carefully pry the vanity light lens from the visor **(see illustration)**.

32   Remove the vanity light bulb from its housing by sliding it out to the left with a pair of small needle-nose pliers **(see illustration)**.

33   To install a new vanity light bulb, carefully insert the bulb into the housing, then, using the needle-nose pliers, slide it to the right, back into the housing, until it's fully seated.

34   Installation is the reverse of removal.

Dome light

Refer to illustrations 17.35a, 17.35b and 17.36

35   Insert a small flat-bladed screwdriver into the notch between the dome light lens and the housing, then carefully pry down the left side (driver's side) of the lens **(see illustrations)**, swing down the lens and allow it to hang from its right edge.

36   Remove the dome light bulb from the dome light housing **(see illustration)**. To install a new bulb, insert the bulb into its socket in the dome light housing until it's fully seated.

28   Remove the reading light bulb from its terminals **(see illustration)**.

29   To install a reading light bulb, push it up into its terminals until its snaps into place.

30   Installation is the reverse of removal.

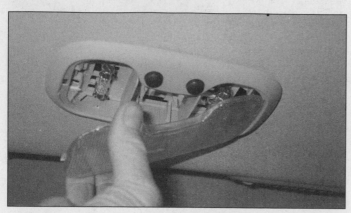

17.35b . . . then swing down the lens for access to the bulbs

17.36 To remove either dome light bulb, simply pull it straight down from its terminals. To install a dome light bulb, push it up into the terminals until its snaps into place

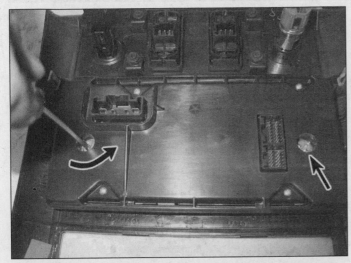

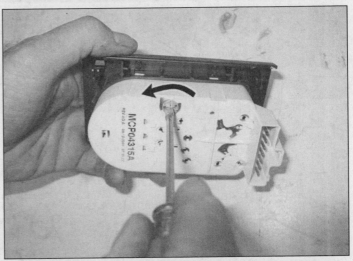

17.39 To replace either illumination bulb for the front heater/air conditioning control assembly, rotate it counterclockwise 1/4-turn, then turn the control assembly upside down and let the bulb fall out. To install a new bulb, drop it into the hole, then turn it clockwise 1/4-turn to lock it into place

17.42 To replace either illumination bulb for the rear heater/air conditioning control assembly, rotate it counterclockwise 1/4-turn, then turn the control assembly upside down and let the bulb fall out. To install a new bulb, drop it into the hole, then turn it clockwise 1/4-turn to lock it into place

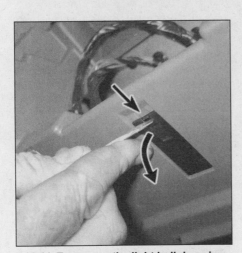

17.44 To remove the light bulb housing from the instrument panel center bezel, pry the retaining latch forward until it disengages from the instrument panel and the housing swings down, then pull the housing down from the instrument panel

17.45 The light bulb for the instrument panel center bezel is housed inside this small plastic box. To open the housing, disengage the lock tab on top and slide the cover (A) off the housing (B)

17.46 To remove the center bezel light bulb, pull it straight out of the housing. To install a new bulb, push it straight in until it stops

37   Installation is otherwise the reverse of removal.

Front heater/air conditioning control assembly illumination bulb

Refer to illustration 17.39

38   Remove the front heater/air conditioning control assembly (see Chapter 3).

39   To remove an illumination bulb from the heater/air conditioning control assembly, insert a small screwdriver into the bulb mounting hole **(see illustration)**, rotate the bulb holder counterclockwise 1/4-turn, turn the heater/air conditioning control assembly upside down and let the bulb fall out. To install a new bulb, insert it into its hole, then rotate it clockwise 1/4-turn until it locks into place.

40   Installation is the reverse of removal.

Rear heater/air conditioning control assembly illumination bulb

Refer to illustration 17.42

41   Remove the rear heater/air conditioning control assembly (see Chapter 3).

42   To remove an illumination bulb from the heater/air conditioning control assembly, insert a small screwdriver into the bulb mounting hole **(see illustration)**, rotate the bulb holder counterclockwise 1/4-turn, turn the heater/air conditioning control assembly upside down and let the bulb fall out. To install a new bulb, insert it into its hole, then rotate it clockwise 1/4-turn until it locks into place.

43   Installation is the reverse of removal.

Instrument panel center bezel light bulb

Refer to illustrations 17.44, 17.45 and 17.46

Note: *The light bulb for the instrument panel center bezel is located on the underside of the instrument panel, directly above the small storage bin in the forward part of the center console, i.e. the bulb is in the "roof" above the bin.*

44   Remove the light bulb housing from the instrument panel center bezel **(see illustration)**.

45   Remove the cover from the light bulb housing **(see illustration)**.

46   Remove the light bulb from the housing **(see illustration)**.

47   Installation is the reverse of removal.

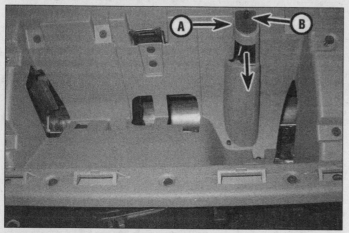

17.48 The light bulb for the glove box is located in the roof of the glove box, on the other side of this plate (A) for the plunger (B). To remove the bulb, grasp it firmly and pull it straight forward, out of its socket. To install a new bulb, push it straight back into its socket until its stops (instrument panel removed and partially disassembled for clarity)

18.2 To remove the horns, remove the horn mounting bracket bolt, remove the horns and mounting bracket as a single assembly, then disconnect the electrical connectors from both horns

Glove box light bulb

Refer to illustration 17.48

48   Open the glove box door and locate the glove box light bulb at the right front corner **(see illustration)**.
49   To remove the glove box light bulb, pull it straight out, toward the front of the vehicle.
50   To install a new glove box light bulb, push it straight back into its socket until it's fully seated.

18   Horn - replacement

Refer to illustration 18.2

Note: *The horns are located behind the left end of the grille, where they're bolted to a frame upright at the left end and in front of the condenser.*

1   Remove the grille (see Chapter 11).
2   Remove the horn mounting bracket bolt **(see illustration)**.
3   Remove the horns and mounting bracket as a single assembly, then disconnect the electrical connectors from the horns.
4   To replace either horn, remove the retaining nut for the horn that you want to replace, then remove that horn from the mounting bracket.
5   Installation is the reverse of removal.

19   Electric side-view mirrors - general information

1   The electric side-view mirrors can be adjusted up-and-down and left-to-right by a driver's side switch located on the left door trim panel. On models with factory-installed dual power mirrors, each mirror is also equipped with a heater grid behind the mirror glass to clear the mirror surface of fog, ice

or snow. On these models, the mirror heater grid is an integral component of each mirror. If a heater grid fails, replace the mirror (see Chapter 11). The heater grid switches and the heated mirror system indicator light are integral components of the heater/air conditioning control panel on the dash. If one of these components fails, replace the heater/air conditioning control assembly (see Chapter 3). The heated mirror relay is located in one of the fuse and relay boxes.
2   The power mirror control switch has a LEFT-RIGHT selector switch that allows you to send voltage to the side-view mirror that you want to adjust. With the ignition switch in the ACC position, roll down the windows and operate the mirror control switch through all functions (left-right and up-down) for both the left and right side-view mirrors.
3   Listen carefully for the sound of the electric motors running in the mirrors.
4   If you can hear the motors but the mirror glass doesn't move, the problem is probably a defective drive mechanism inside the mirror, which will necessitate replacement of the mirror.
5   If the mirrors don't operate and no sound comes from the mirrors, check the fuse in one of the fuse and relay boxes (see Section 3).
6   If the fuse is OK, refer to Chapter 11 and remove the door panel for access to the back of the mirror control switch, without disconnecting the wires attached to it. Turn the ignition ON and check for voltage at the switch. There should be voltage at one terminal. If there's no voltage at the switch, check for an open in the wiring between the fuse panel and the switch.
7   If there's voltage at the switch, disconnect it. Check the switch for continuity in all its operating positions. If the switch does not have continuity, replace it.
8   Reconnect the switch. Locate the wire going from the switch to ground. Leaving

the switch connected, connect a jumper wire between this wire and ground. If the mirror works normally with this wire in place, repair the faulty ground connection.
9   If the mirror still doesn't work, remove the mirror and check the wires at the mirror for voltage. Check with the ignition key turned to ON and the mirror selector switch on the appropriate side. Operate the mirror switch in all its positions. There should be voltage at one of the switch-to-mirror wires in each switch position, except the neutral (off) position.
10   If voltage is not present in each switch position, check the wiring between the mirror and control switch for opens and shorts.
11   If there's voltage, remove the mirror and test it off the vehicle with jumper wires. Replace the mirror if it fails this test.

20   Cruise control system - general information

Note: *The following general information applies to vehicles equipped with a 3.7L V6 or a 4.7L V8. It does NOT apply to vehicles powered by a Hemi engine. On Hemi-powered vehicles the Powertrain Control Module (PCM) controls the cruise control system electronically. If you have problems with the cruise control system on a vehicle with a Hemi, have it checked by a dealer service department or other qualified repair shop.*

1   The cruise control system maintains vehicle speed with a servo motor connected to the throttle body by a cable. The system consists of the servo motor, brake switch, clutch switch (only on vehicles with a manual transmission), the control switches (on the steering wheel on all vehicles) and the wiring and vacuum hoses connecting all of these components. Some features of the system require the use of a scan tool, and diagnostic

procedures that are beyond the scope of the home mechanic. Listed below are some general procedures that may be used to locate common problems.

2   Locate and check the fuse (see Section 3).

3   Visually inspect the vacuum hose connected to the servo and check the control linkage between the cruise control servo and the throttle body and replace as necessary.

4   Test-drive the vehicle to determine if the cruise control is now working. If it isn't, take it to a dealer service department or an automotive electrical specialist for further diagnosis and repair.

21 Power window system - general information

1   The power window system controls the electric motors, mounted inside the doors, that lower and raise the windows. The power window system consists of the control switches, the fuse, the circuit breaker, the motors, the window "regulators" (the scissor-like mechanisms that raise and lower the window glass) and the wiring connecting the switches to the motors. When the ignition switch is turned to ON, current flows through the power window fuse in the engine compartment fuse and relay box to a circuit breaker located in the instrument panel wiring harness (located near the parking brake pedal). From there, current flows to the power window switches.

2   The power windows are wired so that they can be lowered and raised from the master control switch by the driver or by passengers using remote switches located at each passenger window. Each window has a separate motor that is reversible. The position of the control switch determines the polarity and therefore the direction of operation.

3   The power window system will only operate when the ignition switch is turned to ON. In addition, a window lockout switch at the master control switch can, when activated, disable the power window switches on the other doors. Always check these items before troubleshooting a window problem.

4   These procedures are general in nature, so if you can't find the problem using them, take the vehicle to a dealer service department.

5   If the power windows don't work at all, check the fuse or circuit breaker.

6   If only the rear windows are inoperative, or if the windows only operate from the master control switch, check the window lockout switch for continuity in the unlocked position. If it doesn't have continuity, replace it.

7   Check the wiring between the switches and the fuse for continuity. Repair the wiring, if necessary.

8   If only one window is inoperative from the master control switch, try the control switch at the window that doesn't work. **Note:** *This doesn't apply to the driver's door window.*

9   If the same window works from one

switch, but not the other, check the switch for continuity.

10   If the switch tests OK, check for a short or open in the wiring between the affected switch and the window motor.

11   If one window is inoperative from both switches, remove the trim panel from the affected door (see Chapter 11), then check for voltage at the switch and at the motor while operating the switch. First check for voltage at the electrical connectors for the circuit. With the ignition key turned to ON and the connectors all connected, backprobe at the designated wire (see the wiring diagrams at the end of this Chapter) with a grounded test light. Pushing the driver's window switch to the DOWN position, there should be voltage at one terminal. Pushing the same switch to the UP position, there should be voltage at another terminal. If these voltage checks are OK, disconnect the electrical connector at the driver's motor, and check it for voltage when the switch is operated.

12   If voltage is reaching the motor and the switch is OK, disconnect the door glass from its regulator (see Chapter 11). Move the window up and down by hand while checking for binding and damage. Also check for binding and damage to the regulator. If the regulator is not damaged and the window moves up and down smoothly, replace the motor. If there's binding or damage, lubricate, repair or replace parts, as necessary.

13   If voltage isn't reaching the motor, check the wiring in the circuit for continuity between the switches and motors (see the wiring diagram at the end of this Chapter).

14   If you have to replace the main power window switch, pry it out of the door trim panel, then disconnect the electrical connector(s) from the switch.

15   When you're done, test the windows to confirm that the window system is functioning correctly.

22 Power door lock system - general information

1   The power door lock system operates the power door motors, which are integral components of the door latch units in each door. The system consists of a fuse (in the engine compartment fuse and relay box), the instrument cluster, the control switches (in each of the front doors), the power door motors and the electrical wiring harnesses connecting all of these components.

2   The lock mechanisms in the door latch units are actuated by a reversible electric motor in each door. When you push the door lock switch to LOCK, the motor operates one way and locks the latch mechanism. When you push the door lock switch the other way, to the UNLOCK position, the motor operates in the other direction, unlocking the latch mechanism. Because the motors and lock mechanisms are an integral part of the door latch units, they cannot be repaired. If a door

lock motor or lock mechanism fails, replace the door latch unit (see Chapter 11).

3   Even if you don't manually lock the doors or press the door lock switch to the LOCK position before driving, the instrument cluster automatically locks the doors when the vehicle speed exceeds 15 mph, as long as all the doors are closed and the accelerator pedal is depressed. (You can turn off this feature if you don't want the doors to lock automatically. Refer to your owner's manual.)

4   Some vehicles have an optional Remote Keyless Entry (RKE) system that allows you to lock and unlock the doors from outside the vehicle. The RKE system consists of the transmitter (the electronic push-button "key") and a receiver located on the instrument cluster. The RKE receiver, which operates all the time, is protected by a fuse in the engine compartment fuse and relay box. Vehicles are shipped from the factory with two RKE transmitters but, if you want to purchase extra units, the RKE receiver can actually handle up to four vehicle access codes.

5   Some features of the door lock system on these vehicles rely on resources that they share with other electronic modules through the Programmable Communications Interface (PCI) data bus network. Professional diagnosis of these modules and the PCI data bus network requires the use of a DRB III, (proprietary factory) scan tool and factory diagnostic information. At-home repairs are therefore limited to inspecting the wiring for bad connections and for minor faults that can be easily repaired. If you are unable to locate the trouble using the following general steps, consult your dealer service department.

6   Always check the circuit fuses (in the engine compartment fuse and relay box) first.

7   When depressed, each power door lock switch locks or unlocks all of the doors. The easiest way to verify that each door lock switch is operating correctly is to watch the door lock button in each door as you operate the switch. The door lock buttons should all go down when you push the door lock switch to the LOCK position, and go up when you push the door lock switch to the UNLOCK position. Also, with the engine turned off so that you can hear better, operate the door lock switches in both directions and listen for the faint click of the motors locking and unlocking the latch mechanisms.

8   If there's no click, check for voltage at the switches. If no voltage is present, check the wiring between the fuse and the switches for shorts and opens (see the wiring diagrams at the end of this chapter).

9   If voltage is present, but no clicking sound is apparent, remove the switch from the door trim panel (see Chapter 11) and test it for continuity. If there is no continuity in either direction, replace the switch.

10   If the switch has continuity but the latch mechanism doesn't click, check the wiring between the switch and the motor in the latch mechanism for continuity. If the circuit is open between the switch and the motor, repair the wiring.

11   If all but one motor is operating, remove the trim panel from the affected door (see Chapter 11) and check for voltage at the motor while operating the lock switch. One of the wires should have voltage in the LOCK position; the other should have voltage in the UNLOCK position.

12   If the inoperative motor is receiving voltage, replace the latch mechanism.

13   If the inoperative motor isn't receiving voltage, check for an open or short in the circuit between the switch and the motor. **Note:** *It's common for wires to break in the harness between the body and the door because repeatedly opening and closing the door fatigues and eventually breaks the wires.*

23   Power seats - general information

Warning: *The models covered by this manual are equipped with a Supplemental Restraint System (SRS), more commonly known as airbags. Additionally, some models are equipped with seat belt pre-tensioners, which are explosive devices. Always disarm the airbag/restraint system before working in the vicinity of any airbag/restraint system component to avoid the possibility of accidental deployment of the airbag/seat belt pre-tensioners, which could cause personal injury (see Section 25). Do not use a memory-saving device to preserve the PCM's memory when working on or near airbag system components.*

1   Some models feature an optional eight-way power seat system that allows the driver and passenger to adjust the front seats up, down, front up, front down, rear up, rear down, forward and rearward. The system consists of the driver's power seat switch, the passenger power seat switch, the driver's power seat track, the passenger power seat track and, on some models, the optional power lumbar adjusters.

2   The power seat switches are located on the outboard side of the seat cushions, on the seat cushion side panels. If the vehicle is equipped with the optional power lumbar adjusters, the lumbar switches are located on the power seat switch assemblies. Each switch assembly is attached to the seat side panel by two Torx screws. Refer to your owner's manual for instructions regarding switch functions. Individual switches in the power seat switch assemblies cannot be repaired or replaced separately. If one of the switches in a power seat switch assembly fails, replace the entire switch assembly.

3   The seats are powered by three reversible motors that are attached to the upper half of the power seat track assembly. These motors are controlled by the power seat switches on the sides of the seats. Each switch changes the direction of seat travel by reversing polarity to the drive motor. The motors are an integral part of the power seat track assembly and cannot be repaired or replaced separately. If a motor fails, replace

the power seat track assembly.

4   The optional power lumbar adjuster and motor are located on the back of the seat, under the seat trim cover and padding, where they're attached to a molded plastic back panel and to the seat back frame. The power lumbar adjuster and motor cannot be repaired or replaced separately from the seat back frame. If either the adjuster or the motor fails, replace the entire seat back frame unit.

5   Diagnosis is usually a simple matter, using the following procedures.

6   Look under the seat for any object which may be preventing the seat from moving.

7   If the seat won't work at all, check the fuse, which is located in the engine compartment fuse and relay box.

8   With the engine off to reduce the noise level, operate the seat controls in all directions and listen for sound coming from the seat motors.

9   If the motor doesn't work or make noise, check for voltage at the motor while an assistant operates the switch.

10   If the motor is getting voltage but doesn't run, test it off the vehicle with jumper wires. If it still doesn't work, replace it. The individual components are not available separately. The whole power-seat track must be purchased as an assembly.

11   If the motor isn't getting voltage, remove the seat side panel to access the switch and check for voltage. If there's no voltage at the switch, check the wiring between the fuse and the switch. If there's voltage at the switch, check for a short or open in the wiring between the switch and the motor. If that circuit is okay, replace the switch. No further testing is recommended. If the power seat system is still malfunctioning at this point, have the system checked out by a dealer service department.

24   Daytime Running Lights (DRL) - general information

Canadian models are equipped with Daytime Running Lights (DRL). The DRL system illuminates the headlights whenever the engine is running and the parking brake is disengaged. The DRL system provides reduced power to the headlights so that they won't be too bright for daytime use and it prolongs the headlight bulbs' service life. It does this by modulating the pulse-width of the power to the headlights. The duration and interval of these power pulses is programmed into the Front Control Module (FCM), which is located on the instrument cluster. If you want to alter the pulse-width, you must have it done by a dealer service department.

25   Airbag system - general information

These models are equipped with a Supplemental Restraint System (SRS), more

commonly called an airbag system. There are at least two airbags, one for the driver and one for the front seat passenger, on all models. The SRS system is designed to protect the driver and passenger(s) from serious injury in the event of a head-on or frontal collision. The airbag control module is located on the transmission tunnel, right below the center of the instrument panel. Some models are also equipped with optional side curtain airbags. Vehicles with this option can be identified by the "SRS - AIRBAG" logo printed on the headliner above the B-pillar.

Airbag modules

The airbag module houses the airbag and the inflator unit. The inflator unit is mounted on the back of the housing over a hole through which gas is expelled, inflating the bag almost instantaneously when an electrical signal is received from the airbag control module. On the driver's airbag, the specially wound wire that carries this signal to the module is called a "clockspring." The clockspring is a flat, ribbon-like electrically conductive tape that winds and unwinds as the steering wheel is turned so it can transmit an electrical signal regardless of wheel position. The procedure for removing the driver's airbag is part of *Steering wheel - removal and installation* in Chapter 10.

The passenger airbag is located in the top of the dashboard, above the glove box. There's also a passenger airbag ON/OFF switch located at the lower right corner of the center instrument panel bezel. This switch allows you to deactivate the passenger airbag if you're transporting an infant or a young child in a child safety seat. We don't recommend removing the passenger airbag because there is no reason to do so unless it has been activated during an accident and needs to be replaced afterward. Although the electrical connector for the passenger airbag must be disconnected when removing the instrument panel (see *Instrument panel - removal and installation* in Chapter 11), the airbag module itself does not need to be removed.

Optional side-curtain airbags, if equipped, are located on each roof side rail, above the headliner, and they extend from the A-pillar to the C-pillar. Again, we don't recommend trying to remove the side-curtain airbags because there is no reason to do so unless they've been deployed in an accident and must be replaced.

Airbag Control Module (ACM) and Side Impact Airbag Control Modules (SIACMs)

The Airbag Control Module (ACM) is the microprocessor that monitors and operates the airbag system. The ACM checks the system every time the vehicle is started. When you start the car, an AIRBAG indicator light comes on for about six seconds, then goes off, if the system is operating properly. If there is a fault in the system, the ACM stores a Diagnostic

Trouble Code (DTC) and illuminates the AIR-BAG indicator light, which remains on until the problem is repaired and the ACM memory is cleared of any DTCs. If the AIRBAG indicator light comes on at any time other than the bulb test and remains on, or doesn't come on at all, there's a problem in the system. A DRBIII scan tool is the only means by which the system can be diagnosed. Take the vehicle to your dealer immediately and have the system professionally diagnosed and repaired.

The ACM controls the operation of the standard driver and passenger airbags. Vehicles with optional side-curtain airbags are also equipped with Side Impact Airbag Control Modules (SIACMs). There are two SIACMs, one for each side-curtain airbag. The SIACMs are located behind the B-pillar trim, above the outboard front seat belt retractor inside each B-pillar.

Servicing components near the SRS system

There are times when you need to remove the steering wheel, the instrument cluster, the radio, the heater/air conditioning control assembly or other components that are near airbag components. At these times you'll be working around components and wire harnesses for the SRS system. Do not use electrical test equipment on airbag system wires; it could cause the airbag(s) to deploy. ALWAYS DISABLE THE SRS SYSTEM BEFORE WORKING NEAR THE SRS SYSTEM COMPONENTS OR RELATED WIRING.

Disabling the system

Whenever working in the vicinity of the steering wheel, steering column, floor console or other airbag system components, the system should be disarmed. To do this perform the following steps:

a) *Turn the ignition switch to the OFF position.*

b) *Disconnect the cable from the negative battery terminal (see Chapter 5, Section 1).*

c) *WAIT FOR AT LEAST TWO MINUTES before beginning work (during this two-minute interval the capacitor that provides emergency back-up power to the system loses its charge).*

Enabling the system

To enable the airbag system, perform the following steps:

a) *Turn the ignition switch to the OFF position.*

b) *Connect the cable to the negative battery terminal.*

c) *Without putting your body in front of either airbag, turn the ignition switch to the ON position. Note whether the airbag indicator light glows for six seconds, then goes out. If it does, this indicates that the system is functioning properly.*

WARNING: Occupant Classification System (OCS)

The front passenger seat is equipped with a weight sensor module, which is an integral component of the Occupant Classification System (OCS), which is part of the front passenger airbag circuit. The seat weight sensor is a calibrated unit that calculates the weight of the passenger seat occupant. The weight of the person sitting in the passenger seat is a CRITICAL factor in airbag deployment. If you have to remove the front passenger seat for any reason, make sure that you DO NOT ALLOW ANYONE TO SIT IN THE PASSENGER SEAT UNTIL AFTER YOU HAVE DRIVEN THE VEHICLE TO A DEALER SERVICE DEPARTMENT AND HAVE HAD THE AIRBAG SYSTEM AND THE OCCUPANT CLASSIFICATION SYSTEM VERIFIED. Failure to do so could result in serious injury or death to the passenger seat occupant in the event of an accident.

26 Wiring diagrams - general information

Since it isn't possible to include all wiring diagrams for every year covered by this manual, the following diagrams are those that are typical and most commonly needed.

Prior to troubleshooting any circuits, check the fuse and circuit breakers (if equipped) to make sure they are in good condition. Make sure the battery is properly charged and has clean, tight cable connections (see Chapter 1).

When checking the wiring system, make sure that all electrical connectors are clean, with no broken or loose pins. When disconnecting an electrical connector, do not pull on the wires, only on the connector housings.

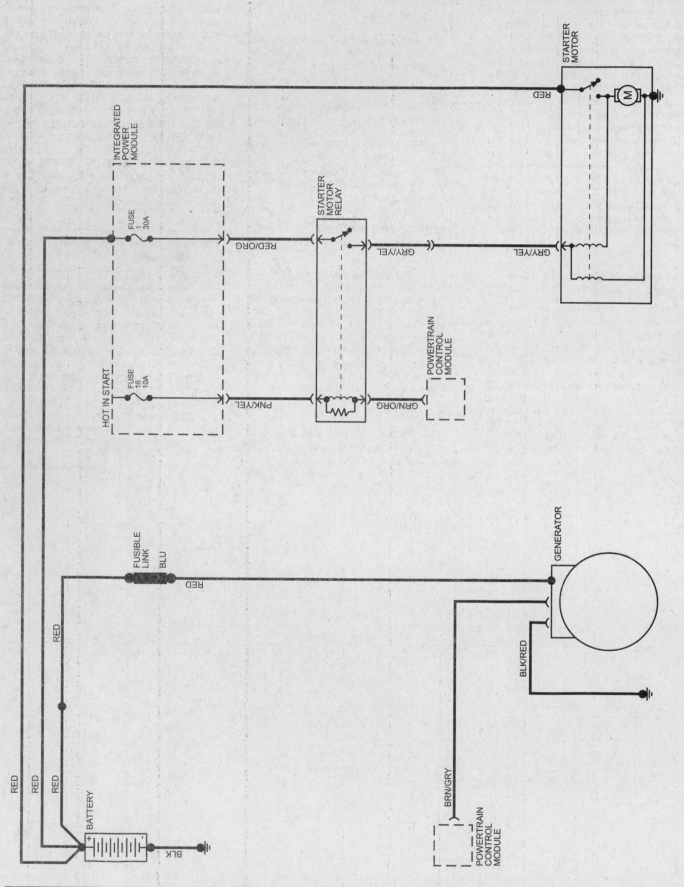

2004-2006 Durango starting and charging systems

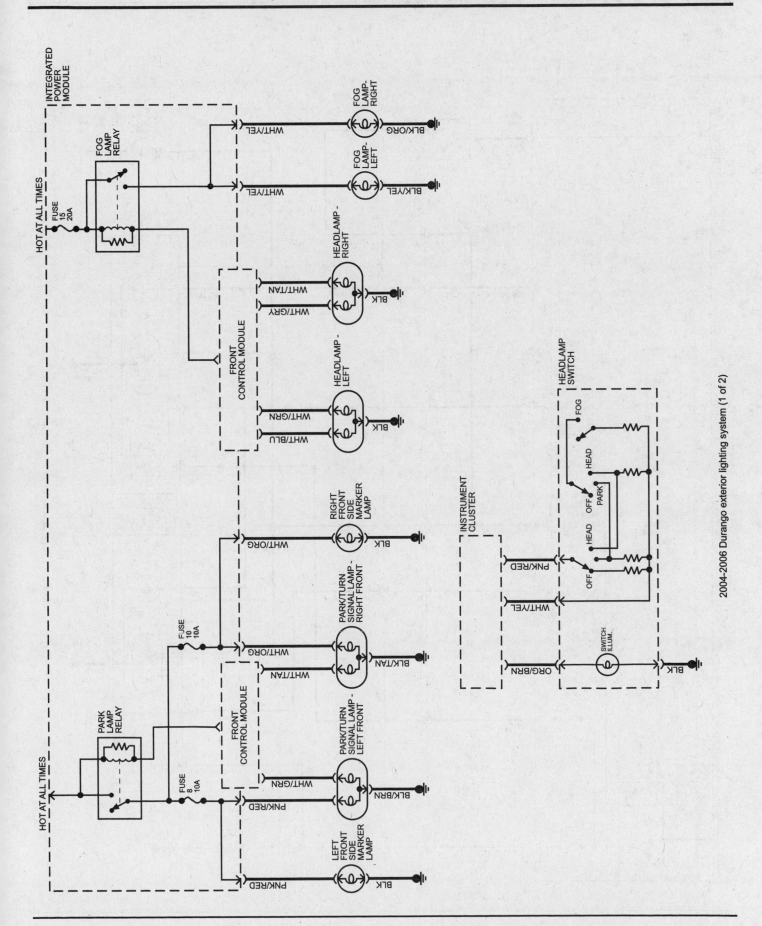

2004-2006 Durango exterior lighting system (1 of 2)

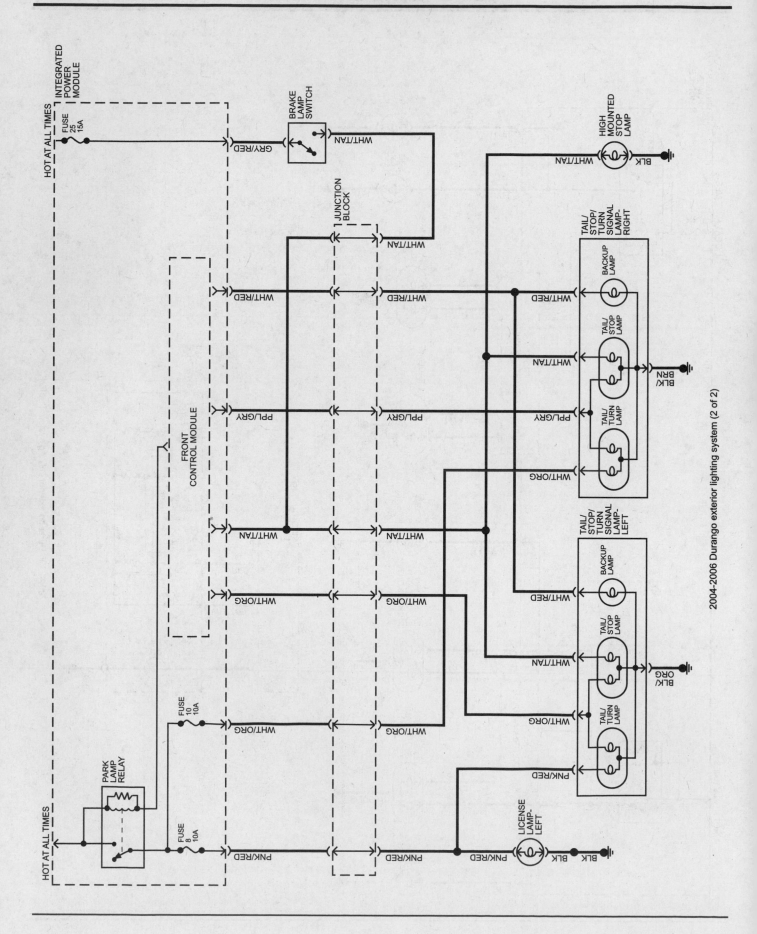

2004-2006 Durango exterior lighting system (2 of 2)

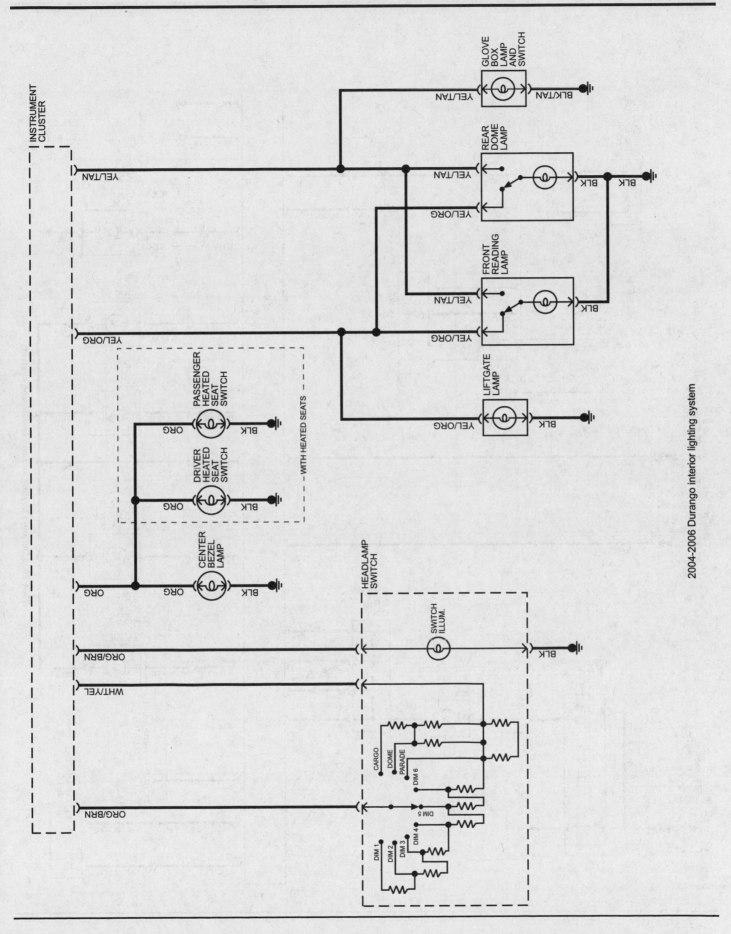

2004-2006 Durango interior lighting system

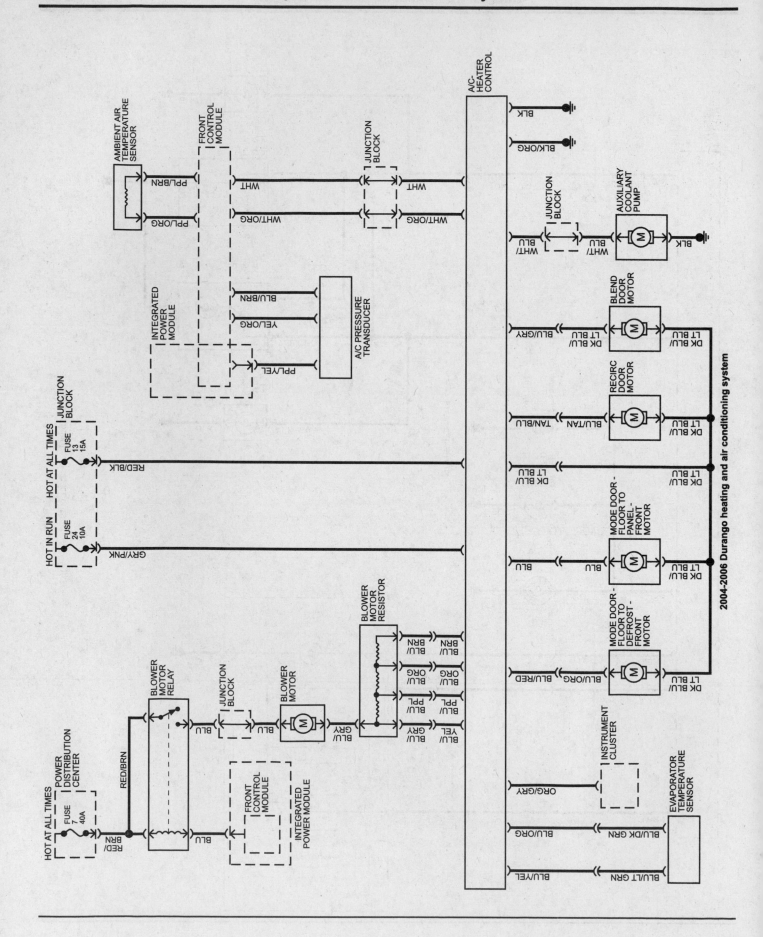

2004-2006 Durango heating and air conditioning system

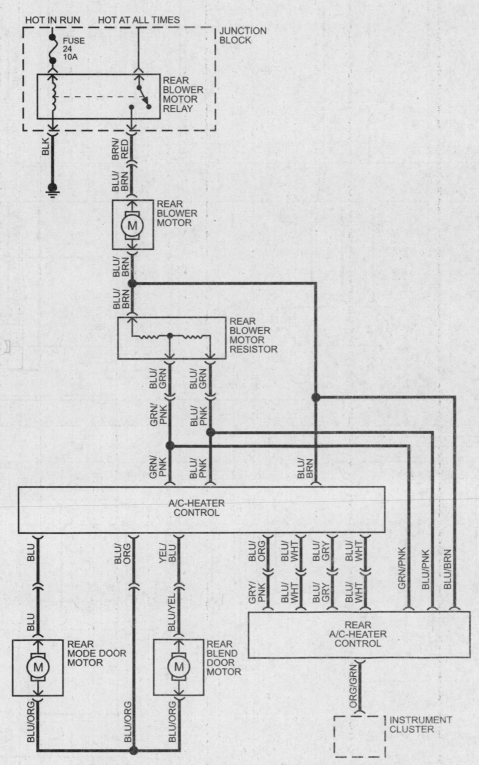

2004-2006 Durango rear heating and air conditioning system

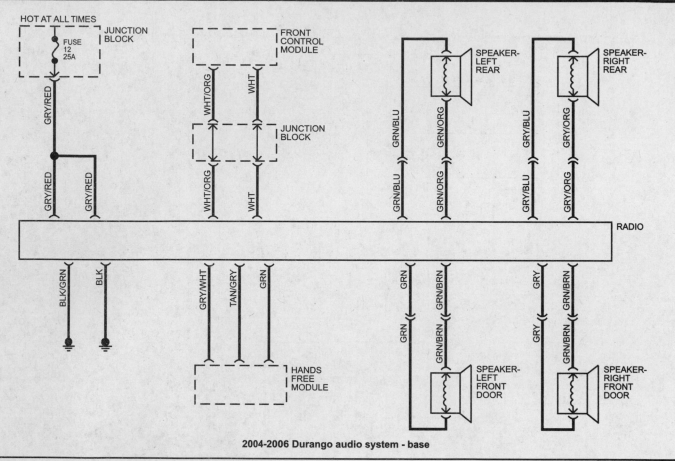

2004-2006 Durango audio system - base

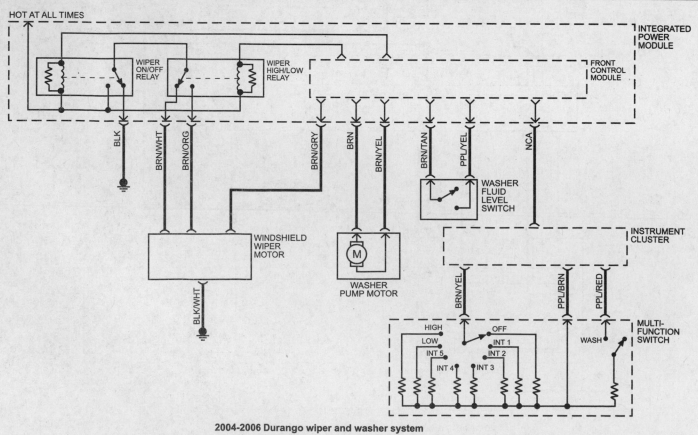

2004-2006 Durango wiper and washer system

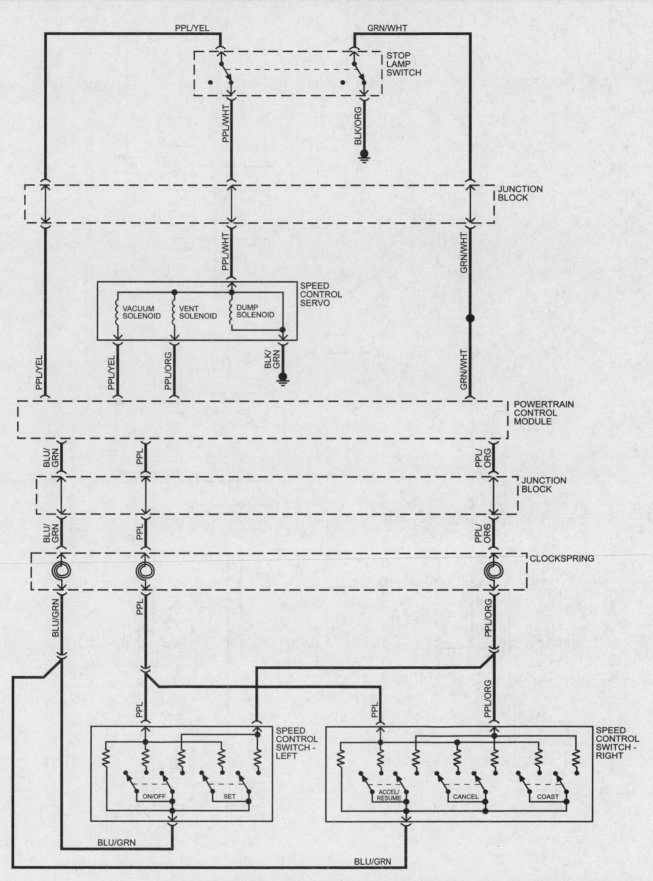

2004-2006 Durango cruise control system

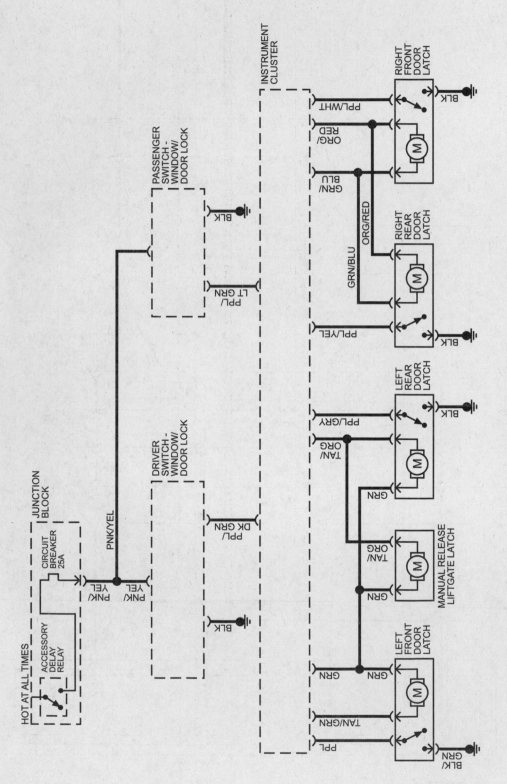

2004-2006 Durango power door locks

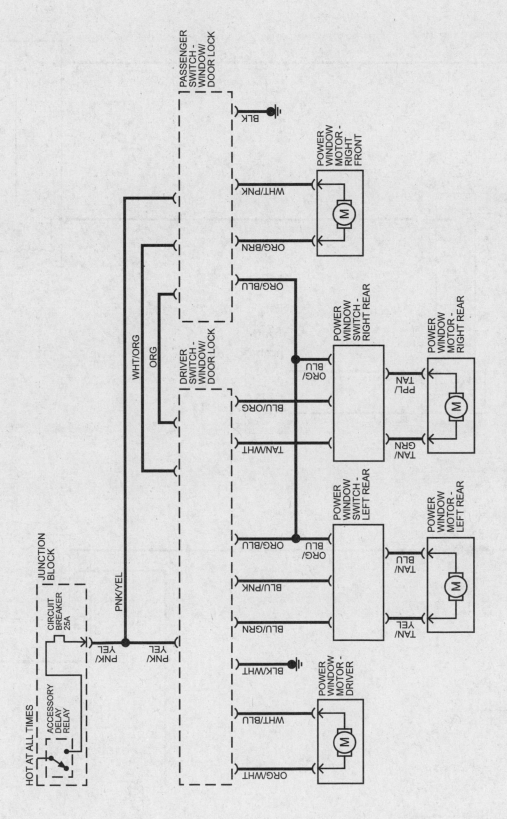

2004-2006 Durango power windows system

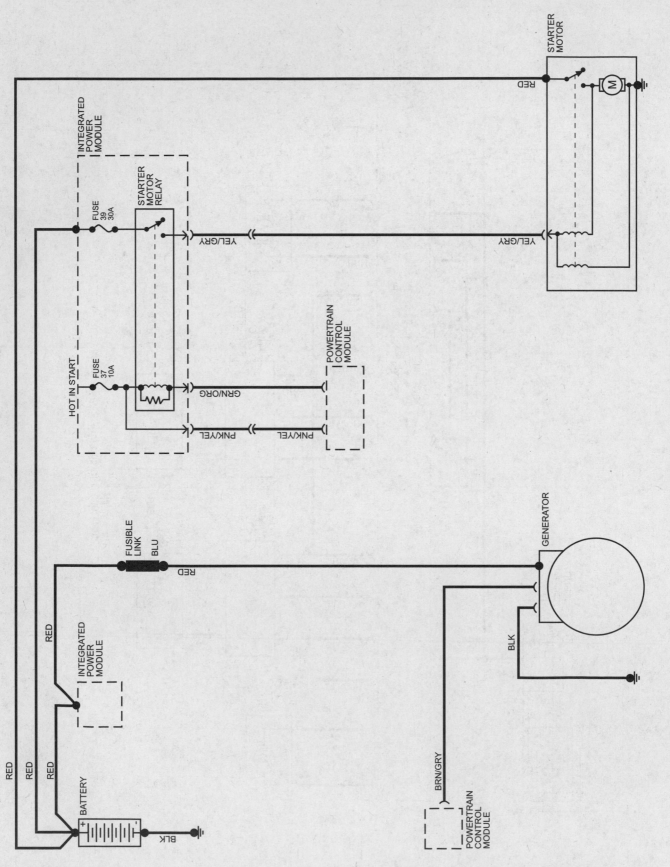

2005-2006 Dakota starting and charging systems

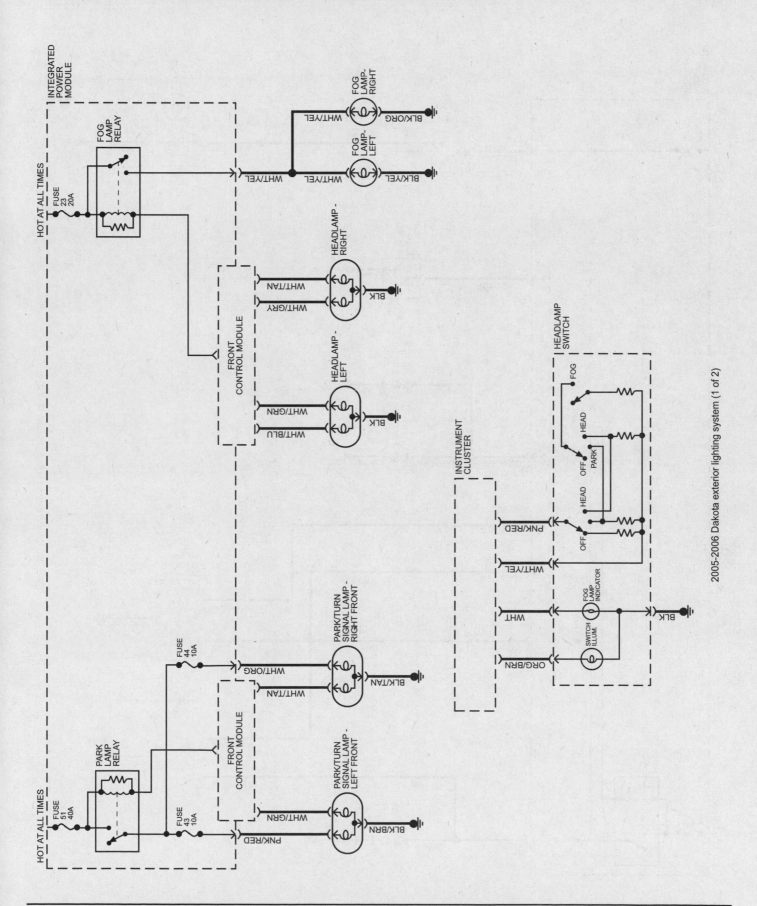

2005-2006 Dakota exterior lighting system (1 of 2)

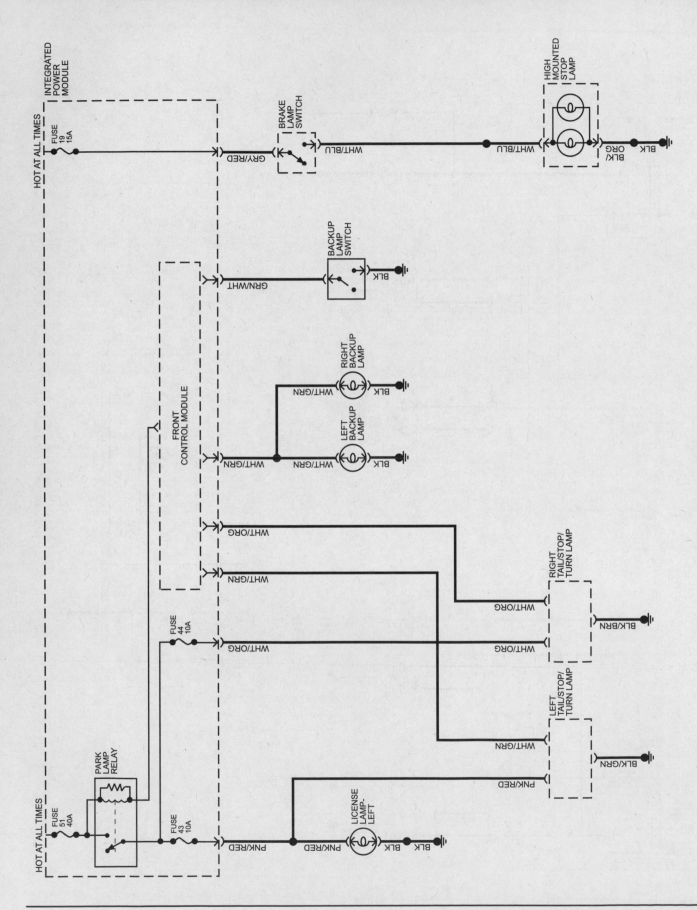

2005-2006 Dakota exterior lighting system (2 of 2)

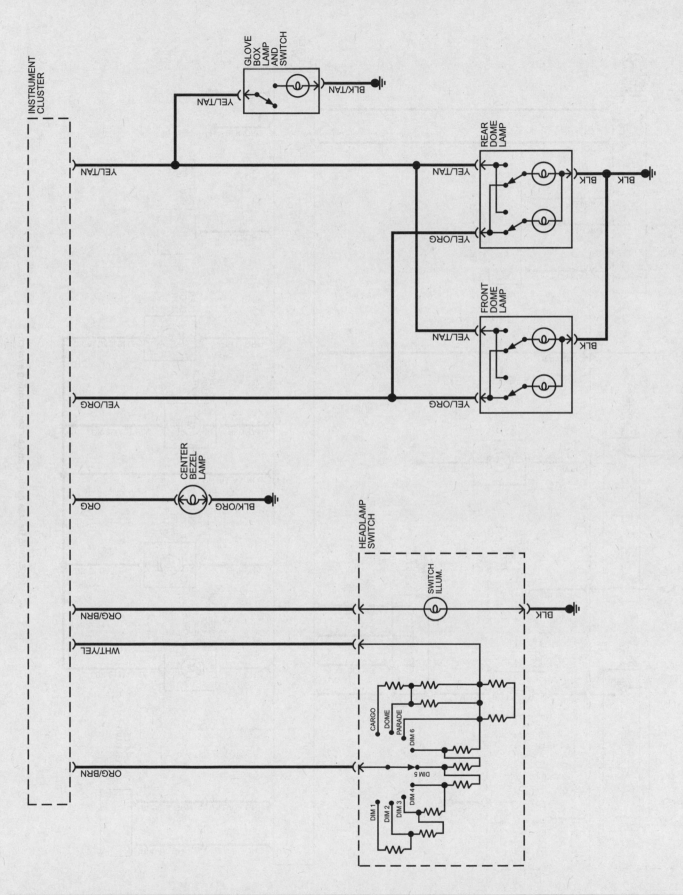

2005-2006_Dakota interior lighting system

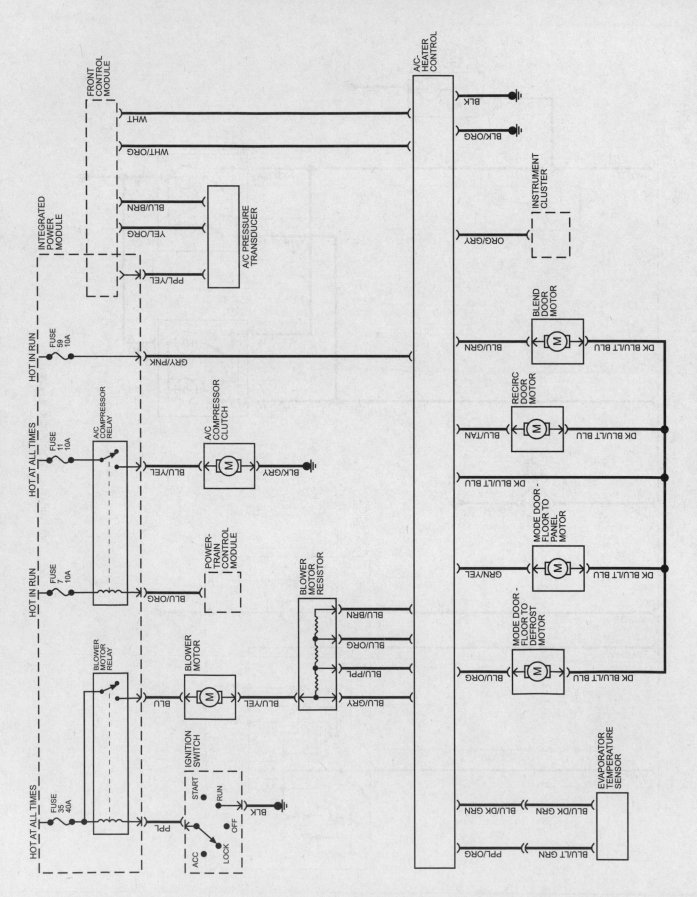

2005-2006 Dakota heating and air conditioning system

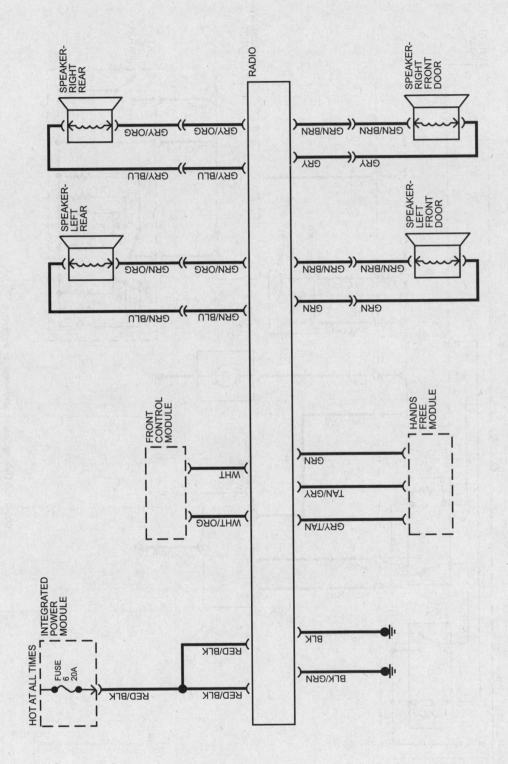

2005-2006 Dakota audio system - base

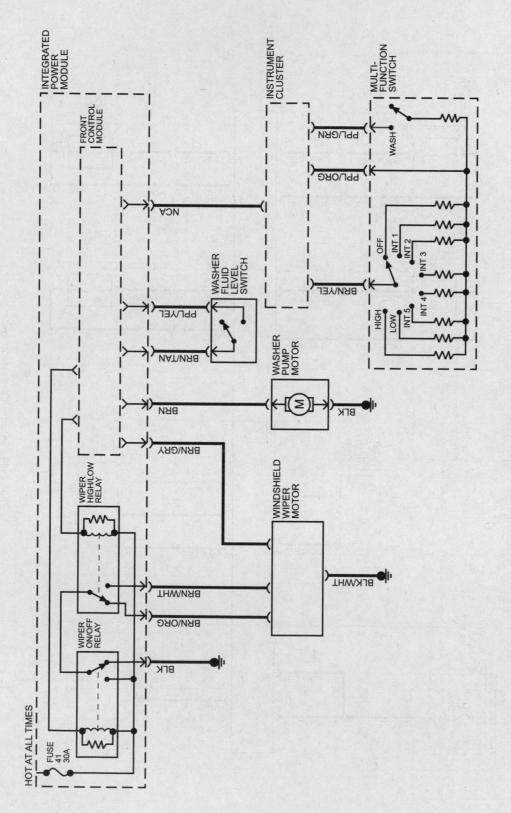

2005-2006 Dakota wiper and washer system

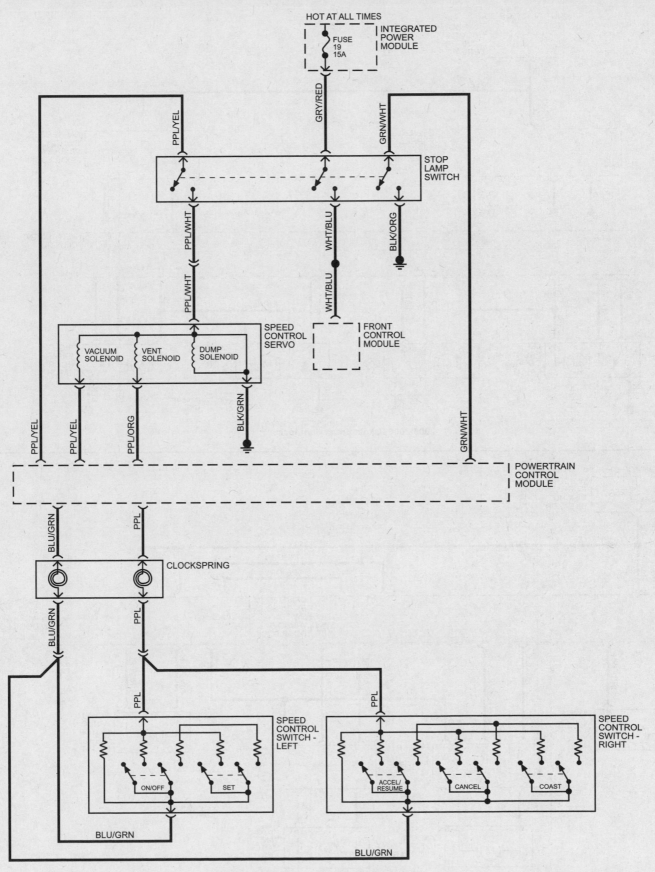

2005-2006 Dakota cruise control system

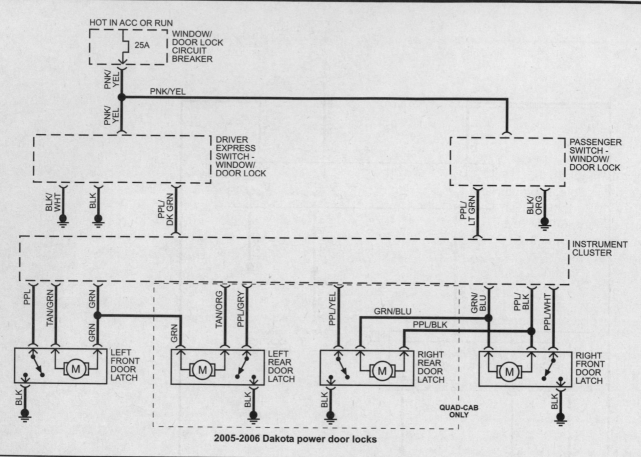

2005-2006 Dakota power door locks

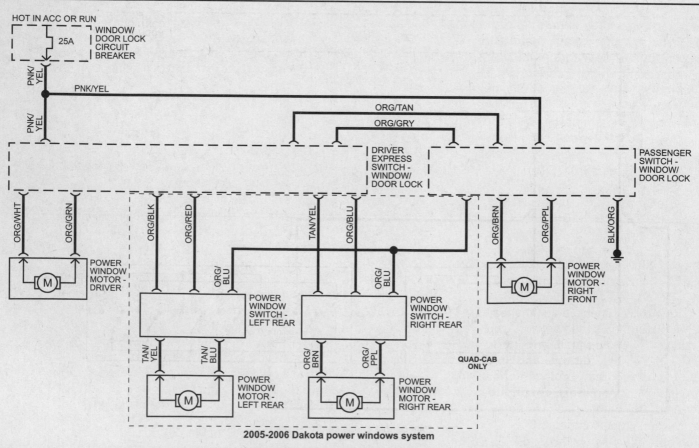

2005-2006 Dakota power windows system

Index

K

Key lock cylinder and ignition switch, replacement, 12-5
Knock sensor(s), replacement, 6-12

L

Leaf spring (Dakota), removal and installation, 10-10
Liftgate (Durango)
   panels, outside handle, latch and support struts, removal and installation, 11-12
   removal and installation, 11-12
Lower control arm, removal and installation
   front, 10-7
   rear, 10-9
Lubricants and chemicals, 0-17
Lubricants and fluids
   capacities, 1-2
   recommended, 1-1

M

Maintenance schedule, 1-6
Maintenance techniques, tools and working facilities, 0-8
Maintenance, routine, 1-1 through 1-26
Manifold Absolute Pressure (MAP) sensor, replacement, 6-13
Manual transmission, 7A-1 through 7A-4
   back-up light switch, check and replacement, 7A-2
   extension housing oil seal, replacement, 7A-1
   lubricant
      change, 1-23
      level check, 1-20
      type, 1-1
   overhaul, general information, 7A-4
   removal and installation, 7A-2
   shift lever, removal and installation, 7A-2
Master cylinder, brake, removal and installation, 9-7
Mirrors
   electric side view, general information, 12-20
   removal and installation, 11-11
Multi-function switch, replacement, 12-5
Multiple Displacement System (MDS), general information and solenoid replacement, 2B-11

O

Oil pan, removal and installation
   3.7L V6 and 4.7L V8 engines, 2A-15
   5.7L V8 (Hemi) engine, 2B-13
Oil pressure check, 2C-4

Oil pump, removal, inspection and installation
   3.7L V6 and 4.7L V8 engines, 2A-16
   5.7L V8 (Hemi) engine, 2B-15
Oil, engine, level check, 1-8
On-Board Diagnostic (OBD) system and Diagnostic Trouble Codes (DTCs), 6-2
Orifice tube, air conditioning, replacement, 3-16
Output Shaft Speed (OSS) and Input Shaft Speed (ISS) sensors, replacement, 6-15
Oxygen sensors, description and replacement, 6-13

P

Pads, disc brake, replacement, 9-3
Parking brake
   adjustment, 9-16
   shoes (models with rear disc brakes), replacement, 9-10
Parts, replacement, buying, 0-8
Pilot bearing, inspection and replacement, 8-5
Pinion oil seal, replacement, 8-12
Pistons and connecting rods, removal and installation, 2C-9
Positive Crankcase Ventilation (PCV) system
   description and check, 6-20
   valve check and replacement, 1-23
Power brake booster, check, removal and installation, 9-8
Power door lock system, general information, 12-21
Power seats, general information, 12-22
Power steering
   fluid
      level check, 1-9
      type, 1-1
   pump, removal and installation, 10-14
   system, bleeding, 10-14
Power window system, general information, 12-21
   Powertrain Control Module (PCM), removal and installation, 6-15

R

Rack-and-pinion, removal and installation, 10-13
Radiator grille, removal and installation, 11-6
Radiator, removal and installation, 3-7
Radio and speakers, removal and installation, 12-9
Rear axle bearing, replacement, 8-9
Rear axleshaft
   oil seal, replacement, 8-9
   removal and installation, 8-8
Rear main oil seal, replacement
   3.7L V6 and 4.7L V8 engines, 2A-17
   5.7L V8 (Hemi) engine, 2B-15

Haynes Automotive Manuals

NOTE: If you do not see a listing for your vehicle, consult your local Haynes dealer for the latest product information.

HAYNES XTREME CUSTOMIZING
11101	**Sport Compact Customizing**
11102	**Sport Compact Performance**
11110	**In-car Entertainment**
11150	**Sport Utility Vehicle Customizing**
11213	**Acura**
11255	**GM Full-size Pick-ups**
11314	**Ford Focus**
11315	**Full-size Ford Pick-ups**
11373	**Honda Civic**

ACURA
12020	**Integra** '86 thru '89 & **Legend** '86 thru '90
12021	**Integra** '90 thru '93 & **Legend** '91 thru '95

AMC
	Jeep CJ - see JEEP (50020)
14020	**Concord/Hornet/Gremlin/Spirit** '70 thru '83
14025	**(Renault) Alliance & Encore** '83 thru '87

AUDI
15020	**4000** all models '80 thru '87
15025	**5000** all models '77 thru '83
15026	**5000** all models '84 thru '88

AUSTIN
	Healey Sprite - see MG Midget (66015)

BMW
18020	**3/5 Series** '82 thru '92
18021	**3 Series** including Z3 models '92 thru '98
18022	**3-Series**, E46 chassis '99 thru '05, Z4 models '03 thru '05
18025	**320i** all 4 cyl models '75 thru '83
18050	**1500 thru 2002** except Turbo '59 thru '77

BUICK
19010	**Buick Century** '97 thru '05
	Century (front-wheel drive) - see GM (38005)
19020	**Buick, Oldsmobile & Pontiac Full-size** (Front wheel drive) see GM (38005)
19025	**Buick Oldsmobile & Pontiac Full-size** (Rear wheel drive) '70 thru '90
19030	**Mid-size Regal & Century** '74 thru '87
	Regal - see GENERAL MOTORS (38010)
	Skyhawk - see GM (38030)
	Skylark - see GM (38020, 38025)
	Somerset - see GENERAL MOTORS (38025)

CADILLAC
21030	**Cadillac Rear Wheel Drive** '70 thru '93
	Cimarron, Eldorado & Seville - see GM (38015, 38030, 38031)

CHEVROLET
10305	**Chevrolet Engine Overhaul Manual**
24010	**Astro & GMC Safari Mini-vans** '85 thru '03
24015	**Camaro V8** all models '70 thru '81
24016	**Camaro** all models '82 thru '92
	Cavalier - see GM (38015)
	Celebrity - see GM (38005)
24017	**Camaro & Firebird** '93 thru '02
24020	**Chevelle, Malibu, El Camino** '69 thru '87
24024	**Chevette & Pontiac T1000** '76 thru '87
	Citation - see GENERAL MOTORS (38020)
24027	**Colorado & GMC Canyon** '04 thru '06
24032	**Corsica/Beretta** all models '87 thru '96
24040	**Corvette** all V8 models '68 thru '82
24041	**Corvette** all models '84 thru '96
24045	**Full-size Sedans** Caprice, Impala, Biscayne, Bel Air & Wagons '69 thru '90
24046	**Impala SS & Caprice and Buick Roadmaster** '91 thru '96
	Lumina '90 thru '94 - see GM (38010)
24048	**Lumina & Monte Carlo** '95 thru '05
	Lumina APV - see GM (38035)
24050	**Luv Pick-up** all 2WD & 4WD '72 thru '82
	Malibu - see GM (38026)
24055	**Monte Carlo** all models '70 thru '88
	Monte Carlo '95 thru '01 - see LUMINA
24059	**Nova** all V8 models '69 thru '79
24060	**Nova/Geo Prizm** '85 thru '92
24064	**Pick-ups** '67 thru '87 - Chevrolet & GMC, all V8 & in-line 6 cyl, 2WD & 4WD '67 thru '87; Suburbans, Blazers & Jimmys '67 thru '91
24065	**Pick-ups** '88 thru '98 - Chevrolet & GMC, all full-size models '88 thru '98; C/K Classic '99 & '00; Blazer & Jimmy '92 thru '94; Suburban '92 thru '99; Tahoe & Yukon '95 thru '99
24066	**Pick-ups** '99 thru '02 - Chevrolet Silverado & GMC Sierra '99 thru '05; Suburban/Tahoe/Yukon/Yukon XL '00 thru '05
24070	**S-10 & GMC S-15 Pick-ups** '82 thru '93
24071	**S-10, Sonoma & Jimmy** '94 thru '04
24072	**Chevrolet TrailBlazer & TrailBlazer EXT, GMC Envoy & Envoy XL, Oldsmobile Bravada** '02 and '03
24075	**Sprint** '85 thru '88, Geo Metro '89 thru '01
24080	**Vans** - Chevrolet & GMC '68 thru '96
24081	**Chevrolet Express & GMC Savana** Full-size Vans '96 thru '05

CHRYSLER
10310	**Chrysler Engine Overhaul Manual**
25015	**Chrysler Cirrus, Dodge Stratus, Plymouth Breeze**, '95 thru '00
25020	**Full-size Front-Wheel Drive** '88 thru '93
	K-Cars - see DODGE Aries (30008)
	Laser - see DODGE Daytona (30030)
25025	**Chrysler LHS, Concorde & New Yorker, Dodge Intrepid, Eagle Vision** '93 thru '97
25026	**Chrysler LHS, Concorde, 300M, Dodge Intrepid** '98 thru '03
25027	**Chrysler 300** '05 thru '07
25030	**Chrysler/Plym. Mid-size** '82 thru '95
	Rear-wheel Drive - see DODGE (30050)
25035	**PT Cruiser** all models '01 thru '03
25040	**Chrysler Sebring/Dodge Avenger** '95 thru '98

DATSUN
28005	**200SX** all models '80 thru '83
28007	**B-210** all models '73 thru '78
28009	**210** all models '78 thru '82
28012	**240Z, 260Z & 280Z** Coupe '70 thru '78
28014	**280ZX** Coupe & 2+2 '79 thru '83
	300ZX - see NISSAN (72010)
28018	**510 & PL521 Pick-up** '68 thru '73
28020	**510** all models '78 thru '81
28022	**620 Series Pick-up** all models '73 thru '79
	720 Series Pick-up - NISSAN (72030)
28025	**810/Maxima** all gas models, '77 thru '84

DODGE
	400 & 600 - see CHRYSLER (25030)
30008	**Aries & Plymouth Reliant** '81 thru '89
30010	**Caravan & Ply. Voyager** '84 thru '95
30011	**Caravan & Ply. Voyager** '96 thru '02
30012	**Challenger/Plymouth Saporro** '78 thru '83
	Challenger '67-'76 - see DART (30025)
30013	**Colt/Plymouth Champ** '78 thru '87
30016	**Colt/Plymouth Champ** '78 thru '87
30020	**Dakota Pick-ups** all models '87 thru '96
30021	**Durango** '98 & '99, Dakota '97 thru '99
30022	**Dodge Durango models** '00 thru '03
	Dodge Dakota models '00 thru '03
30023	**Dodge Durango & Dakota** '04 thru '06
30025	**Dart, Challenger/Plymouth Barracuda & Valiant** 6 cyl models '67 thru '76
30030	**Daytona & Chrysler Laser** '84 thru '89
	Intrepid - see Chrysler (25025, 25026)
30034	**Dodge & Plymouth Neon** '95 thru '99
30035	**Omni & Plymouth Horizon** '78 thru '90
30036	**Dodge and Plymouth Neon** '00 thru'05
30040	**Pick-ups** all full-size models '74 thru '93
30041	**Pick-ups** all full-size models '94 thru '01
30042	**Dodge Full-size Pick-ups** '02 thru '05
30045	**Ram 50/D50 Pick-ups & Raider and Plymouth Arrow Pick-ups** '79 thru '93
30050	**Dodge/Ply./Chrysler RWD** '71 thru '89
30055	**Shadow/Plymouth Sundance** '87 thru '94
30060	**Spirit & Plymouth Acclaim** '89 thru '95
30065	**Vans - Dodge & Plymouth** '71 thru '03

EAGLE
	Talon - see MITSUBISHI (68030, 68031)
	Vision - see CHRYSLER (25025)

FIAT
34010	**124 Sport Coupe & Spider** '68 thru '78
34025	**X1/9** all models '74 thru '80

FORD
10355	**Ford Automatic Transmission Overhaul**
10320	**Ford Engine Overhaul Manual**
36004	**Aerostar Mini-vans** '86 thru '97
	Aspire - see FORD Festiva (36030)
36006	**Contour/Mercury Mystique** '95 thru '00
36008	**Courier Pick-up** all models '72 thru '82
36012	**Crown Victoria & Mercury Grand Marquis** '88 thru '00
36016	**Escort/Mercury Lynx** '81 thru '90
36020	**Escort/Mercury Tracer** '91 thru '00
	Expedition - see FORD Pick-up (36059)
36022	**Ford Escape & Mazda Tribute** '01 thru '03
36024	**Explorer & Mazda Navajo** '91 thru '01
36025	**Ford Explorer & Mercury Mountaineer** '02 thru '06
36028	**Fairmont & Mercury Zephyr** '78 thru '83
36030	**Festiva & Aspire** '88 thru '97
36032	**Fiesta** all models '77 thru '80
36034	**Focus** all models '00 thru '05
36036	**Ford & Mercury Full-size** '75 thru '87
36044	**Ford & Mercury Mid-size** '75 thru '86
36048	**Mustang V8** all models '64-1/2 thru '73
36049	**Mustang II** 4 cyl, V6 & V8 '74 thru '78
36050	**Mustang & Mercury Capri** '79 thru '86
36051	**Mustang** all models '94 thru '03
36052	**Mustang** '05 thru '07
36054	**Pick-ups and Bronco** '73 thru '79
36058	**Pick-ups and Bronco** '80 thru '96
36059	**F-150 & Expedition** '97 thru '03, F-250 '97 thru '99 & Lincoln Navigator '98 thru '02
36060	**Super Duty Pick-up, Excursion** '99 thru '06
36061	**F-150 full-size** '04 thru '06
36062	**Pinto & Mercury Bobcat** '75 thru '80
36066	**Probe** all models '89 thru '92
36070	**Ranger/Bronco II** gas models '83 thru '92
36071	**Ford Ranger** '93 thru '05 & Mazda Pick-ups '94 thru '05
36074	**Taurus & Mercury Sable** '86 thru '95
36075	**Taurus & Mercury Sable** '96 thru '01
36078	**Tempo & Mercury Topaz** '84 thru '94
36082	**Thunderbird/Mercury Cougar** '83 thru '88
36086	**Thunderbird/Mercury Cougar** '89 thru '97
36090	**Vans** all V8 Econoline models '69 thru '91
36094	**Vans** full size '92 thru '05
36097	**Windstar Mini-van** '95 thru '03

GENERAL MOTORS
10360	**GM Automatic Transmission Overhaul**
38005	**Buick Century, Chevrolet Celebrity, Olds Cutlass Ciera & Pontiac 6000** '82 thru '96
38010	**Buick Regal, Chevrolet Lumina, Oldsmobile Cutlass Supreme & Pontiac Grand Prix** front wheel drive '88 thru '05
38015	**Buick Skyhawk, Cadillac Cimarron, Chevrolet Cavalier, Oldsmobile Firenza Pontiac J-2000 & Sunbird** '82 thru '94
38016	**Chevrolet Cavalier/Pontiac Sunfire** '95 thru '04
38020	**Buick Skylark, Chevrolet Citation, Olds Omega, Pontiac Phoenix** '80 thru '85
38025	**Buick Skylark & Somerset, Olds Achieva, Calais & Pontiac Grand Am** '85 thru '98
38026	**Chevrolet Malibu, Olds Alero & Cutlass, Pontiac Grand Am** '97 thru '03
38027	**Chevrolet Malibu** '04 thru '07
38030	**Cadillac Eldorado & Oldsmobile Toronado** '71 thru '85, Seville '80 thru '85, Buick Riviera '79 thru '85
38031	**Cadillac Eldorado & Seville** '86 thru '91, DeVille & Buick Riviera '86 thru '93, Fleetwood & Olds Toronado '86 thru '92
38032	**DeVille** '94 thru '05, Seville '92 thru '04
38035	**Chevrolet Lumina APV, Oldsmobile S & Pontiac Trans Sport**
38036	**Chevrolet Venture, Olds Silhouette, Pontiac Trans Sport & Montana** '97 thru '05
	General Motors Full-size Rear-wheel Drive - see BUICK (19025)

GEO
	Metro - see CHEVROLET Sprint (24075)
	Prizm - see CHEVROLET (24060) or TOYOTA (92036)
40030	**Storm** all models '90 thru '93
	Tracker - see SUZUKI Samurai (90010)

GMC
	Vans & Pick-ups - see CHEVROLET

HONDA
42010	**Accord CVCC** all models '76 thru '83
42011	**Accord** all models '84 thru '89
42012	**Accord** all models '90 thru '93
42013	**Accord** all models '94 thru '97
42014	**Accord** all models '98 thru '02
42015	**Honda Accord models** '03 thru '05
42020	**Civic 1200** all models '73 thru '79
42021	**Civic 1300 & 1500 CVCC** '80 thru '83
42022	**Civic 1500 CVCC** all models '75 thru '79
42023	**Civic** all models '84 thru '91
42024	**Civic & del Sol** '92 thru '95
42025	**Civic** '96 thru '00, CR-V '97 thru '01, Acura Integra '94 thru '00
	Passport - see ISUZU Rodeo (47017)
42026	**Civic** '01 thru '04, CR-V '02 thru '04
42035	**Honda Odyssey** all models '99 thru '04
42040	**Prelude CVCC** all models '79 thru '89

HYUNDAI
43010	**Elantra** all models '96 thru '01
43015	**Excel & Accent** all models '86 thru '98

ISUZU
	Hombre - see CHEVROLET S-10 (24071)
47017	**Rodeo** '91 thru '02, Amigo '89 thru '02, Honda Passport '95 thru '02
47020	**Trooper** '84 thru '91, Pick-up '81 thru '93

JAGUAR
49010	**XJ6** all 6 cyl models '68 thru '86
49011	**XJ6** all models '88 thru '94
49015	**XJ12 & XJS** all 12 cyl models '72 thru '85

JEEP
50010	**Cherokee, Comanche & Wagoneer Limited** all models '84 thru '01
50020	**CJ** all models '49 thru '86
50025	**Grand Cherokee** all models '93 thru '04
50029	**Grand Wagoneer & Pick-up** '72 thru '91
50030	**Wrangler** all models '87 thru '03
50035	**Liberty** '02 thru '04

KIA
54070	**Sephia** '94 thru '01, Spectra '00 thru '04

LEXUS
	ES 300 - see TOYOTA Camry (92007)

LINCOLN
	Navigator - see FORD Pick-up (36059)
59010	**Rear Wheel Drive** all models '70 thru '05

MAZDA
61010	**GLC** (rear wheel drive) '77 thru '83
61011	**GLC** (front wheel drive) '81 thru '85
61015	**323 & Protegé** '90 thru '00
61016	**MX-5 Miata** '90 thru '97
61020	**MPV** all models '89 thru '94
	Navajo - see FORD Explorer (36024)
61030	**Pick-ups** '72 thru '93
	Pick-ups '94 on - see Ford (36071)
61035	**RX-7** all models '79 thru '85
61036	**RX-7** all models '86 thru '91
61040	**626** (rear wheel drive) '79 thru '82
61041	**626 & MX-6** (front wheel drive) '83 thru '92
61042	**626** '93 thru '01, & MX-6/Ford Probe '93 thru '01

MERCEDES-BENZ
63012	**123 Series Diesel** '76 thru '85
63015	**190 Series** 4-cyl gas models, '84 thru '88
63020	**230, 250 & 280** 6 cyl sohc '68 thru '72
63025	**280 123 Series** gas models '77 thru '81
63030	**350 & 450** all models '71 thru '80

MERCURY
64200	**Villager & Nissan Quest** '93 thru '01
	All other titles, see FORD listing.

MG
66010	**MGB** Roadster & GT Coupe '62 thru '80
66015	**MG Midget & Austin Healey Sprite** Roadster '58 thru '80

MITSUBISHI
68020	**Cordia, Tredia, Galant, Precis & Mirage** '83 thru '93
68030	**Eclipse, Eagle Talon & Plymouth Laser** '90 thru '94
68031	**Eclipse** '95 thru '01, Eagle Talon '95 thru '98
68035	**Mitsubishi Galant** '94 thru '03
68040	**Pick-up** '83 thru '96, Montero '83 thru '93

NISSAN
72010	**300ZX** all models incl. Turbo '84 thru '89
72015	**Altima** all models '93 thru '04
72020	**Maxima** all models '85 thru '92
72021	**Maxima** all models '93 thru '01
72030	**Pick-ups** '80 thru '97, Pathfinder '87 thru '95
72031	**Frontier Pick-up** '98 thru '04, Xterra '00 thru '04, Pathfinder '96 thru '04
72040	**Pulsar** all models '83 thru '86
72050	**Sentra** all models '82 thru '94
72051	**Sentra & 200SX** all models '95 thru '04
72060	**Stanza** all models '82 thru '90

OLDSMOBILE
73015	**Cutlass** '74 thru '88
	For other OLDSMOBILE titles, see BUICK, CHEVROLET or GM listings.

PLYMOUTH
	For PLYMOUTH titles, see DODGE.

PONTIAC
79008	**Fiero** all models '84 thru '88
79018	**Firebird V8 models** except Turbo '70 thru '81
79019	**Firebird** all models '82 thru '92
79040	**Mid-size Rear-wheel Drive** '70 thru '87
	For other PONTIAC titles, see BUICK, CHEVROLET or GM listings.

PORSCHE
80020	**911** Coupe & Targa models '65 thru '89
80025	**914** all 4 cyl models '69 thru '76
80030	**924** all models incl. Turbo '76 thru '82
80035	**944** all models incl. Turbo '83 thru '89

RENAULT
	Alliance, Encore - see AMC (14020)

SAAB
84010	**900** including Turbo '79 thru '88

SATURN
87010	**Saturn** all models '91 thru '02
87011	**Saturn Ion** '03 thru '07
87020	**Saturn** all L-series models '00 thu '04

SUBARU
89002	**1100, 1300, 1400 & 1600** '71 thru '79
89003	**1600 & 1800** 2WD & 4WD '80 thru '94
89100	**Legacy** models '90 thru '98
89101	**Legacy & Forester** '00 thru '06

SUZUKI
90010	**Samurai/Sidekick/Geo Tracker** '86 thru '01

TOYOTA
92005	**Camry** all models '83 thru '91
92006	**Camry** all models '92 thru '96
92007	**Camry/Avalon/Solara/Lexus ES 300** '97 thru '01
92008	**Toyota Camry, Avalon and Solara & Lexus ES 300/330** all models '02 thru '05
92015	**Celica Rear Wheel Drive** '71 thru '85
92020	**Celica Front Wheel Drive** '86 thru '99
92025	**Celica Supra** all models '79 thru '92
92030	**Corolla** all models '75 thru '79
92032	**Corolla** rear wheel drive models '80 thru '87
92035	**Corolla** front wheel drive models '84 thru '92
92036	**Corolla & Geo Prizm** '93 thru '02
92037	**Corolla** models '03 thru '05
92040	**Corolla Tercel** all models '80 thru '82
92045	**Corona** all models '74 thru '82
92050	**Cressida** all models '78 thru '82
92055	**Land Cruiser** FJ40/43/45/55 '68 thru '82
92056	**Land Cruiser** FJ60/62/80/FZJ80 '80 thru '96
92065	**MR2** all models '85 thru '87
92070	**Pick-up** all models '69 thru '78
92075	**Pick-up** all models '79 thru '95
92076	**Tacoma** '95 thru '04, 4Runner '96 thru '02, T100 '93 thru '98
92078	**Tundra** '00 thru '02, Sequoia '01 thru '02
92080	**Previa** all models '91 thru '95
92082	**RAV4** all models '96 thru '02
92085	**Tercel** all models '87 thru '94
92090	**Toyota Sienna** all models '98 thru '02
92095	**Highlander & Lexus RX-330** '99 thru '06

TRIUMPH
94007	**Spitfire** all models '62 thru '81
94010	**TR7** all models '75 thru '81

VW
96008	**Beetle & Karmann Ghia** '54 thru '79
96009	**New Beetle** '98 thru '00
96016	**Rabbit, Jetta, Scirocco, & Pick-up** gas models '75 thru '92 & Convertible '80 thru '92
96017	**Golf, GTI & Jetta** '93 thru '98, Cabrio '95 thru '98
96018	**Golf, GTI, Jetta & Cabrio** '99 thru '02
96020	**Rabbit, Jetta, Pick-up** diesel '77 thru '84
96023	**Passat** '98 thru '01, Audi A4 '96 thru '01
96030	**Transporter 1600** all models '68 thru '79
96035	**Transporter 1700, 1800, 2000** '72 thru '79
96040	**Type 3 1500 & 1600** '63 thru '73
96045	**Vanagon** air-cooled models '80 thru '83

VOLVO
97010	**120, 130 Series & 1800 Sports** '61 thru '73
97015	**140 Series** all models '66 thru '74
97020	**240 Series** all models '76 thru '93
97040	**740 & 760 Series** all models '82 thru '88

TECHBOOK MANUALS
10205	**Automotive Computer Codes**
10206	**OBD-II & Electronic Engine Management Systems**
10210	**Automotive Emissions Control Manual**
10215	**Fuel Injection Manual, 1978 thru 1985**
10220	**Fuel Injection Manual, 1986 thru 1999**
10225	**Holley Carburetor Manual**
10230	**Rochester Carburetor Manual**
10240	**Weber/Zenith/Stromberg/SU Carburetor**
10305	**Chevrolet Engine Overhaul Manual**
10310	**Chrysler Engine Overhaul Manual**
10320	**Ford Engine Overhaul Manual**
10330	**GM and Ford Diesel Engine Repair**
10340	**Small Engine Repair Manual**
10345	**Suspension, Steering & Driveline**
10355	**Ford Automatic Transmission Overhaul**
10360	**GM Automatic Transmission Overhaul**
10405	**Automotive Body Repair & Painting**
10410	**Automotive Brake Manual**
10415	**Automotive Detailing Manual**
10420	**Automotive Electrical Manual**
10425	**Automotive Heating & Air Conditioning**
10430	**Automotive Reference Dictionary**
10435	**Automotive Tools Manual**
10440	**Used Car Buying Guide**
10445	**Welding Manual**
10450	**ATV Basics**
10452	**Scooters, Automatic Transmission 50cc to 250cc**

SPANISH MANUALS
98903	**Reparación de Carrocería & Pintura**
98904	**Carburadores para los modelos Holley & Rochester**
98905	**Códigos Automotrices de la Computadora**
98910	**Frenos Automotriz**
98913	**Electricidad Automotriz**
98915	**Inyección de Combustible 1986 al 1999**
99040	**Chevrolet & GMC Camionetas** '67 al '87
99041	**Chevrolet & GMC Camionetas** '88 al '98
99042	**Chevrolet Camionetas Cerradas** '68 al '95
99055	**Dodge Caravan/Ply. Voyager** '84 al '95
99075	**Ford Camionetas y Bronco** '80 al '94
99077	**Ford Camionetas Cerradas** '69 al '91
99088	**Ford Modelos de Tamaño Mediano** '75 al '86
99091	**Ford Taurus & Mercury Sable** '86 al '95
99095	**GM Modelos de Tamaño Grande** '70 al '90
99100	**GM Modelos de Tamaño Mediano** '70 al '88
99106	**Jeep Cherokee, Wagoneer & Comanche** '84 al '00
99110	**Nissan Camionetas** '80 al '96, Pathfinder '87 al '95
99118	**Nissan Sentra** '82 al '94
99125	**Toyota Camionetas y 4-Runner** '79 al '95

Over 100 Haynes motorcycle manuals also available

10-06

Haynes North America, Inc., 861 Lawrence Drive, Newbury Park, CA 91320 • (805) 498-6703